100 GREAT BOOKS

100
Great Books

MASTERPIECES OF ALL TIME

EDITED BY
JOHN CANNING

A CENTURY BOOK
Published by
SOUVENIR PRESS

ISBN 0 285 62127 0

SOUVENIR PRESS EDITION: 1974

MADE AND PRINTED IN GREAT BRITAIN BY
J. W. ARROWSMITH LTD., BRISTOL

Contents

CONTENTS

CONTENTS

7

CONTENTS

CONTENTS

CONTENTS

Illustrations

ILLUSTRATIONS

Introduction

I should make clear in the first instance that the compilation of titles for this volume of *One Hundred Great Books* has not rested with me, though as I glance through the index with its formidable array of names I can find very little to quarrel with. If one had to provide a short list of books which have, in their various ways, moulded the cultural sensibility of Europe and the world one could hardly improve upon this guide. Of course one cannot pronounce upon living authors in so easy a fashion; the books of the great dead, however, still give off the steady glow of their genius.

It is indeed a somewhat chastening experience to confront this log-book of the European voyage; can anyone, one wonders, have really read them all? Yes, undoubtedly. Unfortunately I am not among that happy band; there are several gaps which might have been filled in with a little more conscientiousness had not travel and adventure interfered with planned reading. I have not dealt as honestly with Aristotle as he deserves; my antipathy to Milton has made me fearfully unjust to him because he bores me. Yet, as I say, if I had to make this star-map of international literary genius I would certainly swallow my antipathy and base my choice upon the concensus of informed opinion over the ages. Milton, however tiresome to me, is big and his work blocks the light. He would have to go in.

It is obvious, too, that a compilation of this scope could not be exhaustive without turning into something of encyclopaedic proportions, and it should not be unjustly taken to task for the limitations imposed upon it by the scheme. But within these limitations it provides a ground-plan of its subject with conciseness and accuracy – the plain man's vade-mecum to culture. And it should whet the curiosity of the young reader today.

LAWRENCE DURRELL

Editor's Note

What is a great book? I have used three principles in determining my selection: first, outstanding literary merit; second, the most highly original thinking in various branches of knowledge; third, deep spiritual insight. Here and there, rarely, a work reaches the highest standard in two of these categories; and, even more rarely, in all three. But most are pre-eminent examples of one or other of these divisions. (The accomplishment of being a best-seller has, in itself, counted for nothing in advancing a book's candidature for inclusion.)

With these thoughts in mind, I have endeavoured to make my list as broadly based as possible not only as to time and to territory but also in the range covered: thus novels, history, philosophy, psychology, religion, zoology, essays, biography, allegory, burlesque, satire, politics, economics, sociology and travel all have their place.

I have deliberately excluded from my purview plays and books of poems, but two limitations have imposed themselves upon me.

First has been the number of possible inclusions; even if the figure had been considerably higher than one hundred, I should still have been forced to omit many works of outstanding quality. I am deeply conscious of the omissions; but when one is compiling what is in effect a cosmic literary short list, the competition for places is bound to be very, very severe. As usual, when faced with a choice between books of more or less equal merit, I have chosen the one for which I have a personal preference.

Then there has been the problem sometimes imposed by the material itself. There is no doubt about the importance of, say, *Principia Mathematica* or *The General Theory of Relativity*; but I am afraid these works do not lend themselves to popular exposition, and therefore they find no place in this book.

A word about the inclusions. The reader will sometimes appear to be getting extra value for his money, for here and there a chapter will cover more than one book. I have allowed this when two volumes make up an artistic whole (*Gargantua* and *Pantagruel*); when a work is such a well-known trilogy as *The Forsyte Saga* or such a unique tetralogy as *The Alexandria Quartet*; when a number of volumes make up the whole (Gibbon's *Decline and Fall*); and in the case of the Koran and the two portions of the Bible.

The books are in chronological order of writing and, later, of publication. The only exception to this is The Old Testament, where it seemed to me that logical considerations demanded that somewhat out of sequence it should be placed next to The New Testament.

JOHN CANNING

THE ILIAD

HOMER

WERE THE early epic masterpieces, the *Iliad* and the *Odyssey*, composed by one hand or by many? That is the Homeric Question which has intrigued classical scholars down the centuries. Modern opinion is overwhelmingly in favour of the view that there was, indeed, one outstanding poet named Homer among the throng of minstrels in the Greek-speaking world during the eighth or ninth century before Christ – one genius who selected, refined, and embellished the material from the countless lays available in those far-off times and bound them together to produce the *Iliad* and the *Odyssey* in their present form.

As Homer marks the inevitable starting-point for any serious study of European literature, it is necessary to set the scene in which his two imperishable works were given permanent shape. The greatest event of the ancient Greek world was the siege of Troy by the Achaean Greeks, then the most powerful warriors of the eastern Mediterranean. The traditional date of the fall of Troy to the Achaeans is 1184 B.C. But a century or so later a new wave of invaders from northern Europe (usually called the Dorians) threw the whole of this Mediterranean world into turmoil and those Achaeans who were rich enough fled before the storm, moving east across the Aegean Sea as refugees or émigrés, taking with them their way of life – and their songs.

The Achaeans established new settlements in Ionia and merged successfully with the local population until stable city-states grew out of the amalgam. The old habits were gradually submerged in the new civilization, more peaceful but less glorious. What had once been a confederacy of nobles under one great chieftain as undisputed master now gave way to an aristocracy in which all nobles were equal – in short, the monarchic system of government gave way to the aristocratic.

This background of a declining ruling class looking not forward to a glittering future, but backwards to a glorious past, is the key to understanding how the *Iliad* and the *Odyssey* could develop out of the earlier minstrelsy. The émigré Achaean nobles now making the

17

best of their new life in Ionia still clung to their folk-songs and their minstrels but the subject-matter of the lays had to change because the audience would no longer respond to the songs of the uninspiring present or the not-too-happy recent past. They clamoured to hear of the exploits of their traditional heroes, of the days when their adventurous ancestors were masters of their world.

As the art of minstrelsy was passed down from one generation to the next, a repertoire of short lays about the heroic times was built up. But two special themes made certain appeal to an audience nurtured on memories of a magnificent past: (1) The Siege of Troy which was the supreme glory of their heroic ancestry, and (2) the wanderings oversea forced upon their forebears by the all-conquering Dorians. Every well-born Ionian was familiar with the history of the Trojan War and its sequel. But such a splendid theme could not be worthily expressed in short lays. The grandeur of the subject called into being narrative verse which used the traditional saga as raw material but was composed in epic dimensions, magnifying the two favourite themes far beyond historical fact. By this time, too, the minstrel had developed into a more conscious and sensitive artist and had now the sophistication to weave an imaginative spell around one major incident in the traditional story.

Thus the *Iliad* – literally "poem about Ilion," the capital of Troy – deals with one aspect of the siege: the Wrath of Achilles. It opens with a quarrel over captive women between Achilles, the greatest Achaean warrior, and Agamemnon, Commander-in-Chief of the Achaean army which had for nine years been besieging Ilion to recover Helen, wife of Agamemnon's brother, Menelaus, from her abductor, Paris, son of the Trojan king, Priam.

Agamemnon has given offence to Chryses, a priest of Apollo, by refusing to let him ransom his daughter, who is Agamemnon's slave. Chryses asks Apollo to punish the Greeks and the god sends a plague on them. Achilles calls an assembly and a seer declares that the girl must be restored to her father and an offering made to Apollo. Agamemnon reluctantly agrees but, to compensate himself, seizes Briseis, the slave-concubine of Achilles, who sulkily retires to his tent and refuses to take further part in the war. He appeals to his divine mother, Thetis, who then persuades Zeus, ruler of the gods, to exact vengeance for her son. This is the substance of Book I.

Agamemnon dreams that he will capture Troy with his next assault and confides this to his generals. He decides to make trial of his army's enthusiasm for the siege by offering the soldiery the choice of winning Troy or returning home immediately, and he is horrified when the men make gleeful preparation to depart. His dream, of course, is a trick by Zeus to cut Agamemnon's pride down to size. It takes all the guile of Odysseus to restore the army's discipline (Book 2). This book sets out a catalogue of the Greek and Trojan forces and it is argued that this was an insertion put in later by someone other than Homer.

Now the two armies advance toward each other (Book 3), but the battle is prevented by a proposal from the Trojans, Paris and Hector, that Paris and Menelaus settle the issue by fighting a duel. If Paris is the winner, he can keep Helen and the Greeks must go home; if Menelaus, Helen and all her property are to be restored to the Greeks and peace made. Paris fights, and is defeated by, Menelaus but Aphrodite the goddess of love saves him and returns him to Troy.

The truce which followed the duel is broken (Book 4) and Agamemnon reviews his army but quarrels with Diomedes who distinguishes himself in a desperate engagement with the Trojans, even taking on the goddess Aphrodite when she tries to rescue her son, Aeneas (later immortalized by Vergil), and the god Ares when he rushes to aid the Trojans (Book 5). Hector now appeals to his mother, Hecuba, to intercede with the goddess Athena to support the Trojan cause (Book 6). Hector talks with Helen in Ilion, sends an SOS to Paris to arm himself and sally forth. Finally – in a most moving passage – Hector speaks to his wife, Andromache, and his son, Astyanax, in the tone of a man who knows his days are numbered. In Book 7 Hector and Paris return to the battlefield and Hector challenges any Greek to meet him in single combat. The mighty Ajax is chosen by lot for this encounter and the duel ends inconclusively, with Ajax the winner on points. Another truce follows during which the Trojans propose that Paris be allowed to keep Helen but only on condition that he gives up her property. This peace feeler is rejected with scorn by the Greeks.

Now Zeus comes down on the side of the Trojans and forbids the other gods to take any part in the fray (Book 8). After a day-long engagement, the Greeks retire to their camp. Agamemnon is much discouraged but, on Nestor's advice, sends Ajax and Odysseus to Achilles with a forgive-and-forget offer. The Commander-in-Chief hopes to wheedle his greatest warrior back into the campaign by returning his slave-concubine, Briseis, compensating him for the insult with generous gifts – and the hand of one of his daughters in marriage. But Achilles (Book 9) makes contemptuous refusal of all reconciliation attempts.

Agamemnon, sleepless and worried, calls his leaders into council.

Nestor suggests that two scouts be sent forth to reconnoitre the Trojan position. Diomedes at once volunteers and requests that Odysseus accompany him. On their dangerous patrol they capture a Trojan scout who reveals that reinforcements from Thebes have reached the Trojan army. The intrepid Greek commandos raid the reinforcements under cover of darkness, kill their leader and a dozen others, seize their horses and ride back to the Greek camp (Book 10).

Next morning (Book 11) the Greek army advances again and the Trojans join battle. Agamemnon, Diomedes and Odysseus are all wounded and the Greeks fall back into camp. At last the conscience of Achilles seems to be stirring as he sends his dear friend Patroclus to Nestor's camp for an account of the casualties. Nestor rails at Achilles's obstinacy and appeals to Patroclus to persuade him at least to send his men into action and, indeed, to gird his friend in his armour to deceive the Trojans into believing that Achilles is back in the fight.

Meanwhile the Trojans are attacking the Greek camp and Hector breaches their first line of defence (Book 12), forcing them back to their ships on the beach where Ajax keeps Hector in check (Book 13). Zeus, watching the battle from Mount Ida, is lulled to sleep by Hera, and the Trojans, without their divine supporter, are driven out of the Greek lines (Book 14), Hector being knocked unconscious by Ajax. Zeus awakens to the Trojans' danger and bids Apollo revive Hector to renew the assault. The Greeks are again driven back on their ships (Book 15) and seem to be near defeat when Patroclus hastens back to coax Achilles into lending him his armour. Now fighting with the strength of ten, Patroclus helps the Greeks to thrust back the Trojans but he foolishly pursues the Trojans to their city walls from which he is thrust away by Apollo himself, who stuns and disarms him. Then Hector steps in and kills him, stripping off Achilles's armour and wearing it. The Greeks manage to reclaim the body of Patroclus and beat a desperate retreat back to camp. These see-sawing fortunes of war occupy two books (16 and 17) and the following book (18) deals with the arousing of Achilles, who is crazed with grief at the death of his beloved Patroclus and has to be comforted by his mother, Thetis, who emerges from the sea.

Achilles goes to the limits of the Greek defence-line and scares the Trojans off with his fearsome battle-cry. But Hector is now brimming over with confidence and ignores all warnings by daring the Greeks to come out of camp and give battle. Thetis has persuaded the god Hephaistos (Vulcan to the Romans) to forge new arms and an elaborate shield for Achilles. The following day Achilles is impatient to get to grips with the Trojans but Odysseus insists on his reconciliation with Agamemnon, who apologizes for his own churlish behaviour. The women of the camp lament over the body of Patroclus. Achilles refuses to eat, but his mother, Thetis, puts nectar and ambrosia in his bosom and he arms himself for battle (Book 19).

The climax of the epic is at hand and Zeus calls the gods into council, then gives them permission to support which side they choose. The gods materialize on earth and their intervention confuses the issue, but still the Trojans fall back before Achilles. Aeneas faces up to him but he is snatched away in time by Poseidon (Neptune) because his descendants are destined to become the lords of Troy. It was no doubt this book (20) which decided Vergil to make Aeneas the hero of his epic, the Aeneid. The Trojans are now in full flight and Achilles almost dams up the river Xanthos with their dead. The gods on the rival sides now fight each other (Book 21). Achilles returns toward Troy and finds Hector alone outside the walls, ashamed to enter his city because of the failure of his battle plans. As Achilles approaches him his courage fails and he runs round the walls three times, hotly pursued by the "fleet-footed Achilles" (Homer's standing epithet for him). At last he stands at bay, finally making a desperate last charge on Achilles and falls mortally wounded. He makes a dying prayer to Achilles to return his body to Priam, his father, for burial but the plea is contemptuously rejected. Instead Achilles ties Hector's corpse to the rim of his chariot and rides back to the camp dragging it behind him in full view of the Trojans on the walls, including Hector's widow, Andromache, who did not even know he was outside (Book 22).

That night the ghost of Patroclus asks Achilles for speedy burial that he may enter Hades. Next day a most elaborate funeral is prepared, with twelve prisoners-of-war burned on the pyre – the only case of human sacrifices in all Homer – and athletic contests of all types (Book 23). Achilles presides over these funeral games and distributes prizes. The body of Hector is ceremoniously dragged round the tomb of Patroclus each day for eleven days until the gods decide to intervene to save the body from corruption and mutilation. Priam goes to the Greek camp by night and pleads with Achilles to ransom him his son's body. Achilles is persuaded by Thetis to give way to this plea and he receives the old man with sympathy. The epic ends with a reference to Hector's funeral.

The key books of the *Iliad* are the first, which gives the motive for the action; the ninth, in which Achilles, who had previously had the right of the quarrel with Agamemnon, puts himself in the wrong by scorning a genuine offer of reconciliation; the sixteenth, in which the stubbornness of Achilles really brings about the death of his dearest friend; and the twenty-second, in which Hector is humiliated. It must be noticed that the characters of the epic are real and not sentimental inventions but their stature is larger than life – Achilles and Hector are not romanticized; Helen, who was to become a literary sex symbol in later ages, is given no sex-appeal as such by Homer. In this way the poet heightened the prestige of the descendants of his characters, the rulers of Ionic Greece. But his heroes are drawn with full consciousness of their humanity and feebleness in the face of death.

Above all, the simplicity and integrity of the narrative, the pace of the action and the overall magnificence of the composition impart the highest quality to the *Iliad* and make it one of the world's greatest literary treasures.

HERODOTUS'S *HISTORY*

THE MAN who is called the Father of History was a Greek, although he was born not in Greece but in one of the Greek cities that were then spread out along the coasts of Asia Minor. His name was Herodotus, his birthplace was Halicarnassus, and he was born between 490 and 480 B.C. This was between the first and the second of the two invasions by the Persians of the Greek mainland of which he was to write in his *History*.

When he was born, Halicarnassus was one of the Greek colonies which had been conquered by the Persians, and whose efforts to recover their independence was a prime cause of the great wars with the Persian Empire. When as a consequence of the repulse of the vast army of Xerxes, the Persian emperor, in 480 B.C. these Greek cities were liberated, there ensued a period of political instability, and Herodotus as a young man was forced to go into exile. Since his family was well-off, he had the means for travelling, and for a number of years he travelled in the lands of the eastern Mediterranean, including Egypt and Palestine, and inland as far as Mesopotamia.

At this time he probably had in mind the writing of a history of the great war with Persia, but subsequently he enlarged his plan, and he visited Egypt for a second time, penetrating as far south as Assuan and westwards into Cyrenaica, and also ventured into the region of the Black Sea, where he made contact with the Greek colonies there and also the tribes of Scythian barbarians. He visited Athens on more than one occasion, where he made the acquaintance of Pericles, the great Athenian statesman, and is said to have given in 446 B.C. a public reading of part of his *History*, and to have been awarded a present of ten talents (about £2,000) from the public treasury. In his later years he settled in the Greek colony of Thurii in southern Italy, but he does not seem to have ever visited Rome or any of the Etruscan cities. There is no mention in his book of any event later than 429 B.C., and it is assumed that he died four or five years later.

Much of his life, then, was spent in travelling, and his travels he undertook for the purposes of his *History*. To begin with, as indicated above, he had no idea of extending his theme beyond the great war, but as time went on and his travels extended over a large

23

part of the known world he decided to incorporate in his narrative such information as he could collect on the history, geography, ethnography, religion and social customs, et cetera, of the peoples involved in the great struggle. The result was one of the most extraordinary works of antiquity. Thoroughly deserving as he is of his title of the Father of History, he might equally well be called the Father of Geography. Obviously he was a man of the most inquiring disposition, and almost everything that he heard was grist for his mill. The book is written in Greek, in the Ionian dialect spoken by the Greek colonies on the western shores of Asia Minor, and the style is singularly simple, clear and graceful.

While there were Greek historians before Herodotus, other writers of geographical descriptions, and other tellers of popular tales, it is his distinction that he combined in his composition all three elements. This is well displayed in his first book, which has been given the name of "Clio, the Muse of History".

The book opens with a statement that it is a report of what Herodotus of Halicarnassus has been able to discover, made in order that the great and wondrous deeds performed by both Greeks and Barbarians (that is, by all who were not Greeks) may not be forgotten. Then comes a lengthy account of the establishment of the monarchy in Lydia, the central portion of Asia Minor, followed by the dramatic story of its overthrow by Cyrus, the Persian emperor. Also included in this historical portion is the conquest of the Greek colonies in Ionia by the Persians and of Cyrus's eventual overthrow and death in battle with the Massagetae, a tribe of barbarians in the neighbourhood of the Caspian Sea.

Interpolated in the historical (or professedly historical) matter are a number of excellent stories. But fascinating as they are, these stories are not so valuable as the paragraphs in which Herodotus describes the manners and customs of some of the many peoples which enter into his narrative.

First the Lydians. These folk (we are assured) have customs very like those of the Greeks, except that they bring up their daughters to become harlots. They were the first to mint money of gold and silver, and they were the first traders. They invented games with dice and knucklebones, ball games, and indeed all kinds of games except draughts. And this they did when there was a sore famine in their land, and they had to do something to pass the time and make them forget the pangs of hunger.

Next the Persians. "According to my own knowledge, the Persians observe the following customs." They do not erect images and altars and temples to the gods as the Greeks do, but offer up sacrifices to the Supreme God on the tops of high mountains. Birthdays are celebrated with a feast. They are moderate eaters, but have a partiality for dainties in preference to main dishes. They are much addicted to wine; and they have a very sensible rule, that a man is not bound by any arrangement that he may have made when he was in his cups unless he confirms it in the morning when he is sober again. They have as many wives as they like, and as many concubines as they can afford in addition. They are proud of their large families, and take great pains with the education of their children. They are very straight in their dealings, and consider it most disgraceful to tell a lie. More than any other people that Herodotus knows of, they are ready to adopt any foreign custom that seems to them worth copying.

Of all the cities that Herodotus visited, Babylon was perhaps the most remarkable, and he is most enthusiastic in his account. The fertility of the countryside was such that he refrains from telling all he knows about it, for fear of being disbelieved. As for the people, they wear long linen tunics with a woollen shirt underneath, keep their hair cut short, and anoint their bodies with sweet-smelling perfumes. Each man has his own personal seal, and carries a staff topped with the representation of an apple or a rose or an eagle, or some such thing. Only one feature of Babylonian life he considers shameful. Every native woman (he asserts) was required, once in her lifetime, to repair to the temple of Mylitta, the goddess of love, and offer herself as a prostitute; not until a stranger had put silver in her lap and possessed her was she allowed to return home.

Herodotus's second book is largely taken up with a detailed description of Egypt, a country which he knew well. "It possesses more wonders than any other country," he remarks, "and that is why so much space must be devoted to it." Not only is the climate distinctive, but even more so is the River Nile, on which the life of the country and its people depends. He pays tribute to the excellence of the Egyptian calendar, and praises the people's inventiveness. He acknowledges their deep interest in religion, and allows that the Greeks got their names for the gods from Egypt. He describes their strange animal worships, and goes into detail in his account of the embalming processes. He tells stories (and strange stories they are) of how the Pyramids came to be raised above the desert sands. Then he points out some of the many ways in which the Egyptians differ from other peoples, such as, for example, that the men carry burdens on their heads and women on their shoulders; that women engage in business while their menfolk stay at home and do the weaving; that they write from right to left and have two scripts, one sacred and one for everyday purposes; that they are very fond of cats and dogs and when they die give them a regular funeral; and that while a man wears two garments, usually of linen, a woman has only one.

From this delightfully intimate picture of the Egyptians among whom he had spent so many happy months, Herodotus goes on to describe the conquest of the country by the Persians under Cambyses, from which it is an easy transition to the main theme of his *History*, the policy of aggressive imperialism pursued by Darius after he had succeeded Cambyses on the Persian throne. Three books are devoted to the campaigns of Darius against the Scythians, the Libyans, and the Greek cities of Ionia, and then we are told how, having formed a powerful navy and a vast army, Darius ordered it across the Hellespont into Europe. Thrace and Macedonia were subdued, and Greece was invaded. And then, on the plain of Marathon, a band of 10,000 Athenians under Miltiades, aided by about a thousand from the allied city of Plataea, confronted the Barbarian hordes and utterly routed them. The victors, says Herodotus, "followed the Persians in their flight, cutting them to pieces, till, reaching the shore, they plunged into the sea and attacked the ships". So ended the battle of Marathon (490 B.C.), one of the decisive battles of the world, for if the Persians had been victorious the Greek experiments in political democracy and intellectual liberty would have been impossible.

Enraged at this reverse, Darius planned an even more powerful expedition against the Greek states, but he died when the preparations were far from complete. He was succeeded by his son Xerxes, who decided to lead the invasion in person. An enormous force was assembled at the Dardanelles – Herodotus says that the land forces alone numbered 1,700,000 men – and there Xerxes reviewed them before they passed over into Europe. It is Herodotus who tells us that the emperor wept when he considered that, of all that enormous army, not one would be alive in a hundred years' time, and that he had ordered the Hellespont to be flogged because of a violent storm which had endangered his ships. On the day chosen for the crossing, "Xerxes when the sun was up, poured a libation into the sea out of a golden cup and prayed to the Sun that nothing should prevent him from conquering Europe up to its furthest limits. After having prayed, he threw the cup into the Hellespont, and with it a golden bowl, and a Persian sword, but I have been unable to determine whether he did these things as an offering to the Sun, or because he repented of having scourged the sea and offered these gifts by way of compensation". So the mighty host passed over from Asia into Europe, and Herodotus's description of the regiments and their equipment must have owed a great deal to eye-witnesses' accounts.

In the van were ten thousand Persian cavalry, wearing crowns on their heads, iron breastplates, and "loose trousers". Then on the second day followed a promiscuous host drawn from all the nations of the Persian realm—Medes dressed after the manner of the Persians, Assyrians in brass helmets, Bactrians in turbans, Scythians in pointed caps and trousers, Indians in garments of cotton, Caspians in goatskin mantles, Arabs in girdled cloaks, Ethiopians in lions' skins, curly-haired Libyans in leather jerkins, Phrygians, Thracians, Bithynians ... For seven days and seven nights the host passed over, "without halting at all".

The invaders moved on. Thrace and Macedonia were occupied, and at length Greece itself was reached. And now one day a message reached Xerxes that a band of Spartan Greeks were holding the Pass of Thermopylae. "Xerxes sent a scout on horseback to see how many they were, and what they were doing. When the scout rode up to the camp, the Spartans happened to be posted outside the wall; and some of the men he saw were performing gymnastic exercises, and others were combing their hair." When Xerxes heard this, he was astounded: he did not understand that the Spartans were displaying a sublime contempt for death, and were preparing to sell their lives as dearly as possible. Six thousand Spartans against perhaps four hundred thousand Persians – but their captain was the heroic Leonidas, and they fought and died where they stood.

The Persian war-machine rolled on again, and most of Greece was overrun; Athens was evacuated by its defenders, and the Acropolis was captured and most of the buildings on it burnt. But the Greek fleet was intact, and in a great sea-fight in the narrow waters between Salamis and the mainland the Greek ships under Themistocles put to rout the vast navy of the Persian invader (480 B.C.). "And when the battle was over, the Greeks hauled ashore at Salamis all the wrecks and broken pieces of ships they could find there, and held themselves ready for a renewal of the fight, expecting that the Persian king would make use of the ships that had survived. But Xerxes ..." – well, to put it short, Xerxes had had enough, and went back to Asia, leaving the struggle to be maintained by his generals.

Within a few years, as Herodotus describes in his ninth and final book, they, too, had been worsted, and only a fragment of the original mighty host succeeded in recrossing the Dardanelles. The triumphant Greeks followed hard on their heels, and the *History* draws to its conclusion with an account of the Greek capture of the city of Sestos, the last Persian stronghold on European soil. So the "Persian Wars" that Herodotus described with such dignity and pathos and patriotic fervour came to an end, and Europe was saved. For though the struggle between Greeks and Persians continued for a long time, henceforth it was the Greeks who were the aggressors.

Great wars provide historians with exceptional opportunities, and it may be said of Herodotus that he proved fully equal to his theme. And like all truly great historians he felt that he was describing something more than a conflict of peoples, a clash of empires, the competition of rival systems of government, civilizations and cultures. Throughout his tremendous narrative we are reminded of his firm conviction that over and above the battle broods the spirit of Nemesis, that there is a moral law decreed and enforced by Providence or the gods, against which even so powerful and vainglorious a monarch as Xerxes is opposed in vain.

THE HISTORY OF
THE PELOPONNESIAN WAR
THUCYDIDES

ALL THAT is known about Thucydides, the founder-father of critical history, is what he himself tells us – and that is precious little. It is remarkable that one of the greatest of the Greek immortals should attract a host of classical imitators, but no biographers.

He was an Athenian born between the years 470 and 460 B.C. in the Golden Age of literature, art and thought – the century of Aeschylus, Sophocles, Euripides, Aristophanes, Herodotus and Socrates. Yet in the *History of the Peloponnesian War*, which has earned Thucydides his place in the Pantheon of Greek letters, there is not a mention of the works of these glorious contemporaries. For Thucydides dedicated himself to recording the events of a conflict between tiny states, smaller in size and population than most English counties. He was utterly absorbed in the fortunes and leaders of a handful of towns no bigger than many a London suburb.

But the measure of his greatness as a historian lies in this: that his reader quickly falls victim to the style and method of the work and is almost persuaded that he is participating in current events, so ennobled is the theme by the genius of the writer. And this is because Thucydides had compiled a contemporary history of the drama through which he himself lived. Although he was able to revise some passages after the war, while he was actually describing its course he did not know what the end of the story was to be.

Thucydides was in his thirties when the Peloponnesian War broke out in 431 B.C. between rival alliances led by Athens on the one side and Sparta on the other. In the second year of this twenty-seven-year struggle Athens was ravaged by a great plague. Thucydides himself fell victim to it (almost certainly typhus) but made a full recovery and in 424 he was given command of an Athenian fleet. But he proved to be a failure as a naval tactician. His fleet was defeated by the Spartan, Brasidas. Thucydides was recalled to Athens, put on trial and sentenced to exile – an exile which lasted until the final defeat of Athens and the peace of 404.

29

All that is known of his twenty-year exile is that he visited many of the warring Peloponnesian states collecting material for his history. The work is arranged in eight books and stops in 411 – six to seven years before the war's end. It has even been conjectured that the historian met a violent death because his writing terminates abruptly in the middle of a paragraph. The *History* cannot be classified as a mere chronicle of the war: it is also a political handbook of the times with dissertations on the merits of democracy and imperialism, speeches put into the mouths of political leaders which deal with the great issues of any age: When can war be justified? Is a compromise peace better than unconditional surrender? Is voluntary military service or conscription to be preferred in a democracy?

The twentieth-century student cannot fail to appreciate the aptness of many of the discussions to the great debates of our own times. Thucydides allows the story to tell itself, content to record the events without comment, then bringing on the actors in the drama to unfold the situation as they see it. The historian never intrudes his own opinions but his comments are made through the speeches which are all set in the same style. "I made the speakers say what I thought the occasion demanded," he explains.

Sparta and Athens had led the Greek states against their great invader, Persia, and at one period of the second invasion (Marathon, 490) Athens stood alone. Fortified by her example, the others rallied and the Persians were finally driven off in 480. With the danger past Sparta withdrew from the victorious alliance leaving Athens at its head and, almost inevitably, an Athenian Empire came into being. Many of the larger states became uneasy at the growth of Athenian economic power which seemed to some to threaten the entire Greek mainland. This threat was removed by a thirty-year peace treaty between Sparta and Athens which then left the mainland alone and concentrated on building up her power among the islands and coastal towns which she could control by her command of the sea.

Athens thus became head of the Delian League in which a number of Greek states banded together for defence against the menace of another Persian invasion, taking an oath not to secede from the alliance. But some did secede and Athens reduced them to subjection. Most of the states contributed treasure to the League, the amount being decided by Athens which controlled the treasury. Soon Athens became the religious and intellectual centre of Greece. This attempt at unity under one leadership was new to Greece – and dangerous to Sparta and old-established Greek political institutions.

The Peloponnesian states, particularly Corinth, watched the grow-

ing importance of Athens with increasing jealousy. They pressed
Sparta to assume the leadership of a Peloponnesian alliance which
declared war on Athens in 431.

That, in bald outline, is the background to the events which
Thucydides describes. He contrasts the policy and temperament of
Sparta and Athens through the mouth of the Corinthian delegate
urging Sparta to go to war:

"The Athenians are revolutionary and their designs are characterized by swiftness alike in conception and execution; you have a
genius for keeping what you have got, accompanied by a total want
of invention and, when forced to act, you never go far enough. They
are adventurous beyond their power and daring beyond their judgment and in danger they are sanguine; your way is to attempt less
than your power justifies, to mistrust even what your judgment sanc-
tions and to convince yourself that there will be no end to your
dangers.

"They are prompt, you procrastinate; they are never at home, you
are never from it; they hope by leaving it to extend their acquisitions,
you fear any new enterprise will endanger what you possess. They
are swift to follow up a success and slow to recoil from a reverse;
their bodies they spend ungrudgingly in their country's cause; their
intellect they jealously husband to be employed in her service. A
scheme unexecuted is with them a positive loss, a successful enterprise
a comparative failure. If they fail in some attempt, they compensate
for the miscarriage by conceiving new hopes – unlike any other
people, with them to hope is to have, so quick are they to put an idea
into practice.

"So they toil on in trouble and danger all the days of their life,
with little opportunity for enjoying, always engaged in getting –
their only idea of a holiday is to do what the occasion demands and
to them laborious occupation is less of a misfortune than inaction and
rest. In a word, one might truly say that they were born into the
world to take no rest themselves and to give none to others."

(To many who remember the pre-war tensions this could have
been a speech to the British Parliament about Nazi Germany in
1939.)

Then the Corinthian delegate analyses Sparta:

"Such is Athens, your antagonist. And yet, Lacedaemonians, you
still delay – your principle is to treat others fairly and, while not
harming others, to defend your interests at no expense to yourselves;
you do not realize that men secure peace not by using their power
justly but by making it clear that they will not allow others to wrong

them. Your ways are old-fashioned as compared with theirs. As in the arts, so in politics, the new gets the better of the old; in quiet times conservative and traditional ways are best, but men compelled to meet new situations need to employ new methods. Thus it happens that the vast experience of Athens has carried her further than you on the path of innovation . . ."

Thucydides defends Athens against the charge of empire-building, arguing that there were no provinces under the heel of Athenian governors and that free institutions were not interfered with in the other states. But the causes of war 2,000 years ago were strikingly similar to the causes of war in the twentieth century. Athens did not want war. Nor did Sparta. But Corinth, the commercial rival of Athens with colonies to the west, holding the isthmus between the Peloponnese and the rest of Greece, and with access to two seas, found herself threatened on all sides by Athenian competition. So she proceeded to work up tensions – and tension begets fear and mistrust.

The result was a conflict between two types of Greek – the energetic and inventive revolutionary against the cautious, slow-moving conservative – and Thucydides points up these differences by analysing the characters of four men: Themistocles, the Athenian hero of the Second Persian War, Pericles, Brasidas and Alcibiades.

The historian was also deeply interested in the technical aspects of the war, for instance the limitations of the traditional heavy-armed land fighting – the Greek soldiers being mainly peasant-farmers who dared not be too long away from their fields. The Athenians had the advantage of being able to import all the food they needed. Thucydides also examined other military problems which have intrigued the captains and the kings down the ages: the difficulties of siege warfare, and of landing an army from ships against an enemy on shore.

But the major fascination of Thucydides for the modern mind is the way in which he uses his speeches to explain the motives and ambitions of the leading men in their states. Indeed he proclaims that one of his aims in writing the *History* was the study of the human spirit in time of war. And the summit of his achievement was surely in the "Funeral Oration" delivered by Pericles to the Athenians gathered for the first public funeral of those who had fallen in the war.

Imagine the setting for the occasion. The entire population of the state is come together to do homage to their dead. The bones of the fallen are exposed on a covered platform for three days during which anyone may place personal offerings at their side. On the third day they are laid in ten coffins of cypress, one for each tribe, every war-

Somewhere in the dim beginnings of European literature stands the mysterious figure of the author of those grandest monuments of Ancient Greece, *The Iliad* and *The Odyssey*. Who was this supreme master of poetic creation? Some scholars have argued that the epics were the work of a succession of bards, but the general opinion today is that there was "one Homer" who lived probably in one of the Greek colonies on the western shores of Asia Minor. Traditionally he was blind, as is suggested in this antique bust (*right*). Both poems have for their subject the war between Greeks and Trojans for the possession of the city of Troy, not far from the Dardanelles; and (*above*) we have an imaginative representation by a Renaissance artist of the death of Hector, the Trojan hero. (*Below*) An ancient sculpture of Achilles, the valiant captain of the Greeks.

Among the great books of the world the Bible holds a place of unchallengeable eminence, comprising as it does the holy scriptures of two world faiths, Judaism and Christianity. Within its covers are a number of books of very varying authorship and date and content, and of these there have come down to us some thousands of MSS. Among the most important are the great codices (i.e. books, not scrolls), written in Greek capital letters without breaks between the words; *above* is a page from the Codex Sinaiticus, one of the great treasures of the British Museum. Of the innumerable translations of the Bible, some of the finest are in Tudor English. (*Left*) A reproduction of the title-page from the Great Bible, a copy of which King Henry VIII ordered in 1539 should be placed in English parish churches so that any man might "commodiously resort to the same and read it".

rior's bones in the coffin of his tribe, which are then put on carriages and driven to the grave. One empty bed covered with a winding-sheet is also carried along for the missing whose bodies could not be recovered. By the graveside are gathered the womenfolk of the dead, bewailing. When at last the coffins are laid in the earth, Pericles steps from the graveside on to a high platform built for the occasion so that his voice may carry as far as possible over the crowd.

The words put into his mouth by Thucydides have carried to the ends of the earth and through the centuries. They are among the noblest ever conceived by man. Here is Pericles speaking on the ideal of liberal democracy:

"Our constitution is named a democracy because it is in the hands not of the few but of the many. But our laws secure equal justice for all in their private disputes, and our public opinion welcomes and honours talent in every branch of achievement, not for any sectional reason but on grounds of excellence alone. And, as we give free play to all in our public life, so we carry the same spirit into our daily relations with one another. We have no black looks or angry words for our neighbour if he enjoys himself in his own way, and we abstain from the little acts of churlishness which, though they leave no mark, yet cause annoyance to whoso notes them. Open and friendly in our private intercourse, in our public acts we keep strictly within the control of law. We acknowledge the restraint of reverence; we are obedient to whomsoever is set in authority, and to the laws, more especially to those which offer protection to the oppressed and those unwritten ordinances whose transgression brings admitted shame."

And on patriotism:

"Fix your eyes on the greatness of Athens as you have it before you day by day, fall in love with her, and when you feel her great, remember that this greatness was won by men with courage, with knowledge of their duty, and with a sense of honour in action, who, if they failed in any ordeal, disdained to deprive the city of their services, but sacrificed their lives as the best offerings on her behalf. So they gave their bodies to the commonwealth and received, each for his own memory, praise that will never die, and with it the grandest of all sepulchres, not that in which their mortal bones are laid, but a home in the minds of men where their glory remains fresh to stir to speech or action as the occasion comes by. For the whole earth is the sepulchre of famous men; and their story is not graven only on stone over their native earth, but lives on far away, without visible symbol, woven into the stuff of other men's lives . . ."

But Pericles, perhaps the ablest democratic leader of all time, was, like many another after him, to experience the fickleness of public opinion. With their population scythed by the plague and their lands ravaged by their enemies, the anger of the Athenians welled up against him and, although he dissuaded them from suing for peace with Sparta, they bridled at his policy and fined him heavily after the early reverses. He himself lost two sons to the plague and died two years and six months after the outbreak of the war. The shrewdness of his policy became apparent only after his death.

He had urged the Athenians to play a waiting game, to pin all their faith to their navy, to attempt no new conquests and to buttress their city against any possible assault. But after his death the Athenians did the opposite, allowing (writes Thucydides) "private ambitions and interests to lead them into projects which, if successful, would only conduce to the honour and advantage of individuals and, by failing, brought certain disaster on the country in the war".

Analysing the causes of the Athenian defeat in a passage which was clearly written after the war's end in 404, the historian records: "Pericles, by his rank, ability and known integrity, was able to exercise an independent control over the masses – to lead them instead of being led by them; for, as he never sought power by improper means, he was never compelled to flatter them. On the contrary, he enjoyed so high a reputation that he could afford to anger them by contradiction. When he saw them unseasonably and insolently elated, he would, with a word, reduce them to alarm; on the other hand, if they fell victims to a panic, he could at once restore their confidence. . . . With his successors it was different. More on a level with one another, and each grasping at supremacy, they ended by committing even the conduct of state affairs to the whims of the multitude. This, as might have been expected in a great imperial state, produced a host of blunders. . . ."

Pericles was an aristocrat, a friend of philosophers and scientists whose interests he shared; his successors were drawn from a very different stock – one a flax merchant, another a sheep dealer. Then there emerged Cleon, a tanner, who although hard-headed and in the main honest, had little education and no idealism. Under him the Athenian conception of imperialism became brutalized.

The deaths of Cleon and the great Spartan general, Brasidas, at the battle of Amphipolis in the tenth year of the war brought a peace treaty which was, in effect, a victory for Athens, as under its terms each side recovered what had been lost in the hostilities. Immediately after the peace treaty a fifty-year alliance was signed between Athens and Sparta. But all this did not bring peace. Sparta's allies felt that they had been betrayed and two of the largest, Corinth and Boeotia, refused to acknowledge the treaty. Varying combinations of states attempted to cement alliances, war and peace parties spread throughout all Greece – in Athens the war party was led by Alcibiades who forged new alliances which led to a renewal of the war with Sparta in 418 B.C. and from that date the Athenian Empire and cause crumbled to final defeat.

The sixth and seventh books of the *History* deal mainly with the disastrous Athenian campaign in Sicily. Thucydides reaches the height of his powers in a brilliant exposition of the failure of a tremendous undertaking because of blundering politicians at home and generals abroad. After the retreat and annihilation of the Athenian army at Syracuse, her supremacy at sea was lost, her allies were in revolt and Persia supported Sparta. Nonetheless Athens fought on until 404 when gross carelessness by her naval commanders led to the destruction of her fleet, Sparta succeeded in closing the Dardanelles, cutting off all imports from Athens, and starved the city into surrender.

The eighth and final book of the *History* takes the war to 411 and is generally regarded as the least interesting. It obviously had not been revised by the historian and ends in the middle of a sentence. It is perhaps fitting to leave his masterly work by quoting from it the everlasting principles of historical research laid down by Thucydides 2,400 years ago:

"The way most men deal with traditions, even those of their own country, is to accept them all without applying any critical test – so unlaborious to most is the search for truth, so readily do they accept what comes first to hand.

"The historian must not be misled by the exaggerated fancies of the poets, or by the tales of chroniclers who seek to please the ear rather than speak the truth. Their accounts cannot be tested by him and most of the facts in the lapse of ages have passed into the region of romance. At such a distance of time he must make up his mind to be satisfied with conclusions resting upon the clearest evidence which can be had.

"Of the events of the war I have not ventured to speak from any chance observation or according to any notion of my own – I have described nothing but what I either saw myself or learned from others of whom I made the most careful and particular inquiry. . . .

"My history is an everlasting possession, not the showpiece of an hour."

THE BHAGAVADGITA

FOR TWO thousand years, more or less, the *Bhagavadgita* has been the most cherished of all the sacred scriptures of the Hindu people. The name means The Song of the Lord, and the book forms part of the *Mahabharata*, the earlier and longer of the two great epics that have come down to us from ancient India. But only a very small part, since the *Mahabharata* is the longest poem in the world, about seven times as long as Homer's *Iliad* and the *Odyssey* put together, whereas the *Gita*, as the *Bhagavadgita* is often called for short, is only about the length of St. John's Gospel in the New Testament.

Like all the literature of ancient India, it is anonymous, but its author was almost certainly a Brahmin, a member of the caste which includes men of education and culture and religious vision. Sometimes it is said to have been the work of a certain Vyasa, but this man (if he ever lived) was the compiler of the vast epic in which the *Gita* is embedded. As for its date, the opinions are very conflicting. Up to a generation or so ago it was generally stated that the little book was written after the commencement of the Christian era, and there were some who thought that they could detect in its lines some traces of Christian teaching or influence. But the view now held by most scholars is that it is definitely pre-Christian. Dr. Sarvepalli Radhakrishnan, for instance, the philosopher-statesman who is now President of the Republic of India, states in his translation of the *Gita* that it may be assigned in all probability to the fifth century before Christ, although the text may have received many additions since.

In form the *Gita* is a dramatic poem, something after the manner of the book of Job in the Bible, or the Dialogues of Plato. The chief speaker is Krishna, who is "the Lord" of the title – or, as the term is variously rendered in translation, the Adorable One, the Divine One, the Blessed One, *et cetera*. To begin with, when the poem opens, he is the charioteer of a young Indian prince named Arjuna, who is his cousin, and their conversation takes place in the chariot that has been made ready to engage in battle. But as the poem proceeds there is a gradual revelation of Krishna's real essence, until at length he discloses himself in the full glory of Godhead.

Before we examine the *Gita* in detail we should learn something of the immense epic of which it is a part.

Mahabharata means "the great war of the Bharatas", and the poem tells the story of a war between two celebrated families of Indian princes who all claimed descent from a probably legendary monarch named Bharata. Their country was the great plain of Hastinapura, in northern India, where there was a kingdom ruled over by the head of their house. When the poem opens the kingdom is being ruled by a regent on behalf of his two nephews, Dhritarashtra and Pandu. The former was blind and was therefore deemed incapable of reigning. When they came of age, Pandu became king, but after a time retired into solitude in the Himalaya mountains and there died. Dhritarashtra thereupon became king in his turn, notwithstanding his blindness. He was the father of a hundred sons, commonly called the Kuru princes, all the sons of one mother; they were all bad, and the worst of them all was the eldest, Duryodhana, who was bold, crafty, and malicious. King Pandu had had five sons by his two wives, and the Pandu princes were as good as their cousins the Kurus were evil. But their uncle, King Dhritarashtra, showed them great kindness, bringing them up with his own sons and intending to give them a share in the kingdom when they were old enough. The best of the Pandu princes was Arjuna, the middle one in age, who is the real hero of the *Mahabharata*; he is revealed as a young man of dauntless bravery, yet generous and tender-hearted and easily moved to compassion.

As the two sets of princes grew to manhood there was increasing jealousy and hostility between them, and at length the Pandavas, as the Pandu five were called, were tricked out of their prospects by the wily Duryodhana and were treated with such contumely that they had no alternative but to take up arms against their cousins. This brings us to the end of the fifth chapter, or *parvan* to use the technical term, of the *Mahabharata*, and it is in the sixth that we meet with the *Bhagavadgita*.

War has been declared, and the two contending armies of Kurus and Pandavas are supposed to be drawn up in battle array. The place is the great plain of Kurukshetra, in the neighbourhood of the modern city of Delhi. Prince Arjuna is seated in his war-chariot, with Krishna standing beside him. Krishna, we are given to understand, has refused to take up arms on either side, since he is closely related to all the princes engaged, but he has consented to serve as Arjuna's charioteer and to aid him with his advice. And now all is ready. The trumpets are blowing, the war-cries burst from many a thousand throats, arms flash in the sun. All eyes are on Arjuna, whose responsibility it is to start the battle as the leader of the Pandava host. And at this most critical moment he hesitates . . .

When he was just about to give the word to charge, his heart has been smitten with compunction. In only a few minutes' time (he thinks to himself) so many of those gallant men on his side and on the side facing him will be biting the dust in their death agony – and this in *his* cause, that *he* may perhaps carve a way through to the throne! The very thought fills him with revulsion, and he turns suddenly to his charioteer (whom up to now he has had no reason to suspect is any other than the cousin he knows) and implores him to tell him what to do.

There are a number of English versions of the *Bhagavadgita*, but the best known is possibly that which has endeared itself to more than one generation of readers, the one made by the distinguished Orientalist and man of letters Sir Edwin Arnold and published in 1885 under the title of *The Song Celestial*. It is from this version in blank verse that the following quotations are taken.

> Arjuna. *Krishna! As I behold, come here to shed*
> *Their common blood, yon concourse of our kin,*
> *My members fail, my tongue dries in my mouth,*
> *A shudder thrills my body, and my hair*
> *Bristles with horror; from my weak hand slips*
> *Gandiv, the goodly bow; a fever burns*
> *My skin to parching; hardly may I stand;*
> *The life within me seems to swim and faint;*
> *Nothing do I foresee save woe and wail!*
> *It is not good, O Keshav! (Krishna) nought of good*
> *Can spring from mutual slaughter! Lo, I hate*
> *Triumph and domination, wealth and ease,*
> *Thus sadly won!*

What if they *are* guilty (the young prince goes on), these grand-sires, sires and sons, these brothers, fathers-in-law and sons-in-law, these elders and friends – what if they are as wrong as we have every right to think they are? They are blinded by lust and anger, so that they cannot see how wrong it is to make war on one's own kinsfolk and slaughter them. But with us it is different. "We who perceive the guilt and feel the shame. . . . If we slay kinsfolk and friends for love of earthly power, what an evil fault it were!" Having said which, Arjuna sinks back on the chariot-seat, and "let fall bow and arrow, sick at heart".

To us that will have the sound of a most generous impulse, the workings of a noble spirit, and our hearts go out to the young prince in his honest and honourable bewilderment. But there is a great gulf fixed between the Indian way of looking at things and our own, and Krishna's reply will show how difficult it is to bridge it.

> Krishna. *Thou grievest where no grief should be!*
> *Thou speak'st words lacking wisdom!*

Arjuna, we are given to understand, is worrying his head about things that are really outside his province and certainly beyond his ken. He is taking himself and his problems much too seriously. He has forgotten for the moment one of the most fundamental doctrines of Indian religious belief, that life goes on however often the body that is its vehicle dies and makes way for another.

> *Mourn not for those that live, nor those that die.*
> *Nor I, nor thou, nor any one of these,*
> *Ever was not, nor ever will not be,*
> *For ever and for ever afterwards.*
> *All, that doth live, lives always! To man's frame*
> *As there come infancy and youth and age,*
> *So come there raisings-up and layings-down*
> *Of other and of other life abodes,*
> *Which the wise know, and fear not . . .*

This individual human soul of ours (Krishna continues with his explanation) can never cease to be. It is indestructible. It is not born, nor can it ever die. No dart can pierce it. No flame can consume it, no water drown it, no scorching breezes dry it up. It is eternal, incomprehensible, altogether deathless; why make such a fuss, then, about killing a man, or in getting killed? It is only the body that is involved in the slaying; the spirit goes on to inhabit another body, very much as a man puts off old and worn-out garments in exchange for new.

The end of birth is death, and the end of death is a new birth. All these things are ordained, and there is not the slightest reason why we should bother our heads about them. The part of a brave man is to know his duty and then to try to do it, faithfully and well, just because it is his duty and not because of what he hopes to get out of it. As for Arjuna, he should have not the least difficulty in deciding where his duty lies. He is a Kshatriya, a member of the great Warrior caste, and if he were to throw aside his sword – why, even his friends might suspect that it was fear and not high principle that was his motive. Let him arise then, brace his arm for conflict, nerve his heart to meet whatever comes, victory or defeat, gain or loss.

This is the first of the great teachings of the *Bhagavadgita*, that it is the duty of a man to act always in accordance with the principles of the caste into which he has been born. If he is a Kshatriya, then he should be ready and eager to serve in war and fight valiantly. If he is a Brahmin, then it will be his duty to study the sacred books and expound them. If a Vaisya, let him perform his duty as a merchant or an agriculturist. While if he should be born into the lowest caste of all, the Sudras, let him still take heart and do his best even in the most menial of occupations.

The second great teaching of the *Gita* is bound up with the personality of Krishna. Up to this point in the poem Krishna has been revealed as a man of flesh and blood, the cousin of Arjuna and his companion princes. But in Hindu religion Krishna is an incarnation, or *avatar*, of Vishnu, one of the great gods of the Hindu trinity (the *Trimurti*, the other members being Brahma and Siva). Nor is this all. As the poem proceeds, Krishna is exalted more and more, until he is manifested not as a god merely, not even as an incarnation of Vishnu, not even as Vishnu himself, but as Brahma, the one Eternal God!

But this is only part of the teaching. The heart of the matter is that this stupendous Divine Reality, this God of Gods, this Brahma, is a God to be approached, to draw near to, to be worshipped, and what is more, to be *loved*, with such an intimately passionate love as that of a man for a woman and a woman for a man. And so we reach the final message of the *Gita*, the message spoken by Krishna to Arjuna but one which countless trusting souls have taken to their hearts as addressed to them as a personal revelation:

> *Take My last word, My utmost meaning have!*
> *Give Me thy heart! adore Me! serve Me! cling*
> *In faith and love and reverence to Me!*
> *So shalt thou come to Me! I promise true,*
> *For thou art sweet to Me! Fly to Me alone!*
> *Make Me thy single refuge! I will free*
> *Thy soul from all its sins! Be of good cheer!*

So the great philosophical religious dialogue comes to an end at last, and the two armies are free to fight and slay and be slain. The Pandava brothers are eventually victorious, although the tremendous epic concludes with their renunciation of the kingdom they have won and their ascent to heaven. But all this is comparatively unimportant: the real worth of the ancient poem lies in the little book that is embedded in its mass of myth and marvel. The exaltation of the duties of caste above all other obligations, and the inculcation of *bhakti*, love, of God manifested in human form – these are the two great doctrines of the *Bhagavadgita* that have become incorporated in the spiritual inheritance of the Hindu peoples.

"I find a solace in the *Bhagavadgita*," wrote Mahatma Gandhi, "that I miss even in the Sermon on the Mount. When disappointment stares me in the face and all alone I see not one ray of light, I go back to the *Bhagavadagita*. I find a verse here and a verse there, and I immediately begin to smile in the midst of overwhelming tragedies."

THE DIALOGUES OF PLATO

PLATO, the father of Western philosophy, used to say that he thanked the Gods for three things: one, that he was born a free man and not a slave; two, that he was born a Greek and not Barbarian; and three, that he lived in the days of Socrates. He was not only born a free man but an aristocrat, his father's name being Ariston, a descendant of one of the legendary founders of Athens, while on his mother's side he was related to many wealthy and well-born Athenians. It is thought that he adopted the name of Plato because of his broad shoulders.

In early youth a poet as well as an intellectual, Plato, it is believed, was a great wrestler, and he also served as a soldier. Like all Greeks of the time, the cultivation of the body by sport, gymnastics, dancing and riding went along with the exercise of the intellect, and the philosopher did not lead the retired and studious life which today tends to unfit some intellectuals for ordinary affairs.

The whole of Plato's philosophy is expressed in dialogues and many of the early dialogues preserve an air of having risen from chance conversations in the streets. Plato's philosophy seems to arise directly out of daily life and this is one of its great charms. For this father and fountain-head of philosophy, unequalled in the breadth of his ideas, is also unmatched for the persuasive beauty of his writing. Plato is said to have burnt his poems after he met Socrates and he adopts a very severe view of poets in his *Republic* – but he could not help being a poet himself. He also attacked the Sophists, the new brand of philosopher who, in Athens, were re-examining everything and teaching the people no longer to respect the old ideas on which the city had been founded and whose brilliant speech and witty paradoxes attracted men to them – and yet Plato himself had all the qualities, and often used them, of these enemies of his.

For Plato was a very typical Greek in his love of elegant discussions conducted like a bout of fencing. He might have turned out to be merely the greatest of all the Sophists or he might have turned his talents and his social advantages to politics: but for his friendship with Socrates and particularly for the condemnation of Socrates by the Athenians and Socrates's death by drinking a poison. The death of Socrates inspired Plato with a hatred of the Athenians and of Athenian democracy. It turned him into spiritual exile – and indeed for a short time after the death of Socrates into a physical exile in Megara. It inspired him with a burning hatred for the easy false cleverness of the Sophists. But above all it gave him the strength of purpose to carry out his great work of investigating the nature of things.

Socrates was the contrary of Plato – a man of the people, a sort of poor monk whose teaching, based on questioning and cross-questioning, tended to turn to ridicule the poetry, the eloquence and the metaphysics of which the young aristocratic Plato was a master. Socrates, who always stated that he was only wise because other men thought they knew certain things for sure while he knew he did not know, went about asking very simple questions and using the language and metaphor of the market-place. The work of Plato can be said to be the simple moral teaching of Socrates understood and re-expressed by the most brilliant man of his age who preserved, while being the passionate disciple of Socrates, the qualities of mind he was born with, those of the clever fashionable world. It has the many-sided attraction of thought at its fullest and most elegant combined with an intense moral preoccupation, the preoccupation of getting somewhere, of not being satisfied with the most ingenious argument, the most appealing and attractive arrangement of ideas. Socrates gave Plato inner conviction.

Socrates and Plato lived during the Great Age of Greece; but for their city, Athens, it was an age of political decline. The Great Age of Athens had been that which followed the repulse of the Persians from Greece, the foundation of the Athenian maritime empire and the long rule of Athenian democracy by Pericles from 466 to 428 B.C., during which time the city was rebuilt with unparalleled magnificence and beauty; when flourished the great dramatists Aeschylus, Sophocles and Euripides. Herodotus came to Athens to recount his history and Anaxagoras taught the beginnings of scientific astronomy.

The war between Athens and Sparta, the Peloponnesian War, which began before Pericles died, went well at first for Athens, but in the long run she lost the war, largely because she overreached herself in the disastrous expedition to conquer Sicily. When Plato was twenty-two, in 405 B.C. the last Athenian fleet – Athens ruled the sea and Sparta the land – was destroyed by the Spartans at Aegispotomi, the Long Walls of Athens were destroyed and for a short time Athens was ruled by an oligarchy, the Thirty Tyrants, of whom one of Plato's relations, Critias, was the leader. But if the city was in a political decline, its economic recovery was quick, and though defeated in war Athens was once again very quickly the centre of Hellenism and civilization, and also once more a democracy.

It was an age of questioning, however, without the inner unity of Athenians which had characterized the great years of the rule of Pericles. Socrates was condemned to death (actually the condemnation was a formal one and Socrates's accusers expected him simply to leave the city) as a result of a strange coalition between conservatives, who thought his doctrines were subverting belief in the gods and in the institutions of the city, and his enemies the Sophists, the clever new men who did not believe in the gods or in the city at all. All was in fact confusion in Athens and, after the death of Socrates, both Plato and Xenophon, the soldier-philosopher who was also a disciple of Socrates, turned toward Sparta as a better political ideal. This was understandable but strange, because Sparta had little intellectually to offer.

It was understandable on Plato's part because he saw in Sparta the image of an all-powerful state in which the political disunity and intellectual anarchy which had resulted in the death of the best of men did not exist. In *The Republic*, one of the earliest of Plato's dialogues, he drew his ideal state which was not really very like Sparta though it had resemblances. Plato's ideal republic is collectivist or communist, with the ideal not of promoting the material well-being of the citizens but of making them better through the absence both of poverty and of ambition. Actually, before he died, Plato decided against the abolition of private property as impracticable, but he vested all ownership of land and capital in the family and not in the individual.

It was an idealistic and aristocratic form of communism, in which philosophers were the ultimate rulers and in which men and women are equal before the law and have the same education. Poets and speculative thinkers were banished from the republic. What makes this book much more than a curiosity is the emphasis on the value of mind and on the possibility of curing social and political ills by thinking. Plato in our time has been attacked by Marxists as an enemy of democracy – which he was – and also as, in some ways, the foster-father of the modern corporate or fascist state.

Of course, we do not find in Plato's political work any recognition of the principles of the French Revolution or of other generous impulses which have stirred liberal opinion in Europe. But Plato also shows himself an enemy of any tyranny or dictatorship which, he argues, arises because of the misuse of democracy and because of democracy's incapacity to provide men with what they need.

The method of the dialogues is astonishingly the same throughout; it is that of examining, usually by question and answer, some important idea, the effect of Socrates being to show that what has appeared to his friend or his opponent to be something quite obvious was in reality not so at all; or else – as in the *Symposium* or *Banquet*, where a great number of characters are present – the dialogue takes the form of many speeches on a common subject, love in the *Symposium*, with argument at the end.

Many of the dialogues do not result in any conclusion being reached. Thus in one, the *Loches*, Socrates talks about courage with a general, an ordinary soldier and a citizen and at the end it is left quite undecided whether courage is an effort of the mind or an animal instinct. In one of the most charming of the short dialogues called the *Lysis*, Socrates talks to two boys as they are coming out of school about friendship and also about parents and their behaviour toward children and their authority. They are unable to decide what friendship is at the end. Yet from this dialogue one important Platonic idea emerges: that what is neither good nor evil loves the good because of the presence of evil.

A much more ambitious dialogue, the *Protagoras*, named after one of the best-known and most intelligent Sophists, shows Socrates and Protagoras arguing about the nature of knowledge. Protagoras is a "relativist", yet we find him, in this dialogue, in many ways nearer to Plato's thinking about the nature of wisdom than Socrates appears to be. Yet the final impression, conveyed very subtly, is of Protagoras as a false prophet, because he is self-complacent, always trying to be popular and to avoid the hard questions which Socrates puts to him.

In the *Phaedrus*, devoted to the discussion of the beautiful, Socrates and his friend Phaedrus walk in the country together outside Athens and sit down underneath a cedar in a very beautiful grove. Socrates persuades Phaedrus to read a discourse by a great Sophist whom Phaedrus admires and whose speech he carried with him under his cloak. A young man, according to this discourse, should prefer as friend and mentor someone who is not in love with him, since the lover is liable to be suspicious, self-seeking and unreasonable. Socrates thereupon delivers a better speech on the same theme, that is to say against the idea of accepting as mentor a man who is in love. But, dramatically, Socrates breaks off and says that he has been blaspheming against Eros, the god of love; he develops in a third discourse the theme that love is a condition of the soul and the impulse to love is in one part the remembrance of Absolute Beauty, implanted in the soul by God, as well in part merely human desire. Thus love can lead man toward truth and wisdom and is therefore to be preferred above all feelings and certainly not to be rejected as the Sophists' discourse suggests.

The speech is one of the most imaginative and powerful in all Plato. But after this Socrates is still dissatisfied. All these speeches have something which belongs not to truth but to rhetoric. Before men make speeches on great subjects they must delve deeper. For nature has implanted a love of wisdom in men's minds but it is exceedingly laborious to get to and is not really reached by means of speeches of the kind they have been listening to. Before Socrates and Phaedrus leave the grove, Socrates offers up a prayer to the sylvan deities:

> Beloved Pan, and all other gods who here abide, grant me to be beautiful in the inner man, and all I have of outer things to be at peace with those within. May I count only the wise man rich and may my store of gold be such as none but the good can bear. Phaedrus, need we anything more? For myself I have prayed enough.

As Jowett, the great classical scholar and the translator of Plato, has said: "The germs of all ideas, even of most Christian ones, are to be found in Plato." This is true not only of ideas but of attitudes. Plato was not interested in physical science *per se* – one of his contemporaries was Democritus, the man who first spoke of the atom – but he advocated calculation and experiment against rhetoric; he opposed the fanciful, theological concepts of the gods and of current mythology, yet he was himself to make use of a number of myths to express his ultimate conceptions about the human soul. Out of Plato many mystical schools of thought and spiritualistic philosophies have been developed; and yet Plato stood fundamentally as a unifier of knowledge, a seeker and definer of clear first principles. Plato absorbed and expressed the great many ideas of his time such as the mystical Orphic conceptions of the soul and brought them out of their isolation, freed them from their exaggerations and foibles and related them to the general experience of mankind. It is therefore impossible to sum up Plato's philosophy except in a very general way.

Plato's philosophy is essentially a moral philosophy in that he considers that man is born to perfect himself and that this perfection has to be realized, more or less, in this world. This is the law which man rarely understands and only imperfectly glimpses at times; but on account of this, man feels always that something is lacking in him. If he understood and obeyed this law of his being, he would be completely happy. This is indeed different from the Christian notion of morality which contains the idea that man has to conquer his lower nature and which sees the kingdom of heaven as not of this world. For Plato, man has no higher obligation than to attach himself to teaching perfection; the search for the perfect belongs to his nature; it is not a moral imperative, it is rather the necessary condition of the sane and harmonious development of man's nature. The good is good because it is healthy and because it is beautiful; justice is good because injustice is incoherent, inharmonious and ugly.

Plato's foremost place as a philosopher lies in his conception of unity. He was convinced that truth and goodness exist and are inseparable, and that virtue is one thing and is dependent upon knowledge. On account of this unity of goodness, truth and beauty, Plato considered that the arts – music, literature, poetry, architecture, rhetoric, politics and the practical arts – must be the servants of moral philosophy and only have value in so far as they serve it. There is a false architecture, false music, literature *et cetera* which takes man away from the pursuit of the perfect and helps him to remain ignorant and malformed, and there is the converse. In essence the doctrine of Plato has many similarities with that of Christianity. But it is a doctrine founded on an intellectual view of man and of the soul rather than one based on a belief in God and a Redeemer of mankind. But even for those who can no more accept the Platonic conception of unity than they can the teaching of Christ, the figure of Plato cannot be dismissed. He remains the man who most subtly, most persistently, most attractively, and who at the greatest length and with the greatest thoroughness, argued about the nature of man and of the human soul.

ARISTOTLE'S *ETHICS*

OF ALL the great writers whose works have come down to us from the ancient world, perhaps the most important is Aristotle. Plato is perhaps even more famous, but Plato for the most part wrote with his head in the clouds. Aristotle, on the contrary, had his feet planted very firmly on the ground. He preferred facts to theories, and he thought no time wasted in carrying out experiments. The world was as mysterious to him as it was to Plato, but he saw in its mysteries a challenge. He wanted to find out, and such was the massive scope of his intellect that he wrote on a great variety of subjects – logic and philosophy, natural history and geography, psychology and physiology and anatomy, physics and astronomy, politics and ethics. Much that he wrote has been lost, and a good deal of what has been preserved has been invalidated by the discoveries of modern science. But in one field in particular what he had to say is still regarded as being worthy of consideration and discussion. That field is Ethics.

On the face of it, this is somewhat surprising, since the world in which Aristotle lived was so very different from our own. He was a Greek, but not an Athenian, since he was born (in 384 B.C.) at Stagira, a small Greek colony on the confines of Macedonia. He was the son of a medical man who was appointed a physician-in-ordinary to the Macedonian king; but his father died, and when he was about seventeen Aristotle betook himself to Athens, where he entered as a student in Plato's famous Academy. He stayed with Plato for twenty years, and then, on his master's death, he taught in several towns until 343 B.C. when he accepted an invitation from King Philip of Macedon to be tutor to his son, the future Alexander the Great.

Both Philip and his son seem to have valued him highly, and most liberally seconded his studies in natural science, for which he had inherited his father's predilection. But when Alexander set out on his career of conquest in Asia, Aristotle returned to Athens, where he conducted a school of philosophy in a grove named the Lyceum. This came to be known as the Peripatetic school, from his habit of walking up and down while conversing with his pupils. After the death of Alexander, Aristotle fell out of favour with the new rulers, and he retired to Chalcis, on the Black Sea, where he soon after died (322 B.C.).

But although the conditions – political and economic, social and religious – were so different in that world of small city-states from our own, the problems that confronted Aristotle when he came to talk about the Good Life – which is what Ethics is mostly about – were not altogether unlike those which confront us today. For this reason his writings on the subject have a perennial appeal. They are comprised in two treatises, of which much the more important is the *Nicomachean Ethics*. Nicomachus is the name of a son of Aristotle by a concubine, and it is surmised that the book was addressed to him, or he may perhaps have edited it after his father's death. The other treatise is known as the *Eudemian Ethics*, after Eudemus, a pupil of Aristotle's who is thought to have edited it; some authorities think that Eudemus might be regarded as its author.

In all his writings on philosophy, whether political or ethical, Aristotle reveals himself as a teleologist, that is, as attempting the interpretation of things under discussion in terms of purpose or end (Greek *telos*, end). This is clearly in evidence from the very first statement of his *Nicomachean Ethics*. "Every art and every science," it begins, "and in like manner every action and every moral choice, aims, it is thought, at some good". What that good is depends of course on the things concerned: some activities are undertaken only for what they lead to or produce and bring about, while others are engaged in for their own sakes. But it is surely clear that there must be something that may be fairly described as the Chief Good, that is, the best thing of all. So far as man is concerned, this end must be the Good of Man.

Now, what is this very special Good? There is pretty general agreement that it is *eudaimonia*, a Greek word which is usually translated as Happiness, although a possibly better rendering would be Well-being or Welfare. To use the more common form, "Happiness (says Aristotle) is what both the multitude and the refined few call it, and 'living well' and 'doing well' they conceive to be the same with 'being happy'; but about the nature of this Happiness men dispute, and the multitude do not in their account of it agree with the wise. For some say it is some of those things which are palpable and apparent, as pleasure or wealth or honour; in fact, some one thing, some another; nay, oftentimes the same man gives a different account of it, for when ill, he calls it health, when poor, wealth; and conscious of their own ignorance, men admire those who talk grandly and above their comprehension".

So many and varied are these opinions, that we may come to the conclusion that to call Happiness the Chief Good is a mere truism and what we are looking for is something much clearer – what, in fact, is its real nature. "Now this object may be easily attained, when we have discovered what is the work of man; for as in the case of flute-player, statuary (sculptor), or artisan of any kind, or, more generally, all who have any work or course of action, their Chief Good and Excellence is thought to reside in their work, so it would seem to be with man, if there is any work belonging to him." *If* there is any work . . . but surely it would be unreasonable to suppose that "while carpenter and cobbler have certain works and courses of action, Man as Man has none, but has been left by Nature without a work".

What, then, can this be? It cannot be just life, since that is something that he shares with the vegetables, nor can it be the "life of sensation, since that is common to horses, oxen, and indeed every other animal". It must be something which has most particularly to do with man as a Rational Being, for his distinguishing characteristic is his power to reason. So we arrive at Aristotle's conclusion, that the Good of Man is "a working of the soul in the way of Excellence, or, if Excellence admits of degrees, in the way of the best and most perfect Excellence".

After this rough sketch of the Chief Good, Aristotle proceeds to analyse human excellence into intellectual and moral components, of which the fruit is Virtue. This he defines as a state or condition in which man exercises a deliberate choice, using his reason to choose between extremes, "as a man of practical wisdom would determine". This brings us to that most famous feature of Aristotle's system, the Doctrine of the Mean.

Virtue is a mean (that is, middle) state, he argues: "It is a middle state between two faulty ones, in the way of excess on one side and of defect on the other; and it is so, because the faulty states on one side fall short of, and those on the other exceed, what is right." He then draws up a list or Table, as he calls it, of the principal virtues, and demonstrates how they are, each one of them, a kind of middle way between too much and too little. Courage is the mean state between rashness and cowardice. Self-mastery is the mean state between indulgence and asceticism. Liberality is the mean state between prodigality and stinginess. Meekness is the mean state between violence and abasement. What Aristotle calls "easy-pleasantry" is the mean state between acting the buffoon and the clown. A man who is friendly is practising the happy mean between being a flatterer and a quarrelsome fellow. And so on.

These aspects of Virtue are next examined in detail in the three following books into which the treatise is divided, Books 3 to 5. Beginning with Courage, there are some things which a man who is very properly called brave may still fear – disgrace, for instance. But he ought not to fear poverty, or disease, or even death in all circumstances, even though death is what most people dread most, "because it is the end of all things, and the dead man is thought to be capable neither of good nor evil". A truly brave man has no fear of honourable death in war or other sudden emergencies, nor is a man a coward who fears insult to his wife and children. Dying to escape from poverty, or the pangs of love, or anything that is simply painful is not the action of a brave man but of a coward, "because it is mere softness to fly from what is toilsome, and the suicide braves the terrors of death not because it is honourable but to get out of the reach of evil".

Next, the man who has perfected Self-mastery, in all such bodily pleasures as eating and drinking and sexual intercourse. With regard to all these things he tries to follow the mean, that is to say, he indulges in them "only in moderation, and neither more than he ought, nor at improper times, and so forth; but such things as are conducive to health and good condition of body, being also pleasant, these he will grasp at in moderation and as he ought to do, and also such other pleasant things as do not hinder these objects, and are not unseemly or disproportionate to his means". The Man of Perfected Self-mastery, in short, "regulates his desires by the dictates of right reason".

After some pages descriptive of the Liberal Man, who "will give and spend on proper objects, and in proper proportion, in great things and in small alike, and all this with pleasure to himself", we come to a portrait of the Magnificent Man, which is doubtless based on what Aristotle had observed of the great aristocratic, popularity-seeking spenders of Athens. "The expenses of the Magnificent Man are great and fitting: such also are his works." He will consider how a thing may be done most beautifully and fittingly, rather than for how much. The kinds of expenditure which he will incur will be what are called honourable, "such as dedicatory offerings to the gods, and the furnishing their temples, and sacrifices, and in like manner everything that has reference to the Deity, and all such public matters as are objects of honourable ambition, as when men think it is their duty to furnish a chorus for the stage splendidly, or fit out and maintain a three-decker for the navy, or give a great public feast. . . . It is characteristic of the Magnificent Man to do magnificently whatever he is about."

Now there comes into view a man of "slow motion, deep-toned voice, and deliberate style of speech". He is the Great-minded Man, and what Aristotle has to say about him is thoroughly Greek. Among much else we are told that "he is not a man to incur little risks, nor does he court danger, because there are but few things he has a value for; but he will incur *great* dangers, and when he does venture he is prodigal of his life, since he knows that there are circumstances in which it would not be worth his while to live". He is the sort of man to do kindnesses, but he is ashamed to receive favours – the former give him the feeling of superiority, and the latter put him in the position of feeling inferior. "Further, it is characteristic of the Great-minded Man to bear himself loftily towards the great or fortunate, but towards the people of middle station affably, because to be high and mighty towards those of humble station would be low and vulgar – it would be like parading strength against the weak." One thing more may be noted about him: he is the kind of man who makes a point of acquiring those objects which are beautiful and unproductive – one might almost say, useless – rather than those which may be turned into profit. On the whole, Aristotle's Great-minded Man might well have served as a model for the English nobleman of the eighteenth century who collected pictures and bronzes and Sèvres china because it was the thing for a rich man to do.

A whole book (No. 5) is devoted to an examination of Justice as a component of desirable character. To have a proper understanding of Justice – to know what it is and how it should be applied – was something that every Greek citizen who took a pride in his citizenship would strive to obtain, since he might at any time be called upon to serve as a juryman or arbitrator in the public courts and assemblies. Aristotle distinguishes between three kinds of Justice, namely, Distributive, which decides what each man should receive as his proper share of what there is to be divided; Corrective, the justice of the law courts; and Commercial, which governs business transactions. In the remainder of the treatise (there are ten "books" in all) there are elaborations of various themes that have been discussed earlier.

"Now we have said enough in our sketchy kind of way on these subjects," Aristotle concludes, but this matter of the Good Life is not to be settled by discussion: it has to be lived. "He who is to be good must have been brought up and habituated well, and then live accordingly under good institutions, and never do what is low and mean. Now these objects can be attained only by men living in accordance with some guiding Intellect and right order, with power to back them." In other words, Ethics cannot be properly discussed and decided except in relationship with Politics, and in fact the *Nicomachean Ethics* leads directly to Aristotle's *Politics*. To go back to that first statement about the Chief Good, for the Rational Man such as Aristotle ever has in mind the Chief Good is life lived according to reason, practised according to the Happy Mean, in such a community or state as the Greeks had worked out for themselves in the spring-time of their genius.

THE AENEID

VERGIL

THE *Aeneid* is the great national epic of classical Rome and has been accepted as a literary masterpiece since its publication by order of the Emperor Augustus after Vergil's death in 19 B.C. Yet this heroic poem, written to immortalize the ancient Roman ideals of valour and honour, was composed by a shy, gentle and, indeed, effeminate genius who had won his reputation as a poet for a selection of charming pastorals and who had no taste for martial glory.

Publius Vergilius Maro (there was no such name as Virgilius, therefore it is incorrect to call him Virgil) was born near Mantua on 15 October, 70 B.C. – seven years before the birth of Augustus. He had a learned education but his life of quiet study was disrupted by the series of civil wars which rocked the foundations of the Roman world at that time, particularly the conflicts between Caesar and Pompey and between Octavian and Antony.

When Octavian emerged as the undisputed master of Rome, the eventual demobilization of the armies brought confiscation of lands needed to settle on the returning warriors. Octavian seized a large tract of Mantuan territory for this purpose, including Vergil's own estate. The soldier to whom it was allocated brutally turned out the poet and even threatened his life. Hardly an encouragement for the man who was to sing so nobly of the military virtues. That great patron of the arts, Maecenas, interceded with Octavian and the poet's patrimony was restored to him. After his bucolic poems, "The Eclogues," were read in Octavian's circle, Vergil became a great favourite in Rome.

As soon as Octavian became the Emperor Augustus he decided that the new Rome he was seeking to create should have the inspiration of a heroic poem on the Homeric scale and the project of composing a national epic around Augustus's achievements was made known to every poet of ability. Only one had the depth of learning and the technical power to take up the suggestion – Vergil. He devoted the last eleven years of his life to the *Aeneid*, first composing in prose and converting it into verse piecemeal when the mood took him. Thus he did not follow any particular order of books: he composed slowly and sometimes forgot what he had already written – which accounts for occasional inconsistencies to be found in his work. These blemishes as well as some incomplete lines indicate that he did not live long enough to revise and polish the whole of the *Aeneid*. Indeed, he was so dissatisfied with it that his dying wish was that it should be burned.

Vergil chose his theme from the event which Homer immortalized – the siege of Troy – but the Italian took his story from the legend of the arrival in the west of the Trojan fugitive, Aeneas, and his band of followers. Of course, to Vergil Aeneas represented much more than a man, more than an ordinary epic hero – he was the greatness of Rome and, in a sense, the Emperor Augustus himself: the embodiment of the aspirations and destiny of the greatest power in the known world.

Perhaps because of his sensitive and delicate nature the poet seemed to find the character of his superman the most difficult task of creation and it is conceded even by his devoted admirers that it is also the most glaring weakness in his work – Aeneas, who was meant to be the epitome of the Roman ideal, emerges as brutal rather than strong and fails in his words and deeds to measure up to the adulation of his followers and the admiration of his enemies. Vergil apparently felt it necessary to invest his tale with a love interest, but he draws the character of Dido so sympathetically that the reader is bound to experience a sense of disgust at the hero's treatment of her.

Aeneas, a son of the goddess Venus, is introduced (Book 1) on his voyage from Sicily toward the Italian coast. His implacable enemy, the goddess Juno, persuades the wind god, Aeolus, to bring on a storm and scatter the Trojan fleet which is driven toward the coast of Africa. The god Neptune is persuaded by Venus to intervene and he quells the storm, but not before three of the Trojan ships are sunk; the rest of the fleet land their crews at different spots along the African coast. Aeneas, with his faithful follower Achates – "Fidus Achates", who has become a byword through the centuries for loyalty – heads inland and reaches the site of Carthage, the greatest of Rome's ancient foes. On his way his mother, Venus, warns him that the leader of a new settlement there is the widowed Tyrian princess, Dido, who has fled from her native city after the murder of her husband and is seeking to found a new kingdom with a powerful band of followers. But Dido accords Aeneas a most hospitable welcome and, at a banquet in his honour, asks him to tell the story of his wanderings after the fall of Troy. Aeneas accepts the invitation and (Book 2) recounts how he was warned by Venus to gather his family and household gods (Penates) together and escape from the doomed Troy before it fell into the hands of the Greeks. In the confusion he was separated from his wife, Creusa. During his search for her he came upon her ghost and was told that his destiny was to settle permanently in Italy.

He continues his story in Book 3, telling how he and other refugees built a fleet and sailed off in the spring of the following year. As they approached the coast of Thrace they were warned off by Polydorus, a murdered kinsman of Aeneas, and they then made for Delos where they were told by Apollo's oracle to seek their ancient mother. Anchises, father of Aeneas, presumes Crete is the answer to the oracular advice but the Penates convince Aeneas that Italy is meant. Accordingly they head toward Italy but a storm drives them almost into the hands of the Harpies. They change course yet again and land on the coast of Epeiros where they meet Helenus, now wed to Andromache. Helenus, inspired by Apollo, urges them to go around Sicily and make for the west coast of Italy. They reach the western extremity of Sicily and decide to winter there – and that is where Anchises, Aeneas's father, dies.

Dido is moved by this story and, falling deeply in love with Aeneas (Book 4), goes through a form of marriage arranged by Venus. Aeneas, however, is warned by Mercury that Africa is not his destiny and he tries to sneak off on his travels, but Dido finds him out and makes most eloquent appeal to him to stay. But she fails to persuade him and in despair takes her life. Aeneas sees her funeral pyre as he sails off (Book 5). This book is given over to a description of funeral games, thus complying with the Homeric epic tradition. During the games Juno talks the Trojan women into burning Aeneas's ships. He loses four ships but manages to set sail on the final stage of his voyage, leaving the least sturdy of his followers to found a new town in Sicily. On the way he visits the Sibyl who has a prophetic frenzy and foretells that he will wage wars in Italy for the sake of a new Helen. She advises him to descend into the underworld, first finding the Golden Bough which is the only passport by which the living may enter Hades. Once Aeneas has the Bough the Sibyl conducts him across the Styx (Book 6) to the Elysian Fields where he meets his father's spirit. There, too, he sees a pageant of the souls of future Romans awaiting reincarnation, including Augustus.

This book throws some light on Vergil's own religious views, especially when he makes Anchises expound to Aeneas a philosophy in which a Spirit animates all the world and every living thing in it: it is divine but hampered by defiling material surroundings in which it finds itself – thus it is argued that man's spirit is divine but he is capable of evil passions. The polluted soul must be purified and therefore has to undergo a painful cleansing in a sort of Purgatory. Only a few choice spirits are so freed from all guilt that their wanderings are at an end and they abide permanently in Elysium – most souls must pass into new bodies on Earth, first drinking the waters of Lethe which makes them forget the past. This book is a brilliant adaptation of the visit by Odysseus to Hades in Book 11 of the *Odyssey* and brings to an end the first half of the poem.

The second half was clearly less to Vergil's taste, for he seems ill at ease with many passages, particularly the battle scenes inevitable in the epic. He is at his weakest when describing the carnage of war and at his best dealing with the pathos of death and in the wealth of detail but, throughout, his poetry is highlighted with the most brilliant imagery and similes. At last (Book 7) Aeneas reaches the scene of his future settlement – he and his followers land in the kingdom of Latium, ruled by Latinus, whose daughter, Lavinia, was being wooed by Turnus, prince of the Rutuli. But it was foretold to Latinus that she would not marry a native of his country and, when Aeneas seeks the king's leave to settle in his territory, Latinus realizes that he has found the predestined mate for Lavinia in this chief from across the seas. But his Queen, Amata, much prefers Turnus. The goddess Juno intervenes again and soon the whole kingdom is demanding the expulsion of the foreign invaders.

This book ends with a catalogue of the Italian forces – another feature of the Homeric epic (compare the catalogue of ships in Book 2 of the *Iliad*).

Now (Book 8) Aeneas visits the site of the future city of Rome and the god of the Tiber tells him in a dream that he should seek the help of Evander the Arcadian who has already settled there. He will understand that his dream has been fulfilled when he sees on the shore a white sow with thirty white farrow. Aeneas finds the sow, realizes that the omens are favourable, sails off upstream and comes upon a Festival of Hercules being celebrated outside the settlement on the Palatine Hill which was the primitive Rome. He is given a hospitable welcome by Evander and his son, Pallas, and invited to join the rites to Hercules.

Meanwhile there is plenty of activity on Olympus with Venus persuading her all-forgiving husband, Vulcan (who is *not* Aeneas's celestial father), to beat out heavenly armour for her son. On the shield is wrought a prophetic series of scenes from Roman history ending with the battle of Actium (one of the decisive battles of ancient history, fought in 31 B.C. between the victorious Octavian and Antony and Cleopatra). In this passage Vergil parallels Homer's description of the arms of Achilles.

Now Vergil must recapitulate (Book 9) all that has gone on in Latium during the absence of Aeneas. Turnus has attacked the Trojan camp and set fire to their ships at their moorings. Neptune, however, turns the ships into sea nymphs. The Trojans, obedient to the orders left behind by Aeneas, stay within the walls of their encampment, although Nisus and his friend, Euryalus, make a sortie, hoping to get through the Rutulian lines to warn Aeneas of the attack (in the *Iliad* Odysseus and Diomedes made a similar sortie to spy out the enemy camp). They are killed and the next day Turnus renews his furious assault which breaches the walls. Turnus, however, is cut off and is lucky to escape with his life.

The gods of Olympus decide it is time to hold a council as the war is reaching a decisive stage. After a debate between Juno and Venus (Book 10) Jupiter rules that ultimate victory must be left to fate. Aeneas, on his journey back to his followers, has put himself at the head of an Etruscan army and arrives in time to rescue his hard-pressed Trojans. A fierce battle ends in the defeat of the Rutulians, but Pallas (Evander's son) who has joined up with Aeneas is killed by Turnus. There follows in Book 11 a truce for burying the dead. Aeneas offers to settle the outcome of the war in single combat with Turnus but his enemy prefers to renew the general fighting and again Aeneas and his men emerge victorious.

The final book (12) opens with another truce conditional on the acceptance by Turnus of Aeneas's offer of single combat. Queen Amata is utterly opposed to the duel and Turnus's sister persuades the Rutuli to thwart Aeneas by violating the truce. Aeneas is then treacherously wounded by an arrow in a skirmish but Venus helps his physician to heal the wound. Aeneas rejoins the battle and his followers rout the Latins. Queen Amata takes her own life and Turnus is at last brought to a final confrontation with Aeneas in single combat. There is much celestial interference with the duel, but in the end Turnus is disabled. He asks Aeneas to spare his life, but when Aeneas realizes his adversary is wearing the belt of the slain Pallas as a trophy, he dispatches him at once.

So ends the poem. Although the adventures of Aeneas provide the plot of the *Aeneid*, the glories of Rome-that-was-to-be and the fortunes of the Julian House, of which the Emperor Augustus was a member, are skilfully woven into its texture. The great family of the Caesars are rather fawningly declared to be the descendants of

Aeneas, and his sojourn at the court of Dido, queen of what was to become Carthage, unmistakably hints at the future rivalry of the Romans and the Carthaginians, ending in the eventual triumph of the master race of Rome.

Comparisons between Vergil and his great Greek prototype, Homer, are inevitable, although academic admirers of the Latin poet find them odious, arguing that Homer composed for an audience which knew only the epic on the grand scale and that his poetry was meant to be heard, not read. It is also true that Homer's society was relatively uncomplicated, with a nobility not unlike the barons of England's feudal ages, whereas Vergil's civilization was complex and he wrote for scholarly and thoroughly educated readers. Nevertheless it can hardly be disputed that the poetic merits of the *Aeneid* are far below those of the *Iliad*, lacking the unity of purpose and integrity of construction of the earlier work as well as its truth and simplicity.

Perhaps a model, however masterly, can never quite capture the spontaneous freshness of a glorious original.

PLUTARCH'S *LIVES*

THE MAN from whom so many people learned their ancient history, including Shakespeare and Montaigne, was born around A.D. 46 and lived for most of his life in a comparatively obscure market town, Chaeronea, which is not even the capital of Boeotia – Thebes is that – one of the less brilliant parts of Greece in the time of Greece's glory. Plutarch was for a long time Archon of his town, that is, one of the principal magistrates. He studied in Athens under the philosopher Ammonius; he once travelled to Egypt and later in life, sometime before he was forty-five, he went to Rome probably for the affairs of his native town and gave lectures there which brought him friendships with some Roman intellectuals. He married and had five children and seems to have lived a remarkably happy life as a country gentleman and man of letters.

From his writings and particularly from his *Moralia*, a collection of essays and reflections on all sorts of happenings during his life, we learn much about Plutarch's character even though records are scarce. He was intensely curious about people, all that concerned people, including their money affairs; he was credulous and his aesthetic sense made him believe facts which even if they were not verifiable were picturesque and, as the Italians say, well found (*ben trovato*); he was conservative in politics; and he liked people to behave with dignity and restraint. He tells of how he was once lecturing in Rome when a certain Rusticus in the audience was brought a letter from the Emperor Domitian by a soldier. Plutarch stopped his lecture so that Rusticus could read the letter. "But," writes Plutarch, "Rusticus declined to do so, put the letter aside until I had finished the lecture and the audience had withdrawn; an example of serious and dignified behaviour which aroused much admiration."

The fact of being able to be a historian, and one who embraced the whole of Greek and Roman history in his *Lives*, and yet to live in what was a distinctly backward province, is a tribute to the order and security of the Mediterranean world under the Pax Romana. It is true the great libraries of Athens were not more than a hundred miles or so away; but this was quite a journey. Although the Chinese had invented and used printing, the Romans did no more than employ crude stamps to mark articles of commerce; they might have printed books but for the fact that suitable ink and paper were lacking. Plutarch therefore relied on manuscripts and, of course, on visitors, who gave him accounts of what they knew or had read.

After the civil war which followed the death of Caesar, Octavius Caesar, later known as Augustus, established order throughout the civilized world from Persia and the Middle East to Spain and northwards to the Danube and over most of what is now France. The Empire held together under the successors of Augustus, Tiberius and the somewhat weak Claudius and the profligate Nero who came to Greece around A.D. 67 (Plutarch would then have been twenty and probably studying in Athens). The Empire was not even seriously disturbed by the Praetorian civil wars between Galba, Vitelius and Otho which lasted for some two years after Nero's death. The disturbances and drama of the first seventy years or so of the Roman Empire took place in Rome and largely only affected Rome. A civilized country such as Greece prospered and was quiet. In any case, during most of Plutarch's prime the Empire was governed by relatively good and efficient emperors – Vespasian, Titus, Domitian, Nerva, Trajan and, in A.D. 117, some three years perhaps before Plutarch died, by the great Hadrian.

Plutarch, though a Greek, felt himself in no way lessened through being a citizen of the Roman Empire and his mature outlook on politics and society was optimistic. It was a good time to be alive in. He believed in the great Roman hegemony as a necessary consequence of the inability of the Greeks to make a large Hellenistic state. The Age of Greece was over, her population had shrunk and two centuries ago, at the seige of Corinth, she had finally lost her independence. As Plutarch writes, in his life of Flaminius, of Greek political defects:

> For if we except the victory at Marathon, the sea fight at Salamis, the battles of Plataea and Thermopolae and Cimon's exploits at Eurymedon, Greece fought all her battles against herself and to enslave herself. She erected all her trophies to her own shame and misery and was brought to ruin and desolation almost wholly by the guilt and ambition of her great men.

Yet in Plutarch's view Roman domination of Greece was no tragedy. It was good to belong to a large stable empire. The Greek language and Greek customs were inseparably a part of the Roman governing classes' education and Greeks in the Roman Empire were what would be called today first-class citizens.

Plutarch probably intended *The Parallel Lives*, to give the work its full title, to keep before his own time and posterity the greatness of Greece, that of Rome being sufficiently apparent. Most of the individual lives of Greeks and Romans are compared the one with the other and these comparisons, which were not certainly intended to boost Greek heroes at the expense of Roman, show how similar in many ways was the environment of the great men of both nations. But Plutarch does not like ideological arguments or disquisitions on the course of history. He is a recorder of the glories of the past. As a recorder his achievement is immense, for he covers the whole period of Greek and Roman history from the mythical times of Theseus and Romulus up to his own day; though he has been shown sometimes to have made mistakes about facts and has certainly told many anecdotes which are probably fictitious, his work is a formidable bringing together of knowledge.

The order in which Plutarch composed his *Parallel Lives* is uncertain, but it is fairly certain that he composed the mythical accounts of Theseus and Romulus, the founders of Athens and Rome, and of others, such as Solon or Numa, last. He worked backwards, in fact, from history to myth. The Greeks, whose thinking was so like ours of today and who were the first to practise a scientific approach to history and natural history, did not possess an extended sense of time, and had not even a vague conception of the vastness of history. Thus Plutarch has not much idea when Theseus lived and gives no dates. He says at the beginning of his "Life of Theseus" that it belongs to the province of romances and poets, where nothing is certain or credible. "Let us hope I shall succeed in purifying fable and make her take on the appearance of history."

Plutarch had no idea of the existence of the Minoan civilization of Crete, although he wrote of King Minos and his many ships when Theseus went to Crete to release the seven Athenian youths and maids who formed the tribute which Athens paid to Minos. He tells the beautiful story of a thread laid for Theseus by Ariadne, the daughter of Minos and Queen Pasiphae, to guide him through the labyrinth where lurked the Minotaur. But the world of Theseus and the Bronze Age is a good deal more shadowy to Plutarch than it is today. Yet in his "Life of Cimon", who lived in the fifth century B.C., Plutarch tells how the Delphic Oracle told the Athenians, after the war with the Persians, to bring back the bones of Theseus from the island of Scyros where he had died. And Cimon captured the island and discovered the bones by divine inspiration; he saw an eagle pecking at a sort of mound and when he ordered his soldiers to dig in the mound they found a coffin of gigantic size and lying by it a bronze spear and sword.

To pick out the best lives – that is to say the most exciting and readable – is very difficult because they all abound in curious anecdotes, incidents and Plutarchian observations which are unforgettable. Many people would agree that the lives of Caesar and Mark Antony, Alcibiades, Pericles and Nicias are among the most enthralling. Of Cleopatra in the life of Antony, Plutarch writes:

Plato admits four sorts of flattery; but she had a thousand.

Nobody, not even Shakespeare in *Antony and Cleopatra*, better describes the nature and attraction of Cleopatra—

The crowding mischief that could befall Antony—

as has this provincial moralist from Chaeronea.

When Antony perceives that he cannot outmatch Cleopatra in elegance, splendour and wit, he falls into broad and gross raillery. She, perceiving that he was more a soldier than a courtier, answered him in the same manner without any sort of reluctance or reserve:

For her actual beauty, it is said, was not in itself so remarkable that none could be compared with her, or that no one could see her without being struck by it. But the contact of her presence, if you lived with her, was irresistible; the attraction of her person, joining with the charm of her conversation and the character that attended all she said or did, was something bewitching. It was a pleasure merely to hear the sound of her voice, with which, like an instrument of many strings, she could pass from one language to another.

If one had to pick out the peculiar merit of Plutarch as a writer, it lies surely in his mastery of the perennially interesting and exciting detail. Thus in his life of Pericles, Plutarch notices on the beauty of the buildings, erected in the new, great and prosperous Athens:

So the buildings arose, as imposing in their sheer size as they were inimitable in the grace of their outline, since the artists strove to excel themselves in the beauty of their workmanship. And yet the most wonderful thing about them was the speed with which they were completed. Each of them, men supposed, would take many generations to build. But in fact the entire project was carried through in the high summer of one man's administration ... each building possessed a beauty which seemed venerable the moment it was born, and at the same time a youthful vigour which makes them appear to this very day as if they were newly built. A bloom of eternal freshness hovers over these works of Pericles and preserves them from the touch of time, as if some unswerving spirit of youth, some ageless vitality had been breathed into them.

In his great and unrivalled narrative of the disaster which befell the sole Athenian expedition to Syracuse during the Peloponnesian War between Athens and Sparta, Thucydides describes, in general terms, the dismay which the news caused in the city. Plutarch, however, has this:

When the terrible story first reached Athens it is said people could not believe it, especially because of the messenger who first broke the news. It appears that a stranger landed at the Piraeus, took a seat in a barber's chair and began to talk about the subject as if it were common knowledge. The barber listened to him and then, before the traveller could tell anyone else, ran as fast as he could into the city and rushing up to the Archons, blurted out the news in the open market-place. Naturally enough this caused utter dismay followed by an uproar, and so the magistrates immediately summoned the assembly and brought the barber before them. When he was cross-examined as to how he had heard the story, he could give no satisfactory account and so was promptly condemned as a rumour monger and public agitator. He was fastened to the wheel and tortured until other messengers arrived who reported the disaster in all its details.

One could go on for ever quoting these human curiosities from Plutarch. He is interested in everything except perhaps in describing the obvious, and is a true Greek in his love of new things and the extraordinary invention.

Plutarch's view of history is sometimes said to be that of a moralist. It is true he contrasts in his *Parallel Lives* the virtues and the vices of his heroes. At the beginning of the life of Pericles he writes that he chooses to describe the lives of men of action for he considers that these lives are more likely to make men desire and understand virtue than the lives of poets or painters. But, in the author's opinion, it is better to call him a *humanist*. He is above everything else interested in the character of great men and his heroes are all, to use a phrase of D'Astier de la Vigerie, "Waiting for their places in history". It is on these that he concentrates and he writes:

As portrait painters are more exact in the lines and features of the face, in which the character is seen, than in the other parts of the body, so I must be allowed to give my more particular attention to the marks

Dante's tremendous visions of Hell, Purgatory and Heaven have challenged generations of artists. *Above* is one of the illustrations for the *Inferno* by Gustave Doré. It shows Dante being guided through the subterranean region by the Roman poet Vergil; they have reached the Third Circle, in which gluttonous sinners are exposed to the rending fangs of fearsome hounds. Very different is the atmosphere of *The Canterbury Tales* of Geoffrey Chaucer. Here all is light and laughter, well exemplified in Thomas Stothard's painting (*below*) of the pilgrims setting out from the Tabard Inn in Southwark. In the midst of the gay throng may be picked out the Young Squire on his white horse, and on the far right the Nun and the Lady Prioress. In the van rides the Miller with his dogs, and just behind him comes Mine Host.

Other men in earlier ages had written of their dream cities, but it was left to Sir Thomas More to invent the name of Utopia and to describe this visionary commonwealth in precise and far-sighted detail. The book was published at Louvain in 1516, in Latin, and here (*left*) is reproduced an illustration from this first edition. As is clearly indicated, Utopia was an island, separated from the mainland by a narrow channel. In the middle distance may be discerned the capital city of Amaurot, well built and stately and standing on the banks of a noble river. At the foot we see a ship of the period, such as the one in which Raphael Hythloday is supposed to have sailed with Amerigo Vespucci to the Americas and to have discovered the island of so many wonders.

Don Quixote, as it is called for short, tells of the adventures, generally absurd but highly amusing, of a lanky, crack-brained knight, as he rode about the Spanish countryside accompanied by his faithful squire Sancho Panza. Here (*below, left*) we see the knight after he has tilted at a row of windmills, thinking they were giants, while Sancho Panza scratches his head in bewilderment. Another of the great classics of European literature is Rabelais's *Gargantua*; the illustration (*below, right*) by Gustave Doré represents the birth of Gargantua, giant child of gigantic parents, who as soon as he was born shouted loudly for drink. . . .

and indications of the souls of men, and while I endeavour by these to portray their lives, may be free to leave more weighty matters and great battles to be treated by others.

The *Lives* reflect the interest of a highly intelligent man in life in general – from the supernatural to the way different characters deal with money. The *Lives* constitute also an affirmation of the capacity of men to be great, to separate themselves from their fellow-citizens and to become a mark, for good or ill, in history. Plutarch, precious source for a historian, is also deservedly the most popular of all the historians of the Ancient world. He, for all his dignity as a magistrate and father of a family, is like a faun playing his flute and inviting us go follow him into the dark forest of the soul of man, full of strange creatures, wild desires and half-heard sounds which give delight. He is not a guide to history so much as a temptation to lose oneself in the past.

THE OLD TESTAMENT

ONE HUNDRED years ago simple people would have considered it strange, almost smacking of blasphemy, to write about the Bible as one of the great books of the world. It was The Book, The Holy Scriptures, divinely inspired from Genesis to the Book of Revelation which ends the New Testament. Church-going made passages from the Bible as familiar as the furniture of a house; the Bible was compulsory reading at home also and young men going out to serve in the Empire were given it by their parents and exhorted to study it regularly. Stories from the Old Testament – the Burning Bush from which God spoke to Abraham, Joseph and his coat of many colours, David playing his harp to Saul and slaying Goliath – were more familiar to English people than any other legends or pieces of history from foreign sources.

The Old Testament, less directly the bearer of the Christian message than the New, was by our forefathers considered as much the word of God. It was particularly revered in Protestant countries where people were free to interpret its meaning according to their own minds and consciences. Nowhere was this more so than in England where the first complete translations of the Bible which were printed, those of Tyndale and of Miles Coverdale, were of great literary merit, as was the Prayer Book of Cranmer compiled in the reign of Henry VIII. The English, all through the Tudor period and after, were filled with intense religious enthusiasm and it was not only the extreme Puritans but the nation which devoured the Bible as though it were a vital food of which it had long been deprived.

The appeal of the Bible was not only religious. It must be remembered that no history nor romance nor poetry except the little-known verses of Chaucer, and perhaps of Skelton, existed when Henry VIII ordered the Bible to be set up in churches and read. Then, in the reign of James I, a committee of scholars and ecclesiastics evolved, on the King's orders, the Authorized Version which was a revision and clarification of the Bishop's Bible which had appeared in 1568 and of others but closer to the spirit of the language than any of its models. As the historian John Greene has written, and it is doubtful if anyone would dissent, "the tongue of the Hebrew, the idiom of Hellenistic Greek, lent themselves with a curious felicity to the purposes of translation. As a mere literary monument, the English version of the Bible remains the noblest example of the English tongue. Its perpetual use made it from the instant of its appearance the standard of our language." In spite of the decay in church-going of modern times, the Old Testament, which is much less familiar than it was to most people, still provides an immense number of phrases, idioms, similes and metaphors which are used in ordinary speech and yet which have their origin in the Bible.

The Old Testament is not a single book but a compendium of myths, historical records and writings by individuals which at various periods were collected by Hebrew priests and scholars as expressing the spirit of the nation and its peculiar message. The Old Testament contains books which are in effect poems such as the *Psalms* and the *Song of Solomon* and the *Book of Lamentations*, and short stories such as *Jonah*, *Ruth* and *Esther*, but these, like the many historical books of the Bible, are also more or less directly concerned with the history of the Hebrews as are the works of the Prophets which have no exact parallel in any other literature. So this compendium is concerned largely with history.

Judged by the standards of political influence on world affairs, the Hebrews were certainly not among the important nations of the world. Some time around 1900 B.C., a small semitic clan or group of families under a patriarch called Abraham moved from Ur of the Chaldees, in Mesopotamia, westwards toward Canaan or Palestine. The Bible story shows that the descendants of Abraham in Canaan suffered severely from famine and gradually migrated into Egypt. There they were at first well received until "there arose a King which knew not Israel" and they were enslaved and employed on various kinds of building works. The kings who had, probably, kindly received Joseph were the Hyksos or Shepherd kings who were themselves Semites and had successfully invaded Egypt and would have had a fellow feeling for the Israelites. And the Pharaoh who began to enslave them was probably Rameses II, who revived an indigenous dynasty.

Around 14–1300 B.C. the Hebrew slaves escaped from Egypt led by a Hebrew born in Egypt with a name, Moses, commonly found on the banks of the Nile as Maose. By an indirect route across the desert, the quick route by Gaza and the coast was too closely guarded by the Egyptians, the Israelites came back to Canaan, the land of milk and honey which their forefathers had left some four hundred years ago. After a while the now numerous Israelite tribes elected a king. The story of their getting a foothold in Canaan is one of violence, cunning and trickery, the necessary qualities no doubt of a small self-conscious group of tribes struggling against long-settled, more numerous and more civilized neighbours. It is a record of ferocious struggle for national existence. The Israelites had been ruled by early Prophets such as Joshua, who succeeded Moses, and by Judges. At the time of an intense struggle with the Philistines, the Israelites elected kings. The first was Saul, the second David of the House of Jesse. The story is now firmly rooted in history.

The history must be broken off for a moment to consider an important fact about the Old Testament as history. When Queen Victoria came to the throne it was generally believed that the world was created in 4004 B.C. To the simple-minded then, as in past centuries, the story of the Old Testament appeared as exact, literal history. By the end of the century, when the work of geologists and physicists had begun to enlarge man's knowledge about the beginning of the physical world, the Bible as history began to be considered largely as fable or folk-lore; by Christians it was thought divinely inspired but still basically mythical. But later, when scholars had deciphered the cuneiform inscriptions of Babylon and Assyria, the historicity of a large part of the Old Testament was vindicated. In the last fifty years or so, when so much has been discovered by archaeology about the Middle East and Egypt, the claim of the whole Old Testament story to be a valuable historical record has been more and more accepted. The story of Abraham, for instance, is now seen to be much more than a folk tale, for the discoveries in the 'thirties of the Amorite Kingdom ruled by the smiling-faced Mari kings have unearthed cities such as Harun and Nathor mentioned in the Biblical narrative but totally unknown until they were unearthed. Many of the happenings during the Exodus from Egypt, too, have now been shown to have a basis in hard fact. Thus, in the Old Testament, a great event was the capture of a huge city called Jericho whose walls fell down at the sound of Joshua's trumpet. Archaeology does not confirm the miracle but discoveries reveal the existence of a huge fortified city, perhaps the oldest in the world, and already 2,000 years old when the Israelites came to it. Until the last thirty years, Jericho was known to be mentioned nowhere but in the Bible.

In 1000 B.C. or thereabouts history for the civilized Greeks of the fifth century was still concerned with largely mythical heroes – the date of the siege of Troy is around 1200 B.C. – but King David is a well-authenticated historical personage who reigned from 1000 to 961 B.C.

David was succeeded by Solomon under whom the small kingdom

of Israel prospered and grew rich. Solomon, however, lost the affection of his people on account of his extravagance and of the heavy
taxes he imposed. The kingdom split in two at his death in 922 B.C.,
into a northern realm called Israel or Ephraim and a smaller southern
land called Judah, largely a flat mountainous territory the capital of
which was Jerusalem. It was shortly after the death of Solomon that
the Bible began to be put together. There are, except for the later
Prophets, no means of knowing the names of the authors of the Holy
Scriptures. The tradition according to which Moses was the author
of the first five books of the Bible, known to Jews as the Torah or
the Law, is unlikely to be true. The first real makers of the Bible are
the priests or scholars who began to collect traditional writings in the
ninth century B.C. One such group is called the J source from the fact
that the word Jehovah or Jahveh is used for the name of God. This
source was located in Judah. A slightly later source is called E, from
the preference for the use of the word Elohim for God, and this
source was scholars living in the northern kingdom of Israel. There
is a later source which used the work both of J and E, and a Priestly
source which gathered together and corrected records in the fifth
century.

In 721 B.C. Israel was overwhelmed by the Assyrians who were
building up their short-lived military empire which covered most of
the Middle East. And about 140 years later, when Assyria had gone
the way of many empires, the kingdom of Judah was conquered by
Babylon; Jerusalem was destroyed. Then came the empire of the
Medes and Persians which overthrew Babylon and the great King
Cyrus allowed the Jews to return to Jerusalem to rebuild the city and
reconstitute their kingdom. And so in the fifth and fourth centuries,
at the time for instance of the Golden Age of Athens, the Hebrews
were once more a people living in a land of their own. Conquered
by Alexander the Great in 334 B.C.. the Hebrew way of life and
tradition at first had little to fear from the Greeks, but later, after
Alexander's empire had been divided among his generals, an attempt
was made to interfere with the Jewish religion. Under the Macca-
bees the Hebrews regained their independence for a century or so
until, around 65 B.C., domestic quarrels between rivals for the
throne encouraged Rome to step in. The last great rebellion of the
Jews against Rome led, in A.D. 70, to the destruction of the Temple in
Jerusalem and to the dispersion of the Jews about the world. There
was to be no Hebrew state until A.D. 1947 when the present Republic
of Israel came into being.

Now the history of the Hebrews, though dramatic and moving,

particularly when it is looked at from its beginning around 2000 B.C. until today, would not have become perhaps the best-known book throughout the Christian world were it not for two fundamental reasons. One is that in the Christian religion, the Old Testament fore-shadows the New with the message of Christ. From a Jewish point of view, Christianity itself is the heresy of a sect, a heresy which of course grew to gigantic proportions. As Mr. Robert Davidson, lecturer in Hebrew and Old Testament at St. Andrew's University and the author of a penetrating work on the Old Testament, has written:

Christianity's missionary message was steeped in the faith of the Old Testament. The true Messiah had come in Jesus of Nazareth. He had inaugurated the new covenant. His followers were the new Israel upon whom God had poured out his spirit. In the life, death, and resurrection triumph of Jesus, the Old Testament had come to its full fruition. For the Christian, therefore, the Old Testament should never be an alien or unimportant book. Abraham, Isaac and Jacob, Moses and the prophets are his own ancestors in the faith. He will see the story of a church, the people of God, beginning when Abraham journeyed forth from Ur of the Chaldees. He will see in the story of God's deliverance of his people out of enslavement in Egypt the pattern of all God's gracious dealings with men which reach their climax in that greater deliverance offered in Jesus Christ.

The other fundamental reason cannot be divorced from Christi-anity but it is one with which non-Christians, atheists, agnostics, Buddhists, Mohammedans or believers in any of the religions of the world cannot but be concerned. The Old Testament is the history of a people's relationship with God and it is, in the annals of the world, the only such story. It starts with the covenant which God made with Abraham:

Now the Lord had said unto Abram get thee out of thy country and from thy kindred and from thy father's house unto a land that I will shew thee. And I will make of thee a great nation and I will bless thee and make thy name great.
And I will bless them that bless thee and curse him that curseth thee; and in thee shall all families of the earth be blessed.

From then until the end of the Old Testament, prophets and priests, kings and men of war and the people themselves are really interpreting and re-interpreting this covenant. In the case of the people, they are often trying to get out of it – to return to Egypt

when they are in the desert in 1300 B.C., to worship Baal or the flesh-
pots, or to forsake the new customs and to behave like the more
civilized people around them, as in the days of the Greek domination. But they cannot rid themselves of their destiny which is to be
unable to escape from God and his covenant.

The originality of the Old Testament, that which gives it its
universal validity, is the conception that there is only one God, that
he is a God of righteousness, that he is also the God of all the World.
Jehovah is not the property of the Hebrews, unlike the other Gods of
the Ancient World who belonged to their worshippers. Over and
over again, Jehovah has, painfully, to be understood by the Hebrews
as a God of righteousness who despises burnt offerings and even
prayer unless the spirit is there.

And when ye spead forth your hands, I will hide mine eyes from you.
Yea, when ye make many prayers, I will not hear

says Isaiah.

The God of the Hebrews is the God of all men and not a tribal
God. The Hebrews consider themselves as a people of priests, the
Chosen People who have made a covenant with God from which
they achieve greater gains and also greater disasters than other
people – and this their history shows. The Old Testament is the story
of the relationship of a people with God. If one made a compendium
of the works of Greek literature of about the length of the Old
Testament – with extracts from Homer, Herodotus, Thucydides,
Aeschylus, Sophocles, Euripides, Plato and Aristotle – it would be a
far richer work from a human point of view, far more varied in its
imaginative and intellectual appeal than the Old Testament. Indeed
the Hebrews were neither imaginative nor philosophical. They were
a passionate and practical race, and their writers, when commenting,
as all great writing does on the meaning of life, were really concerned with one aspect of life – the relation of man to the Creator.
But in this narrowness lay their genius. Since this aspect of life is,
after all, one that only the fool in his heart ignores by saying there is
no God, since indeed it is perhaps the most profound of all questions,
the Old Testament, this record of a savage people, without graces
except the fierce ones of the desert, the vineyard and the battlefield,
remains the most profound of all books.

THE NEW TESTAMENT

FOR MANY years after the coming of Christianity into the world, the members of what had started as a Jewish sect had no Scriptures beyond those they shared with the other Jews. There was no reason why they should have. Not only had many of them known Jesus in the flesh and had listened to his discourses, but they believed with the utmost confidence that sooner rather than later he would return to them as their Risen Lord, coming down from heaven in clouds of glory to establish on earth a new age and order of peace and happiness for all the children of God.

But the Parousia – the Second Coming – was delayed, and as year followed upon year the number of converts, both Jew and Gentile, increased. Many of these had no personal knowledge of Christ, and their contacts with the apostles were few and far between. The need for authoritative statements of Christian doctrine and practice became increasingly apparent, and so it was that there came into existence a body of literature that was written over a period of at least fifty years, by a number of writers who differed widely in temperament and background and outlook, as well as in their ways of writing and in their reasons for writing at all. To this literature, after it had been subjected to a lengthy process of selection and editing and reproduction, was given eventually the name of *The New Testament*.

The word Testament comes from the Latin, and is a translation of the Greek word meaning covenant. In the Bible the special relationship of God with His people is generally described as a covenant. The first covenant is the constant theme of the Old Testament; but this proved ineffectual, and a new Covenant was thereupon effected, by and through the incarnation, death and resurrection of Jesus Christ. In Christian belief, the two Covenants are inseparably connected, the one leading up to the other as its culminating climax, and the New Testament is therefore regarded as the end and crown of the Bible.

Greatly superior though it be in theological importance, the New Testament is a very much smaller book than the Old Testament – less than a third as long in fact. And like the Old Testament it is not one book but a collection of books. There are twenty-seven of them, and as they have come down to us they are all written in a special form of Greek. It is not the classical Greek of Plato and Sophocles, nor of the much more nearly contemporary Philo and Josephus, but approaches very closely to that form of Greek, known as *koine*, that was the common vernacular over the eastern parts of the Roman Empire, the language of the home and the market-place, of the great run of the not-very-well-educated mass of ordinary folk. But the most careful study of the surviving papyri has shown that it is not identical with the *koine*. There are numerous slight differences in words and expressions, and it is now generally supposed that these reflect the influence of Aramaic, the language that was the common tongue of the Palestinian Jews and which Jesus himself employed.

None of the twenty-seven books is dated, nor is the internal evidence of such a character as to enable us to arrive at anything like precision in the chronology. It is generally agreed, however, that the books were not written in the order in which they are printed, and the earliest would seem to have been some of the Epistles that are attributed to St. Paul.

While all the dates in the earliest period of Christian history are exceedingly uncertain, the balance of opinion would seem to indicate that the vision on the road to Damascus that transformed that fierce Jewish persecutor of Christians, Saul of Tarsus, into Paul the Christian missionary, took place around A.D. 33, and that the first missionary journey of Paul and Barnabas began in A.D. 46 or 47. Perhaps it was some four or five years later that Paul began to reinforce his spoken word with written letters or epistles.

There is no need to look far for his reasons. Little cells or communities or churches of Christians were coming into existence, many of them as the result of his own preaching, and the new believers were in need of further instruction, of incitement to perseverance in the Christian life, of encouragement, of warning against false prophets and doctrine as well as against conduct that was wrong and sinful and unworthy of those who were making a profession of the Christian faith. Almost certainly the earliest of the Pauline Epistles were those addressed to the Christians in Thessalonica, the great Greek city (the modern Salonika) where Paul and Silas had had such a rough reception at the hands of the Jewish-instigated rabble. The First Epistle to the Thessalonians is usually dated to about A.D. 52, but the Second Epistle raises problems that can hardly be answered. At about the same time Paul is supposed to have written the Epistle to the small band of Christians who had declared themselves in Galatia, in the highlands of Asia Minor. Two or three years later the letters to the Christians in Corinth were prepared and dispatched, and the

Epistle to the Romans may be dated to A.D. 57 or 58. As regards the remainder of the Pauline Epistles, they are generally supposed to have been penned by Paul after his arrival as a state-prisoner in Rome. But when this was (A.D. 60, 61, 62?), how long he lived there in his own hired house, and when he eventually was martyred, cannot be decided with certainty.

There are other Epistles in the New Testament, ascribed to the Apostle Peter, James, Jude brother of James, and John, who may or may not have been the apostle. Some authorities have argued that *James* may well be one of the earliest of the New Testament books, even ante-dating the Pauline Epistles, but others have maintained that it is late, belonging perhaps to the early part of the second century, to which period the other Epistles just mentioned have also been ascribed. *Hebrews* presents problems that are insoluble.

The Epistles were written in the special form of Greek mentioned above on sheets of papyrus (the common writing material of the ancients, made out of the pith of the paper-reed cut into thin strips and pressed together) about five inches by nine inches. Since there was no post in the Roman Empire available to ordinary citizens, they would be sent by hand, in the wallet of some trusted messenger. On receipt they would be read and re-read in the Christian assembly, expounded and talked over, and copied out for wider distribution.

While the Epistles were getting into circulation throughout the Christian world, another and more important and vitally interesting body of New Testament literature was coming into being. This was, of course, the gospels, the four narratives of the "good news" of the life, teaching, death and resurrection of Christ.

No books in all the world have been examined with such care, explored and explained, commented upon, argued about and fought over, as these four short biographies. Which came first? Who was the author of this one, this, that and the other? What were the original sources drawn upon? Were they all written in the first place in Greek, or was at least some part of the gospel story put down in Aramaic, the language of the oral tradition? Libraries have been written on these and cognate problems.

Jesus wrote nothing – at least so far as we know – and for a time those who had been his disciples felt no impulse to write any account of what he had said and done. Why write a biography of one who was so shortly expected to return to their midst? But at length the necessity for an authoritative account of the Lord's deeds and sayings became accepted, and steps were taken to fill the gaps in knowledge. By almost common agreement, the first document telling the story of Christ's life was produced in Palestine round about A.D. 50. It is supposed to have been mainly a collection of sayings of Jesus as they were remembered by some of those who had heard them as they fell from his lips, and was probably composed in the Aramaic vernacular. This hypothetical document is generally referred to as Q, which is short for *Quelle*, German for source, because it is held to have been the source of much of the material that is common to both *Matthew* and *Luke*. But the oldest of the four existing gospels is generally held to be *Mark*, which was traditionally based upon the reminiscences of Peter. It is the shortest of the four, but it was originally a little longer, for some accident happened to the last page or pages and the story breaks off in the middle of a sentence. As to its date, it was written probably between A.D. 65 and 75. *Luke* and *Matthew* are later, possibly A.D. 80–85 and 85–90 respectively. But those Bible scholars who are inclined to favour the theory of an Aramaic original ascribe all four gospels to before A.D. 70, the year in which Jerusalem was taken and sacked by the Romans under Titus.

The first three gospels are so much alike in their essentials that they are styled the Synoptics, a term derived from the Greek words meaning "what can be brought together under one combined view, or synopsis"; but St. John's Gospel is very different, presenting problems which would seem to defy solution. So many are the differences between the Fourth Gospel and its fellows that some scholars have decided that it is not to be relied upon as history, although its value in theology is immense.

Following upon the gospels is the only book of history proper in the New Testament, the *Acts of the Apostles*. This is stated to have been written by one who had prepared a "former treatise of all that Jesus began both to do and teach", and the author in question is taken to have been St. Luke. The book is the first Church history, it covers a period of about thirty years, and its date is perhaps toward the end of the first century, perhaps about A.D. 85. The narrative itself would seem to end about A.D. 62.

Finally, there is the last book in the collection, "The Revelation of St. John the Divine," or *Revelation* for short. This is the only specimen of apocalyptic literature in the New Testament, and it does indeed contain matter that is "covered", matter that is as fascinating as it is mysterious. Speculation has run riot in its interpretation, but the simplest explanation is that the book's lurid prophecies reflect the furious hatred of a Jewish author, who saw in the approaching downfall of the Roman imperial power the occasion for the establishment of a new heaven and a new earth on its ruins. In this case the book may be dated to the reign of Nero, say about A.D. 65, or perhaps thirty years later to the reign of Domitian.

The earliest Christians had no other Bible than what we call the Old Testament, which they shared with the Jews, and there is no reason to suppose that their authors had any idea that they were contributing toward the formation of a New Testament. As the second century wore on, however, we may trace the emergence of a *canon* of New Testament scripture. To begin with there were many more than the twenty-seven books in circulation, but the number was steadily reduced on the grounds of lack of authenticity or theological soundness. There were even more than four gospels claiming apostolic authorship, but the very evident superiority of the four we know soon led to their inclusion in the canon, while their rivals were as definitely excluded. It was not until the close of the fourth century that under the influence of St. Jerome and St. Augustine the New Testament canon was finally settled at the synods of Hippo and Carthage (A.D. 397).

The oldest copy of any part of the New Testament in existence is a tiny papyrus fragment of a second-century *codex* (that is a book, not a roll) containing a few verses of the Gospel of St. John, which is now in the Rylands Library at Manchester. It would seem that the Christians were the first to make use of the papyrus codex, and it may be the case, as has been suggested, that this was because they wished to be able to read the four gospels side by side instead of in four separate rolls. More than 3,000 Greek manuscripts of the New Testament writings are in existence, and the number is being added to almost year by year. Some of these are *uncials*, so called because they are written in capital letters without any break between the words; of these the earliest and the most valuable are the four great codices, viz., Codex Sinaiticus (fourth century) and Codex Alexandrinus (fifth century), both in the British Museum in London; Codex Vaticanus at Rome (fourth century), and Codex Bezae (sixth century) at Cambridge. Of these the Codex Sinaiticus contains the whole text of the New Testament. Then there is a much larger number of MSS. that are called *cursives*, because they are written in a smooth, running hand.

In addition to the New Testament manuscripts we possess a large number of quotations in early Christian writers, from which it is possible to ascertain the text used in their time, and also a number of versions or translations of the New Testament into Latin, Syriac, Coptic and other languages, some of which were made much earlier than our most ancient manuscripts.

For generations now scholars have studied and compared these different witnesses to the text of the New Testament, and the work goes on. A number of variations have been discovered, but the great majority would seem to be of but slight importance. On the whole, then, we are fully justified in holding that in the accepted text of the New Testament we have the authentic record of what the earliest Christians preached and practised as "the glorious gospel of Christ".

THE KORAN

WHEN THE Meccans challenged Mohammed to perform a miracle as proof of his Divine mission, he appealed, boldly and confidently, to the book which was taking shape under his supervision. So wonderful a work (he maintained), written in such superlatively beautiful language and expressing the most profound and majestic of religious truths, could surely not have been written by a mere man, most certainly not by such an unlettered man as he was himself. It was indeed a miracle, the miracle of miracles, this book that had come down from heaven. . . .

The book in question was the Koran, as we generally call it, although a more correct rendering is Quran, which is an Arabic word meaning reading, lecture, or recitation, or perhaps that which ought to be read. For more than thirteen centuries this book has been the sacred scripture – the Bible, if you like – of one of the great world religions, the one which is often called Mohammedanism after the Prophet who preached it, although the name that he himself chose, and therefore the better one for us to use, is Islam, which means submission or surrender to the Will of God, or Allah.

Those who profess Islam – and they constitute a very large portion of the human race, particularly in Africa and Asia – are often called Mohammedans, but they themselves prefer the term Moslems, or Muslims, which word comes from the same Arabic root as Islam, and means believers, or those who have surrendered themselves to Allah. They prefer this term because they feel that Mohammedan suggests that they worship Mohammed, in the same way that Christians worship Christ. But this is completely untrue. Moslems do *not* worship Mohammed, although they hold him in the greatest esteem and reverence as the last and most authoritative of the Prophets who have been commissioned by Allah to proclaim his message among men. The shortest and simplest and most emphatic of the statements of fundamental Moslem belief is, "There is no God but Allah, and Mohammed is the Prophet of Allah".

Even more erroneous, if possible, is the assertion that is sometimes made that Mohammed wrote the Koran. To Moslems this sounds as the most shocking blasphemy, since it is their unquestioned belief that the author of the Koran was none other but Allah Himself. The

78

original volume is believed to have rested, since the beginning of time, on a vast table placed beside the throne of Allah in heaven. A copy, written on paper and bound in silk and adorned with gold and precious stones, was carried down from heaven by the Angel Gabriel, and shown to Mohammed on a number of occasions, generally once a year, but in the last year of the Prophet's mission, twice. Gabriel is further believed to have dictated passages to Mohammed as occasion required, over a period of twenty-three years, and these were repeated by the Prophet to scribes or amanuenses who took down the words as they fell from his lips, or they stored them up in their minds.

Mohammed called the Koran a miracle, and, apart altogether from its religious significance, in a sense it is. It is written in the purest, most classical form of Arabic – and yet before its appearance there was practically nothing in Arabic other than a few martial lays and love songs. It is because the Koran is written in Arabic that Arabic has become one of the most widely used of languages, being spoken not only in Arabia but in many other countries, either as the principal or auxiliary tongue. Wherever there are Moslems – in North Africa and the Near East, in Nigeria, Madagascar, Zanzibar and many other places – the Koran is generally the basis of education, law and political systems, as well as of religion. By Moslems everywhere it is accepted as a completely reliable and authoritative guide in every aspect of daily life.

It is not a very large book; indeed, it is only about three-quarters of the length of the New Testament. According to one Moslem statistician who has taken the trouble of counting the words it has 77,639, although another has made the count 77,934. Someone has even counted the letters, making the total 323,015.

Like the Bible, the Koran is divided into chapters and verses. The chapters are called *suras*, and there are 114 of them, varying greatly in length. In general the arrangement is in order of length, the longest ones being put first; but if a chronological arrangement were adopted, the order would have to be reversed, since in the main the shorter suras date from the early part of Mohammed's missionary career, when he was in Mecca, and the longer ones belong to the period when he had quitted Mecca and was established at Medina.

There is one principal exception to this generalization: the opening chapter of the Koran is one of the shortest, containing only half a dozen lines. It is the Moslem counterpart of the Lord's Prayer, and it is repeated by faithful Moslems everywhere a number of times each day. It is called the *Fatihah* (that is, the preface, introduction, beginning), and here it is in the translation made by J. M. Rodwell:

> *Praise be to God, Lord of the worlds!*
> *The compassionate, the merciful!*
> *King on the day of judgment!*
> *Thee only do we worship,*
> *   and to Thee do we cry for help.*
> *Guide Thou us on the right path,*
> *The path of those to whom Thou art gracious,*
> *Not of those with whom Thou art angered,*
> *   nor of those who go astray.*

This theme is the beginning of the Koran and likewise its end. There is not a page from first to last in which the power and majesty, the goodness and loving-kindness, the mercy but also the terror of the One God are not described. To quote from another chapter, No. 2 (one of the longest, "revealed partly at Mecca and partly at Medina"):

> *Allah! There is no God but He, the Living, the Eternal One!*
> *He neither slumbers nor sleeps.*
> *Everything in Heaven and in earth belongs to Him.*
> *Who shall intercede with Him without His permission?*
> *He knows all that is past and all that is to come.*
> *Men understand nothing of what He knows unless He wills.*
> *Over Heaven and earth extends His Throne,*
> *Their preservation is not the slightest trouble to Him,*
> *The Most-High, the All-Glorious One.*

And then there is the shortest chapter of all, Chapter 112, almost at the very end of the book:

> *Say, God is One, the Eternal God!*
> *He begetteth not, neither is He begotten.*
> *And there is not any one like unto Him.*

The nearest counterpart in the Koran to the Apostles' Creed is contained in Chapter 4: "O true believers, believe in God (Allah) and His Apostle, and the scripture which He hath caused to descend unto His Apostle, and the scriptures which He hath formerly sent down. And whosoever does not believe in God, and His angels, and His scriptures, and His Apostles, and the Last Day, he surely has strayed a very long way from the truth." From this and many other passages in the Koran it is clear that Mohammed did not believe that he was preaching a new religion, but that he had been commissioned by Allah to restore to its original purity the one and only true religion that had been revealed to Adam and Abraham and their successors in the line of Prophets, but which in the course of time had become corrupted.

Twenty-eight of this line of divinely-inspired men are mentioned in the Koran by name, and of these eighteen are drawn from the Old Testament and three from the New (Zacharias, John the Baptist, and Jesus Christ). The last of the glorious line is Mohammed himself – the last and greatest, the Seal of the whole long succession. The "scripture" which Allah had "caused to descend to His Apostle", that is, to Mohammed, is, of course the Koran; and the "scriptures formerly sent down" include the Jewish Torah or Pentateuch, the Psalms of David, and the Gospel of Jesus given in the New Testament. All are part of God's Word, but the only book in which the whole truth is given is the Koran, the latest of those "sent down". From these and many other passages it is clear that Mohammed had considerable knowledge of the Bible, which he probably gathered from Jews and Christians whom he had come across in his trading expeditions to Syria, or in the towns and villages nearer home.

Angels are often mentioned in the Koran. Their home is in heaven, where they hold up the throne of Allah and worship Him perpetually. They act also as His messengers, and from time to time come down to earth to carry out His behests. One of the most important of the angelic host is Gabriel, who was charged with the transmission of the Koran to Mohammed.

Another subject to which much space is devoted is the Day of Judgment and what comes after. Many passages might be quoted, and what follow are from the English translation of the Koran made in 1734 by George Sale, an English oriental scholar, which is specially valuable because of the "Preliminary Discourse" and the copious notes with which it is provided.

"When the sun shall be folded up, and when the stars shall fall, and when the mountains shall be made to pass away; and when the camels ten months gone with young shall be neglected, and when the wild beasts shall be gathered together, and when the seas shall boil; and when the souls shall be joined again to their bodies; and when the girl who hath been buried alive shall be asked for what crime she was put to death" – a reference, this, to the old pagan custom among the Arabs of destroying unwanted girl babies – "and when the books shall be laid open; and when the heaven shall be removed; and when hell shall burn fiercely, and when paradise shall

be brought near; every soul shall know what it hath wrought..."
(Chap. 81).

"The fate of every man have we bound about his neck; and we
will produce unto him, on the day of resurrection, a book wherein
his actions shall be recorded; it shall be offered him open, and the
angels shall say unto him, Read thy book; thine own soul will be
a sufficient accountant against thee this day" (Chap. 17).

Those who appear before the Judgment Seat will be separated into
"the companions of the right hand (how happy shall the companions
of the right hand be!), and the companions of the left hand (how
miserable shall the companions of the left hand be!)" The former
are those "who shall approach near unto God.... They shall dwell
in gardens of delight.... Reposing on couches adorned with gold
and precious stones... youths shall go round about to attend them,
with goblets, and beakers, and a cup of flowing wine; their heads
shall not ache by drinking the same, neither shall their reason be
disturbed.... And there shall accompany them fair damsels having
large black eyes, resembling pearls hidden in their shells.... Verily
we have created the damsels of paradise by a peculiar creation; and
we have made them virgins, beloved by their husbands, of equal age
with them, for the delight of the companions of the right hand....
But the companions of the left hand shall dwell amidst burning
winds, and scalding water, under the shade of a black smoke, neither
cool nor agreeable. For they enjoyed the pleasures of life before this,
while on earth; and obstinately persisted in a heinous wickedness..."
(Chap. 56).

While the Koran is chiefly concerned with doctrine, the distinctive practices of Islam – prayer, almsgiving, fasting, and pilgrimage
once in a lifetime to Mecca – are also described and enjoined. But in
conclusion a few words are necessary about the way – the very
strange way – in which the Koran was compiled and handed down.
There seems to have been no systematic reporting. As the words
were pronounced by the Prophet in his trance-like state they were
scribbled on anything that came handy – scraps of parchment and
leather, camels' shoulder-blades and mutton bones, ribs of palm-
leaves, pieces of board; and then these were flung, higgledy-piggledy,
into a chest or some other convenient receptacle. Quite a number of
the suras were not written down at all, but were memorized by those
standing by.

Only when the Prophet was dead and there could be no more
revelations was the necessity for putting on record what he had said
properly realized. There was nothing, of course, in his own hand-

writing. One of the first acts of Mohammed's successor in the Moslem leadership, his friend Abu Bekr, was to order the young man who had been Mohammed's secretary to turn out the collection of oddments and get them into some kind of order. They were then transcribed, and had added to them what could be gathered from the "hearts of men".

Then about A.D. 650, that is nearly twenty years after Mohammed's death, a fresh version was prepared, which was henceforth regarded as altogether standard and canonical. Three fair copies were made of this version, and one was sent to each of the three military camps – Damascus, Basra, and Kufa – which were established as the capitals of the great new Moslem empire, while the original copy was preserved in the mosque at Medina in which Mohammed was buried. All later manuscripts of the Koran have proceeded from one or other of these four. There is no reason to doubt that in the "Excellent Book", as the Moslems call the Koran, we have the actual words that Mohammed used when, all those many centuries ago, he uttered his pronouncements as the Messenger or Apostle of Allah, the One Most High God.

THE DIVINE COMEDY
DANTE ALIGHIERI

IF A LIMIT may be set to the period of medieval literature, Dante's *Divine Comedy* may be said to have brought it to an end in a glorious climax. Here all the greatest and best in thought and work that flowered in the millennium between the fall of the Roman Empire and the close of the thirteenth century, is given a new vitality and endowed with poetic passion. Of all the great figures who embellish the whole pageant of literature, Dante shares an equal place with Shakespeare. Fortunately, the lack of details available about the life of Shakespeare does not apply to Dante, who is revealed to us as the hero of one of the strangest and most beautiful love stories in the world.

Dante was born in Florence in 1265, the son of an ancient but impoverished family. Having served in the Florentine cavalry at the battle of Campaldino, in 1289, from 1295 onwards he began to take part in political life, and for two months in 1300 was a member of the chief magistracy of the Florentine republic.

At this time Florence was rent with political dissensions. Dante supported the constitutional party that resisted papal intervention. In October, 1301, he went with two others in a delegation to Pope Boniface VIII, to dissuade him from sending Charles of Valois as peacemaker to Tuscany. During Dante's absence, Charles entered Florence, and a general proscription of Dante's party followed. Dante was arrested on a false charge of corruption, sentenced to a heavy fine and two years' exile, and excluded from all public office in perpetuity by a decree of 27 January, 1302. A second decree of 10 March condemned him to be burned alive if he fell into the hands of the governing party.

At first Dante joined his companions in an attempt to return to Florence by force of arms, but he soon broke away from them, wandering "a pilgrim, almost a beggar" through northern and central Italy. During the next eight years he wrote a number of treatises in Latin.

The election of Henry of Luxembourg as Emperor of the Holy Roman Empire in 1310 brought Dante back into active politics, but

Henry's death, two years later, shattered all Dante's hopes, and though a general amnesty of all exiles was declared in 1315, Dante refused to return to Florence on conditions that did not recognize his innocence. Refusing an official summons to Florence, he was again sentenced to death. This virtually condemned him to continued exile.

He had already gained a reputation as a poet with his *Vita Nuova* (*The New Life*) as long ago as 1292. The *Vita Nuova* is a collection of lyrics set in a prose narrative, telling in mystical fashion the story of his love for Beatrice, and closing with the hint of "a wondrous vision" and the promise to "say of her what was never said of any woman". During the last phase of his exile, he began to implement his promise in the *Divine Comedy* which he completed only a few months before his death in 1321.

Dante had first met Beatrice when he was nine, and she was the same age. The children did not speak, but, says Dante, "from that day forward Love quite governed my soul". Nine years passed before the poet saw her again. She was dressed in white and was walking with two older ladies in the streets of Florence.

Again they did not speak, but "she turned her eyes thither where I stood sorely abashed, and by her unspeakable courtesy she saluted me with so virtuous a bearing that I seemed then and there to behold the very limits of blessedness". During the whole of his lifetime he saw Beatrice only once again.

Beatrice, who has been identified as Bice Portinari, married and died when she was thirty-five. Learning of her death, Dante wrote, "When I had lost the first delight of my soul I remained so pierced with sadness that no comfort availed me anything."

The *Vita Nuova* appeared two years after Beatrice's death. In the same year as he declared his passion for her in some of the most beautiful lyrics written in any language, he married a Florentine lady of noble birth, Gemma Donati, by whom he had two sons and two daughters.

His political troubles must be held responsible for his producing no poetry between 1292 and the *Divine Comedy*. Not until he had given up all hope of influencing the political scene was his mind freed and he was able to turn once more to his one absorbing and inspiring passion, his love for Beatrice.

The *Divine Comedy* is a description of heaven, hell and purgatory. Taken in its literal sense, it is a vision of the state of men's souls after death; but it is much more than this, it is an allegory demonstrating man's need of spiritual illumination and guidance.

The poet, having lost his way in a gloomy forest, meets the great poet of ancient Rome, Vergil, whose *Aeneid* also presents a vision of man's life after death from the pagan viewpoint. Vergil promises to show him the punishments of hell, and leads him to the gate of the inferno, above which are inscribed the words, "All hope abandon, ye who enter here".

Within a short distance they reach the entrance hall of hell, a dark plain on which the Spirits of the Selfish and the Idle, stung by wasps and hornets, run for ever behind a whirling flag.

Having crossed the plain, they come to the River Acheron, the Stream of Sorrow, where the ferryman, Charon, a fierce old man with eyes like wheels of flame, is busy transporting across the river crowds of suppliants. On the other side, the souls enter Limbo, the first circle of hell.

In Limbo, Dante finds the souls of the great pagans, who, though they were great and noble in their lives, are confined here because they are not baptized. Among them are the great classical poets, Horace, Ovid and Homer, who welcome Dante as a poet like themselves.

Going on, Vergil leads Dante to the second circle of hell, the entrance to which is guarded by an enormous dog with the face of a man. He is Minos, the Infernal Judge.

Here the famous guilty lovers of past ages are punished, by being tossed about by a mighty wind.

> Now 'gin the rueful wailings to be heard.
> Now am I come where many a plaining voice
> Smites on mine ear. Into a place I came
> Where light was silent all. Bellowing there groan'd
> A noise, as of a sea in tempest torn
> By warring winds. The stormy blast of Hell
> With restless fury drives the spirits on,
> Whirled round and dash'd amain with sore annoy.
> When they arrive before the ruinous sweep,
> There shrieks are heard, there lamentations, moans,
> And blasphemies 'gainst the good Power in Heaven.[1]

Among these "carnal sinners" are Semiramis and Cleopatra, Helen and Paris, Tristan and Isolde, and above all Francesca of Rimini and her lover Paolo. Francesca's account of how they were surprised and killed together by her husband, John the Lame, made

---

[1] From the translation made by Henry Cary, published in 1814, which has become a classic in its own right. The poet Rossetti also made a translation which is not so good.

Dante faint with pity. This is one of the most glorious passages of the whole work.

Having recovered, Dante finds himself in the third circle of hell, where the gluttons lie in mud under a continual rain of hail, snow and filthy water, while the giant dog, Cerberus, barks and snarls at them. In the fourth circle he sees the spendthrifts and misers, who pass their time rolling huge boulders to crash against one another.

Farther on they come to the Styx, the marsh in which the Sullen and Angry writhe and fight. At last they reach a high tower, from which two beacons are shining. Phlegyas, the ferryman, takes them across the lake, to the entrance to Satan's city of Dis, whose gates are guarded by a horde of demons. An Angel, passing across the lake dry-footed, scatters these monsters from the path of the travellers.

Leaving the city by a chasm of shattered rocks, they come to a river of blood, in which stand the Tyrants, while troops of centaurs, led by Chiron, gallop up and down the bank and shoot the Sinners with their arrows. Further on they meet the Suicides, whose spirits have become stunted trees. Beyond the wood lies a naked plain of fiery sand, where the Violent stand under a slow eternal shower of sparks.

Going along the bank of the river of blood, the two poets come to the place where it falls in a cataract into the gulf. Here Vergil throws Dante's girdle into the waters, and at once the monster Geryon swims up to them. They mount him and are carried to the eighth circle, where the Seducers, Flatterers and the False Prophets are undergoing their various vile punishments. From the region of the Hypocrites, Thieves, Evil Counsellors and Schismatics, one of whom, who had rebelled against Henry II of England, holds up by the hair his severed head to talk to Dante, they reach the ninth circle.

Here the sound of a great horn, like thunder, strikes their ears, and they see three giants standing on the edge of the lowest pit of hell. One of them, Antaeus, sets them down on the bottom of the pit, which is a sea of everlasting ice, in which the shapes of the tormented appear like flies in amber.

From here they come to the very depths of hell, the Judecca, the place of the Betrayers. At the very centre of it stands the Arch-Traitor Satan, champing three sinners in his huge jaws, and sending from his vast bats' wings an icy blast which freezes all the sea.

Passing by Satan, the poets go up through a long steep passage,

> *Till on our view the beautiful lights of Heaven*
> *Dawn'd through a circular opening in the cave:*
> *Thence issuing we again behold the stars.*

At last they come out beside the Hill of Purgatory. Unlike other medieval writers, Dante sets purgatory in the open air. Round the steep sides of its mountain run seven circles, each corresponding to one of the Seven Deadly Sins. In the lower terraces are expiated the sins of the spirit, in the fourth, sloth, which is a sin of both spirit and flesh, and in the three upper, the sins of the flesh.

When they have passed through these terraces they enter the Earthly Paradise, where Dante sees the mystical procession which represents the triumphant march of the Church. At the end of this procession, Beatrice appears in a chariot, surrounded by a hundred angels singing and scattering flowers. She is dressed in the mystical colours, red, white and green, and is crowned with a wreath of olive leaves, the symbol of wisdom and peace. When she appears, Vergil vanishes to return to Limbo, from whence he came to guide his fellow-poet through hell and purgatory.

The third part of the *Divine Comedy*, the *Paradiso*, is its crowning glory. With Beatrice as his guide now, Dante passes through nine Heavens which are spheres revolving round our own earth, till he reaches the final motionless heaven, the abode of God. The eight lowest heavens are visible from earth. Above them is the crystalline heaven, which directs by its movements the daily revolutions of all the others. Here nature has its beginnings, from it time and motion and all celestial influences for the government of the world emanate.

Above it, the climax of the vision, is the infinite and motionless sea of divine love where God makes blessed the saints and angels in the Vision of His Essence.

The old commentators on Dante laid much stress on his theology, his metaphysics, his use of allegory and so on. They looked upon him not so much as the great poet as the magician from whose verses they drew oracles. One maintains that Beatrice represents the Church, another that she personifies the love of God. We cannot view it in this way in these modern times, but that does not detract from its true greatness.

The *Divine Comedy* is in fact a bridge between two ages; its conception of morality rather than belief as the basis of goodness was a forerunner of the new ideas of humanism. Above all, it is a grand and mighty poem, a story of immortal joys and sorrows, having no parallel or equal among the literature of the world.

THE CANTERBURY TALES

GEOFFREY CHAUCER

ON AN April morning, many centuries ago, a band of pilgrims set out from the Tabard Inn in Southwark to go to Canterbury. We should not suppose that the fact that they were pilgrims means that they were specially devout. Pilgrimages in the Middle Ages – and the year in question is somewhere in the thirteen-eighties – were a most welcome break in the monotonous round of daily existence, an occasion for seeing the sights and meeting fresh people and exchanging gossip and tales of high life, and of low. There were numerous religious shrines at home and abroad that attracted the pilgrim hosts, but in England by far the most popular was Canterbury, where in the great cathedral stood the magnificent tomb of Thomas à Becket – St. Thomas of Canterbury – hard by the spot where in 1170 he had been brutally slain by four of King Henry's knights.

Of all the seasons of the year the springtime was the most favoured, when the roads, or rather the trackways, had become passable after the floods and snows of winter. So we may imagine them rising from their beds of straw and performing their scanty toilet, partaking of an early breakfast of bread and ale – those men and women who were to become the most famous of all the pilgrim bands of English story. There is the clatter of horses' hooves, the clank of stable chains, the shouts of the ostlers, a medley of "hail" and "well met" and "have we got everything?", while mine host keeps on bustling around with his cups of ale and jingling the pence in his pouch. And somewhere in the background stands one Geoffrey Chaucer, a well-dressed and prosperous-looking fellow who is storing up in his mind's eye who all these people are, and what they look like, and what sort of story they may be able to tell. When he gets back home he will put it all down in black and white on clean sheets of parchment, and his *Canterbury Tales* will keep his memory green for evermore.

The night before, some nine-and-twenty "sondry folk" had arrived at the "Tabard", which was the last of the hostelries of the capital before entering upon the wilds of Surrey. Before they had gone to bed he had spoken with each one of them and made himself acquainted with their characters and station in life. And now he proceeds to tell us something of what he had gleaned, in that *Prologue* which is like nothing else in our literature, a portrait-gallery of human types such as might be encountered in the England of Edward III. The first to be presented to us is one of the gentry, and an excellent specimen he makes.

> *A Knight ther was, and that a worthy man,*
> *That from the tyme that he ferst bigan*
> *To ryden out, he loved chyvalrye,*
> *Trouth and honour, fredom and curtseie.*
> *Ful worthi was he in his Lordes warre,*
> *And thereto had he riden, no man so farre.* . . .

He had fought against the Moors in Spain and North Africa and Egypt, and "ageynst another hethen in Turkye", in fifteen battles altogether, and he had more than held his own in knightly tournaments.

> *He was a verray perfit gentil Knight.*

Then, "to telle you of his array," his horse was good enough, but his own appearance was not particularly smart. Indeed, his hauberk (coat of chain mail) was marked with "ful many a stain, for he was late come from his voyage" when he decided to make the pilgrimage.

> *With him ther was his sone, a yong Squyer,*
> *A lovyer, and a lusty bacheler,*
> *With lokkes curled as if they lay in presse.*
> *Of twenty yeer he was of age I gesse.*

Although so young, he had served overseas in the French wars and had acquitted himself well, so as to be deserving of the favours of his lady-love.

> *Embroidered was he, as it were a mead*
> *Al ful of fresshe floures, white and red.*
> *Syngynge he was, or flutynge, al the day;*
> *He was as fressh as is the month of May.*

A Yeoman comes next, dressed in a green coat and hood and with a sheaf of arrows at his belt. He has a round, nut-like head, and a brown visage, and he is well armed, with mighty bow, sword and buckler,

and a "gay daggere, sharp as poynte of spere". And then we have one
of the ladies of the company, whose portrait is beautifully drawn in
her arch simplicity and coy reserve. This is the Prioress, who has
brought along with her one of her nuns and three priests. Madame
Englentyne, as her name was,

> Ful wel she sang the servises divyne,
> Entuned in her nose ful seemely;
> And Frensh she spake ful faire and sweetely,
> After the scole of Stratford-atte-Bowe,
> For Frensh of Parys was to her unknowe.
> At mete wel i-taught was she in all;
> She let no morsel from her lippes falle,
> Nor wet her fyngres in her sauce deepe.

Very pleasant she was, and a lover of good cheer, and not one to
stand upon her dignity. And she was so kind-hearted that "she wolde
weepe if that she saw a mous caught in a trappe, if it were ded or
bled". Now we are told what she looked like:

> Her nose streight; her eyen grey as glas;
> Her mouth ful smal, and thereto soft and red;
> But certeynly she hadde a fair forheed.

She was wearing a well-fitting cloak, and on her arms a pair of coral
bracelets, from one of which hung a gold brooch engraved with the
letter A and the motto *Amor vincit omnia* (Love overcomes everything).

Next comes a companion picture of a Monk, but one that is
nothing like so pleasing. This "fair prelate" was a sportsman above
all else, with good horses in his stable and "greyhoundes as swifte as
fowl in flight" for hunting the hare. He was completely bald, and
his face looked as though it had been greased, and his bright little
eyes were always rolling in his head. Then there was a Friar, "a
wanton and a merye", who was a great favourite with the ladies; his
tippet "was ay stuffed ful of knyves and pynnes, for to give to fair
wyves", and he had arranged the marriages of many of his "yonge
wymmen, at his owne cost".

Then follows a Merchant, a worthy fellow with a forked beard
and on his head a Flemish beaver hat, who kept a good seat on his
horse and looked as prosperous as he was. Very different was the
appearance of the Oxford student.

A Clerk ther was of Oxenford also,
That unto logik had long tyme i-go.
As lene was his horse as is a rake,
And he was not right fat, I undertake.

His cloak was threadbare, since he was too unworldly to get a benefice or other office in the Church.

For he wold rather have at his beddes hed
Twenty bookes, clothed in blak and red,
Of Aristotil, and his philosophie,
Then robes riche, or fiddle, or psaltery.

Next, a Sergeant of Law, who knew every Statute by heart and was
always busy, "and yet he semed busier than he was". After him
comes a Franklin, or freeholder, of sanguine complexion and with a
beard as white as a daisy, who loved a cup of wine first thing in the
morning and whose table was always loaded with good things. He is
followed by a Haberdasher and a Carpenter, a Weaver and a Dyer,
and a Tapicer (tapestry or carpet-maker), all of them well set up
men of business and good enough to sit on the aldermanic bench.
Next a Cook, who "coude roste, sethe, broile, and frye, make soupe
and brawn and bake wel a pye", while "for blankemange he made
with the beste". Then a Shipman from Dartmouth, who knew all
the harbours from "Scotland to the cape of Fynestere, and every
creek in Bretayne and Spayne", and after him a "Doctour of
Phisik" who "knew the cause of every maladye" and was "a very
parfit practisour". But we must not spend time with these people,
for here comes the most powerfully drawn of all Chaucer's characters, the rude and ribald and richly vital piece of femininity known
as the Wife of Bath.

A good Wif of beside Bathe ther was,
But she was ever somwhat def, allas.
Her kerchiefs weren al ful fyne of grounde;
I dursten swere they weigheden ten pounde
That on a Sonday were upon her hed.
Her hosen were of fyne scarlett red,
Ful streyt y-tyed, and shoes ful moyste and newe.
Bold was hir face, and fair, and red of hewe.
She was a worthy womman al her lyfe,
Hosbondes at churches dore hadde she fyfe,
Withouten other compayne in youthe...

What a woman she was for going on pilgrimages! Thrice had she been to Jerusalem, she had been to Rome and to the shrine of St. James in Spain, to Cologne and to Boulogne. She was no beauty, being a bit big in the tooth, but she rode her nag easily. She was wearing a flowing cloak and on her head a hat as broad as a buckler, "a foot-mantel aboute her hippes large, and on her feet a paire of spurres sharpe". She could laugh and jest with the best, and there was nothing that she didn't know about Love and its mishaps, and the best way to cure them.

Now who comes? A Parson from a town parish, who though poor was rich in "holy thought and werk, a lerned man, a clerk that Cristes gospel gladly wolde preach". He was of no social conse-quence, since his companion was a Ploughman, who was his brother, but a man all the same who always paid his dues promptly and was ever ready with a helping hand, "for Christes sake, withouten hyre, if it laye in his might". There were also a Reeve (estate bailiff), a Miller, a Summoner (official of an ecclesiastical court), and a Par-doner (man who sold indulgences on behalf of the Church author-ities, that were believed to secure the pardon of sins committed), a Manciple (steward), "and my-self, there was no mo".

That night when they were all assembled and had dined well and late, the host – his name was Henry Bailey – first congratulated them on making such a fine show – and then put forward the suggestion that each member should tell two stories, one on the way to Canter-bury and one on the way back; and that he, or she, who told the best should be given a dinner at the expense of all the rest when they re-assembled at the Tabard. The suggestion was acclaimed, and the host volunteered to accompany the pilgrims on their way and act as adjudicator. This, too, was agreed to, and so they repaired to rest, and were up in the morning at cock-crow. Their first stop would have been at St. Thomas's Well, only a mile or two on their way, where they would tighten up their horses' girths, adjust their saddles, and water their mounts. At each halt we may imagine them grouped around the tale-teller, and also at night when they put up at one of the hostelries.

Since there were about thirty in the company, there should have been sixty "tales", but the poem as we have it contains only twenty-three. Several of the pilgrims, the Ploughman and the Yeoman, for example, do not relate tales.

Few if any of the stories were of Chaucer's own composition. Like Shakespeare, he was content to borrow from various sources. "The Knight's Tale" is a shortened version of a story by Boccaccio, and

Boccaccio's *Decameron* is drawn upon for several of the later contributions. Those tales of "harlotrie", as Chaucer calls them, told by the Miller and the Reeve, owe something to the *fabliaux* of the Continent, but Chaucer has given them a gaiety which goes some way to make up for their crude indecency. Alison, the heroine of the "Miller's Tale", is a particularly delightful creation, this eighteen-year-old wife with a body as sleek as a weasel's, her eyes black as sloes, and her mouth as sweet as a store of apples kept in hay.

Of all the contributions to the miscellany the most remarkable is the Wife of Bath's, and that not because of the actual Tale she told but because of her lengthy prologue. This has been called the first autobiography in English fiction, and it reveals a woman ripe and warm and passionate, who "evyr folewed myn owne appetite" and never minded "were he schort, long, blak, or white, how pore he was, so that he liked me".

So tale after tale was told, as the pilgrims drew near to their destination. At length they arrived at Canterbury, and on the morrow joined the throng making for the Saint's tomb in the cathedral. There they made their devotions and laid down their gifts and purchased holy souvenirs. After which they went back to the inn and supped well, and as soon as it was light started on the return journey.

All this was getting on for 600 years ago, and so it continued for 150 years after Chaucer's time. Then came the Reformation, the Martyr's Tomb was broken up and despoiled, and the pilgrims came no longer. But nothing could destroy the stories that had been told on the pilgrim path. The *Canterbury Tales* are the ever-living and precious memorials of the springtime of English poetry.

UTOPIA

SIR THOMAS MORE

OF ALL the cities that men have built in the cloudlands, much the most famous is the one described in a small book written by the English scholar-statesman Sir Thomas More in the beginning of the sixteenth century. It is called *Utopia*, and so famous is it that ever since all similar imaginary commonwealths have been referred to as Utopias.

The word is a made-up one. It comes from the Greek words, *ou* meaning not, and *topos*, a place, and so means literally Nowhere. It was invented by More, and is a reminder of the fact that he was one of the most famous figures of the Revival of Learning that was inspired by the rediscovery of the ancient classical civilizations of Greece and Rome after the long night of the Middle Ages.

At the time he wrote his book More was in his middle thirties, a barrister of Lincoln's Inn with a large practice, and a seat in the House of Commons. In 1515 he was despatched to the Low Countries as ambassador with the special charge of negotiating a fresh trade treaty. It was while he was in Flanders that the idea of *Utopia* came to him, and on his return to England, his mission accomplished, he wrote the book in Latin. It was printed at Louvain late in 1516, and copies were soon on sale in England. The first English translation did not appear until 1551, sixteen years after More had been executed on Tower Hill for having refused to acknowledge Henry VIII as Head of the English Church in place of the Pope of Rome. The translator was one Ralph Robinson, "sometime fellow of Corpus Christi College in Oxford," and as will be seen from the quotations given here, taken from the second and revised edition of 1556, Robinson wrote in a fine, full-flavoured Tudor English.

In the opening sentences we have an impression of More kicking his heels in Antwerp while the negotiations were proceeding in the customary leisurely fashion. Fortunately he had made some good friends in the city, among them Peter Giles, "a man in his talk and communication so merry and pleasant" that More's fervent desire to see "my native country, my wife and my children", from whom he had been separated more than four months, "was greatly abated and diminished". It was Peter who introduced him, one morning when they were returning from hearing divine service in Our Lady's Church, to "a certain stranger, a man well stricken in age, with a black sunburned face, a long beard, and a cloak cast in homely fashion about his shoulders, whom by his favour and apparel forthwith I judged to be a mariner". The man's name was Raphael Hythloday, and it turned out that although he was not a mariner he was a Portuguese who had accompanied Amerigo Vespucci on his last voyage to the Americas, and had been one of the band of twenty-four who were left behind at their own request in a fort established somewhere on the coast of Brazil. After a period of exploration, he arrived back in Europe on a Portuguese ship. It was in the course of this long and venturesome journey that (so More tells us, but of course the story was wholly a romantic invention on his part) he had come across the island of Utopia, situated somewhere south of the equator, and had lived among its people for the space of five years.

More was delighted with his new acquaintance, and we are given a very pleasant picture of the three men going to his lodging, "and there in my garden upon a bench covered with greene turves we sat down talking together". For an hour or two they discussed social and economic conditions in England, and what they had to say takes up the first of the two books into which *Utopia* is divided. "So we went in and dined," continues the narrative, and "when dinner was done, we came into the same place again, and sat us down upon the same bench, commanding our servants that no man should trouble us." And then Raphael, "seeing us desirous and willing to hearken to him, when he had sat still and paused a little while, musing and bethinking himself, thus he began to speak . . ."

"The island of Utopia containeth in breadth in the middle part of it (for there it is broadest) two hundred miles." Within it there are fifty-four "large and fair cities, or shire towns, agreeing all together in one tongue, in like manners, institutions, and laws". The capital is Amaurot, situated in the middle of the island, to which place representatives from all the other cities repair at regular intervals to discuss matters of common interest. At the head of the commonwealth is a prince, who is elected generally for life.

All the cities are built on the same plan and are of about the same size. The streets are twenty feet wide, and are well drained. The houses are built in continuous rows, and are all of three storeys. Each house has two doors, "one into the street, and a postern door on the backside into the garden", and these doors are never locked or bolted, so that "whoso will, may go in, for there is nothing within the houses that is private, or any man's own". Behind each house is a large garden, for the Utopians "set great store by their gardens". In the country round about are numerous farms which are worked by the town and country folk in turn.

Special attention is called to their poultry farms. "They bring up a great multitude of pulleyne (poultry), and that by a marvellous policy. For the hens do not sit upon the eggs: but by keeping them in a certain equal heat they bring life into them, and hatch them." This is a remarkable piece of foresight on More's part, since in his day artificial incubation had never been tried out in practice.

All the Utopians are dressed alike, except that there is some distinguishing difference between men's and women's garb, and that of the married and the unmarried. They wear the same clothes summer and winter, and every family makes its own. When at work they wear garments made of leather or skins, which are expected to last seven years. When they have finished the day's work they "cast upon them a cloak, which hideth the other homely apparel. These cloaks throughout the whole Island be all of one colour, and that is the natural colour of the wool."

Everybody in Utopia, men and women alike, is required to work on the farms and also at a trade or handicraft. The working day is six hours, that is, three hours in the morning and, after a dinner-break of two hours, three hours in the afternoon. They all go to bed at eight, and sleep eight hours. The rest of the time is their own, but they must not waste it. There are numerous educational lectures that they should attend, and there is always something to be done in the gardens. They "exercise themselves in music, or else in honest and wholesome communication", and have "two games not much unlike the chess", but "dice play and such other foolish and pernicious games they know not". Hunting and hawking is also most strongly condemned.

If it be argued that six hours of work a day cannot possibly be sufficient, it is pointed out that in Utopia *everybody* works. There are no rich men living on poor men's labour, no lazy dependants and hangers-on, no thriftless vagabonds, no idle priests, monks and friars, no "sturdy beggars", no "stout bragging rush buckler", that is, swashbucklers. And to crown all, every woman has a job – and "women be the half of the whole number".

So far from a six-hour-day being insufficient, it is sometimes too long, and then the magistrates give order by proclamation "that they shall bestow fewer hours in work". For they see no point in unnecessary labour, but try to arrange matters so that the citizens are left with plenty of time in which they may develop "the free liberty of the mind, and garnishing of the same. For herein they suppose the felicity of this life to consist."

This is one of the Utopian rules for good living. A second is, "to think no kind of pleasure forbidden, whereof cometh no harm".

In Utopia everything needful for subsistence is possessed in common. In the market-places are large warehouses in which the produce of the country is stored, and if a citizen wants anything he has only to go and ask for it. Similarly everything is consumed in common. There is very little home life, but all is done in the full gaze of everybody. Meals are taken in large dining-rooms, where the young people wait considerately on their elders. The men sit upon one bench over against the wall, and the women sit opposite. The cooking is done by the women, but "all slavery and drudgery, and all laboursome toil, and base business, is done by bondmen".

Now we come to their marriage customs. "In choosing wives and husbands they observe a custom which seemed to us", reports More, "very fond (silly) and foolish. For a sad (serious) and an honest matron showeth the woman, be she maid or widow, naked to the wooer. And likewise a sage and discreet man exhibiteth the wooer naked to the woman. At this custom we laughed. . . . But they on the other hand do greatly wonder at the folly of all other nations, which in buying a colt, whereas a little money is in hazard, be so chary and circumspect, that though he be almost bare, yet they will not buy him, unless the saddle and all the harness be taken off, lest under these coverings be hid some gall or sore. And yet in choosing a wife, which shall be either pleasure or displeasure to them all their life after, they be so reckless, that all the residue of the woman's body being covered with clothes . . . so foul deformity may be hid under those coverings, that it may quite alienate and take away the man's mind from his wife, when it shall not be lawful for their bodies to be separate again."

Divorce is allowed for adultery and "the intolerable wayward manners of either party", but a husband is not allowed to put away his wife just because "some mishap is fallen to her body". But there is also what we should call divorce by consent, when "the man and the woman cannot well agree between themselves, both of them finding other with whom they hope to live more quietly and merrily".

The Utopians have few laws and no lawyers. Scholars are held in high repute, and nowhere are physicians regarded with greater honour. In every city there are four hospitals, "so big, so wide, so ample, and so large, that they may seem little towns". And these are so well appointed and comfortable that a man who falls sick would much rather go there than be treated at home. A man who is suffering from an incurable disease, so that his life is "full of continual pain and anguish", may embrace a voluntary death, but otherwise suicide is sternly reprobated.

Nothing in the book can have struck the reader more forcibly than the way in which the glories of war are discounted. The Utopians detest "war or battle as a thing very beastly", and strive to avoid it. If war is forced upon them, they do their best to win, but by methods that other peoples would regard as most unfair and inglorious.

Another Utopian peculiarity is their attitude to the precious metals. The metal they most prize is iron, because of its multiplicity of uses. They eat and drink out of vessels made of clay or glass, but "of gold and silver they make commonly chamber-pots and other vessels, that serve for most vile uses, not only in their common halls but in every man's private house". The chains and fetters with which they load their prisoners and malefactors are also made of gold and silver, so intent are they on associating what other peoples value so highly with "reproach and infamy".

More has a good deal to say about the religion of the Utopians. "Some worship for God the sun; some the moon; some, some other of the planets. . . . But the most and the wisest part believe that there is a certain Godly power unknown, everlasting, incomprehensible, inexplicable, far above the capacity and reach of man's wit, dispersed throughout all the world, not in bigness, but in virtue and power. Him they call the father of all."

The Utopian churches "be very gorgeous, and not only of fine and curious workmanship, but also (which in the fewness of them was necessary) very wide and large, and able to receive a great company of people". In these churches they meet on the first and the last day of every month, and the last day of the year, and give thanks to God and pray that they may have good fortune in the time that is to come. "They kill no living beast in sacrifice, nor they think not that the merciful clemency of God hath delight in blood and slaughter, which hath given life to beasts to the intent they should live." They sing hymns, accompanied by musical instruments, and join with the priest in prayers. And one thing more must be mentioned – "one of the ancientist laws among them: that no man shall be blamed for reasoning in the maintenance of his own religion".

What a terrible thing it is to have to record that More, when he became Lord Chancellor thirteen years later, forgot so completely the tolerant spirit of his Utopians and proved himself a cruel and inveterate persecutor!

But no shadows of a dreadful future fall on the men sitting there in an Antwerp garden, those many centuries ago, listening to the returned traveller's account of "that commonwealth, which verily in my judgment is not only the best, but also that which alone of good right may claim and take upon it the name of a common wealth or public weal". They have been sitting there for hours, no doubt they are stiff with sitting and the grass may be getting damp. And so they go into the house for supper.

THE PRINCE

MACHIAVELLI

ALTHOUGH Niccolo Machiavelli wrote a number of books – histories, literary essays, comedies, treatises on military science – he is chiefly remembered for one only, and that one of the shortest of the world's great books. This book has also the distinction of being one of the most venomously vilified in the whole vast field of literature. Lord Macaulay, for instance, who must have read quite a number of shocking books in his time, declared in his famous essay on Machiavelli that "it is scarcely possible for any person, not well acquainted with the history and literature of Italy, to read without horror and amazement the celebrated treatise which has brought such obloquy on the name of Machiavelli. Such a display of wickedness, naked yet not ashamed, such cool, judicious, scientific atrocity ... principles which the most hardened ruffian would scarcely hint to his most trusted accomplice ..."

What was this dreadful little book? Its name in Italian is *Il Principe*, in English *The Prince*. As for its subject, it is a treatise on political power, dealing in particular with how states or principalities are established in the modern world, and how they may be preserved and aggrandized. It is a carefully composed essay in statecraft. Note that it is concerned with states as they are, not as they might or ought to be: there is nothing of the Utopian idealist in Machiavelli's make-up. One thing more should be said by way of introduction: the book holds an unassailable place as the first important publication in the history of Western political thought.

Machiavelli wrote it in 1513, shortly after he had been sacked from his important position of Chief Secretary to the Government of the Florentine Republic. He had held this post since the summer of 1498, the year in which he had seen the great reformer Savonarola, so recently the darling of the populace, swept from power and burnt alive in the Piazza della Signoria: *that* was something that he never forgot. He had served his masters, the "Council of Ten", with marked ability, and had been employed on a number of diplomatic missions. Then the great family of the Medici had returned to power in Florence, Machiavelli had been arrested on a charge of conspiracy against the State and put to the torture to make him disclose what he knew of the plot (which, he stoutly maintained, was nothing), and subsequently had been allowed to retire into private life. But he might still use his pen, and it was in this saddest period of his career that he wrote the book that has perpetuated his name. Here is his own account of its gestation, given in a letter to his friend, Francesco Vettori:

"Since my last misfortunes I have led a quiet country life, and, all counted, have not passed twenty days in Florence. I spent September in snaring thrushes; but, at the end of the month, even this rather tiresome sport failed me. I rise with the sun in the morning, and go into one of the woods ... to pass some time with the wood-cutters, who have always some troubles to tell me, either of their own or their neighbours. ... Then I betake myself to the inn by the road-side, chat with passers by, ask news of the places whence they come, hear various things, and note the varied tastes and diverse fancies of mankind. There I generally find the host, a butcher, a miller, and a couple of brick-makers. I mix with these boors the whole day, play-ing at cards and dice, which games give rise to a thousand quarrels and much exchange of bad language, and we generally wrangle over farthings, and our shouting can be heard in San Casciano. . . . "

Not a pleasant picture, particularly the bird-snaring and the card-playing with drunken boors. But better is to follow.

"At nightfall I return home, and seek my writing-room, and, divesting myself on its threshold of my rustic garments, stained with mud and mire, I assume courtly attire, and thus suitably clothed, enter within the ancient courts of ancient men, by whom, being cordially welcomed, I am fed with the food that *alone* is mine, and for which I was born, and am not ashamed to hold discourse with them and inquire the motives of their actions; and these men in their humanity reply to me, and for the space of four hours I feel no weariness, remember no trouble, no longer fear poverty, no longer dread death, my whole being is so absorbed in them. . . . And I have recorded that which I have acquired from the conversation of these worthies, and composed a pamphlet ... discussing the nature of princedom, of how many species it consists, how these are to be acquired, how they are maintained, why they are lost . . ."

Much of the earlier part of the book is taken up with an account of the political arrangements in Renaissance Italy, and this will be of interest mainly to the students of political history. For our present purpose all that we need to know is that Italy at this time was still nothing more than a geographical expression, the whole country being divided into a number of petty principalities and city-states, together with the extensive temporal realm of the Popes of Rome – who between them, by their rivalries and quarrels and frequent wars, kept it divided and therefore weak in the face of the great and growing national monarchies of France and Spain. From what may be termed the mechanics of government we turn to consider the Machiavellian principles of statecraft as he had seen them exemplified in his own experience.

To take the most notorious chapter first, this is the one that bears the title, itself full of significance, "In what way princes must keep faith". This is a subject on which the political theorist is inclined to take a high line of moral rectitude. Not so Machiavelli, however. "What a praiseworthy thing it is," he begins, "that a prince should keep his word! And yet the experience of our own times has shown often enough that those princes who have done really great things have been those who have paid least attention to keeping faith. On the contrary, they have rather confused men's minds with their cleverness, and have eventually overcome those who have put their trust in fair dealing." The truly capable ruler, he goes on, must combine the qualities of the lion and the fox, striving to be as brave as the one and as crafty as the other. It is not sufficient to be like the lion only, for lions do not know how to protect themselves from traps, nor like the fox only, for foxes are unable to defend themselves against wolves. Those who wish to be only like lions, he comments sardonically, don't understand this. . . .

"Therefore a prudent ruler ought not to keep his word when by so doing it would be against his interest. If men were uniformly good, this precept would not be a good one, but as they are all bad, and would not keep faith with you, so you are not bound to keep faith with them. Nor are legitimate grounds ever wanting to give colour to a broken promise. Of this I could give any number of modern instances, but I will content myself with one. Pope Alexander VI did nothing else but deceive men, he thought of nothing else, and always found a way of doing it; and yet he was uniformly successful, since he knew all that there was to know about this side of human conduct."

A prudent prince must be a great feigner and dissembler. He should make a point of *seeming* to be pious, faithful, humane, sincere and so on, but he must be prepared when necessary, in order to preserve the state, to act against faith, against charity, against humanity, against religion. The common crowd of people always judge by appearances. The important thing is to be successful; and if the prince can manage that, he will be praised by everyone, no matter how he has achieved his success.

Another chapter that has incurred frequent censure is concerned with "Cruelty and clemency, and whether it is better to be loved or feared". A prince (we are told) while naturally wanting to be considered merciful rather than cruel, must not mind incurring the charge of cruelty if his actions keep his subjects secure and happy. He may thus be far more merciful than a prince who, through excess of tenderness, allows disorders to arise from which may spring murders, rapine and general ruin. For these things affect the whole body of the citizens, whereas the executions ordered by a cruel prince are of a few individuals only. It is only to be expected that a conqueror should be cruel, but he would be well advised to commit all his cruel actions at once, and not repeat them from day to day.

As for the question, whether it is better to be loved than feared, Machiavelli's reply is that a wise ruler will endeavour to be both, but, since this is sometimes difficult to accomplish, "it is much safer to be feared than loved". For men are selfish and are apt to forget their obligations to a ruler when it suits their purpose, but "fear is maintained by a dread of punishment that never fails". All the same, the prince must not overdo it. He should aim at being feared without being hated, and this state of affairs can usually be achieved provided he refrains from interfering with his subjects' possessions and their women. If unpopular acts have to be done, the wise prince will ensure that they are done not by him but by his ministers, while he keeps in his own hands the bestowal of favours and gifts.

There are many who think (says Machiavelli on a later page) that a wise prince should foment some enmity if he has the chance, so that by overcoming it he may augment his greatness. Similarly he may gain a great reputation by deliberately stirring up foreign foes just in order to overcome them in battle.

These are some of the maxims taken from the Machiavellian copybook, and reading them it is not difficult to understand the revulsion that they aroused in such minds as Macaulay's. But to make matters worse, Machiavelli illustrates his theme with a portrait of the kind of prince whom he thinks most worthy of emulation; and the subject of his portrait is none other than Cesare Borgia, one of the most ruffianly figures – perhaps the most ruffianly – of the whole Renaissance period! "I know of no better precepts for a new prince to follow (he writes) than the example of his actions; and if his measures were not successful, it was through no fault of his own but only by the most extraordinary malignity of fortune. . . . Reviewing all his actions, I find nothing to blame; on the contrary, I feel bound to hold him up as an example to be imitated by all who by fortune and force of arms have risen to greatness . . . "

No wonder that the man who could write in such eulogistic fashion of an unprincipled scoundrel should himself become suspect. "We doubt whether any name in literary history be so generally odious as Machiavelli's," to quote Macaulay further, and yet in himself Machiavelli was "a man whose public conduct was upright and honourable, whose views of morality, where they differed from those of the persons around him, seemed to have differed for the better, and whose only fault was, that, having adopted some of the maxims then generally received, he arranged them more luminously, and expressed them more forcibly, than any other writer".

The truth of the matter would seem to lie in the fact that, as indicated above, Machiavelli was a realist. He was also a most sincere patriot, to the extent that we may employ such a term in the Italy of his time. The best years of his life had been spent in devoted service to the Florentine Republic, and he asked for nothing better than that the system of government that he had helped to make work should endure and flourish. But he knew that this was impossible. The day of small city-states was rapidly drawing to a close, in an atmosphere of blood and ruin. What course of action should a wise man then adopt? He could see no other way to the establishment of law and order, of security and peace, than in the rule of a prince who should be strong and if possible enlightened – but strong before all things else.

This is abundantly clear in his concluding words, an exhortation addressed to the Medici prince to whom his little treatise was dedicated and for whose guidance and encouragement it had been written. "Let your Illustrious House," he urges, "take up the cause of liberating Italy from the domination of the barbarians", as he calls the foreign invaders, the French in particular. "May you assume the task with courage and in the hopes inspired by a just cause, so that under your banner our fatherland may be raised up. . . ." Thus the man who had once put his hopes in a Cesare Borgia pointed the way to Mazzini and Garibaldi, to an Italy unified and free.

GARGANTUA *AND* PANTAGRUEL

FRANÇOIS RABELAIS

NOT MANY great humorists have made their contribution to the world's literature, but among the few François Rabelais stands on a lonely eminence. He was a Frenchman, born at Chinon, in the Touraine country, where his father practised law and farmed a small estate. The date of his birth is uncertain; it may have been as early as 1483 or as late as 1495. At a very early age, possibly when he was not yet in his teens, he was placed in a convent, and when he was old enough he became a monk. Such he was for perhaps as long as twenty-five years; and when at length he went back into the world he carried with him a fund of antique scholarship which he had somehow managed to accumulate in the slender libraries of the convents to which he was assigned. In 1530 he was entered as a student in the University of Montpellier, where he took his degrees in medicine and lectured on anatomy. Then in 1532 we find him filling the post of physician to the municipal hospital at Lyons, at that time one of the chief centres of French life and culture. It was while he was walking the wards in the Lyons hospital that he brought out the first volume of the book which placed him among the immortals. This was *Pantagruel*, and it was followed two years later by *Gargantua*.

Although it was the later in point of time, *Gargantua* is a preliminary volume to the other, and it is for this reason that it is always printed first. Both books were translated into English in 1653 by Sir Thomas Urquhart, a Scottish man of letters who was successful in reproducing something of the fantastical quality of the original. The quotations in this article are from Urquhart's version.

Gargantua was originally the name of a giant in French folk-lore, and the Gargantua of Rabelais's novel is likewise a giant, born of gigantic parents, Grangousier and Gargamelle his wife. He had a strange birth, since he made his appearance in the world by way of his mother's left ear, and "as soon as he was born, he cried not as other babes used to do, miez, miez, miez, but with a high, sturdy, and big voice shouted about, some drink, some drink, some drink, as inviting all the world to drink with him". So vast was his size, that seventeen thousand nine hundred and thirteen cows were appointed to furnish him with the great quantity of milk that was needed for his nourishment, and hundreds of yards of various stuffs were required to provide him with apparel.

From the time he was three until five he "was brought up and instructed in all convenient discipline, by the commandment of his father; and spent that time like the other little children of the country that is, in drinking, eating and sleeping: in eating, sleeping and drinking: and in sleeping, drinking and eating". He "wallowed and rolled himself up and down in the mire and dirt; he trod down his shoes in the heel; he wiped his nose on his sleeve; he would drink in his slipper; he sharpened his teeth with a top, washed his hands with his broth, and combed his hair with a bowl. He did eat his cake sometimes without bread, would bite in laughing, and laugh in biting." He would also do a number of other things which it would be far from polite to mention, although they are the sort of things that are responsible for getting "Rabelaisian" into the dictionary.

Several chapters are devoted to an account of the education of the lusty young brute, and these have been taken as a satire on the degraded schools of the Middle Ages. "At the last his father perceived, that indeed he studied hard, and that, although he spent all his time in it, he did nevertheless profit nothing, but which is worse, grew thereby foolish, simple, doted, and blockish." So he was taken away from the schoolmasters whose "knowledge was nothing but brutishness" and sent to Paris, where things were very much better. The students learnt not only from books but from practical work; they not only listened to public lectures but visited the workshops of upholsterers, weavers, watchmakers, printers, goldsmiths and other artificers, and visited the shops of druggists, herbalists and apothecaries. "Thus was Gargantua governed, and kept on in this course of education, from day to day profiting, as you may understand such a young man of his age may, of a pregnant judgment, with good discipline well continued. Which, although at the beginning it seemed difficult, became a little after so sweet, so easy, and so delightful, that it seemed rather the recreation of a king than the study of a scholar." In such passages as this we have an expression of the best and noblest ideas of the Humanist movement.

Gargantua was recalled from Paris by his father, who had become involved in a war with the neighbouring king, Picrochole by name. This war is described at great length and in much detail, and Rabelais takes obvious delight in drawing the portrait of the principal hero on the Gargantuan side, a jovial and highly disreputable cleric of the name of Friar John. At last Picrochole was defeated and peace restored, and then Gargantua set about the establishment of an abbey of which Friar John might be appointed abbot, by way of rewarding him for his prowess in the war just concluded.

The description of this Abbey of Thelema constitutes one of the most elaborate literary passages in the book. Clearly Rabelais had the intention of describing something that was to be in every way the opposite of the sort of monastic houses with which he had been intimately acquainted. "First then, said Gargantua, you must not build a wall about your convent, for all other abbeys are strongly walled and mured about. . . . And because in all other monasteries and nunneries all is compassed, limited, and regulated by hours, it was decreed that in this new structure there should be neither clock nor dial, but that according to the opportunities and incident occasions, all their hours should be disposed of; for, said Gargantua, the greatest loss of time that I know, is to count the hours. What good comes of it? Nor can there be any greater dotage in the world than for one to guide and direct his courses by the sound of a bell, and not by his own judgment and discretion."

Some even more extraordinary items follow. One of these runs: "Because both men and women, that are received into religious orders after the expiring of their noviciate or probation year, were constrained and forced perpetually to stay there all the days of their life; it was therefore ordered, that all whatever, men or women, admitted within this abbey, should have full leave to depart with peace and contentment, whensoever it should seem good to them so to do." And another: "For that the religious men and women did ordinarily make three vows, to wit, those of chastity, poverty, and obedience; it was therfore constituted and appointed, that in this convent they might be honourably married, that they might be rich, and live at liberty." The building itself was a stately mansion, luxuriously furnished and equipped, and the inmates were garbed not in the plain and ugly robes of the monastic orders but in clothes of bright colours and fashionable cut.

And what were the rules of this new-model convent? There was only one that they had all to observe: *Do what thou wilt.* "All their life was spent not in laws, statutes, or rules, but according to their own free will and pleasure. They rose out of their beds when they thought good: they did eat, drink, labour, sleep, when they had a mind to it, and were disposed for it. None did awake them, none did offer to constrain them to eat, drink, nor to do any other thing; for so had Gargantua established it." And if we wonder why he did so, it was "because men that are free, well-born, well-bred, and conversant in honest companies, have naturally an instinct and spur that prompteth them unto virtuous actions, and withdraws them from vice, which is called honour. Those same men, when by base subjection and restraint they are brought under and kept down, turn aside from that noble disposition, by which they formerly were inclined to virtue, to shake off and break that bond of servitude, wherein they are so tyrannously enslaved; for it is agreeable with the nature of man to long after things forbidden, and to desire what is denied us".

In the second book we are introduced to Pantagruel, who is the principal hero of the whole work. It was at the age of four hundred fourscore forty and four years (so it is stated with quaint precision in an early chapter of *Pantagruel*) that "Gargantua begat his son Pantagruel upon his wife named Badebec, daughter to the king of the Amaurots in Utopia" – an interesting reference to Sir Thomas More's *Utopia* which had been published in Latin some forty years earlier – and "so wonderfully great and lumpish" was the infant that his mother died in giving him birth. Like his father before him, Pantagruel when he was old enough was sent to the University of Paris, "where he studied very hard, and profited accordingly, for he had an excellent understanding and notable wit".

While at Paris Pantagruel made the acquaintance of Panurge, in describing whom Rabelais must surely have had in mind some roistering blade of real life. "Panurge was of middle stature, not too high nor too low, and had somewhat an aquiline nose, made like the handle of a razor. He was at that time five and thirty years old, or thereabouts – a very gallant and proper man of his person, only that he was a little lecherous, and naturally subject to a kind of disease, which at that time they called lack of money – it is an incomparable grief, yet, notwithstanding, he had threescore and three tricks to come by it at his need, of which the most honourable and most ordinary was in manner of thieving, secret purloining, and filching, for he was a wicked lewd rogue, a cozener (cheat), drinker, roysterer, rover, and a very dissolute and debauched fellow, if there were any in Paris; otherwise, and in all matters else, the best and most virtuous man in the world; and he was still contriving some plot, and devising mischief against the sergeants and the watch."

Although the third book is headed, "Of the Heroic Deeds and Sayings of the Good Pantagruel", it is most largely concerned with the deeds and sayings of this priceless rogue, and in particular with Panurge's determination to marry. Then in volumes four and five (which were not translated by Urquhart but by Peter le Motteux, a much less happy translator, in 1694) we are told how Pantagruel, Panurge and their friends set out on a voyage to visit the "Oracle of the Holy Bottle". On their way the voyagers met with many strange peoples and adventures and it seems to be established that the narrative is based on the tales brought back by the explorers who had ventured into the Arctic in search of the north-west passage to India. At last they arrived at the Land of the Lanterns, where in a temple underground they were shown the sacred Bottle standing in a fountain of alabaster. Following carefully the instructions of Bacbuc, the "noble priestess" in charge of the shrine, Panurge and Pantagruel consulted the Oracle: "Bottle! Whose mysterious deep does ten thousand secrets keep, with attentive ear I wait: ease my mind and speak my fate." Whereupon, "immediately after this was heard the word trinc," which Bacbuc explained as "a word understood, used, and celebrated by all nations, and signifies drink". For some reason Panurge took this mysterious utterance as a sanction for his marriage, and with this the story comes to an end.

Of the five books composing the whole of *Gargantua* and *Pantagruel*, it is the first two which are chiefly responsible for the coining of the term Rabelaisian, which the dictionary defines as extravagantly humorous, robustly outspoken, coarsely indecent. Rabelais did indeed delight in calling a spade a spade, and he refused to call it anything else. He was principally interested in the primary activities of man, the human animal, in begetting, in eating and drinking, and in the process of digestion. His humour is primarily sexual and excretory in its sources and expressions. Beyond a doubt he was a coarsely-fibred man, and his humour was as coarse as he was. He laughed and laughed at the ridiculous displays of men and women in love, he jested about codpieces and thought cuckolds most delightful figures of fun. He had a very low opinion of women, admitting their usefulness, but for the most primary purposes. But at least it must be allowed that in his humour there is none of the sniggering indecency of Sterne or the fierce nastiness of that other dirty-minded cleric, Dean Swift.

There is another word in our dictionaries for which Rabelais is responsible, Pantagruelism, which he defines in the prologue to his fourth book as a certain jollity of mind, pickled in the scorn of fortune. The description fits him like a glove. He was the first and most characteristic of the Pantagruelians, a man who when he looked out on the world could not but be amused by the extraordinary antics of his fellows, and yet at the same time saw through the shams and falsities and humbug to the solid core of courage and human worth.

MONTAIGNE'S *ESSAYS*

YOUNG PEOPLE obliged to study Montaigne for examinations are liable to find the *Essays* an unpromising book, full of wise remarks but which have become commonplace, and vastly crowded with quotations from Latin and Greek authors. No doubt Montaigne, whose motto, *Que sais-je?* (What do I really know?), was one of the first men to question established beliefs, no doubt he had great independence of mind, that he was in his time enlightened, wrote vigorously against the use of torture, criticized the Spaniards for their barbarities in Mexico and Peru and defended dissection; yet all this does not mean that the *Essays* have really much to tell us today. Then some eminent writers have said that the *Essays* are for the elderly. Andrew Lang, for instance, an admirer of Montaigne, wrote: "He is a man's author, not a woman's; a tired man's, not a fresh man's; we all come to him, late indeed, but at the last we all rest in his panelled library." The picture is thus formed of an elderly recluse meditating on all sorts of subjects from stage-coaches, human vanity, the education of children, full of "wise saws and curious incidents", somewhat bold no doubt in his speculations, but with little to say to a generation which has absorbed outlines of history, Freudian psychology and the daring "black" thinkers of today from Sartre to the young American novelists.

The attitude of the young in demanding that what they read shall have a vital exciting meaning, is absolutely right. The supposition that, in the author of the *Essays*, they will only meet with a respectable and charming wiseacre is absolutely wrong. One small detail of Andrew Lang's sentences quoted above, "at the last we all rest in his panelled library," should be noted. Montaigne was well-off, and he lived in a splendid château near Bordeaux, close to the Dordogne river. But he did not write his *Essays* in "a panelled library", but in a rather dark room, crowded with untidy piles of books, in a tower which was totally separated from his château, where he often slept and, in old age, passed most of his time, even hearing Mass alone. Montaigne liked solitude and wrote: "All the trouble in life is that man cannot be alone with himself for a few hours."

Montaigne was not by nature a recluse at all. On the contrary, he liked society and conversation, was of an impetuous humour (full of fits and starts, now exalted, now depressed), a temperament which often goes with melancholy from which he suffered. Nor had he lived a sheltered life, distilling philosophy learnt purely from books. Born in 1533, his father, Pierre Eyquem de Montaigne, had brought up his eldest son with the aim of avoiding constraint and discipline and allowing him to grow freely and according to his nature. He was also intent on making him a scholar and a wise man. Thus Montaigne was awakened from his sleep by music, never forced to do anything he did not want to do, and given, as god-parents, two peasants from the village near the château in order that he might understand men of every kind. Until the age of six he was never spoken to except in Latin, so this became his first language; even his mother and father had to learn sufficient Latin to talk to their child.

A curious man this enlightened and cranky father, not untypical of the second generation of a family which had become rich and moved up in the world. Montaigne's grandfather had been the last and most successful of a Bordeaux merchant house – which sold herrings among other commodities. When he bought the château at Montaigne he acquired the right to belong to the lesser nobility of the region; a right which his grandson cherished very much. Michel de Montaigne, like Voltaire, was not immune to snobbery and he more or less dropped the patronym of Eyquem which smacked too much of trade. It is interesting that, in the course of the *Essays* in which Montaigne writes so abundantly about himself, there is no word of his mother, Antoinnette de Louppes, of Spanish-Jewish descent, all the more curious in that the mother actually outlived her son.

Michel de Montaigne was sent to the Collège de Guyenne in Bordeaux, one of the best schools at that time in Europe, where his knowledge of Latin, the principal subject of education, quickly put him on a level with his professors. On leaving school he followed his father's example and became one of the State Magistrates at the capital of his province, Perigueux. He made many visits to Paris, where he was received at Court, and this was the period of his many love affairs and of his friendship with Etienne de la Boétie, a gifted young man born like Montaigne in the Perigord, whose death was a calamity for his friend.

Throughout Montaigne's life France was the subject of constant dissension between the extreme Catholics, headed by the Duke of Guise, and the Huguenots or French Protestants which dragged on, intermittently breaking into civil war, with the French monarchy in the middle trying to keep the peace. Montaigne was a Catholic – his father's enlightenment being so great that he allowed one brother and one sister to become Protestants – and belonged to the King's party, being indeed the friend of Charles IX and of Henry III, who was later assassinated by a Jesuit priest after he had had the Duke of Guise assassinated. In 1572, after the massacre of St. Bartholomew, Montaigne tried to mediate between the Duke of Guise and Henry of Navarre, the leader of the Protestants and the brother-in-law of Henry III.

Montaigne was spasmodically, but often intensively, active in his region as leader of the Royal party fighting both the extremists. In 1581 he came back from a seventeen-months' journey in Germany, Switzerland and Italy which had ended in a sojourn in Rome, and found that the King had made him Mayor of Bordeaux, a Royalist city but one threatened by the Catholic League and by the Protestants. He served two terms, in all four years, with great success. During the last year of his term of office, half the inhabitants of the city perished from the plague and Montaigne was taken to task by writers in the nineteenth century for having passed over his duties as Mayor to his successor at a place outside the centre of the city. Montaigne believed in avoiding unnecessary dangers. In 1586 the plague was at the town of Castillon, very near his château, and he and his household had to spend six months living in caravans in the countryside.

The first three volumes of his *Essays* were published in Paris in 1588, the year of the Spanish Armada, and Montaigne went to Paris, being charged also with important business on behalf of Henry of Navarre. He left the Court shortly after Henry III's assassination and he died in 1591 after Henry IV, the King of Navarre, had been proclaimed King of France but before Henry had recaptured Paris from the League and made his celebrated statement that "Paris was worth a Mass". This was something which Montaigne would obviously have approved of. A number of letters from Montaigne to Henry of Navarre show Montaigne in the rôle of an outspoken counsellor. Just as his mother is left out of his *Essays*, so, from reading the *Essays*, one would not guess that the author had taken any part in great affairs. The *Essays* are not memoirs.

To some extent Montaigne's solitude in his tower, as well as his frequent travelling even in relatively old age (he died at the age of fifty-nine), were means of avoiding the cares of marriage and of his household. He had six children from his marriage, "two or three of whom died in childbirth", he writes casually, and of the six only one daughter, with whom he had little in common, survived to adolescence. "Marriage," he wrote, "is a bargain to which only the entrance is free, its continuance being constrained and forced, depending otherwise than on our will." He also wrote: "I am so fond of throwing off burdens and obligations that I have sometimes counted ingratitude, affronts and indignities as profitable ... taking the occasion of the offence as acquittance and discharge of my debt." "With me," he writes, "nearness of kin does not alleviate defects: it aggravates them." He hated household cares and states often that his principal aim in this life is to live it comfortably, relaxedly, rather than busily. The cares of the head of a household were greater in the sixteenth century when living was more dependent on local arrangements than today.

Montaigne had a fortune left him by his father which he never tried to increase, only being content not to use it up too fast. "At home," he writes, "you pry into everything too closely; your perspicacity hurts you. I avoid occasions for examination ... yet I cannot contrive well enough not to be bumping into something at home I do not like." He therefore loved travelling, went often on short and sometimes long journeys, finding the only drawback to travel was its cost. He liked travel not only because it separated him from his family; he thought it was always an advantage to change from a bad state to an uncertain one, that brand-new acquaintances of his own choice seemed to him better than those other common chance acquaintances of his neighbourhood and that "nature has put us into the world free and unfettered; we imprison ourselves in certain narrow districts". He felt himself as much akin to Poles as to Frenchmen, and when abroad and asked if he wanted to be served in the French fashion he would laugh at the idea and make straight for the table thickest with foreigners.

The *Essays* are not memoirs nor are they confessions. Many authors, when they write of themselves, are seeking either to justify themselves and their acts or to confess that they are discontented with their past and to hold up themselves as a noble warning to other people. Not so Montaigne. Montaigne starts from the premise that each of us, if honest, finds nothing more interesting than himself, that the object of his study ought to be what he himself felt, experienced and really wanted in this world, including the means he adopted to obtain the greatest ease, happiness and contentment in this uncertain life.

Montaigne found himself, and man in general, *ondoyant et divers* by nature – that is changing and inconsistent. What Montaigne principally holds up as the cause of man's discomforts are his pretentions, his erection of systems to justify himself or to force himself to walk in a certain path. From this, Montaigne thought, sprang the intolerance and the cruelty which he saw all about him and which characterizes life as much today as then.

The *Essays*, varying in length from a page or two to one of three hundred pages, the "Apology of Raymond de Sebond" is a series of reflections, often very amusing, on the mistake of thinking truth lies in this or that belief or way of conduct and a plea for natural conduct and natural thinking. His creed, if Montaigne can be said to have had one, is summed up at the end of the long essay on "Vanity". He makes the Delphic Oracle condemn those who think they can embrace the cosmos and who scatter their intellects in vain speculations:

> Except for you, oh man, each thing studies itself first, and, according to its needs, has limits to its labours and desires. There is not a single thing as empty and needy as you who embrace the universe; you are the investigator without knowledge, the magistrate without jurisdiction and, all in all, the fool of the farce.

At the end of his last essay on "Experience" he sums up his more positive view of life:

> It is an absolute perfection and virtually divine to know how to enjoy our being rightly. We seek other conditions because we do not understand the use of our own and go outside of ourselves because we do not know what it is like inside. Yet there is no use our mounting on stilts, for on stilts we must still walk on our own legs. And on the loftiest throne in the world, we are still sitting only on our own bottom.

He adds that the most beautiful lives to his mind are those which conform to the common human pattern, with order but without miracle or eccentricity. Old age, he thought, needed to be treated a little more tenderly and ought to be commended to that God who is the protector of health and wisdom, but of gay and sociable wisdom.

The "Apology for Raymond de Sebond" is an exposition of the work of a Spanish theologian who argues that the nature of God can be understood and perceived by reason. Apparently approving of this thesis, Montaigne, in fact, accumulates a huge dossier proving the feebleness, the presumption, the incapacity of man, and above all of man who makes systems and rules, to guide himself. Montaigne's celebrated doubt was essentially applied to the claims of theologians and philosophers. Nevertheless, Montaigne himself remained all his life a practising Catholic, holding that it is foolish to try to settle questions of belief and conduct and that the wise man lives according to those of his country just as he serves his Prince and government, doing both without servility and with all the mental reservations of an intelligent man who is not hoodwinked. It is not necessary, he thinks, to bother about ultimates: there are other more important things in life.

One may disapprove or approve of the attitude of life of this great man but it does not alter the attraction of the *Essays* very much. Great minds such as Shakespeare, who read Montaigne in the English translation by Florio a few years after the book appeared, were certainly very much attracted by Montaigne's thinking. Montaigne charms and interests his intellectual opposites because the *Essays* are a work of good faith and honesty and because in no other book does one get such a full living and real picture of the human predicament. The young, anxious to know about the habits and thoughts which society is usually reticent about, have not to go far in Montaigne to discover much. The titles of the *Essays* are misleading; thus one called "On the Verses of Vergil" is mainly concerned with Montaigne's views of love and sex which are set out with unparalleled frankness, while the essay "On the Powers of the Imagination" would have been enormously censored if it had appeared as an original work in the Victorian age. All in all Montaigne's *Essays* are one of two or three books – Pepys's journal is another – in which a man portrays himself as he really is. Only respect to the public, writes Montaigne, prevented him showing himself entire and wholly naked. Characteristically he begins his book by saying that it is an idle jotting to help his friends remember him:

My defects will here be read to the life and also my natural form. Thus reader I am myself the subject of my book and you would be unreasonable to spend your leisure on so frivolous and vain a subject. So farewell.

DON QUIXOTE

MIGUEL DE CERVANTES

"In a certain village in La Mancha, which I do not wish to name, there lived, not long ago, a gentleman – one of those who have always a lance in the rack, an ancient shield, a lean hack and a greyhound for coursing."

The words were written by a Spanish soldier at the start of the seventeenth century – a man, maimed in battle, who had gone on to lead the most exciting of lives before becoming – more or less – a full-time writer.

And the gentleman of whom he writes bears a considerable resemblance to himself.

The tale of this Spanish gentleman, "verging on fifty, of tough constitution, lean-bodied, thin-faced, a great early riser and a lover of hunting", is one of the world's greatest. Every novel written since then owes something to its example. It is the sort of book one picks up at almost any point and reads a chapter or two of with delight. For Don Quixote, as the Spanish gentleman went on to call himself, is one of the most pathetic, laughable and lovable characters in all fiction. One might almost have said "in history", for the comic exploits of this lantern-jawed, lanky and bogus knight – the first man ever to tilt at windmills and leave us the phrase – are so much a part of life that one finds it no harder to picture Don Quixote getting himself knighted by an exasperated publican than it is to see Lawrence setting off in Arab dress to defeat the Turks.

To begin, then, at the beginning. The Spanish gentleman whose surname was, according to Cervantes, "Quixada or Quesada, there is some difference of opinion among authors on this point –" had, in the intervals of looking after his small estate, spent a lot of time reading books of knight-errantry. He was especially moved by love passages written, Cervantes tells us, in this sort of way: "The reason for the unreason with which you treat my reason, so weakens my reason that with reason I complain of your beauty." He thrilled to the beauty of the words.

And so, in the fullness of time, our hero decided that he must become knight-errant. He would travel the globe in shining armour, mounted on a mettlesome steed, in search of adventure, righting wrongs, rescuing maids in distress. He got hold of an old suit of armour, diligently cleaned it, got as much rust off as he could, and clambered inside. It fitted creakily, lacking only a visor to the helmet, but this he made laboriously out of cardboard. But then, "to see if it was strong enough to stand up to the risk of a sword cut, he took out his sword and gave it two strokes, the first of which demolished in a moment what it had taken a week to make".

He made another visor, reinforced with little strips of iron, and wisely refrained from any further test. (Soon the helmet itself would be replaced, ridiculously, by a gleaming barber's bowl.) He set about saddling his steed.

This pitiful beast – the "lean hack" of our first paragraph, all skin and bones – he named, because he liked the sound, Rocinante. His own title then had to become "Sir Quixote (which sounded better than Quixada or Quesada) from (his district of) La Mancha". And a splendid title it was: "Don Quixote de La Mancha."

Next he needed, as knights do, a fair lady of whom to be enamoured. He had not, at his age, given much thought to such a problem, but now he remembered something which might be suitable. She was a brawny farm-girl he had once rather admired (without bothering to tell her of the fact), and now (again without telling the lady) he gave her the finest name he could invent for a beauteous damsel: "Dulcinea del Toboso."

And off he goes, without telling his household – niece, housekeeper, or gardener's boy. It is a steaming day in July.

He has just begun to swelter in the armour when he realizes, with a pang of horror, that he had never been knighted.

This, though it involves the connivance and help of others, he achieves to his complete satisfaction. He arrives that evening at an inn which he conveniently decides is a castle. Outside it are a couple of ladies of easy virtue whom he greets with a flourish as "beauteous maidens" – a title, Cervantes points out, ill-suited to their profession – and he sweeps on in. Here, after an evening of wildly comic misadventure – he has an hilarious fight with a pair of muleteers and, unlike most of the battles which involve him during the book, wins it – the landlord hastily "knights" him, to get rid of so troublesome a guest.

A knight at last, bursting with pride. Adventure follows adventure at breakneck speed. First of all, he makes a man who is flogging a servant desist by threatening to run him through with his lance. Satisfied with the achievement, he spurs Rocinante, leaves them behind. The man then ties the boy up to a tree for a second time and flogs him nearly to death – but the gallant Quixote is miles away, congratulating himself on this first righted wrong.

He comes upon a group of merchants at a crossroads. As soon as they get within earshot, the old fool shouts out, "Let the whole world stand, if the whole world does not confess that there is not in the whole world a finer lady than the Empress of La Mancha, the peerless Dulcinea del Toboso!"

The merchants have little doubt that he is out of his mind and are on the point of humouring him. Then one of them decides to taunt him, and doubt whether the peerless lady is as fine as he says.

This is too much for Quixote, who "couched his lance and ran at the man who had spoken, with such rage and fury that if Rocinante had not fortunately stumbled and fallen in the road, things would have gone badly for the rash merchant".

But Rocinante *has* fallen: our hero rolls away like a helpless armoured beetle, unable to get up under the weight of his equipment, roaring, "Stay – you slavish crew! It is not my fault, but my horse's, that I lie here."

And, indeed, the merchants and their muleteers do not fly away, but break his lance into convenient bits and beat him with it, like wheat in a mill, while the gallant knight howls threats to heaven.

The merchants exit laughing, and the wretched Quixote, unable to get up because of the weight of armour, the battering of his body, lies there, singing some convenient ballad that has occurred to him about a wounded knight, when a labourer from his own village, passing by, removes the cardboard-and-iron visor, now smashed to pieces, and is horrified to see Master Quxiada in this fancy dress, and grievously hurt. He gently loads the self-styled knight on his own donkey; ties helmet, splintered lance and one or two other loose items to the back of Rocinante, leads the lot home.

Tenderly, his housekeeper removes what equipment is still on the bruised body, and puts him into bed – still shouting nonsense about brigands and ladies fair.

So, after five hilarious chapters of a tale which rollicks on through no less than 126, ends the first expedition of the Knight of the Doleful Countenance. But after a fortnight's convalescence he has secretly made up his mind to go off again. He has been able, this time, to talk a simple yokel into going with him as squire. Sancho Panza, tempted with offers of booty and perhaps the governorship of some island, agrees.

And so, one evening, without farewells to housekeeper or to

Sancho's wife, they set off, knight on bony Rocinante, squire on donkey. Almost straight away, they have the adventure with the windmills: they see thirty or forty of them on the plain, and Quixote insists on believing them giants. Sancho politely insists they are not, but is told to go away and pray, while the gallant knight attacks them.

Commending himself to heaven and his Lady Dulcinea, Quixote charges the nearest windmill.

There is a loud crack as his lance sticks into a whirling sail, is whipped from his hands, and smashed to pieces (our hero is expensive in lances), and he is hurled, complete with horse, halfway across the plain.

Undeterred by this further misadventure, Quixote assures himself – and Panza – that an evil spirit has at the last moment changed the giants into windmills to cheat him of the glory of conquering them.

And on they go. Within an hour they have rescued some unfortunate woman in a coach from the innocent priests who are riding beside her, have urged the frightened lady to go to El Toboso and present herself to the peerless and beautiful Dulcinea, explaining that she has been rescued for Dulcinea's sake. The lady agrees to the request from this armoured lunatic, and we are not told whether she makes any attempt to carry it out. It would be difficult – as there is no Dulcinea.

Adventure succeeds adventure and in almost all of them Quixote is the loser: in very few is he aware of defeat. His second, long, expedition ends many chapters later, with a highly unsuccessful attempt to rescue yet another lady (who, being a statue, is even less anxious than the first) and the return of the two warriors, bruised and bleeding, on a hay cart, while their animals are led behind. Sancho Panza's wife is furious: "What profit have you got out of this squireship? Have you brought me a skirt? Or some pretty shoes for the children?" – but Sancho has brought nothing but experience. Already he has forgotten the hardship, is able to say, with enthusiasm, that "there's nothing so pleasant in the world for an honest man than to be squire to a knight-errant".

But of course this cannot be the end. A whole second part comes from Cervantes's extraordinary imagination, in which the third and final expedition of our knight is detailed at greater – and more comic – length than the first two expeditions put together. There is no space here to recount these extraordinary adventures, which end in the peaceful death of Master Quixana, aware at last that he is not a knight after all. In his will, which he dictates while Sancho Panza weeps at the bedside, he makes certain bequests to the little man and adds, "If, when I was mad, I was party to giving him the governorship of an isle, now that I am sane, I would give him a kingdom, were I able. For the simplicity of his nature and the fidelity of his conduct deserve it."

And as for his young niece, to whom he bequeaths his estate: "She should marry a man of whom she has first had evidence that he does not even know what books of chivalry are."

Miguel de Cervantes, author of this comic novel, was born on 9 October, 1547, the son of a poor Spanish physician and apothecary – poor, unqualified, and almost stone deaf – who was always on the move to escape from his creditors. But by 1566 the family, apparently more solvent, had settled in Madrid.

At the age of twenty-one Miguel wrote, as was the fashion in those days, some verses on the death of Isabel de Valois, wife of Philip II, which were favourably noticed. He might well have become a successful author now, for already he had travelled a great deal, and the bizarre adventures of his own family would have given him material for a lifetime's writing, but he had the misfortune to get involved in a duel: the upshot was that he had to flee from Spain. We next hear of him as private soldier in Rome. A year later, in 1571, he is taking part in the great naval battle of Lepanto. Here he is badly wounded, losing the use of his left hand. A little later, having been granted permission to return to Spain, he is on the way, a day or two out from Naples, when his ship is captured by Barbary pirates. He is taken to Algiers and imprisoned, then sold as a slave. Here he displays great bravery in trying to help others escape.

Eventually, Cervantes was ransomed, in part by his family who had saved and scraped for years to do so, partly by some kindly monks who made up the figure to the required total. In the autumn of 1580 he returned, aged thirty-three, to Spain and a poverty-stricken family. They, for their part, found him a changed person: he was in much the predicament of the soldier home from the wars: he was no longer glamorous, even useful; nobody wanted him.

He began to write verses again, and visited Portugal and – surprisingly – Algiers. He also wrote a great many plays, few of which have survived, and got married, at the age of thirty-eight. Like many writers he found it impossible to keep himself by his pen, and had to take all manner of other work, including helping to requisition supplies for the Armada – a job which made him highly unpopular. Like father before him, he got poorer and poorer – and like his later creation, Sancho Panza, dreamed of being given, if not the governorship of a Spanish island, at least a job in one of them. He applied again and again and was refused.

Throughout these countless frustrations, which included at least two spells of imprisonment, he was working on his *Don Quixote de La Mancha*: as every new misfortune struck him, or each new wild hope raced through his brain, he scribbled it down.

The first part of the book appeared in 1605, was immediately a huge success, was translated into many languages, including English. Overnight, Don Quixote and Sancho Panza had become real people, known to everyone.

He went on with his writing – plays, poems, short stories: then, in the last year of his life, published a brilliant second part to *Don Quixote*, which was as great a success as the first. And deservedly so, for, to most critics, it is far and away the better. High praise indeed.

But – every bit as unlucky as his knightly creation – Miguel de Cervantes, known and honoured all over Europe, died in poverty on 23 April, 1616, and was given a pauper's funeral.

His book, of course, has survived, will always survive, as a splendid memorial. Above all, it is an adventure story, but with more richness of character and background than practically any other. Every single person who enters its pages is carefully, wittily, sometimes touchingly, described, from the fat innkeeper with a passion for story-telling to the original of the "beauteous, peerless, Dulcinea del Toboso", Miss Lorenzo with her delicate moustache and enormous, hooting, voice.

The background, too, is fascinating, and the book would be a masterpiece purely on the merits of the detailed look it gives us at the customs, behaviour, class structure, of sixteenth-century Spain.

As for satire – the book abounds in it: there are attacks which range from gentle nudge to lethal blow. Yet it is not possible to treat the book as a work of social criticism. Cervantes enjoyed himself immensely in poking fun at individuals – but there is no general condemnation of officialdom as a class, or of the Church – even of the Inquisition. Cervantes takes things as they come: he is satisfied in passing them on to us, suitably etched, made plain, for our consideration.

There have been many English translations, from the first, soon after the Spanish originals, of Shelton, to a most excellent one, published in 1950 (by Penguin Books), from J. M. Cohen. But whichever translation, and in whichever one of fifty or so languages the tale is read, the Knight of the Doleful Countenance and his little squire remain two of the most fascinating characters in all fiction.

LA ROCHEFOUCAULD'S *MAXIMS*

THE *Maxims* of La Rochefoucauld have appealed to every generation since they appeared in 1665 and so the author has achieved a
relative immortality on one book. Other men have done this but
none with such a short book – there are only some 700 odd maxims,
the majority of which consist of three or four sentences.

The message of the *Maxims* will be discussed in a moment, but it
should be said straight away that the view of man, his emotions and
his actions, contained in the *Maxims* remains significant and stimulating today because it is entirely based on La Rochefoucauld's meditating on his own experience. There is nothing drawn from books or
from other men's minds; there is no attempt made to erect a system
and even less to propagate a doctrine. Unlike most moralists, La
Rochefoucauld has no desire whatever to convert. He wrote for a
small circle of highly gifted people. His reflections therefore are the
more bold and stark because they were not dressed up for the public.
They are dressed up in a sense because they are written in a prose
which is unmatched and so good that with a little care it easily
remains brilliant in translation. George Saintsbury very aptly compares La Rochefoucauld's prose to work in bronze, to a bronze
medallion, and this applies to the matter as much as to the form.
Nothing, he says, is left unfinished, yet none of the workmanship is
finicky.

Superficially it may be surprising that the life of this French aristocrat, mostly spent – so far as the active part was concerned – in aimless intrigues at the Court and in fighting in the absurd but extremely
damaging civil wars of the Fronde – should have yielded such a penetrating crop of observations which appear valid for mankind in
general. Born in 1613, known as the Prince de Marcillac, the title
borne by the elder son of the Dukes of La Rochefoucauld, he was
married at the age of fifteen to the daughter of an influential courtier
of Louis XIII. This rather weak monarch, the son of the great Henry
IV, allowed the extremely able Cardinal de Richelieu to rule the
kingdom. The young La Rochefoucauld became part of the Queen's
coterie who constantly intrigued against the Cardinal, and at one
period there was a plan by which La Rochefoucauld should remove
the Queen to Brussels and stir up an armed revolt. After a year of

fighting in the French Army in 1635, La Rochefoucauld continued to intrigue against Richelieu and actually spent a week in the Bastille prison. But this excitable young man was not taken very seriously.

When Richelieu died in 1642, Cardinal Mazarin succeeded him, whose ally and, according to many people, mistress the Queen now became. La Rochefoucauld remained, however, the enemy of the man in power. From 1649 to 1653 the wars of the Fronde were in effect the attempts of the great nobles, among whom was La Rochefoucauld, to get rid of Mazarin. They did not mind fighting the royal army or getting help from the Spaniards. Some of the Frondeurs allied themselves with the Parliament of Paris – not a Parliament in the British sense, but rather more an Inns of Court, a collection of lawyers and notabilities who were jealous of the Crown and particularly Mazarin for stealing their privileges. They hated central government.

La Rochefoucauld, like others, changed sides at least twice. He never felt that Mazarin recognized his merits when he had come over to him. In one of the most striking engagements during the war, when the daughter of the King's uncle, the Duke of Orleans, turned the cannon of Paris on the King's army, La Rochefoucauld was shot through the head and nearly lost his sight. Unlike the English Civil War, the Fronde were about no great principles at all and they eventually petered out with Mazarin still at the helm.

La Rochefoucauld, whose father died in 1650, settled down at the Court in 1656 where the star of the young King Louis XIV was rising. Until his death in 1680 he lived a peaceful existence, either in Paris or on his estates in the Poitou. At the Court of the new King he was a respected relic of a past age of disorder and, although still comparatively young, seemed to have no desire to play an active rôle in politics. His great friend was Madame de la Fayette, whose novel, *La Princesse de Cleves*, owes much to La Rochefoucauld's advice. In her salon and in that of Madame de Sable, La Rochefoucauld spent much time with writers such as Molière, Boileau and Corneille, then an ageing man. He was the friend of Bossuet and among the most fervent admirers of the *Maxims* was La Fontaine. The verdict on La Rochefoucauld's active life must be that he was able and intelligent enough to play an important rôle in affairs of State but that he was never destined to be anything but a secondary figure.

A most interesting interior portrait was made of La Rochefoucauld by one of his most intelligent enemies, Paul Gondi, Cardinal de Retz. "There was always about La Rochefoucauld," writes the Cardinal, "a certain *je ne sais quoi*" (a certain "I don't know what").

La Rochefoucauld liked intrigue from his early youth at a time when he had no feeling for petty interests, which indeed never attracted him, and when he did not understand great matters, which as a matter of a fact he never properly understood. "La Rochefoucauld," continues de Retz, "was habitually irresolute. He was very much a soldier but not cut out to be a leader in war; he was never a good party man, though all his life he belonged to parties. He was always rather apologetic in business affairs; it seemed he needed to be. All this," concludes de Retz, "when considered with his *Maxims*, which betrayed too little faith in virtue and his habit of always trying to get out of any serious matter with the same degree of impatience that he entered into it, makes one feel that he would have done much better if he had understood himself better and reduced himself to becoming, as he could have done, the most accomplished courtier of his century."

Not a flattering portrait. De Retz, however, failed to see that the *Maxims* – for all they may not betray a sufficient faith in virtue – removed, by their excellence, his victim from a position in which any attack on his practical ability mattered very much. And having failed to play a successful rôle in life, gave La Rochefoucauld that close insight into the minds of men, including that of the Cardinal, which success might have made no use of.

The basic reflection or observation to which La Rochefoucauld returns time after time in his *Maxims* is the immense importance of self-interest in human actions. "All virtues are directed towards self-interest as rivers flow to the sea," he writes, and this observation leads him to the idea that what men call virtues are really very mixed qualities in which, as he says, "vices form part of virtues as poisons do of medicines". Many of the *Maxims* analyse so-called virtues such as clemency, moderation, love of justice, and bring out the interests which lead to the profession and practise of each of these virtues. Thus of the last he writes that: "Love of justice is usually little more than a strong fear of losing what one possesses; from that comes our consideration and respect for the interests of our neighbours and so too our scrupulous attention not to harm them." And he writes: "People blame injustice not so much from any natural aversion from it as from the damage it could do to them."

Self-interest he sees playing a large part in gratitude which, first of all, he notes, is rare: "Pride dislikes owing and self-interest does not like to pay." For most men who express gratitude it is because of a strong and secret desire to receive greater benefits.

From an exacting analysis of degree to which self-interest mars and

even dominates many so-called virtues, the thoughts of La Rochefoucauld turn to the hollowness of many of the feelings where self-
interest does not seem to play a major part. Of friendship he observes
that: "There is always something which does not altogether dis-
please us in the misfortunes of our friends," an aphorism matched by
the well known: "We have all sufficient strength to bear other
people's misfortunes." Just as La Rochefoucauld traces pity very
largely to compassion for oneself, so "we only follow our tastes and
our pleasures when we prefer our friends to ourselves". Of love La
Rochefoucauld writes: "True love is like the appearance of a ghost.
Everybody talks of it yet few people have seen it." "Love lends its
name to a great number of activities in which it no more plays the
part than does the Doge in all that happens in Venice." Like Stendhal,
La Rochefoucauld is struck by the degree to which vanity plays its
part in love, as in all passions, and just as he says old men give good
advice to console themselves from not being able to give bad examples, so he notes strong feelings and passions are more liable to
leave us than we to overcome them.

The *Maxims*, therefore, tend to analyse good qualities destructively
and to destroy illusions about the nobility of human feelings or
passions. Admired for their style and penetration, they have been
criticized as unduly cynical. But the criticism of La Rochefoucauld,
particularly strong in the eighteenth century with its illusions about
the essential goodness of man's nature and its corruption by society,
has borne on the effects of reading the *Maxims* rather than on the
intrinsic truth of the *Maxims* themselves. It can be said that La Rochefoucauld, in showing that all human acts are mixed with bad, with
self-interest, does not distinguish enough between the different
degrees of egoism – there are some which are indeed nearly as bad as
possible, but others for which the initial good inclination or feeling
subsists. Thus a man who all his life behaves well and honourably for
the pleasure of knowing that he is a good and honourable man may
be an egotist, but he is a much better man than a scoundrel who has
acted as though there was no such thing as goodness or honour. It
can be said too that La Rochefoucauld in his book does not appreciate the practical value of behaving well, of decent conduct and at
least respect for propriety in the life of the world.

All these criticisms, however, take no account of the fact that La
Rochefoucauld does not set himself out to reform mankind, he is not
proposing how man ought to behave or be; he is recording what his
experience has shown him of man and his behaviour. If his experience had been peculiar, if his observations had been one-sided, his

book would not have been read, or would have been read only as a curiosity. But the contrary is the case, and his indictment, if it can be so called, is one which has to be listened to at any time.

La Rochefoucauld is no doubt a pessimist, a man who tends to see the worst rather than the better. But he is not a philosophical pessimist who has concluded that life is not worth living and that evil is more powerful than good. Nor is his pessimism one as it were of the bowels, an irrational hatred of man, which is called misanthropy. Nor is it a sort of attitude deriving from unhappy experiences and cultivated by some writers, artists and sensitive people as a means of self-defence, of avoiding further disappointment. Nor is La Rochefoucauld's pessimism another variety – that of the Christian who wishes to confound man's pride and so bring him to God. La Rochefoucauld is not a Christian; but had he been one it is doubtful if this would have very much altered his observations, for they are remarkably similar to those of other Christians, notably to that of the great writer Pascal. It is to be noted too that La Rochefoucauld's analysis is never brought to bear either on the love of God nor on the love of families or of mother for child.

We return then to the all-important truth that the *Maxims* are read because they are reflections drawn from direct experience. These carefully chiselled aphorisms are, it must be noted, not dogmatic; the words usually, often, almost always, frequently, are precise indications that La Rochefoucauld considered that there were exceptions to his findings. On sincerity we read: "Sincerity is an opening of the heart; few people are capable of it; and that which is seen ordinarily is only a clever piece of dissimulation to attract other people's confidences." But one can and must conclude that the author considers that sincerity *does* exist though it is rather rare. La Rochefoucauld's view of love is a destructive one, but the observer with a pessimistic view of mankind has expressed some thoughts which are certainly not those of a cynic: "There is no disguise whatever which can for long conceal love where it exists or make it appear where it is absent." That La Rochefoucauld believes in the existence of love is shown when he writes: "If there is a love uncontaminated by our other passions, it is that which is hidden in the depths of the heart and which we ignore ourselves." This is a very important maxim, for it shows that La Rochefoucauld believes in the existence of virtues but sees that these are real virtues only when they are spontaneous and uncontaminated by self-consciousness. It makes virtue rare. But that is not a cynical view, and it is the essence of La Rochefoucauld.

PARADISE LOST

JOHN MILTON

IF JOHN MILTON had died in, say, 1640, on the eve of the great Civil War between King and Parliament, he might have been remembered as the author of some exquisite lyrics. If he had died twenty years later, at the time of the Restoration, he might have found a place in the histories of the time as Cromwell's Latin Secretary and as one of the most virulent of the apologists for those formidable characters who had overthrown the monarchy, slaughtered the King in public view, and set up a military dictatorship. But in fact he did not die until 1674, and this gave him time to produce *Paradise Lost*, by common consent the greatest and grandest epic poem in the English language, and perhaps in any other – not to mention the not so very much less remarkable *Paradise Regained* and *Samson Agonistes*.

Everyone knows the story that he made the groundwork of his epic: it is one of the oldest stories in the world, and in the first chapters of the Book of Genesis it is preserved in language of immortal grandeur and beauty. "Of Man's first disobedience," he begins:

> *Of Man's first disobedience, and the fruit*
> *Of that forbidden tree, whose mortal taste*
> *Brought death into the world, and all our woe,*
> *With loss of Eden. . . .*

But it is soon apparent that he has no intention of merely rewriting the Bible story in blank verse; which is just as well, for not even Milton could have improved on the majestic simplicity of the original. No, he has something more in mind. His motive in writing is that –

> *I may assert Eternal Providence,*
> *And justify the ways of God to men.*

What a presumptuous idea! But we may be quite sure that Milton did not think it so. He had an intensely legalistic mind, and he could

Fortunate indeed was Michel de Montaigne in his birth and parentage, for in an age when children were treated as a rule with brutal severity he was brought up by his father in a way that was almost whimsically humane. Thus (as shown in the above engraving) the Seigneur de Montaigne had the boy awakened in the morning by the sound of some musical instrument because he had heard that "it disturbs the tender brain of children to be awakened suddenly". (*Left*) The tower adjoining his chateau near Bordeaux in which, surrounded by his books, Montaigne penned those Essays – witty, deeply reflective, fearlessly critical – which struck a new note in literature. For the last twenty years of his life (he died in 1592, when he was just on sixty) he dwelt here in a happy retirement, more than content to have found an avenue of escape from the vicious intolerance and abominable cruelty of the contemporary world.

Striding through the pages of Milton's *Paradise Lost* is the mighty figure of Satan, chief of the rebel angels who dared to defy the Omnipotent in arms. Even when flung out of Heaven into the abyss of Hell he is undaunted. "Awake, rise, or be for ever fallen!" he cries (*above, left*) to his dispirited followers, and they answer his summons. (*Right, above*) The original articles of agreement for the sale of the copyright in the great poem to Samuel Symons. Equally theological in its theme is John Bunyan's immortal allegory, *The Pilgrim's Progress*. The illustration below shows Christian passing safely between the lions outside the Porter's Lodge.

not help feeling that Adam and Eve had been hardly done by. What after all had they done? On the face of it nothing more than picking a fruit from the forbidden tree, eating it and finding it good! And for this trivial fault they had been condemned to toil and sorrow and eventual death! But was the fault so trivial? Surely there must have been more to it than this, and Milton at length satisfies his sense of right and wrong with a magnification of the apparently trivial misdemeanour into a most heinous sin. So far from having been trivial, the action that the Serpent had instigated was part of a carefully planned and skilfully executed revolt against the authority of the Most High God.

The villain of the piece was the Serpent, whom Milton identifies with "Satan, the Arch-Enemy". Some readers may be surprised to be told that there is no mention of Satan in the *Genesis* account: it was Milton who put him in the story, and it is a tribute to his influence that the Serpent (who in the Authorized Version is not accorded even the capital letter) is so generally identified with Satan or the Devil.

Until recently (we are given to understand) Satan had held an honourable post in the courts of heaven, perhaps even as the second-in-command to the Most High. But when God indicated His preference for "His Only Son", Satan had "raised impious war in Heaven", with the result that he and all the angels who had supported him and had "durst defy the Omnipotent to arms" were

Hurl'd headlong flaming from the ethereal sky,
With hideous ruin and combustion, down
To bottomless perdition. . . .

For nine days and nights "he with his horrid crew Lay vanquish'd, rolling in the fiery gulf", but still he retained his "obdurate pride and steadfast hate". Then he succeeds in raising himself from the fiery deluge and, looking round on the companions of his fall, "with bold words" breaks "the horrid silence".

Already, when we have not turned half a dozen pages, the figure of Satan dominates the stage, as indeed he does almost throughout. The Miltonic conception of the Arch-Fiend has been called the grandest character in the whole world of poetry, and beyond any doubt Satan is the hero of *Paradise Lost* – great in his power to arouse the devotion of his followers and to retain it even when he has led them into what must appear to be irretrievable ruin, mighty in battle and dauntless in defeat, even when he has learnt through bitter pain and loss that their opponent is indeed the Omnipotent. There is never a suggestion of the faint heart or craven in his demeanour.

> *What though the field be lost?*
> *All is not lost; the unconquerable will,*
> *And study of revenge, immortal hate,*
> *And courage never to submit or yield,*
> *And, what is else, not to be overcome....*

When Beelzebub urges him to reconcile himself to defeat or worse may befall, Satan rejoins,

> *Fallen Cherub! to be weak is miserable,*

and he overcomes his lieutenant's remaining objections with the assertion that:

> *To reign is worth ambition, though in Hell:*
> *Better to reign in Hell than serve in Heaven!*

Now "on the beach of that inflamed sea" he "call'd so loud, that all the hollow deep of Hell resounded":

> *Princes, potentates,*
> *Warriors, the flower of heaven! once yours, now lost,*
> *If such astonishment as this can seize*
> *Eternal Spirits! or have ye chosen this place*
> *After the toil of battle to repose*
> *Your wearied virtue, for the ease you find*
> *To slumber here as in the vales of Heaven?*
> *Or in this abject posture have ye sworn*
> *To adore the Conqueror? . . .*
> *Awake, arise, or be for ever fallen!*

Whereupon, "they heard, and were abash'd, and up they sprung". Led and directed by their great Chief, they set about the raising of a palace – Pandemonium by name – where they proceed to hold counsel. Even before their expulsion from heaven they had heard rumours that the "Monarch in Heaven" had planned to create a new world somewhere out in space and "plant it with a generation whom his choice regard should favour equal to the sons of Heaven", and now Beelzebub reminds them of this proposal. "Though Heaven be shut," he says, "this place may lie expos'd". It having sounded good to the assembled peers of hell, Satan with characteristic courage and boldness takes upon himself the dangerous mission to "go in search of this new world" and "confound the race of mankind". After many a strange adventure and encounter he arrives at length on the newborn earth, leaps the wall of Paradise, and from a perch in the boughs of the Tree of Life has his first glimpse of Adam and Eve in the Garden of Eden that God had planted.

> *Two of far nobler shape, erect and tall,*
> *Godlike erect, with native honour clad*
> *In naked majesty seem'd lords of all . . .*
> *His fair large front, and eye sublime, declar'd*
> *Absolute rule; and hyacinthine locks,*
> *Round from his parted forelock manly hung*
> *Clustering, but not beneath his shoulders broad.*
> *She, as a veil, down to the slender waist,*
> *Her unadorned golden tresses wore*
> *Dishevell'd, but in wanton ringlets wav'd*
> *As the vine curls her tendrils, which implied*
> *Subjection, but required with gentle sway,*
> *And by her yielded, by him best receiv'd,*
> *Yielded with coy submission, modest pride,*
> *And sweet, reluctant, amorous delay . . .*
> *So pass'd they naked on, nor shunn'd the sight*
> *Of God or Angel; for they thought no ill:*
> *So hand in hand they pass'd, the loveliest pair,*
> *That ever since in love's embraces met. . . .*

In this ecstatic description of the first human lovers in their heavenly bower was Milton thinking of his own wedding-night in the bedroom in Aldersgate Street? Eve was very unlike the first Mrs. Milton, who was so far from being submissive that she ran away home to her parents after only a few weeks of marriage, and could not be prevailed upon to return for several years. Out of this experience Milton had written a tract in advocacy of divorce (by the husband) that had earned him an unpleasant notoriety. After his first wife's death he had married a second time, and again a third, this time a young woman thirty years his junior, and with them all his experiences seem to have been not altogether satisfactory. Perhaps it is true what Dr. Johnson alleged, that Milton "had something like a Turkish contempt of females, as subordinate and inferior beings. . . . He thought women made only for obedience, and men only for rebellion." The sort of wife he wanted was Eve, and he married Mary Powell. . . . But we must return to the drama that is now about to be played out in the Garden, where Adam and Eve are exposed, in all their inexperienced virtue, to the wiles of the Arch-Tempter. Disguised now as a serpent, Satan first ravishes the girl's ear with his flatteries of her matchless loveliness, and then he induces her to partake of "this fruit divine, fair to the eye, inviting to the taste, of virtue to make wise". And Adam likewise,

> *She gave him of that fair enticing fruit*
> *With liberal hand; he scrupled not to eat,*
> *Against his better knowledge; not deceiv'd,*
> *But fondly overcome with female charm.*

Whereupon, "Earth trembled from her entrails", and "Nature gave a second groan". While as for Adam and Eve, now that their pristine innocence is gone, "in lust they burn . . . to dalliance move," until with the morning their eyes are opened and they make themselves aprons of fig-leaves, "to hide their guilt and dreaded shame".

Meanwhile, "the heinous and despiteful act of Satan done in Paradise" has become known in heaven, and the decree of banishment from Eden is pronounced. The Archangel Michael is dispatched to enforce the sentence, and so the mighty poem reaches its sombre end:

> *They, looking back, all the eastern side beheld*
> *Of Paradise, so late their happy seat,*
> *Wav'd over by that flaming brand; the gate*
> *With dreadful faces throng'd, and fiery arms.*
> *Some natural tears they dropt, but wip'd them soon;*
> *The world was all before them, where to choose*
> *Their place of rest, and Providence their guide:*
> *They, hand in hand, with wandering steps and slow,*
> *Through Eden took their solitary way.*

Paradise Lost was published in 1667. Milton received £5 down, and a further £5 when the first impression of 1,300 copies was disposed of; his widow subsequently parted with all further claims for the sum of £8. These figures have been quoted as an indication of the low esteem in which the poem was held at first; but, as Dr. Johnson maintained, "the sale of 1,300 copies in two years, in opposition to so much recent enmity, and to a style of versification new to all and disgusting to many, was an uncommon example of the prevalence of genius". And from the first the best judges, such as Dryden and later Addison, were most lavish in their praises. Every generation since has agreed that, to quote Milton's own description of a good book, *Paradise Lost* is "the precious life blood of a master spirit".

THE PILGRIM'S PROGRESS

JOHN BUNYAN

THE MORE one studies the history of Bunyan's masterpiece the more of a miracle it appears. Its author, a tinker and son of a tinker, had no education beyond the scant schooling which taught him to read and write. He wrote the book in prison, where he was held twelve years by the authorities for preaching in conventicles. The Puritan ideas he set forth were anathema to the licentious temper of society under the rule of the "Merry Monarch", Charles II. The work got no advance publicity, no sales promotion. Yet it sold edition after edition. In the first ten years its sales totalled 100,000 – and that in a country with about a tenth of today's population, and with a high level of illiteracy among the humbler folk who were its chief purchasers.

Nor was this popularity short-lived. For the next two and a half centuries it remained a best-seller, second only to the Bible in popular esteem. Within the first hundred years some 160 editions of it had been issued. Ere this, it has been translated into more than 200 foreign languages. Though praised by Dean Swift and Dr. Johnson, it was for more than a century ignored or sneered at by most arbiters of literary taste; but at last the spontaneous verdict of the nation was confirmed by the intellectuals. As Southey wrote in 1830: "The opinion of the multitude has been ratified by the judicious." And next year Macaulay classified John Bunyan and John Milton as "the only two great creative minds" of the seventeenth century. Froude, in 1880, included Bunyan among English Men of Letters. Bernard Shaw declared that he was "better than Shakespeare".

What sort of man was he? His family, from the twelfth century, had been small freeholders in Bedfordshire. His father, who described himself as a "braseyer", owned his house and about nine acres of adjoining land. John was born in the autumn of 1628, and christened in the Elstow parish church on 30 November. He early began to assist his father in his trade as a tinker and brazier. He grew up to a time of political and religious strife. In 1642, civil war broke out between Charles I and the Parliament. Two years later, John, just rising sixteen, was conscripted into the Parliamentary army, with which he served till 1647 in the forces garrisoning Newport Pagnell.

Then he was demobilized, and returned to his father's forge.

He was now a tall, big-boned youth, fond of games and village sports, of dancing and dicing, of drinking and horse-play, of cursing and swearing. And yet under this he hid a tender conscience and a troublesome awareness of the unseen, which even in childhood sometimes interrupted his play. He has given, in *Grace Abounding* – his spiritual autobiography – a graphic account of how he was arrested in his profane way of life, and of the long-drawn-out struggles of his soul before he attained to spiritual peace.

At the age of twenty he set up house for himself as an independent craftsman, and married his first wife, Mary, who brought no money but two pious books. A sermon in church against Sabbath-breaking disquieted him. A rebuke by a dissolute woman for his foul cursing staggered him. But the turning-point came when he overheard some poor Puritan women chatting in a Bedford street about the work of grace in their hearts. "Methought they spake as if joy did make them speak."

After passing through many phases of hope and despair, he sought out these women, who put him in touch with their pastor, Mr. Gifford, the Baptist incumbent of St. John's parish church in Bedford. Under the Commonwealth, "Papists and Prelatists" were proscribed and the Prayer Book forbidden, though a wide toleration was extended to other sects, and Presbyterians and Independents took over many livings from which Anglican clergy had been driven. Bunyan became a member of Mr. Gifford's church, a devout Puritan and an untiring student of Holy Writ. Drawn into local preaching, he developed a quite remarkable gift for evangelism, and people flocked to hear him. He also started writing pamphlets against the Quakers, but soon dropped this controversy and turned his pen to expositions of Biblical teaching.

After the restoration of the monarchy under Charles II, the Church of England was re-established, and irregular gatherings and unlicensed preachers banned. On 12 November, 1660, when Bunyan went to preach to a gathering at a farm some thirteen miles south of Bedford, he was arrested and haled before a local justice who committed him to Bedford gaol. Firmly refusing to promise to abandon preaching if released, he was held in gaol for the next twelve years. His gaoler was friendly, and at times during those years he was able to slip out and preach at conventicles; but much driven back on his pen, he wrote a number of pamphlets, and in 1666 he published his first major work: *Grace Abounding*.

This was a vivid narrative of his own spiritual pilgrimage: of his wayward youth, his awakening, his despairing struggles with the assaults of the Devil and his ultimate winning through to an assurance of redemption. Intimate, unreserved, it takes its place, like the Confessions of St. Augustine, among the great documents of spiritual experience.

As he wrote, he found his picturesque mind building up allegorical images of his experiences; of the morasses of despair, the difficult climbs, battles with the tempter, assaults of doubt or soul lethargy; and of the good and evil counsellors he had met, the friends whose companionship he had enjoyed, the trials and persecutions they had shared. At first idly he began to jot down these fancies, then became fascinated by the theme and "set pen to paper with delight". On his release from his twelve years' imprisonment, in consequence of Charles II's Declaration of Indulgence in March, 1672, he brought with him the manuscript of the first draft – not yet complete – of his allegory.

In the previous year, while still officially a prisoner, he had been appointed pastor of the Independent Church in Bedford. He now became extremely active in his ministry to it and to many similar communities. But the withdrawal of the Declaration of Indulgence in February, 1675, brought a fresh warrant for his arrest, and after eighteen months on the run he spent a further nine months in gaol. Here he completed the first edition of his book, and after conflicting advice from his friends decided to publish it. It was licensed on 18 February, 1678, and came out as a small octavo volume, price 1s. 6d. It quickly sold out. A second edition was issued the same year, and a third, to which Bunyan had made some important additions, in 1679. Since then it has sold by the million in many lands. In 1685 he added Part II, the story of Christian's wife, Christiana, and her family and friends, travelling the same road by which the Pilgrim had passed to the Celestial City.

In 1680, Bunyan published *The Life and Death of Mr. Badman*, recording by contrast the downward path of an evil-liver. It was not allegorical. It was in fact the first English novel, a tale of the development of a character. He reverted to allegory in 1682 with *The Holy War*, in which, drawing on his experience as a soldier, he described how the City of Mansoul fell from its first innocence into the power of Diabolus, was rescued by Emmanuel, relapsed into backsliding through the treachery of Diabolonians lingering within its walls, but finally was won back by Emmanuel. Altogether, Bunyan in his lifetime published between forty and fifty books and pamphlets in prose or verse, and left a dozen more to be published after his death.

After his second imprisonment, Bunyan was untroubled by the authorities in his ministry of the Word. He was immensely popular in London. Vast crowds would gather at short notice to hear him preach: 1,200 at 7 o'clock on a cold weekday morning; 3,000 one Sunday to a meeting-house that could hold only half of them. Tireless in his pastoral labours, he at last was laid low by a drenching on a weary ride to Reading and back to reconcile a father and son. He died on 31 August, 1688, in London and was buried in Bunhill Fields.

The Pilgrim's Progress, the work which has set John Bunyan in the front rank of English writers, is couched in the simplest of homely English speech, closely akin to and freely borrowing from that supreme treasury of simple English, the Authorised Version of the Bible, a book which he studied and knew, and could quote from by chapter and verse. His narrative moves swiftly, with a marked economy of words; graphic, lively, gripping the attention and carrying the reader with eagerness to see what happens next.

Its theme is the pilgrimage of Christian from his home in the City of Destruction to the Celestial City. He calls it a dream that came to him in his prison cell. "As I walked through the wilderness of this world I lighted on a certain place where was a denn, and laid me down in that place to sleep; and as I slept, I dreamed a dream." So he begins, and the dream excuse lifts the story into the realms of fantasy, where things incredible in real life become natural.

Christian, the Pilgrim, appears at once as a man in rags, with a book in his hand and a burden on his back, desperate with the realization that his home city is doomed to destruction. He vainly tries to persuade his wife and family to join him in flight, and is directed by Evangelist to the wicket gate through which he can enter the narrow way to eternal life. Rejecting the appeals of family and friends, he stops his ears and runs.

Two neighbours pursue him, Obstinate and Pliable. One of the delightful features of the book is that the character of everyone is stamped on them by their name, with no need for further explanation. Obstinate, unmoved by Christian's urging, goes back, but Pliable comes on till they plunge into the Slough of Despond, when he, too, retreats. Christian struggles on, is diverted into peril by the counsel of Worldly Wiseman and rescued by Evangelist, and so reaches the wicket gate and is set by Goodwill on the straight and narrow way.

He calls first at the House of the Interpreter, where various lessons are taught him by picture and parable. Then he reaches "a place somewhat ascending; and upon that place stood a Cross, and a little below, in the bottom, a Sepulchre". At the sight, the burden falls from his shoulders and rolls down to the Sepulchre, "where it fell in, and I saw it no more".

Rejoicing, he goes on his way; meets Simple, Sloth and Presumption, who reject his advice, as also do Formalist and Hypocrisy, who soon come to a bad end. Then he has to climb the Hill Difficulty, where he gets into trouble by sleeping and mislaying the Roll – his ticket of admission to the Celestial City – which had been given him at the Cross. Late at night he comes to the House Beautiful, to find lions in the way. (Bunyan was all too familiar with the dangers besetting those who made their way to meeting-places of faithful dissenters.) In the House Beautiful he passes some three days, instructed by Piety, Prudence and Charity, and leaves it clad in the armour of salvation.

Down he goes into the Valley of Humiliation, to be challenged by Apollyon. Bunyan, once a soldier, knew something about fighting. Shakespeare himself never achieved so savage a call to combat as Apollyon's shout: "Prepare thyself to die; for I swear by my infernal den that thou shalt go no farther; here will I spill thy soul!" The desperate fight that follows is vigorously described. Then Christian has to thread his way by night through the horrors and perils of the Valley of the Shadow of Death.

In the morning he overtakes another pilgrim, Faithful, who recounts his own adventures to date along the narrow way. They are joined by Talkative, who charms Faithful by his glib religious talk, till Christian, who knows the man, gives warning that the common people describe him as "A saint abroad, and a devil at home". Faithful then soon finds out by searching questions the hollowness of Talkative's professions, who breaks away from their company. They come on to Vanity Fair, where the traders find their piety intolerable. They are put in a cage, marched round in irons, set in the stocks, and brought to trial before Lord Hate-good. Bunyan had ample experience through his own trials to aid him in describing this scene. Faithful is condemned, tortured and burnt at the stake. Christian is remanded, and presently escapes.

He is joined by Hopeful, who has been converted by Faithful's testimony and becomes his companion for the rest of the journey. They hold disputations with By-ends, Hold-the-world, Money-love and Save-all, who end disastrously in the silver mine of Demas. Beguiled by By-path Meadow, they are taken captive by Giant Despair and imprisoned in Doubting Castle till Christian remembers his key, called Promise, which unlocks their doors, though the outer iron gate's lock "went damnable hard".

They come to the Delectable Mountains, where the shepherds give them counsel. Then Ignorance comes in by a side road, very sure of himself. They fall into the Flatterer's net, keep awake on the Enchanted Ground, and enter the Land of Beulah. So they reach the dark river, which Hopeful aids Christian to ford, and are received by the Shining Ones into the Celestial City.

In the second part of *The Pilgrim's Progress*, Christian's wife and children, accompanied by a young neighbour, Mercy, set out to follow by the road he had taken. They come to the Interpreter's House, where they see a new set of symbolic tableaux and object-lessons. On leaving, they are granted the escort of Mr. Great-heart as their guide and protector.

In the arbour halfway up Hill Difficulty, Christiana leaves her bottle of spirits, as Christian had left his Roll. At the summit, by the gate to the House Beautiful, a giant, Grim, is reinforcing the lions, but Great-heart cuts him down. They are welcomed with music at the House, where Prudence, Piety and Charity catechise Christiana's three boys. Mercy is wooed by a Mr. Brisk, who abandons his suit when he finds that she spends her time on works of charity. Matthew falls sick from eating evil fruit, but he is cured with a potion made, says Bunyan, *ex carne et sanguine Christi*. (He adds, apologetically, "The Latin I Borrow.")

The Valley of Humiliation is green and cheerful for them, and they come safely through the Valley of the Shadow of Death. Indeed, their pilgrimage is throughout a gayer and easier journey than Christian experienced. Giants are met with, but Great-heart slays them. Christiana's sons get married, and we read of music and dancing. They gather companions on their way: Honesty, Feeble-mind, Ready-to-halt, Despondency, Mrs. Much-afraid, Valiant-for-Truth, Standfast.

So the pilgrims win to the bank of the last river, and one by one the older ones, Christiana first, pass safely over, leaving legacies and messages to their friends. Most triumphant of all is Valiant-for-Truth, whose words might be Bunyan's own testament:

"My sword I give to him that shall succeed me in my pilgrimage, and my courage and skill to him that can get it. My marks and scars I carry with me, to be a witness that I have fought His battles who will now be my rewarder."

"So he passed over, and all the trumpets sounded for him on the other side."

THE ARABIAN NIGHTS'
ENTERTAINMENTS

SOMETIMES IT is called *The Arabian Nights' Entertainments*, and sometimes it is given the rather more correct title of *The Thousand and One Nights*. But whatever the name we know it by, the book is the most celebrated and popular collection of tales that has ever been presented to the story-loving public.

They are all Eastern tales, written in Arabic in the first place; and they first became generally known in Europe through a French translation that was made of them, or some of them, early in the eighteenth century by Antoine Galland, a French scholar who had travelled in the East and was thoroughly at home with Arabic and other Oriental languages. Galland's version appeared in a number of volumes between 1704 and 1717, and it had a most enthusiastic reception. A number of pirated editions appeared in various languages, and as early as 1707 an English translation of the first four volumes was published. It was by one of those literary gentlemen who are somewhat contemptuously referred to as Grub Street hacks, but in course of time other and very much better translations were made and became deservedly popular. Perhaps the most famous of these is the one made by the English traveller and Orientalist, Sir Richard Burton, which was first issued in a limited edition at Benares, in India, in 1885.

Galland obtained the manuscript on which he based his translation from Syria, and this seems to have been written, of course in Arabic, about a hundred years earlier in Egypt. But the tales are very much older than that, although it is impossible to say just how old. The earliest mention of them that has been traced is in a kind of historical encyclopaedia that was produced by an Arab named Masudi in about A.D. 950. According to Masudi, there were current among the Arabs of his time a number of books which had reached them in translation from Persian, Indian, Greek and other sources, and among these was one entitled *Hezar Afsane*, "a title which, translated from Persian into Arabic, means 'the thousand tales.'" The popular name given to the book was *The Thousand and One Nights*, and it got this name from the story that it contained, of a Persian king who was in the habit of killing his wives on the morning after the consummation of the marriage, and how a very clever young princess who was next on the list managed to escape execution by telling a story on her wedding-night that by morning had reached such an interesting point that the king agreed to spare the narrator for one night more in order that she should finish it. And so it continued for night after night as the wily girl played upon the king's very natural desire to learn "what happened next", as we should say.

This story is what is styled the "master tale", and it opens the collection as we have it. Here it is in brief outline, as told more or less in Sir Richard Burton's sometimes quaint language.

In time of yore and in time long gone before, there was a king of the kings in the islands of India and China whose name was Shahryar. One day he happened to catch his queen and her handmaidens in a gross act of infidelity with some handsome white slaves, and he was so shocked that he became as one distraught and cried out, "Only in utter solitude can man be safe from the doings of this vile world! By Allah, life is naught but one great wrong." Then he sat upon his throne and sent for his Chief Minister. "I command thee," he said, "to take my wife and smite her to death, for she hath broken her plight and her faith." Whereupon the Chief Wazir or Minister carried the queen to the place of execution and slew her, after which King Shahryar repaired to his seraglio and slew all the guilty concubines and their handmaidens. He also sware himself by a binding oath that whatever wife he married he would abate her virginity at night and slaughter her in the morning to make sure of his honour: "for," said he, "there never was nor is there one chaste woman upon the face of the earth. . . ." Then Shahryar commanded his Wazir to bring him the bride of the night that he might go to her; so he produced a most beautiful girl, the daughter of one of the emirs, and the king went unto her at eventide, and when morning dawned he bade his Minister strike off her head; and the Wazir did accordingly for fear of the Sultan.

On this wise the king continued for the space of three years; marrying a maiden every night and killing her the next morning, till folk raised an outcry against him and cursed him, praying Allah utterly to destroy him and his rule; and women made an uproar, and mothers wept and parents fled with their daughters, till there remained not in the city a young person of a sufficient age for marriage.

Presently the king ordered his Chief Wazir, the same who was charged with the executions, to bring him a virgin as was his wont; and the Minister went forth and searched and found none; so he returned home in sorrow and anxiety, fearing for his life from the king. Now the Wazir had two daughters, named Shahrazad and Dunyazad, of whom the elder had perused the books, annals and legends of preceding kings and the stories, examples, and instances of bygone men and things; indeed, it was said that she had collected a thousand books of histories relating to antique races and departed rulers. She had perused the works of the poets, and knew them by heart; she had studied philosophy and the sciences, arts and accomplishments; and she was pleasant and polite, wise and witty, well read and well bred.

Now on that day she said to her father, "Why do I see thee thus changed and laden with care?" Then the Wazir related to her, from beginning to end, all that had happened between him and the king. Whereupon she said, "By Allah, O my father, how long shall this slaughter of women endure? Shall I tell thee what is in my mind in order to save both sides from destruction?" "Say on, O my daughter," quoth he; and quoth she, "I wish thou wouldst give me in marriage to King Shahryar; either I shall live, or I shall be a ransom for the virgin daughters of Moslems and the cause of their deliverance from his hands and thine." "Allah upon thee!" cried he in wrath exceeding, "O scanty of wit, expose not thy life to such peril! How durst thou address me in words so wide from wisdom and unfar from foolishness? Know that one who lacketh experience in worldly matters readily falleth into misfortune...." "Needs must thou," she broke in; "make me a doer of this good deed, and let him kill me and he will; I shall only die a ransom for others." "O my daughter," asked he, "and how shalt that profit thee? When thou shalt have thrown away thy life?" And she answered, "O my father, it must be, come of it what will!"

Thereupon the Wazir, being weary of lamenting and contending, persuading and dissuading her, all to no purpose, went up to King Shahryar and, after blessing him and kissing the ground before him, told him all about his dispute with his daughter from first to last, and how he desired to bring her to him that night.

The king wondered with exceeding wonder, for he had made an especial exception of the Wazir's daughter, and said to him: "O most faithful of counsellors, how is this? Thou knowest that I have sworn by the Raiser of the Heavens that after this night I shall say to thee on the morrow's morning – 'Take her and slay her!' – and if thou slay her not, I will slay thee in her stead without fail." "Allah guide thee to glory and strengthen thy life, O King of the Age," answered the Wazir, "'tis she who hath so determined: all this I have told her and more; but she will not hearken to me, and she persisteth in passing this coming night with the King's Highness." So Shahryar rejoiced greatly and said, " 'Tis well; go get her ready, and this night bring her to me."

Then Shahrazad told her younger sister Dunyazad, "Note well what directions I entrust to thee! When I have gone in to the king I will send for thee, and when thou comest to me and seest that he hath had his will with me, do thou say to me, 'O my sister, and thou be not sleepy, relate to me some new story, delectable and delightsome, the better to spend our waking hours!; and I will tell thee a tale which shall be our deliverance, if so Allah pleases, and which shall turn the king from his bloodthirsty custom."

When evening came the Wazir took his daughter and went with her into the presence of the king, who was overcome with happiness. But when he was about to take the young girl she began to weep, so that he asked, "What ails thee?" She answered, "O my king, I have a little sister and I would say my farewells to her." Whereupon the king sent for Dunyazad and she came and threw herself upon her sister's neck and then lay down behind the bed.

When it was midnight Shahrazad awoke and signalled to her sister, who sat up and said, "Allah upon thee, O my sister, relate to me some new story, delectable and delightsome, wherewith to while away the waking hours of our latter night." The king had chanced to be sleepless and restless, and therefore he was pleased with the proposal of hearing a story. "Tell on," quoth he to Shahrazad. So Shahrazad rejoiced, and in this way, on the first night of the Thousand and One Nights, she began with the story of the Merchant and the Jinn.

This story is the first in the collection in all the versions that have come down to us, and it may be briefly summarized. It tells of a rich merchant who went on a journey, and one day, when he was sitting under a tree to take his midday repast of dates, he threw the stones behind him and had the misfortune of killing the son of a fearsome jinn or demon, who happened to receive some of them on his breast. The jinn threatened the merchant with immediate death, but he begged for time in which to proceed home and settle his affairs, after which he would return and submit to his fate. This he did, but when he was waiting for the appearance of the jinn three sheikhs arrived, one after the other, who all listened to the merchant's tale and lamented over his hard fate. At length they concocted a plan whereby he might be saved. When the jinn appeared, they suggested to him that they should each tell a story, which, if it pleased him, should be rewarded with a third of the merchant's blood. The jinn agreed ... and the first story was in progress when wily little Shahrazad noticed that the dawn was approaching and discreetly fell silent. Her sister urged her to continue, and the girl replied that there was nothing she would like better than to finish the tale, if she were still alive and the king spared her, the following night.

On hearing this the king said to himself, "By Allah! I will not slay her until I have heard from her lips the rest of her story." Then the king and Shahrazad – in English her name is generally spelled Scheherazade – spent the remainder of the night in each other's arms, and the Wazir was filled with amazement when he arrived at the palace the next morning, carrying the shroud for the daughter whom he believed was as good as dead. The procedure thus begun was followed for night after night, until Shahrazad bore the king a son, when she summoned sufficient courage to tell him of her device. He admired her intelligence so greatly that he spared her life and made her his favourite.

What were the stories that Scheherazade told in order to keep her head on her shoulders? It would seem that they are unlikely to have been any that are contained in the present collection, with the exception of the opening tale which sets the pattern. The collection seems to have varied from century to century, even country to country, new ones being added and old ones dropped to suit the fancy or the convenience of the compiler. It was not until the tales were printed in Galland's French translation that the text may be said to have become finalized.

Some of the most famous stories in the collection do not appear in the oldest manuscripts. Among them is the story of Aladdin and the Wonderful Lamp, and that of Ali Baba and the Forty Thieves. A real historical character who features in quite a number of the tales is Haroun al-Raschid – Haroun the Magnificent, as he was called – who reigned as Caliph of the Moslem world from A.D. 786 to his death in 809; and indeed so many have their scene of action in the capital of the Caliphs that it has been surmised that a primary source was a book of tales that was compiled in Baghdad in its days of greatest prosperity.

A very marked feature of the *Nights* is their erotic flavour, which is one of the reasons why in the East they are not generally considered to belong to what may be described as polite literature, but as the sort of thing that men may amuse each other with when gathered round the camp-fire or sitting over their coffee-cups in the bazaar. Sir Richard Burton remarked on this stumbling-block to universal approbation in his Translator's Foreword, distinguishing between "the simple, naive, and child-like indecency which, from Tangier to Japan, occurs throughout general conversation of high and low", of which he was inclined to take a kindly view, and "an absolute obscenity, sometimes, but not always, tempered by wit, humour, and drollery," which he strongly condemned.

All in all, however, we may be inclined to agree with Burton that "the general tone of the *Nights* is exceptionally high and pure. The devotional fervour often rises to the boiling-point of fanaticism. The pathos is sweet, deep and genuine; tender, simple and true. The morale is sound and healthy." Whatever its faults (and each reader will make his own list), this extraordinary collection of Oriental tales of strange adventures and voyages, moral and historical anecdotes, animal fables, philosophical and religious disquisitions, and romances with a high love interest, for generations has delighted readers in East and West and may be confidently expected to delight them for generations to come.

ROBINSON CRUSOE

DANIEL DEFOE

THE SON of a London tradesman, Daniel Defoe was born in 1660 and was nearly sixty when he wrote his immortal *Robinson Crusoe* – universally accepted as the greatest of all desert island tales. He was given a good education at the Rev. Charles Morton's dissenting Academy at Newington Green, and though intended for the Ministry, chose instead to enter the world of commerce.

He married, at twenty-four, the daughter of a rich merchant, who brought him a dowry of £3,700. Within a year, thirst for adventure led him to take part in the Monmouth rebellion. On his return, he ran into financial difficulties and, after a spell in a debtors' prison, started up as a brick- and tile-maker at Tilbury. Then, turning to journalism, he wrote a variety of pamphlets, one of which, "The Shortest Way With Dissenters", again landed him in jail.

After much miscellaneous writing he produced *Robinson Crusoe*, an instant success, which he followed with a succession of other exciting tales.

A lively journalist, with a retentive memory and a discerning eye for detail, he imparted verisimilitude to all his first-person stories. As in *Robinson Crusoe*, he had the knack of getting inside the skin of every character into whose supposed words he put his narratives. Alexander Pope declared: "There is something good in all he has written."

Though much wealth passed through his hands, Defoe died penniless.

For most readers, young or old, the true story may be said to begin at the moment when Crusoe, sole survivor of a shipwreck, clambers desperately ashore on an island that is to be his world for the next twenty-eight years. Thenceforth the reader shares every anxious, adventurous moment with the resourceful castaway; shares all his emotions, his innermost thoughts, his fears, his hopes, his soul-searching, his despair, his endless battles against loneliness, against all the elements; his triumphs over difficulties and dangers . . . and his ultimate exultation on rescue.

At the moment of landing the outlook is grim indeed.

Crusoe has nothing but a knife, a tobacco pipe and a little tobacco in a box.

He swims to the wreck and begins to equip himself with everything useful. He builds a raft and stocks up with provisions first – bread, rice, Dutch cheeses, some goat's flesh and some corn. He helps himself to liquor from the Captain's stock; then gathers together clothes and tools, sagely noting that the carpenter's chest was more valuable to him than gold. His next care is for arms and ammunition.

Ashore again, he climbs a hill for a quick survey of his domain to find that the island is uninhabited. For his second night he constructs a rough kind of hut by barricading himself round with chests and stores.

In repeated trips to the wreck he adds to his miscellaneous possessions – nails, spikes, powder and shot, sailcloth, scissors, charts, cables, ironwork, knives, forks, razors, ropes and much else. His inventories have a fascinating ring.

His next concern is to erect a tent in front of a small cave. This retreat he encloses in a double semi-circle of stout stakes, inside which he erects a strong barrier with more stakes and cables. Patiently he carries all his provisions and stores into this retreat. Inside this "fortress" he feels he can settle to sleep in peace.

Gradually, with much labour, he enlarges his cave, using the excavated earth and rock to construct a small terrace. A sudden storm, with blinding lightning flashes, at once makes him think of his gunpowder, so he loses no time in dividing it up into small packets in bags and boxes.

Two weeks pass before he thinks of scoring the date of his landing, 30 September, 1659, upon a post; but thereafter he cuts notches to record days, weeks and months.

Among his miscellaneous salvage he has pens, ink and paper, three or four compasses, mathematical instruments, charts, books on navigation and three Bibles. He has also been able to rescue the ship's dog and two cats.

He starts a diary, and one day he draws up a kind of balance sheet of his situation, philosophically noting that every evil can be offset by some advantage. Though alone on a "horrible desolate island", he reflects: "But I am alive, and not drowned as all my ship's company was" and: "He that miraculously saved me from death can deliver me...."

He experiences the terrors of an earth tremor and a hurricane, afterwards being struck down with fever. He doses himself with tobacco steeped in rum; but he also begins to pray, though not hitherto a religious man. He reflects on the mystery of life, looks out one of the Bibles salved from the wreck and dips into it daily. The fever passes and he feels moved to do what he has never done before – to kneel, and give thanks in prayer.

After being on the island about ten months he gathers enough nerve to explore a little. He comes upon a fertile region where everything is green, with a spring of fresh water in its midst. As he gathers limes, lemons and grapes he feels uplifted by the thought that he is lord of the whole island. The valley appeals so strongly that he spends a lot of time there and builds himself "a little kind of bower", surrounded at a distance by a high fence. He beguiles himself with the conceit that he now has "a country house" as well as his "sea-coast house". His morale is high.

On the first anniversary of his landing Crusoe keeps a solemn fast and spends much time in prayer.

Now, much more sure of himself, he plans an ambitious survey of his island from shore to shore, taking his gun, a hatchet, his dog and a sufficient stock of provisions. When he reaches the far shore he sights land some way off, but the thrill is momentary, and fear of the unknown and the possibility that the land on the horizon may harbour savages, enables him to convince himself that he is well enough off where he is.

In fact, this side of the island strikes him as being far pleasanter than his main base, for there are woods and fields and flowers and grasslands. The woods are full of parrots and he catches a young one with the intention of teaching it to talk. On this excursion he makes leisurely progress of about two miles a day, usually sleeping in trees. He finds turtles, penguins and fowls of all kinds. He enjoys a variety of food – goat's meat, turtles, pigeons, grapes and other fruits. His survey takes in a twelve-mile strip of beach, and he erects a pole to mark the limit of his journey for guidance on future excursions.

On the way back he acquires another pet, a young kid, for which he makes a collar of rope.

After a fruitless attempt to repair the ship's boat, which had been washed ashore badly damaged, he sets about making a canoe. But he is too ambitious, for it is so large and heavy that he cannot get it to the water.

The years pass. His clothes wear out. He would go without, but needs protection from the fierce sun. He contrives to fashion an umbrella from skins of animals he has shot, and makes clothes of sorts as well, wryly commenting that if he was a bad carpenter he was a worse tailor. His ability to laugh at himself also helps his morale.

Anyway, his carpentry improves sufficiently for him to construct a smaller canoe with sails.

Crusoe is never idle; always making things; a potter's wheel; baskets, furniture of sorts. He plants corn, husbands his stores; practises trapping against the day when his powder and shot must run out.

Then, midway through his absorbing chronicle of discovery and endeavour comes the great, dramatic moment when he comes suddenly upon the print of a man's naked foot upon the seashore. He can find no other impression. "I stood as one thunderstruck, or as if I had seen an apparition. I listened, I looked around me. I could hear nothing, nor see anything. . . . When I came to my castle . . . I fled into it like one pursued. . . . I slept none that night. . . ."

This incident fills him with frightening ideas. "Sometimes I feared it must be the Devil. . . ." His great fear banishes his religious hope until he suddenly recalls words from the Scriptures: "Call upon Me in the day of trouble. . . ."

He prays earnestly and, opening his Bible at random, reads: "Wait on the Lord, and be of good cheer, and He shall strengthen thy heart. . . ." He comments that he was no more sad – at least "not on that occasion". Still, he stays in for three days.

When seeking a suitable site for penning some of his livestock he makes a still more horrific discovery – a stretch of shore strewn with remnants of a cannibal feast. This moves him to look for a hiding place on a hill from which he can keep a sharp lookout, and this, in turn, leads to the discovery of a vast cavern, with a roof twenty feet high, to which he hastily transfers most of his arsenal.

Then, one day, he spies the light of fires, and from his vantage point on the hill he watches nine naked savages sitting round feasting, their two canoes hauled up on the beach. When they leave on the ebb tide he investigates and is sickened by the grisly remains of flesh and blood and bones. . . .

On another night he hears gunfire at sea which he suspects comes from a vessel in distress. He lights a beacon and in the morning there is a wreck upon the rocks. He hopes that at least one of her crew may have survived, so great is his craving for companionship. But there is no sign of life and only the corpse of the ship's boy is washed ashore. "He had nothing in his pocket but two pieces of eight and a tobacco pipe," comments Crusoe, adding: "The last was to me of ten times more value than the first."

A trip to the wreck in his small canoe takes him two hours. He finds a Spanish vessel firmly wedged by the bows, with the stern "all beaten to pieces". He takes off the ship's dog and some miscellaneous cargo, liquor, kettles and pots, a powder-horn and some gold and a little clothing, also two pairs of shoes from the feet of drowned seamen.

After this he falls back into his old routine, though more wary. Then comes the dramatic rescue of a young native fleeing from two cannibals. As he kneels in gratitude before his rescuer, Crusoe realizes that at last he has a companion. He christens him Friday, the day of his rescue, and starts to teach him simple words.

Friday also has a bright, sunny disposition. He learns quickly. Crusoe weans him from cannibalistic tendencies by cooking choice meals of goat's meat. And as Friday's vocabulary increases Crusoe undertakes his religious instruction. Friday's searching questions sometimes baffle the teacher, and Crusoe confesses that his own theological ideas are enriched in trying to answer his innocent companion. He also makes clothes for Friday and finds his tailoring improved.

They set about building another canoe, but more cannibals land. Armed with muskets, pistols, swords and hatchets, Crusoe and Friday rout the intruders and rescue two prisoners. One, a Spaniard, is a survivor from that last wreck; the other turns out to be Friday's father. "I thought myself very rich in subjects," records Crusoe, "and it was a merry reflection."

The Spaniard sets off with Friday's father to try and rescue some other survivors, and in their absence an English vessel anchors off the island and sends a boat ashore. Some intuition warns Crusoe to lie hidden. It is well, for eight seamen land with three bound prisoners. When the captors have dispersed in the woods Crusoe and Friday approach the captives and find them to be the ship's captain, his first mate and a passenger, victims of mutiny. Crusoe arms them all; they kill the ringleaders and make the others captive. But there are still twenty-six mutineers on the anchored ship. When more come ashore to investigate Crusoe lures them across the island by a trick while others are overpowered. All the mutineers are rounded up piecemeal and Crusoe finally sails for England, taking as souvenirs of his long isolation his goat-skin cap, his umbrella; one of his parrots and the money found on the Spanish wreck, which at long last promises to be of some use. He records that he left in December, 1686, twenty-eight years and two months after his landing. After a long voyage he lands in England with Man Friday "as a perfect stranger to all the world as if I had never been known there".

It is doubtful if any book has appeared in more versions or in more editions than has *Robinson Crusoe*. In one form or another it has been read avidly for nearly two hundred and fifty years. Every reader is completely enthralled by the magic of Defoe's pen, for just as the author succeeds in identifying himself with Alexander Selkirk, the Scottish castaway on whose real life adventure he based his deathless classic, so every reader is able to identify himself with Robinson Crusoe.

Although the full version is of immense length, Defoe's plain, straightforward style makes it easy to read. This, apart from the natural appeal of any tale of a desert island and man making the best of things in a lone battle against nature, probably explains the perennial popularity of Robinson Crusoe with young people.

Under Defoe's masterly delineation, Robinson Crusoe becomes such an endearing character, so frank, so candid, so ready to smile at himself – as in his quiet references to his botched carpentry and tailoring.

And he never sits and repines for long. He is up and doing, meeting the challenge of his situation; and though he is by nature a naive, simple soul, his courage and resource shine through repeatedly, and even his philosophic musings are of the kind the youngest reader can appreciate and the oldest will applaud.

He is a very human character, and his care for his pets – his dogs, cats, parrots and goats – tends to move every reader to feel glad that Robinson Crusoe is not wholly alone in his long, long years of exile.

Then there is Man Friday, the first human being to enter his island life, another simple, endearing character in his own right.

Curiously enough, interest fades at the moment that their rescue seems assured. Defoe, shrewdly anticipating this reaction, strives hard to offset it by making the final rescue scenes as lively and exciting as possible. But it is vain. The island's peace is shattered for Robinson Crusoe and Man Friday – and for the reader, too. The recording of Crusoe's subsequent adventures after he has reached home safe and sound is an anti-climax.

On his island Crusoe reigned supreme for twenty-eight years and two months, with every reader under his sway. Those years are the core of this enchanting book.

GULLIVER'S TRAVELS

JONATHAN SWIFT

THE STORY gets under way with tremendous speed: within a page, Master Lemuel Gulliver has explained his own background to us (he had been to Emmanuel College, Cambridge, gone on to study medicine, then been made surgeon of a ship) and has set sail, "on May 4th, 1699", for the south seas.

A hundred words later on, it is November and he has been shipwrecked on a foreign shore. He lies down to rest, and "when I awaked, it was just daylight. I attempted to rise, but was not able to stir, for as I happened to lie on my back, I found my arms and legs were strongly fastened on each side to the ground; and my hair, which was long and thick, tied down in the same manner. I likewise felt several slender ligatures across my body, from my armpits to my thighs.

"In a little time, I felt something alive moving on my left leg, which advancing gently forward over my breast, came almost up to my chin; when, bending mine eyes downwards as much as I could, I perceived it to be a human creature not six inches high, with a bow and arrow in his hands, and a quiver at his back. In the meantime I felt at least forty more of the same kind (as I conjectured) following the first. I was in the utmost astonishment and roared so loud that they all ran back in a fright; and some of them, as I was afterwards told, were hurt with the falls they got by leaping from my side upon the ground. However, they soon returned. . . ."

And so Lemuel Gulliver finds himself in the Land of Lilliput. The tiny inhabitants take kindly to him, though he is imprisoned at first. Soon the Emperor comes to see him.

"His dress was very plain and simple, the fashion of it being between the Asiatic and the European, but he had on his head a light helmet of gold, adorned with jewels, and a plume on the crest. He held his sword drawn in his hand, to defend himself if I should happen to break loose; it was almost three inches long. His voice was shrill, but very clear and articulate——"

Gulliver addresses the Emperor and the rest of the Court who have come along, in all the languages he knows: Dutch, Latin,

French, Spanish, Italian; but to no avail, and the Emperor retires. Several of the little people have fired arrows at him, and now the guard which has been mounted over him hands these malefactors over to Gulliver for whatever punishment he cares to inflict. "I took them all in my right hand, put five of them into my coat pocket; and as to the sixth, I made a countenance as if I would eat him alive. The poor man squalled horribly, and the Colonel and his officers were in much pain, especially when they saw me take out my pen-knife: but I soon put them out of fear, for looking mildly, and immediately cutting the strings he was bound with, I set him gently on the ground and away he ran. I treated the rest in the same manner, taking them one by one out of my pocket; and as I observed, both the soldiers and people were highly obliged at this mark of my clemency, which was represented very much to my advantage at Court."

From now on, this "Man Mountain", as the little people style him (he soon picks up their language), is a very popular figure indeed. His liberty is granted him under conditions which state, among other things, that he will not depart from the Emperor's dominions without permission; he will not lie down in cornfields (thereby destroying them); he will take the utmost care not to trample on citizens. He will also hold himself in readiness to act as high-speed conveyance for messages, taking both messenger and horse in his pocket, to wherever the Emperor requires such message sent.

He will also, by pacing its perimeter, map the Emperor's empire.

And "upon his solemn oath to observe all the above articles, the said Man Mountain shall have a daily allowance of meat and drink sufficient for the support of 1728 of our subjects."

Not long after this, Gulliver saves the people of Lilliput from an invasion by their enemies on Blefuscu, "an island situated to the north-northeast side of Lilliput, from whence it is parted only by a channel of eight hundred yards wide". He wades into the water and, to the consternation and dismay of the Blefuscans, the delight of Lilliput, gathers together the tiny anchor chains of the enemy fleet, waiting to set out, and drags it captive to a Lilliputian harbour.

But all this adventure is but an excuse for Jonathan Swift, the real "Gulliver" of these highly imaginary travels, to give us his views on mankind in general, his suggestions for the better running of our world. For example: "Although we usually call reward and punishment the two hinges upon which all government turns, yet I could never observe this maxim to be put in practice by any nation except that of Lilliput. Whoever can there bring sufficient proof that he has

strictly observed the laws of his country for seventy-three moons,
hath a claim to certain privileges, according to his quality and condition of life, with a proportionable sum of money out of a fund
appropriated for that use."

And, "In choosing persons for all employments, they have more
regard to good morals than to great abilities."

Every one of these suggestions – for they are simply that, Swift's
ideas for you and me the running of our affairs – is thought-provok-
ing: many of them, like the institution of crêches and boarding
schools, have been implemented. We may perhaps quarrel with the
idea that "ingratitude is among them a capital crime——" but there
is more than a grain of common sense in the theory that fraud is a
greater crime than theft, or that any man unfairly prosecuted, and
shown to be, should be "quadruply recompensed for the loss of his
time, for the danger he underwent——"

But this moralizing is so intermingled with the excitements of life
on Lilliput that we accept it with delight. Gulliver leaves Lilliput
when he overhears details of a plot among a few jealous citizens to
accuse him of high treason. He escapes to Blefuscu and its own royal
family, where, "I lay on the ground to kiss His Majesty's and the
Empress's hand——"

But he soon makes his departure from here in a small boat (vast by
Lilliputian or Blefuscan standards) which has been washed up from
a shipwreck. He persuades 500 of the tiny people to make him a sail
for it, and off he goes.

Soon he is picked up by an English merchantman. The captain
and crew think him raving mad, but when he takes a few tiny sheep
and cattle out of his pocket they realize he must indeed have visited
some strange land.

A little later, and our hero is in a stranger one. He spends a scant
two months with wife and family, then ships away again. The vessel
in which he travels this time casts anchor off an unfamiliar coast: he
disembarks with a few others and then is surprised to see them
legging it as fast as they can, for the boat.

He wonders why; then sees "a huge creature walking after them
in the sea, as fast as he could: he waded not much deeper than his
knees, and took prodigious strides: but our men had the start of him
by half a league, and the sea thereabouts being full of sharp pointed
rocks, the monster was not able to overtake the boat".

And so, a little later, he finds himself a prisoner of these giants in
Brobdingnag. They, once over the shock of seeing someone built on
such a tiny scale, are as courteous as the Lilliputians.

More adventures follow, and it is interesting to see that all the trees, flowers, birds and animals which Gulliver encounters in Brobdingnag are – just as they were in Lilliput – perfectly in scale. Where a Lilliputian sheep is the size of a mouse, a thrush or a linnet in Brobdingnag has to be tackled, in self-defence, with both hands. "This linnet, as near as I can remember, seemed to be somewhat larger than an English swan."

There is again much thought and discussion of the merits of English life as against these alternatives. He explains to the giant king the construction of cannon and shell, and His Majesty is appalled, "struck with horror at the description I had given of those terrible engines, amazed how so unimportant and grovelling an insect as I (these were his expressions) could entertain such inhuman ideas".

But in the fullness of time, Gulliver leaves even this pleasant and attractive country, where he has been treated as a rare and priceless doll. His accidental departure is distressing to both king and Gulliver – but as you will see if you read the tale, nothing can be done about it.

Soon, on his next voyage – for Lemuel Gulliver is unwilling ever to stay at home for more than a month or two – he is captured by pirates and set adrift in a canoe. He drifts to the land of the Laputians who are able to float in thin air, whose island in fact floats like a cloud. After an exciting time with these folk he moves on; visiting, very briefly, a number of other strange places, culminating in Japan – which in those days was hardly better known than Lilliput.

But it is on his last recorded voyage, "the 7th day of September 1710", he sets sail from Portsmouth, that Gulliver meets the beings which impress him most. It is in the land of the virtually unpronounceable Houyhnhnms that we find his praise most heartfelt. For the Houyhnhnms are in every way superior to man – in fact they keep as slaves a type of sub-human called a Yahoo – but they have the appearance of horses.

Of the beings Gulliver has met in his extraordinary travels, these are the most superior. He is looked after by a benevolent master, and "I freely confess that all the little knowledge I have of any value was acquired by the lectures I received from my master. When I thought of my family, my friends, my countrymen, or the human race in general, I considered them as they really were, Yahoos in shape and disposition".

Eventually, and with the greatest sorrow, he has to leave this pleasant land. After more adventures he reaches England "on the 5th of December, 1715. My wife and family received me with great surprise and joy, because they concluded me certainly dead; but I must freely confess, the sight of them filled me only with hatred, disgust and contempt".

The book ends with Gulliver beginning at last "to permit my wife to sit at dinner with me at the farthest end of a long table. Yet, the smell of a Yahoo continuing very offensive, I always keep my nose well stopped with rue, lavender or tobacco leaves".

A strange tale, with a strange conclusion – but because it is told with verve and tremendous imagination, one that has fascinated young and old for over 200 years. Shorn of its reflections on different customs among the English and the other beings Gulliver meets, it has become a classic among children's books. (And Swift abominated children.) Told in its entirety, it is one of the most savage, telling attacks on the English way of life (which has changed remarkably little in 200 years) ever written.

Jonathan Swift was of English descent, but born in Dublin, in 1667. He was brought up in the greatest poverty and – for lack of any better employment, it seems – took Holy orders at the age of twenty-seven, being granted a small living near Belfast. It was while he was there that he wrote two successful satires, *The Tale of a Tub* (dealing with "corruption in religion and learning") and *The Battle of the Books* which described vividly the age-old battle between ancient learning and modern.

He spent much time travelling between Ireland (which, though he worked hard in his parish, he disliked) and England, where he spent much time in the company of literary men like Addison, Steele and Congreve. But by 1714 he had given up all hope of ultimately settling in England and resigned himself to ending his days in Ireland.

He had, throughout much of his life, a complicated relationship with two women, whom he refers to as "Stella" and "Vanessa", and his *Journal to Stella* shows him in a very odd light. Probably Swift married his "Stella" when he was forty-six, but this is by no means certain, any more than it is certain he ever lived under the same roof with her. At the same time he kept up a lively correspondence with "Vanessa".

He wrote much, little of which remains, but in 1726 – the year before "Stella" (probably the only person he ever loved) died after a long illness – he published his best-known work, *Gulliver's Travels*.

He became more and more of a recluse, haunted by the fear of insanity – and not without reason, for he gradually lost the use of all his faculties before he died, insane, at the age of seventy-eight.

Swift is one of the oddest, most paradoxical, figures in English literature. (To take one small example, could a man who hated children – and he did – write such a wonderful child's book?) He set himself out to be a successful author for the position it would give him, much as another man might set out to become a millionaire on the Stock Exchange. Yet he refused to be a professional writer, which would have been socially degrading: only once did he receive payment for any of the countless things he wrote for publication. His ambition, to be a great and literary man, ruled out marriage: hence his strange relationship with both "Stella" and "Vanessa".

Not, it must be said, an attractive character. But a man with an extraordinary talent, a fantastic comic power – allied to great moral indignation. By the time he got round to writing *Gulliver* the power, the indignation, had been channelled: the humanity he could be so light-hearted about in earlier work was no longer a joke.

His complicated life – being involved with two women at once, neither of whom he seemed to want physically; trying to win promotion in the Church, and, quite sincerely, to help the peasants who worshipped there; trying (and succeeding) at being a wit and a literary figure – petered out, so that from 1742 he was virtually out of his mind. He remained that way, dying on 19 October, 1745.

Perhaps the epitaph, written by himself, in Latin, and which now stands above his grave, gives a fair summing-up of the man who wrote one of the most sparkling, odd books of all time:

"The body of Jonathan Swift, Doctor of Divinity, is buried here, where fierce indignation can tear at his heart no more. Go traveller, and imitate, if you can, one who strove his utmost to champion human liberty."

TOM JONES
HENRY FIELDING

TOM JONES was published in 1749 and, although it is by no means the first English novel, it is the first to embrace a great number and variety of characters and to constitute a full picture of English society, ranging from peasants, landladies, schoolmasters, country squires and women of fashion. It is a vast delineation, neither tragic nor comic, of its period, full-blooded and rumbustious even.

Tom Jones is a foundling, placed on the doorstep of a virtuous, wealthy English country gentleman, Allworthy, who brings him up together with his sister's child, Blifil. Tom Jones falls in love with Sophia Western, the daughter of Squire Western, a roaring drunken hunting man, falls into disgrace with Allworthy, leaves to join the King's army then confronting the Jacobite rebellion of 1745, and after many adventures goes to London where he has a number of love affairs, one of which with a lady of fashion brings him to prison through a duel. He is rescued by Allworthy, who discovers that Tom is his sister's illegitimate child and not a mere bastard. Tom, therefore, inherits wealth and marries Sophia, and the villain, Blifil, who concealed the facts about Tom from Allworthy, is disgraced. The dramatic narrative and the sub-plots are arranged with extreme skill and there is none of the slight sense of tedium which affects some picaresque novels of the period, a tedium due to the fact that some of the episodes do not really matter. But the technical skill of *Tom Jones*, great as it is, is by no means the most important quality which goes to make it a great book.

Tom Jones is the first, and still perhaps the only, hero in English fiction who from top to bottom is thoroughly credible and, to most people, but not to all, thoroughly likeable. He is a good-looking, strong, intelligent though far from intellectual young man with a good heart, whose inclination to indulge in the careless pleasures of the flesh is usually more powerful than his better feelings. Tom Jones accepts money from his fashionable mistress in London – a common enough thing to do at any time but less censored in the eighteenth century than in the nineteenth; he is an adventurer and there is no account given of any particular industry on his part except that of living his life as amusingly as possible. Then, for all his constant passion for the heroine, Sophia Western, whom he loves as a boy and finally marries under the best of circumstances, he can never resist a skirt. One June evening walking in a grove, with nightingales singing nearby and a running stream, his heart is full of love for his dear Sophia. He has a penknife in his hand and is about to carve her name on a tree. When suddenly he sees a peasant girl with whom he had slept, and out of whose way he was keeping, approaching him.

"And at these words he started up and beheld – not his Sophia – no, nor a Circassian maid richly and elegantly attired for the Grand Signor's Seraglio. No, without a gown in a shift that was somewhat of the coarsest and none of the cleanest, bedewed likewise with some odoriferous affluvia, the produce of the day's labour, with a pitch-fork in her hand, Molly Seigrim approached. The girl coming near him, cried out with a smile, 'You don't intend to kill me, squire, I hope.' – 'Why should you think I would kill you', answered Jones. 'Nay', replied she, 'after your cruel usage of me when I saw you last, killing me would, perhaps, be too great kindness for me to expect.'

"Here ensued a parley which, as I do not think myself obliged to relate it, I shall omit. It is sufficient that it lasted a full quarter of an hour, at the conclusion of which they retired into thickest part of the grove."

Tom Jones's love for Sophia though not proof against temptation was all the same great and constant – not the least of the high-spirited Sophia's attractions is that she never considered that Tom was unworthy of her. Right at the beginning of the English novel, then, Fielding has done what no other English writer has done – created a character who is very much "the ordinary sensual man" – though a most agreeable variety of it – and made him the centre and hero of a novel.

Tom's far from virtuous nature, together with the realism of the book, did not please some people in the, on the whole, tolerant and civilized eighteenth century. Dr. Johnson, for example, did not like Fielding's work. Later, in the nineteenth century, there were some critics who deplored Fielding's immorality, and a female novelist expressed the feelings of many people at that time when she said that, in her enlightened age, Fielding's novels were "vanishing like noxious exhalations". Such, fortunately, is not the verdict of posterity and it should be said straight away that the novel won a great success when it appeared, that Gibbon among other writers of the time considered it a very great work indeed and that Scott and Thackeray, though not uncritical, recognized Fielding's genius, the latter indeed admitting, in criticism of his own period, that "*Tom Jones* was the last book in which an English novelist was allowed to depict a man".

Apart from the character of Tom Jones, there are various excellent aspects liable to attract different people to greater or lesser degrees. Without ever being comic for the sake of raising a laugh, without being satirical in order to convey that the people satirized are empty and dull, Fielding contrived to make people comic and ridiculous, because of what they are led to do under certain circumstances. What is more at once touching and yet absurd than the letter written to the charming Mr. Jones by the widow of a rich Turkey merchant whose "very good health, warm constitution and a good deal of religion" made it necessary for her to marry again.

"Sir,
From the first day I saw you I doubt my eyes have told you too plainly that you were not indifferent to me; but neither my tongue nor my hand should have ever avowed it, had not the ladies of the family where you were lodged, given me such a character of you and told me such proofs of your virtue and goodness, has convinced me that you are not only the most agreeable, but the most worthy of men. I have a fortune sufficient to make us both happy but which cannot make me so without you. In thus disposing of myself, I know I shall incur the censure of the world; but if I did not love you more than I fear the world, I should not be worthy of you. One only difficulty stops me; I am informed you are engaged in a commerce of gallantry with a woman of fashion. If you think it worth while to sacrifice that for the possession of me, I am yours; if not, forget my weakness and let this remain an eternal secret between you and
Arabella Hunt".

Then there is what one must call the atmosphere or the poetry of the novel. The house of Squire Western is surrounded by neighing horses and yelping hounds, its back passages smelling of cider; and the female parts of the house, the simple luxury of Sophia's room and the apartments of the curious sister of Squire Western, whose talk is all of politics, defend themselves with difficulty from the masculine, invading disorder. The landladies on Tom's journey are each unique, and yet alike in a curious mixture of sycophancy, hypocrisy, basic vitality and humour, a mixture which seems characteristic of such people in the eighteenth century.

In the middle of the novel there is the strange episode of the Old Man of the Hill, in which a misanthrope who has deserted humanity and lives in a house on a steep hillside in the Mendips, tells Tom

Jones his life story. The Old Man had fought for Monmouth at Sedgemoor in 1685 and its incident welds *Tom Jones* into its fabric of English history. And there is Tom Jones's rescue, on the same wet, wooded hillside of the Mendips, of Mrs. Waters, an attractive young woman who is being assailed by a villainous officer and who has had the upper part of her clothing torn off her.

For the present writer an abiding fascination of Fielding's work lies in certain moments when, following conversations and incidents which flow along slowly and agreeably, one suddenly realizes that this serio-comic picture of human nature in action adds up to something much more. Tom, Blifil and Sophia are still children; Sophia has a bird which Tom had given her and which she had tamed, which bird Blifil asks if he might hold for a moment and, being given it by Sophia, deliberately lets it fly away. Tom climbs a tree on which the bird is perching; just as he is about to rescue the bird, the branch breaks and Tom falls head-over-heels into a canal below. Two pedagogues, Square and Thackum, who live on Squire Allworthy and who protect and flatter the hypocritical Blifil and run down Tom, Mr. Allworthy himself, Squire Western and a lawyer who happen to be there, discuss the incident at length. Thackum says Blifil acted according to a Christian motive – do as you would be done by – in freeing the bird. Square, a Deist, says that to confine anything is against the law of nature, since everything has a right to liberty which is a part of the "Eternal fitness of things". The philosophers quarrel, though they agree about the goodness of Blifil; the mild Allworthy opines that Tom may have done wrong in seeking to recapture the bird but that he will not punish him for he acted from a generous motive. The lawyer says that if Blifil had set free a partridge he might have been wronging Squire Western as it was a piece of property, but since it was a mere singing bird, a thing of base nature, which Blifil has set free, there is no offence in law. Squire Western sums up by telling the company to drink a bout and stating that he doesn't understand a word of what people have been saying:

> "It may be learning and sense for ought I know: but you shall never persuade me into it. Per. . . . you have neither of you mentioned a word of that poor lad who deserves to be commended: to venture breaking his neck to oblige my girl was a generous spirited action: I have learning enough to see that. Damn it, here's Tom's health! I shall love the boy for it the longest day I have to live."

One suddenly realizes here that Fielding has delivered a great

Who that loves a good story does not know the three books that are illustrated here? First, *The Arabian Nights*, the collection of Oriental tales that wily little Scheherazade told to her lord and master, and so managed to keep her head on her shoulders. The tale illustrated (*left*) is that of the Fisherman and the Genie. (*Below*, *left*) A scene from Dean Swift's *Gulliver's Travels*: Gulliver is playing the piano to the gratification of the king and queen of that race of giants, the Brobdingnagians. (*Below, right*) A reproduction of the frontispiece to the first edition, published in 1719, of Daniel Defoe's *Life and Strange Adventures of Robinson Crusoe*

For more than two hundred years *Tom Jones* has kept the interest of generations of readers, and in our own day it has provided the film-makers with an immensely popular subject. Two of George Cruikshank's illustrations to the novel are given here: the battle in the church-yard (*above, left*), when that stalwart young hussy Molly Seagrim puts to flight those who had been casting aspersions (not, it must be admitted, undeserved) on her virtue; and (*above, right*) the philosophic humbug Square caught in the most compromising circumstances in Molly's room. Much less robust but none the less appealing is Oliver Goldsmith's *Vicar of Wakefield*. The drawing below shows the worthy parson rebuking his wife and daughters for "dressing up" far above their station when about to accompany him to church.

judgment on the character of man and the nature of his impulses, a judgment more potent and attractive in that it springs naturally from idle disquisitions by idle men about a childish action.

The depth of Fielding's understanding of human nature, high and low, was derived from the magnanimity of his intellect and also from his varied experience of life. Fielding was born into an aristocratic Somerset family at Sharpham Park, in 1707. Colonel Fielding, his father, lived in impoverished circumstances, managed to send his son to Leyden University in Holland, but had difficulty in paying his son's fees and allowance. Trained as a lawyer, the high-spirited Henry Fielding became a man of the theatre, wrote many plays and lived a thoroughly precarious, Bohemian life. At the age of twenty-eight, he changed his way of life by marrying an heiress to a small fortune, whom he loved passionately and who is the origin of Sophia. He also at this time inherited a small estate from his mother. But all his money was quickly spent in luxurious living in the country and he returned with his wife to London, the theatre, and journalism.

He produced his first great novel, *Joseph Andrews*, and then the satirical *Jonathan Wild*. Shortly after this, the great calamity of his wife's death fell on Fielding. And then a new Act was passed in Parliament regulating theatrical performances, severely hitting the small theatre for which Fielding wrote and produced; his career as a dramatist came to a sudden end.

His legal studies, his commonsense and his humanity and knowledge of the seamy side of life gave him the ideal qualities for the post he received from the Government of stipendiary magistrate at Bow Street. This post, doubled with that of Chairman of the Quarter Sessions, enabled him to play an important part in suppressing some of the more dangerous gangs of criminals then infesting the metropolis. He worked with extreme diligence and courage at his rather unsavoury task of cleaning up crime. He married his wife's maid, Mary Daniel, who looked after the children of his first marriage. But Fielding, by 1751, when his last novel *Amelia* appeared, was worn out with the dissipations of his youth and the toil both as writer and magistrate, of his middle years. In 1754 he sailed to Lisbon with his family to restore his health but died there in October of that year and was buried in the cemetery of Estrella, a beautiful half-rural suburb of that city.

Without doubt the elements of Fielding's life equipped him to draw human nature in its variety and its depth. The pastime of discussing which is the greatest novel in the English language may be a vain one, but it is not perhaps uninteresting. Thackeray's *Vanity*

Fair, Dickens's *Oliver Twist* or *Bleak House* would find many partisans and so might some work of Jane Austen, or Thomas Hardy. Were agreement reached, someone might suddenly ask: "What about *Tom Jones?*" – and straight away the company would be forced to reconsider its verdict. For *Tom Jones* has many claims to excel all other English novels. There is in the writing of Fielding a quality of universality, of complete mastery of the world he is describing, an absence of prejudice, sentimentality or limitations as to the capacity to understand man or woman of whatever class they belong to, which is possessed only by Shakespeare. Fielding lacks Shakespeare's profound poetic impulse; he has not the tragic touch. But every one of the several scores of characters in *Tom Jones* is created with a fullness and ripeness which makes them immune from criticism or doubt as to their being. Fielding, like Shakespeare, cannot introduce the most insignificant character without creating a completely living and breathing character. George Saintsbury, one of the greatest of English critics, has written an excellent, quiet and final commendation of *Tom Jones*: "Everybody in *Tom Jones* does what he or she ought to have done – I do not mean morally, which might subject me to the censure of the Church and the Schools alike, but according to the probabilities of human nature and the requirements of great art."

THE AGE OF LOUIS XIV

VOLTAIRE

THERE ARE many kinds of written history – the kinds vary from theological history, such as is found in the Old Testament, to histories in works such as the *Cambridge Modern Histories* in which numbers of scholars write sections and are concerned with collecting and relating all the known facts about a given period. Mankind, in general, most prizes the history – whether it be on a comparatively small scale, such as Thucydides's account of the Peloponnesian War or immense in scope like *The Decline and Fall of the Roman Empire* – in which the character of the historian shines through the material. The words "shines through" are used advisedly because the great historian does not attempt to impose a pattern on his subject; his first task is to serve truth and his mortal sin to falsify facts. Humanity gives the highest honour to men like Thucydides, Gibbon, Caesar, Tacitus, Froissart, Michelet, Macaulay and John Greene because, in reading their work, one is in contact not with a fact-collecting intellect but with a great mind.

Now Voltaire's history of Louis XIV may not be one of the greatest of the world's histories, though purely considered as history it is a book of the first rank. It lacks the detachment, the profound thinking about events which it describes, which characterizes the very great history. Voltaire in this book accepts some material which is probably untrue and sometimes gives rein to his prejudices. As is customary in his writing, he is not at all averse to giving a slap at what he most dislikes in his own time. But the book has the supreme merit of being alive, from beginning to end. It is enriched and made amusing by an immense number of anecdotes which he had learnt at first hand from men and women who had played a role in the events he describes.

Voltaire's history ends more or less with the death of Louis XIV in 1715; he himself was born in 1694 and was therefore able to know many men such as Marshal Villars, one of the few good generals of Louis XIV's declining years, and from many sources to gather an immense amount of tell-tale incidents. Voltaire once said that history was largely playing tricks with the dead and that it was "a gross piece of charlatanry to pretend to paint the portrait of a man with whom you have never lived". In many ways, Voltaire's *The Age of Louis XIV* is the first history which does not despise gossip. It is also, and this is much to the taste of our time, a restless, impressionistic work, flitting rapidly from subject to subject, but always leaving a memorable impression after its brief impact. There is a good example of the finely turned phrase in a brief sketch of England at the time of Louis XIV's minority when he describes Oliver Cromwell as ruling England "the Bible in one hand and a sword in the other, wearing the mask of religion on his face, and disguising in his government the crimes of a usurper under the qualities of a great king".

Voltaire was the fifth child of his parents, François Arouet, a Paris notary, and a mother of whom little is known, who died when Voltaire was seven, but who was of noble birth and responsible for the young Arouet's early introduction to fashionable society. Voltaire received a sound education from the Jesuits and, at the age of seventeen, already something of an *enfant terrible*, he decided that his career was literature. As an adolescent he mixed in rather disreputable literary society from which his father tried to wean him. Taken up by the Duchesse de Maine as a promising writer, he composed a number of political squibs while supposedly studying law, composed various lampoons and libels on Louis XV and, in 1718, was sent to the Bastille for a few weeks. Records from that prison already show him calling himself Arouet de Voltaire, the origin of which name is uncertain, Voltaire claiming that it belonged to his mother's family.

The pattern of feud with authority was to last throughout his life, and he was to be alternately honoured and then disgraced and exiled for some, at the moment, unforgivable insult or satire against the King or the Church or society in general. The regular pattern of quarrel and friendship marked his relationship with his friend, and alternately his bitter enemy, Frederick II, King of Prussia, known as Frederick the Great. His periods of exile were practically always comfortable and rarely long. From early youth he was interested in money and by speculation and other means he always managed to have plenty of it, and he always managed to have highly placed friends and protectors. His wandering life lasted until his death in 1778 when he returned to Paris for the last time from exile with well-meaning Louis XVI on the throne.

He started collecting reminiscences for his *Age of Louis XIV* from very early youth, but he did not write the book until between 1743 and 1746, and it did not appear in Paris. It is essentially therefore a work of maturity and made after his long visit to England between 1726 and 1729, during which period Voltaire's mind matured considerably. Well known in France as a brilliant playwright and political poet before the English visit, he returned a much wiser man as well as a much richer one. His acquaintances and friends in London had numbered Congreve, Pope, Bolingbroke and the Walpoles and he acquired a great love of England as the home of toleration, free thought and "the land of veritable liberty". While in England he composed his historical work on Charles XII of Sweden which had to be surreptitiously printed in France.

The great merit of *The Age of Louis XIV* is that it really is the portrait of an age and not merely a political history enlivened with anecdotes. It is not, he writes, "merely the life of Louis XIV that we propose to write; we have a wider aim in view. We shall endeavour to depict for posterity, not the actions of a single man, but the spirit of men in the most enlightened age the world has ever seen". Voltaire considered that there were three other great ages in the world – that of Pericles which saw Athenian civilization at its height, that of Caesar and Augustus Caesar, and that of the Italian Renaissance. The age of Louis XIV he considered most important, because France gave an example to the world of civilization and order combined with great creativity in the arts and sciences. "For nine hundred years," he writes, "the genius of France had almost continually been cramped under a gothic government, in the midst of partitions and civil wars, having neither laws nor fixed customs: her nobles undisciplined and acquainted solely with war and idleness; her clergy living in disorder and ignorance; and her people without trade, sunk in their misery". If these ills are to be avoided, if the State is to be powerful, if the arts and sciences are to flourish – and this is the thing which Voltaire considers of supreme value – "either the people must enjoy a liberty based on the laws or the sovereign power must be affirmed without contradiction".

Voltaire rejoiced that as a result of the reign of Louis XIV French civilization – boudoirs, buildings, social manners, all the arts and particularly literature, and military organization – became the example which Europe followed. Politically, Voltaire always preferred English government to the Absolute Monarchy; but what struck him as an historian above all was the fact that when Louis XIV – for long the ruler under the shadow of the great Cardinal Mazarin, as the weak Louis XIII had ruled under Richelieu – began to rule France himself, he inaugurated the reign of order and clarity.

To what extent this order and clarity in government and society favoured the development of literary genius in France is a matter no one can dogmatize about. It is certain that Louis XIV, on whom the eyes of the nation were riveted for so long, was a man of good taste, that he encouraged and supported against their many and powerful detractors and enemies writers such as Racine and Molière, for example. The centralization of French aristocratic life in the Court at Versailles produced a critical, highly intelligent, enthusiastic audience for artistic productions of all kinds which was no doubt highly favourable to the development of talent. But even if one may have doubts about the effects of society on the development of great artists, there is no doubt that the age of Louis XIV was astonishingly rich in such men. In literature alone there flourished during the long reign of Louis XIV, to mention only the best known – Pascal, Corneille, Madame de Lafayette, La Rochefoucauld, Boileau, Bossuet, Molière, Racine, La Fontaine, La Bruyère and Saint Simon. "Nature after the age of Louis XIV went into a condition of repose and produced no more geniuses," writes Voltaire, certainly not without malice toward his contemporaries such as Jean-Jacques Rousseau who considered themselves very highly and put themselves on a level with the men of the Great Century.

The book is so full of anecdotes that it gives the reader the impression that it is written by a contemporary. Some of the character sketches bear the mark of Voltaire's prejudices but these are often splendid passages, as witness that concerning James II who arrived in 1688 as an exile from England and who was received with his wife and son with the greatest generosity by Louis XIV. "Never had Louis appeared to greater advantage, nor James to less. The inhabitants of courts and cities who decide men's reputations had little esteem for him. He saw few people but Jesuits. He told them that he was himself a Jesuit and the most remarkable thing is that it was true. Such baseness in a prince, together with the way in which he had lost his crown, rendered him so contemptible that the courtiers' daily amusement was to compose songs about him. Driven from England, he was mocked in France. He gained no favour for being a Catholic. The Archbishop of Rheims, brother of Louvois, loudly exclaimed in his ante-chamber at Saint-Germaine, 'there goes a simpleton who has lost three kingdoms for a Mass'. From Rome James received only indulgence and pleasantries. In short, during the whole revolution his religion did him little service. It was a noteworthy sight to see James touching the sick at the little English convent in Paris; perhaps the English kings claimed this singular prerogative as pretenders to the throne of France, or else this ceremony has been established since the time of the first Edward."

There is a most restrained portrait of the pious but highly intelligent Madame de Maintenon, the last of Louis XIV's mistresses, who became his morganatic wife and who profited so little from her exalted position. Toward the end of Louis's life the Court became rather gloomy; the King had lost many of his heirs from disease and the war of the Spanish succession had gone very badly. Voltaire has this magnificent touch concerning the King's mistress. "Madame de Maintenon, whose only care was the monotony of her life with a great king, said one day to her brother: 'I cannot bear it any longer, I wish I were dead.' His reply to her was: 'You have then been promised the Almighty as a husband?'"

Voltaire's main judgments about the age which he considered such a glorious one are by and large those which most people have today. He considered the persecution of the French Protestants which culminated in 1685 with the revocation of the Edict of Nantes as the gravest of errors, all the more in that the French Protestants had lost their aristocratic leaders whom they had had in the sixteenth century and were, on the whole, becoming good and industrious citizens of France. Louis XIV was persuaded to persecute them, says Voltaire, by the incessant protests of the clergy, by the insinuations of the Jesuits, and by the influence of Rome which Louis was normally careful to resist. Voltaire's views about the uselessness of war, his abhorrence of militarism, are extremely vigorously illustrated. Voltaire's great quarrel with the Catholic Church was based above all on the Church's refusal to denounce war. About priests he wrote: "Miserable physicians of souls, you declaim for five quarters of an hour against the mere pricks of a pin, and say no word on the curse which tears us into a thousand pieces. Philosophers and moralists, burn your books ... what concern to me are humanity, benevolence, modesty, temperance, gentleness, wisdom, piety, so long as half an ounce of lead shatters my body, and I die at twenty in torments unspeakable surrounded by five or six thousand dead or dying."

Louis XIV was a man who considered that war was the proper business of kings. He nearly ruined France by the wars he led her into, although, as Voltaire points out, the only one which did not end victoriously for France was the last, the War of the Spanish Succession, and this was forced on Louis XIV. Voltaire's portrait of Louis XIV is the *pièce de résistance* of his book. Since the end of the eighteenth century many historians of note, French and foreign, have attacked the memory of the Great Monarch, the Sun King as he was called. The French historian Seignobos sees him as a man of many pretensions without great qualities, the amateur historian Churchill loathed him, while the Victorian, John Richard Green, described him as bigoted, narrow-minded, commonplace and insatiably vain. Louis XIV might well have been anathema to Voltaire – perhaps he would have been if Voltaire had been born fifty years earlier and been one of his subjects. But as it is, Voltaire builds up a picture of Louis which is very convincing and favourable.

One of the most common accusations against Louis was that of overwhelming vanity. The King certainly liked to appear with all the appendages of majesty and he lived his life in part as a ceremony. But this, even if it was overdone, was certainly a part of the technique of being an absolute monarch. But along with this love of magnificence, Louis disliked flattery, liked the conversation of sensible men and did not mind being put right, possessed an admirable self-control and was invariably courteous and amiable to all men or women, high or low born. For all his gallantries, his many mistresses and his love of hunting, the King invariably put business before pleasure. Voltaire admired Louis XIV above all for his professional qualities as a king. His commonsense made him practically always choose good ministers, and though he very carefully controlled them and never allowed them to become too great in their own eyes, he supported them faithfully against all intrigues. The Louis XIV who wrote "the profession of a king is great, noble and delicious" was a man after Voltaire's own heart. Voltaire criticized Louis only for some of his too great expenditure, particularly that on the Palace of Versailles which he created out of a tract of waste land. Voltaire thought the King should have preferred to spend his money on the Louvre and on Paris. He writes of Louis: "It follows from what we have related, that in everything this monarch loved grandeur and glory. A prince who, having accomplished as great things as he, could yet be of plain and simple habits, would be the first among kings and Louis XIV the second."

It is a sensible epitaph, typical of most of the judgments in a book which, with all its occasional extravagances and prejudices, is also one in which good sense predominates.

THE SOCIAL CONTRACT

J.-J. ROUSSEAU

WHAT AN audacious declaration it is, this of Jean-Jacques Rousseau, that "Man is born free; and everywhere he is in chains!" When he first spat it out, it shocked and shattered the complacency of the eighteenth century, and it has been an inspiration and encouragement to the young and hopeful ever since. No matter that the critics in every generation have insisted that the first part of the declaration is untrue, since men come into the world carrying a heavy burden of heredity; and that as for the second part, there are quite a lot of places in the world nowadays where chains have long ceased to form part of the political machinery. No matter: it has a splendid, fine-sounding ring about it, and our political philosophy would be ever so much duller without it.

The statement will be found on the first page of Rousseau's most influential book, *The Social Contract*, of which the first edition – of course in French – appeared in 1762. Rousseau was then a man of fifty, and in the full flood of his literary activity. His novel *La Nouvelle Héloïse* had been published the year before, and *Emile* appeared a few months after *Le Contrat Social*. His *Confessions*, the book by which he is best known to the general reader, did not appear until 1781, three years after his death, although it had been completed in 1765.

These bibliographical details may be supplemented with some personal description. He was born at Geneva in 1712, at a time when that Swiss city was an independent republic, which it remained until the French Revolution; this fact is specially important, since it coloured all his political thinking. His father was a watchmaker, of sentimental disposition and dissipated habits, and very early Jean-Jacques was left in the care of relatives. At thirteen he was apprenticed to a notary, who soon, however, returned him since he found him so utterly incompetent. Next he was apprenticed to an engraver, and for three years he was bullied and half-starved and made utterly wretched. Then one evening in 1728, when he was sixteen, he stayed out too late with some of his young companions, and rather than face his tyrant's wrath he decided to run away. So began his vagrant and vagabondish career which he describes with such un-inhibited charm in his *Confessions*.

Among his chance acquaintances was a young woman – twenty-eight when he first knew her – named Madame de Warens. She was a rather equivocal character, and it has never been decided whether her pension from the King of Sardinia was in respect of her services as an accredited political agent or as a spy. But she was charming and clever and warm-hearted, and she exercised a civilizing influence over Jean-Jacques. He was found some sort of a job in her villa on the Lake of Annecy, and for several years he was happy enough in his double capacity of servant and lover, until in 1741 he decided to seek his fortune in Paris as a man of letters. He found it difficult, for although he was soon admitted a member of the society of the *Encyclopédistes*, he revealed a gift for personal rancour that made him many enemies. No doubt his disappointment had something to do with the discovery that he made about this time, that civilization was a sham and a degradation, and that the really happy man was the savage, in his primeval state of ignorance and simple poverty.

As mentioned earlier, *The Social Contract* was published in 1762 – not, however, in Paris, but (in order to escape the French censorship) in Amsterdam. What he had had in mind in writing it he explained in an introductory note. "I wish to inquire," it runs, "whether, taking men as they are and laws as they can be made to be, it is pos-sible to establish some just and certain rule of administration in civil affairs. In this investigation I shall always strive to reconcile what right permits with what interest prescribes, so that justice and utility may run together. I shall be asked, whether I am a prince or a legis-lator, to write on politics? I make answer, that I am neither, and that is why I am setting about it. For if I were in fact a prince or a legis-lator I should not waste my time in saying what *ought* to be done: I should do it, or hold my peace."

Then he goes on: "Having been born a citizen of a free state, and a member of the body that is sovereign within it, I feel that, however feeble an influence my voice may have in public affairs, the right to exercise a vote on them imposes on me the duty of improving my-self in my knowledge of them; and I feel happy, whenever I medi-tate upon governments, to discover ever fresh reasons for loving the constitution of my own country."

Rousseau was writing as a citizen of the republic of Geneva, in which government was in the hands of a small body of burghers. He liked to think that Geneva was a city-state after the model of Sparta in the days of ancient Greece, and no doubt hoped that his eulogistic reference would be appreciated by his fellow-citizens at home. There he was mistaken, however, since the rulers of Geneva were staunch upholders of the severest forms of Protestant dogma and practice, and were not in the least inclined to acknowledge Jean-Jacques as a "favourite son".

After this exordium, we come to the famous claim that "Man is born free . . ." The passage continues: "Many a man believes that he is the master of others, and yet in fact he is a greater slave than they are. How has this come about? I don't know. Is there anything which can render it legitimate? That is a question which I think I *can* answer . . ." To express it perhaps rather more plainly, what Rousseau is driving at, is to discover, not so much why people *do*, but why they *should*, obey the governments under which they find themselves.

This is a question which could hardly arise in the earliest of all societies, which was the family. In this, the only "natural" form of society, the children remain attached to the father only so long as they need him for their protection; as soon as this need is no longer felt, they proceed to form families of their own. In this "first model of political societies" the father is the ruler and the people are his children, and since all are born free and equal, they alienate their liberty only when it suits them. But there is one great difference between the family and the state. In the former, the father is repaid for the care he takes of his children by their affection, but in the latter the ruler cannot be expected to love his people as a father loves his children but instead is actuated by the pleasure of commanding.

The ruler of a state expects to be obeyed by his subjects, for the good reason that he wields the power and authority. But, so Rousseau maintains in effect, Might does not make Right. "Obey the Powers that be" – by all means: it is something that we all do, when "the powers that be" have the means of making us do it – the fact is so obvious that it is hardly worth mentioning. There is no "right" about it, however. "A brigand surprises me at the edge of a wood, and he compels me to deliver up to him my purse; but if I can think of a way of withholding it, am I in conscience bound to give it up?" If Might means Right, then the answer would be, Yes, for "certainly the pistol he holds in his hand is might". But to repeat, Might is *not* Right. The only powers that we are under an obligation to obey are legitimate ones.

Now Rousseau assumes that we are discussing a state of society in which "the obstacles that endanger their preservation in the state of nature" are greater than can be tackled and overcome by an individual acting on his own. Now, as men cannot create any new forces but only combine and direct those that already exist, they must combine together and work in concert. Here, however, we come up against a serious difficulty. "The problem is, to find a form of association which will defend and protect with the whole force of the community the person and property of each associate, and by means of which, each man, by uniting himself with all the rest, may nevertheless obey himself alone, and remain just as free as he was before."

This is the fundamental problem, and the solution to it is provided by the "Social Contract". The clauses of this contract are so determined by the nature of the act that the slightest modification would make them vain and ineffective. These clauses, rightly understood, may be reduced to one, namely, the total alienation of each associate, with all his rights, to the whole community; for, in the first place, since each gives himself up absolutely, the conditions are equal for everybody; and the conditions being equal for all, no one has any interest in making them burdensome to others. Moreover, the alienation being made without reserve, the union is as perfect as it can be, and no associate has anything more to demand: for, if any rights were left to the individuals, since there would be no common superior who could judge between them and the public, each, being on some point his own judge, would soon claim to be so on all; the state of nature would still continue, and the association would necessarily become tyrannical or useless. In short, each man, in giving himself to all, gives himself to nobody; and as there is not one associate over whom he does not acquire the same rights which he concedes to others over himself, he gains an equivalent for everything that he loses, and all the more power for the preservation of what he has. So, stripping the social compact to its bare essentials, we find that it reduces itself to the following terms: "Each of us puts his person and all his power in common under the supreme direction of the general will; and in return we receive in our corporate capacity an indivisible part of the whole".

Thus there is brought about, in place of the individual personalities of all the contracting parties, a moral and collective body, composed of as many members as the assembly contains voices, or voters, and which receives from this act of association its unity, its common self or identity, and its will. This body, this public person, which is thus formed by the union of all the individual members, formerly took the name of *city*, and now takes that of *republic* or *body politic*; it is called by its members *State* when it is passive, *Sovereign* when it is active, and *Power* when it is compared with others like itself. While as regards those who are associated in it, they take collectively the name of *people*, and are called *citizens* as sharing in the sovereign power, and *subjects* as being all subject to the laws of the State.

This is the theory of *The Social Contract*, as given in Rousseau's own words. He did not invent the theory. The doctrine that society is founded on a compact agreed between the people and their ruler or government has been traced to the political philosophers of the Middle Ages, and it was often expressed in the great constitutional struggles of the sixteenth to the eighteenth century. A very clear expression of it may be found in the declaration made by the Convention Parliament of 1688, in which James II is accused of having broken "the original contract between king and people". But this was in England, and since an English sovereign had been made to mount the scaffold in 1649 it was generally agreed on the Continent that English theory and practice in political matters was far too original and drastic for emulation. But Rousseau was if not a Frenchman a good European, and what he had to say was listened to and heeded wherever French was understood. His doctrine had an immense influence on the development of political ideas in all the more advanced countries, France in particular – indeed, he has been called the principal intellectual parent of the French Revolution of 1789, and perhaps he was: certainly his book was adopted as the gospel of the extreme democratic party that had its leader in Robespierre.

But as with other great political theorists, men turned to his pages to find what they wanted to find, and a good deal of what they professed to find was not really there. Rousseau was no out-and-out democrat, and his doctrine of the General Will (expounded in some of the later chapters in his book), as being something which may be different from the will of all the members of the State, is sufficiently muddled to have provided encouragement to the dictatorships of a later day, from Louis Napoleon (Napoleon III) to Hitler. He believed in the censorship of opinions. He never contemplated giving anything like equal rights to women. He professed an ardent belief in religious toleration, and yet declared that a State would be justified in punishing with death all those who, after publicly recognizing the dogmas constituting its definition of religion, subsequently repudiated them. These are blots on his teaching, and there are others.

During his lifetime he was generally poor, often reviled, bitterly hated, and he had no compunction about biting the hands of the men who fed him. But at bottom he was a genuine soul, a fiery particle of revolt, who hated tyranny and pitied his fellow men.

THE VICAR OF WAKEFIELD

OLIVER GOLDSMITH

"ONE MORNING" – it is Dr. Johnson speaking – "I received from poor Goldsmith a message that he was in great distress, and as it was not in his power to come to me, begging that I would come to him as soon as possible, I sent him a guinea, and promised to come to him directly. I accordingly went as soon as I was drest, and found that his landlady had arrested him for his rent, at which he was in a violent passion. I perceived that he had already changed my guinea, and had got a bottle of Madeira and a glass before him. I put the cork into the bottle, desired he would be calm, and began to talk to him of the means by which he might be extricated. He then told me that he had a novel ready for the press, which he produced to me. I looked into it, and saw its merit; told the landlady I should soon return, and having gone to a bookseller, sold it for sixty pounds. I brought Goldsmith the money, and he discharged his rent, not without rating his landlady in a high tone for having used him so ill."

The novel which was thus ushered into the world was *The Vicar of Wakefield*. It was published in 1766, and, as Macaulay put it in his essay on Goldsmith, it rapidly obtained a popularity which is likely to last as long as our language.

Dr. Primrose is the hero of the story, and he tells it in the first person. He is described in the preface as one who "unites in himself the three greatest characters upon earth: he is a priest, a husbandman, and the father of a family". There is a decided touch of whimsicality about him, but he is pious and good-hearted, thoroughly honest and upright, a sincere patriot and a firm friend. In the book's very first sentence we are told of his opinion, that the honest man who marries and brings up a large family does more service than he who continues single and only talks of population. He had therefore scarce taken Holy Orders a year, before he had thought seriously of matrimony; and he had chosen his wife as she did her wedding-gown, not for a fine glossy surface but such qualities as wear well. She was a good-natured woman, we are told; she could read any English book without much spelling; and for pickling, preserving and cookery there was none to equal her.

Although the parson's living was but a poor one, they had a pleasant house, situated in charming country and a good neighbourhood. Much of their time was spent in visiting their rich neighbours, and relieving such as were poor. As they lived near the road, they often invited a traveller or stranger to taste their gooseberry wine, for which they had a great reputation; and, the parson tells us complacently, "I profess, with the veracity of a historian, that I never knew one of them find fault with it".

Four sons and two daughters made up the Primrose family. George was the eldest, then came Olivia and Sophia, and after them three more boys, Moses, Dick and Bill. "It would be fruitless to deny my exultation when I saw my little ones about me; but the vanity and the satisfaction of my wife was even greater than mine. When our visitors would say, 'Well, upon my word, Mrs. Primrose, you have the finest children in the whole country,' – 'Ay, neighbour,' she would answer, 'they are as heaven made them, handsome enough if they be good enough; for handsome is as handsome does'. And then she would bid the girls hold up their heads; who, to conceal nothing, were certainly very handsome." Olivia, who when the story opens is about eighteen, is described as possessing "that luxuriancy of beauty with which painters generally draw a Hebe", while Sophia's features, though not so striking at first, often did more certain execution, for they were modest, soft and alluring. "The one vanquished by a single blow, the other by efforts successfully repeated. Olivia wished for many lovers, Sophia to secure one."

For some years the Primroses had been living in a state of much happiness. The profits of Dr. Primrose's living were but £35 a year (and even this he made over to the support of the widows and orphans of clergy of the diocese), but he had private means, much more than sufficient for their modest needs. Then things took a turn for the worse, and it was Dr. Primrose who was responsible for the first reverse. He was a crotchety fellow, and he had one "peculiar tenet", viz., that it was unlawful for a clergyman, after the death of his first wife, to take a second, "or, to express it in one word, I valued myself upon being a strict monogamist". Now George, who had been to Oxford and was destined for one of the professions, had set his heart on marrying Miss Arabella Wilmot, the daughter of a neighbouring clergyman who was a dignitary of the Church. She was beautiful and rich, and fully returned his affection, but unfortunately her father was a widower three times over and was now courting his *fourth* wife! He and Dr. Primrose got into fierce argument over the matter, tempers were lost, and the proposed match was already in jeopardy when the news came that Dr. Primrose had lost most of the money that he had invested with a London merchant, and was unable therefore to settle on his son the amount that had been agreed as a wedding portion. The match was broken off, and George was sent off to London to seek his fortune.

Now the Primrose family were obliged to leave their pleasant home and remove to a distant village. The value of the new living was only £15 a year, but the vicar proposed to increase it by managing a small farm. For a time all went well again, and we may agree with Macaulay that these early chapters "have all the sweetness of pastoral poetry, together with all the vivacity of comedy".

The place of their retreat was a community of small farmers, who tilled their own fields and were equal strangers to opulence and poverty. They wrought with cheerfulness on days of labour, but observed festivals as intervals of idleness and pleasure. They kept up the Christmas carol, sent true-love knots on Valentine morning, ate pancakes at Shrove-tide, showed their wit on the first of April, and religiously cracked nuts on Michaelmas Eve. The Primroses' nearest neighbour was Farmer Flamborough, who with his bouncing daughters would often pay them a visit, and there was a blind piper who also sometimes called. When the day's work was done the worthy parson and his wife would sit together on a bench before their homely dwelling, and "drank tea which had now become an occasional banquet". Or the girls would sing to the guitar, and "while they thus formed a little concert, my wife and I would stroll down the sloping field, that was embellished with blue-bells and centaury, talk of our children with rapture, and enjoy the breeze that wafted both health and harmony".

With such delightful touches as these Goldsmith painted the "sweetness" in the picture. The "comedy" may be best illustrated by the incident of young Moses and the Green Spectacles. Mrs. Primrose had urged upon her spouse the desirability of making a better show on Sundays, and had at length got him to agree to selling their colt and buying a horse instead, on which the ladies might ride together to church. Moses goes off to the fair with the colt, and returns at nightfall, with no horse but lugging a great box in which he tells them there is a gross of green spectacles! He had sold the colt, it appeared, for three pounds five shillings and twopence, and was walking about the fairground looking for a suitable horse when he had been invited by a reverend-looking man into a tent, where they had met another man who was trying to borrow twenty pounds on some green spectacles, with silver rims, in shagreen cases. He wanted the money, he said, and would dispose of the spectacles for a third of their real value. "The first gentleman, who pretended to be my friend, whispered me to buy them, and cautioned me not to let so good an offer pass. I sent for Mr. Flamborough, and they talked him up so finely as they did me, and so at last we were persuaded to buy the two gross between us." The silver rims alone would sell for double the money, the youth added. But alas, the vicar had already discovered that the rims were "no more silver than your saucepan, they are only copper varnished over . . ."

There were two other visitors who have a prominent place in the Primrose story. The first was a Mr. Burchell, a man of about thirty, of somewhat modest appearance but obviously cultured and well educated. They made his acquaintance on their way to their new home, and indeed he had put them deeply in his debt for he had rescued Sophia from death by drowning when they were traversing a deep ford. The other was a much more lively figure – their land-lord, young Squire Thornhill, against whom Dr. Primrose had been warned as being "particularly remarkable for his attachment to the fair sex" so that "there was scarce a farmer's daughter within ten miles round but what had found him successful and faithless". He made himself so pleasant, however, that the simple-minded vicar thought that he must have been greatly maligned, while Mrs. Prim-rose saw in him already a very suitable husband for Olivia – who, for her part, seemed to welcome his addresses. Sophia seemed drawn to Mr. Burchell; but when that gentleman displayed a marked anti-pathy to Squire Thornhill and his two lady companions, the Lady Blarney and Miss Carolina Wilelmina Amelia Skeggs, who had so kindly offered to take the two Primrose girls back with them to London and find them good situations there, he was most rudely shown the door.

With Burchell out of the way, Squire Thornhill showed his true colours. Not marriage but seduction was his object, and one evening the Primroses were sitting round the fire when little Dick came run-ning in with the astounding news that "my sister Livy is gone off with two gentleman in a post-chaise; and one of them kissed her, and said he would die for her, and she cried very much, and was for coming back; but he persuaded her again, and she went into the chaise, and said, 'Oh, what will my poor papa do when he knows I am undone?' "

What "poor papa" did was to call for his pistols, and shout that he "would pursue the traitor – while he is on earth, I'll pursue him – the villain – the perfidious villain!" Calmer thoughts prevailed, and in the morning he did set out to pursue his "darling Olivia", but without the pistols.

On the road he fell ill, and was laid up in a wayside inn for some weeks. Then he decided to return home, and on the way fell in with a band of strolling players, among whom he met, of all people, his son George! The young man's story of his adventures since he had left home to make his fortune make up the chapter on "The History of a Philosophic Vagabond", in which Goldsmith is believed to have drawn very largely on his own experiences when, as a young man, he wandered about the Continent with not much in the way of possessions beyond his flute.

After this interesting excursion, we are brought back to the story of the Primrose family, and perhaps we shall agree with Macaulay that the latter part of the tale is unworthy of the beginning, since as we approach the catastrophe the absurdities lie thicker and thicker and the gleams of pleasantry become rarer and rarer.

When not far from his home, the vicar discovers Olivia lying ill in a wayside public house, and takes her back with him in melancholy triumph. But a whole host of fresh calamities now assails him. Since he is unable to pay his rent, his cruel landlord, Squire Thornhill, gets a distraint on his cattle, and then the vicar is cast into a debtors' prison. George challenges his sister's seducer – for it is indeed the Squire who has "undone" her – and seriously injures one of Thornhill's hangers-on, for which he is thrown into the same prison with his father. Then comes the tidings that Sophia too has been carried off, and, to crown all, that Olivia has died, worn out by her distresses and grief. The only bright spot in this chapter of woes is the vicar's determined efforts to relieve and reclaim the prisoners among whom his lot has been cast. This is the occasion for some severe questioning of the horribly cruel penal laws of the age, which bore so heavily upon the poor.

And now the tide begins to turn. A letter to Sir William Thornhill, the uncle of the Squire, whose reputation for benevolence is almost proverbial, brings that gentleman to the vicar's succour – and great is the latter's amazement when he discovers (what the reader must have guessed long before) that Sir William is none other than the Mr. Burchell who had been turned so unceremoniously from his door! Then George gets his release, Olivia is not really dead and was legally married to Squire Thornhill (although he had intended otherwise), a large part of the vicar's fortune is recovered from the defaulting merchant, and Sophia has been rescued from her abductors by "Mr. Burchell"! George marries his

Arabella, Sophia becomes Lady Thornhill, and Olivia is given a third part of her disreputable husband's fortune. "She still remembers him with regret," the vicar tells us, "and she has told me that when he reforms she may be brought to relent."

So the book, which has so happy a beginning, comes to a happy ending. "As soon as dinner was over, according to my old custom, I requested that the table might be taken away, to have the pleasure of seeing all my family assembled once more by a cheerful fireside. My two little ones sat upon each knee; the rest of the company by their partners. I had nothing now on this side the grave to wish for: all my cares were over; my pleasure was unspeakable: it now only remained that my gratitude in good fortune should exceed my former submission in adversity."

THE WEALTH OF NATIONS

ADAM SMITH

IT IS a very big book, running to as many as a thousand pages, and closely printed ones at that. It is big also in another sense. On the subject of Economics it is, almost without question, the most important book ever written. The only possible rival is Karl Marx's *Capital*, and it is not too much to say that Marx could not have written his criticism of the capitalist system if Adam Smith had not, nearly a century before, produced *The Wealth of Nations*.

Before we tackle the book it may be as well to spend a few minutes with its author. Adam Smith was a Scotsman – he would have written it Scotchman – and he had in a marked degree the typically Scottish quality of canniness. So much so, indeed, that it is in evidence on almost every page of his book. Some critics have maintained that only a Scotsman could have written it, and they have meant nothing in the least derogatory.

Born in 1723 in the little seaport town of Kirkcaldy, on the east coast of Scotland, he was the son of a writer to the signet – what in England would be called a solicitor – who died some months before he was born. He was brought up by his mother, who seems to have been the only woman he ever really loved. He went to the burgh school where, after the good old Scottish custom, he sat at the same desk with the laird's son and the fisherman's and the collier's. Even as a boy he seems to have shown a keen interest in the industrial activities of the little place. He won an exhibition to Balliol College, Oxford, but after a very unprofitable four years there returned home to Kirkcaldy, where for some time he was at a loose end. Then he was asked to give a course of public lectures on English Literature at Edinburgh, and these proved so successful that in 1750 he was appointed to the chair of Moral Philosophy at Glasgow College, or University. For fourteen years he was a professor, and he made an excellent impression not only in the classrooms but in the busy, bustling city that lay just beyond the college windows.

In the middle of the eighteenth century Glasgow was still a small provincial city, but by 1760 it had supplanted Bristol as the principal tobacco port, and its "tobacco lords" were fine men of business.

Adam Smith cultivated their acquaintance, and felt highly honoured when he was invited to join their weekly dining-club. From them he obtained a mass of information on business matters that came in exceedingly useful in writing his book. He may well have felt that his career was fixed, but then in 1764 he was invited to accompany the young Duke of Buccleugh on the customary "grand tour" of the Continent. He accepted, and for the next two years was in France where, particularly at Paris, he mixed with the leading figures in the worlds of literature and politics. It was a period of intense intellectual excitement, and Adam Smith listened carefully and occasionally took a part in the discussions himself. The most profitable of his acquaintances was François Quesnay, who was the acknowledged head of the new school of thinkers known as the *Economistes*.

Already, it appears, the idea of writing a book on what was then called Political Economy had entered his mind, and when at length he was able to return to Kirkcaldy he devoted himself entirely to its production. It was published in March, 1776, under the title: *An Inquiry into the Nature and Causes of the Wealth of Nations*; and although at first it was slow in selling, it then "caught on". Five editions were published in Adam Smith's lifetime, it was translated into the chief European languages, and numerous editions have appeared since his death (in 1790, at Edinburgh).

Let it be said at once that it is not an easy book to read, at least right through. Still less is it an easy book to master. While the serious student of Economics can hardly do anything else but start at the beginning and work on steadily to the last page, the "ordinary reader" may well feel intimidated by a glance through the Contents, with its five Books and thirty-two Chapters, a number of which proliferate into Parts, Articles, Appendixes, and even Digressions, and will not venture to make so much as a trial dip – which would be a pity. For his encouragement it may be pointed out that its contents may be conveniently dissected and re-arranged under three main themes or subjects, namely: (1) a description of the economic system of Britain (and to a lesser extent of France and some other countries) in the middle of the eighteenth century; (2) a philosophy of human nature; and (3) a programme of (mainly political) action.

So far as the first be concerned, it should be understood that Adam Smith was writing before – but only just before – the Industrial Revolution. The economic set-up that he describes is that of the times of Hogarth and Dr. Johnson and *Tom Jones*. It is the real "Olde England" that we see reflected in its pages. Down the road comes rumbling the "broad-wheeled waggon, drawn by eight horses, attended by two men," which, if all goes well, will manage to "carry and bring back between London and Edinburgh near four ton weight of goods" in about six weeks. It is a world in which labourers earn between four and five shillings a week, and, as Goldsmith said in a famous line, curates are "passing rich on forty pounds a year". Leather shoes, we are told, are a "necessary of life" in England, so that even the poorest person of either sex would be ashamed to be seen in public without them, but in Scotland women (but not men) of the working classes may walk about barefoot. It is a society in which the Scots poor live almost entirely on oatmeal, but in England butcher's meat and white bread are quite common: while as for Ireland, the common people there are generally fed with potatoes.

If Adam Smith had been writing only a few years later he might have supported his argument by descriptions of the new cotton mills that Mr. Dale was erecting at Falls of Clyde, or Roebuck's great ironworks at Carron or Boulton & Watt's establishment at Soho, Birmingham; but as it was, the illustrations he chose were drawn from a pin-manufactory and a "nailery" such as he had seen as a boy in Kirkcaldy. Even so, these were sufficient to provide him with material for a classic account of the workings of that economic process that he styled – and he was among the first writers to do so – "division of labour", and which we today may prefer to describe as "specialization".

Yes, this "division of labour" is a wonderful thing, but we should not make the mistake of thinking that it is the fruit of human wisdom. "It is the necessary, though very slow and gradual, consequence of a certain propensity in human nature which has in view no such extensive utility: the propensity to truck, barter, and exchange one thing for another." (A few lines lower down the page is the delightfully characteristic remark that "Nobody ever saw a dog make a fair and deliberate exchange of one bone for another with another dog".)

In this way we are introduced to Adam Smith's theory of human nature. It is a very down-to-earth one, and (so some of his critics alleged) a very low one. According to him, men are always what we might describe as "on the make". He refers appreciatively to "the desire of bettering our condition, a desire which . . . comes with us from the womb, and never leaves us till we go into the grave". For the life of him he could not see that there was anything reprehensible in such an attitude; he rejected the idea altogether that there was something low and degrading about it; any sensible man must agree that it was what actually took place. He scoffed at those people who professed to be in business for some other motive than making a profit: "I have never known much good done by those who affected to trade for the public good". He pointed out that "while man has almost constant occasion for the help of his brethren, it is in vain for him to expect it from their benevolence only . . . It is not from the benevolence of the butcher, the brewer, or the baker, that we expect our dinner, but from their regard to their own self-interest".

Now a few words on the third of the main themes of *The Wealth of Nations*, the one which is of greatest practical interest and importance – what may be described as his policy or programme of action. It will be found for the most part in his fourth Book, where we have a lengthy, detailed, and highly critical examination of the "Commercial or Mercantile System" that was the accepted ideology of the principal governments of his time. The Mercantilists held that wealth consists primarily of money, and mercantilist governments strove to foster home industries and encourage the export of as large an amount of goods as possible, and to import as little possible, when the difference would have to be made up in cash or bullion.

Under the influence of Mercantilist ideas, Adam Smith declared, "nations have been taught that their interest consisted in beggaring all their neighbours . . . Commerce which ought naturally to be, among nations as among individuals, a bond of union and friendship, has become the most fertile source of discord and animosity". A few lines later in the same page, and we read that "In every country it always is and must be the interest of the great body of the people to buy whatever they want of those who sell it cheapest"; and a few pages earlier comes the argument that "If a foreign country can supply us with a commodity cheaper than we ourselves can make it, better buy it of them with some part of the produce of our own industry, employed in a way in which we have some advantage".

Here we have the case for Free Trade put by the greatest economic thinker of his age, but it is only part of Adam Smith's programme. Summed up in one word, his whole policy was one of *Freedom*. Freedom of trade, yes; but freedom also for the individual whose abilities and energies were so often frustrated by interfering authorities of one kind and another. A man should be able to choose his job, and not have to submit to the long apprenticeship that was insisted on by the "corporations". Well did he remember the day when young James Watt had come knocking at the door of the College in Glasgow, and had complained that he had been prevented from setting up as an instrument-maker by the Corporation of Hammermen, whose members insisted that they held the monopoly in this business. Adam Smith had taken up his complaint, and the College faculty had provided Watt with a workshop in their premises, where in due course he carried out the experiments that led to his invention of the steam-engine. A man should be able to move about, and not remain tied to the place in which he had been born just because the parish authorities were afraid that he might become a charge upon their funds. Away, then, with all such restrictions and restraints! Down with the "wretched spirit of monopoly"! Let "the simple system of natural liberty" establish itself, when every man may be free, so long as he does not violate the laws of justice, to pursue his own interest in his own way.

There is very much else in Adam Smith. Those four "Maxims of Taxation", for instance, which ever since he framed them have been accepted as what every Chancellor of the Exchequer ought to aim at: (1) "the subjects of every state ought to contribute towards the support of the government, as nearly as possible in proportion to their respective abilities"; (2) "the tax which each individual is bound to pay, ought to be certain, and not arbitrary"; and (3) "levied at the time, or in the manner, in which it is most likely to be convenient for the contributor to pay it"; and (4) "every tax ought to be so contrived as both to take out and to keep out of the pockets of the people as little as possible over and above what it brings into the public treasury of the state". Governments, wrote Adam Smith, "are the greatest spendthrifts of society. Let them look well after their own expense, and they may safely trust private people with theirs".

Mention should be made, too, of the many pithy sayings that ought to find a place in every dictionary of quotations; for example, "the delightful art" of gardening, "the desire for food is limited by the narrow capacity of the human stomach", "a man is of all sorts of luggage the most difficult to be transported", and "When you have got a little money, it is often easy to get more: the great difficulty is to get that little". All these things are of secondary importance, however. The really important thing about Adam Smith is that it was he who mapped out the ground and prepared the way for Economics to become what it is today, one of the most interesting, stimulating, and vitally important of the sciences that are the instruments of human progress.

THE DECLINE AND FALL OF THE ROMAN EMPIRE

EDWARD GIBBON

"WHAT'S THIS, Mr. Gibbon," grumbled the Duke of Gloucester when the historian presented him with a copy of his latest published volume, "another d—— square, thick book! Always scribble, scribble, scribble! Eh! Mr. Gibbon?"

Perhaps Mr. Gibbon smiled: his Royal Highness must have his little joke. Perhaps he winced, although that would have been difficult to see on his pudgy little countenance. Most likely he reached for his snuffbox and took a pinch. But he may have been more than a little put out by the Duke's choice of words. "Scribble" indeed! That, surely, was hardly the way to describe the labour of so many years, the persistent plodding through such countless volumes, the concentrated thought, the relentless search for just the right word and phrase, the continuous pruning and polishing, the writing and re-writing until at last it was ready for the printer. "Scribble, eh?" We may imagine him taking another pinch. . . .

When had it all begun? Long years before, in that summer of 1751 when as a feeble boy of fourteen he had accompanied his father – the wealthy son of a City financier, who had lost one fortune in the South Sea Bubble and had lived long enough to make another and a larger one – on a visit to Mr. Hoare's country seat in Wiltshire. He had been taken round the estate and languidly admired all that he was expected to, but, as he wrote years later in his *Autobiography*, "I was less delighted with the beauties of Stourhead than with discovering in the library the continuation of Echard's *Roman History*. To me the reigns of the successors of Constantine were absolutely new; and I was immersed in the passage of the Goths over the Danube, when the summons of the dinner-bell reluctantly dragged me from my intellectual feast". This "transient glance" at the ancient Romans "served rather to irritate than to appease" his curiosity. He raided the bookshops at Bath, and brought home a book which revealed to his astonished gaze Mohammed and his Saracens; and from there he was led on from one book to another until before he was sixteen he had exhausted all that could be learned in English of the Arabs and Persians, Tartars and Turks. He had made a beginning with the books in French and Latin when he was despatched to Oxford.

For fourteen months he was at Magdalen, and "they proved the most idle and unprofitable of my whole life". There followed his sojourn in a Swiss pastor's home at Lausanne, and his romantic attachment to the pretty and lively young Suzanne Curchod, that came to such an unromantic end when, in face of his father's stern disapproval of such a match, he "sighed as a lover, and obeyed as a son".

Back in England, he established himself comfortably enough in his father's house at Buriton, near Petersfield, where the library was his peculiar domain. He joined the Hampshire Militia, and for two and a half years performed adequately if not always enthusiastically the duties of a captain; the time was not altogether lost, since "the discipline and evolutions of a modern battalion gave me a clearer notion of the phalanx and the legion; and the captain of Hampshire grenadiers (the reader may smile) has not been useless to the historian of the Roman Empire". When the war with France came to an end the regiment was disbanded, and Gibbon crossed the Channel to Paris and eventually to Rome. And "it was at Rome, on the 15th of October, 1764, as I sat musing amidst the ruins of the Capitol ... that the idea of writing the Decline and Fall of the city first started to my mind...."

After the labour of seven years he published in February, 1776, the first volume – a handsome quarto, priced at a guinea – of *The Decline and Fall of the Roman Empire*. Success was immediate. "My book was on every table," he tells us, "and almost on every toilette; the historian was crowned by the taste or fashion of the day." He confesses to a friend in Switzerland that the compliments he was receiving very much pleased him, particularly those from young and pretty women ...

If some of the later chapters are prolix and too detailed, there can be no complaints about the three opening chapters in which Gibbon describes in the most masterly fashion the stage on which the great drama was to be played out. "In the second century of the Christian Era," he begins, "the Empire of Rome comprehended the fairest part of the earth, and the most civilized portion of mankind." The Empire was then at its greatest extent, reaching from the Wall of Antonius (in Scotland) to Mount Atlas and from the Western Ocean (the Atlantic) to the Euphrates; its population, according to an "imperfect calculation", amounted to one hundred and twenty millions, "the most numerous society that has ever been united under the same system of government"; and it was defended and order was maintained by a military establishment of not more than 450,000 men.

As Gibbon describes it, this was a kind of golden age set between two ages of barbarism. "If a man were called to fix the period in the history of the world," he writes, "during which the condition of the human race was most happy and prosperous, he would, without hesitation, name that which elapsed from the death of Domitian to the accession of Commodus (A.D. 96–180). The vast extent of the Roman Empire was governed by absolute power, under the guidance of virtue and wisdom. The armies were restrained by the firm but gentle hand of four successive emperors, whose characters and authority commanded involuntary respect." The two Antonines, Antoninus Pius and Marcus Aurelius, are worthy of special commendation. "Their united reigns are possibly the only period of history in which the happiness of a great people was the sole object of government."

Nevertheless, these monarchs, who had "the exquisite delight of beholding the general happiness of which they were the authors . . . must often have recollected the instability of a happiness which depended on the character of a single man. The fatal moment was perhaps approaching, when some licentious youth, or some jealous tyrant, would abuse, to the destruction, that absolute power which they had exerted for the benefit of their people". And so it soon proved. Marcus Aurelius was succeeded by Commodus, a man in whom "every sentiment of virtue and humanity was extinct . . . who valued nothing in sovereign power except the unbounded licence of indulging his sensual appetites". Truly an abominable fellow, as Gibbon portrays him with mordant particularity, but he had many an infamous successor on the imperial throne. As we turn the pages we may feel almost inclined to agree with his pronouncement that "History is little more than the register of the crimes, follies, and misfortunes of mankind".

A brighter prospect opens when we reach the chapter describing the most important of the barbarian peoples that hovered about the borders of the Empire and eventually brought about its downfall – those German tribes who, "without either cities, letters, arts, or money found some compensation for this savage state in the enjoyment of liberty". Other chapters relate the invasions of the Goths, and Gibbon's pen races as he encounters again those fierce warriors whose war-cries had prevented him hearing the dinner-bell at Buriton. So far so good, thought the critics as they followed the lively chronicle, but now they were brought up sharp by the chapters, the famous fifteenth and sixteenth, in which Gibbon describes the rise and progress of the Christian Church within the Empire.

Hitherto the history of Christianity had been generally placed in a category by itself, as something too sacred to be treated in the same rough and critical way as the history of secular governments and movements, and indeed other religions. But Gibbon had set himself the task of explaining the why and wherefore of the Church's triumph in the Roman world, and, while professing to acknowledge the "convincing evidence of the doctrine itself, and the ruling providence of its great Author", he advanced five "secondary causes" of the new religion's rapid growth, namely: (1) The inflexible, and the intolerant, zeal of the Christians; (2) The doctrine of a future life; (3) The miraculous powers ascribed to the primitive Church; (4) The pure and austere morals of the Christians; and (5) The union and discipline of the Christian republic, which gradually formed an independent and increasing state in the heart of the Roman Empire.

Gibbon professed to be greatly surprised by the tremendous agitation that these two offending chapters aroused. He was himself a typically urbane, cultivated, rational-minded product of the eighteenth century, and for the life of him he could not understand why the origins of Christianity and the Christian Church should not be investigated with the critical detachment that befits a philosophic historian. If his chapters were to appear today, it is probable that they would be received with little surprise, certainly without vigorous denunciation. That in itself is an indication of the success of the Gibbonian technique.

As his work progressed, Gibbon found that he had taken what he called an inadequate measure of the space demanded, and in fact six quarto volumes were required, of which the last two were published in 1788. In whatever edition they may be had, they make an imposing show, but even those readers who are set on following the example of Silas Wegg in Dickens's *Our Mutual Friend*, "going straight across country at everything . . . taking all the hard words, biographical and geographical," may feel after a time that in the several thousand pages there are too many jumps for even the most persistent galloper. To them the exercise of a judicious discrimination may perhaps be recommended.

In this case we may take a hint from Gibbon's statement, toward the end of his final volume, that "I have described the triumph of barbarism and religion". Here are two themes, related but possible to disentangle, which we may follow through, concentrating on those chapters of outstanding interest. "Barbarism": here we may begin with the chapter (No. 9) on Germany before the Barbarian invasions, and then join the bands of invaders who through the centuries crossed the far-flung frontiers to challenge the might of Rome, in particular the Goths under Alaric (Chapters 30 and 31), the Vandals in North Africa (33), the Huns under Attila (34 and 35), the Franks in Gaul and the Saxons in Britain (38), and finally the Seljuk Turks (57). "Religion": on this theme the obvious starting-point is Chapter 15, on "the progress of the Christian Religion, and the sentiments, manners, numbers, and condition of the primitive Christians", and the chapter following on the successive persecutions of the Christians by the Roman government. From here we may move on to the story of the Emperor Constantine's conversion (20), and thence to Julian's unsuccessful attempt to restore the ancient faith (23), the final destruction of Paganism (28), and the beginnings of the monastic system (37). Then the remarkably full and fair chapters (50 and 51) in which Gibbon relates the career of Mohammed and the rapid spread of the religion of Islam, lead up to his account of the wars between Cross and Crescent that we know as the Crusades (58 and 59). At last we arrive at the Fall of Constantinople to the Turks in Chapter 68, but there are still three more chapters bringing the history of the city of Rome up to the middle of the fifteenth century.

Why did Rome "decline and fall"? Gibbon's answer to this very obvious question will be found not in his final chapter but in Chapter 38. "The decline of Rome was the natural and inevitable effect of immoderate greatness," he there writes. "Prosperity ripened the principle of decay; the causes of destruction multiplied with the extent of conquest; and as soon as time or accident had removed the artificial supports, the stupendous fabric yielded to the pressure of its own weight." Then after suggesting that "instead of inquiring *why* the Roman Empire was destroyed, we should rather be surprised that it had subsisted so long", he goes on to state that "the victorious legions who, in distant wars, acquired the vices of strangers and mercenaries, first oppressed the freedom of the republic, and afterwards violated the majesty of the Purple. . . . The vigour of the military government was relaxed. . . . The Roman world was overwhelmed by a deluge of Barbarians. . . ." In conclusion he allows that, while the conversion of Constantine to Christianity may have hastened the Empire's decline, "his victorious religion broke the violence of the fall, and mollified the ferocious temper of the conquerors".

In another famous passage in his *Autobiography* Gibbon describes how he wrote the last lines of his "History" in a summer-house in the garden of his house at Lausanne, beside the Lake of Geneva. "It was on the day, or rather night, of the 27th of June, 1787, between the hours of eleven and twelve . . . After laying down my pen, I took several turns in a covered walk of acacias, which commands a prospect of the country, the lake, and the mountains. The air was temperate, the sky was serene, the silver orb of the moon was reflected from the waters, and all Nature was silent. I will not dissemble the first emotions of joy on the recovery of my freedom, and perhaps the establishment of my fame. But my pride was soon humbled, and a sober melancholy was spread over my mind by the idea that I had taken an everlasting leave of an old and agreeable companion, and that whatsoever might be the future date of my History, the life of the historian must be short and precarious."

The life of the historian had another seven years to run; the future date of the History is still indeterminable. In the nearly two hundred years that have elapsed since Gibbon laid down his pen much has been discovered about the city and empire whose fortunes he related with such matchless charm and dignity. We have manuscripts that he never saw, inscriptions that he never read, archaeological sites that he never explored. But there has been no "decline and fall" in the reputation of the man or his work. Among historians all the world over, Gibbon stood, and stands, supreme.

THE CRITIQUE OF PURE REASON

IMMANUEL KANT

IMMANUEL KANT was born in Königsberg (now Kaliningrad) in what was formerly East Prussia on 22 April, 1724. He was the fourth child of a master harness-maker. Educated first in the elementary school attached to St. George's Hospital, within a short time he entered the Collegium Fredericianum, the Protestant high school, where he quickly showed outstanding promise. Though the Frederici-num had acquired a certain fame, the general education it had to offer was somewhat meagre, and it was not until Kant entered the university in 1740 – a step made possible by the kindness of a well-off uncle – that his education may be said to have begun.

At the university Kant studied classics, physics and mathematics, and on leaving in 1747 he became a private tutor, a profession he followed until 1755, when he obtained his doctorate with a natural philosophic treatise entitled *De Igne* (*Concerning Fire*). At the con-ferment ceremony, he delivered a Latin address on *The Simpler and More Fundamental Exposition of Philosophy*, which greatly impressed all his learned audience and was an important factor in his being offered the post of Reader in mathematics, physics and philosophy in the university. This post he held until 1770 when he accepted the Professorship of logic and metaphysics, an appointment which he filled until old age compelled him to resign, in 1797.

His final seven years, like the sixty-odd which had preceded them, were regulated with clockwork precision and were absolutely un-eventful. He never married, and was never more than forty miles from his city, where he died.

In contrast to this unadventurous existence, which might with some justification be called humdrum, was the impact he made upon the science of philosophy, to which he rendered great service by his endeavour to find a bond of union between realism (materialism) and idealism, each of which had been claimed by its exponents to be the only true system. The realists regarded matter, the idealists mind (the Ego), as the absolute; the former regarded the Ego as entirely *dependent* on the world of sense, the latter as entirely *independent* of the world of sense. Kant, while admitting that experience alone furnishes us with the matter of knowledge, asserts that there exists *a priori* in the mind certain notions independent of experience, ready to be applied to the matter furnished by experience.

The preceding paragraph, simple though it is in philosophical expression, is nevertheless sufficient to show the non-philosophic student that, like all sciences, philosophy has acquired its own particular jargon which only the initiated can understand with ease. If a really outstanding example of non-communication were ever to be sought, scarcely a better one could be cited than that of philosophy. Here, perhaps even more importantly than with any other science, the scientist has created a barrier of terms by which to express thoughts and ideas about matters affecting us all – the origins of knowledge and wisdom – but which effectively cuts off the ordinary man from the thinker, the man who by terming himself philosopher clearly looks upon himself, as the word implies, as the fount of wisdom.

Unfortunately, as with most sciences, the would-be interpreter of philosophy finds himself becoming involved in almost insoluble complications of expression if he does not use some of the jargon, the special terms by which philosophers convey, in a kind of shorthand, their own particular thoughts to their professional colleagues. In this particular case, when the object is to explain as simply as possible philosophical theories which have placed their originator alongside the Olympian philosophers, Plato and Aristotle and their true descendants through the ages, to avoid this pitfall it is intended to introduce the specific subject with a brief general explanation of the aims of philosophy and the definition of a few essential terms, the minimum necessary for the avoidance of complications.

What is the objective of philosophy? Philosophy seeks to co-ordinate the general results of thought and of the individual sciences into a unified view of the world and of life, and to examine the pre-suppositions of all sciences, in so far as these lie within man himself. From time immemorial there have been men who have been attracted to carrying out such investigations, and new investigations are always being undertaken. Many of them, for one reason or another, never reach a conclusion, for, as another great German philosopher, Schopenhauer, once wrote, "Philosophy is a high alpine track. Its only approach is a steep path over sharp stones and piercing thorns. It is a lonely path, and the higher one goes, the more barren it becomes; whoever follows it must know no fear, but forsaking everything confidently blaze his own trail through the cold snow".

Philosophy deals, above all, with three major problems – Truth,

In an age of great thinkers and writers Voltaire – so sceptical in mind, so comprehensive in knowledge, so undaunted in face of a hundred foes – showed that the pen could be mightier than the sword. In the above drawing we see him (the animated little figure in the centre, with his hand upraised) sitting at a table with some of his intellectual companions. Hardly second to him in influence and reputation was Jean-Jacques Rousseau (*left*). If any man has a right to be called the "Father of the French Revolution" it was surely this quarrelsome, often malicious and deeply resentful but most richly gifted man of letters, who found among his dumb friends a simple happiness so generally denied him in human relationships.

A sociable man on the whole was Dr. Samuel Johnson, notwithstanding his occasional fits of misanthropy, and he liked nothing better than an evening with congenial acquaintances in some Fleet Street tavern. Here we see him taking his ease at the "Mitre". As usual, he seems to be arguing his point; the ladies do not seem to be altogether convinced, but Oliver Goldsmith, who was so often the butt of the Doctor's heavy humour, sips his punch with unassuming ease.

For ten years Samuel Pepys before he retired to rest at night entered up his Diary in primitive shorthand. Many characters appear in the book's pages, but there is none more appealing than that of the young girl whom he married in 1655, when she was fifteen, and who died in 1669, the same year in which failing eyesight made him close his Diary for ever. Elizabeth Pepys was half-French, and she was not only beautiful but had the tastes and spirit of a woman of culture and elegance. "My wife this day put on first her French gown," runs one entry, "called a sac, which becomes her very well" (*below*).

Goodness and Beauty. With regard to Truth, it seeks to answer the questions: Does true cognition (the act or faculty of knowing, or a piece of knowledge) exist? How is true, correct and universally valid cognition achieved? Where do its boundaries lie?

With regard to Goodness it asks: What are the principles governing good, morally right conduct? What are the guiding lines of human conduct, and by what criteria are morals to be valued? While of Beauty it asks: Are there laws which objects of nature and art must satisfy in order to be aesthetically valuable, that is, beautiful? What is the nature of the beautiful, the aesthetic?

Kant made a detailed analysis of all these problems, and by so doing founded a new philosophy. The first of three great works in which he investigates the nature, limits and extent of human knowledge is the *Critique of Pure Reason*.

Kant's intellectual development, which may be said to have begun in 1740, was at first naturally dependent upon the systems of other philosophers. Between 1740 and 1760 he was chiefly attracted to the generally accepted doctrine of the times as expounded by the work of the German philosophers Liebnitz and Wolff, with which he also combined the natural philosophy of Newton. From 1760 to 1770 he concentrated on the thought of the English philosophers, mainly Locke and Hume, though, when he saw their weaknesses, he passed beyond their empirical philosophy, that is, their philosophy derived from their own experience. In the numerous short papers he published during this time it is clear that he was deeply attracted to the contemporary philosophical doctrine known as the Spirit of Enlightenment.

There were two conflicting views of the origin of our knowledge and our cognition at this time. The first was the Empiricism of John Locke, who held that all knowledge, all cognition, springs from experience, that is, there are no innate ideas or notions. The understanding contains nothing which has not previously been in the senses, but works over these impressions acquired through the senses, compares, differentiates and combines.

The second was the Rationalism of Descartes, who held that all cognition springs from the human mind, that is, from the *ratio* or reason. Thus it is possible to evolve all truths from pure thought, independently of experience.

The antithesis which these two theories represented had led philosophical development to an impasse from which there seemed no way out, since neither of the solutions provided by Empiricism and Rationalism seemed entirely satisfactory. For ten years Kant devoted all his intellectual powers to a consideration of the problem of cognition, and then, in 1781, he produced the results of his thoughts and his conclusions in the *Critique of Pure Reason*.

(By *reason* in this context Kant means the "faculty of cognition", using the word *cognition* in the sense defined above as "the act or faculty of knowing".)

The question to be answered is: What parts do experience and understanding (the Kantian *reason*) play in our cognitions? In other words, what are cognitions?

Kant answers that cognition is a *necessary* judgment, a judgment, that is to say, which is certain and beyond all doubt. All cognition is expressed in the form of judgments; for example, the water is hot, the box is heavy, the night is dark, and so on. Verbally, judgments are contained in predications.

All the above judgments, however, are derived from experience, and consequently are neither *necessary* nor *universal*. When you say, "This water is hot", you really ought to say, "This water seems to me to be hot", because what you may find hot another may find cool. These judgments, then, are based on personal feeling (subjective), and are, therefore, neither universal nor necessary, but *contingent* (or accidental) since the night is not always dark, nor the water always hot.

Necessary, universal judgments, that is, judgments which are recognized to be true and correct by everyone at all times, exist in physics, mathematics and, above all, in geometry. The statement that when one straight line meets another the angles formed are equal to two right angles is an example of this kind of judgment, since it is recognized as correct without reference to experience, universally and "from the first" (*a priori*). We know for certain, in advance, that this, and all similar propositions, possess universal validity; and they achieve this because they are creations of our own faculty of intuition. (By *intuition* is meant something apprehended through the senses, without reasoning.)

From this it can be successfully argued that geometry proves that cognition of the world need not necessarily be a product of experience, of the functioning of the senses. From the senses we certainly obtain immediate intuitions or ideas, but these in themselves would be blind, dead things, in relation to which our minds would be entirely passive. They contain the raw material of cognitions, but do not, by themselves, constitute cognitions. These blind intuitions become true cognitions through the productive activity of the mind, which, by means of thought, creates *concepts*.

Every science operates with concepts. But concepts are products of the human mind, of thought, which do not exist in reality. The concept "circle" is a flat area bounded by one curving continuous line. A circle possessing these characteristics *alone* is inconceivable, for it exists only by thought and for thought.

The person not trained in philosophy or lacking in critical faculty imagines the world and its contents to be as he sees and experiences them. Kant shows that we do not know at all what the object, the "thing-in-itself", is, but only how it appears to us on the basis of the laws governing our intellectual constitution, which are present *a priori* ("from the first"), and to which experiences are added *a posteriori*. (*A priori* here does not imply inborn; *a priori* cognitions are those which come into being independently of experience, while *a posteriori* cognitions are cognitions having their source in experience.) "It cannot be doubted," says Kant, "that all our cognition begins with experience, for how else should the faculty of cognition be awakened into activity. . . . That all our cognition starts *with* experience does not, however, imply that it originates *from* experience."

So, cognition springs from two sources working in collaboration – from the functioning of the senses and understanding (Kantian *reason*). Objects are given us by the former, but *conceptually* thought by the latter. Without the senses we should not become aware of any object; but without understanding we should form no conception of it.

All our intuitions have a dual nature; objects appear to be outside ourselves and externally co-existent in *space*; and they also seem to exist within our own minds, either *simultaneously* or *in succession*, and so, in *time*. Thus *space* and *time* are the two forms to which all our intuitions are bound, and as they are ideas directly related to objects, they are themselves intuitions.

The reason why all our intuitions are bound up with these two forms lies in the manner in which our faculty of imagination receives the impression of objects. Space and time, then, are pure intuitions, which are present *a priori* in advance of any real sensation, inherent in the faculty of imagination in our souls, and are thus only necessary ideas *a priori*, underlying all intuitions.

The idea that space derives *a priori*, and not from experience, is clear from the fact that space is infinite, which no one can experience or demonstrate. Space is not a universal concept of the relationship of things in general, but a pure intuition, deriving from thought, a necessary mode of intuition *a priori*.

Nor is time a concept derived from experience. It is but the form of the intuition of ourselves and our inward condition. It is a necessary idea underlying all intuitions. As with space, it is possible to conceive the absence of phenomena from time, but not the absence of time itself, which, therefore, is given *a priori*.

The basic idea which Kant consistently drives home in the *Critique of Pure Reason* is that our minds are living, actively operative organisms, drawing the material for their functioning from without, through the senses and through experiences, but shaping this material according to their own laws and so forming their cognitions themselves.

He demonstrates that it is the active functioning of our minds themselves which establishes these laws on the basis of the vast number of outer impressions. The order which rules in the world, and rests upon the principles of cause and effect, has its foundations in our thinking, which, by organizing our cognitions, leads to the sciences. The general principle of the sciences originates from the laws of thought, from the constitution of our minds.

The human mind, however, is not satisfied merely to give to the impressions which reach it through the senses their proper places in space-time. The development of unitary cognition, out of the chaotic confusions of sensations and perceptions, require the latter to be linked together by concepts (synthesis). All impressions are judged according to certain rules whose validity is assumed *a priori*, quite apart from experience. Kant defines twelve of these connective concepts, or categories, arranging them under four heads:

Quantity	*Quality*	*Retention*
unity	reality	inheritance and subsistence
plurality	affirmation	causality and dependence
totality	or	community or
	negation	reciprocity between the
	limitation	active and passive.

Modality
possibility and impossibility
existence and non-existence
necessity and contingency.

The categories are applicable only to phenomena within our consciousness. So, it is we who prescribe laws to nature, not nature that gives them to us. Our constructive understanding forms the world from the grand total of impressions, according to its own laws of thought. Hence, our picture of the world is not an image of reality, corresponding exactly to the original. We can never know and can never learn the nature of the world "in itself".

Nevertheless, there must be some connexion between sensibility and understanding, and, indeed, this is already proved by the possibility of experiment in the natural sciences. Since the results of reflection and calculation can be tested practically by experiment, there must exist common ground between the sensuous and the understanding.

But there are also universal and necessary cognitions of supersensory things. For example, is it possible to prove the existence of God, or is this a matter only for belief?

It is true that such things can be thought, but cannot be made sensible. Supersensory things are only thinkable, or "intelligible". Yet there must be something intrinsic to the constitution of the human mind which leads to the constant preoccupation in theology as in philosophy, with supersensory things.

According to Kant, reason, recognizing the connexion between external phenomena, draws the conclusion that the things of the outer world must also form an absolute whole and have an absolute cause. This reflection leads to the notion of the *universe*. But the inner and outer world – soul and nature – together cause the assumption of an ultimate common basis, embracing both of them. This leads to the notion of *God*, who holds and unites everything.

The notion of God derives equally from a need of reason. There are no rational proofs of the existence of God. God is a useful and necessary notion to which reason requires us to cling. We are compelled to believe in God and immortality for practical reasons, for no science and no intelligence will ever succeed in demonstrating the untenability of these notions. Reason impels us to act *as if* God and immortality were facts.

It is at this point that practical reason steps in, and in his following work, the *Critique of Practical Reason*, Kant argues that if theoretical reason, in the matter of knowledge, is conditional and controlled by experience, practical reason transcends – goes beyond – experience. Certain truths which theoretical reason denied, or was unable to prove – the immortality of the soul, the freedom of will, the existence of God – are established by the principles of practical reason.

The *Critique of Judgment*, the third great work, deals with the sublime and the beautiful, and the order of nature (teleological judgments). These judgments are the kind of middle term between pure and practical reason.

Kant introduced a new epoch in philosophical thought. No one concerned with philosophy can afford to overlook his theories, th development of which continues to this day. Of particular import ance is his high valuation of moral duties and the emphasis he place on the dignity of man.

He was, however, more than a great philosopher. He was a trul ethical personality whose convictions sprang from the nub of hi constant and noble character.

THE LIFE OF SAMUEL JOHNSON
JAMES BOSWELL

On 16 may, 1763, James Boswell, a young Scot, son of Lord Auchinleck, sowing his wild oats in London on a small allowance, met Dr. Samuel Johnson in a back parlour of a bookshop in Russell Street, Covent Garden. The doctor, then fifty-four, was the acknowledged great lion of literary London, the friend of Gibbon, the historian, of Sir Joshua Reynolds, Burke, David Garrick, the centre of the Literary Club which met in Soho, where gathered all the well-known wits as well as the serious scholars of the time.

Dr. Johnson was not at all an elegant eighteenth-century figure, with his twitching eye, his rolling gait and heavy stomach, and, above a great craggy face, his worn periwig and dirty linen. Indeed he belonged in appearance and habits not to the brilliant world in which he now lived but to the Grub Street of his early life, in which he had many a time fasted for want of money and, on one occasion, eaten behind a curtain at the house of a friend because his clothes were too worn for him to appear in public.

Boswell, nervous and often sycophantic, twice was put in his place by the Great Man, once for apologizing for being a Scot and a second time for making a silly remark about the actor David Garrick, a boyhood friend of Johnson. Boswell persisted in wooing the Doctor and Johnson was won over. A few months later, Boswell going on a tour of Europe at his father's orders, Johnson accompanied him all the way to Harwich. The reasons for the friendship which was to bind the two men until Johnson's death in 1883 are many. Johnson liked men of noble families, he found Boswell amusing and was touched by his obvious admiration. Boswell was an excellent foil to his wit and quite often a victim of it. Then Johnson had a very kind heart and was also deeply religious; he knew he could exercise a strong influence on his young friend. Johnson once explained to Boswell why he liked him:

"Sir, I love the acquaintance of young people; because, in the first place, I don't like to think myself growing old. In the next place, young acquaintances must last longest if they do last; and then Sir, young men have more virtue than old men; they have more generous sentiments in every respect. I love the young dogs of this age; they have more wit and humour and knowledge of life than we had; but then the dogs are not so good scholars".

Johnson also realized, probably unconsciously, that his biography, for which Boswell was openly collecting material, was not merely in good hands, but in those of genius. Boswell, like many other young men of his generation, thought that Samuel Johnson was the greatest man of his time. He yielded himself entirely to his influence and as it were basked in his favour. But he was dimly aware too that if he, Boswell, had talents, they were those not of a lawyer, a calling which was forced on him by his father, but of a writer; and furthermore a writer whose *forte* was self-revelation. Before meeting Johnson he had decided that keeping his *London Journal* (which for reasons of tact he never showed to Johnson) was his most important activity. Now Johnson quickly became Boswell's other and better self, and so Boswell, in a manner of speaking, revealed himself in Johnson, or perhaps one should say found his greatest self-expression in writing about the great man.

In Boswell's book we can hear the Doctor gulping his tea, or devouring greedily veal cutlets and fish sauce; we can hear his voice thickening with port wine; in company, someone contradicts him, we wait for the staggering *riposte* in his heavy sentences; we experience too with vivid understanding the Doctor's melancholy fits, his fear of death, the hypochrondria which afflicted him all his life and was accompanied by strange habits such as having to touch every post in a street where he walked. The truth is that this supreme example of biography is very near to autobiography. It is of supreme interest because both Boswell and Johnson in their different ways were extraordinary men, towering above the average.

Samuel Johnson was born in 1709, in the reign of Queen Anne, at Lichfield, the son of an unsuccessful bookseller, who eventually went bankrupt. A boy with a phenomenal memory and early knowledge of Latin, the most important part of education in those days, Samuel Johnson left Pembroke College, Oxford, without a degree, having quarrelled with the benefactor who had helped to pay his living while there. He tried his hand at schoolmastering, one of his few pupils being David Garrick, also born in Lichfield. Early in life he married a widow, a Mrs. Porter, twenty years older than himself, whom he always referred to as Tetty. It was a love match between two physically ungainly characters. She died in 1752, after sharing

Johnson's poverty and also the beginning of his fame. For while she had not seen his great *Dictionary of the English Language* published and had mainly witnessed his struggles, by hack work and translations, to earn a pittance, he had published his great poem on London which had been praised by Pope, the greatest poet of an age before, and his essays in *The Rambler* had already earned him a great reputation.

He had become the mouthpiece of high-Tory, high-Anglican thought and was for long a Jacobite. The tide of his fortunes turning with his *Dictionary*, which appeared in 1754, he was given a pension by George III. Johnson once had a long private conversation with the King, whom he described as a perfect gentleman and as fit to be a king as Charles II or Louis XIV.

Johnson was a man of many prejudices and inconsistencies. A believer in ghosts, in second-sight, in the spiritual importance of customs – he criticized himself severely for once drinking hot coffee on Good Friday – respectful of all sorts of out-dated civil and religious notions, he showed, on the other hand, an extreme scepticism and loved to tear to pieces things told him by other people. Thus he demolished as total nonsense a description of a hurricane in the West Indies and refused absolutely to believe that, at the siege of Gibraltar in 1789 to 1793, the British gunners set fire to French and Spanish ships by using red-hot cannonballs. "Johnson," said Hogarth, "is like King David, he says all men are liars." His prejudices were sweeping. He hated the Scots and the Americans – "I am willing to love all mankind except an American," he once said – and he of course supported George III in the war against the American colonists. He could not either be considered a good judge of the literature of his time, for while he admired Pope and Dryden, he could see nothing in *Gulliver's Travels*, nor in Sterne's *Tristram Shandy*, and never apparently read Fielding's *Tom Jones*. To such works he preferred the dullness of obscure Latin poets and prose writers.

How was it that with his strange appearance and habits, his follies and his prejudices, he was generally regarded as the master of intellectual society in his time? The reasons are many. His extreme opinions were always delivered with a force, a power of reasoning and a readiness of wit which left him the master of the great game of conversation so much enjoyed in that leisurely period. On the whole it was more a battle than a game and Johnson had emerged victorious from so many thousands that his friends, even when they disagreed with him, delighted in the spectacle of his power. His superiority over other learned men, and often men of greater learning than he, lay in the ability of being able immediately to summon up all the powers of his mind: he was able to express himself on any subject with an unusual verbal distinction and felicity. "Sir," said he of a woman preaching, "it is like a dog walking on his hind legs. It is not done well; but you are surprised to find it done at all." In the course of a conversation, a gentleman was referred to who, after one unhappy marriage, had married again. Johnson said at once this represented the triumph of hope over experience.

But there was more in Johnson than a witty conversationalist. He was a man of achievements – his great *Dictionary* and his *Lives of the Poets* were deservedly admired. He was a good scholar in an age which respected scholarships. He was also a representative figure of the eighteenth century and expressed views typical of his time. His opinion that forms of government little influence the happiness of mankind and his dislike of those who sought the prosperity of the State at the expense of the individuals who composed it were widely felt. "Patriotism," he wrote, "is the last refuge of a scoundrel." He wanted stability at home which he associated with monarchy and peace abroad. He mistrusted those who regarded liberty as an end and not as a means. He was full of robust common sense, as many of his best remarks show, and he had a deep hatred of cant. This was a sort of mania with him. Once at the house of Mrs. Thrale, the wealthy, beautiful blue-stocking whom he adored, Mrs. Thrale who, with her dog Presto at her feet had just made a hearty meal, spoke in a piteous tone about a young cousin whose head had been knocked off by a cannon-ball in the American war. Johnson, whose feelings were much aroused by the fact that most of his friends, including Mrs. Thrale, were against the war, exclaimed: "Prithee, my dear, have done with canting. How would the world be worse for it, I may ask, if all your relations were at once spitted like larks and roasted for Presto's supper?" He invariably refused to admit that private conduct was much influenced by public affairs.

Johnson made his mark above all as a great character who had suffered from poverty and neglect and risen triumphant and who was also a man of deep convictions. All his life he had feared going mad and also dying. One evening, when the company had gone, Boswell tactlessly pressed Johnson about the subject of death. Boswell records:

"To my question whether we might not fortify our minds for the approach of death, Johnson answered in a passion: 'No Sir let it alone. It matters not how a man dies, but how he lives. The act of dying is not of importance, it lasts so short a time.' He added with an earnest look: 'A man knows it must be so and submits. It will do him no good to whine.'

"I attempted to continue the conversation. He was so provoked that he said, 'Give us no more of this,' and was thrown in to such a state of agitation that he expressed himself in a way that alarmed and distressed me, showed an impatience that I should leave him and when I was going away called to me sternly, 'Don't let us meet tomorrow'."

His religious convictions made him practise charity. He succoured all in real distress and his house in London was always full of dependants. There was the blind and often tiresome Mrs. Williams, who tried to order his life without the least right to do so; Robert Levet, a penniless and feckless apothecary whom Johnson had brought in from the streets; at times the mother and daughter of an old friend lived on him, and a slut called Polly Carmichael whom Johnson lodged for a long time, he knew not why. Then there was his Negro servant, Frank Barber, to whom he left his money. No wonder there was, as he said to a friend, "anarchy in my kitchen". His friends loved as well as admired him, for in spite of his belligerent nature he had a genius for friendship. "You have always been too good to me," murmured Burke by Johnson's death-bed.

As a thinker and a writer and as a Christian, Johnson may seem far away from the present world. But thanks to Boswell, we are able to live with this intellectual dinosaur as though we conversed with him every day, and enjoyed his intellectual dexterity and knew, behind it all, his courage, his fears and his greatness of spirit. A great man, he called forth a great book. Boswell, not naturally a modest man, said of his *Life of Johnson* that it was "more of a life than most". The view of the world rates it much higher and Lord Macaulay, if he misjudged Boswell, did not misjudge his book when he wrote:

"The life of Johnson is assuredly a great, a very great work. Homer is not more decidedly the first of heroic poets, Shakespeare is not more decidedly the first of dramatists, Demosthenes is not more decidedly the first of orators than Boswell is the first of biographers. He has no second. He has distanced all his competitors so decidedly that it is not worthwhile to place them. Eclipse is first and the rest nowhere."

A VINDICATION OF THE RIGHTS OF WOMAN

MARY WOLLSTONECRAFT

IT WOULD be hard to think of a more important book that has ever been written by a woman than Mary Wollstonecraft's *Vindication*. Not that it is anything much as literature; on the contrary, it is slapdash, high-flown, gushing, and bears all the marks of having been written in haste, with a pen that once started found it hard to stop. But looking back on it in the light of history it shows the indubitable marks of a genuine work of genius, the manifesto which heralded one of the greatest revolutions in human relationships.

The book's full title is *A Vindication of the Rights of Woman*, and in 1792, when it was published, that had a dangerously novel sound. But Mary Wollstonecraft was a woman of ideas, and not in the least afraid of expressing them. There was nothing of the weak, clinging, affectionately submissive female about her: all her life she had been used to standing on her own feet and making her own way in the world. For years she had been the main support of her parents and brothers and sisters, enduring the humiliations of a governess and the near slavery of schoolteaching until at last she had managed to secure a foothold in the world of letters. Under the guidance of a friendly publisher she had come to London, where she succeeded in keeping herself afloat by writing articles for the magazines and doing translation work – something that few women before her time had even attempted, and which most people looked upon as improper to say the least. When she sat down in her dingy and out-of-the-way rooms to write her book, she was in her early thirties, but still possessing the good looks that make her so attractive in Opie's portrait of her. These few facts will be sufficient to indicate that when she wrote about the hardships of woman's life she knew what she was writing about. It was out of her own experience that she made her passionate protest and pointed the way to a better order of things.

What probably impelled her to put pen to paper was the revolutionary changes then being effected in France. The *ancien régime* had fallen and a new constitution was being worked out in Paris, and among its authors was Talleyrand, who had been wont to complain that "one half of the human race" had been excluded from all participation in government. In the new constitution they were drawing up this defect would be remedied, so that even the poorest citizen might have a share in the public administration. But not the citizeness: oh no, to give the franchise to women would never do! "And why not?" was the very pertinent question posed by Miss Wollstonecraft.

The *Vindication* is dedicated to Talleyrand, and in the dedicatory note she appealed to him "as a legislator, whether, when men contend for their freedom, and to be allowed to judge for themselves respecting their own happiness, it be not inconsistent and unjust to subjugate women, even though you firmly believe that you are acting in the manner best calculated to promote their happiness? Who made man the exclusive judge, if women partake with him of the gift of reason?"

Who indeed? We are not told what reply Talleyrand made, if any; and in any case Mary Wollstonecraft did not stay for an answer but made "her pen to dart rapidly along to support what I believe to be the cause of virtue". And let him not think that she is but concerned to ventilate a personal grievance. "I plead for my sex, not for myself. Independence I have long considered as the grand blessing of life, the basis of every virtue; and independence I will ever secure by contracting my wants, though I were to live on a barren heath."

As already suggested, the *Vindication* is a very badly arranged book; so badly that one can hardly avoid the suspicion that its author jotted down in the fury of composition the first idea that came into her head. But it is possible to discover that there are several main themes, to which she recurs again and again. The first that may be picked out is her resentment at the customary subordination of the female sex to the male.

The rights of humanity have been confined to the male line from Adam downwards, she complains bitterly, and for this she is inclined to put the blame very largely on "Moses's poetical story", although she finds it difficult to believe that "few who have ever bestowed a serious thought on the subject can ever have supposed that Eve was, literally speaking, one of Adam's ribs".

"I love my fellow," she confesses, "but his sceptre, real or usurped, extends not to me, unless the reason of an individual demands my homage; and even then, the submission is to reason, and not to man."

In only one respect does man seem to have a natural superiority over woman, his bodily strength, and with some show of reason he may boast of it; but is that any reason why women should be expected to be proud of their weakness? She insists that "woman was not created merely to gratify the appetite of man, or to be the upper servant, who provides his meals and takes care of his linen". The divine right of kings had been swept away; it was surely time that the divine right of husbands, "who are often only overgrown children", should be made to follow suit.

Following upon this, is her protest against women being kept in ignorance and denied proper education. "I wish to see women neither heroines nor brutes," she says in a footnote, "but reasonable creatures." She allows that "the education of women has of late been more attended to than formerly", but even so, "they are still reckoned a frivolous sex, and ridiculed or pitied by the writers who endeavour by satire or instruction to improve them. It is acknowledged that they spend many of the first years of their lives in acquiring a smattering of accomplishments; meanwhile strength of body and mind are sacrificed to libertine notions of beauty, to the desire of establishing themselves – the only way women can rise in the world – by marriage. And this desire making mere animals of them, when they marry they act as such children may be expected to act – they dress, they paint, and nickname God's creatures. Surely these weak beings are only fit for a seraglio! Can they be expected to govern a family with judgment, or take care of the poor babes whom they bring into the world?" Time and again she makes this point, that ignorant mothers make bad mothers, and bad mothers are likely to have poor and weak children. Of course she acknowledges that women who have had their understanding enlarged will not be so ready to display a blind obedience to their husbands. But "blind obedience is ever sought for by power, and tyrants and sensualists are in the right when they endeavour to keep women in the dark, because the former only want slaves, and the latter a plaything".

Mary Wollstonecraft was by no means lacking in feminine attraction, but she resented deeply being looked upon as man's plaything. "I lament that women are systematically degraded by receiving the trivial attentions which men think it manly to pay to the sex, when, in fact, they are insultingly supporting their own superiority. So ludicrous do these ceremonies appear to me that I scarcely am able to govern my muscles when I see a man start with eager and serious solicitude to lift a handkerchief or shut a door, when the *lady* could have done it herself, had she only moved a pace or two."

Elsewhere she remarks sardonically, "I have seldom seen much compassion excited by the helplessness of females, unless they were fair..."

Of course men – some men at least – like their women to be "fragile" and to look up to them for every comfort, and the women make the required response. "In the most trifling dangers they cling to their support, with parasitical tenacity, piteously demanding succour; and their *natural* protector extends his arm, or lifts his voice, to guard the lovely trembler – from what? Perhaps the frown of an old cow, or the jump of a mouse; a rat would be a serious danger. In the name of reason, and even common sense, what can save such beings from contempt – even though they be soft and fair."

This sort of thing aroused Mary Wollstonecraft's intense disgust. She deplored "the sexual weakness that makes woman depend on man for a subsistence, which leads a wife to purr about her husband as she would about any man who fed and caressed her". She knew full well that "men are often gratified by this kind of fondness, which is confined in a beastly manner to themselves; but should they ever become more virtuous, they will wish to converse at their fireside with a friend after they cease to play with a mistress".

Out of her own hard and sometimes bitter experience of life Mary Wollstonecraft protested against the generally held view that a woman need look no further than securing a husband and then obeying him in all things. She was not married until toward the end of her life; and yet from girlhood she had been forced to shoulder the responsibilities of a family. Not all women (she pointed out) manage to get a husband, and some would prefer not to marry even when they could. Then there were innumerable women who were left widows and were faced with the problems of keeping themselves and their children in a world in which the openings for female employment were so few and far between. What could a woman do? She might become a milliner or a mantua-maker, and of course, if she had had some slight education, she might become a governess. ... Even educated gentlewomen, she writes, are sometimes forced into situations in which they are exposed to humiliations and a fall in life. How many women waste away their lives who might have run a farm, managed a shop, and stood erect, supported by their own industry! Women should certainly study the arts of healing and be physicians as well as nurses and midwives. There should be openings in business, so that they would be able to earn their own subsistence and not be driven to marry just for support, or be driven into prostitution.

Nor was this enough. "I may excite laughter," she writes, but "I really think that women ought to have representatives, instead of being arbitrarily governed without having any direct share allowed them in the deliberations of government".

Then there are her views on education, in which she is similarly shown to have been a long way ahead of her time. When she wrote, the vast majority of the nation's children, boys as well as girls, were left in ignorance, and the authorities in Church and State willed that it should be so, since a man who could read and write might be politically dangerous. But Mary Wollstonecraft had no such apprehensions, and in her book she proposed that there should be established in every parish throughout the realm a day-school in which the children of rich and poor, high and low, should be given instruction not only in reading, writing and arithmetic, but in the elements of botany, astronomy and mechanics, natural history, and what she called natural philosophy but what today would be included under the heading of science. Furthermore, the elements of religion, history, anthropology and politics might also be imparted in the form of question and answer. But these pursuits should never be allowed to encroach on the time that should be allotted for gymnastic play in the open air in the "large piece of ground" with which she urged every school should be surrounded.

After the age of nine, boys who would have to earn their livings in the mechanical trades and girls destined for domestic employment should be removed to other schools where they would be given instruction of a special character; in the mornings the two sexes would be taught together, but in the afternoons the girls would attend classes in plain sewing, millinery, et cetera. The young people of superior ability or station in life might go on to schools where they would be taught the dead and living languages, the elements of science, and continue their studies of history and politics on a more advanced scale. These suggestions were revolutionary, and it is not too much to claim that they contain the germ of the secondary modern and grammar schools of our present system.

But the really astounding proposal was that of co-education. "Girls and boys together, I hear some readers ask? Yes."

Very much more could be quoted to good purpose from this extraordinary book, for on almost every page there is a gem of good sense, of pregnant thought and far-reaching reflection buried in the mass of flowing verbiage. But space must be found for her contention that women are human beings just as men are. "Women as well as men," she writes, "ought to have the common appetites and passions of their nature, they are only brutal when unchecked by reason; but the obligation to check them is the duty of mankind, not a sexual duty." She firmly repudiated the idea of the double standard in morality. Morality, she insisted, should rise above sexual differences, and its precepts apply to men and women alike and with equal force.

In its own day the *Vindication* received nothing like the attention it should have done, but later generations of women have found in its pages the ammunition with which they have assailed the age-old fortress of male domination. And experience has proved, and is proving, how right she was when she urged that "would men but snap our chains, and be content with rational fellowship instead of slavish obedience, they would find us more observant daughters, more affectionate sisters, more faithful wives, more reasonable mothers – in a word, better citizens".

ESSAY ON THE PRINCIPLE OF POPULATION

T. R. MALTHUS

AT THE present time the population of the world is estimated at something over three thousand millions. By 1975, according to the statisticians of the United Nations, it will be nearing four thousand millions, and by the end of the century it will be over six thousand millions. In other words, there is taking place what is well called a "population explosion", and the great question is, How are all these people to be fed?

The question is not a new one: ever since men first appeared on this planet they have had a hard struggle to keep alive. But it was never so pressing as now, when the population is increasing at an unprecedented rate. In these circumstances it is not surprising that attention is being redirected to a book, first published in 1798, by an English clergyman, the Rev. T. R. Malthus, in which the problems arising from a rapidly increasing population constantly pressing upon the available food supply are explained and discussed with remarkable force and ingenuity. The book's full title is *An Essay on the Principle of Population as it Affects the Future Improvement of Society*. A completely revised edition appeared in 1803, and this was again revised by Malthus several times before his death.

Malthus was born in 1766 and he lived until 1834. He was the son of a small landowner in Surrey, and on coming down from Cambridge he was ordained in the Church of England and appointed to a curacy at Albury. Whenever he could he took time off to travel on the Continent, and in 1805 he married (very happily) and was made Professor of modern history and political economy at Haileybury, the college near Hertford at which cadets were trained for the East India Company's service. He held this post for the rest of his life.

To begin with, the *Essay on Population* was intended as a reply to certain views that Malthus had heard expressed at his father's house. Malthus senior was an ardent and undiscriminating disciple of Rousseau, and of Rousseau's English disciple, William Godwin. The latter is remembered today chiefly as the father-in-law of Shelley, but in his own day he was famous for his book *Political Justice* (1793), in which he expounded a philosophy of universal benevolence. According to him, men's characters originate in their external circumstances; change these circumstances for the better, and the characters will change likewise, with the result that wars will become ever less frequent, despotism will be abolished, poverty eliminated, crime done away with. Even the passion between the sexes, with all its uncomfortable accompaniments, might be extinguished!

Malthus listened to the arguments and read the book, and came to the conclusion that Godwin's belief in the perfectibility of human society and of man himself was just eyewash. He did not believe a word of it. He scoffed at the idea of inevitable progress, and could find no evidence for the claim that, since human institutions are the source of all evil, by changing them you will set men free to march along the road to perfection. So oppressed was he with a sense of the wrong-headedness of Godwin's theory that he set himself to writing a book to prove it.

On the first page of his *Essay* he tells us what he has in mind. "The principal object of the present essay is to examine the effects of one great cause intimately united with the very nature of man ... the constant tendency in all animated life to increase beyond the nourishment prepared for it." It has been observed by Dr. Franklin (he goes on) that there is no bound to the prolific nature of plants and animals but what is made by their crowding and interfering with each other's means of subsistence. "This is incontrovertibly true. Through the animal and vegetable kingdoms Nature has scattered the seeds of life abroad with the most profuse and liberal hand, but has been comparatively sparing in the room and the nourishment necessary to rear them. The germs of existence contained in this earth, if they could freely develop themselves, would fill millions of worlds in the course of a few thousand years. Necessity, that imperious, all-pervading law of nature, restrains them within the prescribed bounds. The race of plants and the race of animals shrink under this great restrictive law; and man cannot by any efforts of reason escape from it."

Malthus had next to no statistics to go by, but had to form his conclusions on the basis of his (admittedly wide) reading. He thought it safe to conclude that population, when it is unchecked, goes on doubling itself every twenty-five years. The rate of increase of the means of subsistence is more difficult to determine; but in Britain, notwithstanding the great improvements in agriculture, the utmost we can allow is that the produce might be increased every twenty-five

years by an amount equal to what it at present yields. So far as
the earth as a whole is concerned, such an increase is unquestionably
much greater than what any possible exertions of mankind could
effect.

The ultimate check to population appears, then, to be a want of
food. But this ultimate check operates only in cases of actual famine.
There are other checks which are constantly operating with more or
less force in every society, which keep down the number of population to the level of the available means of subsistence. These checks
are of two kinds: preventive (of children being born), and positive
(reducing the number of those who have been born).

Taking the positive check first, these are "extremely various, and
include every cause which in any degree contributes to shorten the
natural duration of human life. Under this head, therefore, may be
enumerated all unwholesome occupations, severe labour and exposure to the seasons, extreme poverty, bad nursing of children,
great towns, excesses of all kinds, the whole train of common diseases and epidemics, wars, plague, and famine".

Preventive checks may be said to be peculiar to man. The increase
in plants and irrational animals is involuntary, but man is a reasoning
animal. Before he gets married and starts a family, he may ask himself such questions as, Will he lower his rank in life and be obliged to
give up his former habits? Does any mode of employment present
itself by which he may reasonably hope to be able to support his
children? Will he be able to transmit to them the same advantages of
education and improvement that he himself has enjoyed? Does he
fear that if he has a large family he will not be able to save them from
rags and squalid poverty, and he will be obliged to apply to the
"sparing hand of Charity" for support? The first of the preventive
checks is, then, restraint from marriage; others in this category are
"promiscuous intercourse, unnatural passions" – we may assume that
here homosexuality is meant – "violations of the marriage bed, and
improper arts to conceal the consequences of irregular connections".
By "improper arts" we may suppose that Malthus has in mind not
only abortion but anything in the nature of contraception.

Perhaps the reader will be surprised at this, since in common
speech "Malthusian" has come to be applied to birth-control practices and the like. But Malthus was never a Malthusian in this sense;
indeed, the very idea of any artificial prevention of the natural result
of sexual intercourse would have filled him with intense revulsion
and disgust. What he advocated was what he calls Moral Restraint,
the first of the "preventive checks" enumerated above.

This sounds, perhaps, as though Malthus were inclined to be cold-blooded, But in fact few economists, few serious writers indeed, have had so much to say about Love, and have said such nice things about it. "Virtuous love," he rhapsodizes, "exalted by friendship, seems to be that sort of mixture of sensual and intellectual enjoyment, particularly suited to the nature of man, and most powerfully calculated to awaken the sympathies of the soul, and produce the most exquisite gratifications. Perhaps there is scarcely a man, who has once experienced the genuine delight of virtuous love, however great his intellectual pleasures may have been, who does not look back to that period as the sunny spot in his whole life, where his imagination loves most to bask, which he recollects and contemplates with the fondest regret, and which he would wish to live over again."

The passion between the sexes is, indeed, one of the principal ingredients of human happiness. "The evening meal, the warm house, and the comfortable fireside, would lose half their interest, if we were to exclude the idea of some object of affection, with whom they are to be shared."

Such happiness is likely to be enhanced if it has to be worked for and waited for. "The passion of love is a powerful stimulus in the formation of character, and often prompts to the most noble and generous exertions; but this is only when the affections are centred in one object, and generally when full gratification is delayed by the difficulties." A man should not embark upon marriage unless and until he is in a position to keep his wife, and any family that may come, in a state of accustomed comfort. "Late marriages taking place in this way would be very different from those of the same name at present, where the union is too frequently prompted solely by interested views, and the parties meet, not unfrequently, with exhausted constitutions. and generally with exhausted affections." At present late marriages are usually effected by men, who prefer to take a young wife when they do marry, with the result that "a young woman without fortune, when she has passed her twenty-fifth year, begins to fear, and with reason, that she may lead a life of celibacy; and with a heart capable of forming a strong attachment, feels, as each year creeps on, her hopes of finding an object on which to rest her affections gradually diminishing, and the uneasiness of her situation aggravated by the silly and unjust prejudices of the world".

If it became the general rule to marry later, "however impatiently the privation might be borne by the men, it would be supported by the women readily and cheerfully". If these, "the more virtuous half of society," could look forward with confidence to getting married when they were twenty-seven or twenty-eight, they would probably much prefer to do so, rather than to be burdened with the cares of a family at twenty-five.

A man's duty is plain: it is merely that he is not to bring beings into the world for whom he cannot find the means of support; and if he marries in the face of the fair probability that he shall not be able to do so, then he is guilty of all the evils which he thus brings upon himself, his wife and his offspring. Clearly it is in his interest, then, to defer marrying until he is in a position to support the children that he may reasonably expect from his marriage. In the meantime he must refrain from gratifying his passions outside wedlock.

"If a man cannot support his children they must starve." Malthus really meant this. He objected to the exercise of private benevolence and the distribution of parish relief that took the edge off what he considered to be the well-deserved penalty of improvidence, and he said so in a way that could not be misunderstood. As a result he was stigmatized as an unfeeling monster.

He was not a monster. In personal character he was kind and considerate, and he had a most sincere desire to improve the condition of the working classes. In his book he advances enlightened proposals for popular education, and the establishment of savings-banks in which people might put their savings against a rainy day and for their postponed marriages. But as a political economist – and he wrote one of the classic works on Political Economy that ranks him with Marx and Ricardo and Mill – he was convinced that there could be no permanent improvement in the lot of the mass of the people until the supply of provisions – the means of subsistence – was made to match the population. As things are (he maintained), the number of consumers more than keeps pace with the increased product of agriculture. This is like setting the tortoise to catch the hare. "Finding, therefore, that from the laws of nature we could not proportion the food to the population, our next attempt should naturally be to proportion the people to the food. If we can persuade the hare to go to sleep, the tortoise may have some chance of overtaking her."

In retrospect, it is easy to see that a good deal of what Malthus maintained was fallacious. He did not allow sufficiently for the unprecedented improvements in agriculture, which enabled a far greater population than ever before to come into existence and flourish. He did not foresee the spread of colonization to Australia and the Canadian prairies and the opening up of the Middle West of America. An immense population lives and grows on lands which in his time were unpeopled wastes and deserts. And yet at root his doctrine is sound. There *are* limits to increased production, even though they have been proved to lie far ahead of where he placed them; and there do not seem to be any limits to the fecundity of the human race. For generations the tortoise has been catching up on the hare, but the hare has not gone to sleep and today is very much awake. Or to express it in the other terminology that he used, the increase in population is pressing on the means of subsistence, and disaster lies ahead. There is nothing about the "population explosion" that we could teach Malthus, but it may well be that he has a good deal to teach *us*.

PRIDE AND PREJUDICE
JANE AUSTEN

JANE AUSTEN was the younger daughter of George Austen, Rector of Steventon, a village in Hampshire, where she was born on 16 December, 1775. She began writing stories at an early age, and liked writing burlesque, nonsense and satire. She lived at Steventon until she was twenty-six and had a placid, uneventful life, leaving home only for short visits to Bath and even rarer visits to London. But out of this small, provincial environment she brilliantly portrayed her own life and times as no other writer has done.

Pride and Prejudice was her first completed work, which she started writing under the title *First Impressions* in 1796, finishing it in August, 1797. Her father was so impressed that he offered it for publication to Thomas Cadell and their disappointment must have been great when he promptly rejected it. Jane Austen then revised a former novel, calling it *Sense and Sensibility*. In 1798–99 she was working on her third novel, *Northanger Abbey*, a satire on the Radcliffian school of romancers, which she sold to Richard Crosby for £10, but he put it in a drawer and left it there for a number of years, eventually reselling it to her in 1816.

In 1801 George Austen retired and the family went to live at Bath. During the next ten years Jane Austen wrote very little. Perhaps she lost heart, having three unpublished novels on her hands. After her father's death in 1805, Mrs. Austen, Jane and her sister Cassandra went to live at Southampton; but it was not until 1809, when settled in Chawton on brother Edward's Hampshire estate, that Jane Austen began once more to take up writing seriously, and after some revisions had *Sense and Sensibility* published at her own expense, with modest success. She then rewrote *First Impressions*, changing it to *Pride and Prejudice*, and during that time, in 1811, also began work on a new novel, *Mansfield Park*, which was completed in 1813, a few months after the publication of *Pride and Prejudice* in January, 1813, and which she sold outright. *Emma* followed and was published by John Murray in December, 1815, and during that year, in failing health, she was at work on her last novel, *Persuasion*. But she was never to see it in print, nor did she live to see the publication of

Northanger Abbey. Both were published in 1817 after her death. Her final work was never finished. It was "Fragment of a Novel", known now as *Sanditon*.

Jane Austen died at the age of 42, on 18 July, 1817, at Winchester where she had gone to receive medical attention and where her memorial window is to be seen in the Cathedral.

Elizabeth, the charming heroine of *Pride and Prejudice*, was the second daughter of Mr. and Mrs. Bennet of Longbourn. Her mother's main object in life was to get her five daughters married. When a single young man of fortune took Netherfield Park, Mrs. Bennet quickly informed Mr. Bennet that "it will be a fine thing for our girls", and that he must call on Mr. Bingley as soon as he comes to the neighbourhood.

Mr. Bennet was therefore among the earliest who waited on the new tenant at Netherfield. Mr. Bingley had brought a party from London for the ball at the Assembly Rooms which included his two sisters, his brother-in-law, Mr. Hurst, and another young man who "soon drew the attention of the room by his fine, tall person, handsome features, noble mien".

It was soon observed, however, that his manner did not conform to his looks, for Mr. Darcy was discovered to be "proud, above his company and above being pleased, also unworthy to be compared with his friend, Mr. Bingley", who was lively and unreserved and danced every dance. Mr. Darcy danced only once with Miss Bingley and once with Mrs. Hurst, and declined to be introduced to any other lady. Once when Elizabeth Bennet had been obliged to sit down owing to the scarcity of gentlemen, Mr. Bingley left the dance to press Mr. Darcy to join in, with Elizabeth as his partner. Elizabeth could not help but hear his reply.

"She is tolerable, but not handsome enough to tempt me; and I am in no humour at present to give consequence to young ladies who are slighted by other men."

Mrs. Bennet's dislike of him was sharpened into resentment by his having slighted one of her daughters. However, Mr. Bingley had danced twice with her elder daughter Jane, and had described her as "the most beautiful creature he had ever beheld", while Mary had heard herself mentioned to Miss Bingley as the most accomplished girl in the neighbourhood.

When an invitation came for Jane to dine at Netherfield, Mrs. Bennet was delighted. It was going to rain, and Jane, obliged to go there on horseback, would surely be asked to stay the night. But poor

Jane was caught in the rain on her way there, and developed such a bad cold that she had to stay for a few days. Elizabeth walked the three miles to see her sister, and Jane was so reluctant to let her go that Miss Bingley invited Elizabeth to remain at Netherfield with her sister.

During her stay there, Mr. Darcy began to see that there was more to Elizabeth's character and looks than he had at first realized. Miss Bingley noticed how often Mr. Darcy's eyes were fixed upon Elizabeth, and, suspecting his increasing admiration for her, she tried to provoke him into showing his dislike of her guest. But "Darcy had never been so bewitched by any woman as he was by her. He really believed, that were it not for the inferiority of her connexion, he should be in some danger."

When Jane was well enough to go downstairs, she received every attention from Charles Bingley, and Elizabeth was amazed at the gallantry of Mr. Darcy, who seemed quite changed.

The two sisters returned home on the day that their father's cousin was expected. Mr. Collins had written to say that he would like to visit them, and that he wished to make every possible amend for the fact of his being next in the entail of the Longbourn estate. He had received ordination at Easter and had been fortunate enough to be distinguished by the patronage of Lady Catherine de Bourgh, "whose beneficence has preferred me to the valuable rectory of this parish". Mr. Collins was an absurd mixture of servility and self-importance, and it was soon realized that his idea of making amends was to marry one of the Bennet girls. His first choice was Jane, but on hearing from Mrs. Bennet that she was about to become engaged, his thoughts turned to Elizabeth. Lady Catherine de Bourgh had condescended to advise him to marry as soon as he could, provided he chose with discretion, and he was sure that his patroness would approve of either young lady.

The next day Mr. Collins accompanied the girls to Meryton to visit their aunt, Mrs. Phillips, who was often visited by the younger girls, Catherine and Lydia. On their way they met one of the officers of the militia regiment recently arrived in Meryton, a Mr. Denny, who introduced them to his friend, Mr. Wickham, who had just accepted a commission in the corps. The party were standing talking together when Darcy and Bingley were seen riding down the street on horseback. They stopped to inquire after Jane's health, and Wickham touched his hat – a salutation which Mr. Darcy just deigned to return. Elizabeth saw both faces change colour and wondered what could be the meaning of it.

She learned part of the answer when next she met Mr. Wickham, who was invited to a party given by Mrs. Phillips, and where he singled out Elizabeth for his attentions. She found him extremely agreeable, and he told her that he had been connected with the Darcy family from infancy. The late Mr. Darcy had been his godfather and he considered him to be the best of men, but this Mr. Darcy had behaved scandalously toward him.

"The Church ought to have been my profession," he said. "I was brought up for the Church, and I should at this time have been in possession of a valuable living, for the late Mr. Darcy bequeathed me the next presentation of the best living in his gift. He thought to provide for me amply, but when the living fell it was given elsewhere." Consequently they had not been on friendly terms. Elizabeth also learned that Lady Catherine de Bourgh was Mr. Darcy's aunt.

When Mr. Bingley gave a ball at Netherfield, Elizabeth hoped to meet Mr. Wickham again, but she was disappointed to learn that he had been "obliged to go to town". During a dance with Mr. Darcy she tried to get him to talk about Wickham, but he refused to do so. Later on Miss Bingley took great pleasure in telling Elizabeth that George Wickham was the only son of the late Mr. Darcy's steward, and that far from using him ill, Mr. Darcy had been remarkably kind to him.

Jane and Mr. Bingley spent most of the evening happily in each other's company, and at supper a delighted Mrs. Bennet talked freely to Lady Lucas on the advantages of such a desirable marriage. Her smug remarks could be heard by everyone, including Mr. Darcy, much to Elizabeth's mortification. For the rest of the evening Elizabeth was attended by Mr. Collins, and had cause to be grateful to her friend, Charlotte Lucas, who often engaged him in conversation, thus giving Elizabeth some relief from his tedious attentions.

The next day Mr. Collins made his declaration to Elizabeth, and Mrs. Bennet was most annoyed at her daughter's rejection of his suit. However, Mr. Collins only suffered from hurt pride, and soon found consolation in the company of Charlotte Lucas, and before he took his leave of them he had become engaged to her. When she heard the news Mrs. Bennet was thoroughly upset, and when Jane heard that Mr. Bingley had left Netherfield "without any intention of returning", Mrs. Bennet's cup of bitterness was full.

Mr. Collins and Charlotte were married soon after Christmas, and the following March Elizabeth accepted an invitation to visit them at Hunsford. She was affectionately received by Charlotte, who appeared to be quite happy and contented, and Mr. Collins's triumph was complete when they were all invited to dine at the Rosings, with Lady Catherine de Bourgh.

Lady Catherine was a large woman with strongly marked features, while her daughter was small, pale and insignificant. Her mother did most of the talking. Elizabeth gave a good account of herself when she had the opportunity, and her ladyship seemed quite astonished that so young a person should give her opinions so very decidedly.

The invitation to the Rosings was repeated twice a week, and at Easter Mr. Darcy came to visit his aunt. Mr. Collins lost no time in going to pay his respects to the visitor and great was the surprise of the womenfolk when he came back accompanied by Mr. Darcy and a Colonel Fitzwilliam, the younger son of Darcy's uncle. When the opportunity presented itself Elizabeth informed Mr. Darcy that her sister had been staying in town these three months. Mr. Darcy was unaware of it.

When next they went to the Rosings, Colonel Fitzwilliam made himself agreeable to Elizabeth, as did Mr. Darcy. After that evening both gentlemen called regularly at the parsonage, and Mr. Darcy often met Elizabeth unexpectedly while she was out walking in the park. One day she met the Colonel and during conversation he told her what good care Mr. Darcy took of his friend Bingley, and that he had saved him from an unfortunate marriage! Elizabeth realized that her informant could only be referring to Bingley's attachment to her sister, Jane.

That evening Elizabeth asked to be excused from going to the Rosings, saying that she had a headache. Mr. Darcy had ruined every hope of happiness for Jane, and she did not wish to see him again. However, Mr. Darcy called to inquire after her health, and despite the fact that she received him coldly he told her how ardently he admired and loved her. She refused his offer of marriage, denouncing him for parting Jane and Bingley, and for his ill-treatment of Wickham.

The next day she received a long letter from Darcy in which he apologized for putting an end to Bingley's attachment to her sister, of "whom he thought from his own observation of her that her feelings for his friend were indifferent". Wickham had refused the living when offered to him, preferring to take instead a settlement of £3,000. He had also persuaded his (Darcy's) sister Georgina, when she was but fifteen years old, that she was in love with him, and an elopement was planned. Fortunately Darcy had arrived in time to stop it. The letter gave Elizabeth much to think about when she returned home to Longbourn.

The militia was leaving Meryton and going to Brighton. Lydia was heartbroken but her spirits were soon revived when she was allowed to accept an invitation to stay in Brighton with her friends, Colonel and Mrs. Forster. Elizabeth had an invitation to spend a holiday in Derbyshire with her aunt and uncle, a Mr. and Mrs. Gardiner. They went to visit Darcy's home, Pemberly, while its owner was away, and Elizabeth was charmed by its beauty. The housekeeper showed them around and surprised Elizabeth by describing her master as being "the sweetest-tempered, most generous boy in the world". Afterwards, when they were viewing the gardens, the owner suddenly arrived in their midst, and a blushing Elizabeth introduced her aunt and uncle, who having heard all about him were surprised to find him so agreeable.

Soon afterwards Darcy took his sister Georgina to visit the Gardiners and Elizabeth found her to be a shy, unassuming girl. Bingley also called and Darcy invited them to dine at Pemberly. Elizabeth once again met Mr. and Mrs. Hurst and Miss Bingley, who jealously noticed Mr. Darcy's anxiety for his sister to get better acquainted with Elizabeth.

The next time Darcy visited the Gardiners, he found Elizabeth alone and in a distressed condition. He was most concerned and she imparted the dreadful news to him that she had just received in letters from Jane. Lydia had run away with Mr. Wickham, her family knew not where they had gone, and, even worse, they were sure they were not married. Mr. and Mrs. Gardiner were out and a servant was dispatched to ask them to return with all speed. Though Darcy was sympathetic, he also appeared to be deep in thought as he paced the room, and when he left Elizabeth doubted if she would ever see him again.

Their return to Longbourn was arranged immediately and Mr. Gardiner promised to assist Mr. Bennet in looking for the guilty pair in London. Wickham had left behind him gaming debts of over £1,000. Mr. Bennet returned with no other news, but two days later a letter from Mr. Gardiner informed them that he had seen Lydia and Wickham. They were not married, but he hoped that it would not be long before they were. An assurance was needed from Mr. Bennet that Lydia would receive her equal share of a legacy of £5,000 after her parents' decease, and during their lifetime an allowance of £100 per annum. He went on to say that Mr. Wickham's circumstances were not as bad as at first believed and there would be a little money over when all his debts were discharged. From this Mr. Bennet realized that Wickham must have received financial help and he wondered how he would ever be able to repay his brother-in-law.

Lydia and Wickham were married and they came to Longbourn on a short visit. Elizabeth learned from her sister that Darcy had attended their wedding. When they had gone, Elizabeth wrote to Mrs. Gardiner asking for the truth of the affair, and her aunt wrote back immediately telling her that Mr. Darcy had found Lydia, and he had paid Wickham's debts, thus enabling his marriage, but at Mr. Darcy's express wish this information must go no further. Mrs. Gardiner finished her letter by saying how much she liked Mr. Darcy, and that all he needed was "a little liveliness which a prudent wife could easily teach him".

When Mr. Bingley returned to Netherfield, he came to visit Longbourn accompanied by a silent and apparently indifferent Mr. Darcy, much to Elizabeth's disappointment. Charles Bingley and Jane became engaged soon afterward, and a day or so later Lady Catherine de Bourgh called expressly to see Elizabeth. She demanded to know if it was true that not only was her sister Jane on the point of being most advantageously married, but that Elizabeth herself would very soon be united to her nephew, Mr. Darcy.

Elizabeth coloured with astonishment, but she declined to answer, and her ladyship was indignant, saying that such a match could never take place. Elizabeth must promise that she would never enter into an engagement with Mr. Darcy, who was already engaged to her own daughter. Elizabeth refused to give any such promise and her ladyship took her leave saying that she was seriously displeased, and that Elizabeth's ambition would never be gratified.

The next time Mr. Darcy came to Netherfield and called at Longbourn with his friend he talked to Elizabeth for a long time. He was annoyed at his aunt's interference and denied that he had ever been engaged to his cousin. His second proposal came soon after, and was this time accepted.

"Happy was the day when Mrs. Bennet got rid of her two most deserving daughters."

Pride and Prejudice is generally considered to be Jane Austen's best work, and in this tale of middle-class provincial family life, comedy reigns supreme. The author's great talent is her ability to make ordinary happenings interesting by her unique, descriptive style. Her character studies of women are particularly perceptive and lifelike, enhancing the youthful gaiety of this work, which is a masterpiece of exact timing and nicely measured understatement.

The heroine has a thoughtful and critical disposition, and incidents occur which deepen her prejudice, while the hero, haughty and patronizing, is humbled by the triumphant femininity of the girl he loves.

Delectable comedy is provided by the quaint and silly Mr. and Mrs. Bennet, the ridiculous cleric Mr. Collins and the formidable snob Lady Catherine de Bourgh, as well as a fascinating gallery of lesser personalities.

IVANHOE

SIR WALTER SCOTT

FROM THE publication of *Waverley*, the first of his novels, in 1814, Sir Walter Scott enjoyed what he himself described as "an unabated course of popularity". In five years he produced nine novels, nearly all of which are still included among the masterpieces of fiction. He was immensely popular, and yet in his heart of hearts he was not satisfied. In all his books he had showed himself a master of Scottish manners, Scottish dialect and Scottish characters, and the great reading public had come to look upon him as a Scottish novelist pure and simple. He rather resented that opinion. He knew that he had it in him to extend his field far beyond the Scottish scene, and he decided to prove it. The result was *Ivanhoe*, published in 1819.

As a historical romance the book at once secured a deservedly high place, and English readers appreciated it all the more because of the absence from it of those tiresome Scotch words and people. It is all English, and the period of its narrative is one rich in English folklore, the period of Robin Hood and his Merry Men in the greenwood, of Friar Tuck and that most romantically ruffianish of English kings, Richard the Lion-Hearted. There are bold knights in it, and some of them are bad as well as bold, and when they are bad they are very, very bad; and there are fair ladies, or rather, there is one who is fair and another who is dark, and whether we prefer the Saxon Rowena to Rebecca the Jewess we must all agree that they are both good as well as beautiful. There is romantic love in it and brutal lust, there are grim scenes of war and rapine, drunken carousals and sick-bed watchings, plotting nobles and the simple-hearted devotion of humble serfs. No wonder that *Ivanhoe* is still among the most often read of Sir Walter's novels.

When the tale opens the year is 1194, just halfway through the reign of Richard I, Coeur-de-Lion, when that "negligent absentee" of a monarch, as Trevelyan calls him, was far away on the Third Crusade, and his brother Prince John was ruling England in his stead. For some months nothing had been heard of the King beyond that on his way back from the Holy Land he had been taken prisoner by his bitter enemies in Austria and was being held captive; and nothing

Among the most successful of historical romancers was Sir Walter Scott, who in more than a score of novels made what had seemed to be the dead past live again. Perhaps the most successful of his "English" novels was *Ivanhoe*, a scene from which – the fierce combat of Ivanhoe with the Norman-French baron Bois-Guilbert in the lists at Ashby – is illustrated *above, right*. Among French practitioners in this field a most prominent place is held by Victor Hugo, who in *Notre Dame de Paris* builds a dramatic tale about the great Gothic church. The most powerful character in the book is the Hunchback Quasimodo, here seen (*left, above*) sporting among the gargoyles. Then another great French master of the historical novel was Alexandre Dumas, who in a series of novels, packed with exciting incident, describes the adventures of the *Three Musketeers (below)*.

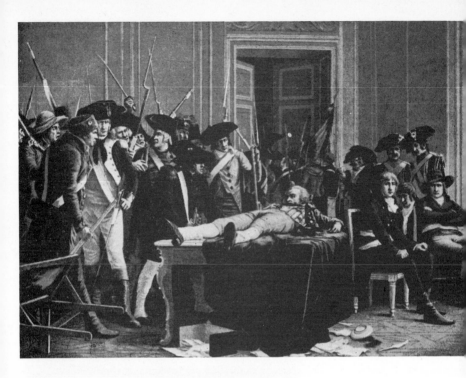

Libraries of books have been written about the French Revolution that began with the Fall of the Bastille on the ever-memorable 14th of July, 1789, but there have been few to rival, in essential truth of representation and intensity of feeling, the book by the struggling Scottish writer Thomas Carlyle that appeared in 1837. So vivid is the fashion in which the dramatic scenes are reported, so intimately portrayed are the characters that move across the death-dominated stage, that generations of readers have been made to feel that they were, and are, actually present as the fires of revolution leaped and roared until they were extinguished by Napoleon's "whiff of grapeshot". (*Above*) Robespierre, the chief architect of the Terror, laid out after being guillotined. (*Left*) Thomas Carlyle as an old man, sitting in the garden of his home at Chelsea.

would have pleased Prince John and his following of self-seeking nobles more than the news that Richard had been done to death in some foreign dungeon. But in fact he had fixed up a deal with his captors, and was actually in England in disguise – a disguise which the reader will have little difficulty in penetrating, and that when the tale is only just getting into its stride.

Like all Scott's novels, *Ivanhoe* is slow in getting started, and half a dozen chapters must be gone through before we reach the first of the novel's peaks of exciting interest. This is the account of the great tournament at Ashby-de-la-Zouch, in which Scott very successfully captures the glamour and glory of the age of chivalry. It was on the second day of the tournament, when those taking part were enlisted in two opposing bodies, that there rode on to the field "a champion in black armour, mounted on a black horse, large of size, tall, and to all appearance powerful and strong, like the rider by whom he was mounted". This knight bore on his shield no device of any kind, and for a time he took very small part in the struggle, beyond beating off with apparently the greatest of ease the few attacks that were directed against him. But when the leader of the party to which he had attached himself became of a sudden hard bested, the attitude of the "Black Knight", as he is styled, was transformed. Setting spurs to his horse, he came to his assistance like a thunderbolt, and within a few moments the bluff Norman baron Front-de-Boeuf got such a crack on the head from the Black Knight's sword that horse and man rolled together on the ground; and the bulky Saxon thegn, Athelstane of Coningsburgh, who was assailing the leader from the other side, was felled by a mighty blow delivered with his own battle-axe that the Black Knight had snatched from his hand. After which the conqueror returned calmly to his own end of the lists, and remained there until the tourney was over for the day, when without attracting any notice he turned his horse's head and rode silently away into the forest. The reader will know that the Black Knight is none other than Coeur-de-Lion, and he will be thinking that Prince John must have been pretty slow not to know it likewise.

The man whom the Black Knight rescued on that "memorable field, one of the most gallantly contested tournaments of that age", was also nameless to begin with, bearing on his shield nothing more than the device of a young oak tree pulled up by the roots, with the Spanish word *Desdichado*, "disinherited," underneath it. Here again the reader who knows his novelist will be quick to recognize him, for the "Disinherited Knight" is the hero after whom the book is named.

Ivanhoe (we are told) was the son of Cedric, one of the Saxon nobility who had managed to retain some of their possessions and privileges in a land that had been overrun by the Norman conquerors. His seat was at Rotherwood, in the Don valley in Yorkshire, where he lived in rustic pomp amid his retainers, and indulged in foolish dreams of a restoration of the Saxon monarchy that had gone down on the fatal field of Hastings, more than a century before. Cedric the Saxon, as he was universally styled, had the wardship of a beautiful young Saxon, the Lady Rowena, who was of higher blood than even he pretended to, being descended from King Alfred himself, and he schemed to marry her to Athelstane of Coningsburgh, whom Cedric envisaged as the future monarch when the Saxons should have ejected the Normans and declared their independence. Rowena did not share these proposals in the least; and so far from being dazzled by the prospect of an alliance with Athelstane, who was a big, brave, lazy and gluttonous lump, she had set her heart on marrying Cedric's son Wilfred, named Ivanhoe, after the manor with which he had been invested. Cedric was deeply incensed against his son, the more so when the youth offered his services to King Richard and set off with him on the Crusade.

Like his royal master, Ivanhoe came back to England by stealth, and in the opening chapters of the book he is disguised as a palmer, or pilgrim, returning from the Holy Land. As such he took part in the tournament at Ashby, and in the successive combats covered himself with glory. His identity remained undisclosed until he was called upon to receive from the Queen of the Tourney, the Lady Rowena, the chaplet of honour which his valour had so richly deserved. The marshals obliged him to remove his helmet, and Rowena recognized him with a faint shriek. Then she recovered her composure and placed the chaplet on his drooping head. "I bestow on thee this chaplet, Sir Knight, as the meed of valour assigned to this day's victor," she said; "and upon brows more worthy could a wreath of chivalry never be placed!" The knight, now revealed as Ivanhoe, knelt to kiss his lady's hand, and then suddenly collapsed at her feet. It transpired that he had been grievously wounded in the combat in which he had so greatly distinguished himself.

Ivanhoe would have died but for the skilled attention that was given him by a beautiful young Jewess, Rebecca, daughter of Isaac of York. She and her father had been befriended by Ivanhoe some days earlier; and now, when Ivanhoe fell to the ground, she bade her servants lift him up and carry him to their lodgings. Arrived there, she examined his wound, and applied to it a "healing balsam" that she kept in her private medicine-chest. For "the beautiful Rebecca had been heedfully brought up in all the knowledge proper to her nation", and "her knowledge of medicine and of the healing art had been acquired under an aged Jewess, the daughter of one of their most celebrated doctors, who loved Rebecca as her own child. . . ."

Rebecca is the most interesting as she is the most original character in the novel, and in drawing so uniformly favourable a portrait of the young Jewess, Scott delivered a most powerful blow at anti-Jewish prejudice. "The figure of Rebecca", he writes, "might indeed have compared with the proudest beauties of England. Her form was exquisitely symmetrical, and was shown to advantage by a sort of Eastern dress, which she wore according to the fashion of the females of her nation. Her turban of yellow silk accorded well with the darkness of her complexion. The brilliancy of her eyes, the superb arch of her eyebrows, her well-formed aquiline nose, her teeth as white as pearl, and the profusion of her sable tresses, which, arranged each in its own little spiral of twisted curls, fell down upon as much of a lovely neck and bosom as a simarre (tunic) of the richest Persian silk, exhibiting flowers in their natural colours embossed upon a purple ground, permitted to be visible – all these constituted a combination of loveliness which yielded not to the most beautiful of the maidens who surrounded her."

This was as she appeared at the Ashby tournament, and Prince John, who was a connoisseur of women, exclaimed that "yonder Jewess must be the very model of that perfection whose charms drove frantic the wisest king that ever lived!" Unfortunately for Rebecca, it was not long-dead Solomon with whom she had to deal but the fiercely passionate Brian de Bois-Guilbert, one of the military monks of the Order of Knights Templars. This bold ruffian carried her off to the castle of Torquilstone, where he insulted her with his professions of love. She spurned his advances, and when he refused to accept her jewels and a princely ransom, exclaimed, "What wouldst thou have of me if not my wealth? We can have nought in common between us; you are a Christian, I am a Jewess. Our union were contrary to the laws alike of the Church and the synagogue."

"It were so indeed," replied the Templar, with a laugh. "Wed with a Jewess! *Despardieux!* Not if she were the Queen of Sheba! And know besides, sweet daughter of Zion, that were the most Christian king to offer me his most Christian daughter, I could not wed her. It is against my vow to love any maiden, otherwise than *par amours*, as I will love thee. I am a Templar. Behold the cross of my holy order."

"Darest thou appeal to it," rejoined the spirited girl, "on an occasion like the present?"

Very obviously the Templar dared. "Thou art the captive of my bow and spear," he reminded her, "subject to my will by the laws of all nations; nor will I abate an inch of my right, or abstain from taking by violence what thou refusest to entreaty or necessity."

"Stand back," cried Rebecca; "stand back, and hear me ere thou offerest to commit a sin so deadly! My strength thou mayest indeed overpower, for God made women weak and trusted their defence to man's generosity. But I will proclaim thy villainy, Templar, from one end of Europe to the other. . . ." Scornfully the villain remarked that "loud must be thy voice if it is heard beyond the iron walls of this castle", and the Jewess prepared to fling herself out of the window into the moat.

Rebecca was saved for the present, however, for the Templar was called away to take his part in the defence of the castle when it was besieged by a horde of outlaws, merry men of the greenwood, led by Robin Hood and the Black Knight. Scott's description of the siege and capture of the castle shows his powers of martial narrative at their best, but justice cannot be done to it in a paragraph or two. We follow the Templar as he snatches up Rebecca and bears her off through the disordered ranks of the attackers to the stronghold of the Templars at Templestowe. There, still besotted by his lust for her, he repeats his offers of an alliance: what if he were expelled from his order? He would carve out a principality of his own in the Orient, and Rebecca should reign there as queen. . . . Again the Jewess spurns his approaches, and nothing that Bois-Guilbert can do may preserve her from being put on trial for witchcraft, since not only had she saved the life of Ivanhoe by magic arts but she had bewitched this most noble knight of the Temple. . . . She is sentenced to be burnt alive at the stake, but one avenue of escape lies open: she may claim, through a champion of her choice, to defend her innocence in the lists. Bois-Guilbert is ordered to serve as the accusers' champion, and at the last moment Ivanhoe appears to champion the Jewess. They fight, and both fall. Ivanhoe is quickly on his feet and points his sword at the Templar's throat. But Bois-Guilbert is already dead, "victim to the violence of his own contending passions". So Rebecca was saved from the stake by what that superstitious assembly concluded was indeed the judgment of God.

And then, of course, she married Ivanhoe? "The character of the fair Jewess" – did Scott forget that he had given her sable tresses and a dark complexion? – "found so much favour in the eyes of some fair readers, that the writer was censured because, when arranging the fates of the characters of the drama, he had not assigned the hand of Wilfred (Ivanhoe) to Rebecca, rather than the less interesting Rowena. But, not to mention that the prejudices of the age rendered such a union almost impossible, the author may, in passing, observe, that he thinks a character of a highly virtuous and lofty stamp is degraded rather than exalted by an attempt to reward virtue with temporal prosperity...."

Well, that is as it may be, and even Scott would seem to have been not altogether satisfied with his lofty line of argument, for on his last page he remarks that "it would be inquiring too curiously to ask whether the recollection of Rebecca's beauty and magnanimity did not recur to Ivanhoe's mind more frequently than the fair descendant of Alfred might altogether have approved".

THE DIARY OF SAMUEL PEPYS

SAMUEL PEPYS died in 1703 at the age of seventy, in his country house at Clapham where he had been retired for many years, leaving behind him the memory of a much respected great official of the Crown who could claim to be one of the finest organizers who had ever served the British Navy, a patron of music, a President of the Royal Society in 1684, a friend of John Evelyn and of Dryden.

Born of an ancient family of yeomen which had risen into the ranks of the gentry in the county of Huntingdon, Samuel Pepys's father, a younger son who had been forced to go into trade, was a tailor in London. Fortunately for Samuel Pepys's career, he was related to the Montagues of Huntingdon. Edward Montague, a friend of Oliver Cromwell, became an Admiral of the Commonwealth Fleet after the Civil Wars, and once Samuel Pepys came down from Cambridge, to which university he had won scholarships, Edward Montague made him his private secretary and manager of his household affairs. He had also secured him what was a minor job in the Civil Service at that time, a clerkship of the Exchequer.

Montague, on Cromwell's death, quickly decided to work for the return of the monarchy. In May, 1660, he himself sailed to Holland to fetch Charles II back to England and took with him his young secretary. The King was grateful and Montague shortly after was made a Knight of the Garter and later the Earl of Sandwich. His young cousin protégé secured an office as Clerk of the Acts, in effect a post on the Board of Admiralty, an immense sudden climb toward power, for it was the equivalent of a permanent Under-Secretaryship in the modern Civil Service. It was also a climb toward wealth, for Pepys, like all officials of the time, used his position, in which he could grant favours to high and low, to enrich himself. He accumulated a considerable fortune by means which were then considered fair. If he made money out of his office, he gave good service and very quickly came to be known as one of the ablest of Charles II's officials. With the constant patronage of the Duke of York, afterward James II, a man with a strong concern for the Navy, Pepys successfully introduced better systems of supply of materials for the King's ships and fought hard in favour of the trained naval officer against the amateur.

After the disgraceful event in 1667 when most of the fleet was burnt by Dutch ships who entered the Medway, more regular funds were obtained for the Navy and the Duke and Pepys could work more effectively. Pepys was Minister for the Navy, in effect, under James II, but the glorious Revolution of 1688, with James II forced to flee to France and the accession of William and Mary, ended the official career of Pepys.

The son of a Puritan who had, as a schoolboy, witnessed and approved the execution of Charles I, he was in later life accused of Popery and in 1690 was briefly imprisoned on a charge of Jacobite plotting. Such small reverses, however, were common to public men of that time and the career of Samuel Pepys was a most successful one on the whole, showing the way in which, with a little luck, a man of undoubted ability but born without material advantages could rise to the top in Stuart times.

But, of course, Samuel Pepys is not for us "a much respected figure"; he is among the immortals, for a reason quite other than his contemporaries would have imagined. He left, on his death, a valuable library of books to his old college in Cambridge and among them were six volumes of manuscript bound in vellum, a diary written between 1659 and 1669. In 1818, the head of Magdalene decided that the Diary ought to be published, no doubt because John Evelyn's Diary had not long ago appeared and been welcomed by the critics.

Pepys's Diary was written in a very small hand and in a comparatively simple system of shorthand invented in 1641, so simple indeed that Pepys, who did not intend that anyone about him should be able to read his Diary, had introduced various Latin, French and Portuguese words to make it harder to read certain passages he particularly wanted unread. The Diary took some time to decipher. Those who had access to the full text before the first edition of the Diary was published in a very abbreviated form in 1825 realized that what appeared before their eyes was something far more than an interesting record of public affairs. The Diary revealed a human being almost uncomfortably fully, who describes himself and his doings in a garrulous, racy prose with an absence of reticence such as no autobiography has ever equalled. In Victorian times it was quite understandable that the first editor should acknowledge that he had cut out details which were "too minute" and it was not until the end of the century that the nine-volume edition of the Diary, a reasonably complete version, appeared.

Now Pepys's Diary is in no way a confession, a work in which the author lays the accent, deliberately, on his frailties which he wishes

to excuse or explain. It is, on the contrary, an honest record of day-to-
day life during the ten years 1659–69, recording his triumphs at the
Admiralty, his struggle to produce order out of chaos in naval affairs,
political and social intrigues in which he participated, his great
pleasure in his increasing prosperity – in the fine clothes he was able
to buy himself and his wife, in the fine meals he delights to give his
friends and useful acquaintances, in his first coach and pair. We meet
an unusually vigorous man, content to live in his time, and what is
unusual a man who is, in spite of occasional moods, happy although
ambitious. Not a brave man physically, Pepys remained at his post
throughout the terrible summer of 1665 when the great plague
struck London. Being constantly in touch with the Court and with
the Royal officials he was well aware of the terrible ravages of the
plague which in one week in August killed over 7,000 people. He
once took a Hackney-carriage and the driver was suddenly stricken
with the disease; he stumbles on a corpse in an alley at night and
vows not to go out again in the dark. "Lord," he remarks, "how
everybody looks, and discourses in the street are of death, and
nothing else, and few people going up and down, and the town is
like a place distressed and foresaken." Great and important matters
concerning the Fleet occupy his mind during the Plague period as
they do during the Great Fire of London which took place in the
following year, 1666. Pepys is fascinated by this monstrous event and
as the fire gradually approaches his own house he sends his gold and
best goods to the house of a friend in Bethnal Green. His descriptions
are dramatic, exact and written by someone with a superb literary
eye.

On the first day of the fire, 2 September, he records that some of
his maids sitting up late last night to get things ready for the next
day's eating, called him up about three in the morning to tell us of
a great fire which they saw in the city. All that first morning and
afternoon he busied himself with watching the fire; he went to see
the King and suggested that houses should be pulled down in front
of the growing flames; he went to the Lord Mayor who described
himself as powerless to do anything at that moment, such was the
panic. Later in the evening he writes:

> So near the fire as we could for smoke; but all over the Thames, with
> our faces in the wind, you were almost burnt with a shower of fire
> drops. This is very true; houses were burnt by these drops and flakes of
> fire, three or four, nay, five or six houses, one for another. When we
> could endure no more upon the water, we to a little alehouse on Bank-
> side, over against the Three Cranes, and there stayed till it was night

almost, and saw the fire grow, and as it grew darker, appeared more and more, and in corners and upon steeples, and between the churches and houses, as far as we could see up the hill of the city, in a most horrid malicious bloody flame, not like the fine flame of an ordinary fire.

Pepys's passion for music, stronger even than his passion for the theatre, was first aroused by his Puritan father who taught him to play the violin. Pepys, we see, leaves the King and great business to go home at midday and before returning to the office sings catches in his garden with friends and with others, usually female ones, in the arbours of Vauxhall gardens (Fox-Hall in the Diary) at night. There is intense pleasure to be gained from the Diary simply because it enables one to escape into the gay, highly coloured world of the Restoration.

But the abounding fascination of the Diary lies in the extraordinary candid, self-revelations of this ambitious, able, sensitive man who, however, could take advantage of a poor young woman, come to demand arrears in her husband's pay, to seduce her. Women were at least, during the ten years of the Diary, Pepys's great temptation and relaxation, taking the place, as it were, of hunting or other field sports. Only a couple of days after the Great Fire, when he obviously had many pressing household cares, including the repatriation of his valuables, Pepys could indulge in two love affairs in one day – in the morning *tout ce que je voudrais* (all I want) with a certain Betty Martin and in the afternoon with a Mrs. Bagwell, the widow of a naval carpenter.

He is tireless in his amours, and in addition to his many seductions he never ceases to fondle and kiss young women of every kind on whom he can lay his hands. His passion for women is not merely gross, although gross it is also. One of his favourite diversions is gazing at women. At a play, he sits next to Mrs. Palmer, subsequently Lady Castlemain, one of Charles II's mistresses, and as he writes "filled my eyes with her, which did much please me". Church was a great occasion for gazing, and at the French Protestant church in London he notes, "much pleased with the three sisters of the parson, very handsome, especially in their noses, and sing prettily". Sometimes in his own church he "entertained myself with my perspective glass up and down the church by which I had the great pleasure of seeing a great many fine women and what with that and sleeping I passed away the time until the sermon was done".

Strangely enough, Pepys with all this shows himself something of a Puritan. He despises women who yield to him too easily and prizes modesty even in his victims. He made it clear quite candidly that he considers licentious behaviour inexcusable when it causes public scandal and, for instance, blames his patron, the Earl of Sandwich, for a liaison with a well-known whore. He frequently deplores the conduct of Charles II for doing precisely what he does himself. He criticizes sometimes a new play for being "very smutty" and excuses himself, even in his Diary, for reading a French book which he describes as "lewd and bawdy" because "it is not amiss for a sober man once to read over such a book to inform himself in the villainy of the world". Incidentally, he records that he burnt this book.

Pepys married Elisabeth Le Marchant, the daughter of a French Huguenot, shortly after he left Cambridge – a love match and an act of great lack of worldly sense since she and he were both penniless. It was a love match from the start and, until his wife died on 16 November, 1669, the marriage was based on mutual love and liking. His wife was exceedingly handsome and Pepys was, quite without cause, liable to be insanely jealous of any male acquaintances. She was decidedly impractical, and a bad household manager, for which Pepys frequently quarrelled with her, once indeed blacking her eye and kicking the cook. He treated her like a child, and was sometimes mean with her, sometimes generous, particularly the latter during the last few years of the Diary when his fortune was considerable. He writes:

> "This evening my wife did with great pleasure show me her stock of jewels, increased by the ring ... and, with this and what she had, she reckons that she hath about £150's worth of jewels of one kind or another; and I am glad of it, for it is fit that the wretch should have something to content herself with."

The phrase "my wife, poor wretch" is one of the best known in the Diary. It's a complex phrase, implying that Pepys felt some guilt about his neglect of his wife and his infidelities, but on the whole it means rather "my little wife" than any notion of Elizabeth being a wretch. For once again one can observe in these years, 1659–69, when we know the real Pepys, the two, apart from having the same interests in getting on in the world together and growing richer, clearly spent some of their best moments together. Over and over again, Pepys expresses his "mighty contentment" with evenings spent with "his poor wife" and refers to the long and laughing conversations they frequently hold together. Their violent quarrels were always quickly made up. No, "always" is wrong. Pepys managed to conceal ninety per cent of his infidelities and his wife was mainly jealous of various actresses and singers with whom Pepys's relations were not more than sentimental. But, once, she discovered him undressing and fondling her young maid, known as Deb in the Diary, of whom Pepys saw and remained fond long after she had been dismissed in disgrace from the house. But after this misadventure, Pepys suffered many weeks of fears that his wife would leave him, their marriage be broken, and he exposed to the ridicule of the world.

Pepys loved writing this Diary and on the 31 May, 1669, it is with immense regret that he states that his eyesight is such that he can no longer keep his "journall".

"And thus ends all I doubt I shall ever be able to do with my own eyes in the keeping of my journall. And so I betake myself to that course, which is almost as much as to see myself go into my grave: for which, and all the discomforts that will accompany my being blind, the good God prepare thee."

It turned out that he was unduly pessimistic about his eyes, but, no matter, the Diary had had its end. People had been much puzzled as to why it was ever written in such a form as to include incidents which undoubtedly put him in such a bad light. Indeed, the extreme frankness has made experts feel sure that Pepys never intended that anyone but himself should see the Diary. It is possible that when he died and bequeathed his library and his bound diaries to Cambridge, he may have given instructions that it was never to be published and that these instructions were somehow forgotten or overlooked. But there is no positive evidence of this and the hypothesis is possible that, on the contrary, Pepys was a broad-minded man and quite willing that his Diary should appear at a decent interval after his death. It is even possible that he surmised that it would be the cause of his name and nature being more famous to us than almost anybody else in his time.

For just as Boswell's *Life of Johnson* is unique as a biography, so is Pepys's journal unique as a self-revelatory document. Montaigne, in a more circumspect and intellectual way, revealed himself very frankly in his *Essays* and the man interested in human nature can find more about the real nature of man in Montaigne and Pepys than in any other works of literature. In Pepys's journal we have a faithful record of ten years of the life of a man who is at once typical and extraordinary. He was near what one can call the average man in his love of money, pleasure and excitement, his desire of advancement, his joy in success, his promises to himself to mend his ways and his constant breaking of them, in a good deal of commonsense, in dominating whoever is weaker than himself, and in decent loyalty to his family and his employers. He is far above average in the strength of his animal instincts, in his diligence and capacity to work, in his mental development and in his sensibility above all to music. All told, Pepys emerges from his Diary not only as a rare phenomenon in literature of someone who has told almost the whole truth about himself, but as a basically likeable and endearing character. Thank God, we can say, for Samuel Pepys.

SCARLET AND BLACK

STENDHAL

"He is a type of mentality much more than a man of letters. He cannot be reduced to a writer." (Paul Valery).

THE PARIS newspapers dismissed Stendhal's sudden death in 1842 with a three-line note of the facts – he had a seizure in the street one evening, was carried into a shop and then, a friend chancing by, was taken home where he died in the early hours of the morning. Only three friends attended the funeral. Yet this classic writer was perhaps the world's finest analyst of the heart and its passions, an area of man's experience that it had long been the pride of French literature to explore and elucidate.

Henri Beyle – known as Stendhal, a pseudonym (one of the fifty or so he used) taken from the name of a small German town – has a reputation now which compensates easily for the almost total neglect of his contemporaries during his lifetime. He always said that he would not be understood before 1880, and he used to imagine he was writing not for his own times, which he considered insensitive, prejudiced and intellectually limited, but for the twentieth century and for the generations of enlightened people to come. He was at a disadvantage, his feelings, his judgments, his attitudes of mind were all in advance of his time, he was a realist in an age of romantics. Today most critics agree that Stendhal – who was closer in feeling to the eighteenth century even than to the nineteenth, born into the liberalism of Rousseau, brought up on the glories of Napoleonic conquest, and in addition a free-thinker – was in tone and treatment the first truly "modern" novelist; and most great writers of the last hundred years have acknowledged him as a master and spoken of their debt to his work.

Henri-Marie Beyle was born in Grenoble in 1783, only six years before the storming of the Bastille. His father was a successful provincial lawyer. His mother died when he was seven and by his treatment in the next few years at home the boy was inspired with an intense hatred for his father that stayed with him all his life. At sixteen Henri went to a post at the War Ministry obtained by a powerful cousin, and he was subsequently engaged in most of Napoleon's campaigns – in Italy, Germany, Russia and in Austria. He was seventeen in 1800, Napoleon was moving to the height of his power, and all was glory and grandeur . . . until the Emperor's defeat in 1814 deprived Henri of official favour for a while. The next fifteen years he has summed up himself as consisting of "travel, great and terrible loves, consolation in writing". He retired to Italy and began to write books – the first were on the history of painting, on travel and on music. Then came an impressive half-psychological half-philosophic study – *On Love*, 1821 – and after its publication he visited England to write a comparison of the merits of *Racine and Shakespeare*.

Though one or two fellow-authors recognized the qualities of Stendhal's writing, these books were largely ignored. His next work was a novel, *Armance*, where he first brought his brilliant powers of analysis to bear on personal motives and social behaviour. This was in fact a private campaign he engaged in against society, a campaign on behalf of, in particular, the under-privileged individual driven to struggle against all the corruptions and villainies that money and power are able to put in the way of his advancement. *Scarlet and Black*, the second novel, published in the autumn of 1830, is the most forceful statement of Stendhal's view of this conflict between the poor man of talent and a society that seems specially designed to keep from him profits and pleasures enjoyed by those of noble birth.

The revolution of 1830 brought Stendhal back into State service, this time as French Consul at Trieste for a very short time and then at Civita Vecchia, where he stayed until, in 1841, a stroke left him unable to fulfil his duties and he asked to be recalled. Two more strokes followed with an interval of only a few months; the third was fatal and he died on the 23 March, 1842. On the headstone of his grave in the cemetery of Montmartre were, inscribed the words he had written as his own epitaph:

Arrigo Beyle, Milanese
Visse, scrisse, amo.

(Henri Beyle, of Milan; he lived, he wrote, he loved.)

Stendhal wrote several books during his last years in the diplomatic service. They include two more novels (*The Charterhouse of Parma* and *The Abbess of Castro*), a number of short stories and a general work, *Memoirs of a Tourist*. He also left a number of manuscripts, in the main autobiographical, some of which were edited and published many years after his death – a *Diary*, the *Memoirs of an Egotist*, and *The Life of Henri Brûlard* (a thin disguise for Henri Beyle).

Scarlet and Black is Stendhal's masterpiece and fully illustrates his genius. This novel, of which the plot came from an incident in the police reports, is a magnificent picture of the period and at the same time a deeply moving study of the feelings of a young man of talent and ambition, born to low estate, who at every turn is blocked by the built-in injustices of the society of his day.

Julien Sorel, a carpenter's son in the small provincial town of Verrières, near Besançon, attracts the notice of a local abbé because of his prodigious memory for Latin. Through the abbé's influence Julien becomes the tutor to the children of the Mayor. Julien is a young man of powerful emotions but little tact, calculating but generous, honest in his feelings but careful not to let them show as he is always concerned with the impression he is making on others. He sees that the accident of birth opens or closes all doors in the world and he discovers that a little hypocrisy in the hands of a clever man can go a very long way. He harbours a deep and bitter resentment about his lowly station in life and Stendhal gives us the following view of Julien's first entry into the Mayor's wealthy entourage:

". . . he felt nothing but loathing and abhorrence for the distinguished company into which he had been admitted, though he only sat at the humblest end of the table – which may help to explain his abhorrence and loathing."

However, the Mayor's beautiful and virtuous wife, Madame de Rênal, sadly neglected by her silly, pompous husband, soon finds a strange pleasure in the company of this sensitive and intelligent young man who has now joined their household. After her husband has treated him with considerable contempt, Julien regards it as a point of honour, and decides he owes it to his pride in his own exceptional gifts, to make advances to Madame de Rênal. He feels revenge is his right, and before long, in spite of her endless moral misgivings, she becomes his mistress.

After some storms and stresses in their relationship Julien begins to love Madame de Rênal seriously. She is in fact his ideal woman and this liaison is just what both his nature and his ambition require. He tells himself ecstatically – "she is of noble birth and I am a workman's son, but she loves me all the same." At times Madame de Rênal is a little indiscreet, nevertheless; an anonymous letter to the

Mayor denounces the liaison and says it is the talk of the district. Madame de Rênal succeeds in calming her husband's jealousy but Julien is sent off to a seminary, thanks once again to the influence of the abbé. This section of the novel concerned with Julien's stay in the seminary is written with exquisite irony, for it is here, living with the clergy when their defences are down, that he learns how necessary and effective dissimulation always is.

Julien is aflame with desire for distinction and success, though he knows all the social dice are loaded against him and his class. He realizes that one of the only avenues to power available for a commoner is offered by the Church and he decides to use it for his purpose. Beneath a cloak of piety he quickly wins the trust of the Director of the seminary, and when this pious man is himself promoted to Paris, Julien is offered a post as secretary to one of the most powerful men in the state, the Marquis de la Mole. Here he blossoms rapidly into a successful diplomatic aide.

Julien has now acquired some experience and social polish; after a time in Paris he discovers that the Marquis's daughter Mathilde, a girl of fierce pride in her class and its values, has fallen desperately in love with him. The treatment of this turn in the story is typical of Stendhal's irony: nothing is ever either as simple or as complex as it appears to be – he shows us the many-sidedness of motives, the frequent contradictions in behaviour and how natural it is for us all to be tortuous and straightforward at one and the same time. Julien is not at first attracted by Mathilde and when she makes advances to him suspects a trap, planned by his well-born rivals and aimed at making an utter fool of him. He therefore evades her. Mathilde is terrified she has made a mistake and chosen a coward, so she challenges Julien to climb to her bedroom in broad moonlight. Julien feels his honour is now at stake and accepts . . . but he goes armed, expecting an ambush. His fears are groundless, Mathilde's feelings are justified by this proof of his courage and she becomes his mistress. The Marquis, informed by his daughter that she is pregnant and intends to marry Julien come what may, reluctantly agrees to accept this brilliant commoner into the family to avoid open scandal.

At this juncture, before he has announced this alliance which he hates but cannot avoid, the Marquis receives a letter from Madame de Rênal accusing Julien of being an adventurer and of seducing her. Julien is just enjoying the realization of his lifelong ambitions – he has been given a title and a fortune in property and been made an officer in the Hussars. When told of the letter he feels that his honour requires him to destroy his betrayer; he hurries to Verrières resolved to shoot Madame de Rênal but the face of the woman he had once loved so dearly makes him feel he can never carry out his design. Standing only a few feet behind Madame de Rênal's pew where she is praying fervently, his hand trembles at the thought of what he wanted to do . . .

"At that moment, the young clerk who was serving at Mass rang the bell for the Elevation of the Host. Madame de Rênal bowed her head, which for an instant was almost entirely hidden by the folds of her shawl. Julien was no longer able to see her plainly. He fired a shot at her with one pistol and missed her. He fired a second shot; she fell."

Madame de Rênal is discovered to be merely wounded and she recovers in a few days, but Julien has been arrested and is put on trial. Madame de Rênal now repents her action in sending the letter and does her utmost to save Julien, whom she still loves. The Marquis's daughter also devotes herself to buying his pardon. All the possible influences of the society and privilege he has always so much hated are brought to bear on the judge and the jury to acquit this would-be murderer – but this time privilege does not work as it should; Julien is condemned and dies on the guillotine.

Though primarily a study of the motives of passion (asked once what he was, Stendhal answered "an observer of the human heart") this strange love story is based on class feeling. There is a tense current of political unrest running through the book. Julien is by nature passionate and honest, but the corruption of society and church forces him into hypocrisy – even his sincere loves are falsified.

In all those stormy years he had passed in the field both of battle and diplomacy Stendhal had had a number of unhappy love affairs. His friend, Prosper Mérimée (author of Carmen), said of him: "I have never known him not in love, or not believing himself to be." It is to his lack of success in love perhaps that we owe the penetrating irony of his observation in both the political and psychological areas of this novel of manners. It has a most distinctive flavour – double-edged and ambivalent, the reader feels he is running with the hounds as well as the hare. "A writer should be romantic in his ideas but classical in his style," said Stendhal, and he created for us Julien Sorel who is as clever, ambitious, courageous and successful in society and in love as any hero of romance, but who is presented with such clarity and such a dry, analytic precision that a mere account of an incident of passionate revenge has been turned into a classical masterpiece of ironic storytelling.

Added to his scintillating handling of the material of his story is the glory of Stendhal's style – so true that you feel the author is enchantingly present on every page. He was the first great exponent of a colloquial, intimate, wholly genuine style, a style that has an effervescent spontaneity, simple charm, profundity without pretence, a touch of delicious impertinence in its constant irony with no fine phrases or heroics but an unfailing ring of truth. "I do not admire the style now in fashion, I have no patience with it," he wrote of the Romantics. "I see but one rule: *to be clear*. If I am not clear, all *my world* crumbles to nothing. . . ." Stendhal is one of the few writers of all time who never use a superfluous word; he is the despair of many readers, who find they cannot skip a line or they miss a touch of genius in the simplest of phrases. Everything is so real that one does not read, one lives the book.

This quality of sincerity was something that was alien to his time. The first review of any importance of Stendhal's work was written in 1840 and brought Stendhal a small amount of belated recognition just before the end of his life. It was Balzac who wrote it; he said of the recently published *The Charterhouse of Parma*:

"I am by no means astonished at the absolute silence with which such a book has been greeted. That is the lot that awaits all books in which there is nothing vulgar. The secret ballot, in which superior minds which make the fame of such works vote one by one, and slowly, is not counted until long afterwards."

The superior minds have since registered their votes and Stendhal has been elected to his place among the world's greatest literary artists.

NOTRE DAME DE PARIS

VICTOR HUGO

AT THE age of fourteen, Victor Hugo declared, "I wish to be Chateaubriand or nothing". He did not become a Chateaubriand, but he did carve for himself a niche among the great writers of France.

Hugo was born on 26 February, 1802. His father was a general who, having attached himself to Joseph Bonaparte, accompanied his patron to Madrid when he was elevated by his brother to the throne of Spain. For his fidelity, King Joseph made General Hugo Governor of Madrid.

The general had taken his family to Spain with him, and so it was that his son Victor became a pupil at the College of Nobles, a circumstance which did more than merely educate him. The prevailing aristocratic environment of the College was to have a profound effect on his later demagogic tendencies.

Unfortunately, the general died shortly after the collapse of the Bonaparte world. The Bourbons, however, granted his widow a pension, and she and Victor lived together in Paris. When she died in 1821 the pension ceased, and Victor, left entirely without financial resources, lived for a time in extreme poverty. But not for long.

Presently he began to publish volumes of verses. His poems were classical in form, and so pleased the conservative critics; while in sentiment they were strongly Royalist, and so pleased the Court, which had been their writer's main intention. Indeed, Louis XVIII liked Hugo's verses so much that he granted him a pension of one thousand francs, and conferred on the twenty-three-year-old poet the distinction of Chevalier of the Legion of Honour.

Now, somewhat curiously, Hugo's sentiments began to change. In 1827, 1829 and 1830 he published three dramas, *Cromwell*, *Marion Delorme* and *Hernani*, which showed that his political leanings were becoming distinctly republican.

By now his writing had matured, and he was already beginning to claim for himself the rôle of high-priest of French romanticism. *Hernani* established his claim, and for the next fifty years he occupied this position, pouring out plays, novels and poems.

In 1845, Louis-Philippe created Hugo a peer. He had for some time been considering himself as one of the leaders of humanity, and as his new honour automatically gave him a seat in the House of Peers he decided to enter active politics so that he might bring his influence to bear on the fate of his fellow-men in a more practical way.

The revolution of 1848, however, abolished the House of Peers, but Hugo was elected to the Assembly under the Second Republic. Once again his rôle of legislator was to be short-lived, for the *coup d'état* of Napoleon III in 1851 deprived him of his position, and he fled to Brussels.

In exile he began to inveigh against the new regime in such terms that the Belgian authorities ordered his expulsion. So from Brussels he went, in 1852, to the Channel Island of Jersey, where, four years later, the same thing happened. This time he found refuge in the neighbouring island of Guernsey, where he bought Hauteville House and where he lived until the Franco-Prussian War of 1870 vindicated all he had been preaching. When the war was over, the French authorities withdrew the ban on him, and he returned to Paris in triumph. Here he died on 22 May, 1885, and was buried in the Panthéon.

From the great mass of his work three of his novels – *Notre Dame de Paris* (1831), *Les Misérables* (1862) and *Toilers of the Sea* (1866) – have assured him a permanent place in literature. *Notre Dame*, indeed, must be considered one of the greatest popular historical romances of all time.

The story opens on 6 January, 1482, with fifteenth-century Paris celebrating the Feast of the Kings and the Fools. The celebrations also coincide with the arrival of a Flemish embassy who have come to arrange the marriage of Margaret, daughter of the Archduke Maximilian of Austria, to the dauphin.

The arrival of the Cardinal of Paris, followed by that of the embassy, has interrupted the performance of a "mystery", commissioned from a poverty-stricken poet called Pierre Gringoire. Gringoire makes several attempts to restart the "mystery", but no one seems interested, especially when one of the Flemings proposes to the crowd that they shall elect their Pope of the Fools without delay by the method used by his fellow-townsmen of Ghent – by deciding which of the candidates can make the ugliest face.

While the competition is in progress there comes on the scene a grotesque figure. "We shall not attempt to give the reader an idea of that tetrahedron nose – that horse-shoe mouth – that small left eye overshadowed by a red bushy brow, while the right eye disappeared entirely under an enormous wart – of those straggling teeth with breaches here and there like the battlements of a fortress – of that horny lip, over which one of those teeth projected like the tusk of an elephant – of that forked chin – and, above all, of the expression diffused over the whole – that mixture of malice, astonishment and melancholy. Let the reader, if he can, figure to himself this combination."

As if the ugliness of the face were not enough, the whole of the rest of the body matched it. "His large head, all bristling with red hair – between his shoulders an enormous hump, to which he had a corresponding projection in front – a framework of thighs and legs so strangely gone astray that they could touch one another only at the knees – monstrous hands – and yet, with all that deformity, a certain gait denoting vigour, agility and courage."

The crowd recognize this deformed dwarf as Quasimodo, the bell-ringer of the cathedral of Notre Dame. They also recognize that no one could make a face uglier than his was naturally, and he is unanimously elected Pope of the Fools.

When the Fools' procession has set off, and the crowd with it, poor Gringoire does not dare to go home, as he owes six months' rent, which he has been planning to pay from the fee for his "mystery". He is quite certain now that he will not receive the fee. As he wanders penniless through the streets, wondering where he will find somewhere to sleep and something to eat, he comes upon a beautiful young gipsy girl called La Esmeralda, dancing for a crowd, and then putting her pretty little white goat, Djali, through some amazing tricks. As she gives her performance a priest calls down imprecations on her. Gringoire recognizes him as Dom Claude Frollo, the archdeacon. The gipsy girl is so frightened by what Dom Frollo has said that she stops her performance. The crowd, annoyed by this, turn on the priest. But at that moment the Fools' procession comes into the square, and Quasimodo springs to the priest's defence.

In a flash-back, it is now revealed that Quasimodo had been left in Notre Dame, a foundling. According to custom, he was exposed by the priests in the hope that some woman would adopt him. He was so ugly, however, that no one would, and as he was about to be sent to an orphanage, a young priest – Dom Frollo, now archdeacon – says that he will undertake to bring up the misshapen object. That had been sixteen years ago, and now the ugly hunchback, at twenty, was principal ringer of the bells of Notre Dame, made absolutely deaf by their clangour. Because of Dom Frollo's kindness to him, he worships the priest.

During the disturbance in the square, Esmeralda slips away. Believing that she must have a room to go to, Gringoire decides to follow her in the hope of persuading her to share it with him. As they are going through a dark narrow street, Quasimodo suddenly darts out of the shadows and seizes Esmeralda, obviously intending to carry her off. Fortunately, a detachment of the watch is at hand, and while their captain, Captain Phoebus de Chateupers, rescues the girl, his men arrest the hunchback. The girl asks the captain his name, and then, before he can stop her, she slips from his horse and disappears.

Gringoire, determined not to be mixed up in the affair, has taken to his heels, and in his running presently finds himself in the Court of Miracles, "into which no honest man had ever penetrated at such an hour". The Court of Miracles was that part of Paris traditionally inhabited by a vast army of vagabonds, collectively known as the Truands.

Recognized at once as a stranger, he is seized and hauled before the King of the Truands. Nothing can save him from immediate death except that he agrees to join the Truands and that one of the women will take him as her husband. When it seems that none will, he is saved by Esmeralda saying that she is prepared to have him.

Next day, Quasimodo is brought before the magistrate, and condemned to be flogged for an hour in the pillory in the Place de Grève and to remain there for a further hour. He takes his severe punishment calmly, but when it is over he cries out for something to drink. Instead the crowd hurl abuse at him and pelt him, until up the steps of the pillory Esmeralda is seen mounting with a jug, from which she gives the hunchback a drink. As she does so a terrible voice cries out, "Cursed be thou, daughter of Egypt! cursed! cursed!"

The voice, a woman's, has come from a kind of cave in a corner of the square, where a recluse, known as Sachette, has shut herself up for many years. In her youth, Sachette had been a famous prostitute, Pâquette-la-Chantefleurie. When she had become worn out by her profession she had longed for some object to love, and had somewhat miraculously become pregnant. She had given birth to a most beautiful baby girl upon whom she lavished all her love and devotion. When the child was four years old it had been stolen by gipsies, and she had withdrawn to the cave, filled with hatred for all gipsies.

Now, Captain Phoebus is engaged to be married to Damoiselle Fleur-de-Lys de Gondelaurier. He is calling on her one day in her mother's house overlooking the Place du Parvis, one side of which is formed by the cathedral of Notre Dame, when Esmeralda is dancing in the square. Fleur-de-Lys and her companions are interested in her and Phoebus calls her and her goat up. During the scene which follows, the little goat, Djali, while playing with one of the younger girls, spells out *Phoebus* from an alphabet which she carries in a small bag tied round her neck. Esmeralda is greatly embarrassed by this discovery of her secret and leaves hurriedly. The captain, unwilling to let the possibility of some pleasant dalliance slip, follows her, and she agrees to an assignation.

Dom Frollo, the archdeacon, is revealed as a very sinister figure indeed. He dabbles in alchemy; but worse, he has formed a guilty and sinful passion for Esmeralda. Learning of Phoebus's assignation with Esmeralda, he persuades the naïve captain to let him hide in the room while they are making love.

When Esmeralda arrives, she is torn between her love for Phoebus and her great desire to find her parents again – for she, too, is a foundling – which she has been warned she will never do if she surrenders her virginity. (For this reason, she has refused to consummate her "marriage" to Gringoire.) However, her love for Phoebus proves too strong, and she agrees; but as he is preparing to make love to her, she sees over his shoulder a black figure spring across the room and plunge a dagger into the captain's back.

She faints, and when she comes round she finds herself and Djali under arrest on charges of murder and sorcery. Under examination she refuses to confess to stabbing Phoebus, and when her trial opens she is at once condemned to be tortured. Under torture she agrees to confess, and back in the court-room she is sentenced to do penance before Notre Dame and then to be hanged in the Place de Grève, and Djali with her.

While awaiting execution, she is kept in a foul dungeon, where she is visited by the archdeacon – who had made the attack on Phoebus – who tells her that if she will become his mistress, he will save her. He assures her that Phoebus is dead, and implores her to go with him, but she drives him away saying that if Phoebus is dead she has no desire to go on living.

Next day she is taken out for execution, and for the first part of the sentence is brought to the main entrance of Notre Dame in a tumbrel. Phoebus, in fact, is very much alive, and is visiting his fiancée when the tumbrel clatters into the square. He has no further interest in Esmeralda and tries to persuade Fleur-de-Lys not to watch the ceremony of penance, but she insists and makes him stand by her side to watch, too.

As the recitation of the prescribed Psalms – performed by the archdeacon – comes to an end, Esmeralda happens to glance up and sees him on the balcony beside Fleur-de-Lys. She calls out his name; he hears her and withdraws hastily indoors. Seeing this, Esmeralda suddenly has the idea that he must think she tried to kill him and the thought makes her fall senseless.

But there has been another watcher of the ceremony. Up among the buttresses of Notre Dame, Quasimodo has been following the proceedings. Though he cannot hear, he knows that this ceremony of penance precedes execution, and that the victim is the beautiful girl who risked the violence of the crowd to give him a drink while he stood in the pillory. He has loved her ever since.

As the executioner's assistants are about to lift the senseless Esmeralda back into the tumbrel, the hunchback comes scaling down the outside of Notre Dame by a rope which he has attached to a gallery, gathers the girl under one arm, and, the little goat at his heels, leaps with her into the church, crying "Sanctuary!" It has all been so sudden and unexpected that no one has been able to prevent him.

For several weeks he looks after Esmeralda with the most touching devotion. But the authorities are determined to remove the girl from her sanctuary, and the only legal means by which this can be done is by a special Parliamentary bill. On the eve of the bill coming into force, the Truands decide to rescue Esmeralda. Unfortunately Quasimodo, misunderstanding their intentions, keeps them at bay.

During the attack on the cathedral, the archdeacon, accompanied by her "husband" Gringoire (since he knows that she will have nothing to do with him if he approaches her alone), goes to Esmeralda and persuades her to follow them to safety. Once outside the church, however, Gringoire disappears, and the archdeacon makes one more attempt to get her to become his mistress. When she refuses he seizes hold of her, and takes her to Sachette, the recluse and gipsy-hater of the Place de Grève, for her to hold while he summons the guard.

While he is absent, Sachette recognizes the amulet at Esmeralda's throat, and knows that she is not a gipsy, but her kidnapped daughter. She tries to save her from the guard, but both of them are dragged from the cell, the old woman falls dead while Esmeralda is hanged on the spot.

After telling the guard where Esmeralda is to be found, the archdeacon returns to Notre Dame, and goes up on to the roof from where he can see the gibbet from which Esmeralda is being hanged. He is so intent on the scene that he is not aware that Quasimodo – who has seen him taking the girl away – is beside him. Quasimodo realizes that the archdeacon has made execution possible, and at the moment that the ladder is pulled away from Esmeralda he pushes the priest over the balustrade, to his death in the square below.

Quasimodo was never seen again, but when a year or two later the charnel-house into which Esmeralda's body had been thrown was opened up, two skeletons were found with their arms entwined. One was of a girl who had been hanged, about whose throat were the remains of an amulet; the other of a man with a deformed spine and chest.

Notre Dame is a very long book. It contains extensive passages giving in great detail descriptions of historical places, events and customs, much of which, to the modern taste, seems both cumbersome and extraneous. This fondness for romantic detail, added to his great output, inevitably deprives much of Hugo's writing of depth and creative force. But if his prose works, with the possible exception of *Toilers of the Sea*, do not find with the modern reader the favour they found with his more leisured contemporaries, he still merits the reputation he achieved during his lifetime, and *Notre Dame* remains one of the greatest examples of the historical romance.

OLD GORIOT

HONORÉ DE BALZAC

THE NAME Balzac is liable to provoke mixed feelings. There are
endearing accounts of this paunchy, cherubic creator, in his white
monastic robe with a gold chain as girdle, writing week after week
for twelve hours at a stretch, sustaining his powers with jugs of black
coffee and visualizing his characters so vividly that they seemed more
real than living people and he imagined they came to tea with him.
On the other hand, we remember his novels: the tortuous style,
microscopic descriptions of all the material paraphernalia of life,
learned dissertations interrupting the action on philosophical, scientific or psychological subjects, inordinate financial detail, characters
declaiming long set speeches, the product of a congested mind evok-
ing a strange and not always congenial world. Even in France
opinion about him has always been divided and his faults as a writer
are considered just as striking as his virtues. But no one in any
country denies his power, the extraordinary accuracy of his insight
into human nature or the fidelity of his portrait of French society
drawn in his monumental, sixteen-volume panorama, "The Human
Comedy".

Balzac was born of peasant stock in Tours in 1799. He died of
overwork in 1850. Into his short life he crammed a gigantic literary
output, perpetually in debt, incessantly borrowing to cover the
expenses of his flamboyant social life, but forever planning and writing the novels which mirrored the entire world already existing, as
he said, in his brain. There never has been, perhaps, a more zestful
creative genius.

The title, "The Human Comedy", was intended as an over-all
description of novels in which Balzac's object was, as he wrote, "to
trace in its infinite details the faithful history, the exact picture of the
manners of our modern society". The volumes were divided into
sections: scenes of private life, provincial life, Parisian life, political
life, military life and country life. The whole comprises what one
French critic has called a Record Office filled with archives, so exact
is the picture it gives of all strata of French society under the July
Monarchy, at a time when careerism and the lust for money were at

their height; the middle class, emancipated by the French Revolution, was continually rising in importance, and new social, political and economic ideas were heralding the advent of change. All this, and the more traditional life of the countryside, Balzac reflected in his novels with immense gusto and accuracy of observation, combining the precision of a scientific observer with the creative power to hold whole groups of people in his mind.

He had originally intended to include upwards of 4,000 characters in "The Human Comedy"; he succeeded in creating around 2,000 drawn from all sections of society and carefully observed. He knew the world of fashionable Paris from personal experience and also the lives of journalists, students and lawyers' clerks: he had been all three himself. Businessmen, artists, actors, peasants, commercial travellers, gaol-birds, bohemians, usurers and the human vermin that lurked in the purlieus of Paris are recreated down to the smallest detail of dress, speech, background, even of their income and expenditure. Those classes of people whom he did not know personally Balzac used to study with the zeal of a zoologist, tracking isolated specimens sometimes through the streets, listening to their conversation, absorbing their cast of mind until, as he said, his soul entered theirs.

But Balzac was not content merely to describe, he sought to understand. He called himself a doctor of the social sciences, meaning that he wished to grasp the mainsprings of human action and the forces at work in society. Human beings, he believed, are driven by a combination of passion and self-interest. Beneath a veneer of convention and respect for the law they pursue their own ends with egotistic fervour, obsessed with the lust for gain, or with ambition, with their sensual appetites, with collecting pictures or insects, with any and every kind of monomaniac idea which drives them through life, often to their destruction. Many of his characters are people of this type, sharply defined, cast in a single block, tragic, pathetic or odious according to their temperaments. In addition, a tendency to seek out the ugly, the vicious, the sordid aspects of life in preference to the beautiful, an inclination to violence and brutality, a sort of pessimistic realism fill most of Balzac's novels. The total effect is at once powerful and somewhat depressing. But one has to admit that they ring true. He forces us to accept his world and therein lies his genius. All this applies to what some critics consider to be the best novel in "The Human Comedy", *Old Goriot*.

The story begins with a description of a typical Balzacian setting, a gloomy boarding house in the Latin Quarter, the grimmest area of Paris, presided over by Madame Vauquer, a mercenary widow. She is not fussy about her boarders so long as they pay their rent, and they are a mixed lot: Madame Couture, widow of a Commissary-General, Victorine Taillefer, a consumptive adolescent, an old man waiting to die, described as a "drudge of the social treadmill", Mlle Michonneau, a shrivelled and elderly spinster who wears a dirty green taffeta eye-shade. All these people, with the exception of Victorine, to whom a suitable young man could still bring awakening, are small-minded and nondescript. But then there is Monsieur Vautrin, with his powerful frame and yet more powerful personality – black wig, dyed whiskers and hearty laugh. The boarders like him, but nobody knows quite what he does and his gleaming eyes which seem to penetrate to the very depths of the soul are awe-inspiring. The general verdict is that Vautrin "is a man", though whether his heart is quite human is another matter. Another boarder, a temporary one, is the young and handsome law-student, Eugène de Rastignac, strong-willed, clear-headed, with a compulsive ambition to succeed in Paris society. Finally there is Old Goriot himself, called significantly in French, Père Goriot.

When the story opens, in December, 1819, Goriot, with his moon-like, foolishly simple face, has been living for six years in the Maison Vauquer. A retired vermicelli-maker, he arrived with a well-stocked wardrobe, a lot of household silver and plenty of money. To start with, he dined out once or twice a week, then these outings stopped, he sold some of his silver and after two years asked to be given a cheaper room. This aroused rumours among the lodgers that he gambled on the Stock Exchange, alternatively that he lavished money on women. This story gained plausibility when he was visited at a short interval by two fashionably dressed ladies. There seemed no doubt then that Old Goriot was a rake, though when Madame Vauquer asked him insolently one day what he took her house to be, he replied meekly that the two ladies were his daughters. Daughters indeed! No one believed him. Then, after three years, he reduced his expenses still further, took a yet smaller room, neglected his clothes. There were no more visits. "Don't those daughters of yours come to see you any more?" asked Madame Vauquer maliciously. "They come sometimes," he replied in a quaking voice. . . .

Behind these events lies a pathetic story supplying one of the two main themes in the book. Old Goriot is another of Balzac's obsessional figures, the obsession in this case being paternal love. An early widower, he lavished affection and money on his young daughters, Delphine and Anastasie. Nothing was too good for them, no demand of theirs was ever rejected, for "to be happy", he said, "fathers must always be giving; it is ceaselessly giving that makes you really a father". The girls were, in fact, the whole universe to him, they were the clue by which he found his way through creation. In due course he found husbands for them, a French aristocrat and a rich German banker, both attracted by the prospect of huge dowries. For a time the old man was welcomed in both daughters' homes in fashionable Paris, then, when the husbands saw that no further money was to be got out of him, the doors were firmly closed. But the girls still saw him occasionally. They both had lovers, the lovers ran into debt and Goriot sold his spoons, cut down on his own living to save them from embarrassment. Cheerfully he gave up tobacco, sold his last investments in return for a smile from Delphine or Anastasie. "I would sell the Father, Son and Holy Ghost to save either of them a tear!" He got no love in return, but he had always allowed his daughters to trample on him. Indeed, to suffer for their sakes was part of his pleasure. To touch their dresses occasionally, to catch a glimpse of them as they got into their carriages for a fashionable ball was reward enough. He was, he said, "a wretched old carcase whose soul is wherever my daughters are". And he did not expect love. Only one illusion was necessary to his happiness: he had to believe that behind their occasional smiles, the pleasure they felt when he gave them money was some sort of feeling for himself. A little twinge of affection, that would be enough. We can see, even at the start of this story, the bitter disillusionment that awaits him.

But there is another theme in the book, the career of young Eugène de Rastignac. He comes from a poor country family who scrape to send him money so that he can cut a dash in society. Through a cousin he gains entrance to fashionable houses in Paris, among them the homes of Anastasie and Delphine. He quickly discovers their stony-hearted indifference to their father, the state of their unhappy marriages, the savage egotism that rules their lives and he is temporarily disconcerted. But ambition revives and with it the realization that to succeed in society he must have much more money than his family can provide. Where can it be found? Here the tempter Vautrin appears at his elbow. He has already been preaching that success is virtue and Eugène now feels that he is right. Professing a keen interest in the young man's affairs, Vautrin makes a proposition and so doing reveals his own cynical and ruthless character. "I stand alone against organized society," he says, "and I beat it hollow." His plan is simple. Victorine Taillefer has a brother who has inherited a fortune. Vautrin will arrange for the brother to be killed in a duel, Victorine will inherit and Eugène will marry her. A million francs! All Vautrin asks for his services is twenty per cent. Eugène is outraged at the suggestion, but cannot quite rid his mind of the dazzling prospects it opens.

We follow Eugène's progress in the fashionable world, incidentally hearing Balzac's indictment of the corruption and egotism which rule there, we watch his friendship with Goriot growing with his passionate attachment to Delphine. Goriot finally ruins himself by paying for an apartment where Eugène can be near his mistress, but he is amply rewarded by her smiles and temporary permission to see her again. Vautrin, the Devil's advocate, goads Eugène in his spendthrift career until the evening, ever memorable in the annals of the boarding house, when news comes that Victorine's brother has been killed and soon afterward nemesis overtakes Vautrin himself. Here Balzac breaks into melodrama. Vautrin is an escaped convict with great power in the Paris underworld, known as Cheat-Death. The police have at last got on to his track. They persuade Mlle Michonneau, the spinster with the eye-shade, to dope his drink and then, under pretext of bringing him round, confirm that he bears the convict's brand-marks on his shoulder. This is done, the police invade the boarding house dining-room to arrest him, manhandling him so that his black wig is torn off to reveal close-cropped, bright-red hair. The face now seems transformed, giving "a shocking suggestion of strength combined with cunning. At that moment the soul and spirit of the man were apparent, as if he stood in a lurid glare thrown by the flames of hell. . . . The blood rose to his face, his eyes glittered like a wildcat's." After an unrepentant speech, pouring scorn on humanity at large, Vautrin is led away.

The story now builds to a climax. Eugène and Old Goriot are preparing to move permanently from the boarding house when Delphine arrives in a state of near-collapse. Her entire fortune has been appropriated by her husband, the German tycoon, to help finance his business – a crooked one, she suspects – and he will only allow her to keep her lover on condition that he retains the money. So all Goriot's savings which he lavished on his daughter have gone with the wind. Soon Anastasie arrives with a similar tale. She has sold the family diamonds to pay her lover's gambling debts. Her husband has found out and has blackmailed her into signing over all her property to him. But that is not all. She still needs 12,000 francs and appeals to her father for the money. But he has nothing left. His last 12,000 went on furnishing the apartment for Eugène. . . . This news provokes a violent quarrel between the daughters, the old man tries in vain to calm them, then collapses on his bed crying: "Children, I shall die if you go on like this!" Anastasie promptly flees the room; that night, Delphine is not deterred from going to the opera with Eugène by news that her father is seriously ill. It is late next day when the lovers remember him, and then only Eugène returns to see how he is. He finds the old man considerably worse, having got up that morning to sell his last remaining silver to buy Anastasie a new dress. In semi-delirium he is now dreaming of making another fortune in Odessa to hand over to his daughters. . . .

That night, Eugène receives a note from Delphine, complaining that he is neglecting her. Meeting her later, he tries to persuade her to visit her father, but she insists on him accompanying her to a ball. Meanwhile, in his miserable garret Old Goriot is sinking, after suffering a stroke. He is still lucid though, and next day when he hears that neither of his daughters will come to see him he realizes what he has secretly suspected for the last ten years: they have no affection for him at all. But Old Goriot, the archetype of all doting fathers, blames himself rather than his daughters. "They are innocent," he says. "Tell everyone that." He spoilt them, he humbled himself in the dust for them. He resigned his rights. The result was that unwittingly he corrupted his own children. "I am the cause of their unfilial conduct. I always indulged them in all their childish whims. They had a carriage of their own when they were fifteen! Nothing was denied them. I, and I only, am to blame; but I sinned through love of them. Their voice melted my heart. . . ."

Then the mood of the dying man suddenly changes. In a rage he demands that his children be sent for. It is their duty to come; the law demands it. They must be forced, if necessary by troops of the line, to do their duty. He calls them vile, stony-hearted women. He curses them. He abhors them. . . . A few moments later he is mumbling again of going to Odessa to earn a million for them. Then he rails against his sons-in-law, believing that it is they who have prevented his daughters from coming. Then, sinking fast, he murmurs: "Not to see them – there is death's sting. . . ." Finally Eugène goes to fetch them, and comes back with promises only from Delphine. But she is a long time in coming and Old Goriot dies with only Eugène and a medical student beside him, touching their heads, believing them to be his daughters', his last words: "Ah! My angels!"

He is given a third-class funeral as no money is forthcoming from either of the wealthy households. His daughters do not attend. The only mourners are Eugène and a servant from the boarding house. The service lasts only twenty minutes. So Old Goriot is laid to rest, and the servant speaks his epitaph: "A good, kind man who never said one word louder than another; he bothered nobody and never did any harm."

Has Eugène been cured of his yearnings for High Society? He sheds a tear "the last tear of his youth", over Goriot's grave and then his eyes turn to the lights of Paris gleaming below the hill where the cemetery stands.

That night – and here is Balzac's ironic touch, opening vistas of a new story to be pursued in another volume – he is dining with Delphine again.

THE FRENCH REVOLUTION

THOMAS CARLYLE

OF ALL the great events of world history, one of the best known is the French Revolution of 1789. And the reason why it is so well known is very largely because its history was written by an obscure, struggling, but exceedingly gifted Scottish journalist named Thomas Carlyle.

Why Carlyle should have chosen the subject requires some explanation. He had no French connexions or interests. He had no personal knowledge of France or the French, and his acquaintance with the language was but slight. The idea probably first came to him when, on one of his occasional visits to Edinburgh from his wife's farm at Craigenputtock, where they were then living, he was looking for material in the city libraries for an article on the affair of the Diamond Necklace that some years before the Revolution had involved the French Court, and Queen Marie Antoinette in particular, in an atmosphere of scandal and trickery.

Carlyle wrote his article – it was reprinted in his *Essays* – and then turned to an examination of the French Revolution as a whole. What had caused it? Why did it break out when it did? Who were its chief characters? And might there be detected in its course the operation of the great moral laws of which Carlyle was always conscious? These were some of the questions he asked, but he soon found that the materials for answering them did not exist in Edinburgh. He decided, therefore, to remove to London; and in June, 1834, he and his wife established themselves in the house in Cheyne Row, Chelsea, which was his home until his death nearly half a century later.

In London he made a number of useful acquaintances and some friends, including John Stuart Mill, the brilliant young writer who was the exponent of the Utilitarian philosophy and a good deal else.

The first volume was finished in five months, and Carlyle sent it to Mill for his comments. Mill took it to his bosom friend, Mrs. Harriet Taylor, upon whose literary judgment he had come to rely. And while the MS. was in her possession it was accidentally burned by the servant girl, with the exception of the last four or five pages.

Mill was staggered at the disaster, and insisted on Carlyle's acceptance of a cheque for £100 – he had tried to make it £200 – to cover Carlyle's household expenses while rewriting the destroyed MS. Carlyle had no copy, and few notes, but with dogged courage he set to work, and the book was finished early in 1837. On 12 January he wrote to his wife to tell her that the work was done. "What they will do with this book, none knows, my Jeannie lass; but they have not had, for a two hundred years, any book that came more truly from a man's very heart; and so let them trample it under foot and hoof as they see best." "Pooh, pooh!" replied his gallant wife, "they cannot trample that".

Six months later the book was published, and it was soon clear that Mrs. Carlyle's judgment had been sound. It was very favourably received, and henceforth Carlyle's future was assured. And, notwithstanding Carlyle's grotesque style, *The French Revolution* has retained its place as the most generally readable of all the books written in English about that epoch-making struggle. For Carlyle had something that is all too often lacking in historians: a sense of history as being not something that is over and done with but as something that is still living, still going on. Such was the power of his imagination that he could recapture the past and recreate it, and as we read his pages we are *there*, sharing the ardours and the dangers, the disappointments, and the excitements of triumph, in one of the great turning-points of history.

It is a long book, and the story is slow in getting started. The first chapters describe the disgusting death-bed of Louis XV – Louis the Well-Beloved, as he was once styled, and not in jest – and the terrible state of the country over which he ruled and which he had bled almost to death with his wars and debaucheries. Royalty was on its way out. The nobility wasted the rents they managed to extract from their tenants in dressing gracefully and eating sumptuously and exhausting themselves in depravities unequalled since the most infamous days of the Roman emperors. The Church was in eclipse. The *Philosophes* were the guides of educated opinion. And the people? "They are sent for, to do statute-labour, to pay statute-taxes; to fatten battlefields with their bodies, in quarrels which are not theirs; their hand and toil is in every possession of man; but for themselves they have little or no possession. Untaught, uncomforted, unfed; to pine stagnantly in thick obscuration, in squalid destitution and obstruction: this is the lot of the millions. . . ."

Slowly, chapter by chapter, the story is continued, as slow as what it has to record, the tottering decline of the *ancien régime* into the abyss. As we draw near the brink, the pace quickens, and now Carlyle shows what he is capable of.

Morning has dawned, of a day and date that all the generations to come will remember: 14 July, 1789. "The bustlings and preparings, the tremors and menaces; the tears that fell from old eyes! This day, my sons, ye shall quit you like men. By the memory of your fathers' wrongs, by the hope of your children's rights! Tyranny impends in red wrath: help for you is none, if not in your own right hands. This day ye must do or die." *A la Bastille!*

Within the walls of the grim old fortress the governor, old De Launay, is "hampered, as all military gentlemen now are, in the saddest conflict of uncertainties". Emissaries from the popular headquarters at the Hôtel de Ville have invited him to admit "National Soldiers, which is a soft name for surrendering", but on the other hand His Majesty's orders are precise. No surrender then, but his garrison is but eighty-two old Invalides, reinforced by thirty-two young Swiss. True, his walls are nine feet thick, he has cannon and powder; but he has only one day's provisions. And outside is a city in arms.

"De Launay gives fire; pulls up his drawbridge. A slight sputter; – which has *kindled* the too combustible chaos; made it a roaring fire-chaos! Bursts forth Insurrection, at sight of its own blood (for there were deaths by that sputter of fire), into endless rolling explosion of musketry, distraction, execration – and overhead, from the Fortress, let one great gun, with its grapeshot, go booming, to show what we *could* do. The Bastille is besieged!

"Let conflagration rage; of whatsoever is combustible! Guard-rooms are burnt, Invalides mess-rooms. . . . Blood flows; the aliment of new madness. The wounded are carried into houses of the Rue Cerisaie; the dying leave their last mandate not to yield till the accursed Stronghold fall. And yet, alas, how fall? The walls are so thick!

"How the great Bastille Clock ticks (inaudible) in its Inner Court there, at its ease, hour after hour; as if nothing special, for it or the world, were passing! It tolled One when the firing began; and is now pointing towards Five, and still the firing slakes not. Far down, in their vaults, the seven prisoners hear muffled din as of earthquakes.
. . For four hours now has the World-Bedlam roared. The poor Invalides have sunk under their battlements, or rise only with reversed muskets: they have made a white flag of napkins. . . . Sinks the drawbridge, Usher Maillard bolting it when down; rushes in the living deluge: the Bastille is fallen! *Victoire! La Bastille*

est prise!" Late that night the Duke de Liancourt gains access to the royal apartments at Versailles, and unfolds to the King what has happened that day in Paris. *"Mais, c'est une révolte!* Why, that is a revolt!" says poor Louis XVI. "Sire," answers Liancourt, "it is not a revolt – it is a revolution."

Comparable with this as a most vivid piece of historical reconstruction is Carlyle's account of the royal family's misguided and ill-fated flight from Paris with a view to joining the loyal troops under Bouillé on the north-east frontier. They make their getaway in a berline (four-wheeled covered carriage) – a *new* berline. It lumbers along, lurchingly with stress, at a snail's pace; noted of all the world. ... Stoppages occur, and breakages. . . . "With eleven horses, and double drink-money, it will be found that Royalty, flying for life, accomplishes Sixty-nine miles in Twenty-two incessant hours. Slow Royalty! And yet not a minute of these hours but is precious: on minutes hang the destinies of Royalty now."

Evening draws on, and in the little village of Sainte-Menehould "wearied mortals are creeping home from their field-labour; the village artisan eats with relish his supper of herbs, or has strolled forth to the village street for a sweet mouthful of air and human news". And at the last door of the village stands a man "in loose-flowing night-gown – an acrid, choleric man, rather dangerous-looking, still in the prime of life – Jean Baptiste Drouet, Master of the Post here". Into the village rolls the berline, and Postmaster Drouet steps up to take a good look at the arrivals. That lady in slouched gypsy hat, that gentleman in round hat and peruke, who keeps on poking his head out of the window – there is something familiar about them surely? A new assignat (paper-money) is hurriedly produced, and the King's head on it compared with that of the man in the carriage: "you might say the one was an attempted Engraving of the other!"

The berline moves on. The thick shades of night are falling now. Postilions crack and whip. They are safe through Clermont, and the royal party "sinks every one of them into a kind of sleep". But in the meantime Drouet and his companion the town clerk have been spurring, and when the berline rumbles up to the entrance to the village of Varennes they find the road blocked by a furniture wagon, and muskets are levelled through the coach doors. "Mesdames, your Passports?" With Drouet standing by, the travelling party are ever so courteously invited to rest in M. Sausse's grocer's shop "till the dawn strike up!" Louis steps out, they all step out, and are conducted to the room above the shop. "Where straightway his

Majesty 'demands refreshments'. Demands refreshments, as it is written; gets bread-and-cheese with a bottle of Burgundy; and remarks, that it is the best Burgundy he ever drank!" And then in the morning they take the road back to Paris – and the guillotine.

Carlyle is at his superlative best in describing such incidents, when time seems to stand still and the air is heavy with expectancy. His portraits of the chief actors in the drama are sometimes superb. Take his picture of Charlotte Corday, for instance, the girl "of stately Norman figure, in her twenty-fifth year, of beautiful still countenance", as on Tuesday, 9 July, 1793, she takes her seat in the *diligence* with a place booked for Paris. "None takes farewell of her, wishes her Good-journey; her Father will find a line left, signifying that she is gone to England, that he must pardon her, and forget her." But it is not to England that she is gone but to Paris, to the squalid room in which Marat, the all-powerful instrument of the Terror, "sits now in slipper-bath; sore afflicted; ill of Revolution Fever – of what other malady this History had rather not name. Excessively sick and worn, poor man: with precisely elevenpence-halfpenny of ready-money in paper; with slipper-bath, strong three-footed stool for writing on, the while. 'Citizen Marat, I am from Caen, the seat of rebellion, and wished to speak with you.' – 'Be seated, *mon enfant*. Now what are the traitors doing at Caen? What Deputies are at Caen?' – Charlotte names some Deputies. 'Their heads shall fall within a fortnight,' croaks the eager People's-friend, clutching his tablets to write: *Barbaroux*, *Pétion*, writes he with bare shrunk arm, turning aside in the bath: *Pétion*, and *Louvet*, and – Charlotte has drawn her knife from the sheath; plunges it, with one sure stroke, into the writer's heart".

When she was charged before the Revolutionary Tribunal, Charlotte Corday was beautiful and calm. "I killed one man," she said, "to save a hundred thousand; a villain to save innocents; a savage wild beast to give repose to my country. I was a Republican before the Revolution: I never wanted energy." The sentence of death was passed, and that same evening, "from the gate of the Conciergerie, to a City all on tiptoe, the fatal Cart issues: seated on it a fair young creature, sheeted in red smock of murderess; so beautiful, serene, so full of life; journeying towards death. . . . Many take off their hats, saluting reverently; for what heart but must be touched? Others growl and howl."

Less than a year later, the Revolutionists were slaughtering each other. "At the foot of the scaffold, Danton was heard to ejaculate: O my Wife, my well-beloved, I shall never see thee more then!' –

but, interrupting himself: 'Danton, no weakness!' He said to
Hérault-Seychelles stepping forward to embrace him: 'Our head
will meet *there*,' in the Headsman's sack. His last words were to
Samson the Headsman himself: 'Thou wilt show my head to the
people; it is worth showing.' "

Very different was Robespierre's end, when the Revolution was
burning itself out. As the tumbril carried him along to the guillotine
"the Gendarmes point their swords at him, to show the people which
is he. A woman springs on the Tumbril; clutching the side of it with
one hand; waving the other Sibyl-like; and exclaims: 'The death of
thee gladdens my very heart, *m'enivre de joie*'; Robespierre opened
his eyes; '*Scélérat*, go down to Hell, with the curses of all wives and
mothers!' – At the foot of the scaffold, they stretched him on the
ground till his turn came. Lifted aloft, his eyes again opened; caught
the bloody axe. Samson wrenched the coat off him; wrenched the
dirty linen from his jaw: the jaw fell powerless, there burst from him
a cry; hideous to hear and see. Samson, thou canst not be too
quick. . . ."

So scene is added to scene, until the last scene of all, when a young
artillery officer named Napoleon Bonaparte gives the order for that
"whiff of grapeshot" that strewed the street with the bodies of the
last of the revolutionaries. And so, "the thing we specifically call
French Revolution is blown into space by it, and becomes a thing that
was!"

DEAD SOULS

NIKOLAI V. GOGOL

NIKOLAI VASSILYEVITCH GOGOL was born at Sorotchinetz in the Ukraine and belonged to a Cossack family. When a sensitive, romantic youth of nineteen he went to St. Petersburg where he became a humble copy-clerk in a Government office. During his brief term of service he developed a bitter and lasting hatred of the bureaucratic rule which exercised such a stranglehold on the Russia of his day, and determined to seek his fortune in America. He resigned his job, borrowed money from his mother and set off but turned back at Lübeck, having persuaded himself that he possessed the ability to become a great actor; and for the next six months he trailed vainly round St. Petersburg's many theatres.

It was a humiliating experience. Gogol protested to his friend, the poet Pushkin, that it was grossly unfair of managers to say his voice was too weak; but the truth was his whole appearance was against him. According to a contemporary he was "a little man with legs too short for his body. He walked crookedly; he was clumsy, ill-dressed and rather ridiculous-looking, with his long lock of hair flapping on his forehead, and his large, prominent nose".

The disconsolate Gogol was comforted by Pushkin, who introduced him to the circle of young intellectuals forming the nucleus of the movement that was to grow until it swept Russia into revolution nearly a century later. Under their stimulus Gogol wrote the brief prose epic *Taras Bulba*, and several superb short stories, the most famous being *The Cloak*, to which Dostoevsky always referred as the tree out of which the Russian novel grew.

Most Russians can get drunk on tea and talk: Gogol was no exception. Night after night he and his companions discussed the iniquities of their country's huge and corrupt Civil Service until he became convinced that it was his duty to expose its evils. Still in thrall to the theatre, he did so in his brilliant satiric comedy *The Inspector-General* which Zhukovsky, the poet who tutored the young Tsarevitch, had the temerity to show to Tsar Nicholas I. To the amazement of all, the martinet Tsar was so delighted that he ordered the play to be produced at the Imperial Theatre on 19 March, 1836. He occupied the Royal box, laughed uproariously throughout and as the curtain fell declared: "Everyone has received their due, myself most of all."

To say that the play caused a sensation would be an understatement. Yet even as the critics lauded it and the public besieged the box-office, the all-powerful Civil Service chiefs met in secret conclave and came to the unanimous decision that this monstrous N. V. Gogol must be removed forthwith. Aware of the Tsar's interest in him they had to move stealthily, but so relentless was their persecution that before the year was out the sensitive Gogol fled to Rome, where he lived on a small allowance which he believed came from his friends but was in reality provided by Nicholas I.

During the early 1830s Gogol had made a rough draft of an immensely long novel he proposed to call *Dead Souls*. Though the story was witty and satiric the underlying theme was so tragic that when he read it aloud to Pushkin the latter cried out at the end: "God! What a sad country Russia is!" and later told friends: "Gogol invents nothing: it is the simple truth, the terrible truth." In Rome Gogol set to work on the draft but progress was slow. Pushkin's death in a duel in 1837 affected him profoundly, and his own exile preyed on his mind so much that he suffered prolonged bouts of melancholia. Not until 1842 was the first volume published, and despite several hiatuses in the narrative it became renowned as the great prose classic of Russia. The second volume, alas, was never issued as Gogol burnt the unfinished manuscript years later in a fit of despair.

Dead Souls is a pungent satire on the subject closest to Gogol's heart, the corruption fostered and stimulated by bureaucratic rule, and the central figure is an engaging rogue called Chichikov, whose career as a Government Customs officer has ended in ignominy. He hits on a brilliant scheme to recoup his fallen fortunes. At that time every Russian landowner owned serfs or "souls" on each of whom he had to pay an annual head-tax. As the Government only took a census every ten or twenty years and mortality was high the owner often had to pay tax on dead souls, which he considered grossly unfair. Chichikov's plan is to travel the country buying up dead souls very cheaply, then presenting his list of purchases to the local Governor who, presuming them to be live souls (for nobody in his senses would buy dead ones), would sign a deed of transfer. Armed with this document Chichikov could go to any bank and raise a substantial loan on his souls. With this money he would buy a small property in a distant province and some real live souls to work on it.

In high spirits Chichikov arrives at the town of N—— in his

britchka (a light carriage drawn by three horses) with his coachman Selifan and his servant Petrushka. He quizzes the waiter at the inn about the civic dignitaries; then sallies forth to call upon each one of them, an elegant figure with rosy, smooth-shaven cheeks, a bilberry-coloured silk frock-coat and a handkerchief scented with *Eau de Cologne*. He is an expert name-dropper, and his casual references to the great combined with his admiring remarks on the way the town is run and his charming habit of addressing everybody as "Excellency" make a tremendous impression on his listeners. Before the day is out the Governor has invited him to a grand reception the following night and his diary is filled with luncheon and dinner engagements for a week ahead.

Everyone is captivated by the visitor and there is a storm of protest when he announces he must depart for a short time. But Chichikov is adamant, alludes mysteriously to a mission he must fulfil and drives off, leaving the town agog with rumours that he is a high Government official engaged on important secret work.

We now follow his successful and often hilarious progress round the countryside. From his new friends in N—— he has acquired valuable information concerning the characters and idiosyncracies of the landowners in the district, so knows who to cajole, flatter or bully into doing business with him. True, some of those he interviewed thought him a harmless lunatic, while others thought him a saintly philanthropist, but all were so eager to make something for nothing that they agreed to his proposal and in a very short time Chichikov was the proud owner of hundreds of dead souls.

But success makes Chichikov greedy and he decides to call on a very rich landowner many miles away. Unfortunately Selifan has had too much vodka the night before and takes the wrong road. They are hopelessly lost when a violent thunderstorm breaks, the horses take fright and the *britchka* overturns in the mud. Eventually Chichikov is put up for the night by Madame Korobotchka, a rich, eccentric and miserly widow who, after much haggling, sells him a large number of her dead souls. Next morning Chichikov again sets out, halts for refreshment at an inn and is hailed by the boisterous Nozdrev, whom he first met in N—— It is a disastrous encounter. Nozdrev is exceedingly drunk and has been to a local fair where he has lost money gambling. He insists on sweeping Chichikov back to his home and plies him with food and wine, but when his guest broaches the subject of souls Nozdrev refuses to sell him any, saying that instead he will wager his horses, his dogs and many other possessions at any game Chichikov cares to choose. Chichikov demurs, whereupon Nozdrev flies into a violent rage, denounces him as a charlatan and is about to have him thrown out when a superintendent of police arrives to arrest Nozdrev on a charge of assaulting a neighbour.

Thankful to escape unscathed, Chichikov orders Selifan to make for N—— with all possible speed. Once arrived, he goes straight to the President of the local Council, presents his lists of souls and has the deeds of transfer duly signed and sealed. In triumph he retires to the inn, where the Governor's servant calls upon him with an invitation to a ball the following night.

When he arrives at this function the local bigwigs crowd round him in welcome and he is enjoying himself hugely when he sees a beautiful girl at the far end of the room. Eagerly he asks her identity and, on being told she is the Governor's daughter, secures an introduction to her. Henceforth he has eyes for nobody else (although the damsel evinces no least interest in him), and this offends the other ladies, while the menfolk are chagrined by his sudden lack of interest in them and their affairs. Then Nozdrev appears, deplorably drunk as usual, and, in ringing tones which carry the length of the ballroom, denounces Chichikov as a scoundrel who buys up dead souls for some illegal and nefarious purpose of his own.

Chichikov leaves the scene hurriedly – but the harm is done. By next morning the town seethes with gossip, and when Nozdrev calls at the inn to humiliate him further by accusing him of planning to abduct the Governor's daughter, Chichikov sees the game is up and decides to fly while there is yet time. As the *britchka* jolts southwards he reflects bitterly on man's inhumanity to man.

But he is a resilient creature and by the time he reaches a region of wooded mountains and fertile valleys he has regained his natural optimism. By good fortune his first call is on the liberal-minded Tientietnikov, who is soon convinced that in his guest he has met a kindred spirit. Chichikov strikes an excellent bargain with him and, again the possessor of some dead souls, moves on to interview the eccentric General Betristchev, who ridicules his proposal and calls him a fool. He has his uses, however, for henceforth Chichikov keeps alluding to "my benevolent patron, General Betristchev" with great effect. Next he visits landowner Pietukh, whose estates are mortgaged to the hilt, but to offset this disappointment he meets there one Platon, who takes him to stay with Kostanzhoglo, an immensely rich liberal who runs his estates in the most modern and successful way.

Astute man of business though he is, Kostanzhoglo thinks Chichikov such a fine fellow that he offers to advance him a considerable sum with which to purchase a property! Naturally, Chichikov accepts with alacrity, buys some land from a harassed owner and orders new clothes, including a smoke-grey-shot-with-flame-colour frock-coat. Now all his troubles are at an end, and as he swaggers around in his new finery he boasts to a wise and important man named Murazov of his grandiose plans for the future.

But the sands are running out. A new Governor-General has been appointed to the province, and by the worst possible stroke of luck he is the same man who once had Chichikov drummed out of the Customs Service for fraud. On his first visit to the district this Prince— is besieged by a host of people who produce irrefutable evidence that Chichikov has swindled them. Consequently, just as he is preening himself on his success Chichikov is arrested and marched into the presence of the Prince. When he hears the indictment Chichikov grovels on the ground and babbles he is innocent. But the Prince coldly tells him his true character, adding that he has never made a *kopeck* "by aught but shameful methods of trickery or theft, the penalty for which is Siberia and the knout".

Chichikov struggles with the guards who seize him but is no match for them and is thrown into a dank cell in the town gaol. His beautiful coat is in tatters, his body a mass of bruises; worst of all his accusers have taken the precious despatch-box in which all his ill-gotten gains are stored. Within the hour he is visited by Murazov, who out of his wisdom realizes that the real blame lies not with Chichikov but with the corrupt system which has made him what he is. Having extracted a solemn promise from the prisoner that he will lead an honest life in future, he intercedes with the Prince on his behalf, pointing out that innumerable Government officials are equally guilty because they profited by his nefarious schemes. Reluctantly, the Prince sets the culprit free, gives him back his despatch-box and orders him to leave the town forthwith. He then summons the officials and gives them a long lecture while Chichikov orders himself a new smoke-grey-shot-with-flame-colour frock-coat and drives off joyfully to seek fresh woods and pastures new.

It is a measure of the novel's greatness that although it is unfinished it is still regarded, over a hundred and twenty years later, as a masterpiece of fictional writing. As Pushkin said: "Behind Gogol's laughter you feel the unseen tears", and here, underlying the wit, the satire and the superb descriptions of the countryside, there is a well-nigh perfect analysis of that haunting, melancholy something which, for want of a better term, we may call the Russian soul.

But at the time of publication it was Gogol's sympathetic

treatment of Chichikov's character that gave rise to a storm of controversy, and he received thousands of letters imploring him to ensure that this villain received his deserts in the second volume. To the hypersensitive Gogol, already enduring the torment of exile from the Russia he adored, these letters were the last straw. He wrote to friends and critics alike that he would make Chichikov a reformed creature; but his growing mental derangement prevented him from achieving more than fragments of the second volume. An incurable restlessness led him to wander from place to place, and in 1848 he made a pilgrimage to Jerusalem. Finally, he returned to Russia with no possessions save a small bag containing pamphlets and press-cuttings which savagely attacked his work. He distributed these haphazardly and spent his last days praying and fasting. In 1852, on his death-bed, he cried wildly for "A ladder! Quick, a ladder!", this being supposedly the "spiritual ladder" asked for by Jeremiah in the Greek translation of the Old Testament. A few faithful friends arranged for his burial and had one of his favourite sayings: "I shall laugh my bitter laugh", carved on his gravestone.

THE THREE MUSKETEERS

ALEXANDRE DUMAS

THE TWO most famous historical romances in all literature are Alexandre Dumas's *The Three Musketeers* and *The Count of Monte Cristo*. Both these fabulous stories have survived for well over a century and are still favourites all over the world. Who has not heard of Edmond Dantes and the Château d'If, of Athos, Porthos, Aramis and d'Artagnan and has not, hovering at the back of his mind, surviving perhaps from childhood, a series of pictures: desperate duels, the Musketeers, in capes and plumed hats, carousing at some wayside inn, horses' hooves thundering in a midnight dash under a flickering moon, the sinister figure of Cardinal Richelieu planning the downfall of the Queen, phials of poison, secret messages and the four inseparables, fighting, laughing and conspiring together in deeds of chivalry and daring? Who has not been charmed by the freshness and naïvety of *The Three Musketeers*, its speed and gusto and the whole-hearted enjoyment which Dumas obviously finds in telling his adventurous story? It is Dumas himself who enchants us in this tale of plot and counter-plot in the reign of Louis XIII, and a few words about him will help to convey the flavour of his book.

Dumas was born in 1802, grandson on his father's side of a minor Norman aristocrat and a Haitian Negress. His father was one of Napoleon's generals, a man of immense physical strength who died when his son was three. After early happy-go-lucky years spent with his impoverished mother in the country, Dumas moved at the age of twenty-one to Paris where his only saleable asset, good handwriting, got him a clerk's job in the offices of the Duke of Orleans. The young man with frizzy hair and thick, negroid lips was shockingly ignorant, but a friend saw to his literary education and an urge to write was born in him. They collaborated in vaudevilles which were dismal failures and it was not until he was twenty-seven that his first serious work, an historical verse drama in the Romantic style, earned him a moderate success. Fame, however, was waiting around the corner and in 1829 his play, *Henri III et sa Cour*, brought him instant recognition. The true Dumas, the genial lover of life, spendthrift, ebullient, kind to all the world, then began to emerge and he lost no time in acquiring an eyeglass, a vivid waistcoat, a horse, a valet and palatial apartments. Success filled him with childish delight. He talked, he cracked jokes, he beamed on friends and enemies alike. Stirring in him was the precious gift of creative genius which in later years was to make him the Lion of Paris and the demigod of literary France, the natural phenomenon, *Hercule bon enfant* as he was called, Papa Dumas who was read from one end of the civilized world to the other, and first and foremost, as he frankly confessed, by himself.

From 1830 until his death at the age of seventy Dumas's life story is one of colossal literary output, tremendous extravagances, riotous living and immense success. Everyone, with the exceptions of Hugo, de Musset and Balzac, whose hate sprang from jealousy, found him lovable. Even his terrific vanity was acceptable because it was so naïve. He loved adventure and excitement and the morbid fantasies of current Romantic fiction left him cold. In his joyous acceptance of all life had to offer he was an eternal child. Much of this refreshing outlook comes over in the pages of *The Three Musketeers*, which was written at lightning speed at the end of 1843 and first published in serial form in 1844. The story was an immediate success, so startling that Dumas himself was surprised, for there is no profundity of thought here, no distillation of experience in subtle prose, no scenes, even, which move the reader with their pathos. The book is simply a hotchpotch of history and fiction, fast moving and written to entertain, and the manner in which it was compiled underlines the fact that this popular best-seller could never have been a literary masterpiece.

Dumas had many collaborators – which led a venomous critic to speak of his "fiction factory" – and chief of them was Auguste Maquet, a young writer and scholar who did much research for him and fed him with ideas and draft material for his novels. In 1843, when preparing to write a historical work on the age of Louis XIV, Dumas had come across a book entitled *Mémoires d'Artagnan*, a soldier of fortune who had lived in the early seventeenth century. Dumas drafted out some ideas, sent them to Maquet for his opinion, then the collaborators met to discuss the character of the novel-to-be. Throughout the subsequent writing of *The Three Musketeers* Maquet appears to have done much of the spade work in supplying historical material and even some of the key chapters, though these were amended and given colour and life by Dumas. At any rate, one can say that while the great man was sitting with rolled-up sleeves and an open-necked shirt in his bare work-room, hammering away like a village blacksmith, Maquet was kept busy supplying him with suitable lengths of iron. The result was a highly readable romance, no more no less, memorable as a whole rather than for its individual parts, unevenly written, but brimful of Dumas's zest for living.

The historical setting for a novel of cape and sword was admirably chosen. No period of French history has been more full of unrest and intrigue than the reign of Louis XIII (1610–43), when only the firm hand of Cardinal Richelieu was able to produce a semblance of strength and unity in a country riven with internal dissensions due to a feeble monarch, fractious nobles and bitter religious strife between Catholics and Huguenots. Armed bands and private armies roved the country. Duelling, though officially abolished, accounted for hundreds of deaths every year. Morals, in a disrupted society, were at their lowest ebb. Never had there been such a chance for a resolute young man to fight his way to fame, fortune and the favours of beautiful women. One such, as the source-book related, was Monsieur d'Artagnan, officer in the King's Musketeers. Dumas saw his chance and seized it with both hands. First, from his various sources he extracted the historical background and some of the key figures who would play a part in his story: the feeble and petulant Louis XIII, his beautiful but unhappy Queen, Anne of Austria, the ever-alert and universally feared Richelieu, the Duke of Buckingham, Charles I's showy and incompetent favourite, leader of the unsuccessful expedition to relieve the Huguenots beseiged in La Rochelle and allegedly in love with the French Queen.

With these characters ready to play their part in the plot, Dumas began his story. D'Artagnan, an eighteen-year-old Gascon nobleman, athirst for glory and ever ready to avenge insults with his sword, sets out to seek his fortune in Paris on a sorry old nag with nothing but fifteen crowns in his pocket and a box of miraculous ointment for healing wounds. In Paris, after being promised eventual employment in the royal bodyguard of Musketeers, he meets three of these men and after becoming involved with each one of them in a duel seals with them a pact of eternal friendship. So the three Musketeers, Athos, a *grand seigneur* with a romantic cast of mind, Porthos, a vain, portly but good-natured fool, and Aramis, former clerk in holy orders who longs to re-enter the Church and writes theological theses in his spare time, get involved with their new-found friend in a series of brawls with Richelieu's guards, between whom and the Musketeers perpetual warfare rages in the streets of Paris.

The scene now switches to high politics. Richelieu, an unsuccessful applicant for the Queen's favours, knows of Buckingham's secret love and lures him to Paris with a pretended message from her. Louis has given his wife a set of twelve diamond studs and these she presents to Buckingham in return for his promise to return at once to England. Richelieu hears of the gift and plans to discredit the Queen by persuading Louis to announce a ball at which he will require her to wear the studs. Richelieu guesses that she will send post-haste to get them back from Buckingham and arranges for a female agent to go to London and steal two of the studs so that when the Queen appears at the ball there will be ten instead of twelve. This agent, known as Milady, is a leading character in the book, a figure of pure melodrama complete with beautiful face and wicked heart, separated wife of Athos, later bigamously married to an Englishman and branded by the public executioner in France for various youthful misdeeds. She is described as half-serpent, half-lioness. The serpent-cum-lioness duly steals two studs and is closely pursued to England by d'Artagnan and the three Musketeers who have been commissioned by the Queen to recover the set from Buckingham. On the journey, other agents of Richelieu try to lay low the band of brothers, but their motto is "one for all and all for one", and as Porthos, Aramis and Athos are successively involved in affrays they urge d'Artagnan to leave them and press on to his goal. He reaches England, recovers the studs from Buckingham who has two replicas made to replace the stolen ones and in due course the Queen appears at the ball wearing the complete set. Richelieu and the King have been foiled.

Another stage in the plot now opens. The brothers in arms are called to the siege of La Rochelle and while they are there two attempts engineered by Milady are made to murder d'Artagnan, who has had an assignation with her and discovered the secret of her brand-mark. Near the military camp Richelieu has an interview with Milady which is overheard by Athos. She is to go to England and try to deter Buckingham from relieving La Rochelle by threats from the Cardinal that he will reveal the Duke's relations with the Queen and ruin her. The four Musketeers – d'Artagnan has by now been enrolled – discuss how to counter this move in the intervals of defending a bastion captured from the Huguenots.

They decide to warn Lord de Winter, Milady's English brother-in-law who has reasons for hating her, that she is coming to England. On arrival at Portsmouth she is taken into custody by de Winter, who is governor of the city, and lodged at his castle under a naval guard headed by a Lieutenant John Felton. Several chapters describe how, under threat of being deported to a lonely island by her brother-in-law, Milady discovers that Felton is a fanatical Puritan, feigns a kindred passion, throws in a story for good measure that the wicked Buckingham once raped her, and persuades Felton to help her escape to France. The historical scene is then described, much altered, in which Felton assassinated the Duke at Portsmouth. But in France nemesis awaits the wicked schemer. A serving woman of the Queen with whom d'Artagnan is desperately in love has been immured in a convent on Richelieu's orders. Milady visits her, gains her confidence and plans to put her permanently out of the way. But d'Artagnan and his friends are on her trail, and after Milady has poisoned the serving woman rather than let her fall into friendly hands, she is captured, tried for her numerous crimes and beheaded in a midnight scene of rough justice. All this comes to the ears of Richelieu. He summons d'Artagnan and toys with the idea of trying him for high treason. But the young man's record of resource and daring, his intelligence and his frank demeanour persuade the Cardinal that here is indeed a useful servant of the King, and potentially of himself, and he gives him a Lieutenant's commission in the Musketeers.

This is the bare outline of Dumas's tale. A multitude of intriguing incidents has been omitted, all the humour, many excellent minor characters. Above all, only a reading of the book can convey its speed, its freshness and, to my mind, the conception which has made it so famous: the band of brothers who fight for their suffering Queen, half out of chivalry, half from sheer devilment, the young soldiers of fortune, living by their swords, gallant to their mistresses, implacable to their foes, full of laughter and generosity toward their friends. They drink deep, they sleep sound, they love life, and in the age of Louis Philippe when *The Three Musketeers* was first published, as in our own, such men have an eternal appeal.

VANITY FAIR

W. M. THACKERAY

AMONG THE Victorian novelists – and what a collection they are, unsurpassed in any other country and age – Thackeray holds a position of superiority that is only challenged by Dickens, and some excellent critics have maintained that he has nothing to fear even from *that* comparison. While one or two of his novels seem to have been written rather against the grain, he displayed the master's touch in *Henry Esmond* and its sequel *The Virginians*, in *Pendennis* and *The Newcomes*, but never more surely and triumphantly than in *Vanity Fair*. This was the first of his novels to be published (originally in monthly numbers, commencing in 1847), and it made his reputation. For more than a hundred years now it has been pretty sure of a place in any list of the supremely great masterpieces of fiction.

Vanity Fair, he tells us on an early page, is a very vain, wicked and foolish place, full of all sorts of humbugs and falsenesses and pretensions, but to begin with he shows us nothing that is so very dreadful. The book opens on a sunshiny morning in June, before the great iron gate of Miss Pinkerton's academy for young ladies on Chiswick Mall – and who that ever had that formidable lady's acquaintance could ever suspect that there was anything about her that was not of the highest respectability? Why, she boasted of the friendship of the great Dr. Johnson, who had once honoured the establishment with a personal visit, and a copy of his *Dictionary* was solemnly placed in the hands of every departing pupil. Miss Pinkerton's young ladies were models of decorum and the most ladylike behaviour, and when they went home for the holidays it was to the mansions of City magnates or the country seats of landed proprietors. But as with most things there was an exception. There was an odd man out – girl rather: a seventeen-year-old girl who is described as small and slight in person, pale, sandy-haired, and with eyes habitually cast down – but when they looked up they were very large, odd and attractive. They were *green* eyes, and that surely is enough to put us on our guard.

Vanity Fair has the sub-title "a novel without a hero", and indeed the men in the story are nothing to shout about. George Osborne, spendthrift son of a wealthy father with a house in Russell Square, is a foolish young cub, and his best friend Dobbin is a blundering ass. Jos Sedley, home on leave from his appointment in His Majesty's East Indian service, so proud of his waistcoats and his taste in curries, is a slow-moving lump; while as for the Crawleys, of Queen's Crawley, in the county of Hants, Sir Pitt is a mean old reprobate, doling out the candles and dining on bread and cheese, and of his sons, Pitt is a narrow-minded prig and Rawdon is a military man with a bad reputation for gaming and duelling and other high-class vices. No, there is no hero in *Vanity Fair*. But there is a heroine, if we are prepared to extend that term to include one who is perhaps the most brilliant, and most shameless, little adventuress in English fiction. Rebecca Sharp her name is – Becky for short; and – yes, you have guessed it – she is the green-eyed little minx already referred to. Heroine or no, she is the centre of interest from beginning to end, and indeed there would have been no *Vanity Fair* without her.

"I think I could be a good woman if I had five thousand a year," Thackeray makes her say. "I could dawdle about in the nursery if I were a country gentleman's wife, and count the apricots on the wall. I could water plants in a greenhouse, and pick off dead leaves from the geraniums. I could ask old women about their rheumatisms, and order half-a-crown's worth of soup for the poor. I shouldn't miss it much out of five thousand a year. I could go to church and keep awake in the great family pew, or go to sleep behind the curtains, with my veil down, if I only had practice. I could pay everybody, if I had but the money . . ." But as it was, Miss Becky was the daughter of an artist with a great propensity for running into debt and a partiality for taverns, who when he was drunk – which was pretty often – used to beat his wife and daughter, and the next morning, with a headache, would rail at the world for its neglect of his genius. She inherited her father's brains, but she had also the "dismal precocity of poverty". Many a dun had she talked to and turned away from her father's door, and many a tradesman had she coaxed and wheedled into good humour and the granting of just one meal more. Her father was very proud of her wit, and she used to sit beside him at his carousings and hear the talk of many of his wild companions – talk which we may well believe was often but ill-suited for a girl to hear. But her mother had had some education somewhere, with the result that Becky learnt to speak French with a purity and a Parisian accent that in those days was rather a rare accomplishment; and on the strength of it she was promoted from charity-pupil to the post of French mistress at Miss Pinkerton's academy. But when that majestic lady, thinking to save herself the expense of a music master, intimated to her that she would be required to instruct the juniors in music in future as well as in French, the girl refused point-blank. "For five and thirty years," said Miss Pinkerton, "I have never seen the individual who has dared in my own house to question my authority. I have nourished a viper in my bosom." "A viper – a fiddlestick," rejoined Miss Sharp to the old lady who was almost fainting with astonishment. "You took me because I was useful. There is no question of gratitude between us. I hate this place, and want to leave it. . . . Give me a sum of money, and get rid of me – or, if you like it better, get me a good place as governess in a nobleman's family – you can do so if you please."

Miss Pinkerton *did* please, although the place she obtained for her was only at a baronet's, but she sternly refused to present the girl with a copy of the *Dictionary*. Her sister, Miss Jemima, was made of kinder stuff, however, and as the carriage that was taking away Becky and her dear friend Amelia Sedley was about to start, that kind creature thrust a parcel through the window. "It's some sandwiches, my dear," she told Amelia, who was a favourite among the pupils, "you may be hungry, you know; and Becky, Becky Sharp, here's a book for you that my sister – that is, I – Johnson's *Dictionary*, you know; you mustn't leave us without that. Good-bye. God bless you!" And lo, just as the coach drove off, Miss Sharp put her pale face out of the window and actually flung the book back into the garden!

After a stay in London with the Sedleys – when she set out to entrap Jos Sedley, Amelia's brother, and might well have hooked him if he had not got shockingly drunk at a party at Vauxhall Gardens – Becky took up her appointment at Queen's Crawley. Here she made up to everyone who was likely to be of any advantage to her – to dirty, cynical, thoroughly disreputable old Sir Pitt Crawley, to his wealthy sister Miss Crawley, who luxuriated in the attentions engendered by the possibility of a mention in her will, to his fox-hunting brother of a parson, and also to his sons, Pitt and Rawdon, who were so strongly contrasted in character and pursuits. Very soon she was twisting the baronet about her little finger, and before long we are witnesses of a truly extraordinary scene, in which old Sir Pitt (whose wife has so lately died that the funeral has not taken place) goes down on his knees before the little governess, making her an offer of marriage. "Say yes, Becky. I'm an old man, but a good'n. I'm good for twenty years. I'll make you happy, zee if I don't. You shall do what you like; spend what you like; and 'av it all your own way . . ."

In the course of this history (writes Thackeray) we have never seen Rebecca lose her presence of mind; but she did now, and wept some of the most genuine tears that ever fell from her eyes. "Oh, Sir Pitt!" she said. "Oh, sir – I – I'm *married already*." If only she had waited, she reflected in bitter exasperation: she might have been Lady Crawley, but she had married Rawdon, the younger son . . .

In complete contrast with Becky Sharp is her dear friend already mentioned – Amelia Sedley, a pretty little thing, with "such a kindly, smiling, tender, gentle, generous heart of her own, as won the love of everybody who came near her". This is Thackeray's view of her, but it is to be feared that Thackeray liked his women to be soft and cling- ing. Less well-disposed persons might have thought Miss Sedley to be an insignificant little chit – and what on earth could handsome young Captain Osborne have seen in her they could not imagine. . . . To his credit as a worthy citizen of Vanity Fair, if not as the gentle- man which he would have liked to be, he was not at all eager to marry her when her father went bankrupt following upon Napo- leon's return from Elba, and George's disagreeable old father forbade the match. It was Dobbin who, being himself hopelessly in love with Amelia and not being able to stand her tears, at length goaded George to carry out his promise and marry the girl, his father notwith- standing.

Now we come to what many readers, perhaps most, must regard as the most interesting chapters in the whole long novel. The cam- paign of Waterloo was about to open, and Osborne and Dobbin, and likewise Rawdon Crawley, joined their regiments in Brussels. Becky and Amelia accompanied their husbands, as was the strange custom of those days; and whereas Becky drew all men to her, from the general to the youngest subaltern, Amelia was already the neglected wife. Osborne was among Becky's "flames", and it was only on the battle-eve that his heart smote him for his treatment of his girl-bride. Their final parting is most movingly described, and then Osborne hurried away to join his men. As he marched past at the head of his company he looked up at Amelia standing at the window of their lodging, "smiled and passed on, and even the sound of music died away". Then a few pages later we have the battle of Waterloo summed up in a few paragraphs, concluding with a superlatively fine piece of economical writing.

"No more firing was heard at Brussels – the pursuit rolled miles away. Darkness came down on the field and city; and Amelia was praying for George, who was lying on his face, dead, with a bullet through his heart."

After Waterloo the Crawleys (on whom we must concentrate, although Amelia and Jos Sedley and Dobbin and many another all clamour for their share of attention) accompanied the British army of occupation to Paris, where Mrs. Rawdon was courted by all the men and most heartily disliked by almost all the women. Then after living two or three years on nothing more substantial than credit and what the Colonel could make at the card table and at billiards, they found it necessary to make a quick and quiet removal. Eventually they settled in London and lived for some years there, very comfortably, on "nothing a year", or in other words, at other people's expense. Becky moved in high society, though not in the most respectable; she was presented at Court, and had lots of aristocratic acquaintances. One in particular, the Most Honourable the Marquis of Steyne. He was a battered old lecher, but he had rank and influence and great possessions, and he admired her wit and beauty and laughed at her scrapes and wheedlings. Until one night . . .

"Rawdon opened the door and went in. A little table with a dinner was laid out – and wine and plate. Steyne was hanging over the sofa on which Becky sat. The wretched woman was in a brilliant full toilette, her arms and all her fingers sparkling with bracelets and rings; and the brilliants on her breast which Steyne had given her. He had her hand in his, and was bowing over it to kiss it, when Becky started up with a faint scream as she caught sight of Rawdon's white face. At the next instant she tried a smile, a horrid smile, as if to welcome her husband; and Steyne rose up, grinding his teeth, pale, and with fury in his looks . . . 'I am innocent, Rawdon,' she said; 'before God I am innocent'. She clung hold of his coat, of his hands; her own were all covered with serpents, and rings, and baubles. 'I am innocent. Say I am innocent', she said to Lord Steyne. He thought a trap had been laid for him. 'You innocent! Why, every trinket you have on your body is paid for by me. I have given you thousands of pounds which this fellow has spent, and for which he has sold you . . .' 'You lie, you dog!' said Rawdon. 'You lie, you coward and villain!' And he struck the peer twice over the face with his open hand, and flung him bleeding to the ground . . ."

Was she guilty? "She said not; but who could tell what was truth which came from those lips?" Who indeed? And that thousand-pound note that Rawdon found in his wife's desk in her bedroom looks decidedly suspicious. Thackeray leaves the matter open so that the reader may come to what conclusion he will. But that Becky was not wholly bad is clear enough from her kindness to Amelia in the last chapter of the book.

And what happened to Becky in the end? Did she sink lower and lower in the social scale? Did she apply herself to the rouge-pot and the brandy-bottle more and more until at length she arrived at a lonely, miserable, and neglected old age? Oh dear me no; that's not the way things happen in Vanity Fair, not to the Becky Sharps. The last picture we are given of Rebecca, Lady Crawley (as she called herself, although she had no strict right to do so), is of her living in most comfortable circumstances in Bath or Cheltenham, where (we are told) a very strong party of excellent people consider her to be a most injured woman. "She has her enemies. Who has not? Her life is her answer to them. She busies herself in works of piety. She goes to church, and never without a footman. Her name is in all the Charity Lists. The Destitute Orange-girl, the Neglected Washerwoman, the Distressed Muffin-man, find in her a fast and generous friend. She is always having stalls at Fancy Fairs for the benefit of these hapless beings . . ." Yes, that's the way it is, in Vanity Fair.

JANE EYRE

CHARLOTTE BRONTË

AT HAWORTH parsonage, on the edge of the Yorkshire moors, they had their dinner midday, and one afternoon in 1847, when the things had been cleared away, the eldest daughter knocked rather timidly at the door of her old father's study and, entering, handed him a book together with a few newspaper-cuttings.

"Papa," she began, "I've been writing a book."

"Have you, my dear?"

"Yes, and I want you to read it."

"I am afraid it will try my eyes too much."

"But it is not in manuscript; it is printed."

"My dear! You've never thought of the expense it will be! It will be almost sure to be a loss, for how can you get a book sold? No one knows you or your name."

"But, Papa, I don't think it will be a loss; no more will you, if you will just let me read you a review or two, and tell you more about it." Whereupon the young woman – she was not so very young, in fact, being one-and-thirty – sat down and read some of the reviews to her father; and then, having given him the copy of her book, left him alone to read it. A few hours later, when he made his appearance at the tea-table, he said, "Girls, do you know Charlotte has been writing a book, and it is much better than likely?"

That is Charlotte Brontë's own description of the way in which she broke the news to her father that she had written *Jane Eyre*, as recorded by Mrs. Gaskell in the biography which is still the best of all the "lives" of her that have been written, since she knew Charlotte Brontë as a personal friend.

Jane Eyre is a penniless orphan, who has been left to the care of her aunt, Mrs. Reed, as unpleasant a specimen of the middle-class matron as may be found in English fiction. Ten years old when the story opens, little Jane is harassed and bullied and generally pushed around by her aunt's own children, until the ill-treatment to which she is subjected leads to an outburst on her part of passionate resentment, and she is thereupon consigned to a charitable institution for the education of orphan girls. Lowood Institution it is called in the novel, and it has been identified with an establishment at Cowan Bridge, beside the road that runs from Leeds to Kendal, where Charlotte Brontë was herself a pupil for some years, as well as her sisters.

From her description it must have been a dreadful place, at least in its early years. The site was unhealthy, the conditions poor, the food abominable, and the teachers (with the exception of the superintendent, Miss Temple, who is portrayed most sympathetically) incompetent, harsh and unfeeling. The controller of the school was a local clergyman, called in the book Mr. Brocklehurst but identified in real life with the Rev. Carus Wilson.

The two eldest of the five Brontë sisters went to Cowan Bridge in the summer of 1824, and Charlotte and Emily followed a few months later. A low fever broke out in the school, and Maria and Elizabeth, little girls of eleven and ten respectively, sickened and were taken home to die. Maria Brontë is the Helen Burns of the novel, and we are assured by Mrs. Gaskell that Helen "is as exact a transcript of Maria Brontë as Charlotte Brontë's wonderful power of reproducing character could give. Her heart, to the latest day on which we met, still beat with unavailing indignation at the worrying and the cruelty to which her gentle, patient dying sister had been subjected" by the teacher who is given the name of Miss Scatcherd.

Jane Eyre took with her to the school the worst of testimonials from her aunt, and for a time she was victimized by the sanctimonious and overbearing Brocklehurst. But her character was cleared eventually by Miss Temple, she did well at her studies, and for the last two years of her time at the school she acted as a pupil-teacher. Then having attained the age of eighteen she went out into the world as a governess.

Having advertised in the county newspaper for a post, Jane Eyre received the offer of one from a Mrs. Fairfax, writing from Thornfield Hall, some seventy miles away, near the large manufacturing town of Millcote. The situation was one "where there is but one pupil, a little girl, under ten years of age; and where the salary is thirty pounds per annum". Jane accepted by return, and arrived in due course at Thornfield Hall, where she was welcomed warmly enough by Mrs. Fairfax, who however turned out to be only the housekeeper. Her employer was Mr. Edward Rochester, the owner of the mansion, who was a wealthy bachelor and away a good deal; and her charge was to be this gentleman's ward, who, Jane soon discovered, was the daughter of a French opera dancer who had been Mr. Rochester's mistress in Paris.

Mr. Rochester did not put in an appearance at the Hall for some weeks, and then he *rode* into Jane Eyre's life with a crash. She was taking a country walk one afternoon in December when she was overtaken by a great black and white dog, that suggested some spectral hound, and a man on a powerful horse. The rider tore past, and then, "a sliding sound, an exclamation of 'What the deuce is to do now?' and a clattering tumble arrested my attention. Man and horse were down; they had slipped on the sheet of ice which glazed the causeway". She hurried up and gave what assistance she could, and with a few words of thanks the man dashed away. "He had a dark face, with stern features and a heavy brow; he was past youth, but had not reached middle age; perhaps he might be thirty-five. I felt no fear of him, and but little shyness . . ."

When she got back to the Hall, she found everything in a bustle. Mr. Rochester had just arrived, Mrs. Fairfax told her; he had had an accident; his horse had slipped and fallen, and his ankle was sprained. One of the men-servants had gone for a surgeon.

The following evening Jane and her little pupil, Adele, were invited to take tea with Mr. Rochester in the drawing-room. She found his manner brusque and a bit overwhelming at first, but soon got used to it. So far from being repelled, she was most powerfully drawn to him; and he, for his part, showed signs of finding something in her, notwithstanding her plain looks and simple unaffected ways, that appealed to his better nature. Soon he was taking her into his confidence, and even telling her of some at least of his youthful misdemeanours. And she – "Was Mr. Rochester now ugly in my eyes? No, reader; gratitude, and many associations, all pleasurable and genial, made his face the object I best liked to see; his presence in a room was more cheering than the brightest fire."

All the same, there was much that she did not understand – about him, and about the house, and about one of its inmates in particular, a woman named Grace Poole who did the sewing and had her own quarters up a back stair on the third floor.

When she had been at Thornfield Hall two or three months there was an extraordinary occurrence that brought Jane and her master very near together. She was wakened one night by a lugubrious murmur coming apparently from the room above hers; then ghostly fingers scratched at her door, and after the clock in the hall had struck two there was a demoniac laugh! Hurrying on some clothes, she went out into the passage, and found it filled with smoke coming from Mr. Rochester's room. She thrust open the door, and saw his bed was alight. "Wake! wake!" she cried, and shook him violently, but he was stupefied with the smoke. Then she seized the water-jug and deluged bed and occupant. Mr. Rochester awoke then. "Is there a flood?" he demanded. "No, sir," she replied with unconscious humour, "but there has been a fire".

When he had heard her account of what had happened, he did not seem to be half so surprised as she felt he ought to have been. Placing her, well wrapped up, in his chair, and bidding her to be quiet as a mouse, he took the candle and went upstairs to the attics. He was away a long time, and when he came back he was pale and gloomy. "I have found it all out," he said, "it is as I thought." That odd laugh that she had heard – hadn't she heard it before, or something like it? "Yes, sir; there is a woman who sews here, called Grace Poole – she laughs in that way. She is a singular person." "Just so," replied Mr. Rochester; "Grace Poole – you have guessed it. She is, as you say, singular – very."

On the day following this eventful night, Jane was more than surprised to find Grace Poole calmly sewing new rings on Mr. Rochester's bed-curtains, while another of the servants was cleaning up the mess made the night before when, she was informed, master had fallen asleep while reading in bed and the curtains had got alight; fortunately he had woken in time, and had managed to put out the fire with water from the ewer on the washstand. . . . Jane's bewilderment was increased when Mrs. Fairfax told her that Mr. Rochester had suddenly taken it into his head to join a house party at a country seat some ten miles the other side of Millcote, where one of the other guests would be the Honourable Blanche Ingram, a strikingly beautiful girl who had been the belle of the ball last Christmas at Thornfield Hall. Jane's spirits sank lower and lower, and she called herself a fool for daring to think that her master was in the least interested in *her*.

A few days later, Mr. Rochester returned the hospitality, and a gay party assembled under his roof. Jane was pushed into the background and treated by the guests as very much the poor governess. Then occurred another extraordinary scene in the dead of night. A terrible cry awoke the house, the gallery was filled with ladies and gentlemen in their night clothes, and everyone was asking, "Where is Mr. Rochester?" Where indeed? At first he was among his guests, allaying their fears and getting them all to go back to bed. And then, some little time later, there he was knocking at Jane Eyre's bedroom door. She opened it, and he urged her to accompany him to the third floor. Here in one of the attics, lying on an antique bed, she was amazed to see a man, a visitor who had put in an appearance only the evening before, and who had seemed to be as unexpected as he was unwelcome. His name was Mason. Now here he was, covered with blood, scratched and torn – and bitten! He seemed at death's door, but Jane tended him while Mr. Rochester surreptitiously departed to fetch a doctor. Then while it was not yet light and everyone else was sleeping, they got him out of the house.

"You have passed a strange night, Jane," said Mr. Rochester in the morning; "were you afraid when I left you alone with Mason?" "I was afraid of someone coming out of the inner room," she rejoined; "will Grace Poole live here still, sir?" "Oh, yes," rejoined Mr. Rochester coolly, "don't trouble your head about her . . ."

Soon after Jane was called away to her aunt's, and found her dying and full of remorse for having told a wealthy uncle of Jane's, living in Madeira, that she had died when a pupil at Lowood. On her return to Thornfield Jane soon forgot the fortune that might have been hers, for the brightest of futures seemed to lie before her. She was still the governess, but the Honourable Blanche had disappeared from the scene altogether, and it was *she*, Jane Eyre, whom Mr. Rochester asked to be his bride! Of course she accepted him, since by this time he "was becoming my whole world, and more than the world; almost my hope of heaven . . . I could not, in those days, see God for his creature, of whom I had made an idol . . ."

The month of courtship that had been agreed upon soon passed, and then on the last night before the wedding eve Jane experienced yet another nocturnal adventure. She woke to find someone in the room; the cupboard in which she had hung her wedding-dress and veil stood open, and the someone, whoever it was, took them out and held them aloft. Then she – for now Jane could see that her visitor was a woman, with thick dark hair hanging down her back, a woman she had never seen before – threw the veil over her own head, and then tore it off, flung it to the ground and trampled on it.

A few hours later, Jane and Edward stood side by side in the village church, about to be made man and wife. But when the clergyman put the formal question about "any impediment", a man stepped forward and announced that he knew of an impediment, in that Mr. Rochester had been married before, and his wife was still living. The man (he proved to be a London solicitor) proceeded to read an affidavit to the effect that Rochester had married one Bertha Mason, fifteen years earlier, at Spanish Town, Jamaica; and then he produced a witness, the mysterious Mr. Mason whom Jane had tended on that night of blood and terror. "Mrs. Rochester," he said, "is now living at Thornfield Hall; I saw her there last April".

A grim smile contorted Mr. Rochester's lips. Then he briefly announced that there would be no wedding that day, and led the party back to the house, up the stairs to the third floor, and into one of the attics. "You know this place, Mason," he said; "she bit and stabbed you here." In a room beyond they came upon Grace Poole cooking something in a saucepan, and "in the deep shade, at the further end of the room, a figure ran backwards and forwards. What it was, whether beast or human being, one could not, at first sight, tell: it grovelled, seemingly, on all fours; it snatched and growled like some strange wild animal, but it was covered with clothing and a quantity of dark, grizzled hair, wild as a mane, hid its head and face". Jane recognized at once the mysterious visitant who had ripped up her wedding veil. "Take care, sir! for God's sake, take care!" cried Grace Poole. The lunatic sprang – she was a big woman and corpulent – grappled at Mr. Rochester's throat viciously and laid her teeth to his cheek. They struggled, and at length she was mastered, her arms pinioned, and she was tied to a chair.

Mr. Rochester turned to the spectators. "That is *my wife*," he said. "Such is the sole conjugal embrace I am ever to know. And *this* is what I wished to have," laying his hand on Jane's shoulder, "this young girl, who stands so grave and quiet at the mouth of hell, looking collectedly at the gambols of a demon . . ."

Later in the day, Jane and Rochester discussed the situation that had arisen. For hours and hours they talked, as he explained how he had been trapped into marrying that dreadful woman upstairs, when he was a young man and altogether unaware that there was insanity in her family. He had brought her back with him to England and kept her hidden, and sought his pleasures elsewhere. Then Jane Eyre had come into his life, and all had been changed. He wished to marry her, and he still wished it! They might still marry in all but the form. They might go abroad, they would be so happy, all would be well.

But Jane would not have it. She let him know in no uncertain fashion that she loved him – and it was her open expression of a deep sexual feeling that so shocked the Victorian reader. She knew in her heart of hearts that what Rochester was proposing was wrong and that no good would come of it. He urged, pleaded, raged and almost wept. "He turned away; he threw himself on his face on the sofa. 'O Jane! my hope – my love – my life!' broke from his lips. Then came a deep strong sob. I had already gained the door; but, reader, I walked back . . . I knelt by him; I turned his face from the cushion to me; I kissed his cheek; I smoothed his hair with my hand. 'God bless you, my dear master!' I said; 'God keep you from harm and wrong –

direct you, solace you – reward you well for your past kindness to me.' He held his arms out, but I evaded the embrace, and at once quitted the room. 'Farewell!' was the cry of my heart as I left him. Despair added, 'Farewell for ever!' "

Strong stuff, this, and what follows hardly lives up to it. On fleeing from Thornfield Hall, Jane was for some days destitute and desperately ill, but by a most preposterous coincidence she was befriended by a young clergyman and his sisters who turn out to be her cousins. *Almost* she had agreed to marry the young clergyman, even though what he wanted was not a wife but a companion in the missionary career that he planned; but in the nick of time she thought she heard a voice calling her, "Jane! Jane! Jane!" Without hesitating a moment she hurried back to Thornfield Hall, and found it a blackened ruin. At the village inn she was told that the place had been set on fire by a maniac woman who was hidden there, and who had flung herself to death from the battlements. And Mr. Rochester? He had been maimed and burnt in trying to rescue her, and he was now living, practically blind, in his other country seat. Jane hastened there, and in a moving scene made herself known. Yes, he avowed later, he *had* called her name, at the very hour when she had heard it; and her voice had replied, "I am coming; wait for me . . ."

When he told her this, they were walking together in the grounds of the old house where he had found refuge. "Then he stretched out his hand to be led. I took that dear hand, held it for a moment to my lips, then let it pass round my shoulders: being so much lower of stature than he, I served both for his prop and guide. We entered the wood, and wended homeward."

WUTHERING HEIGHTS

EMILY BRONTË

WUTHERING HEIGHTS is the name given to one of the wildest, strangest, and most luridly magnificent works in the whole vast range of English fiction. It was written by Emily, the next to Charlotte in the doomed sisterhood of the Brontës, and it was published at the end of 1847, when she had only another year to live.

It is not at all the sort of novel that one would expect so deeply retiring and reticent, so spinsterish a female, to write – and she was a country parson's daughter at that. When Charlotte read the book in manuscript she "shuddered under the grinding influence of natures so relentless and implacable, spirits so lost and fallen", and sympathized with the complaints that "the mere hearing of certain vivid and fearful scenes banished sleep by night, and disturbed mental peace by day". Over the book, she confessed, there broods a "horror of great darkness", and it is difficult to breathe in an atmosphere so storm-heated and electrical.

If this were all, reading the book would be a torturing experience rather than a pleasure. But it is not all. Here and there, now and again, the sun breaks through the clouded daylight, and we are at large on the moor, where the moths go fluttering amid the harebells, and the scents of summer flowers are carried along on the breeze.

Generations of critics have attempted the exploration of the recesses of Emily Brontë's mind, and precious little good has come of it. Much more to the point is her literary craftsmanship. It must be said that the book is very ill-arranged, so that it might be supposed that she tried to make it as difficult to follow as possible. It opens with what is almost the end of the story, and that story, extending over some thirty years up to 1802, is told in first-hand narratives that dodge back and forth in time. To add to the reader's confusion, there are two heroines, mother and daughter, and they are both named Catherine. But holding the story together is one male character – we can hardly call him the "hero" – who is as commanding an expression of the devil in human shape as Milton's Satan. In following this man Heathcliff's career we shall come to appreciate the terror, and the redeeming pity, of this stupendous novel.

The book opens with a date: 1801, and the first narrator is a young man named Lockwood who has just taken a short lease of Thrushcross Grange, a house on the moors of West Yorkshire. One morning he walks across the moor some four miles to see his landlord, Mr. Heathcliff, whose own dwelling is called Wuthering Heights. "Wuthering," explains Lockwood for our benefit, is "a significant provincial adjective, descriptive of the atmospheric tumult to which its station is exposed in stormy weather", and it is easy to guess the power of the north wind sweeping over the edge by the excessive slant of a few stunted firs and a range of giant thorns all stretching their limbs one way, as if craving alms of the sun. But the house is stoutly built of stone, and is well capable of keeping wind and rain at bay.

If we follow Lockwood over the threshold, we shall have our first glimpse of Mr. Heathcliff. "He is a dark-skinned gipsy in aspect, in dress and manners a gentleman: that is, as much a gentleman as many a country squire: rather slovenly, perhaps, yet not looking amiss with his negligence, because he has an erect and handsome figure; and rather morose. Possibly, some people might suspect him of a degree of under-bred pride ..."

When Lockwood pays a second visit to the old farmstead the next day he realizes that there are strange deeps in this man's character that must require a great deal of fathoming. On this second occasion Lockwood meets a mysterious pair, a young man and a girl, who seem to share the place with Heathcliff. Who these are, and what they are doing there, are questions that need not detain us at present. Now let us turn to halfway through Chapter 4, when Mrs. Nelly Dean, who is the principal of the series of narrators, starts her story.

Nelly was a girl of thirteen or fourteen when it opens, and she was always at Wuthering Heights, the ancient farmstead that was the home of the Earnshaw family, "because my mother had nursed Mr. Hindley Earnshaw, and I got used to playing with the children: I ran errands too, and helped to make hay, and hung about the farm ready for anything that anybody would set me to". One fine summer morning, at the beginning of harvest, the "old master", as Nelly calls him, came downstairs, dressed for a journey, and told his children – Hindley and Catherine, about fourteen and six years old respectively, as they sat with Nelly eating their porridge, that he was going on a journey to Liverpool, "sixty miles each way, that is a long spell!", and asked them what they would like him to bring back. Hindley named a fiddle, and Miss Cathy a whip, for even so young she could ride any horse in the stable. Three days later he returned,

Described by its author as a "novel without a hero", Thackeray's *Vanity Fair* has at least a near-approach to a heroine in that clever, scheming little woman, Becky Sharp, who married Rawdon Crawley when she might have married the Baronet his father. (*Above, left*) She flings back the copy of Dr. Johnson's Dictionary into the garden of Miss Pinkerton's Academy at Chiswick; and (*right*) she and her husband and little boy are made welcome at Queen's Crawley by the younger Pitt Crawley and his family.

Born in India, where his father held some small appointment in the Government service, William Makepeace Thackeray was sent back to England as a youth to be educated at Charterhouse and Cambridge. He tried to make a living as a miscellaneous writer and book illustrator, but he had no great success until his novel *Vanity Fair* began to appear in instalments in 1849. Discerning judges then realized that a new master of the novel was in the making, and his fame was consolidated by *Pendennis*, *Henry Esmond* and its sequel *The Virginians*, and *The Newcomes*. He liked to think of himself as a humorist, but his humour was heavily charged with the most compassionate and deep understanding of human follies and frailties.

Some of the finest writers have been women, and this notwithstanding the fact that, as was bitterly complained of by Mary Wollstonecraft (*above, right*, in John Opie's portrait) in her book *A Vindication of the Rights of Woman*, they were completely subordinate to the male sex in every walk of life. Jane Austen (*above, left*) was not in the least concerned with such matters: hers the incomparable art of making the insignificant details of very ordinary lives assume an absorbing importance. (*Below*) we see two of the doomed sisterhood of the Brontës, those strange products of the sheltered loneliness of a Yorkshire parsonage. Emily (*left*, from the portrait group painted by their gifted brother Branwell) wrote *Wuthering Heights*, most awe-inspiring work of genius, and Charlotte, the eldest sister, produced among much else *Jane Eyre*, perhaps the most melodramatic contribution to Victorian fiction.

tired almost to death, and it soon appeared that he had lost the whip on the way, while as for the fiddle – he opened his greatcoat and there it was, "crushed to morsels". But he had brought something else: "a dirty, ragged, black-haired child; big enough both to walk and talk, yet when it was set on its feet, it only stared round, and repeated over and over again some gibberish that nobody could understand". Mrs. Earnshaw was ready to fling it out of doors, demanding of her husband what he was thinking of to bring "that gipsy brat" into the house. But old Earnshaw threw himself into a chair, laughing and groaning, and all the explanation they could get out of him was that he had found the boy starving and homeless and as good as dumb in the streets of Liverpool. It was in this way that Heathcliff (as they named him after a son who had died in childhood – and whether it was intended as a Christian name or surname, he was given no other) entered into the home and family that he was to dominate and ruin. The year was about 1771.

A sullen, patient child Heathcliff turned out to be, tremendously strong in physique and ferocious in character. No one knew his exact age, but he was probably six or seven when he was picked up, and before he was halfway through his teens he was almost a grown man. Hindley hated him as an interloper and treated him cruelly, until the lad was big enough to hit back; but Catherine seemed drawn to him almost from the first. She was a wild, wicked, slip of a girl, according to Nelly Dean; but she had the bonniest eye, the sweetest smile, and the lightest foot in the parish. And she became much too fond of Heathcliff. "The greatest punishment we could invent was to keep her separate from him," while he for his part followed her about with the dumb devotion of a dog.

Perhaps if old Earnshaw had lived, the two might have been allowed to marry, but he died in his chair one October evening about two years after Heathcliff's arrival, and Hindley became master in his stead. When Heathcliff had reached the age of sixteen or so he had acquired a slouching gait and ignoble look, his naturally reserved disposition had been exaggerated into unsociable moroseness, and continual hard work on the farm had obliged him to abandon the ideas he had once had of being a companion to Catherine in her studies. He was a graceless young ruffian; and yet, notwithstanding, the girl felt for him an extraordinary affection. "Nelly," she told the astounded Mrs. Dean one evening when they were sitting together before the kitchen fire, "I *am* Heathcliff! He's always, always in my mind: not as a pleasure, any more than I am always a pleasure to myself, but as my own being . . ."

But she had no intention of marrying Heathcliff when she was old enough. "It would degrade me to marry Heathcliff now," she said, when he had been brought so low by her brother, "the wicked man in there". The man she was going to marry was Edgar Linton, who lived with his parents at Thrushcross Grange; he had just proposed, and she had accepted him. Edgar was young – about four years older than she was – he was handsome, and cheerful, and rich; he loved her, and his parents made no objection. There was another reason for the match. "Nelly, I see now, you think me a selfish wretch; but did it never strike you that if Heathcliff and I married, we should be beggars? whereas, if I marry Linton, I can aid Heathcliff to rise, and place him out of my brother's power."

Unknown to them both, Heathcliff had been listening to their conversation, but he had slipped away before he heard that last of Catherine's reasons, and that night he left Wuthering Heights in rage and disgust. Catherine was greatly perturbed by his sudden departure, but she had quite made up her mind to marry Edgar Linton, and the wedding took place in the spring of 1783, when she was eighteen. And then, Heathcliff came back, on a mellow evening in September. He had grown into a tall, well-formed and athletic man. His manners, too, were greatly improved, "quite divested of roughness, though too stern for grace".

Without troubling to ask leave, Heathcliff established himself at the Heights, where Hindley Earnshaw (whose wife had died some time before, leaving him with a little boy named Hareton) was rapidly drinking himself to death in surroundings of increasing impoverishment and squalor. But even on the evening of his reappearance Heathcliff managed to obtain admission to Thrushcross Grange. Catherine welcomed him with transports of delight, and her young husband thought it best to humour her, since she was expecting a baby, although in his heart he was filled with the deepest apprehensions. He had, indeed, good cause to worry, for in one thing Heathcliff was unchanged: his resolute desire for vengeance. Soon to Edgar's horror he learned that his sister Isabel, a flighty young girl of nineteen, had become fatally enamoured of Heathcliff. A few weeks later they eloped. Heathcliff's motives in carrying her off were clear enough: Isabel was her brother's heiress unless Catherine should bear him a son, and that matter would be decided in a very few weeks now. Heathcliff treated his bride with savage brutality, and on their return to Wuthering Heights lost no time in assuring Catherine that it was she, and only she, that he loved – that it was for her sake he had gone away, and had returned, and had allowed himself to be made her brother-in-law. Linton forbade him the house, but he thrust aside all opposition.

When news reached him that Catherine was desperately ill, Heathcliff induced Nelly Dean to bear her a note, and he slipped into the house when Edgar and the servants were at church. Heathcliff pushed open the door of her room, and in a moment he had grasped her in his arms. "Why did you betray your heart, Cathy?" he moaned. "You loved me – then what *right* had you to leave me? What right – answer me – for the poor fancy you felt for Linton? Because misery and degradation, and death, and nothing that God or Satan could inflict would have parted us, *you*, of your own will, did it. I have not broken your heart – *you* have broken it; and in breaking it, you have broken mine . . ."

"Let me alone. Let me alone," sobbed Catherine. "If I have done wrong, I'm dying for it. It is enough! You left me too; but I won't upbraid you! I forgive you. Forgive me!"

About twelve o'clock that night – if you are interested in the date it was Monday, 20 March, 1784 – Catherine gave birth to a child, a girl, who was named Catherine after her; and two hours later she died.

What may be considered the second part of *Wuthering Heights* extends from Chapter 18 to Chapter 30. The narrator is Nelly Dean as before, and it is concerned chiefly with the second Catherine, the child who was born on that night of terror and anguish. Probably most readers will find in it a falling off from the sustained melodrama of the first part, and think Catherine the Second a rather tiresome little creature, shockingly spoilt, vain, foolish and self-willed. She has only herself to blame when at seventeen she is entrapped by Heathcliff into marrying his son, Linton, by Isabel (who left him after only a few weeks of marriage), a poor, puny, snivelling, self-pitying little fellow, for whom Catherine had however conceived some kind of compassionate affection. Edgar Linton dies soon after receiving this final blow at Heathcliff's hands, and then the boy-husband also dies. So Heathcliff is left the absolute master of both the Grange and Wuthering Heights, in which latter place he lives with Hareton Earnshaw, now in his early twenties, and Catherine. These, then, were the two young people whom Lockwood encountered on his visits to Wuthering Heights in 1801.

Now back to Chapter 3, in which Lockwood tells of the night he had to spend, snowbound, at Wuthering Heights. He was put to bed in a kind of cupboard up against the window; it was cold and comfortless, and he dreamed – what dreams! Someone was rattling at the window; he thrust his arm through the broken glass, and it was clutched by the fingers of a little, ice-cold hand! "Let me in! – Let me in!" sobbed a most melancholy voice. "Who are you?" he asked. "Catherine Linton," it replied shiveringly; "I'm come home: I'd lost my way on the moor!" "Begone," he shouted; "I'll never let you in, not if you beg for twenty years!" "It is twenty years," mourned the voice: "twenty years. I've been a waif for twenty years!" With that he awoke, yelling in a frenzy of fright. Heathcliff rushed in, cursing and yet horribly agitated, and as Lockwood hurried from the room he saw his landlord kneeling on the bed and wrenching open the lattice. "Come in," he sobbed, "Cathy, do come! Oh do – *once* more! Oh! my heart's darling! hear me *this* time, Catherine, at last!"

A year later, Lockwood visited the Heights again, as is told in the final chapters. Hareton and Catherine were there, and it was clear that they were very much in love; Nelly Dean too, and she told him that Heathcliff was dead some months – she had found him one morning, "dead and stark", stretched on the bed in the box-like chamber that Lockwood knew so well. For some days before his end he had seemed strangely agitated, as though he were expecting something, and had refused food and drink. Yet he was not ill, and the doctor was perplexed to pronounce of what disorder he had died. They buried him in the churchyard at evening as he had demanded, in the grave next to that of the woman he had loved so passionately years before, and Nelly remembered what he had told her he had done on the occasion of Linton's funeral. "I got the sexton, who was digging Linton's grave," he had said, "to remove the earth from her coffin-lid, and I opened it . . . I saw her face again – it is hers yet! . . . I struck one side of the coffin loose, and covered it up: not Linton's side, damn him! I wish he'd been soldered in lead. And I bribed the sexton to pull it away when I'm laid there, and slide mine out too . . ."

There were tales told of him in the countryside. "I was going to the Grange one evening – a dark evening, threatening thunder," Nelly told Lockwood, "and, just at the turn of the Heights, I encountered a little boy with a sheep and two lambs before him; he was crying terribly. 'What's the matter, my little man?' I asked. 'There's Heathcliff and a woman, yonder, under t' nab,' he blubbered, 'un' I darnut pass 'em.'"

"*They* are afraid of nothing," Lockwood grumbled, as they saw the lovers returning from their evening ramble. "Together they would brave Satan and all his legions."

As Lockwood walked back to the Grange he stepped aside to visit he churchyard. "I sought, and soon discovered, the three headstones n the slope next the moor: the middle one grey, and half buried in eath: Edgar Linton's only harmonized by the turf and moss creep- ig up its foot: Heathcliff's still bare. I lingered round them, under hat benign sky; watched the moths fluttering among the heath and arebells, listened to the soft wind breathing through the grass, and vondered how anyone could ever imagine unquiet slumbers for the eepers in that quiet earth."

THE HISTORY OF ENGLAND

LORD MACAULAY

ALTHOUGH THERE have been many "histories of England" sinc
Lord Macaulay's, there has never been one to equal it in popula
appeal. There is no mystery about this: the reason is plain. He mad
history interesting. "I shall not be satisfied," he wrote in 1841, whe
he was industriously filling his six pages of foolscap every mornin;
"unless I produce something which shall for a few days supersed
the last fashionable novel on the tables of young ladies". Seven yea
later, when the first volumes were published, he knew within
matter of a few days that he had succeeded, and not only with th
young ladies. Everybody was reading his *History* who could get hol
of a copy, and the later volumes repeated the success of the first. A
the years have passed, edition after edition has appeared, and it
probably true to say that no other serious work of the kind has eve
been in such great and sustained demand.

The book's title is *The History of England from the Accession*
James II, and Macaulay's original intention was to cover the perio
from this date of 1685 "down to a time within the memory of me
still living", by which he seems to have meant the death of Georg
III in 1820. On the scale that he projected, this was a tremendou
undertaking, and would have required as many perhaps as fift
volumes. As things turned out, he lived only long enough to take th
story up to the death of William III in 1702. Which is a pity, for
would have been good to have his account of the great war in whic
Marlborough won such splendid triumphs, and of the foundation c
the British Empire in North America and in India.

But we must not be ungracious. As it is we have sufficient t
justify his belief that "the general effect of this chequered narrativ
will be to excite thankfulness in all religious minds, and hope in th
breasts of all patriots.... Those who compare the age on which the
lot has fallen with a golden age which exists only in their imaginatio
may talk of degeneracy and decay: but no man who is correctl
informed as to the past will be disposed to take a morose or despond
ing view of the present".

Doubtless it was with the intention of correcting some of thes misguided notions that, after a couple of chapters describing in rapid but most brilliant fashion the history of England up to the close of Charles II's reign, he wrote the chapter which many readers, past and present, have considered the best thing he ever did. Social history is so very general today that it must come as something of a shock to learn that in writing this chapter on the state of England in 1685 Macaulay was venturing on an almost virgin field. It is not too much to claim that in so doing he was the Father of Social History, and even of Local History worthy of the name. And although a number of excellent writers have followed in his footsteps, there is not one who has been able to evoke the past with such intimacy of detail and sympathetic comprehension. Those timid souls who may feel "put off" by the sight of the set of closely printed volumes on the library shelves would be well advised to make a beginning with this third chapter of the *History*; and even though they read no further, they will have acquired an insight into the daily lives and circumstances of our forefathers that no other piece of historical writing may give.

The first point Macaulay makes is the smallness of the population. Since the first census was not taken until more than a hundred years later, the number of English subjects of James II cannot be stated with any degree of accuracy, but the most likely figure is between five million and five million five hundred thousand. Since 1685 the greatest increase has taken place in the northern districts, a large part of which, down to the eighteenth century, was in a state of barbarism. . . . The magistrates of Northumberland and Cumberland were authorized to raise bands of armed men for the defence of property and order. The parishes were required to keep bloodhounds for the purpose of hunting the freebooters. Sportsmen who wandered in pursuit of game to the sources of the Tyne found the heaths "peopled by a race scarcely less savage than the Indians of California, and heard with surprise the half-naked women chaunting a wild measure, while the men with brandished dirks danced a war dance". Only about half the country was under cultivation, the remainder being moor, forest and fen. Within a few miles of London thousands of wild deer roamed through the glades of Enfield Chase.

After describing the country gentlemen whose "chief pleasures were commonly derived from field sports and an unrefined sensuality", and parsons who could barely read their Prayer Books and whose status was such that in marriage they could seldom aspire to the hand of any woman above a squire's housekeeper or cast-off mistress, Macaulay proceeds to describe the changes which have come over the towns and cities.

London was far larger in comparison than it is now. In the days of Charles II the population of the metropolis was more than seventeen times the population of Bristol or Norwich, the next largest towns. Bristol had a population of just under 30,000, and was the first seaport, but most of its streets were so narrow that they were inaccessible to coaches and carts, and goods were conveyed about the place in trucks drawn by dogs. Norwich was the principal seat of the woollen manufacture, the chief manufacture of the realm, and its population was a little below Bristol's. Next came York, the capital of the north, and Exeter, the capital of the west; neither can have contained much more than 10,000 inhabitants. Leeds was already the chief seat of the Yorkshire woollen manufacturers, yet its population did not exceed 7,000 souls; Birmingham buttons were just beginning to be known, but of Birmingham guns nobody had yet heard, and the population did not reach 4,000. Seaside resorts there were none, but the gentry and lovers of gay life repaired to Cheltenham, Tunbridge Wells and Buxton, where in the last-mentioned place "they were crowded into low, wooden sheds, and regaled with oatcake, and with a viand which the hosts called mutton, but which the guests strongly suspected to be dog".

The highways connecting the towns were abominable. "Often the mud lay deep on the right and the left, and only a narrow track of firm ground rose above the quagmire. It happened, almost every day, that coaches stuck fast, until a team of cattle could be procured from some neighbouring farm, to tug them out of the slough." Then the travellers, unless they were numerous and well armed, ran the risk of being stopped and plundered by highwaymen, "about whose names a romantic interest attached, and perhaps still attaches". The common folk "eagerly drank in tales of their ferocity and audacity, of their occasional acts of generosity and good nature, of their amours, of their miraculous escapes, of their desperate struggles, and of their manly bearing at the bar and in the cart" on the way to the gallows.

Macaulay, wrote Thackeray once, "reads twenty books to write a sentence; he travels a hundred miles to write a line of description", and as we turn the pages of this wonderful chapter we may well believe it. It is tempting to quote further, in particular from those in which he writes of the intellectual life of the time. The theatres, for instance, in which "the fascination of sex was called in to aid the fascination of art, and the young spectator saw, with emotions unknown to the contemporaries of Shakespeare and Jonson, tender and sprightly heroines personated by lovely women". And the scientific discoveries, as a result of which "phantoms which had haunted the world through ages of darkness fled before the light". But this chapter is only No. 3, and there are twenty-two more to come. Only toward the end is there a slackening of the interest, a weakening of the great master's descriptive powers attributable to the illness that carried him off at the age of fifty-nine. There is not a chapter without its incomparably realistic pictures of a long-ago past made vividly present.

One scene that sticks in the memory is that of Charles II's palace at Whitehall on the evening of Sunday, 1 February, 1685. "Some grave persons who had gone thither, after the fashion of that age, to pay their duty to their sovereign, and who had expected that, on such a day, his court would wear a decent aspect, were struck with astonishment and horror. The great gallery was crowded with revellers and gamblers. The King sat there chatting and toying with three women, whose charms were the boast, and whose vices were the disgrace, of three nations. ... While Charles flirted with his three sultanas, a handsome boy warbled some amorous verses. A party of twenty courtiers was seated at cards round a large table on which gold was heaped in mountains. Even then the King had complained that he did not feel quite well. He had no appetite for his supper: his rest that night was broken ..."

Charles II died, and his brother James II reigned in his stead. Like his brother, he was a pensioner of the King of France and was quite happy at being so; but unlike Charles, he was bigoted and cruel and, above all, an opinionated fool. He was the first Roman Catholic to sit on the throne since "Bloody Mary" more than a hundred years before, and he planned to subvert the Church of England and the English constitution in the interests of his own Church. Very early on in his reign he had to encounter the rebellion of the Duke of Monmouth, one of the bastard sons of his brother King Charles but a darling with the mob because of his handsome presence and winning ways and professed championship of the Protestant cause. Macaulay is at his best in this chapter (Chapter 5) in which he relates the tragic history of that adventurer's bid for the throne, his incompetence, his collapse into utter ruin, and then the fearful harvest of judicial slaughters that followed the revolt's suppression and Monmouth's execution.

As was his custom, Macaulay went down into Somerset and explored the ground at Sedgemoor where was decided, on 6 July, 1685, the last battle to be fought on English soil. Monmouth to begin with did "his part like a stout and able warrior. He had been seen on foot, pike in hand, encouraging his infantry by voice and by example. But he was too well acquainted with military affairs not to know that all was over. His men had lost the advantage which surprise and darkness had given them. . . . He saw that if he tarried the royal cavalry would soon intercept his retreat. He mounted and rode from the field. Yet his foot, though deserted, made a gallant stand. The Life Guards attacked them on the right, the Blues on the left; but the Somersetshire clowns, with their scythes and the butt ends of their muskets, faced the royal horse like old soldiers. . . . But the struggle of the hardy rustics could not last. Their powder and ball were spent. Cries were heard of 'Ammunition! For God's sake ammunition!' But no ammunition was at hand. And now the King's artillery came up. . . . The pikes of the rebel battalions began to shake; the ranks broke; the King's cavalry charged again, and bore down everything before them; the King's infantry came pouring across the ditch. Even in that extremity the Mendip miners stood bravely to their arms, and sold their lives dearly. But the rout was in a few minutes complete. Of the rebels more than a thousand lay dead on the moor."

Monmouth was captured, and died at the hands of a bungling executioner on Tower Hill, while the infamous Lord Jeffreys made the West Country a horrid shambles. Seventy-four rebels were hanged at Dorchester, and in Somersetshire 233 prisoners were in a few days hanged, drawn, and quartered. "At every spot where two roads met, on every market-place, on the green of every large village which had furnished Monmouth with soldiers, ironed corpses clattering in the wind, or heads and quarters stuck on poles, poisoned the air, and made the traveller sick with horror. In many parishes the peasantry could not assemble in the house of God without seeing the ghastly face of a neighbour grinning at them over the porch." But Chief Justice Jeffreys, "laughed, shouted, joked and swore in such a way that many thought him drunk from morning to night . . ."

Equally dramatic in its telling is Macaulay's account (Chapter 8) of the trial of the seven Bishops who had refused the royal command to have read in the churches of their dioceses the Declaration of Indulgence, which they thought, and rightly, was a deadly blow aimed at the place and prestige and possessions of the Church of England.

So we come to the end of James II's reign, his abdication and flights, the accession of his son-in-law William III and his daughter Mary II. The highlights in the succeeding chapters are the battle of the Boyne (Chapter 16), in which William crushed James's army in Ireland, and the massacre of Glencoe (Chapter 18), when one Highland clan committed a horrible crime against another. When the great piece of historical narration comes to an end, the curtain is falling on King William, who dies just when he is about to lead a great European coalition against the French king. Ahead lie the victories of Marlborough, but Macaulay did not live to record them. On him, too, the curtain falls – seated in his easy chair in the library in his house in Kensington, with a book on the table beside him, open at the page he had been reading when he died as he had always wished to die. He was buried in Westminster Abbey, but his greatest and most enduring monument is the *History* in which he told, in such a way that ordinary people can understand, the story of that great Revolution that ended the tyranny of the Stuarts and introduced the era of profound yet peaceful change that won Britain so commanding a position in the modern world.

DAVID COPPERFIELD

CHARLES DICKENS

AS A NOVELIST, Dickens cannot be classified, for he holds a place in fiction, and in his readers' affections, entirely his own. As a creator of character, he is unrivalled; few other novelists, if any, have given us so extensive and wide-sweeping a portrait gallery. Though each generation will naturally tend to prefer novels depicting the life and times they know, it is quite certain that the novels of Dickens will endure so long as the English language lasts, for the vividness, the variety, the humour and the sympathy with which he evokes the life and characters, especially of the middle and poorer classes, of mid-Victorian times.

Of the eighteen great books which Dickens wrote, critical opinion generally acclaims *David Copperfield*, which first appeared in serial form in 1849, and in book form in the following year, as his masterpiece. It is based to a large extent on the events of his own life.

His father was a clerk in the Navy Pay Office, his mother the sister of a fellow-clerk. When Charles was two, the family moved from Portsea to London, and later to Chatham. Seven years later, when the boy was eleven, they moved back to London. Here they were soon in grave financial difficulties, and the undersized sickly boy was used as a household drudge. Before he was twelve he was put to work in a blacking factory for six shillings a week.

Eventually Dickens senior's creditors had him committed to the Marshalsea debtors' prison, where he settled in with his family, except Charles, who was placed in the care of an old woman.

At twelve he was sent to school in Camden Town, and from there passed to a solicitor's office. But he had no liking for the law, and on acquiring a knowledge of shorthand he became a reporter. In 1836 he abandoned journalism for literature, and married. The success of the *Pickwick Papers* in this year brought his unhappy days of financial worry to an end.

In his domestic life he was less fortunate. The difference in temperament between husband and wife led to their separation in 1858, after they had produced ten children. For the remainder of his life his sister-in-law kept house for him.

This extremely brief outline of Dickens's own life will, it is believed, help the reader to a deeper understanding of *David Copperfield*, for the actual experience upon which the author draws gives to the novel qualities which are lacking in many of his other books, qualities which are responsible for making *David Copperfield* the most impressive of all the novels. The device of writing the story in the first person, thus giving it the appearance and form of a real autobiography, adds to the illusion of reality, which is one of the most striking features of the story.

David Copperfield opens with the birth of David, on a Friday, just as the clock was striking midnight. His father had died six months earlier, and Mrs. Copperfield lived alone except for Peggotty, whom she had engaged as the baby's nurse.

The three of them lived a quiet, happy life together until David was seven. Then one day Peggotty asked him if he would like to go on a visit to her brother, who lived in a converted boat at Yarmouth. Here they passed a happy fortnight, but on arriving home David learned that he had a new father, a Mr. Murdstone, who had called on his mother on several occasions and to whom he had taken an instinctive dislike.

Murdstone and his sister, who came to live with them, completely dominated Mrs. Copperfield, and were determined to discipline her spoiled son. Both the mother and the boy were extremely unhappy.

The climax of the relationship of Murdstone and David was reached when Murdstone expressed his intention to beat the boy for "not knowing his lessons". In his fear, the boy bit Murdstone on the hand. After being kept in his room for several days as a punishment, David was sent to board at Salem House, near London, whose sadistic headmaster, Mr. Creakle, kept sixty boys in terror. Here he was befriended by Steerforth, a boy six years his senior, who helped and protected him.

Returning home at the end of the term, David found that he had a new brother. One day during the following term he learned that his mother and her baby had died.

Murdstone, now unwilling to bear the expense of David's education, took him from school and set him to work in a wine-bottling factory in London. Here he was expected to feed himself on his seven shillings a week wages, while Murdstone paid for his lodging with a Mr. Micawber and his family.

Mr. Micawber was always in debt, but always had plans for making money, none of which was ever successful. A supreme optimist, he was constantly waiting "for something to turn up", but it never did, and eventually he was put in the debtors' prison, where his family joined him. Here they remained until a relative paid their debts, and on coming out of prison they set off for Portsmouth "to start a new life".

Left alone, and miserably unhappy at the factory, David decided to run away. He remembered that he had an aunt, an eccentric lady called Miss Betsy Trotwood, who lived at Dover with a companion, the "mad Mr. Dick". He would ask for her help, and wrote to Peggotty, who was now married, for the loan of half a guinea for the coach fare.

When this was stolen from him, he set out to walk, and after an adventurous journey arrived at Miss Trotwood's cottage. When she heard his story, she decided to look after him.

Presently, he was sent to school in Canterbury. As there was no place for him as a boarder, he lodged with Aunt Betsy's solicitor, Mr. Wickfield, a widower, who lived in a large house with his daughter Agnes, who was about David's age.

Mr. Wickfield's clerk was a sinister, ingratiating creature called Uriah Heep, whom David found late one night studying law books in Mr. Wickfield's office. When he remarked to Heep, "I suppose you are a great lawyer," he heard for the first of many times what may be described as Heep's refrain, "Oh, no! I am a very stupid person and much too 'umble to become a real lawyer."

At the Wickfields' and at school, David was happier than he had been since Mr. Murdstone had entered his life. As the days passed, he became head boy. He was seventeen by this time, and wore a gold watch and chain, and a ring upon his little finger.

On leaving school he embarked upon the career he had chosen for himself, and entered the law office of Spenlow and Jorkins in London.

He had been in London only a few months when he received a message from Agnes Wickfield, in London on a visit, asking him to go and see her. He found her in some distress. For some time her father had appeared to be ill; now he was worse, and Uriah Heep had been looking after the business. Heep, she had learned, was demanding to be taken on as a partner.

When David exclaimed angrily at this news, she begged him to be polite to Heep when they met, lest he should hurt Mr. Wickfield in some way.

Heep had come up to London with Agnes, and next day he and David met. Heep told David that Mr. Wickfield had been very unwise, and but for him would have been professionally disgraced.

David said nothing, but watched Heep's cunning face and his evil little eyes.

Heep went on to divulge another secret. "I know I am a very 'umble sort of person," he said, "but I have always had a great affection for Miss Agnes and I hope one day she will be my wife."

David was so angry that he almost struck Heep. He left at once, and after a sleepless night he concluded that his best course for the time being was to say and do nothing.

Meanwhile the days and weeks slipped by. Then one day he was invited for a few days to the country home of Mr. Spenlow, one of his employers. Here he met Dora Spenlow and was greatly surprised to find Miss Murdstone to be the girl's governess. After dinner on the first evening, Miss Murdstone took him on one side and suggested that they should forget the past, to which David agreed.

David saw a good deal of Dora Spenlow, and by the end of the visit had fallen in love with her.

On his return to London he decided to look up an old friend from the Salem House school days, Tommy Traddles. During conversation, he learned that Traddles was in love with a Miss Micawber. Even before he had finished speaking, the door opened and Mr. Micawber walked in. He was the same old Micawber. Beset with difficulties in the West Country, he had brought his family back to London, and was still waiting "for something to turn up".

Once more David was invited to visit the Spenlows, and this time he told Dora how much he loved her and wished to marry her. They thought, however, that as she was still a little young to marry, they would keep their engagement secret. But they met often at the house of a friend of Dora's.

His new great happiness was soon to be dashed, however, by the news that Aunt Betsy Trotwood had lost all her money. To help, he asked Mr. Spenlow to allow him to leave his office and find a job so that he could support his aunt and "mad Mr. Dick". Spenlow was reluctant to do this, and on the advice of Agnes Wickfield he continued his training in law, and in the mornings and evenings he earned money acting as secretary to his old Canterbury headmaster, Dr. Strong, who had set up a coaching establishment in London. Mr. Dick also earned a little by copying legal documents.

Two days after these changes had been made in his life, David received a visit from Mr. Micawber, who surprised him by telling him that "something had turned up" at last; he had been engaged as a clerk by Wickfield and Heep, and was moving his family to Canterbury.

When the new plans were working well, David went to Dora and asked if she could marry a poor man. She would not at first believe that he was poor, but when he had convinced her, she said that she loved him still, and that somehow they would manage.

But now came another shock. On going to the office one morning, David was met by Mr. Spenlow and Miss Murdstone. Looking very serious and speaking coldly, Mr. Spenlow handed David one of the love-letters he had written to Dora. Miss Murdstone, he was told, had found Dora's little dog Jib playing with it, and though she had promised to be his friend, had taken it to Mr. Spenlow.

David admitted writing the letter, told Mr. Spenlow of his love for Dora and apologized if he had behaved badly keeping their engagement secret.

"You are not engaged to my daughter," Spenlow exclaimed, "and you never will be. You must promise me never to see Dora again or write to her."

"I cannot give such a promise," David told him.

On arriving at the office next morning, David learned that Mr. Spenlow had died suddenly the previous evening. He had left no will, his affairs were in great disorder, and Dora was now as poor as David was. She was taken to live with aunts on the other side of London.

Aunt Betsy, having become seriously perturbed by her nephew's misery, sent him to Dover to inspect her cottage, which she had let. On the way home he called upon Agnes Wickfield in Canterbury.

After dinner that evening, Uriah Heep, in David's presence, announced his desire to marry Agnes. Mr. Wickfield was so greatly shocked it seemed for a time that he was going out of his mind.

Back in London, David followed Agnes's advice and wrote to Dora's aunts asking permission to visit them. They invited him to call upon them as soon as he wished. Though they would not agree yet to his marrying Dora, he could call for tea twice a week, an invitation which completely restored his spirits.

The weeks, the months, the seasons passed, and after a time the Misses Spenlow agreed to David and Dora getting married. He was now twenty-one and he had discovered that he had the gift of writing. Newspapers bought all he wrote and in consequence he was earning a thousand pounds a year and more.

So the wedding day came. He and his beloved Dora settled in a comfortable little house, prepared for them by Peggotty. Dora proved an unskilful housekeeper, but her failures and her frailness seemed to make David love her even more.

Some months after he had married, David received a letter full of mysterious remarks from Mr. Micawber, who wished to meet him secretly.

Curious, David agreed, and at the meeting, though hesitant at first, suddenly Mr. Micawber exclaimed with a rush, "Heep is a villain, a cheat, a liar and a thief!" If they would all go down to Canterbury, he concluded, he would show them.

He would say no more then, so David, his Aunt Betsy and his friend Traddles went to Canterbury, and in their presence Micawber confronted Heep with the accusation that he had stolen Mr. Wickfield's and his clients' money, including Aunt Betsy's, and could prove it.

Heep was compelled to repay the money, and leave the Wickfields.

Presently they received news that the Micawbers had decided to emigrate to Australia. David went to see them off, and on arriving home he found Dora ill. Aunt Betsy came to live with them to nurse Dora, but all her skill and attention could not bring Dora back to health, and in a short time she died.

To recover from the shock of his wife's death, David went to live in Switzerland, where he presently wrote a novel which made him famous. At the end of three years he found that his grief had calmed and he remembered only his wife's beauty and charm. Suddenly he decided to come home.

While he had been away he had thought a good deal about Agnes Wickfield. Now he realized that he loved her.

He went to stay with Aunt Betsy in the cottage at Dover, where Peggotty was also living. While there he visited Canterbury and told Agnes of his love for her.

Smiling through her tears, laying gentle hands upon his shoulders, and looking calmly in his face, she, too, confessed: "Dearest, I have loved you all my life."

In the telling of this story Dickens has excelled in the chief characteristics of his prose writing – simplicity, emotional quality and the frequent use of humorous turns of phrase. The emotional and lyrical quality is chiefly found in David's ecstatic descriptions of Dora. One of the salient features of the novel is the great proportion of dialogue to narrative. The dialogue is natural, varied in tone and made to suit each character. In *David Copperfield*, too, to a greater degree than in most of the other novels, can be seen Dickens's great powers of observation.

Among a number of remarkably fine descriptive passages, such as those of Peggotty's house, the schoolroom at Salem House and the interior of the emigrants' ship off Gravesend, the really outstanding one is that relating the storm at Yarmouth. The claim of many critics that this may compare with the most impressive descriptive passages in the English language can be justified.

Dickens was a sentimentalist, and in most of his novels there are passages in which he was betrayed into overwriting the pathos – for example, in the death scenes of Little Nell (*The Old Curiosity Shop*) and of Paul Dombey (*Dombey and Son*). In *David Copperfield*, however, Dickens has achieved several passages of genuine pathos where this defect is avoided – the sadness of David's isolation at Blunderstone and his mother's divided loyalty between him and her new husband, but pre-eminently in Dora's realization of her failure as a wife.

The greatest strength of the story is the development of David's character. Dickens always presented a great number of characters in his stories, the large majority of whom are unreal in the sense that they are either utterly good or utterly bad. They do not change and develop as the story progresses, although they all have a remarkable fictional reality, the result of the vividness with which Dickens conceives them and the dramatic way in which he makes them behave and talk.

David does not fall into this category. He is a finished, rounded creation; his good points and his weaknesses are revealed; and as the story develops, so David develops from boy to young man to mature adult. He is a whole character, and this can be said of practically no other of Dickens's main characters.

Despite the achievement, however, it would be wrong to present *David Copperfield* as a flawless masterpiece. There are blemishes – in structure, style and characterization – but these are outweighed by the genuine humanity which so brilliantly illumines this great work of fiction.

THE SCARLET LETTER

NATHANIEL HAWTHORNE

BORN OF Puritan ancestry in 1804, at Salem, Massachusetts, Nathaniel Hawthorne's early life was devoted to solitary introspection. It is significant that he chose "Solitude" as the subject for an essay he published when only sixteen. It is also significant that he shut himself away as a virtual recluse in a lonely room to brood upon life and to write and write and write in a determined effort to master the difficult art of transferring his innermost musings to paper.

He was at Bowdoin College, Brunswick, Maine; a contemporary of Longfellow and Franklin Pierce, who later became President of the United States, and a staunch friend.

In 1842, his marriage to Sophia Peabody (a happy union) ended his aimless brooding and moved him to devote himself to more ambitious writing. He took a post as weigher in the Boston Customs House and wrote children's stories in his spare time. He had already published two series of *Twice Told Tales*, and in 1846 appeared *Mosses From An Old Manse*, though he was far from being able to survive on writing alone. A job as Surveyor of Customs at Salem lasted for three years, and when this ended abruptly through political pressures, sheer necessity forced him to set to work upon *The Scarlet Letter*. Into this tale he now put everything he knew of the human heart and spirit. In a sense it was "the pay off" for those twelve long years of self-imposed solitude and self-training in the writer's craft.

The Scarlet Letter was published in 1850, when its author was forty-six. It established him as a master. Other books followed swiftly: *The House of the Seven Gables* in 1851; *The Blithedale Romance* in 1852; *Tanglewood Tales* in 1853.

Having written a campaign note of Franklin Pierce, he was rewarded by being appointed U.S. Consul in Liverpool; but shyness held him back from seizing the opportunity of making acquaintances among British or European writers, though he did spend a year and a half in Italy.

When he returned to America in 1860 his powers were in decline, and he died suddenly in his sixtieth year.

In all his works he achieved nothing to equal *The Scarlet Letter*. Nor was it necessary. That work is monument enough.

No heroine, surely, ever made a less propitious entry into any novel than Hester Prynne's first appearance in the opening pages of Hawthorne's masterpiece? She is led from a prison gate to stand exposed before the pillory, clasping her illegitimate infant to the bosom of her gown on which she has been forced to embroider the scarlet letter "A", signifying "Adulteress". The fact that the needle-work is at once artistic, with flourishes of gold thread, gives a clue to the wearer's independence and skill. The woman is tall, elegant, with dark, abundant hair, "so glossy that it threw off the sunshine with a gleam". She has beautiful, regular features, a rich complexion and deep black eyes. She is graceful and ladylike. Yet she is being compelled to parade her shame in public. The scene is seventeenth-century Boston under implacable Puritan rule.

The author enters no special plea for this elegant heroine in her ignominious plight, and merely chronicles the facts. Two years before she had been sent out from England by her ageing husband, whose intention was to join her. The father of her child is unknown to her fellow-citizens. She refuses to divulge his name. Hence her sentence to stand exposed for three hours on the platform of the local pillory, her infant in her arms, the accusing letter on her bosom.

Though the populace is in ignorance, the author makes the reader aware that the two other principals in this eternal triangle are among the spectators in the market-place. Hester's wronged husband, newly arrived in Boston under the name of Roger Chillingworth, watches from the edge of the crowd; her craven lover, the Rev. Arthur Dimmesdale, a Calvinistic minister, is on the church balcony, overlooking the pillory, with the eldest clergyman in Boston beside him.

Dimmesdale leaves it to his senior cleric to admonish the young mother, though while the reader is thus apprised of his weakness of character it is noteworthy that Hawthorne ventures no strictures upon anyone. He presents his characters and the situation in which they find themselves, leaving the reader perfectly free to marshal his own views and feelings.

A first reaction might well be that here is a trite tale of an ageing husband deceived by an ardent young wife, herself deceived by a worthless young lover; but as the narrative unfolds it is rapidly revealed as a deeply-etched study of human strength and frailty with universal implications.

The very setting seems symbolic. The early settlement of New England, pent between the great unknown forestland of the unexplored American continent and the vast Atlantic Ocean which cuts off the settlers from their English homelands. A new setting and new values. It is in this confined settlement that the three principal characters are pinned down like butterflies while the discerning author examines their every characteristic with unhurried and detached precision.

It gradually dawns upon the reader that these three hapless humans are trapped even more relentlessly in the narrow world of Puritanism and the escape-proof prisons of their own personalities. Hester with her self-imposed determination to keep her silence and to expiate her one lapse by lifelong devotion to good works. Her ageing husband, warped in body and in mind, with one obsession – to exact a subtle and protracted vengeance from her cowardly lover. Arthur Dimmesdale with his guilty secret weighing more heavily upon him with every passing day.

With masterly insight into human foibles and intellectual and spiritual attributes, Hawthorne slowly but surely reveals these characters in depth. In advance of the psycho-analysts or psychologists he probes their minds, their characters, their very souls. And, in so doing, he broadens his canvas and contrives to present a fable with subtle undertones of good and evil. In his eternal triangle all accent is on the eternal. His characters are not exceptional, specially-drawn-to-suit-the-plot puppets. They are flesh and blood human beings, feeling the force of destiny, a destiny they have fashioned for themselves; and just as they have created the problems that enmesh them, so he makes it clear that any solution must likewise be worked out by them.

How these three will resolve their individual problems provides the thread of interest that leads the reader on and on through Hawthorne's pages of carefully wrought prose, a prose that is often poetic in quality. And interest is cleverly sustained by his masterly construction and deftly drawn characterization.

In an early meeting between Hester and her husband after her release she remains steadfast in her refusal to reveal the secret of her lover's identity. Chillingworth, who has already divined the truth, binds her also to similar silence concerning himself. Hester makes the vow of silence he demands, and thus we have the interesting situation that while Chillingworth suspects, rightly, who has wronged him, Dimmesdale has no conception that Hester's husband is not still in England.

Hester's one thought is to retain her own independence. She withdraws to a lonely cottage on the fringe of the settlement and busies herself with needlework to earn a livelihood while giving the rest of her time to good works and to bringing up her daughter, Pearl.

When, as her daughter begins to grow up, an attempt is made by the authorities to take the child away from her, she appeals to the Rev. Dimmesdale to speak up for her. He does so and tells the Governor of the settlement: "This child of its father's guilt and its mother's shame hath come from the hand of God, to work in many ways upon her heart, who pleads so earnestly, and with such bitterness of spirit, the right to keep her. It was meant for a blessing, the one blessing of her life! It was meant, doubtless, as the mother herself hath told us, for a retribution, too; a torture to be felt at many an unthought-of moment; a pang, a sting, an ever-recurring agony, in the midst of a troubled joy! . . . For Hester Prynne's sake, then, and no less for the poor child's sake, let us leave them as Providence hath seen fit to place them."

Present while this impassioned plea is being spoken is Roger Chillingworth, who, smiling at the speaker, comments: "You speak, my friend, with a strange earnestness." His suspicions of Dimmesdale's guilt are confirmed.

The plea is successful. Hester is allowed to keep her child and to devote herself to the life she has chosen. Arthur Dimmesdale, still concealing his own shame, finds his health declining under the strain of maintaining the deception, a fact that is not lost to the designing Chillingworth. A scholarly man, with some pretensions to medicine, he deliberately sets out to win the minister's friendship and confidence, even inducing him to share his home. Dimmesdale, still wholly ignorant of Chillingworth's true identity, submits himself, under subtle pressure, as the mystic's patient. Chillingworth could desire nothing better. He now has the weak-willed betrayer under his own roof and completely under his domination. He is thus able to prey upon the harassed, nerve-racked creature and, in Hawthorne's words: "He now dug into the poor clergyman's heart like a miner searching for gold; or, rather, like a sexton delving into a grave, possibly in quest of a jewel that had been buried in the dead man's bosom, but likely to find nothing save mortality and corruption. Alas for his own soul if that were what he sought."

To keep his theme continually in focus, Hawthorne rings the changes, sometimes devoting an entire chapter to each character in turn; sometimes depicting them in varying combinations. A few chapter headings must serve in this brief summary of the story to indicate the clever way in which the author contrives to keep the reader informed about the four principal characters and to keep the narrative moving at the same time – Hester at Her Needle; Pearl; The Elf-Child and the Minister; The Leech; The Leech and His Patient; the Minister and his Vigil; Another View of Hester; Hester and Pearl. . . . In this way, the characters and their relationships with each other as the years slip past are rounded and developed.

Then come three chapters which suddenly give an entirely new twist to the story. Hester, with Pearl, encounters Arthur Dimmesdale in the forest, and while the child plays innocently in a sunlit glade, Hester and Arthur have a heart-to-heart talk. Seven years have passed; in the forest, close to Nature, they feel free to plan a happier future.

> Such was the sympathy of Nature – that wild, heathen Nature of the forest (writes Hawthorne), never subjugated by human law, nor illumined by higher truth – with the bliss of these two spirits! Love, whether newly born, or aroused from a deathlike slumber, must always create a sunshine, filling the heart so full of radiance that it overflows upon the outward world. Had the forest still kept its gloom, it would have been bright in Hester's eyes, and bright in Arthur Dimmesdale's!

As the outcome of this idyllic reunion it looks to the reader as if the sombre story may also be illumined by a flood of sunshine; that a happy ending for father, mother and child is in prospect. They can secretly join a ship shortly bound for England. Hester has paved the way. They can escape from the Puritanical setting and all the cramping circumstances that enmesh them, return to England as a united family and start life anew. In a stroke, all sympathy is focused upon these three; one feels that every reader will exult. . . .

But Hawthorne is too sincere an artist to sanction such a facile solution to his tale. It may be logical enough that the lovers would think of such a course; though deeper reflection must show that it would solve nothing. Human beings can never arrest the consequences of their actions merely by running away to fresh scenes. They still have to live with themselves, whatever the backcloth may be. So the tale is given another sudden twist. Arthur, Hester and Pearl are all ready to set sail when they learn with consternation that Chillingworth likewise plans to return to England. And on the same boat!

Again, the story might well have been brought to a conclusion with this shattering piece of irony; but, again, this would have offered no solution. The drama must be played out. The reader must be kept in suspense, and only a few more pages of the book remain. How will this tale of human passion and spiritual conflict end?

Summoning all his artistry, yet stoutly preserving his literary integrity, Hawthorne draws in his threads and so contrives it that the climax shall be enacted at the place where his tale began – on the pillory platform in the market square.

Dimmesdale, finally broken by the accumulated anxiety and strain, is taken desperately ill on the very spot where he held his cowardly silence seven years before. And there, to a crowd assembled to hear an Election sermon, and in defiance of Chillingworth, who seeks to restrain him, he makes a full confession of his guilt. He expires with his head upon Hester's bosom and with Pearl beside them.

Chillingworth, who had thriven only while able to exercise his subtle vengeance, breaks up completely, leaves for England and passes from the book. Hester devotes her remaining days to good works and succeeds in winning back the respect and affection of her neighbours. The reader is given a hint that Pearl, having inherited property in England, grows up there and makes a happy marriage. The author gives a brief glimpse of Hester busily plying her needle to fashion an exquisite baby garment. Life goes on. . . .

The haunting quality of this fable of the effect of guilt upon four different people is unique. Long after the reader has laid the book aside his mind is likely to recall the imagery and atmosphere of many scenes, and though Hawthorne at no time rams his moral lessons down the reader's throat, a great wealth of inspired moral philosophy is implicit in the conception and presentation of this masterpiece.

The sole moral that Hawthorne actually puts into words in his closing pages is this: "Be true! Be true! Show freely to the world, if not your worst, yet some trait whereby the worst may be inferred."

One thinks instinctively of Polonius. "To thine own self be true, and it shall follow as the night the day, thou canst not then be false to any man." If the characters in *The Scarlet Letter* had been true to themselves, how differently might things have turned out. But then there would have been no tale for Hawthorne to tell; no scope for his incisive study of the psychological effects of evil on the human heart and spirit. As it is, each stage of development in *The Scarlet Letter* follows as surely as the night the day. The whole story is full of moral philosophy and almost every page reveals deep, thoughtful, sympathetic understanding of the human heart.

Hawthorne does not set himself up in judgment; he records the actions of his characters and the consequences of those actions. In the process he fills a broad canvas with a masterly picture of the New

England setting, its atmosphere and influences under Puritanism.

Henry James considered Nathaniel Hawthorne to be America's first great literary artist, and *The Scarlet Letter* is generally acknowledged to be his masterpiece. It is certainly evident that Hawthorne wrote this book with the greatest care and precision, infusing immense artistry into its creation.

There is linked artistry in the introductory essay which serves as a kind of foreword and describes the author's own experiences when employed in the Customs House at Salem. Readers should be wary of skipping in eagerness to get to the book itself, for embedded in this essay is the explanation of how the author got his title and found the basic ingredients for his story when rummaging among documents found in an old cask.

Some critics have said that Hawthorne merely added the essay to fill out the volume. If that is so one must still respect the artistry that links the two, and the book should be read as a whole. Arnold Bennett voiced the opinion that *The Scarlet Letter* came "as near perfection as it is granted a man to bring his achievements".

If, by modern standards, the story may sometimes seem slow moving, the complete picture that Hawthorne presents so painstakingly makes increasing impact upon the reader, until finally it leaves an impression that is wellnigh indelible – the true acid test of a masterpiece.

MOBY DICK

HERMANN MELVILLE

THE SON of a merchant, whose early death changed the family fortunes, Hermann Melville, born in 1819, shipped before the mast to Liverpool at eighteen. A native of New York City, he followed the sea for many years, absorbing the knowledge and experience he was later to use as material when he took to authorship.

On a voyage to the Pacific, when twenty-one, he jumped ship at the Marquesas Islands to escape a brutal Captain; was captured by cannibals on the island of Nuku Hiva and, being well treated, remained with them for four months before being rescued by an Australian whaler.

When he again reached America he put his experiences into *Typee*, published in 1846. In the following year he published a second book, *Omoo*, and married, his bride being the daughter of the Chief Justice of Massachusetts.

His first two books had been successful, but his third, *Mardi*, proved disappointing, but he went on writing and, in 1849, visited London to confer with his English publishers. The idea for *Moby Dick* was germinating and he was encouraged by his friend Nathaniel Hawthorne to press on with it. He did so and it appeared in 1851. The effort left him exhausted, but the book did not even earn the small advance he had obtained. Some critics were baffled; the public seemed indifferent.

Worried at his failure to make a living by his writing, he suffered a breakdown in health. But his pen could not remain idle. He kept up the flow, with *Pierre*, 1852, *Israel Potter*, 1855, *The Piazza Tales*, 1856, and *The Confidence Man*, 1857. Then followed a lecture tour of numerous American and Canadian cities in which he chose the South Seas as his subject.

Between 1866 and 1885 he was employed in the New York Customs House. When he died in 1891 an unpublished manuscript was among his literary effects. It did not appear until 1924. It was *Billy Budd*.

"Call me Ismael," are the opening words. The author says whenever he finds himself "growing grim about the mouth" he knows it is time to go to sea. He makes for New Bedford, the whaling port where "fathers give whales as dowers to daughters". He puts up at The Spouter Inn, where he falls in with a tattooed Pacific Islander, son of a king, named Queequeg, lover of beefsteak done rare, inseparable from his favourite harpoon – he even removes the head and uses it for shaving. Hearing that Ismael plans to join a whaler, he says he will go with him.

They board a schooner to take them to Nantucket. As they move down the Acushnet River, Queequeg teases a young novice. While the Captain remonstrates, the boom swings free and sweeps the youngster overboard. Queequeg deftly makes fast the boom and then dives to the rescue. When the pair stand dripping on deck, Queequeg is fêted as a hero. "From that hour," says the author, "I clung to Queequeg like a barnacle."

At Nantucket, the companions seek berths on the *Pequod*, under Captain Ahab, a skipper whose leg was "devoured, chewed up, crumbled . . ." by a monstrous whale. The Captain, who does not appear at first, is described as "A queer man, but a good one. Grand, ungodly, god-like . . . been in colleges as well as among canni- bals . . . Got his name through foolish, ignorant whim of his crazy widowed mother. . . ."

They encounter the chief mate, Starbuck, a native of Nantucket, to whom "courage was not a sentiment, but a thing"; the second mate, Stubb, "an easy going, unfearing man"; and the third mate, Flask, "short, ruddy and pugnacious concerning whales", nicknamed "King Post", being in form like a square timber of that name in Arctic whalers.

They learn of the system of "Knights and Squires" on the whaler. Starbuck chooses Queequeg as his squire; Stubb takes a mixed Indian, Tashtego; while little Flask selects a big, coal-black Negro, Daggoo, the third harpooner.

They are several days at sea before Captain Ahab appears on deck; then, the reader is told, "reality outran apprehension", for "His whole, high, broad form seemed made of solid bronze, and shaped in an unalterable mould, like Cellini's cast Perseus". A livid scar runs from his grey hair down his "tawny scorched face and neck" to disappear in his clothing. No one knows whence it came.

The Captain's lost limb is replaced by an ivory peg made from polished bone of a sperm whale's jaw. His habit is to wedge it in a knot-hole to steady himself. He stands erect, looking out ahead, full of determination. Then he calls the ship's company aft and, with melodramatic gesture, nails a sixteen-dollar gold piece to the mast. This, he says, is for the first man who raises a white-headed whale with three holes in his starboard fluke. The whale is known as "Moby Dick"; the one that maimed Ahab on an earlier trip. Queequeg knows the monster and declares that it has three irons, twisted like corkscrews, in its hide.

Captain Ahab thirsts for vengeance. It is almost an insane obsession. He orders a ritual drinking to the project, ordering the harpooners to draw their poles and quaff their spirit from the harpoon sockets. "Death to Moby Dick!" he cries. "God hunt us all if we do not hunt Moby Dick to his death!" He sees the white whale as "the monstrous incarnation of all those malicious agencies which some deep men feel eating in them, . . ."

As the quest proceeds Ahab spends much time studying his charts. He knows a lot about the migratory habits of whales; and there have been reports of Moby Dick's movements for several consecutive years. There is no mistaking his distinctive white hump.

A day comes when a school of whales is sighted and the traditional cry is raised: "There she blows! there! there! there! she blows! she blows!"

The first lowering of all four of the ship's boats is disastrous, for in the chase one of them is run down by their own vessel in a thick mist, though no lives are lost.

Captain Ahab's zeal is in no way crushed. If anything, he increases his preparations for the ultimate encounter. Although the whaleboats have been made ready for service he takes a hand in working on additional items. At other times he stands, ivory peg wedged in its customary hole, gazing "dead to windward" while squalls of sleet or snow "all but congeal his very eyelashes". Even when weariness forces him below he does not take to his hammock. Starbuck finds him on occasion still in his dripping clothes, his closed eyes still facing the cabin compass.

Though Moby Dick is not sighted there are several lowerings and pursuits. Stubb kills one whale, and he and Flask claim another. There is nearly tragedy when Tashtego falls into a whale's severed head, which Melville likens to the great tun at Heidelburgh. Once again Queequeg proves himself a hero, for, regardless of his own safety, he plunges to the aid of his shipmate and, by superhuman efforts, brings him safely out.

There are several encounters with other ships, and always Ahab demands: "Hast seen the White Whale?" After many disappointments an English captain displays a false ivory arm. "Man my boat!"

cried Ahab; and he is soon alongside the stranger. Ahab plies the Englishman with excited questions, and learns of an epic tussle with a huge white whale in which the Captain received a wound from one of his own harpoons, resulting in the loss of an arm. There is no doubt that the whale was Moby Dick.

Ahab presses on with greater intensity. One night, in the midwatch, he sniffs the air, orders the ship's course to be slightly altered, and the sail to be shortened. At daybreak he yells: "Man the mastheads! Call all hands!" While being hauled aloft himself, he gives the warning: "There she blows – there she blows! A hump like a snow-hill! It is Moby Dick!"

Boats are lowered and Captain Ahab leads his crews in the attack; but Moby Dick, full of fighting tricks, rolls over, crushes the gunwales of Ahab's boat in its mighty jaws and flings them all into the water. Ahab is too handicapped to swim, but he contrives to keep afloat and has the presence of mind to yell to the *Pequod* to sail on the whale and drive it off.

The command is promptly obeyed and Moby Dick moves off sullenly. Ahab and the others are hauled safely aboard. The Captain claims the gold piece as the first to have sighted the whale; but he tells his crew: "I shall let it abide here till the White Whale is dead." Magnanimously he repeats his offer that whoever raises the whale on that day shall have the gold piece; but he adds that if he is again the one to make the first sighting he will divide ten times that sum among them all.

At daybreak next day the pursuit is resumed. The crew is imbued with Ahab's fanatical zeal. They act as one man, not thirty. Excess of zeal leads to one false sighting; then Moby Dick suddenly looms up less than a mile ahead. All boats are lowered and Moby Dick comes straight at them, churning himself into furious speed. Three harpoons are planted, but the whale weaves and manoeuvres incessantly and tangles the lines. Some are cut, but in the mix-up Moby Dick charges Ahab's boat, overturns it and makes off, trailing the intertangled lines behind him.

For a second time Ahab and his disgruntled men are rescued by the *Pequod*, some with strained shoulders, wrists and ankles and other injuries. Ahab's ivory leg has been snapped off, leaving one sharp splinter. He can only stand with Stubb's aid. But his determination is undiminished.

Moby Dick, he concedes, has floated for two days, but "Tomorrow will be the third. Aye, men, he'll rise once more, but only to spout his last!"

As dusk descends, Moby Dick is still in sight to leeward. His pursuers toil by lantern light to overhaul the spare boats and to sharpen fresh weapons for the morrow. Using the broken keel of Ahab's wrecked boat, the ship's carpenter makes a new leg for his Captain.

In two fierce encounters all honours have gone to Moby Dick. Will the third day prove decisive? Will Ahab's boast that the great White Whale will spout his last be justified?

That day dawns fresh and fair. Look-outs take over from the solitary night watcher, but Moby Dick is not in sight. Ahab is also hoisted aloft in a hempen basket. Impatient, after a long vigil, he comes down again and has his boat lowered, grasps Starbuck's hand in a dramatic leavetaking and, ignoring warnings of sharks, pulls away, followed by the other boats.

Suddenly Moby Dick, bedraggled with trailing ropes and harpoons, rises ahead and swims off rapidly. But soon his pace slackens; Ahab relinquishes the helm and is helped up to the bows to hurl a harpoon into the monster's hide. The *Pequod* is bearing down upon them and the giant whale turns its attention to this new enemy, butting it in the starboard bow. The ship shudders and water streams into the breach made by the force of the charge. Moby Dick dives right under the *Pequod* and comes up close to Captain Ahab's boat. Ahab hurls a second harpoon, but the line runs foul. He stoops to clear it and succeeds, only to be caught round the neck and whipped overboard. The heavy eye-splice at the rope's end causes it to sink, dragging Ahab to his doom. The *Pequod*, too, is sinking, and soon disappears beneath the waves. Moby Dick has triumphed in the end.

This craggy monument of a book grows upon the reader with compelling fascination. Some commentators, among them Nathaniel Hawthorne, who was a friend and neighbour of Melville, have sought to read into its prolix pages some kind of inner meaning or allegorical significance. Certainly, the book's 500 crowded pages, consisting of 135 chapters and an epilogue, provide plenty of food for thought and much scope for speculation. Those who enjoy seeking subtle interpretations of every piece of literature can here give themselves an occupation for life. But the normal reader will enjoy the thrilling story itself, the striking characters and all the great wealth of colour and excitement and suspense that Melville provides for their entertainment.

There are innumerable occasions when he wanders into interminable digressions on whales and whaling, packing his pages with every conceivable detailed fact he has been able to discover, either from personal experience, the yarns of whaling men he had met, or from painstaking historical research. The effect is an untidy, rambling volume with, sometimes, a disconcerting variation in narrative style. Nevertheless, it is a book in which a reader may lose himself completely and there is something to be learned on every page.

In spite of the seeming digressions, the central theme of the quest for Moby Dick (based upon the story of a famous white whale, Mocha Dick, reputed to have caused the deaths of at least thirty whaling men) is never lost, and the sheer excitement of the ultimate encounters and the highly dramatic climax must hold nearly everyone enthralled.

Somewhere Melville hints that this book is merely a draft – and not even a draft, rather the draft of a draft, though, as mentioned, it runs to great length. The modern reader, accustomed to having his fiction presented to him in terse, fast-moving form, will need all his staying power to follow the author in his changing moods and styles through to the end; those who stay the course find the experience wholly rewarding. There has been no other book quite like this great saga of whaling; nor will there ever be.

LAVENGRO

GEORGE BORROW

NEVER WAS there such a man for strange encounters as George Borrow. He seems to have gone about collecting strange characters with the same ease as he acquired a mastery of the most out-of-the-way languages; and, such were his powers of narration, he described them in such a way as to make even the most improbable take on the appearance of likelihood. All this is most clearly seen in his two books, *Lavengro*, and what may be regarded as its sequel, *The Romany Rye*.

"Lavengro" in gipsy language means "philologist", and "Romany Rye" means "the gipsy gentleman". These are terms which were applied to Borrow in his youth by the gipsy who makes a frequent appearance in the two books as Jasper Petulengro, and whose real name was Ambrose Smith. Taken together, the books constitute a more or less exact autobiography, covering the period from Borrow's birth in 1803 to the end of August, 1825, although they were not written until long after the event. *Lavengro* was first published in 1851 and *The Romany Rye* six years later.

On his father's side George Borrow was of Celtic descent, the Borrows being an old family long established in Cornwall, while his mother was the strikingly handsome daughter of a Norfolk farmer of French Huguenot stock. To this combination of ancestries may doubtless be ascribed a good deal of his characteristic strangenesses. Mr. Borrow was quartermaster in the West Norfolk Militia, and in those stirring times of the Napoleonic wars the boy accompanied the regiment as it was moved about from place to place in answer to the varying threats of invasion, from Norfolk to the Midlands, then to Scotland and eventually to Ireland. Wherever he went, he became involved in strange happenings which aroused the deepest concern in his simple-minded parents.

When he was seven or eight he made the acquaintance of an old snake-catcher and herbalist, who used snake-fat in his concoctions. The two became fast friends, wandering the heaths and fields together, and when the old man left that part of the country he presented the boy with a viper which he had tamed and rendered harmless by removing its fangs. This came in useful one day when George

Best-loved, and probably still the most widely read, of all English novelists is Charles Dickens, and of his many books *David Copperfield* retains its position of first favourite. *Left*, is one of the illustrations drawn by "Phiz" (Hablot Knight Browne), showing Barkis and Peggotty driving off to their wedding, with David and Little Emily sitting behind, while Mr. Peggotty, Ham and the ever-snivelling Mrs. Gummidge wish them good-luck. Behind is the upturned boat that was the Peggottys' home on the beach at Yarmouth. (*Left*, *below*) A heavily corrected page in Dickens's original MS. of *David Copperfield*. (*Below*) A drawing by the celebrated artist Daniel Maclise of Charles Dickens reading aloud from one of his compositions – the date was 2 December, 1844, when Dickens was thirty-two – in the Lincoln's Inn Fields home of his friend and biographer John Forster (seen on the extreme left). On Dickens's right is Thomas Carlyle, and in the group of listeners in the foreground is Maclise himself.

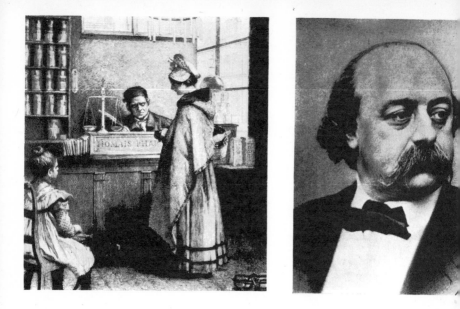

Competent judges have considered Gustave Flaubert to be the most remarkable French novelist of the second half of the last century, and of his books the most generally regarded is *Madame Bovary*, the tragic tale of a young French girl of some education and strong aspirations after culture and elegance, who was condemned to be the wife of a commonplace country doctor and tried to find in a succession of lovers the realization of her amorous imaginings. *Above, left* is a drawing of her by a French artist, consulting the apothecary Homais in his shop at Yonville. *Above, right*: Flaubert in middle age, when his literary reputation was at its height; and *below*, the pavilion at Croisset in which he wrote his novels.

ell in with a band of gipsies, and their hostility turned to supersti-
ious reverence when, to counter their malevolence, he suddenly
roduced the viper from his shirt. The gipsies were still further im-
ressed when he showed them he could read, and the man called to
is son to be introduced. This is the first appearance of Jasper Petu-
engro in the story. "A queer look had Jasper; he was a lad of some
welve or thirteen years, with long arms . . . he wore drab breeches,
vith certain strings at the knee, a rather gay waistcoat, and tolerably
vhite shirt; under his arm he bore a mighty whip of whalebone with
brass knob, and upon his head was a hat without either top or
rim."

"I say, Jasper," said the man, "here's a young sap-engro (snake-
atcher in the gipsy language) that can read, and is more fly than
ourself. Shake hands with him: I wish ye to be two brothers."

"Can he box, father?" replied the youth, surveying George rather
ontemptuously; "I should think not, he looks so puny and small."

"Hold your peace, fool!" said the man: "he can do more than
aat – I tell you, he's fly; he carries a sap about, which would sting
ninny like you to dead."

"What, a sap-engro!" said Jasper, with a singular whine; and,
ooping down, he leered curiously into George's face, kindly, how-
ver, and then patted him on the head. "A sap-engro," he ejaculated;
lor!"

George soon showed him that he could box as well as catch
nakes, and a strange comradeship developed between them, that
as renewed whenever they happened to meet in the course of their
vanderings. Jasper was a bit of a gipsy philosopher, as will be seen
om what is perhaps the most often quoted passage from *Lavengro*.
he two have met again after some long interval, when Borrow is
ow seventeen.

"What is your opinion of death, Mr. Petulengro?" said Borrow,
s he sat down beside him.

"My opinion of death, brother. . . . When a man dies, he is cast
ato the earth, and his wife and child sorrow over him. If he has
either wife nor child, then his father and mother, I suppose; and if
e is quite alone in the world, then, he is cast into the earth, and there
an end of the matter."

"And do you think that is the end of a man?"

"There's an end of him, brother, more's the pity."

"Why do you say so?"

"Life is sweet, brother."

"Do you think so?"

"Think so! There's night and day, brother, both sweet things
sun, moon, and stars, brother, all sweet things; there's likewise th
wind on the heath. Life is very sweet, brother; who would wish to
die?"

After some very scattered schooling, Borrow was articled to
worthy solicitor in Norwich, but instead of learning law he spent hi
time in acquiring languages, the more remote and professionall
useless the better – Welsh, Arabic, Danish, Armenian. . . . Realizing
that he was not cut out to be a lawyer, and his father having died and
left him to his own resources, he went to London with the intention
of becoming an author. But no publisher showed the least interest in
his manuscripts, and he became a hack writer in the employ of Si
Richard Phillips, who had a publishing business off Bedford Row
Sir Richard put him to work on the compilation of six volumes of
the lives and trials of famous criminals. This book, referred to in
Lavengro as the "Newgate Lives and Trials", was at length com
pleted and published in 1825, and although it cost him a tremendou
effort Borrow confessed that he liked it best of all the tasks tha
Phillips imposed on him.

"The trials were entertaining enough," he wrote; "but the lives –
how full were they of wild and racy adventures, and in what racy
genuine language were they told. What struck me most was the ar
which the writers, whoever they were, possessed of telling a plai
story."

How to tell a plain story: that was something that Borrow knew
how to do, and none better. Take for example his account of his firs
encounter with the old apple-woman on London Bridge. "Slowly
advancing along the bridge, I came to the highest point, and there
stood still, close beside one of the stone bowers, in which, beside a
fruitstall, sat an old woman, with a pan of charcoal at her feet, and
a book in her hand, in which she appeared to be reading intently
. . . As I stood upon the bridge, gazing into the jaws of the pool, a
small boat shot suddenly through the arch beneath my feet. Ther
were three persons in it; an oarsman in the middle, whilst a man and
a woman sat at the stern. I shall never forget the thrill of horror
which went through me at this sudden apparition. What! – a boat –
a small boat – passing beneath that arch into yonder roaring gulf! . .
A monstrous breaker curls over the prow . . . the boat, which
appeared to have the buoyancy of a feather, skipped over the threat
ening horror, and the next moment was out of danger, the boatman
– a true boatman of Cockaigne that – elevating one of his sculls in
sign of triumph, the man hallooing, and the woman, a true English

woman that – of a certain class – waving her shawl. . . . I was so
excited, that I strove to clamber up the balustrade of the bridge, in
order to obtain a better view of the daring adventurers. Before I
could accomplish my design, however, I felt myself seized by the
body, and, turning my head, perceived the old fruit-woman, who
was clinging to me. 'Nay, dear! don't – don't!' said she. 'Don't fling
yourself over – perhaps you may have better luck next time!' "

When his hack work for Phillips was completed, and being by
this time completely disillusioned in his prospects of a literary career,
Borrow left London toward the end of May, 1825, and took the road
to the south-west. For some weeks he wandered about the country,
doing twenty to twenty-five miles a day on foot, until he arrived in
Shropshire, where a chance meeting in a wayside inn with a travel-
ing tinker named Slingsby led to his purchasing the man's cart and
pony and tinker's gear and embarking on the trade himself – and
this although he had been warned by Slingsby that the reason why
he was giving it up was because he had been threatened by a big bully
of a man known as "the blazing tinman", who "likes nobody but
himself, and wants to be king of the roads". Having paid the honest
tinker £5 10s. for his outfit, Borrow pitched his little tent in one of
Slingsby's former camping-grounds, where he was poisoned by a
cake which had been specially made for him by old Mrs. Hearne, the
ebee, or grandmother, of the Petulengro family, who hated him for
having managed to learn so much of the gipsy lore and language.
Borrow nearly died, and would have done so if he had not been
rescued by a Welsh preacher and his wife who tended him with loving care. They pressed him to accompany them into Wales, but the
young man declined and moved back into Staffordshire, where he
established himself in "a deep hollow in the midst of a wide field",
with "shelving sides overgrown with trees and bushes", and a steep
winding path leading down into its depths. The name of this retreat
is given as Mumper's Dingle, and it has been located as being near
the town of Willenhall. And here the Flaming Tinman caught up
with him.

"I do not remember ever to have seen a more ruffianly-looking
fellow; he was about six feet high, with an immensely athletic
frame. . . . I did not like the look of the man at all." He was accompanied by two women: one, about forty, stout and vulgar-looking,
and the other – note her well, for she supplies the chief feminine
interest in Borrow's books – "an exceedingly tall woman, or rather
girl, for she could scarcely have been above eighteen; she was dressed
in a tight bodice, and a blue stuff gown; hat, bonnet or cap she had

none, and her hair, which was flaxen, hung down on her shoulders unconfined; her complexion was fair, and her features handsome with a determined but open expression." Her name? Isopel Berners.

Borrow had by no means recovered from the effects of the gipsy's poison, and he played for time. He pointed out that he was not Slingsby and that he had paid for the pony and trap and the rest. But the man came for him, growling, and – "Mind your eyes Jack," shouted the girl. "There, you've got it. I thought he was chaffing at you all along."

"Never mind," said the vulgar woman. "You know what to do – go in." And go in he did. Borrow went down, and the Flaming Tinman seized his throat. He gave himself up for dead, and probably would have been had not the girl caught hold of the handkerchief which the fellow wore round his neck. "Do you call that fair?" she said. The Flaming Tinman was nearly throttled, relinquished his hold of Borrow and aimed a blow at "my fair preserver". She avoided it and said coolly, "Finish t'other business first, and then I'm your woman whenever you like; but finish it fairly – no foul play when I'm by – I'll be the boy's second, and Moll can pick you up when he happens to knock you down".

The battle during the next ten minutes raged with fury, and now it was Borrow who got knocked down, six times in succession. "I can never stand this," he said as he sat on Belle's knee; "I am afraid I must give in: the Flaming Tinman hits very hard", and he spat out a mouthful of blood. "Now, will you use Long Melford?" said Belle. "I don't know what you mean by Long Melford," Borrow rejoined. "Why, this long right of yours," said Belle; "if you do, I shouldn't wonder if you yet stand a chance". On the man came again, and aimed a blow which would doubtless have ended the battle if he had not slipped and it hit a tree with terrific force. "Before the Tinman could recover himself I collected all my strength and struck him beneath the ear, and then fell to the ground completely exhausted, and it so happened that the blow which I struck the tinker beneath the ear was a right-handed blow. 'Hurrah for Long Melford!' I heard Belle exclaim. . . ."

So ends what has been called the finest description of a fight in English literature. And what follows is all of a match. Is there a reader who has not been moved by the story that the brave, sternly independent and high-principled girl told Borrow when – the Tinman and his moll having gone off, swearing horribly – they sat beside the fire in the dingle? Bearing the name of one of the noblest of ancient families – her mother's name, for she was illegitimate and born in a workhouse – she casts a glow over Borrow's pages as warm and bright as the colour of her hair. How far is the story true? Surely he cannot have made it all up, for from what he tells us he treated the poor girl with a cruel insensitiveness. Seated together in that lonely hollow, the young man and the handsome girl – what did they say and do? He insisted on trying to teach her Armenian!

Lavengro ends with extraordinary abruptness, and equally strange and sudden is the opening of *The Romany Rye*, in which we are told all that Borrow chose to tell of the Isopel Berners episode. He tricked her into saying "I love you, I love you," in Armenian, and when the girl burst into tears he assured her that there was no reason why they should not go off together to America, "where we will settle down in some forest, and conjugate the verb *siriel* conjugally". "Conjugally?" said Belle. "Yes," he replied, "as man and wife in America." "You are jesting as usual," said Belle; and when she had been brought to believe that he really meant it she said she must have time to consider the proposal.

The next day Borrow had engaged to go to a fair with Jasper, and, "on arriving at the extremity of the plain, I looked towards the dingle. Isopel Berners stood at the mouth, the beams of the early morning sun shone full on her noble face and figure. I waved my hand towards her. She slowly lifted up her right arm. I turned away, and never saw Isopel Berners again."

MADAME BOVARY

GUSTAVE FLAUBERT

MADAME BOVARY is the story of a country doctor's wife who find
no happiness in her marriage, has two lovers and finally commit
suicide when a moneylender and merchant, with whom she has ru
up debts, forecloses and puts the bailiffs in her house. The book wa
first published in 1856 and, Victorian prudery being as strong i
France as in England, the author, Gustave Flaubert, and the pub
lishers were prosecuted for producing an indecent work. At mucl
the same time, Baudelaire was brought before the same court an
obliged to suppress a number of poems in *Les Fleurs de Mal*. Flauber
was more fortunate, and though the judgment expressed some dis
pleasure at some aspects of *Madame Bovary* it stated that *Madam
Bovary* was unlike "certain works written with the sole aim of givin
satisfaction to sensual passions, to the spirit of licence and debauch
or of turning into ridicule things which ought to be respected b
all".

No doubt as a result of this scandal Flaubert's book had consider
able sales as well as the success with literary critics which it wa
bound to have. It was the first important and entirely realistic nove
written in France, or for that matter anywhere else, a study o
provincial life and the people concerned – doctors, a priest, a chemist
a lawyer's clerk, a tax-collector, a small landowner – belonged to th
order of society usually neglected in favour of the aristocracy or o
picturesque adventures, criminals or bandits as in Balzac an
Stendhal, who were realists in a manner of speaking, or the leisure
middle classes as in Jane Austen. Further, the world of Madam
Bovary was painted with apparent objectivity, from a distance an
without any favourable prejudice for any intrinsic virtues it migh
have – indeed it was drawn very coldly indeed, the author, in th
course of his six years of arduous work on this book, frequentl
complaining of having "to immerse himself in mediocrity".

Last of all, this book, with its somewhat sordid subject-matter, wa
written in a style of never-equalled perfection. The author had se
himself to write a novel in which not a sentence or even a word wa
unimportant. He wrote as an artist and not, as did Dickens an

Balzac, great geniuses as they were, as writers pressed to produce copy. Flaubert said he sometimes spent eight days composing a single page. He intended his writing to be a perfect vehicle of expression, for every object, place, circumstance and person. Everything he wrote had to pass the test of being read aloud, so that the rhythm and movement of his phrases might appear perfect. He said "a phrase is what it should be only when it corresponds to all the necessities of breathing – bad sentences weigh on the chest, impede the beating of the heart and are thus lifeless".

Still, after a hundred or more years, the quality of Flaubert's writing, the vividness of his perceptions, the exact detail of his descriptions give to the often distressing episodes of this book a quality of memorability. Who can forget, for instance, Emma Bovary's second "fall" when she keeps her assignation with the lawyer's clerk, Léon, in Rouen Cathedral, where they are pursued by the beadle with his tiresome patter about the Cathedral's history, and when finally Emma is bundled into a cab by Léon and the cabman is told to drive where he likes. When he stops he is urged by an angry voice and so he drives about all the afternoon until evening, aimlessly, a symbol of the disorder in Emma's life.

"And on the quay-side, in the midst of the drays and casks, and in the streets, at the corners, the good folk opened large, wonder-stricken eyes at this sight, so extraordinary in the provinces, a cab with blinds drawn and which appeared thus shut more closely than a tomb, and tossing about like a vessel.

"Once in the middle of the day, in the open country, just as the sun beat more fiercely against the old plated lanterns, a bare hand slipped beneath the small blinds of yellow canvas, and threw out some scraps of paper that scattered in the wind, and further off lighted like white butterflies on a field of red clover in full bloom. About six o'clock the carriage stopped in a back street, and a woman got out; she walked away with her veil down, and without turning her head."

Emma Bovary was the daughter of a Normandy farmer who gave her a superior education in a convent. She had a quick intelligence and answered, best of all the class, the priest's questions on the Catechism. Her nature was formed, however, before she had left home, and, in her first religious phase, she loved the sick lamb and the bleeding heart and image of Jesus sinking beneath the Cross but did not attend to the Mass. She invented little sins at confession in order that she might prolong her attitude of kneeling in the shadow, her hands joined together against the grating, listening to the

whispering of the priest. At the convent there had been an old maid
who came to mend the linen who knew the songs of the last century
told the girls stories of gallant love affairs and brought them romanti
novels and stories about persecuted ladies fainting in lonely pavilions
horses ridden to death by frantic lovers, summer forests, vows, sobs
tears, nightingales in shady groves and gentlemen brave as lions yet
gentle as lambs.

A model child at first, when her father took her away from the
convent the nuns were not sorry to see her go. "This nature," writes
Flaubert, "loved the church for the sake of the flowers, and music
for the words of the songs, and literature for its passional stimulus
rebelled against the mysteries of faith as it grew irritated by discip
line, a thing antipathetic to her constitution". Emma emerged from
the convent as the complete romantic of the mid-nineteenth century

It was her fate to marry Charles Bovary, the local doctor, an un
imaginative feeble character who could make no appeal to Emma
who could in no way correct the romantic exaggerations of his
wife's emotional nature – indeed he did not even know of their
existence. Emma needed to admire her husband – but he had nothing
to make himself even respected; he was a poor doctor who, on a
least two occasions, was deservedly humiliated by colleagues he had
had to call in. An important incident was an invitation to a ball to
the young married couple by a local nobleman where Emma saw the
rich in their luxurious clothes and danced with elegant young men:

> "They had the complexion of wealth – their clear complexion height
> ened by the pallor of porcelain, the shimmer of satin, the veneer of ol
> furniture, and which an ordered regiment of exquisite force maintain
> at its best. Their necks moved easily in their low cravats, their lon
> whiskers fell over their turned-down collars, they wiped their lips o
> handkerchiefs with embroidered initials that gave forth a subtle per
> fume. Those who were beginning to grow old had an air of youth
> while there was something mature in the faces of the young. In their
> unconcerned looks was the calm of passions daily satisfied and throug
> all their gentleness of manner pierced that peculiar brutality, the resu
> of a command of half-easy things – the management of thoroughbre
> horses and the society of loose women."

This experience had opened a yawning fissure in her life, a fissur
like one of those great crevasses which a storm will sometimes mak
on a mountainside in the course of one short night. Emma was lik
a shipwrecked sailor turning a despairing gaze on the solitude of he
life, seeking some white sail in the far mists of the horizon. She gav
up her drawing and music and bought a map of Paris. She neglecte

her house and herself, took to wearing grey cotton stockings and bought the cheapest yellow tallow candles.

Something happened. They moved to Yonville, a larger village near Rouen, and Emma met Léon – a young notary's clerk, somewhat effeminate, a kindred romantic soul. They both loved seas, mountains and travel, and he played the guitar. This sentimental companionship satisfied them both. Léon, however, went to Paris to pass his exams, and once more Emma's life was empty. She was nearly thirty. She has a young child, a girl, who in no respect offset her romantic cravings. Then arrives M. Rodolphe Boulanger, a well-off small landowner with much experience of women. He decides to seduce her – for in spite of her husband, the brat, and the gossip of the neighbourhood, he really dotes on pale women with piercing eyes. At last I have a lover, she says to herself, and as Flaubert writes: "The legion of adulteress women began to sing in her memory, enthralling her with the charm of their voices."

Rodolphe's technique of seduction included knowing how to adopt the right kind of attitude to please women and he indulges her illusions for a while as they ride together through the woods. He gets bored. She, more and more in love, is anxious to elope. He yields to her desire and they plan to go to Venice. He sends Emma at the last moment a letter of "Renunciation of his great love". Emma falls violently ill. Rodolphe had satisfied her above all because he had been clever enough to answer her demand for a lover out of the ordinary. She had interpreted his boredom as being like that of Byron, and his brutality as that of a tempestuous lover. His loss therefore was a wound to Emma's soul, not merely the misfortune of ending an agreeable experience. She recovered slowly, her insatiable romanticism finding, for a short time, some consolation in playing at piety, religious exercises and charity. She bought herself a Gothic prayer-stool.

But this does not last for long. Léon has returned to practice in Rouen. Although, technically, it is Léon who seduces her in the cab it is she who leads the game, and she is the dominating partner in their love affair. From her stupid husband Emma obtains permission to go once a week to Rouen for music lessons. Léon and she live out their idyll in a hotel in the quarter reserved for theatres, taverns and whores. She has made Bovary give her a power-of-attorney over his affairs and quickly runs through a small legacy. She gives free rein to her desires for every kind of dress and luxury and, at home, for rich carpets and curtains in keeping with her mood of exaltation.

L'Heureux, a typically plausible and rapacious tradesman who lives at Yonville, gives her unlimited credit and of course robs her. As her love affair begins to lose its emotional freshness, as she begins to find in adultery the old commonplaces of marriage, her financial affairs get worse. She is to be sold up. Desperately on the day the bill of sale is fastened on her door, all pleading with L'Heureux being useless, she runs to the local notary to borrow 8,000 francs; he tries to seduce her and she refuses; to the tax-collector and finally to Rodolphe in his comfortable château. It is all in vain. She swallows a handful of arsenic and her death agony is described in great detail by Flaubert, including the kiss she implants on the crucifix, followed by a reaction in which, her convulsions ceasing for a few seconds, she looks at herself in a hand-mirror and weeps.

It has been pointed out by some critics that Flaubert's book shows an exaggerated cynicism and an unwarranted degree of hatred for the bourgeoisie. It is unnatural, these critics say, that Emma should have had such immensely bad luck – to have married Charles Bovary, to have been seduced by so selfish a man as Rodolphe and then in Léon, the effeminate "sister soul", to have met another lover who is useless for her inner needs. Then she is surrounded by people, who if they are not evil – and indeed there are no characters which can be described by that word – are dull, lacking any insight whatever into a sensitive nature – selfish, grasping, small-minded. The chemist Homais is a wonderfully drawn figure of the small town, anti-clerical intellectual. He is not an unkind man; but merely superficial and unperceptive. Should she not have met with at least one or two people who understood her?

Emma Bovary's life is not a tragedy, for it lacks inevitability – her romanticism only led to a tragic end through the misfortunes of her marriage and to a large extent the fortuitous events of her life, the absence of any nobility in what surrounded her. The book is what we call today "a slice of life", seen in great depth. Emma is an intensely living character. Emile Faguet, the great French critic, has written of her: "Madame Bovary, the immortal Madame Bovary, is the most complete portrait of a woman which I know in all literature, including Shakespeare and including Balzac. For her Flaubert has not been content to suggest a biography; he has made an entire biography minutely, patiently, year by year, sometimes day by day, with the feeling and the intelligence at once of the necessary evolution of a character and of all the successive changes which it can undergo and of the end which is bound to happen. It is the entire life of a soul which unwinds itself before our eyes with the immanent logic which presides over the progress of the human soul."

Her romantic disease, if one may call it so, consists in being always determined to live beyond the horizon. It consists of being incapable of extracting from the things which surround us, their savour, their grace, their agreeable qualities and their poetry. The romantic disease consists in believing that savour, grace, agreeableness, poetry and happiness are always where one is not. It is perhaps for this reason that Flaubert, who had a strong romantic vein in his nature, which was made creative through his devotion to art, said of his heroine, "Madame Bovary, *c'est moi*".

BARCHESTER TOWERS

ANTHONY TROLLOPE

A SHAMBLING, incredibly dirty schoolboy cold-shouldered by his classmates, a schoolboy who blotted and smeared his exercises and was invariably at the tail-end of the form: this was Anthony Trollope at fifteen.

The fourth and youngest son of Thomas and Frances Trollope, Anthony was born at 6, Keppel Street, Bloomsbury, on 24 April, 1815. His father was a brilliant barrister, but as he was arrogant, quarrelsome and self-opinionated, he did not prosper, hence he became increasingly embittered and morose.

In 1816, Mr. Trollope moved his family from London to the handsome estate he had leased near Harrow which he called Julians, after the magnificent Julians near Royston[1] he expected to inherit from his wealthy bachelor uncle. Unfortunately, the old man married a young wife, and the fortunes of the Trollope family were thus hopelessly compromised.

At seven, Anthony, awkward and seemingly stupid, became a despised day-boy at Harrow. In 1825, he was sent to a boarding school in Sunbury where he felt less of an outcast although "I never had any pocket-money and seldom much in the way of clothes". Two years later, he obtained a place at Winchester.

Mr. Trollope could no longer afford Julians, and he moved his family to a more modest estate which he named Julians Hill. He now committed his crowning folly by making a bid for fortune in the New World; the Grand Bazaar he opened in Cincinatti was a disastrous failure that engulfed his remaining capital, and he returned to England where he sank into degradation. He leased a squalid farm, took Anthony from Winchester and sent him back as a day-boy to Harrow. Anthony plodded three long miles to school along narrow, filthy lanes, and not unnaturally he was shunned by all when he arrived covered with dust or mud. "For eighteen months I endured what was possibly the worst period of my life," Trollope wrote in his autobiography.

[1] Now owned by the Hon. Mrs. Pleydell-Bouverie.

The situation was temporarily saved by the return of Frances Trollope and the publication of her book: *Domestic Manners of the Americans*. It became a best-seller, and with the money it brought her she paid off the most pressing debts and reinstated the family at Julians Hill. But in 1834 she realized that the ship was well and truly sunk; she persuaded her husband to go to Ostend, and herself took Anthony and her other children to Bruges, leaving the sheriff's officers in possession of Julians Hill.

Anthony was now nineteen, with no qualifications, no prospects. In the autumn of 1834 he returned to London to take up the junior clerkship in the Post Office his mother had obtained for him.

Friendless, semi-starved, hating the work which he scamped, Anthony nevertheless developed a power for observation as he lounged in taverns or walked alone through the crowded streets. In 1841 his dread of being chained to a desk for the rest of his life drove him to apply for the post of surveyor's clerk in Banagher. This lowly position he duly obtained.

Ireland completely transformed Anthony. He was enchanted by the Irish, he enjoyed his work which took him out and about, and did it well; he married, had two sons, gained promotion, and now that he was happy, genial and contented, he turned his thoughts to writing. The three books he produced were published, but died still-born, and it was not until 1851, when he was summoned to England to organize rural postal deliveries in the south-west counties, that the foundations on which his genius was to build were laid. During the two years the work took him, he acquired an unrivalled knowledge of the English scene and of the gradations of its society; above all, he learnt to appreciate to the full the immense power exerted by the upper clergy. It was while he was wandering round Salisbury Cathedral that he conceived the idea for *The Warden*. He completed the book in 1854, and the following year it was published by Longman, Brown, Green and Longmans.

Trollope's first Barset novel concerns Mr. Harding, Precentor of Barchester Cathedral, who is the Warden of Hiram's Hospital, an almshouse for twelve old men. He is paid £800 a year, and lives with his younger daughter Eleanor (his older daughter is the wife of Archdeacon Grantley) in the comfortable house provided for him rent-free. A reforming young surgeon, John Bold, accuses the Church of misusing the Charity's funds, and decides to bring a case; Mr. Harding, a good and upright man, feels that he *is* overpaid, but as he has no means of his own on which to support Eleanor, he allows the worldly Archdeacon Grantley to overrule his scruples. Eleanor and

John Bold have fallen in love, and she persuades him to drop the case. By the time she reaches home, however, her father, driven by his conscience, has already left for London where he hands in his resignation. Eleanor marries John, and Mr. Harding takes the tiny living of St. Cuthberts where he lives contentedly on £75 a year. Poor Eleanor is widowed before her son is born, but she is left handsomely provided for, she is young and charming; the future may bring her consolation for her present grief. . . .

Barchester Towers, the sequel to *The Warden*, was published in 1857, and a great English novelist was well and truly started on his long career.

Dr. Proudie, a Low Churchman, has just been appointed to the vacant see of Barchester. He, poor, weak man, is dominated both by his formidable wife and the chaplain she has chosen for him, the Rev. Obadiah Slope. Mr. Slope has greasy red hair, an even redder face "like bad beef", a sweaty forehead and clammy hands; behind his oleaginous, obsequious manner lies a lust for power. The chaplain, in short, is determined to rule the Bishopess, as well as the Bishop, to become Cock of the Diocese.

When Archdeacon Grantley and Mr. Harding call at the Palace, Mr. Slope's insolent manner incurs the former's hatred and the latter's distaste. On the occasion of the Bishop's enthronement in the Cathedral, his chaplain preaches the sermon in which he denounces even intoning as a "Popish" practice; outraged, the Archdeacon and all the upper clergy swear war on him.

The grand inaugural reception at the Palace is ruined for Mrs. Proudie when the self-styled Signora Vesey-Neroni is borne in and deposited gracefully on a sofa where she is instantly surrounded by a host of admiring gentlemen. The lady is the flighty younger daughter of Dr. Vesey Slope, the prebendary; after a short-lived marriage to an Italian scoundrel, she had returned home crippled for life, but with her beauty unimpaired. From then on she has found ample consolation in wielding her irresistible charms over male hearts; she instantly captivates Mr. Slope. Her shameless behaviour outrages Mrs. Proudie, who has the misfortune to ruin her train by catching it on the sofa. She rebukes Mr. Slope very sharply indeed for paying ardent attention to the Signora.

There has been no warden at Hiram's Hospital since Mr. Harding's resignation. Parliament now regularizes the affairs of the Charity; provision is to be made for twelve old women and a matron in addition to the twelve old men, and the warden's salary is reduced to £450 a year. It is taken for granted that the new bishop will reappoint Mr. Harding, and indeed Dr. Proudie does decide in his favour, but Mr. Slope, who transmits the offer, does not intend that any of the Old Guard shall get preferment. He therefore lays such unpleasant stress on the new duties the warden will be expected to perform that Mr. Harding is driven into saying: "Under these conditions, you may tell the Bishop I decline." Dr. Proudie is surprised and sorry; not so his spouse. "The whole set of clergy are determined to defy your authority," she tells him, and advises him to appoint as warden the lowly Rector of Puddingdale, Mr. Quiverful, who has fourteen children and but £300 a year. "He is far more worthy than Mr. Harding and will be useful to us at the Palace," she declares. The Bishop says resignedly that Mr. Slope had better see Mr. Quiverful.

Naturally, Mr. Quiverful is overjoyed. "Mr. Harding doesn't want the Hospital – his daughter, the Widow Bold, has £1,200 a year," he tells Mr. Slope. That gentleman instantly changes direction. Why should he not marry the Widow Bold and make the prize his own? To win the daughter, however, he must procure the wardenship for her father.

Mr. Slope begins his courtship of the unsuspecting Eleanor by praising Mr. Harding skyhigh, and beseeching her to prevail on him to revoke his decision. Eleanor cannot like Mr. Slope, but she believes him to be sincere. His visits become more and more frequent.

Mr. Slope is not the only aspirant to Eleanor's hand. Charlotte Stanhope, the Signora's older sister, has made friends with Mrs. Bold, as only a wealthy wife can save her brother Bertie, a charming ne'er-do-well, from ruin.

Unauthorized, Mr. Slope visits Mr. Quiverful, tells him that Mr. Harding has *not* declined the wardenship, and gets the poor man to stand down. In despair, Mrs. Quiverful rushes off to implore Mrs. Proudie to intercede. The Bishopess confronts the Bishop who is in his sanctum with Mr. Slope, and demands an explanation. Mr. Slope says he has advised His Lordship that there will be great ill-will if Mr. Harding is not reappointed. Mrs. Proudie, furious at his unwarrantable interference, demands to see the Bishop alone, and adds imprudently: "Either Mr. Slope or I will leave the room at once!" Whereupon His Lordship murmurs: "Well, my dear, Mr. Slope and I are very busy. . . ." Routed, Mrs. Proudie sweeps out, seething with hate for the victorious Slope, to assure Mrs. Quiverful her husband *shall* have the Hospital.

Archdeacon Grantley strengthens the Anti-Slope contingent by persuading his friend, the brilliant Mr. Arabin, to accept the humble living of St. Ewolds. Mr. Arabin is a bachelor and despite his complex character a most likable man; he has quite erroneously persuaded himself that he does not wish for preferment, that earthly happiness and marriage are not for him. When he and Eleanor meet, however, it is obvious that they are made for one another.

Eleanor goes to stay with her sister and brother-in-law, and Archdeacon Grantley, who has noted with growing alarm Mr. Slope's frequent visits to Eleanor, asks her outright if she means to marry him, adding: "Mr. Arabin agrees with me that as Mrs. Slope you could no longer be received in this house." The innocent Eleanor is both astounded and furious; she instantly terminates her visit, but before she leaves Mr. Arabin begs her to forgive him for presuming to give her advice. "Answer me just one question: you do not intend to marry Mr. Slope?" he asks imprudently. "It is a question you have no right to ask," replies Eleanor haughtily, and Mr. Arabin, who knows nothing about women's hearts, thinks all is lost.

The Dean of Barchester has a stroke and lies dying. Mr. Slope instantly aspires to the Deanery, and readily drops the affair of the wardenship to canvass support for himself. Mr. Quiverful is officially appointed warden, and Archdeacon Grantley tries in vain to get Mr. Harding to put up a fight. The Archdeacon then asks Dr. Gwynne, the all-powerful Master of Lazarus, to speak to the Bishop, but nothing comes of his request.

Miss Thorne, sister of Squire Thorne of Ullathorne, gives a grand party to afford the nobility and gentry and all the tenantry the opportunity of meeting Mr. Arabin. Due to Charlotte Stanhope's machinations, poor Eleanor is forced to drive to Ullathorne with Mr. Slope – Mr. Arabin is deeply upset when he sees them arrive together. He hovers round the Signora, fascinated by her beauty, and she cleverly leads him on to disclose his secret to her: his love for Eleanor. She resolves that if Bertie does not succeed in winning her, she will do Eleanor a good turn and Mr. Slope a bad one.

Poor Eleanor is utterly taken aback when Mr. Slope follows her to a quiet part of the garden, clasps her to his bosom and proposes. Furious and disgusted, she boxes his ears soundly, and flies to Bertie Stanhope for protection. Out of the blue, Bertie himself pops the question – the party is completely ruined for Mrs. Bold.

Dr. Gwynne visits the Bishop, and as a result the Deanery is offered to Mr. Harding. He is so overwhelmed that he asks for time to think over his decision. Meanwhile, the Signora, after a delicious scene when she mocks Mr. Slope for aspiring to the Deanery and forces him to confess that he has been rejected by the Widow Bold, sends for Eleanor and tells her that Mr. Arabin adores her. Miss Thorne, who does not approve of unmarried rectors, now takes a hand and invites Eleanor to stay at Ullathorne. Eleanor thus meets Mr. Arabin again; he implores her to forgive him, her eyes fill with tears, and her expression tells him that his love is returned. Miss Thorne, Mr. Harding and the Grantleys are delighted when they announce their engagement. Mr. Harding finally decides he is too old to be Dean of Barchester, so he puts forward another candidate for preferment, a candidate who meets with the full approval of the Bishop and Dr. Gwynne. He is, of course, none other than the Rector of St. Ewolds, Mr. Harding's son-in-law to be, Mr. Arabin.

Both the Bishop and the Bishopess have had enough of Mr. Slope, and he is dismissed from his post. "What, my lord, has been my fault?" he demands, whereupon Mrs. Proudie thunders: "The Signora is one fault, and a very abominable fault she is! Fie, Mr. Slope, fie! You an evangelical clergyman indeed!" When Mr. Slope retaliates by saying that he will publish abroad that Dr. Proudie has dismissed him at her bidding, she retorts: "You may publish what you please. Clergymen have been unfrocked for less than what you have been guilty of!" Mr. Slope realizes that he has lost the day, and his cup of humiliation is full when Mrs. Proudie says: "If you wish to remain in the neighbourhood and will solemnly pledge yourself never to see that woman again, the Bishop will mention your name to Mr. Quiverful who now wants a curate at Puddingdale!"

No résumé can do justice to such a book as *Barchester Towers*, to Trollope's brilliant portrayal of the English scene as it was in his day. The "sports" at Ullathorne, for instance, deliciously illustrate the rigid caste system under which the sheep, the nobility and gentry, were strictly separated from the goats, the common herd. How outraged are the former, how indignant the latter when Mrs. Lookaloft, the farmer's wife who thinks herself as good as her betters, stalks triumphantly into the drawing-room! Trollope describes the many minor characters with as much care as he lavishes on the major ones, and so well did he understand human beings that even the odious Mr. Slope, the formidable Mrs. Proudie and the shameless Signora each have a saving grace: Mr. Slope is sincere in his religious beliefs, Mrs. Proudie has a heart, albeit small, within her stiff-ribbed bodice, a heart to which Mrs. Quiverful gains access, while the Signora does at least perform one good action. Mrs. Proudie is one of the great comic creations of literature, and it is our loss that Trollope overheard two members of his club expressing their boredom with her. He went over to them, remarked "I will go home and kill her in a week", and was as good as his word. While some of the Barchester characters reappear in later books, we hear no more about the bishopess after *The Last Chronicle of Barset*.

In all, Trollope wrote 47 novels, the best-loved of which are surely the six that make up the Barchester series: *The Warden, Barchester Towers, Doctor Thorne, Framley Parsonage, The Small House at Allington* and *The Last Chronicle of Barset*. A particular interest attaches to *The Small House at Allington*, for when he created the character of the luckless Johnny Eames, Trollope was recalling his own experiences when he was a Post Office clerk in London, struggling to exist on £90 a year. This wretched period following an equally wretched boyhood might have left him permanently scarred; thanks, however, to the balanced and genial maturity which he attained through peace and contentment in Ireland, he was able to write of the past, not with bitterness, but with that detached and gentle amusement which typifies all his work.

ON LIBERTY

JOHN STUART MILL

UP TO 1859 most people, when they talked about liberty, had in mind protection from political tyranny. After that year many of the thinking part of mankind had a much larger and deeper conception. This was because they had had the opportunity of reading a small book concisely named *On Liberty*, written by John Stuart Mill and published in the year in question.

At this time Mill was at the height of his intellectual and literary powers. Born in 1806, he was the son of James Mill, only second to Jeremy Bentham as the spokesman of the Utilitarian philosophy. He had had one of the most extraordinary educations on record, never going to school or university but being taught at home by his father, starting to learn Greek at the age of three, and then arithmetic, history and Latin. Through his father's influence he obtained a clerical post in the head offices of the East India Company in London, and his career was that of a bureaucrat until his retirement in 1858. His employment left him plenty of time for outside interests, and he wrote books on logic and political economy that were very highly regarded. Then after a small book on Utilitarianism, in which he adopted a much more humane view of that rather arid philosophy than his father had done, he wrote his essay *On Liberty*. In its production he was assisted, as he had been in most of his earlier books, by Mrs. Harriet Taylor, the really remarkably intelligent and cultured woman whom, after a platonic love affair extending over some twenty years, and when she had become a widow, he married in 1851. She died from consumption in 1858, to his great but not unutterable grief.

In his *Autobiography* (which, notwithstanding his lifelong and most sincerely held rationalism, must take a high place among "spiritual" autobiographies, and remains the most generally popular and readable of all his books, *On Liberty* possibly excepted) he writes of her with the deepest affection and admiration. She had been specially helpful in writing *On Liberty*. When the little book was published it bore the dedication, "To the beloved and deplored memory of her who was the inspirer, and in part the author, of all that is best in my

339

writings – the friend and wife whose exalted sense of truth and right was my strongest incitement, and whose approbation was my chief reward...."

Let us begin our examination of the book with an assertion: Mill added a new dimension to the concept of Liberty. He was not concerned with political liberty: that, in the England of the middle of the last century, had been practically achieved. And yet there was still tyranny, plenty of it, the "tyranny of the majority", of class and professional interests, of custom and social convention and generally accepted prejudices. It was this kind of tyranny that he proceeded to stigmatize and assail with all the power of a well-trained and disciplined pen and of an intellect that was among the finest in a generation of fine intellects.

"The object of this Essay," he tells us on an early page, "is to assert one very simple principle ..., that the sole end for which mankind are warranted, individually or collectively, in interfering with the liberty of action of any of their number, is self-protection. That the only purpose for which power can be rightfully exercised over any member of a civilized community, against his will, is to prevent harm to others. His own good, either physical or moral, is not a sufficient warrant. ... The only part of the conduct of any one, for which he is amenable to society, is that which concerns others. In the part which merely concerns himself, his independence is, of right, absolute. Over himself, over his own body and mind, the individual is sovereign."

Of course Mill allows for certain exceptions. His doctrine is meant to apply only to human beings in the maturity of their faculties, not to children and young persons, nor to those backward races that should be regarded as fortunate if they may find an Akbar or a Charlemagne to undertake their improvement. But it does apply to all those who have attained the capacity of being guided to their own improvement by conviction and persuasion, and these are the only people with whom we are now concerned.

The "appropriate region of human liberty" is, then, first the inward domain of consciousness, demanding liberty of conscience, liberty of thought and feeling, absolute freedom of opinion and sentiment on all subjects, practical or speculative, scientific, moral or theological. Necessarily allied with this is the liberty of expressing and publishing opinions of whatever kind. Secondly, the principle requires liberty of tastes and pursuits – of framing the plan of our life to suit our own character, of doing as we like subject to such consequences as may follow, without impediment from our fellow creatures so long as what we do does not harm them, even though they should think our conduct foolish, perverse or wrong. Thirdly, from this liberty of each individual, follows the liberty, within the same limits, of combination among individuals – freedom to unite for any purpose not involving harm to others, the persons combining being of full age and not forced or deceived.

"No society in which these liberties are not, on the whole, respected, is free, whatever may be its form of government ... The only freedom which deserves the name, is that of pursuing our own good in our own way, so long as we do not attempt to deprive others of theirs, or impede their efforts to obtain it."

In his second chapter Mill concentrates on one particular aspect of the problem, that of liberty of thought and discussion. Here what he is up against is the widely held opinion that a government that has been popularly elected and may be considered, therefore, as representing the will of the people, is entitled to exercise some power over what the people shall be allowed to know and say and do, simply because this is in accordance with the popular or majority voice. "But I deny the right of the people to exercise such coercion, either by themselves or by their government. The power itself is illegitimate. The best government has no more title to it than the worst. It is as noxious, or more noxious, when exerted in accordance with public opinion, than when in opposition to it." Then follows a most eloquent and often quoted passage, containing the kernel of Mill's gospel.

"If all mankind minus one were of one opinion, and only one person were of the contrary opinion, mankind would be no more justified in silencing that one person, than he, if he had the power, would be justified in silencing mankind."

If an opinion were a personal possession of no value to anyone other than its owner, it might make some difference, perhaps, whether the injury of its suppression were inflicted only on a few persons. But this is not the case. "The peculiar evil of silencing the expression of an opinion is, that it is robbing the human race; posterity as well as the existing generation; those who dissent from the opinion, still more than those who hold it."

There are three possibilities that we should bear in mind. First, that the opinion which it is attempted to suppress by authority may possibly be true. Of course, those people who want to suppress it do not think so, but then they are not infallible. History affords only too many instances when the arm of the law has been employed to root out the best men and the noblest doctrines. Mill mentions only two, but they are of surpassing importance, and he relates them in passages of the most persuasively moving prose.

"Mankind can hardly be too often reminded, that there was once a man named Socrates," begins the first. "Born in an age and country abounding in individual greatness, this man has been handed down to us by those who best know both him and the age, as the most virtuous man in it." And what happened to him? The tribunal before whom he was tried, "there is every ground for believing, honestly found him guilty, and condemned the man who probably of all then born had deserved best of mankind, to be put to death as a criminal".

The second case is even more impressive. "To pass from this to the only other instance of judicial iniquity, the mention of which, after the condemnation of Socrates, would not be an anti-climax: the event which took place on Calvary rather more than eighteen hundred years ago. The man who left on the memory of those who witnessed his life and conversation, such an impression of his moral grandeur, that eighteen subsequent centuries have done homage to him as the Almighty in person, was ignominiously put to death, as what? As a blasphemer."

Supposing, on the other hand, that the opinion that it is desired to suppress be an error? Then it may, and very commonly does, contain a portion of truth, and it is only by the collision of adverse opinions that this remainder has any chance of being supplied.

Then there is the third possibility, that the generally held belief be not only true but the whole truth. Even so, unless it is suffered to be vigorously and earnestly contested, it will be little better than a prejudice, a dogma, a mere formal profession, of no use to anybody and preventing the growth of any real and heartfelt conviction.

At the back of all this argument, this eloquent pleading for the right of individuals to form their own opinions and work out their own way of life for themselves, lies Mill's profound belief in the worth of human personality. "It really is of importance, not only what men do, but also what manner of men they are that do it. Among the works of man, which human life is rightly employed in perfecting and beautifying, the first in importance surely is man himself. Supposing it were possible to get houses built, corn grown, battles fought, causes tried and even churches erected and prayers said, by machinery – by automatons in human form – it would be a considerable loss to exchange for these automatons even the men and women who at present inhabit the more civilized parts of the world, and who assuredly are but starved specimens of what nature can and will produce. Human nature is not a machine to be built after a model, and set to do exactly the work prescribed for it, but a tree, which requires to grow and develop itself on all sides, according to the tendency of the inward forces which make it a living thing."

In a later chapter Mill summarizes the principles worked out above into two "maxims", namely (1) that the individual is not accountable to society for his actions, in so far as these concern the interests of no person but himself: advice, instruction, persuasion and avoidance are the only measures by which society can justifiably express its dislikes or disapprobation of his conduct; (2) that for such actions as are prejudicial to the interests of others, the individual is accountable, and may be subjected either to social or legal punishment, if society is of opinion that the one or the other is requisite for its protection. From these maxims it will be seen that Mill was no extreme libertarian. Society must not tyrannize over the individual, but the individual has duties and responsibilities toward society which he is bound to perform.

By way of illustration, Mill applies these maxims to problems of everyday life, and sometimes leaves the matter open. If a man likes to gamble, then let him do so; but should a man be permitted to keep a gambling-house? A man may get drunk if he likes, but "I should deem it pefectly legitimate that a person, who had once been convicted of any act of violence to others under the influence of drink ... if he were afterwards found drunk should be liable to a penalty". Offences against public decency must of course be punished. Fornication must be tolerated – but should a person be free to act as a pimp? A man should not be forbidden to purchase dangerous drugs, but he should be warned of what he is buying. Parents should be held responsible for the proper education of their children; indeed, it should be recognized that "to bring a child into existence without a fair prospect of being able, not only to provide food for its body, but instruction and training for its mind, is a moral crime, both against the unfortunate offspring and against society".

Mill's attitude toward women is most fully expressed in another of his books, *The Subjection of Women*, published in 1869, but it may be mentioned that in the *Liberty* he writes that "the almost despotic power of husbands over wives need not be enlarged upon here, because nothing more is needed for the complete removal of the evil, than that wives should have the same rights, and should receive the protection of law in the same manner, as all other persons".

There is a great deal more in this little volume that it is impossible even to refer to here. *On Liberty* is a book to read, and read again and again. Some of it dates, but most of it has retained its original freshness. Perhaps its message is specially telling in our present age, when the power of creating and manipulating public opinion is to a greater extent than ever before in the possession of those forming or controlling the Government. The State is all-powerful, or almost, what with education for all provided at the public expense, social security, planned employment, the regulation and provision of broadcasting and television, and so on. It is a commonplace that the individual is at a discount, and the weight of public opinion bears heavily on the human spirit. In these circumstances, it is well to be reminded of what Mill wrote in the last paragraph of his book: "The worth of a State, in the long run, is the worth of the individuals composing it. . . ."

ORIGIN OF SPECIES

CHARLES DARWIN

IF EVER a book worked a revolution in human thought it was Charles Darwin's *Origin of Species*. Before its publication in 1859, evolution was an interesting idea, indulged in by some speculative thinkers who were not altogether satisfied with current explanations. After it had appeared, most educated men who were able to understand the issues involved and to weigh up the arguments had come to the conclusion that Darwin had triumphantly demonstrated the *fact* of Evolution, and had furthermore outlined a way in which it may well have taken place and, more likely than not, did actually take place.

How have all the different species of living things – animals and plants, fishes and insects and even man himself – come to be what they are? Up to Darwin's time the generally accepted belief was that they had all been specially created in the way they are now. Each species was the result of a special act of creation. True, there had been some philosopher-scientists in antiquity, such as Aristotle among the Greeks and Lucretius among the Romans, and some of a much later date, such as the eighteenth-century French scientist Lamarck and his contemporary the English Erasmus Darwin, Charles Darwin's grandfather, who had fumblingly outlined some suggestions of an evolutionary theory, but their ideas had completely failed to convert the great majority, who preferred to continue to put their trust in the Bible statement that "in the beginning" all things had been brought into existence by Divine command.

This was Charles Darwin's belief in 1831, when as a young man of not quite twenty-three he joined H.M.S. *Beagle*, a naval surveying vessel under the command of Captain Fitzroy, R.N., and set sail on a voyage of scientific discovery round the world. He considered himself highly fortunate in his new appointment, as indeed he was. Son of a wealthy doctor in Shrewsbury, who had married a daughter of the great Staffordshire potter Josiah Wedgwood, he had had an inglorious career at Shrewsbury School, and later at Edinburgh University, where his intentions of becoming a doctor like his father were put an end to by his complete inability to stand the blood and

345

the screaming patients in the operating-theatre. He *almost* became a clergyman, and was sent to Cambridge with that in view. But he found it hard to swallow some of the things that he would be required to preach, and besides, his real interests had begun to show themselves, in natural history and geology. Even as a schoolboy he had dearly loved collecting beetles, and the passion never left him. So it was with intense relief that he heard that his professor had recommended him to Captain Fitzroy to accompany him on his voyage as an unpaid naturalist.

The voyage in the *Beagle* turned out to be, as Darwin himself declared, the most important event by far in his life; they were away until 1836, and visited not only the coasts of South America but a number of out-of-the-way islands in the Atlantic and the Pacific, as well as Australia and New Zealand. Everywhere Darwin went he kept his eyes open and his notebook handy, for already he had formed the ambition of "adding a little to Natural Science". Now let us turn to see what he has to tell us on the first page of the *Origin*, as we may call his famous book for short.

"When on board H.M.S. *Beagle* as naturalist, I was much struck with certain facts in the distribution of the organic beings inhabiting South America, and in the geological relations of the present to the past inhabitants of that continent. These facts ... seemed to throw some light on the origin of species – that mystery of mysteries, as it had been called by one of our greatest philosophers. On my return home, it occurred to me, in 1837, that something might perhaps be made out on this question by patiently accumulating and reflecting on all sorts of facts which could possibly have any bearing on it. After five years' work I allowed myself to speculate on the subject, and drew up some short notes; these I enlarged in 1844 into a sketch of the conclusions, which then seemed to me probable: from that period to the present day I have steadily pursued the same object. I hope that I may be excused for entering on these personal details, as I give them to show that I have not been hasty in coming to a decision."

No, "hasty" is hardly the word. He had spent twenty years in investigating the subject, and he might have gone on considering the problem if he had not been shocked by a letter that the postman delivered to his home at Downe, in Kent, on the afternoon of Friday, 18 June, 1858. The letter was from a professional collector of natural-history specimens named Alfred Russel Wallace, who wrote from a sick-bed in an island of the Moluccas, in the East Indies. Enclosed with the letter was a little essay entitled, "On the tendency of Varieties to depart indefinitely from the Original Type," and a glance at it was sufficient to show that Wallace had not only been working on the same problem as Darwin but had reached the very same explanation of why the variations occurred!

Darwin's first reaction was to wish to scrap his own work and let Wallace have the whole glory, but his friends at length persuaded him to agree that he and Wallace should prepare a joint paper to be presented to a meeting of the Linnean Society in London. This was done, the paper was read, on 1 July, 1858, and the thirty or so fellows of the Society who heard it (neither of its authors was present) were not greatly impressed.

But Darwin now pressed ahead with his own book, and this was at last published in November, 1859, under the title, *The Origin of Species, by means of Natural Selection, or the Preservation of Favoured Races in the Struggle for Life*. "It is no doubt the chief work of my life," wrote Darwin years after it had first appeared. What now, is it about? Let Darwin himself first state the problem.

"In considering the Origin of Species, it is quite conceivable that a naturalist, reflecting on the mutual affinities of organic beings, on their embryological relations, their geographical distribution, geological succession, and other such facts, might come to the conclusion that species had not been independently created, but had descended, like varieties, from other species. Nevertheless, such a conclusion, even if well founded, would be unsatisfactory, until it could be shown how the innumerable species inhabiting this world have been modified, so as to acquire that perfection of structure and co-adaptation which justly excites our admiration. Naturalists continually refer to external conditions, such as climate, food, etc., as the only possible cause of variation. In one limited sense ... this may be true; but it is preposterous to attribute to mere external conditions, the structure, for instance, of the woodpecker, with its feet, tail, beak, and tongue so admirably adapted to catch insects under the bark of trees. In the case of the mistletoe, which draws its nourishment from certain trees, which has seeds that must be transported by certain birds, and which has flowers with separate sexes absolutely requiring the agency of certain insects to bring pollen from one flower to the other, it is equally preposterous to account for the structure of this parasite, with its relations to several distinct organic beings, by the effects of external conditions, or of habit, or of the volition of the plant itself."

This was the problem, and now we shall read of the way in which Darwin set about its solution. At the commencement of his observations (he tells us), it seemed to him probable that a careful study of domesticated animals and of cultivated plants might throw some light on the subject. Thus his first chapter is devoted to a study of domesticated animals, pigeons in particular. It is in this chapter that Darwin makes his famous confession of ignorance, that "the laws governing inheritance are for the most part unknown". They were to remain unknown until the end of the century, when at long last the results of the experiments with peas and bees that had been carried out by an obscure Austrian abbot named Gregor Mendel were given to the world. As it was, he did not know (and never did know) how variations in plants and animals are carried down from one generation to another, but he had arrived at one important conclusion so far as domesticated breeds are concerned. "The key," he said, "is man's power of accumulative selection; nature gives successive variations; man adds them up in certain directions useful to him. In this sense he may be said to have made for himself useful breeds."

This is what happens under domestication, he felt sure, and now he asked himself, What happens under Nature? Well, here again selection was at work, but in a way far more powerful and effective than when it is being exercised by man. How does it operate? Through the "struggle for existence", the importance of which he had first learnt from reading in 1838 Rev. T. R. Malthus's book on *The Principle of Population*, published forty years earlier. Throughout the whole world of nature (writes Darwin) "a struggle for existence inevitably follows from the high rate at which all organic beings tend to increase. ... There is no exception to the rule that every organic being naturally increases at so high a rate, that, if not destroyed, the earth would soon be covered by the progeny of a single pair. Even slow-breeding man has doubled in twenty-five years, and at this rate, in less than a thousand years, there would literally not be standing-room for his progeny."

This is something that we do not always realize, and yet "unless it be thoroughly engrained in the mind, the whole economy of nature ... will be dimly seen or quite misunderstood. We behold the face of nature bright with gladness, we often see superabundance of food; we do not see or we forget, that the birds which are idly singing round us mostly live on insects or seeds, and are thus constantly destroying life; or we forget how largely these songsters, or their eggs, or their nestlings, are destroyed by birds and beasts of prey; we do not always bear in mind, that, though food may be now superabundant, it is not so at all seasons of each recurring year".

Owing to this constant struggle, "variations, however slight and from whatever cause proceeding, if they be in any degree profitable to the individuals of a species, in their infinitely complex relations to other organic beings and to their physical conditions of life, will tend to the preservation of such individuals, and will generally be inherited by their offspring. The offspring, also, will thus have a better chance of surviving, for, of the many individuals of any species which are periodically born, but a small number can survive. I have called this principle, by which each slight variation, if useful, is preserved, by the term Natural Selection, in order to mark its relation to man's power of selection".

Following this exposition of Natural Selection comes a short but very interesting section on what Darwin calls Sexual Selection. This form of selection, he explains, "depends not on a struggle for existence in relation to other organic beings or to external conditions but on a struggle between the individuals of one sex, generally the males, for the possession of the other sex. The result is not death to the unsuccessful competitor, but few or no offspring. Sexual selection is, therefore, less rigorous than Natural Selection." It is Natural Selection that is most powerfully and constantly in operation throughout the whole world of nature. "I am convinced," declares Darwin, "that Natural Selection has been the most important, but not the exclusive, means of modification".

There are many other chapters in the *Origin*, in which Darwin expands his theory, explains it further, and examines in the most serious and conscientious manner a number of objections that may be brought against it. Many people then, including quite a number who were well qualified to judge the evidence, remained unconvinced of the truth of Darwin's theory, at least in its entirety. There are many still who hold much the same position. But here a distinction must be drawn between Darwin's theory of Natural Selection and that of Evolution as a process that has continued through all the ages that have gone, is happening now, and will, so far as we may judge, continue in operation for all the ages that may lie ahead. This is a truly revolutionary idea, and that it is nowadays part and parcel of the mental furniture of educated men and women everywhere is very largely attributable to the effect of Darwin's book.

"I see no good reason why the views given in this volume should shock the religious feelings of any one," he writes in his final chapter. "When I view all beings not as special creations, but as the lineal descendants of some few beings which lived long before the first bed of the Cambrian system was deposited, they seem to me to become ennobled." And here are some eloquent sentences from his concluding paragraph.

"It is interesting to contemplate a tangled bank, clothed with many plants of many kinds, with birds singing on the bushes, with various insects flitting about, and with worms crawling through the damp earth, and to reflect that these elaborately constructed forms, so different from each other, and dependent upon each other in so complex a manner, have all been produced by laws acting around us. . . . There is grandeur in this view of life, with its several powers, having been originally breathed by the Creator into a few forms or into one; and that, whilst this planet has gone cycling on according to the fixed law of gravity, from so simple a beginning endless forms most beautiful and most wonderful have been and are being envolved."

THE MILL ON THE FLOSS

GEORGE ELIOT

DORLCOTE IS the mill's name, and a pleasant place it is with its walls of warm red brick and its roof of yellow thatch. Below the bridge is the river that has come down from the Midlands plain and now rolls on and on, through the pastures and the fields of dark brown earth to the quays of St. Ogg's and thence to the not-so-distant sea.

It is the river that gives a unity to this story of humble folk caught up in the relentless streams of emotion, of young loves and innocent passion and at last a turmoil of torn-up lives. You will not find its name on the map, but it is there all the same, for the Floss is the Trent, and St. Ogg's is Gainsborough on the Lincolnshire levels. And while we are penetrating disguises, we may as well mention that George Eliot was the pen-name that Miss Mary Ann Evans chose for herself when she set up as a novelist.

And there she is, that little girl standing on the bridge over against the mill, watching the great wheel go round and round. Yes, that little girl with the mane of dark hair that will keep on flicking her big black eyes is Mary Ann herself. But in the book she is Maggie Tulliver.

When the story opens Mr. and Mrs. Tulliver are discussing the matter of their son's education. "It seems a pity as the lad should take after the mother's side instead o' the little wench. She's twice as 'cute as Tom. Too 'cute for a woman, I'm afraid. It's no mischief while she's a little un, but an over-cute woman's no better nor a long-tailed sheep – she'll fetch none the bigger price for that."

"You talk o' cuteness," replies Mrs. Tulliver, "but I'm sure the child's half an idiot i' some things; for if I send her upstairs to fetch anything, she forgets what she's gone for, an' perhaps 'ull sit down on the floor i' the sunshine an' plait her hair an' sing to herself like a Bedlam creatur', all the while I'm waiting for her downstairs."

"Pooh, nonsense!" says Mr. Tulliver, "she's a straight black-eyed wench as anybody need wish to see, and she can read almost as good as the parson."

"But her hair won't curl all I can do with it."

"Cut it off – cut it off short," rejoins Mr. Tulliver rashly. . . .

Mrs. Tulliver was the youngest of the four Dodson sisters and the most simple-minded (that is why Mr. Tulliver chose her). They were a formidable family, the Dodsons, specially when united against the outside world. Mr. Tulliver was definitely "outside", as is shown clearly enough on the occasion of the family council called to discuss his proposal to send Tom to be taught by a country parson, who has already in charge Philip Wakem, the son of the lawyer with whom the miller has had some unpleasant and uniformly unsuccessful lawsuits over the supply of water to his mill. "Wakem's as big a scoundrel as Old Harry ever made," says Mr. Tulliver, "but tell me who's Wakem's butcher, and I'll tell you where to get your meat."

"But Lawyer Wakem's son's got a hunchback," says Mrs. Pullet, "it's more nat'ral to send *him* to a clergyman."

Mr. Glegg, husband of the eldest sister, considers this a sound point: "Wakem's son isn't likely to follow any business. Wakem'll make a gentleman of him, poor fellow."

"Mr. Glegg," counters his wife, "you'd far better hold your tongue. Mr. Tulliver doesn't want to know your opinion nor mine neither. There's folks in the world as knows better than everybody else."

"Why, I should think that's you, if we're to trust your own tale," says Mr. Tulliver.

"O, I say nothing," rejoins Mrs. Glegg sarcastically; "my advice has never been asked, and I don't give it."

"It'll be the first time, then," says Mr. Tulliver . . .

Tom takes after the Dodsons; one of the few things he is clear about is that he "would punish everybody who deserved it; why, he shouldn't mind being punished himself, if he deserved it; but then, of course, he never did deserve it". He is self-centred and grasping, an ill-educated, or mis-educated, lout. Maggie on the other hand is a Tulliver, a charming little piece of impulsive mischievousness. But she is absolutely devoted to Tom, just as Mary Ann Evans was devoted to her brother Isaac – who, there is reason to believe, served her for Tom's portrait.

Harum-scarum though she was, she was the apple of her father's eye, and as she grew in girlhood increasingly his stay and support. Certainly he needed one, as his pigheaded obstinacy caused his affairs to go from bad to worse. He lost another suit against Wakem, and the discovery that his mill had been mortgaged to his enemy brought on a stroke from which he was slow in recovering. When he did recover, he learnt that he had been made a bankrupt, and to

As heavy in appearance as the soil of the English midlands from which she sprang, Mary Ann Evans produced, under the pen-name of George Eliot, a succession of novels that are unsurpassed for their acute perception, their intense earnestness, and yet at the same time their appreciation of the lighter side of human character. *Above* is illustrated the first page of her MS. of *The Mill on the Floss*, in which the relationship of brother and sister is most movingly related; and *left, above* is an illustration of the novel's final scene, when Maggie Tulliver and her far less appealing brother are swept to destruction by the overcharged waters of the river Floss. The chalk drawing on the left suggests well George Eliot's brooding intelligence combined with a tender capacity for warmth of friendship.

An Oxford don and author of number of abstruse mathematic treatises – this was Charles Lu widge Dodgson in the dr reality of everyday life. But "Lewis Carroll" he was t author of some of the mc popular books for children ev written, *Alice's Adventures Wonderland* and *Through Looking-Glass*. Originally the were written for the delectatic of the little daughters of D Liddell, Dean of Christ Chur College, and *above, right* we s the original Alice, with one of h sisters dressed up in Orient costume for some party. T books had the advantage of bein illustrated by Sir John Tenni and one of the drawings is show here – the Trial Scene in *Alic Adventures*. Then (*left*) we s Lewis Carroll himself, the ma who could turn his brain fro mathematical reasonings and ca culations to the creation juvenile fancies that have arous the admiration not only generations of children but countless grown-ups.

keep a roof over his head he had to engage as the mill manager under Wakem. But his heart was filled with bitter hatred, and one evening he called for the family Bible and made Tom swear on it to "remember what Wakem's done to your father, and make him and his feel it, if ever the day comes".

"O, no, father," cried Maggie, "you shouldn't make Tom write that." "Be quiet, Maggie," says Tom, "I *shall* write it."

Several years of penurious dullness pass, in course of which Tom works hard at a job in St. Ogg's and saves every possible penny toward paying off his father's debts. Then one morning Philip Wakem rides into the mill-yard beside his father, and by slow degrees something in the nature of a love affair grows up between him and Maggie. They meet, unknown of course to their parents, in a lonely spot called the Red Deeps. They talk and talk, they exchange books, they hold hands, and are good friends – the relationship is the happiest thing that Maggie, now at sixteen already the young woman, has ever known.

But the insufferable Tom gets to hear of it, and in a tone of insolent brutality orders Philip to keep away from his young sister. "If you dare to make the least attempt to come near her, or to write to her, or to keep the slightest hold on her mind – your puny, miserable body shall not protect you. I'll thrash you – I'll hold you up to public scorn. Who wouldn't laugh at the idea of *your* turning lover to a fine girl?"

"Tom, I will not bear it – I will listen no longer," cries Maggie in disgust and fear and humiliation. "I don't want to defend myself," she tells Tom later; "I know I've been wrong – often, continually. But yet, sometimes when I have done wrong, it has been because I have feelings that you would be the better for, if you had them. If *you* were in fault ever . . . I should not want punishment to be heaped on you. But you have always enjoyed punishing me – you have always been hard and cruel to me. . . . You have no pity. . . . You are nothing but a Pharisee. . . ."

But Tom was quite unmoved, and not long afterward he had his hour of triumph, when he was able to repay every penny that his father owed. And precious good that did the old man, for on his way home from the creditors' meeting he encountered Wakem, and savagely assaulted him. It was Maggie who rescued the lawyer as he was being thrashed, who dragged her father away and helped to put him to bed. He was dying, and the girl implored him to say, "you forgive him – you forgive everyone now?" "No, my wench," came the reply, "I don't forgive him . . . I can't love a raskill."

With Mr. Tulliver's death the old home was broken up, and Maggie obtained a post at a girls' school some distance away. But she used to go back to St. Ogg's at holiday time, staying at her cousin Lucy Deane's, and it was there that she renewed her friendship with Philip Wakem, although Tom was still coldly disapproving. Philip was as deeply in love as ever, but Maggie's attitude toward him had changed. Her feelings for him had always had more of pity in them than love, and now another and very different man invaded her life and stampeded her affections.

Stephen Guest his name was, and he was young and handsome, well-bred and well-off. He and Lucy Deane had been for years as good as engaged, but from his very first meeting with Maggie Stephen was most powerfully attracted by her beauty, and perhaps more, by her strong intelligence. Maggie's senses were equally stirred; indeed, there sprang up between them a passion that was ardently sexual, although they both did their best, out of loyalty to gentle little Lucy, to keep it within bounds. One day, however, Stephen took Maggie for a row on the river in his boat; they drifted and drifted, until it was too late to return that day. They spent the night on the deck of a Dutch trading vessel that had picked them up, and in the morning Stephen urged upon Maggie that they had gone too far to go back now. Maggie must be his! They would get married at once, and go abroad until the tongues at St. Ogg's had done clacking. Maggie was *almost* persuaded, but at the last moment she refused her lover's impassioned pleadings. She loved him, yes, she acknowledged it; but she knew full well that love bought at the price of another woman's happiness would not be worth having.

"Good God, Maggie!" cried Stephen; "you rave. How can you go back without marrying me? You don't know what will be said, dearest." "Yes, I do," replied the girl; "I will confess everything. Lucy will believe me – she will forgive you, and – and – O, *some* good will come by clinging to the right. Dear, dear Stephen, let me go! – don't drag me into deeper remorse. My whole soul has never consented – it does not consent now." So they parted, he to go abroad, and she to return to St. Ogg's, where indeed the tongues clacked with a vengeance. Tom, being Tom, turned her out of *his* house; and when Isaac Evans read that, in this book by a certain George Eliot, he knew at once who the author was, for Tom had done just what he would have done in similar circumstances.

Maggie found refuge in the riverside cottage of a poor pedlar to whom she had been kind in days gone by. To that cottage beside the Floss came one day a messenger bearing a letter from Philip, a letter illed with nothing but sympathy and understanding and undying devotion. "God comfort you – my loving, large-souled Maggie. If everyone else has misconceived you, remember that you have never been doubted by him whose heart recognized you ten years ago." And one evening Lucy Deane came to the cottage. "Lucy," Maggie assured her with a tremendous effort, "*he* struggled too. He wanted to be true to you. He will come back to you. Forgive him – he will be happy then." The two girls clung together, and when they parted Lucy sobbed, "Maggie, you are better than I am."

Then one night Maggie was sitting in the gloom with the rain beating against the windows. It had been raining steadily for days and the Floss was rising fast, so that old men were shaking their heads and recalling ominously the terrible floods of sixty years before. Maggie was intent on the letter from Stephen Guest that had just reached her. "Write me one word," he implored her; "say, 'Come'!" It was her darkest hour, and as she put the letter in the candle flame she muttered to herself, "I will bear it, and bear it till death. ... But how long will it be before death comes! I am so young, so healthy. How shall I have patience and strength?" She was on her knees when she felt "a startling sensation of sudden cold about her knees and feet". Water was flowing in under the door, and she knew that it was the flood!

Swiftly the story moves to its climax, as swiftly as the river that is now rushing everything to destruction. After seeing her good friend and his family safely into a boat, Maggie pushed off in another to see what help she could render to those at the old mill. She found her mother had already gone to safety, but Tom was still there. He reached the boat and stumbled in. "They sat mutely gazing at each other: Maggie with eyes of intense life looking out from a weary, beaten face – Tom pale with a certain awe and humiliation," until at last "a mist gathered over the blue-grey eyes, and the lips found a word they could utter: the old childish – 'Magsie!'"

A few minutes later the Floss had swept them against a huge mass of floating fragments of broken buildings. "It is coming, Maggie," Tom said, in a deep, hoarse voice, loosing the oars and clasping her in his arms. "The next instant the boat was no longer seen upon the water – and the huge mass was hurrying on in hideous triumph. But soon the keel reappeared, a black speck on the golden water. The boat reappeared, but brother and sister had gone down in an embrace never to be parted: living through again in one supreme moment the days when they had clasped their little hands in love, and roamed the daisied fields together."

THE CLOISTER AND THE HEARTH

CHARLES READE

SOME EXCELLENT critics have maintained that Charles Reade's *The Cloister and the Hearth* is the finest historical novel in the English language. However that may be, it is indeed an exciting story, packed with incident, an adventure on almost every page. If you want to know what life was like in that rugged and riotous age when the Renaissance was just coming into flower, you will find it here, most brilliantly and vividly described and portrayed.

Reade wrote it first as a magazine story, but he was far from satisfied with it as it stood. For some time past he had been reading about the life of Erasmus, the great Renaissance scholar and humanist, and he had gone on to Erasmus's own sometimes lively writings and Froissart's *Chronicles* and Luther's tracts and treatises. Having thoroughly soaked himself in the atmosphere of those stirring times, he rewrote his story to novel length. The book was published in 1861, and it achieved instant success.

When the story opens, it is in Holland, not long past the middle of the fifteenth century. In the little town of Tergou lived Elias and Catherine his wife. He was a trader in cloth, silk and leather, and the couple would have been quite well off if they had not brought into the world a brood of nine children. Even the biggest loaf from the baker's just seemed to melt away when it was placed on *their* table. The pressure was somewhat relieved when the elder sons left home to seek employment, and then, as the parents quite got into the habit of saying, "Thanks to St. Bavon and all the saints, there's Gerard".

Gerard was one of the younger sons, and on him all the family's hopes were centred: not that they were very great hopes, nothing more than that his love of reading and natural gift for penmanship would obtain for him a minor post in the Church. To begin with Gerard fell in with his parents' ideas, but then one day he went to Rotterdam to take part in a competition between young painters and scribes, and there he happened to encounter an old man, poorly dressed but dignified, and his daughter. It was the girl of course who attracted his attention, and he never forgot this first glimpse of her. She was dressed in a gown of plain russet cloth, "yet snow-white

wn covered that part of her neck the gown left visible, and ended
alf-way up her white throat in a little band of gold embroidery;
.stead of hiding her hair in a pile of linen or lawn, she wore an
pen network of silver cord with silver spangles at the interstices:
. this her glossy auburn hair was rolled in front into two solid
aves, and supported behind in a luxurious and shapely mass". Her
ame was Margaret Brandt, and she was the daughter of a poor
holar, who knew so much more than his simple-minded neigh-
ours that he was suspected of sorcery.

Young Gerard won a prize in the competition for a piece of manu-
cript, and royal patronage was promised in the way of obtaining
or him a benefice when he was old enough – at present he was only
lector, at the bottom of the ladder of the clerical profession. But
hen he started for home, it was "with fifteen golden angels in his
urse, a golden medal on his bosom, and a heart like a lump of lead".
or he knew full well that there would be the strongest opposition to
1y proposal that he should abandon the career that had been planned
or him, of a priest vowed to celibacy. But there was not the least
oubt in his own mind that this was what he would have to do. He
oved Margaret, and Margaret returned his love, and what more was
1ere to say?

A very great deal, as things turned out. When Gerard told his
.ther of his intention to abandon the Church as a career and of his
etrothal to Margaret, the old man sternly forbade the match.
erard urged Margaret to accompany him to Italy, where, so he
ad been told, there were wonderful opportunities for young crafts-
1en; but the girl could not leave her father, and so they decided to
et wed forthwith and then retire to Flanders until the storm should
ave blown over. But as they stood together in the church at Seven-
ergen, "he radiant with joy, she with blushes," the happiest young
ouple in Holland, the constables of Tergou hurried up the aisle and
rrested Gerard; "this young man would marry against his father's
vill," they informed the priest, "and his father has prayed our
urgomaster to deal with him according to the law". Gerard was
1arched off to the town prison, and was soon involved in a series
f extraordinary adventures – escape, recapture, escape again. . . .

There was "one terrible night", when he "grazed the prison and
1e grave". Sought for everywhere by the burgomaster's officers he
ad taken refuge in Margaret's home, and there the constables caught
p with him. They forced their way in, and searched every room,
ven Margaret's, where "they found the beauty of Sevenbergen
eeping on an old chest, not a foot high, and no attempt made to

cover it; but the sheets were snowy white, and so was Margaret
linen. Presently she awoke, and sat up in the bed, like one amazed
then, seeing the men, began to scream faintly. . . ." Shamefaced, th
men beat a hasty retreat; and "no sooner had they retired tha
Margaret stepped out of bed, and opened the long chest on whic
she had been lying down in her skirt and petticoat and stockings, an
night-dress over all . . . and whispered tenderly, 'Gerard!' Gerar
did not reply. She laid her hand upon his shoulder – 'Gerard!' N
reply. 'Oh, what is this?' she cried, and her hands ran wildly over h
face and his bosom. She took him by the shoulders; she shook hin
she lifted him; but he escaped from her trembling hands, and fe
back, not like a man, but like a body. A great dread fell on her. Th
lid had been down. She had lain upon it. The men had been som
time in the room. With all the strength of frenzy she tore him out c
the chest. She bore him in her arms to the window. . . ."

Gerard was not dead, however; and when he came to, he foun
his head pillowed on Margaret's arm, and heard the woman l
adored murmur new words of eloquent love, as she showered tea
and tender kisses and caresses on him. "They wreathed their arn
round each other, and trouble and danger seemed a world, an ag
behind them. They called each other husband and wife. Were the
not solemnly betrothed? And had they not stood before the alta
together? Was not the blessing of Holy Church upon their unior
. . . Poor things! they were happy. Tomorrow they must part. Bt
that was nothing to them now. . . ."

After this, their marriage night, the two had to separate, Margare
returning to her father's house, and Gerard taking the road int
Germany and thence to Italy and Rome, where he hoped to obtai
employment for a year or two. He had not gone far when he me
with a Burgundian soldier, a good-hearted fellow named Deny
brave and resolute and with an ever-open eye for a pretty girl. I
those early days, before he had become hardened to the sort of con
pany that thronged the roads by day and filled the inns at nigh
Gerard would very likely have soon fallen a victim to treachery an
murder but for the aid afforded by the rather ruffianly Denys. Th
most exciting incident in the book discloses the pair imprisoned in
room in a country inn, when they have been informed by a friendl
maidservant that the innkeeper had slipped away into the woods t
fetch a band of robbers.

"In their room at the top of the stairs the two awaited the assaul
They took their posts. Denys blew out the candle. They could he;
each other's hearts thump at times. . . . When they were almo.

tarved with cold, and waiting for the attack, the door on the stairs opened softly and closed again. Nothing more. There was another narrowing silence. Then a single light footstep on the stairs; and nothing more. Then a light crept under the door; and nothing more. Presently there was a gentle scratching, not half so loud as a mouse's. The door swung gently open. The candle was held up, and shaded from behind by a man's hand. The man glided into the apartment. But at the first step something in the position of the cupboard and chair made him uneasy. He ventured no farther, but put the candle on the floor and stooped to peer under the chair; but as he stooped an iron hand grasped his shoulder, and a dagger was driven so fiercely through his neck that the point came out at his gullet. . . ."

Denys closed the door and bolted it, and then told Gerard to help him to set the dead man up in a chair. "What for? Frighten them! Gain time." And while saying this, Denys had whipped a piece of string round the corpse's neck and tied it to the chair, and there the ghastly figure sat, facing the door. "Denys, I can do better!" said Gerard, "saints forgive me!" He busied himself about the corpse, and Denys was amazed to see a luminous glow spreading rapidly over the white face. Gerard blew out the candle; and on this the corpse's face shone still more like a glow-worm's head. Denys shook in his shoes, and his teeth chattered. "What, in Heaven's name is this?" he whispered. "Hush! 'tis but phosphorus," rejoined Gerard, "but 'twill serve. . . ."

The first man who came up the stairs got no farther than the door: Denys nailed his hand to the post with a bolt from his arbalest and then sliced it off with his sword. Then the chief of the robber band, a huge villain known as "the Abbot", suddenly appeared in the doorway, a colossus with a glittering axe. "He saw the dead man with the moon's blue light on half his face, and the red light on the other half and inside his chapfallen jaws; he stared, his arms fell, his knees knocked together, and he crouched with terror. *'La Mort!'* he cried, in tones of terror, and turned and fled. In which act Denys started up and shot him through both jaws. . . ." But he was soon back again, with two of his men. "Wild with rage and pain, he spurned his dead comrade, chair and all, across the room, then, as the men faced him on each side with kindling eyeballs, he waved his tremendous axe like a feather right and left, and cleared a space, then lifted it to hew them both in pieces. . . ." Denys went staggering back covered with blood. Gerard had rushed in like lightning, and, just as the axe turned to descend on him, drove his sword so fiercely through the giant's body that the very hilt sounded on his ribs like

the blows of a pugilist, and Denys, staggering back to help hi
friend, saw a steel point come out of the Abbot behind. The stricker
giant bellowed like a bull, dropped his axe, and shook Gerard like
child. Then Denys with a fierce snarl drove his sword into the giant'
back. Thus horribly spitted, the Abbot gave a violent shudder, an
his heels hammered the ground convulsively. . . . Still he was no
killed, and Denys and Gerard were preparing to thrust him throug
again when he "leaped full five feet in height and fell with a tremen
dous crash against the door below, carrying it away with him like
sheet of paper"; and through the aperture the gallant pair saw th
gleam of torches as a band of soldiers fetched by the maidservan
burst into the inn in rescue.

Who that has read this piece of spirited bloodletting as a youngste
can ever have forgotten it? – and what has been found room for her
is only a part of what is spread over a dozen pages and more. No
does it stand on its own. There are numerous episodes in the boo
which are its rivals in the gusto of the telling. Adventure is pile
upon adventure, until with the arrival of Gerard at Rome the not
changes. From being a novel of exciting incident it becomes a sa
tale of broken hopes and twisted lives.

A letter reached the young man from a friend in Holland – a fals
letter as it turns out, written by those who for bad reasons of thei
own were his enemies – to the effect that Margaret was dead. Th
blow was a terrible one. If he had stayed at home, he might hav
saved her: such was his thought, and in a fierce revulsion of feelin
he plunged into "wine, women, gambling, whatever could procur
him an hour's excitement and a moment's oblivion". Then on
night he was about to fling himself into the Tiber when he was save
from suicide by the very man who had been charged, by a woma
he had repelled, with his assassination. Again he experienced
revulsion of feeling, and this time it carried him into religion as
friar of St. Dominic. He made his mark as an impassioned preacher
and in the course of his missionary journeyings went back to Hol
land, where one day Father Clement, as he now was, looking dow
from the pulpit in Rotterdam met the eyes of the woman whom h
had loved, and lost – and still loved! But what had he, a priest, nov
to do with the love of woman? For him "the Hearth" was dead
only "the Cloister" remained.

In the situation he had evolved not even Charles Reade coul
provide his readers with a happy ending such as the Victorians wer
accustomed to expect, but he did his best. After a terrific outburst c
anger at those who had engineered the ruin of his hopes, Gerard – o

Father Clement – became a hermit, but Margaret tracked him down, and the two were brought together again by the little boy, her son and his, who had been conceived on that night when he had "grazed the prison and the grave". Again through Margaret's loving instrumentality, he exchanged his hermit's cell for the parsonage of Gouda, where for years he carried out the duties of parish priest.

"History itself," writes Reade, "though a far more daring story-teller than romance, presents few things so strange as the footing on which Gerard and Margaret now lived for many years. United by present affection, past familiarity, and a marriage irregular but legal; separated by Holy Church and by their own consciences, which sided unreservedly with Holy Church; separated by the Church, but united by a living pledge of affection, lawful in every sense at its date. . . ."

"History?" says the reader, who has perhaps become a little drowsy over the account of his hero's and heroine's last days, "what has History to do with it?" Only this, that "the yellow-haired laddie" who was their son grew up to become none other than the great Erasmus.

FATHERS AND SONS

IVAN S. TURGENEV

IVAN SERGEYEVICH TURGENEV had already won fame both a
dramatist and poet before he wrote *Fathers and Sons*, the nove
which provoked more bitter, deep and lasting controversy than an
other work of fiction has ever done in any country. In his ow
words: "I will not enlarge on the effect produced by this novel. I wil
only say that everywhere the word Nihilist was caught up by
thousand tongues. . . . A shadow lay on my name. I don't deceiv
myself. I know that shadow will remain."

The Turgenevs were landed gentry, but Ivan's childhood was no
a happy one as his father had married his mother for her money an
she, resenting his lack of affection, tyrannized over her family an
the serfs. To the dreamy, idealistic boy the constant atmosphere o
strife was highly upsetting and he withdrew more and more int
himself. His greatest solace was reading and he eagerly devoured th
works of Pushkin, Gogol and Lermontov, the leading liberal writer
of their day. Like them he was passionately devoted to Russia: lik
them he realized also that she must be given the chance to expand
and develop as other European countries had done.

In his late teens Turgenev was sent to university, first in Moscow
then in St. Petersburg. No mean scholar, he threw himself into hi
studies with zest and with his new-found freedom from family
restraint the latent genius within him quickened, then burgeoned
His mother, proud of her son's academic attainments, allowed him to
move on to the University of Berlin in 1839, and during his two
years' stay there his horizons widened yet further. He returned home
full of enthusiastic ideas about the necessity of Westernizing Russia,
but these suffered a rude shock when he entered the Civil Service to
start the career chosen for him by his ambitious mother. Like his hero
Gogol before him he found its bureaucratic methods intolerable and
after stormy family scenes he resigned.

During the 1840s Turgenev's poems were lauded by the critics and
his plays met with instantaneous success, among them being that
masterpiece *A Month in the Country* which is still produced in many
lands today. He won added fame with his brilliant *A Sportsman's*

Sketches, issued between 1847 and 1852, and before his mother died in 1850 she had the satisfaction of knowing that her son was regarded as one of Russia's foremost writers.

She left Turgenev her considerable fortune, thus enabling him to travel extensively in Europe, where he met many progressive intellectuals with ideas akin to his own and also fell in love with the famous singer Pauline Garcia (Mme Viardot), for whom he was to cherish a hopeless passion his life through. A hiatus in his wanderings came in 1852, when he was exiled to his estates near Orel for writing a glowing obituary of Gogol. His enforced seclusion gave Turgenev the opportunity of studying the problems of the serfs and he resolved to devote all his energies to fighting for their cause. He wrote no more plays but a few years later published *On the Eve*, the great novel in which he describes the end of the Crimean War and the tremendous upsurge of vitality which occurred throughout Russia with the death of the despotic Nicholas I and the emancipation of the serfs by his successor, Alexander II. It was this book which made him the idol of the younger generation.

Fathers and Sons, which was to send him crashing from his pedestal, first appeared in 1862 in Katkoff's *The Russian Messenger*, a paper known as "the organ of the younger generation". The novel foretells the great spread of the Liberal movement which was to take place in the Russia of the 1860s, and its central figure, Bazarov, is the prototype of that terrifying creature just visible on the political horizon – the Nihilist. About him Turgenev wrote later: "I have never attempted to create a type without having, not an idea, but a living person, in whom the various elements were harmonized together, to work from. . . . At the foundation of the principal figure, Bazarov, was the personality of a young provincial doctor. He died not long before 1860. In that remarkable man was incarnated to my ideas the just rising element, which, still chaotic, afterwards received the title of Nihilism."

Bazarov is the aggressor, destroyed even as he destroys; the iconoclast against whom his followers revolt; the man of science perpetually in conflict with the man of faith. He is a brave man who glories in living dangerously; a man who always stands alone; a man who believes in nothing, not even in the masses for whom he has striven so mightily because he knows they are cowards at heart.

We first meet Bazarov as he arrives with his ardent disciple, Arkady Kirsanov, to spend a holiday with the latter's father, Nikolai, at his country home. Tall and lean, with penetrating green eyes under a broad forehead and a sardonic expression emphasized by drooping sandy whiskers, Bazarov is an arresting figure in his long, rough coat. Nikolai is delighted to welcome any friend of his son, but is a shade disconcerted by the guest's laconic speech and surly manner. From Arkady's chatter he learns that Bazarov is a brilliant student who has won a degree in natural science and hopes to graduate in medicine the following year.

Nikolai Kirsanov is a kindly, anxious man who prides himself on his progressiveness, for he has divided his estate of Maryino between his emancipated serfs, only retaining four acres on which he has built a modest wooden house with a red tin roof. But he is inefficient and lets his bailiff swindle him, so he often has to accept help from his elder brother Pavel, who lives with him. . . . Worried by his affairs and lonely without his lately dead wife he has taken a mistress, a girl of humble origin named Fenitchka, by whom he has had a baby son. In a shamefaced way he tries to explain this moral lapse to Arkady and is relieved when the boy says he thinks it an excellent arrangement. Nikolai also feels more at ease with Bazarov, who treats Fenitchka with courtesy and advises her on baby Mitya's teething troubles.

For his part Bazarov thinks Nikolai a good-hearted old muddler and is not surprised that the peasants nickname Maryino "Poverty Farm". His real antagonist is Pavel, the stiff-backed, aristocratic ex-officer who wears English suits and looks with scorn at a young man who spends his days dissecting frogs and his meal-times gulping down food so fast that he only answers in monosyllables when addressed. And there is a deeper cause for their mutual dislike: Pavel is secretly, passionately in love with Fenitchka and Bazarov is the only one who senses this. So Pavel deliberately airs his reactionary ideas, thus goading Bazarov into voicing his Nihilistic views until the atmosphere is so electric that poor Nikolai sighs thankfully when Bazarov announces he must visit his parents some sixty miles away and Arkady decides to accompany him as far as the town which lies on his route.

There they are hailed by Sitnikov, a silly and rich young fop who chases madly after every new movement and at present professes to be a follower of Bazarov. He greets them joyously and insists they visit his "emancipated" friend, Mme Evdoksya Kushkim, who prattles happily about the *avant-garde* and plies them with champagne. Bazarov is extremely rude to her, a fact she is too stupid to notice. The next evening, at the Governor's ball, Arkady meets the striking Mme Anna Odintsov, who asks him to bring Bazarov to see her as she wants to meet "the man who has the courage to believe in nothing". A strange three-cornered relationship ensues. Arkady falls headlong in love with Anna; she regards him as a pleasant boy but is tremendously intrigued by Bazarov and is oddly stimulated by his conversation; Bazarov recoils from the lure this cool, serene woman has for him even as he strives to convert her to his Nihilistic views.

Anna invites them to stay at her country home, where they meet her eager young sister Katya and a desiccated old princess who is her aunt. The house is luxurious and beautifully run, the very epitome of all that Bazarov seeks to destroy. And the more he learns about Anna the more he despises her way of life. On the death of her father, a handsome nobleman who gambled his fortune away, she deliberately married the rich, middle-aged Odintsov. A few years later he died, leaving her his wealth, and for the past three years she has remained on her estate, making no effort to use her riches to help anyone save her aunt, Katya and herself.

Yet despite himself Bazarov falls in love with this ice-cold beauty, and as the warm summer days slip by his whole being is filled with the desire to change her into an ardent, pulsating human being who will return that love. He takes her on long botanical expeditions; talks to her at length about the regeneration of Russia; rouses her interest in modern science; spends the evenings studying her in silence, his green eyes fixed upon her face. Meanwhile poor Arkady is disconsolate. Katya tries to cheer him by her piano-playing and in the process grows to love him, although all his thoughts are centred on her sister.

Things come to a head one hot evening when Anna tells Bazarov she is sure they are destined to become close friends, but she wishes he would confide in her more. He asks if she would care to know the reason behind his reticence and she says she would. Then the words burst from him: "Let me tell you that I love you like a fool, like a madman. . . . There, you've forced it out of me." Tenderly she uses his Christian names for the first time, "Yevgeny Vassilyevitch!" and he turns, snatches her hands and draws her to his breast. She does not struggle, but somehow melts from his embrace and the next instant is standing in the far corner of the room, her eyes wide with horror. He rushes to her but she whispers in alarm, "You have misunderstood me," and he turns and leaves the room.

Next day he leaves for his home after telling Anna bitterly that she is incapable of loving him or anybody. His old parents give him a joyful welcome, but within a few days Bazarov feels stifled by their cossetting, their fussing, their constant following him around and abruptly takes the road back to Maryino. But he finds no peace there. Arkady is no longer the admiring friend for, like Bazarov himself, he is tormented by memories of Anna and presently he returns to her home. Nikolai is distraught with financial troubles and Pavel's sarcastic allusions to Nihilism are intolerable. Climax comes when he accuses Bazarov of trying to entice Fenitchka away from his brother and challenges him to a duel. Pistols are used and Pavel receives a flesh wound. Bazarov gives him expert medical care, but Nikolai is so upset and the atmosphere so strained that he leaves Maryino and returns to his home. This time he forces himself to suffer their loving care, and to still his mental torment over Anna throws himself into dealing with a typhus outbreak among the peasants. While doing a post-mortem he cuts himself and becomes infected with the disease.

Bazarov's grief-stricken parents nurse him, but the father, formerly an army doctor, has no knowledge of modern methods and is forced to watch his son's life ebbing away. Aware of every symptom of the disease, Bazarov knows that soon he will sink into unconsciousness and asks his father to send a message to Anna. He does so and she arrives with a German doctor who examines Bazarov, then tells Anna and the father there is nothing anyone can do.

Anna goes into the sick-room alone and sits beside the bed. Bazarov gazes at her out of sunken eyes: "Noble-hearted!" he whispers. "Oh, how near, and how young and fresh and pure. . . . Well, good-bye! Live long, that's the best of all, and make the most of it while there is time. You see a hideous spectacle; the worm half-crushed, but writhing still. And, you see, I thought too: I'd break down so many things . . . there were problems to solve, and I was a giant! And now all the problem for the giant is how to die decently. . . ." Suddenly he tries to sit up: "Listen . . . you know I didn't kiss you then. . . . Breathe on the dying lamp, and let it go out. . . ."

Anna kisses him on the forehead and he sinks back. "Enough!" he murmurs. "Now . . . darkness. . . ." He speaks no more and lies in a coma until his death the following day.

Six months later there is a dinner at Maryino to celebrate the weddings of Nikolai and Fenitchka and Arkady and Katya. Toasts are drunk to the happy couples, also to Pavel who is going to live in Dresden. Nobody mentions the man who influenced them all save Katya, who whispers as she clinks glasses with Arkady: "To the memory of Bazarov!"

When the book was published Turgenev received thousands of

furious letters from young Russians to whom he had been an idol, demanding to know how he had dared to "caricature" a character who symbolized their cause. At the same time he received more thousands of letters from older Slavophils and reactionaries praising him warmly for his courage in denouncing that appalling modern phenomenon, the Nihilist. He argued in vain with his detractors and admirers alike: the storm continued to rage about his head. Later he wrote: "The whole ground of the misunderstanding lay in the fact that the type of Bazarov had not time to pass through the usual phases. At the very moment of his appearance the author attacked him. It was a new method as well as a new type I introduced – that of Realizing instead of Idealizing. . . . The reader is easily thrown into perplexity when the author does not show clear sympathy or anti-pathy to his own child. The reader readily gets angry. . . . After all, books exist to entertain."

Like most great artists Turgenev was a highly sensitive creature. Like a snail he retreated into his shell and moved away, eventually settling in France, where he became the close friend of Flaubert and was much sought after by de Maupassant and other younger writers. But, as he had foretold, the shadow on his name remained, and the violent denunciations of his work by Dostoevsky and Tolstoy wounded him deeply. His devotion to Russia had not altered and in 1880 he paid his last visit to the country he loved. By this time the storm had died and Nihilism had grown in power, so that people realized how truly he had portrayed the future in *Fathers and Sons*. It is good to record that his journey through his native land was a triumphal progress which wiped out memory of the sufferings he had endured for almost twenty years.

WAR AND PEACE

LEO TOLSTOY

COUNT LEO TOLSTOY, an aristocratic landowner who lived in a large house on his family estate in central Russia, was born in 1828 and began to write *War and Peace* when he was thirty-five. The finished product, a huge work containing 700,000 words and no less than 539 characters, started publication in instalments five years later. Today, after being translated into dozens of languages, it is recognized as perhaps the greatest novel in world literature.

But to call this immense, panoramic book a novel is misleading. Most of the novels that we read take a small slice of life, present a handful or so of characters and pursue a recognizable plot. Tolstoy does none of these things.

Admittedly, the book begins with a small scene: an evening reception given by a society lady in St. Petersburg, in July, 1805. A few months previously, Napoleon had been proclaimed Emperor of the French. He had already annexed Genoa, seized Hanover from the British and been crowned King of Italy. England was his enemy. Now he threatened Austria and, remotely, Russia itself. Plans were afoot for an alliance between these three countries and on this evening in St. Petersburg tempers are raised against the "Antichrist", the barbarian who had murdered the Duc d'Enghien, heir to the Bourbons, and now threatened the whole of Europe.

All this is talked about at the *soirée*, mingled with gossip and the affected courtesies exchanged in high society. We get to know various individuals. None of them seems very remarkable, though there are clear differences between them. One is a bulky young man with spectacles, shy and rather too explosive in speech for the mannered atmosphere of the salon. His name, we learn, is Pierre and he is the illegitimate son of one of the wealthiest of Russian princes. Another young man, Prince Andrew, is handsome, cynical and aloof. Other families, too, are represented this evening and we meet their womenfolk. There is nothing very sensational in this – we feel baffled and perhaps even bored.

But soon the scene widens, other families are brought into the story and we get to know the characters more intimately: their home life, their ambitions, their loves, their jealousies. Gradually a whole picture of the aristocratic life of those days is brought before our eyes: the nobles in their palaces sustained in their fabulous wealth by thousands of serfs working for them on their country estates and waited on in their life of idleness by myriads of servants. But, different as they are from ourselves in their background, the more we know them, the more their ordinary human characteristics appear. These are real people, very individual, some of them very likeable, delightful when they are young, full of life and busily living, as we do, by guess and by God. So by the time we have read the first hundred pages we still do not know where Tolstoy is leading us, but these characters are all becoming important to us and our hearts begin to beat with theirs.

But meanwhile war has come between Russia and France, and the Russian army, with many of the young men we have met in St. Petersburg serving in it, has advanced into Austria to join hands with its ally. With great realism – he himself had served in the Crimean War – Tolstoy describes the movements of the army and the military atmosphere, always with the stress on individuals (of whom many more are now introduced) and their reactions to events. Chapter by chapter, the narrative skips from one scene to another, from big decisions and preliminary battles to the talk of humble soldiers and the pranks of junior officers, until we dimly discern the author's aim in his epic narrative. On the one hand, he is going to depict the whole flavour of the great patriotic war against Napoleon which began in earnest with the invasion of Russia in 1812 and ended, after the French army had spent six weeks in burning and deserted Moscow, with its retreat and the escape in December of the exhausted remnant over the Beresina. On the other hand, Tolstoy will pursue the threads of his domestic narrative by placing the young nobles who are the chief characters in the book in the Russian forces and by viewing the war through their eyes trace their own development in the midst of the national struggle.

But still we have not reached the core of this highly complex and varied book. Tolstoy's double aim is certainly ambitious, but it does not entirely account for the lavish outpouring of incident or for the choice of the incidents themselves. World events such as the battle of Austerlitz are followed by seemingly trivial family affairs. The spotlight shifts continually, from one family to another, from a scintillating ball to a quiet conversation between two people, from love affairs to hunting scenes, Pierre's initiation into Freemasonry, a vignette of an irascible old prince who tyrannizes over his unmarried daughter, high politics, youthful joys and sorrows, the near-seduction of an innocent girl, Christmas mummers, engagements and marriages – a welter of the most brilliantly conceived but apparently disjointed scenes all taking place in the interlocking aristocratic circles. What is the meaning of it all? Where does it lead?

One might ask the same question of life itself, and here we are getting nearer to the core of the book and the clue to its greatness. Tolstoy was an intense lover of life and in writing *War and Peace* he created a facsimile of the real thing: its untidiness, its disjointedness, its extreme variety, its crowd of struggling, lonely human beings and its seeming lack of purpose. But into this facsimile he also infused his own vitality so that, like real life, we accept and enjoy it for its own sake. He recreates for us the big phenomenon with which we all have to cope, the great river without beginning or end which bears us all toward an unknown destination.

Now let us return to the twin aspects, war and peace. In the first half of the book, before Russia is invaded, they are separate. There are the soldiers at the front and the civilians at home and when the soldiers go on leave they pass from war to peace, that is, the young nobles bring their experiences with them and, disgusted, inspired or enlightened as the case may be by what they have seen and done, they look on their families and friends with new eyes. Perhaps they have matured, perhaps not, at any rate they have changed, and these changed men provoke new ripples in the aristocratic pond and provide fresh scenes in the book. Domestic relations move forward on to new planes and we still get the impression that individuals can be the masters of their fate.

But then the cataclysm breaks. Napoleon invades and the whole country is at war. Closely following historical sources, Tolstoy portrays the conqueror, the man who believes that it is really he alone who controls events and has set a million feet marching into Russia. He also portrays Kutuzov, the Russian Commander-in-Chief. Kutuzov does not think for a moment that in this greatest of wars individual men can achieve much by calculation. To him this struggle is decreed by providence. All that he can do is to work with providence toward the final outcome which he senses will be the defeat of the invader. It is here that a new element comes into the book. In his portrayal of this vast event – the capture of Smolensk, the battle of Borodino, the evacuation of Moscow, its occupation by the French, their withdrawal and retreat, harried by the Russians – Tolstoy consciously contrasts the futility of those ambitious men on both sides who thought they could decisively influence events and those who submitted to them with simplicity, courage and faith. Life, Tolstoy is saying, is bigger than any of us. How it treats us personally does not much matter. The important thing is to accept it positively. So in this war section of the book with its huge panorama of tragedy and suffering he concentrates on the men of instinctive wisdom – Kutuzov whose motto is "patience", the peasants who go cheerfully into battle, putting on clean shirts to meet their death because they are going to their Maker, the Russian prisoner of the French who, amidst squalor and starvation, smiles at some private vision of his own.

The book is full of faith and an awareness of spiritual reality. It is positive, optimistic and loving toward men, animals and nature. After the French retreat, when the last soldier has gone limping back over the frontier, the threads are gathered up again on this spiritual theme. Some of the characters that have been with us all through the book are no more. A boy hussar, full of the ardour and beauty of youth, has gone to his death, gallantly charging the French. Prince Andrew, whom we met as a cynical young man in the first chapter, has been seeking all through these years for some experience that would give meaning to life and peace to his mind. It comes to him on a sick-bed when, after a mortal wound in battle, he dreams that he is alone in a room and death is trying to get in. He attempts to bolt the door, but the bolt sticks. He tries to hold it shut, but gradually it is pushed farther and farther open. Then death comes into the room. . . . At that moment, in real life, an orderly tending him says: "Wake up" – and he awakes with the wonderful realization that death is an awakening from life. From that moment on his life ebbs slowly, in perfect peace, to the end.

At last now we get to the core of the book, the real message which the whole vast epic, this throbbing facsimile of life, contains for us. The main characters have all been of a special kind, people of greatly differing temperaments, but all united in the search for spiritual truth. They cannot be happy unless they acquire some insight into the meaning of life and human destiny. They cannot be reconciled to the trivialities of daily existence unless they can catch some glimpse of the Power that rules over all. This spiritual awakening comes to them in different ways and can never be forced. They are seekers, but however hard they seek the moment of enlightenment will choose its own time. But to them, Tolstoy's *élite*, that enlightenment is essential. They cannot really *live* without it, and to all such people, today as in his own time, his message seems to be: "Seek, and ye shall find."

That is something very positive. But it does not imply that salvation can be found in mysticism, by turning away from life. On the contrary, Pierre, who is the chief character of the whole book, is a busy, bustling individual. His appetites are strong and he indulges them. As a civilian he finds his way to the battlefield of Borodino to see what is going on. In burning Moscow he rescues a child – and gets arrested by the French for incendiarism. It is in captivity that the moment of truth comes to him, in talk with his fellow-prisoner, the man with instinctive wisdom. And then he realizes that God is here and everywhere. God is under his very nose, *in* life, not outside it.

There is something extremely touching in the groping of these main characters for the bread of life and the fact that some of them survive the war and no hardship, toil or suffering has deflected them from their search stresses another view of Tolstoy's: however severe outward events may be, our centre of gravity lies within ourselves and it is our spiritual life which really matters.

But not all the characters are "seekers". Among the three families whose affairs are in the forefront of the book, almost all are worthy people in their way, that is, they possess fundamental goodwill. But most of them are content to ask no questions of life; they do not try to open their eyes to a wider horizon. They feel no need for it. Among these people are some charming individuals: an old Count, head of a large family, rather ineffectual, but always ready to make sacrifices for others. His daughter Natasha, a sensitive, joyous, attractive girl, very conscious of her charm and eager to give love and receive it. Nicholas, her brother, a literal-minded young man, practical, resolute and warm-hearted.

Most of the younger people find their place in life toward the end, and the closing chapters, which portray them on their country estates surrounded by their families, breathe an air of calm after the storm. Tolstoy originally thought of calling his book "All's Well that Ends Well", and by "well" he meant devotion to simple country tasks, the rearing of children, the mutual support of husband and wife – all those things which give people a stake in life, a centre for their existence, a field of constructive activity.

But the word "end" in the title would have implied a cut-and-dried quality in the book which is the very opposite of its atmosphere. In *War and Peace* there is no real beginning and no end. All is change, variety and flux, particularly in the relations between individuals, and in the last few pages, to underline the perpetual movement of life, Tolstoy portrays a fifteen-year-old boy, the orphaned son of Prince Andrew whom he has never seen, who dreams of his father and swears, on waking, to "do something with which even *he* would be satisfied".

For modern readers accustomed to taut plots and strenuous efforts by authors to claim and sustain their interest *War and Peace* is a difficult book to read, and not merely because of its length. There are no cheap effects. Melodrama is entirely absent. There is no stimulus for the nerves. The reader has to persevere, but if he does the reward is great. The book is full of life, variety and memorable characters and in the last resort it is not the great battle scenes which one remembers, but an eager young girl at her first ball, an old man dying, a declaration of love, a boy hussar joyfully sharpening his sabre, the shouts of children, the tremulous voices of old age, the great spaces of Russia – and behind all the powerful spirit of Tolstoy who loved life and longed to understand it.

ALICE'S ADVENTURES IN WONDERLAND

LEWIS CARROLL

THE REVEREND CHARLES LUTWIDGE DODGSON was an Oxford don, a lecturer in mathematics and author of sundry books on Euclid and Logic; a bachelor, methodical, precise, indeed pernickety in his habits. Yet he wrote *Alice's Adventures in Wonderland*.

On the surface it seemed a most improbable feat. *The Times*, in its obituary notice of his death on 14 January, 1898, remarked: "Few would have imagined that the quiet, reserved mathematician, a bachelor, who all his life was remarkable for his shyness and dislike of publicity, possessed the qualities necessary to produce a work which has stood the test of more than 30 years" (today one can say with equal truth, "of a century") "and still captivates young and old alike by its quaint and original genius."

In the author's lifetime the book sold by scores of thousands in Britain and America, and was translated into several European languages. With the expiry of its copyright in 1907, its sales have gone on mounting into the millions, and it has been translated into Chinese and Japanese. It still sells steadily, year by year. Its charm is timeless.

Charles Lutwidge Dodgson was born on 27 January, 1832, of a long-established north country family with a tradition of service to the Church. His father, Charles Dodgson, a parson, incumbent of Daresbury, later became Rector of Croft and Archdeacon of Richmond. A great-grandfather and a great-great-grandfather had been bishops. They were a big family. Charles junior was the third child and eldest son in a family of eleven – seven girls and four boys. Thus as a child he had a bevy of little girls for playmates. His lifelong passion for amusing little girls, to which we are indebted for *Alice's Adventures in Wonderland*, no doubt owes its origin to this circumstance.

As a young boy he showed a love of the dramatic; made marionettes (he had clever hands) and wrote and produced puppet plays for them; wrote and illustrated manuscript magazines. He was educated by his scholarly father till at the age of twelve he went to Richmond

Grammar School, where he showed marked ability in mathematics. He passed on in a year and a half to Rugby, where he was miserable, for he was hopeless at athletic games. He was that unpopular figure, a clever swot, collecting a variety of prizes. He went into residence at Christ Church, Oxford, on 24 January, 1851. Shy and hampered by a stammer, he made few friends among his fellows, but did brilliantly in his studies, and on Christmas Eve, 1852, was nominated to a Studentship – the title given at Christ Church to a Fellowship. This he could retain so long as he remained unmarried if he went on to take Holy orders. He was a Student of Christ Church till his death.

Officially his concern was mathematics. He got a First in Mathematics in 1854, and next year started coaching pupils in that subject, and then became Mathematical Lecturer (that is, Tutor) and Master of the House. His residence and income were henceforth assured. He did not take Deacon's Orders till 1861. Priest's Orders he never took.

To his mathematical competence and his logical mind he added a strong artistic sense. He sketched throughout life – mostly figures. He was a devotee of the theatre. He loved poetry, and wrote much verse, mostly humorous. Apart from writing, his supreme hobby was photography, then in its infancy. It was an exhausting business, for the operator had to prepare his own wet plates and take a mass of paraphernalia round with him. It suited Dodgson with his meticulous attention to careful detail. He was supreme in his day as a photographer of children.

He was blissfully happy in the society of children – especially of little girls. Most little boys bored him. But while shy and retiring with adults, he expanded in the company of little girls, where the playful, comic side of his mind could flow forth unembarrassed, awakening and responding to their simple-hearted delight.

When Dr. Liddell became the new Dean of Christ Church in 1855, Dodgson came to know his family – a boy, Harry, and three little girls, Lorina, Alice and Edith. He tried to photograph them, but their formidable mother, who seems to have rather disliked him, disapproved. Despite her, he managed to build up a warm friendship with the children. He used to tell them stories, and would give them copies of his comic verses, printed in *College Rhymes*, an Oxford periodical of the time. Their governess sometimes brought them to tea in his rooms in Tom Quad.

Unawares came that great day on 4 July, 1862, when the three little girls, brought round by their governess and left with Dodgson and another clergyman, Robinson Duckworth, Fellow of Trinity, went down with picnic baskets to Folly Bridge and embarked for a boating trip up the Isis. As they rowed, Dodgson began to tell a rambling story to Alice, who was coxing the boat. Trying to find an original opening, he sent his heroine down a rabbit-hole, with no idea what would happen next. Near Godstow they rested by a haycock on the bank, where they had tea and Dodgson went on with his story. When they arrived back at the Deanery, Alice begged him to write out the story for her, and he sat up nearly all night, jotting down as much as he could recall of the story he had spun. On 6 August he took the three again to Godstow, accompanied this time by the Senior Student of Christ Church, A. G. Vernon Harcourt, and was compelled by their insistence to go on with his tale of Alice's Adventures Underground.

His meetings with Alice Liddell became less and less frequent after this, because of her mother's objections, and in 1864 they were stopped altogether. But at an encounter in November, 1862, she had reminded him of his promise and in February, 1863, he completed the revision of his notes. He then started to illustrate his manuscript for Alice. Meantime he had decided to print the story. He extended the copy for the press to nearly twice the original size, and succeeded in getting John Tenniel, the Punch artist, to undertake the illustrations.

Its original title, "Alice's Adventures Underground," sounded too like a lesson book about mines, and after much thought he made it *Alice's Adventures in Wonderland*. As for the author's name, he realized that *Dodgson* was prosaic, so he took his two Christian names, *Charles Lutwidge*, reversed their order and reshaped them as Lewis Carroll.

The first edition was printed in July, 1865, but Tenniel was dissatisfied with the printing of the pictures, and Dodgson, always a perfectionist about everything he touched, had the edition stopped when only the first 48 copies had been given away or sold. The unbound sheets were disposed of to an American firm, which published them as the Second Edition. The real Second Edition was published by Macmillan in November, 1865, but bore the date 1866.

Though it delighted its readers, the book's popularity was not at first spectacular; but edition succeeded edition, and it never looked back. French and German translations appeared in 1869; Italian in 1872. Dozens of other translations have followed. It is read by children and their elders. Advertisers quote from it with the certainty that it is universally familiar.

There is an apocryphal story that Queen Victoria, after reading *Alice*, asked to see the author's next book. But Dodgson's next publication was a mathematical treatise entitled: *Condensation of Determinants*. He later denied that he sent this to Her Majesty. He was an indefatigable writer, and continuously poured out books and pamphlets on mathematical subjects, notably on Euclid; but though these had some brief success in his lifetime, they are forgotten today. Euclid has given place to other forms of Geometry.

As Lewis Carroll, however, he went on writing fantastic tales for his young friends. In 1868 he secured Tenniel's promise to illustrate a sequel to *Alice's Adventures in Wonderland* which he had resolved to write; and after much back-and-forth work over the illustrations, *Through the Looking-Glass* came out by Christmas, 1871. To the first impression of 9,000 copies, Macmillan had at once to add another 6,000. In twenty-two years more it had sold 60,000, and was firmly wedded in people's minds with the original *Alice* book. Today they are so blended that many would be unsure whether a particular incident, character or poem is in *Wonderland* or the *Looking-Glass*.

The Hunting of the Snark, a narrative poem of comic characters sailing in quest of an elusive monster, was published in 1876. Its author later admitted that its last line stuck in his mind: "For the snark *was* a Boojum, you see." And he wrote the poem to lead up to that climax. He wrote it for children, but its wit appeals much more to adult readers. After a slow start it sold edition after edition, in Britain and America.

For years he worried over the composition of another story for children, with fresh characters. At last, in 1889, it appeared with the title: *Sylvie and Bruno*. Rather a patchwork effort, it lacks the smooth coherence of the *Alice* books, and little of it lives in public memory beyond the acrobatic gardener's sudden bursts of verse on the theme of "He thought he saw ..." such as:

> *He thought he saw a banker's clerk*
> *Descending from a bus.*
> *He looked again, and saw it was*
> *A hippopotamus.*
> *"If this should stay to dine," he said,*
> *"There won't be much for us!"*

Dodgson's life held no great romance. His intense love of little girls was the innocent affection of an uncle. Friends record that his love of Ellen Terry, whom as a little girl he devotedly admired, might have ripened to romance and marriage, but when their friendship was renewed she was already married, and though the marriage had broken down, he as a clergyman could not seek her hand. He continued to cultivate friendships with young girls; busied himself with the internal affairs of Christ Church; disagreed with his fellow dons; and perpetually found fault with the college servants and the cooking. In January, 1898, he had an attack of bronchitis, and on 14 January he passed away, shortly before his 66th birthday. By his orders, the funeral was a very simple one.

Few remember C. L. Dodgson; but all the world will hold dear the name of Lewis Carroll, who lives for their endless delight in those fantasies of genius, *Alice's Adventures in Wonderland* and *Through the Looking-Glass*. They are read, laughed over and re-read by millions, young and old. Their phrases and characters have passed into common speech.

Alice's Adventures in Wonderland is told as the story of a dream, and this sets it free to indulge in any kind of incredible happening. Alice is drowsily resting beside her sister on a sunny bank, and dozes off to see a white rabbit hurriedly consulting its watch and plunging down a rabbit-hole. She follows, dropping slowly down an interminable well and finding herself in a long hall, surrounded by locked doors. At length she spies a little door which she opens with a golden key that was lying on a glass-topped table. Through the passage she sees a lovely garden, but is far too big to go through the tiny doorway to it. On the table is a little bottle labelled "Drink Me". She does so and becomes quite small, but the key is now out of reach on the table. Under the table is a cake labelled "Eat Me" and this makes her open up like a telescope. This curious result of eating or drinking and growing bigger or smaller recurs again and again as she wends her way through Wonderland.

A happy feature of the story is the way in which Alice talks aloud to herself in an artless fashion about her strange predicaments, and spills out delicious parodies of familiar verses when she tries to recite them. Here, where she is weeping tears in bucketsful about her overgrowth, she essays the nursery rhyme about the busy bee, and finds herself saying:

> *How doth the little crocodile*
> *Improve his shining tail . . .*

She has grown small unawares, and swims in the pool of her tears, along with a mouse and a Dodo and other animals and birds. They dry themselves with a "Caucus Race", and then she goes to the White Rabbit's house, where another bottle makes her grow immense and fill the room. The Rabbit and his gardener cannot eject her, and she sends Bill, the Lizard, flying when he tries to come down the chimney. Smaller again, she escapes into a wood and finds a caterpillar sitting on a mushroom, smoking a hookah. At his demand she repeats an unintended parody of "You are old, Father William". She arms herself on his advice with bits from each side of the mushroom, and henceforward can make herself bigger or smaller at will.

Invading the Duchess's house, she finds the Duchess nursing a baby, the cook scattering pepper, and the Cheshire Cat grinning. She takes the baby, which turns into a pig, and the Cheshire Cat directs her to the March Hare's house. Here she meets him holding a Mad Tea Party with the Hatter and the Dormouse – a delicious episode. Leaving them, she finds herself back in the long hall, and this time opens the little door and passes into the beautiful garden.

Its occupants are all members of a pack of cards. Three gardeners, the Two, Five and Seven of Spades, are painting red the white roses of a tree. Soon there enters a grand procession, escorting The King and Queen of Hearts. The Queen is an irate dame whose favourite command is "Off with his head!" But Alice declines to be beheaded, and is summoned to a chaotic game of croquet, with hedgehogs for balls and flamingoes for mallets. Here the Cheshire Cat and the Duchess amusingly reappear, and the Queen takes Alice to hear the story of the Mock Turtle, escorted by the Gryphon. This occasion brings in some more grotesque parodies of familiar songs.

The conclusion is reached with the trial of the Knave of Hearts for his theft of tarts. Alice, returning to her normal size, tells the assembly they are nothing but a pack of cards, and wakes to find dead leaves fluttering down on her face.

The wit, the simplicity and unexpectedness of the story carry its readers on eagerly from one surprise to another.

Lewis Carroll's sequel, *Through the Looking-Glass*, is also contrived as a dream, but its framework is more rigid, for it is set round a game of chess. Alice becomes a pawn, who has to move through square after square to reach the eighth, where she turns into a Queen. Each square brings her a new landscape and another set of characters. The animals and insects talk as freely and unexpectedly as those in *Wonderland*, and several of them, especially Tweedledum and Tweedledee, Humpty Dumpty, and above all, the White Knight, have established themselves firmly in popular affection.

Lewis Carroll poured into this book a number of the nonsense verses he had stored in his notebooks. Among these are "Jabberwocky", begun many years before as a parody of Anglo-Saxon poetry, which has contributed such new words as "chortle" and

"Galumph" to the English language; "The Walrus and the Carpenter," Humpty Dumpty's song "In Winter, When the Fields are White," and the White Knight's "The Aged, Aged Man". Alice is the only character who retains her own name and identity through both books, except for her cat, Dinah. But the March Hare and the Mad Hatter of Wonderland re-appear in Looking-Glass Land as the White King's messengers, Haigha and Hatta, feeding him with ham sandwiches and hay. There is also an echo of Wonderland's Frog Footman in the Frog Gardener who meets Alice outside the royal dining-hall at the end of the Looking-Glass story.

As we close these books we reflect that C. L. Dodgson, the erudite mathematician, treasured in his complex nature the heart of a little child. Lewis Carroll recorded its fancies for our undying delight.

CAPITAL

KARL MARX

KARL HEINRICH MARX was a German Jew. He was born at Treves, in the Rhineland, in 1818, and was the son of a lawyer of liberal leanings, who some years after Karl's birth abandoned his ancestral Jewish faith and adopted that of Protestant Christianity. Karl was sent to the universities of Bonn and Berlin with the intention of becoming a lawyer like his father, but he preferred to study history and philosophy and began to take a small part in democratic activities. For some months he edited a political sheet in the Rhineland, and then in 1843, shortly after his marriage to Jenny von Westphalen, who was said to be of aristocratic Scottish descent, he moved to Paris and engaged in the kind of literary activity that occupied him for the rest of his life – activity that was arduous, poorly paid, usually unappreciated, and often giving rise to intense antagonism. Very shortly he had become a convinced revolutionary, and in 1845 he was expelled from France and took up his quarters in Brussels. There in association with Engels he wrote the famous *Communist Manifesto* of 1848, which was intended as the programme of the working classes in that "year of revolutions", and concludes with the words, "Let the ruling classes tremble before a Communist revolution. The workers have nothing to lose but their chains. They have the world to win. Workers of the world, unite!"

But the *Manifesto* fell on deaf ears, and Marx, almost penniless and again under a sentence of banishment, at length crossed the Channel and found refuge in England. For the remainder of his life, until his death in 1883, he lived in London, spending most of the hours of every working day in the reading-room of the British Museum. He was fortunate in his wife, a woman of sterling character and good sense, who kept the home and family together. He was fortunate also in his friends, among whom Frederick Engels takes pride of place. Engels had a job in his father's cotton factory in Manchester, which enabled him to give substantial financial assistance to Marx when he needed it most.

After many years of close study in the British Museum, in the course of which he acquired a remarkably wide and intimate knowledge of the economic literature of modern Europe, Marx published the first volume of *Capital* in 1867. As he declared it in the preface to the first German edition of the book, his final purpose was to reveal "the economic law that moves modern society", and the primary subject of study was, therefore, the capitalist method of production and the relations of production and exchange that were appropriate to that method.

Here it is of the utmost importance to keep the book's date in mind. The capitalist system that Marx writes about is not the capitalist system of the latter part of the nineteenth century and the beginning of the twentieth, still less is it that in which we live and have our beings today. It is the largely uncontrolled and irresponsible capitalism of the earlier part of the last century, which was already in process of modification and supersession when Marx wrote.

In Marx's mental picture, the capitalist system is mostly composed of a large number of small and highly competitive business units or firms, owned and controlled and managed by one man or by a small group of men who are primarily concerned with their own personal enrichment. Limited liability companies were already in existence when he wrote, but they had not yet supplanted the small firm as the normal unit of industrial organization, and their inherent possibilities were quite unrecognized. The "managerial revolution" that has given birth to a huge army of business executives and administrators was beyond Marx's vision and outside his imagination. He thought of the "workers" as a downtrodden mass of wage-slaves, as "the Proletariat"; and although he was an active supporter of the new trade unions he can hardly have expected very much from their development. Himself a man of the middle class, a bourgeois (to use one of his favourite terms), he looked forward with the utmost confidence to the great day when there would be only two classes – masters and men, employers and employed, capitalists and workers, bourgeoisie and proletariat – and out of their inevitable clash there would arise, just as inevitably, a new socialist order and society, in which the "workers" would be all in all.

Unfortunately for Marx's readers, *Capital* does not open with a description of the capitalist system that he knew but with a highly abstruse account of his ideas about Value. These are so hard to grasp that libraries have been written to explain them, and still we cannot be sure that we know what Marx really meant. It is not generally understood that the theories that Marx expounds are not his own, but were taken over from the "classical" economists of the generations before his time. Thus he cannot be held responsible for the

Labour Theory of Value", that is, that the value of a commodity depends upon the amount of human labour that has been put into its production; nor for the kindred theory, that the wages of labour tend to settle around subsistence level, that is, at what it costs to keep the worker in a reasonably fit state of health and efficiency, and to enable him in due season to produce the next generation of "wage slaves" who will take over when he has been worn out and thrust on the rubbish dump. If there is anything in these early chapters that bears the marks of originality, it is the theory of "Surplus Value". This is explained as follows.

The capital employed in the productive process is of two kinds, "constant" and "variable". By variable capital Marx means the sums expended on the employment of labour, that is, as wages, and by constant capital all the other kinds. The distinction between the two lies in the fact that variable capital not only produces the equivalent of its own value but also something over and above, varying according to circumstances. This excess is what Marx terms Surplus Value. Only human labour can produce it, and (according to Marx) the whole of it is appropriated by the capitalist employer.

This theory of Surplus Value is Marx's special contribution to economic ideology, and it is no wonder that it made a strong appeal to the workers, especially those engaged in factory production in the industrialized countries of Europe and America. The important place that it occupies in Marx's system is shown by the hundreds of pages that he devotes in *Capital* to its elucidation and illustration. Most of his supporting material is drawn from English practice, for the very good reason that it was in England that the capitalist system had mainly originated and had reached its most advanced development. But nowhere do we find any indication that Marx had ever been inside a cotton-mill or down a coal-mine, that he had ever visited a pottery or ironworks or railway shed; and all the detail with which his pages are filled was what he could collect from seat No. 7 in row G in the British Museum reading-room.

From what he tells his readers, they might believe – and only too many of them did believe, in Paris and Berlin and Moscow and New York – that the British workers as a class were the victims of the most complete and heartless exploitation. He talks of "little children who had been butchered for the sake of their delicate fingers, just as cattle had been butchered in South Russia for the sake of their skins and tallow", and quotes what a far from reliable writer had written more than thirty years before of "the cupidity of mill-owners whose cruelties in the pursuit of gain have hardly been exceeded by those perpetrated by the Spaniards in the conquest of America in the pursuit of gold".

He writes of capital as dead labour which like a vampire can keep itself alive only by sucking the blood of living labour, and "the more blood it sucks, the more vigorously does it live". He writes of railwaymen whose working day had been extended to 14, 18, even 20 hours, and who, when excursion trains had to be run, had to work for from 40 to 50 hours without a break. He has a phrase about free trade in adulterated foodstuffs, and tries to turn the Londoner's stomach with his account of bread made out of dough that has been moistened with a certain quantity of human sweat and mixed with the discharge from abscesses, cobwebs, dead cockroaches and such "pleasant mineral ingredients" as sand and alum. He lifts from the columns of his daily newspaper the report of a coroner's inquest on a young girl of twenty, Mary Anne Walkley by name, who had been taken ill and died after working in Madame Elise's respectable dressmaking establishment for $26\frac{1}{2}$ hours without a pause on making dresses for the fine ladies who had been invited to the ball in honour of the "newly imported" Princess Alexandra.

In every case Marx quotes chapter and verse, whether in the text or in the copious notes with which the text is accompanied, but some of his quotations are taken from books and papers published years before, reflecting conditions that had long been improved out of recognition; others are taken out of context; and all when added together give nothing like the whole truth. His readers were no doubt impressed by the fact that he relied largely upon the reports of Government inspectors and commissioners, but they were given no inkling of the fact that these very reports were an indication that the Victorian social conscience was very much alive. The 1860s were by no means a period of misery and degradation and oppression of the working classes; on the contrary, they were marked by tremendous advances in housing and public health, in industrial safety, and in the general improvement of the workers' lot. The new trade unionism dates from that very period, and it was in 1867, the year in which *Capital* first saw the light, that the working man of the towns was granted the Parliamentary franchise.

Following upon the section devoted to a study of Surplus Value come several chapters on Wages, and then we arrive at the final group of chapters, concerned with the Accumulation of Capital. Here again Marx, drawing upon a great mass of miscellaneous writings, paints a uniformly depressing picture of the evolution and present state of the English masses. His general thesis is, that "as

"Science fiction" may be said to have begun about a century ago in the novels of Jules Verne, in which the most thrilling adventures are related against a background of scientific fantasy and fact. One of the illustrations from the most famous of the series – *Round the World in 80 Days* – is reproduced here; it shows the Inspector of Police, one of the chief characters. Very different were the "Wessex Novels" of Thomas Hardy, in which the life and scenery of south-western England are described as they were in the last century. Perhaps the best is *Tess of the d'Urbervilles*, which tells of the short and tragic life of a Dorset peasant-girl; in the picture by Hubert Herkomer (*below*) we see her sleepwalking husband carrying her on their wedding-night to a grave in the adjoining churchyard.

In the last century Russian writers first began to make an impact on the wider world, and of them perhaps the greatest – certainly the best known – was Count Leo Tolstoy. Born to wealth and high position, he revolted against the artificial standards of his class and upbringing, and strove to share the hard and harsh conditions of the common people. In the above painting we see him ploughing the fields just as a peasant would do. Largely contemporary with Tolstoy was Feodor Dostoevsky, who in *The Brothers Karamazov* and *Crime and Punishment* enlarged the horizons of the novel by exploring the dark places of the human spirit. (*Below, right*) He is portrayed in characteristically meditative mood. Very different was the American writer Samuel Langhorne Clemens (*below, left*), known to fame under his pen-name of Mark Twain. He was a master of humorous fiction, and many readers have failed to understand that beneath his smile lay a profound appreciation of the problems of human existence.

apital accumulates, the condition of the worker, be his wages high
r low, necessarily grows worse" – note the "necessarily". Put more
hortly, "poverty grows as the accumulation of capital grows".

Before the modern system of capitalist enterprise could come into
xistence there had to be what Marx calls the stage of "primary
ccumulation", which he defines as "the historical process whereby
he producer was divorced from the means of production" .This was
ffected through the spoliation of the property of the Church at the
eformation, the subsequent alienation of the State domains, the
ansformation of feudal property and the property of the Scottish
ans, by a system of ruthless terrorism, into modern private property.
hese were "the idyllic methods of primary accumulation", which
eared the ground for capitalist agriculture and provided urban
dustry with the requisite number of "masterless proletarians".

Then followed the discoveries of gold and silver in America, the
xtirpation or enslavement and entombment of the natives, the
eginnings of the conquest of the East Indies, the transformation of
frica into a source of the raw material of the slave trade – these
ere the incidents that characterized the "rosy dawn of the period of
apitalist production". Hard upon their heels came the commercial
ars between the great European powers, fought over the whole
urface of the globe, of which a recent sequel had been the opium
ars against China.

One of the most powerful stimuli to the accumulation of capital
 its earlier stages had been the creation of the public debt under the
anagement of the Bank of England. Before long other countries
ere linked with Britain in the financial network. "A great deal of
he capital which makes its appearance in the United States without
y birth certificate, was yesterday in England the capitalized blood
f children."

On his concluding page Marx describes the United States and
ustralia as following in Britain's footsteps: in the one "capitalist
roduction is advancing with giant strides", and in the other there
e constant complaints of the labour market being glutted with
urplus workers. In the New World as in the Old (he says), political
conomy has discovered a "great secret" and then proclaimed it from
e housetops, that "the capitalist method of production and accum-
lation, in short capitalist private property, demands as its fund-
mental condition the expropriation of the worker".

Capital was published originally in German; the first English trans-
tion (of Volume 1) was published in 1886, three years after Marx's
ath. Engels wrote a preface for this, and he was able to state that

"*Das Kapital* is often called, on the Continent, 'the Bible of the work ing class'." This was probably true enough of the Continent, but was never true of Britain. There is a large measure of truth in th saying, that the British Labour movement has owed more to th Methodists than to Karl Marx.

Marx believed that his book would provide the lever with whic the capitalist system would be overturned by the proletariats of th industrialized countries of the world. He was right in thinking th Capital was political and economic dynamite. But in the event it w not in one of the great, highly capitalized countries that the revolu tion came at last but in that one of the great powers in which capita ism was least advanced, least developed – in the Russian empire the Czars. Among the books that must be ranked as makers of histor Karl Marx's *Capital*, because of its influence on the Russian Revolu tion of 1917 and later, holds a position of unassailable superiority.

LORNA DOONE

R. D. BLACKMORE

RICHARD DODDRIDGE BLACKMORE (1825–1900), although a prolific and popular novelist during his life, is remembered today as the author of a single book – *Lorna Doone*. His other novels were not failures. Indeed, some of them achieved a certain distinction. It was *Lorna Doone*, however, that made him famous and it is *Lorna Doone* that is forever linked with his name. There are various reasons for the book's success, but perhaps the most notable one is its primitive human quality, a quality that must have belonged to Blackmore himself. Few other novels illustrate so decisively that the style is the man.

Just as Kingsley loved Devon, and as Hardy and Phillpotts loved Wessex and Dartmoor respectively, so did Blackmore love that enchanting region of Exmoor where Devon rubs shoulders with Somerset. As a boy, living at Newton Nottage on the coast of Glamorganshire, he studied Exmoor's rocky outline across the Severn estuary. When his father, a country curate, moved to Devon, young Richard first attended the King's School, Bruton, and then Blundell's School at Tiverton, absorbing in both establishments something of the authentic magic of the West Country. During his frequent visits to his grandfather's house at Parracombe he must have listened to many a local legend concerning the exploits of a band of outlaws who operated from a stronghold near Exeter in the reign of Charles II. At the same time he would be storing up images of the countryside, coming into contact with interesting characters, registering the colourful dialects of Devon and Somerset and noting such effective expressions as "goyal", "eyesen", "toesen", "yelloon" and "circumfere".

Even when he moved on to Exeter College, Oxford, he was always within reach of the simpler pleasures of the countryside, while his classical studies, together with a genuine passion for the Bible and the works of Shakespeare, were helping to provide the vast treasure-house of words, phrases and felicitous allusions that contribute toward the poetical character of his masterpiece, *Lorna Doone*.

As Blackmore's first ambition was to be a poet, it is not altogether surprising that some of the descriptive passages of *Lorna Doone* have an almost lyrical intensity. Ferns growing beside a brook, for instance, are seen by Blackmore to be "pluming, stooping, glancing, glistening, weaving softest pillow-lace, coying to the wind and water, where their fleeting image danced, or by which their beauty moved".

But *Lorna Doone* has not won fame as a novel because of its Theocritean and Vergilian echoes, nor yet because it has all the dignity and grandeur of an epic. It has been read and re-read by generations of readers because it does something that E. M. Forster, in his *Aspects of the Novel*, tends to deprecate.

Lorna Doone tells a story. . . .

John Ridd's story begins at Blundell's School, Tiverton, in the year 1673. Even at twelve John enjoys a reputation as a fighter. In fact his set-to with Robin Snell on his last day at school establishes right away the unyielding tenacity and obstinate courage that John displays throughout the book in his long and bitter conflict with the Doones. He beats the bigger boy, as he beats the Doone giants later, "partly through my native strength and the Exmoor toughness in me", as he himself says, "and still more that I could not see when I had gotten my bellyful".

John's schooldays end abruptly because his father has been murdered by one of the Doones, a family of outlaws and robbers who live in a deep valley carved out of the mountains marking the Devon-Somerset border. On his way home, John sees a party of thirty or more Doones returning from a raid. "Heavy men, and large of stature, reckless how they bore their guns, or how they sat their horses, with leathern jerkins, and long boots, and iron plates on breast and head, plunder heaped behind their saddles." They have stolen sheep and deer, and one of the band has a small child flung across his saddle-bow.

Incensed by the Doones' callousness, John's mother goes to their lair and puts her case before their leader, Sir Ensor Doone, an apparently gracious old man who greets her courteously and sends for Counsellor Doone, their legal expert. The grey-bearded Counsellor square-built and powerful, gives a distorted account of the murdered man's encounter with the Doones, insinuating that John's father had been the aggressor. Dazed and grief-stricken, Mrs. Ridd goes back home to Plover's Barrows Farm.

John, spurred on by thoughts of vengeance, teaches himself how to handle a gun. He also visits Mr. Pooke of Porlock to buy powder

nd a chunk of lead for making shots. He is still only a boy, but even
hen he is determined to avenge his father's death.

One day, when his mother is ill and off her food, John decides to
atch some loaches for her. Armed with a three-pronged fork
ttached to a rod with cord, he climbs up a water-course which
rings him to the Doone valley. There he meets and is enchanted by
n eight-year-old girl who tells him she is Lorna Doone.

Years later his mother's uncle, Reuben Huckaback, a wealthy
hopkeeper from Dulverton, sets out to visit the Ridds. When he
ails to arrive at the appointed hour, John goes to seek him. He finds
hat the Doones have robbed Uncle Reuben, stolen his horse and
oped him to the back of a mountain pony. John frees the old man
nd carries him down to Plover's Barrows.

When Uncle Reuben fails to obtain legal redress locally, he
ecides to approach Judge Jeffreys, but first John has to show him the
Doones' mountain stronghold. While Reuben is planning a military
ttack on the glen, John catches a glimpse of Lorna in the distance
nd feels that his destiny is linked with hers. After Uncle Reuben's
eparture, he visits Lorna's secret bower and the girl, who is now
fteen, tells him her story. She is virtually a prisoner in Glen Doone.

With the coming of spring, Jeremy Stickles, a King's Messenger,
rrives at the farm. He brings a royal invitation for John, requiring
im to give evidence against the Doones before the Justices at
Westminster. Consequently John goes to London, where he comes
p against the law's delays and eventually is questioned by Judge
effreys, who asks him about the Doones and if there are any rebels
n the West Country. Satisfied with John's answers, the Judge tells
im he is free to go.

Soon after his return, John makes his way up the watercourse to
Glen Doone. He sees Lorna, who confesses that she is beginning to
ove him. She also informs him that she is expected to marry Carver
Doone, who would like to take her by force but dare not make a
nove as long as Sir Ensor remains at the head of the clan. Somewhat
eassured, John agrees to stay away from Glen Doone for two
nonths.

Meanwhile, harvest is fittingly celebrated. John and his sister
Annie slip away from the revels and Annie tells him that she is in
ove with Tom Faggus, their highwayman cousin. In his turn John
onfides in her, admitting that he too has lost his heart – to Lorna
Doone. When they rejoin the festivities, they find that Uncle
Reuben and his grand-daughter, Ruth Huckaback, have arrived.

Everybody wonders why Uncle Reuben has come to Plover's

Barrows at a time when he would normally be busy in Dulverton His lonely trips over the moors each day arouse even greater curiosity. He is followed as far as the Wizard's Slough, a horrible quagmire in the neighbourhood, but his business there remains a mystery at least for the time being.

When the two months expire, John goes to Glen Doone every evening for a fortnight, but there is no sign of Lorna. An early morning visit proves more rewarding, however, for at last Lorna declares her love for him. At the girl's request he hurries home to tell his mother everything. Mrs. Ridd, who has just learned that Annie proposes to marry Tom Faggus, is upset when she hears that her son is in love with a Doone, but she accepts the situation philosophically.

For the first time John enters the Glen by the Doone-gate and penetrates as far as Sir Ensor's house. He talks with Lorna through a window. She promises that if serious danger ever threatens she will signal to him.

Soon after this visit, Lorna's maid brings a message to John. Sir Ensor Doone is dying and wants to see him. The maid takes John to the valley by a secret path and conducts him to the old man's room. Although at first Sir Ensor advises John never to see Lorna again, he finally seems to relent and gives Lorna a valuable necklace before he dies. After his funeral, John returns to Plover's Barrows.

A harsh winter, with heavy snowfalls and biting frosts, puts an end to John's visits to Lorna. His younger sister, Eliza, suggests that John should make snow-shoes. He makes a pair, learns to use them and sets out for Glen Doone. He reaches Lorna's house safely, but discovers she is to be starved until she consents to marry Carver Doone. John immediately decides to get her away from Glen Doone.

He goes home to warn his mother and sisters that Lorna will soon be with them, and then he drags a pony sled all the way to the valley. He arrives just in time to save Lorna from the drunken advances of Charleworth Doone and his friend. Putting Lorna and her maid in the sled, John pulls it across the snow and back to the farm.

Torrential rains and floods follow the heavy winter. Jeremy Stickles comes to Plover's Barrows and plans are made to repel an attack by the Doones. Some days after the expected assault has been beaten off, Counsellor Doone calls at the farm and by a clever trick gains possession of Lorna's necklace. John learns from Jeremy Stickles that Lorna is not a Doone but the Countess of Dugal, daughter who was carried off by the Doones years ago. John remembers that as a boy he actually saw the child lying across the raider's saddle-bow.

John and Jeremy, with a motley army, set out to do battle with the
Doones. Despite their superior numbers, they are driven back and
Jeremy is badly wounded.

Not long after this Doone victory, John discovers what Uncle
Reuben was seeking near the Wizard's Slough. Old Huckaback,
under the impression that he has found a gold-mine, takes John to
inspect it. John, who is not particularly interested, goes to Bodmin
to wrestle with a Cornish giant in answer to the champion's challenge. With his winnings – a hundred pounds – he hastens back to
the farm. Lorna, he finds, has gone to London, compelled by the
Court of Chancery to live with her uncle and guardian, Earl Brandir,
until she is twenty-one.

Close upon the heels of this disappointment comes news that Tom
Faggus, who is now Annie's husband, has joined Monmouth and
his rebel army. Annie implores John to go and bring Tom home
again. During his search for Faggus, John sees the rebels beaten at
Sedgemoor. He locates Tom, who is severely wounded, and manages to get him safely away. He himself is in danger of being hanged
by Kirke's "Lambs", but Jeremy Stickles comes to his rescue.

Fortunately for John, the barrier of rank that lies between him and
Lorna is removed when he is knighted and given a coat of arms for
apprehending two traitors. Sir John goes home and is promptly
given the job of dealing with the Doones once and for all. He gathers
his little "army" and storms Glen Doone, firing the houses and
finally settling accounts with his enemies. The Counsellor, after
handing over Lorna's necklace, is granted his freedom. Carver
Doone, the man who killed John's father, contrives to escape.

On the death of Earl Brandir, Lorna is allowed to return to
Plover's Barrows to marry John. At the end of the ceremony, Carver
Doone appears and shoots Lorna. Believing her dead, John pursues
Carver and catches up with him near the Wizard's Slough. Carver
fires and hits John, but John wrestles with him on the brink of the
quagmire. Thoroughly beaten, Carver falls into the slimy pool and is
sucked under.

Little Ruth Huckaback nurses Lorna and John back to health and
all ends happily.

There, then, are the bare bones of Blackmore's West Country
romance. There are long descriptive passages – most notably the
chapters devoted to the long and terrible winter; there are sub-plots,
digressions, historical references and local legends; there are classical
allusions, satirical observations and occasional moralizings. But

holding everything together in an artistic whole is the love story of John Ridd and Lorna Doone. Physically and morally John emerges as one of the most likeable heroes in fiction, a true Englishman *sans peur et sans reproche*. Lorna, with her dark hair, "flowing from a wreath of white violets", gentle, beautiful, modest and very feminine, proves a fitting mate for him. These two, so far apart and yet so close together, tower above the other characters and move toward their destiny with a majestic inevitability.

Unforgettable among the lesser characters are that ebullient highwayman and pleasant rogue, Tom Faggus; the knowledgeable sophisticated and courageous Jeremy Stickles; the cautious money loving Reuben Huckaback; the unctuous seemingly pious Counsellor Doone; old Ensor Doone, dignified and authoritative to the last and, among the women, Mrs. Ridd, still comely, simple, valiant living only for her children; sweet-tempered, domesticated Annie the book-loving Eliza, so apt to play the critic; and little Ruth Huckaback, so understanding and tender-hearted.

As for the manner in which all these diverse characters are presented, even the most captious critic must concede that Blackmore's style, although sometimes turgid (especially in the love scenes), can attain to a sinewy strength that is wholly masculine. The account of the storming of Glen Doone, for example, is a powerful piece of writing – expressive, vivid and exciting. The tale is also illuminated from time to time with sudden flashes of humour. When schoolboy John is reluctant to exchange blows with Robin Snell, Blackmore slyly comments that "the principal business of good Christians is beyond all controversy, to fight with one another". And later, after Uncle Reuben has balanced his accounts, he sets "the writs running against defaulters, as behoves a good Christian at Christmastide".

And finally, in plenary control of the whole work, Blackmore's creative imagination is everywhere evident. Essentially a warm hearted, unassuming, robust man of the West Country, Richard Blackmore has set the seal of his own rich personality on *Lorna Doone*. In love with this green and pleasant land himself, he awakens in his readers a nostalgic longing for those days that were "full of warmth and fine hearth-comfort, which now are dying out".

ROUND THE WORLD IN EIGHTY DAYS

JULES VERNE

EVERY NOW and again the human race produces a specimen who seems to be endowed with an extraordinary vision of the future. Such a one was Leonardo da Vinci, whose fertile imagination forecast the coming of the aeroplane, the parachute and the tank. Another was H. G. Wells, whose science-fiction stories foretold the Space Age which we are now entering. Yet a third was Jules Verne, whose fantastic science fantasies told of developments, which when he wrote them seemed the wildest flights of fancy, but which were to become fact in a relatively short time.

Jules Verne was born on 8 February, 1828, in Nantes, where his father, Pierre Verne, was a successful lawyer. At sixteen Jules entered his father's law firm, and in 1848 he went to Paris to complete his law studies.

Already, however, he was nursing ambitions to become a dramatist, and having made the acquaintance of Alexandre Dumas, through the latter's kindness, his one-act play, *Broken Straws*, was produced in 1850.

Forsaking the law, he supported himself by freelance work, writing scientific-historical stories for the journal *Musée*, and the libretto for a light opera, which was successfully produced in 1853.

After resisting the temptation to join in the Californian gold-rush, he conceived the idea of writing a series of science-fiction books. His aim was to achieve for himself in this field the position held by his friend Dumas as an historical novelist. He was convinced that the whole future of man lay with science.

By easing his financial position in becoming secretary to the Théâtre Lyrique, he was able to devote his spare time not only to writing his stories and articles, but to reading every book about exploration and discovery on which he could lay hands, in preparation for his project. But presently he fell in love with a young widow, Honorine Morel, and married her. Since he believed that for marriage to be successful it must be largely based on financial security, to everyone's great surprise he abandoned writing and became a stockbroker.

But he was the born writer, and soon found that the inner compulsion was too great to be resisted. So he made time to be both a successful stockbroker and a man of letters.

In 1863 his first real literary success came his way with the publication of *Five Weeks in a Balloon*, an adventure story based on his ideas about the future of ballooning. It was the first of the great series of *Extraordinary Journeys* which were to come from his pen for several years thereafter.

Consequent upon the success of his books, in 1865 he left the Bourse, and moved to a cottage at Crotoy, on the Somme estuary. For almost all the remainder of his life he lived by or on the sea, for he bought a series of yachts, each more grander than the last.

It was on board one of these boats that he wrote *Twenty Thousand Leagues Under the Sea*, which, when published in 1870, achieved an astounding success and established Verne as one of the most popular writers in France. In 1873 his fame was further enhanced by the publication of *Round the World in Eighty Days*.

The success of Verne's stories depended almost entirely on the verisimilitude with which he was able to clothe even his most fantastic fantasies. This talent is particularly demonstrated in *Round the World in Eighty Days*.

Phileas Fogg lived in London in the house in which the great English playwright Sheridan had died. Little was known of Fogg, except that he was "one of the most perfect gentlemen of good English society". Clearly he was rich, and he had the air of a man who had travelled widely. He was a bachelor and was looked after by a young French servant, Jean Passepartout.

Fogg was a member of the Reform Club, where he was accustomed to taking lunch and dinner. One day during a conversation among some of the members concerning a daring robbery recently committed at the Bank of England, the whereabouts of the thief were discussed. One man said that he might be anywhere, "the world is big enough".

"It was formerly," said Phileas Fogg.

"How formerly? Has the world grown smaller perchance, because the tour of it can now be made in three months?"

"In eighty days only," said Phileas Fogg.

"But not including bad weather, contrary winds, shipwreck, running off the track, etc."

The robber now forgotten, the conversation turned into an argument about the possibility of going round the world in eighty days, in which Fogg maintained that practically it was possible, while other members maintained that it was not.

The upshot was that Fogg was challenged to prove his contention by going round the world himself in eighty days. Fogg accepted the challenge, for a wager of £20,000, and on leaving the club went home, where he announced to a startled Passepartout that they were leaving in ten minutes for a trip round the world. When the servant protested that ten minutes were not enough to pack the necessary luggage, Fogg told him that all that was necessary was a carpet-bag containing two woollen shirts and three pairs of stockings for each of them. In ten minutes they left the house for the train to Dover, from where they crossed to Calais.

The news of Fogg's acceptance of the challenge and his departure quickly became known throughout London, and his journey became the talk of the town and a principal subject of discussion in the news-papers. The weight of popular opinion was against his succeeding, and bets were laid at two hundred to one in this sense, until all wagering ceased, when, seven days after his departure, the Com-missioner of Police at Scotland Yard received a cable from Suez: "I have the bank robber, Phileas Fogg. Send without delay warrant of arrest to Bombay, British India. (Signed) Fix, *Detective.*"

What had happened was this. From Calais, Fogg and Passepartout had travelled by train to Brindisi, where they had arrived without incident. There they had boarded the P & O steamer *Mongolia* bound, via the Suez Canal, for Bombay. Fix was one of several detectives sent to various ports throughout the world to watch for the bank-robber.

When the *Mongolia* arrived at Suez, Fix's intuition told him that Fogg was the man he was looking for, and though he had not a shred of evidence he cabled to London for a warrant, and himself boarded the *Mongolia*, to follow Fogg to Bombay. Conditions in the Red Sea and Indian Ocean proved so favourable that the steamer arrived at Bombay two days ahead of schedule, much to Fogg's delight.

From Fix's point of view, this early arrival was most unfortunate, for there had not been time for the warrant to arrive from London. Fogg was therefore able to take the train for Calcutta, which he did at eight o'clock the same evening.

(Verne uses these chapters, as he does all the later ones, to describe the sights and customs of the countries through which Fogg passes. The descriptions lend the book a great deal of its appeal, and for Verne's contemporaries were particularly interesting.)

Up to this point, Fogg's journey had been uneventful. Halfway to Calcutta, however, it emerged that a fifty-mile section of the line between Kholby and Allahabad had not been completed, and the passengers were expected to find their own transport between the two towns.

All the conventional means of transport had already been reserved by knowledgeable passengers, but the resourceful Fogg bought an elephant from an Indian, and accompanied by a travelling acquaintance, General Sir Francis Cromarty, he and Passepartout set out through the forests for Allahabad.

This part of the journey gives rein to Verne's interest in the unusual, and he describes with great relish the scenery through which Fogg passes and the people encountered.

Twelve miles from Allahabad they came upon a splendid procession which turned out to be the funeral of a rajah. Accompanying it was the late rajah's beautiful young wife, who, Sir Francis explained, was to be burned alive on her husband's pyre according to the barbarous custom of *suttee*.

Fogg, appalled, planned to rescue the unhappy woman from her fate. They tried to free her from the pagoda in which she was confined for the night, but failed, and she was eventually saved after the ceremony had begun the following morning, by Passepartout, who having made his way through the smoke was mistaken by the crowd for the corpse come to life. While the spectators prostrated themselves in fear, he snatched the widow from the pyre, and with her and his companions escaped into the forest, just as the priests realized what had happened. Allahabad was eventually reached in safety.

As the widow would be hunted down, Fogg offered to take her with him as far as Hong Kong, where, she had told him, she had relatives.

On their arrival in Calcutta by train, they were met by the police and arrested. Though no charges were preferred, they were told that they were to be brought before the magistrate. In court they learned that the charge was one of sacrilege, arising out of an incident in Bombay when Passepartout had inadvertently entered a Hindu temple with his boots on. The magistrate imposed imprisonment and a heavy fine. Since the delay would have ruined his schedule, Fogg asked for bail, which was granted. Having deposited £2,000, they boarded the steamer *Rangoon*, bound for Hong Kong. Also on board was Detective Fix, who had traced them to Calcutta.

All went well on this part of the journey until they were a few days from Hong Kong, when a great storm blew up. Fogg was most concerned by possible delay, which might cause them to miss the steamer from Hong Kong to Yokohama, and this was what happened. Twenty-four hours were lost, and the connexion clearly missed.

On arrival at Hong Kong, however, they found that the *Carnatic* had been held up for repairs, and was not due to sail until the following day. They reserved berths and while Fogg went ashore with Mrs. Aouda, the widow, to find her relatives, Fix revealed to Passepartout his mission. Naturally, the servant refused to believe that his master was a thief, and so that he should not warn Fogg, Fix drugged him, and then went ashore to keep an eye on his quarry.

Mrs. Aouda's relatives had left Hong Kong, so Fogg suggested she should go on with them. When they returned, accompanied by Fix, who had introduced himself as a fellow passenger, they found that the *Carnatic* had sailed. Her repairs had been completed earlier than estimated and her master had weighed anchor at once without waiting for any passengers who might be ashore.

Undaunted, Fogg chartered a pilot-boat to take them to Shanghai, where he hoped to catch up with the *Carnatic*. During the night they ran into a bad storm which slowed them down, but they were able to stop an American steamer bound for Yokohama, whose captain agreed to take them on.

Meanwhile Passepartout had regained consciousness in the *Carnatic* and found himself alone *en route* for Yokohama. Arrived in Yokohama, Passepartout decided to work his passage across the Pacific to America, but while watching a troupe of Japanese acrobats he was reunited with his master.

From Yokohama they sailed for San Francisco, accompanied by Fix. When they entered the Golden Gate, Fogg was dead on schedule, having neither lost nor gained a single day.

After a brief look at San Francisco, they boarded an express train to take them across to the east coast. On this journey they met with many adventures, in one of which Passepartout was captured by Sioux Indians who attacked the train. Fogg led a detachment of passengers and went after the Indians and rescued Passepartout, but when they returned to the station they found the train had gone.

This time Fix came to their aid by procuring a sledge in which the four of them travelled to Omaha, where they caught a train for Chicago, and from there to New York. Having missed the steamer for Southampton, they boarded a cargo ship bound for Liverpool.

On arrival at Liverpool Fix found the warrant awaiting him, and, somewhat reluctantly now, arrested Fogg and gaoled him. Next day, however, news arrived that the robber had been arrested three days earlier, and Fogg was freed. By chartering a special train Fogg calculated he could still reach London in time. Unfortunately the train was delayed and drew into the London depôt at ten minutes to nine, five minutes late.

Believing that he had lost his wager, and since he had deposited his cheque for £20,000 at the Reform Club, he decided to stay at home. After dinner the following evening, realizing that he was in love with Mrs. Aouda, he asked her to marry him, and on her accepting, proposed that they should get married the next day.

Passepartout was sent to a near-by clergyman to make the necessary arrangements. In three minutes he returned with the news that Fogg had miscalculated, that today was not Sunday as he thought, but Saturday, and that, this being so, if he could reach the Reform Club in ten minutes, he would still win the wager.

On checking Fogg discovered that he had forgotten to make allowances for crossing the International Date Line.

He arrived at the Reform Club on the stroke of quarter to nine, to the delighted surprise of the members gathered there.

Even in these more sophisticated modern times, when it is possible to make the journey round the world by air in half the number of hours that it took Fogg days, the story still has the power to interest, excite and thrill. It must continue to do so for as long as books are read.

The descriptive details and the careful and interesting characterization with which Verne achieved his verisimilitude are as valid today as they were nearly a century ago. This is the great strength of all Verne's work. Like Wells, he took the trouble to create interesting situations and characters. Wells, with his concern with social and human problems, was perhaps more profound, but Verne's narrative mastery and attention to detail make him the equal still of his successor in the field of science-fiction, and the superior of all but him.

THE ADVENTURES OF
TOM SAWYER

MARK TWAIN

HUMOUR HAS become one of the outstanding features of American literature, but it developed late. This is not surprising when the conditions under which this literature was born and developed are considered. The people of the English-speaking colonies of North America were a hardy, down-to-earth people engaged in a fierce material struggle for existence.

Only when conditions of life were considerably less harsh did humour begin to emerge in literature. It made its first significant appearance in Washington Irving's satirical extravaganza, *A History of New York*, which appeared in 1809; and was sustained by the more mature *Sketch Book* (in which he introduced Rip Van Winkle) and *Bracebridge Hall*.

Irving's influence, however, seems to have been limited. The humorists who followed him, though they employed the same form – the short sketch and essay – showed a tendency toward grotesque burlesque and a raw localism of accent, as, for instance, is found in the Canadian Thomas Haliburton's creation "Sam Slick". Indeed, the river of true American humour of universal appeal ran dry, and was not to flow again until after the Civil War, the termination of which at last seemed to remove the barriers which had confined all degrees of boisterousness within a kraal of sobriety constructed of tragic reality.

A number of considerable humorists now began to emerge, writers like Charles Leland, John Hay and Joel Harris, whose work contained a quality of tenderness. It was the tenderness of disillusioned idealists, but it entitled many of their pages to rank with those of Irving for their universal note.

The outstanding of the post-Civil-War humorists was Mark Twain. He outlived practically all the rest of the group, and even before his death in 1910 it had become clear that his work would also outlive theirs.

Mark Twain was a pseudonym. His real name was Samuel

Clemens, and he was born at Florida, Missouri, on 30 November, 1835.

On leaving school he became apprenticed to a printing works, and later worked as a compositor on newspapers in St. Louis, New York and Philadelphia. But he was unable to settle and returning to St. Louis in 1857 he asked Captain Bixby, the most famous pilot on the Mississippi, "to teach him the river". Two years later he obtained his licence, and worked as a co-pilot until the outbreak of the Civil War when he joined a cavalry company in the Confederate army.

Invalided out after only a few months, he returned to newspaper work, now as a reporter. But he still could not settle, and wandered from job to job until in 1866 he accompanied an expedition to Hawaii as correspondent for the *Sacremento Union*.

On his return, wondering what to do next, he decided to lecture about his Hawaiian experiences. His lectures were a great success, and believing that he had at last found his real métier he decided to make lecturing his career, and came to Europe to find material.

Out of this tour, however, came not only material for lectures, but his first book, *Innocents Abroad*. It made an immediate hit with the American public, and when published in England a little later achieved an even greater success.

As a result of this success he now devoted his time to writing books. *Roughing It* and *The Gilded Age* further enhanced his reputation as a humorist, but it was with his fourth book, *The Adventures of Tom Sawyer*, that he was hailed as a humorous genius, and the book a humorous masterpiece, a reputation it has sustained ever since.

In writing *Tom Sawyer*, Twain set out to write a story for boys, but his descriptions of the lawless side of boyhood inevitably struck sympathetic chords of memory in countless men, who were able to identify themselves with the characters. The appeal of the book was, therefore, universal and indestructible. Much of it is based on incidents in his own childhood.

Tom Sawyer and his brother Sid were brought up by their elderly Aunt Polly. Tom was a typical small boy, stealing jam, playing truant, hating work, extricating himself from difficult situations with the special cunning with which small boys are endowed. In fact, "he was not the model boy of the village. He knew the model boy very well, though, and loathed him." But no matter what scrapes he got into, what punishments he received from his aunt, he bore no malice, his memory was short.

As a punishment for disobeying her orders, his aunt resolved "to turn his Saturday holiday into captivity at hard labour", the latter to take the form of whitewashing the garden fence. It was a beautiful morning, not the kind of day which gave whitewashing a fence any appeal whatsoever to a small boy.

As he set about his task, however, Jim, the Negro boy-of-all-work to Aunt Polly, came out to fetch a pail of water from the pump. Tom tried to bribe him to relieve him, and was on the point of succeeding when Aunt Polly made an unsignalled appearance, to Jim's discomfiture and Tom's despair.

Presently, however, Ben Rodgers came along, impersonating a steamboat. Tom pretended not to see or hear him, until the boy spoke to him directly, teasing him about having to work on a nice day. Not stopping his whitewashing, Tom replied that what he was doing was not work but pleasure. Before Ben realized what he was doing he was whitewashing, while Tom was lazing in the sun, munching the apple with which Ben had bribed him. By the time Ben was tired, other boys had come along, whom Tom allowed to bribe him with a kite, a dead rat, a key, a one-eyed kitten, a dog-collar and other useless articles which have a special value to a boy. In no time at all the fence was finished. Tom had done little of it and he had had company as well as help.

Released by Aunt Polly, he ran out to play, "hooking" a dough-nut on the way. He made his way to the village square, where two groups of boys had met by previous appointment to stage a battle. Tom was general of one group, Joe Harper, a bosom friend, general of the other. After a long and hard-fought struggle, Tom's army secured the victory.

As Tom passed the house where Jeff Thatcher lived, on his way home, he saw a new girl in the garden. "The fresh-crowned hero fell without firing a shot." He pretended she was not there, and began to show off in all sorts of absurd ways in order to win her admiration. Presently the girl went into the house. Later he returned and repeated his antics, hoping in vain that she would reappear.

A fight with his brother Sid at the supper table, when his aunt was not present, a fresh assault from Aunt Polly, and bed ends a representative day in Tom's life.

Troubles at school, at Sunday school and in practically every other aspect of existence, Tom treats in the same way; with a mixture of boyish cunning leavened with naïvety, with a stoic acceptance of any retribution that is meted out to him, and always with an undercurrent of joy in living, no matter how black things are. He is in a constant state of rebellion against authority in the shape of grown-ups.

One incident occurred, however, that brought into the lives of Tom and one of his friends unusual excitement and an element of danger. After his aunt was safely asleep one night, Tom got up and crept from the house to keep an assignation with Huck Finn in the graveyard, where they were to bury a dead cat which Huck had acquired. Huck was the son of the village drunk, a tatterdemalion of a boy, with no book-learning but a vast store of the lore of the countryside, and the envy of all the other boys because of his absolute freedom from parental control; and conversely, regarded by all parents as an undesirable companion for their sons.

While the boys were making preparations for their ceremony they heard men approaching. From their hiding place they watched the village doctor accompanied by Muff Potter, another drunk, and a sinister character, a half-breed known as Injun Joe, open up the latest grave and remove the body of its occupant.

This done, the two ruffians demanded of the doctor more money before they would agree to carry the body to his surgery. The doctor protested that he had already paid them well, and when Potter became aggressive, defended himself. In the scuffle that followed, the doctor knocked Potter unconscious, and Injun Joe picked up Potter's knife, rushed at the doctor and stabbed him in the heart. The half-breed then put the knife in the still unconscious Potter's hand, and when he came round Potter believed that he had killed the doctor.

When the two men had run off, the two boys discussed what they should do, and eventually decided that they would tell no one, in order to avoid getting into trouble themselves. An investigation followed the discovery of the doctor's body, but no sign was found of his assailants, though Potter was known to be one of them since he had carelessly left his knife beside the corpse. Soon the boys had put the incident out of mind.

Not long afterward, having been assaulted by Aunt Polly, which Tom had some justification in feeling he had not deserved, he decided to teach his aunt a lesson by running away. On his way to carry out this unspoken threat he met his bosom friend, Joe Harper, who was in the same frame of mind, after being cuffed by his mother for drinking cream, not a drop of which he had tasted. Joe said he would join Tom. A little farther on they met Huck Finn, who said he would go with them.

The three boys took a skiff and rowed over to a small island in the middle of the river, and there diverted themselves by pretending to be a band of pirates. They had forgotten food, however, and after dark Tom returned to his aunt's house and raided her larder.

For two days the boys enjoyed themselves immensely. On the third day they heard men's voices on the river and realized that the river was being searched for their bodies. A reconnaissance informed them that they were believed to be dead, and that a funeral service was to be read for them in the church.

This experience reminded Joe that, despite his mother's discipline, he loved her very much, and he became homesick. Tom persuaded him not to go home, as he wanted to, because he had a plan. Reluctantly Joe agreed to stay, though Tom would not divulge his plan.

On the evening that the funeral service was to be held Tom took his friends secretly to the church, where they hid in the deserted gallery, and from where they listened to a panegyric preached by the minister, in which he praised them highly. At the climax of the service Tom led his friends up the aisle, and so great was the relief at their still being alive, Mrs. Harper and Aunt Polly forgave them.

Time passed, during which Tom and his friends sustained their rebellion against adult authority. Then one day it was learned that Potter had been caught, and was lodged in the village cell to await trial for murder.

The news put Tom in a quandary, for he knew that Potter was not guilty. After some heart-searching and serious discussion with Huck Finn, Tom decided to go to Potter's lawyer and tell him what he and Huck had seen.

Injun Joe had come forward to give evidence against his former companion, and so was in court when Tom was called. "Every eye fixed itself upon him; with parted lips and bated breath, the audience hung upon his words. . . . The strain upon pent emotion reached its climax when the boy said, 'And as the doctor fetched the board around and Muff Potter fell, Injun Joe jumped with the knife and——'

"Crash! Quick as lightning, the half-breed sprang for a window, tore his way through all opposers, and was gone!"

As a result of the part he had played at the trial, Tom was "the glittering hero . . . the pet of the old, the envy of the young". A hue and cry was raised after Injun Joe, but had no success. Tom realized that so long as the half-breed was free, he must keep out of his way. This did not prevent him, however, from conceiving a "raging desire to go somewhere and dig for hidden treasure".

Having failed to find Joe Harper or Ben Rodgers to ask them to go with him, he had to settle for Huck Finn. For several days the search for treasure kept them occupied.

But for Tom the most exciting diversion of all was his invitation to join a picnic arranged by Judge and Mrs. Thatcher. In the party was to be Becky, Tom's present love, and this was the cause of his delight.

The place chosen for the picnic was a vast labyrinth of underground caves, and when they had eaten everyone went to explore them, Tom taking Becky with him. When the party reassembled, however, Tom and Becky were missing. Search parties were at once organized, but no sign of the children was found. For three days and nights the search went on.

During this time Tom was himself trying to find his way out of the caves, and at last he was successful. To prevent anyone else getting lost in them, the caves were boarded up. Tom did not know this until a fortnight later, and then he told Judge Thatcher that he was sure Injun Joe was hiding in the caves. A party at once went to the caves, and found the half-breed dead beside the blocked-up opening. He was buried near by.

While Tom was lost, Huck Finn had also been having his experiences. He had overheard Injun Joe and another man planning to rob Widow Douglas, and had given the warning. He had then been taken ill, and in gratitude for saving her from injury and loss the Widow Douglas had taken him in, nursed him back to health, and then insisted upon his making his home with her. Before his illness, however, he had continued his search for treasure alone, and had actually found a cache of 12,000 dollars. Judge Thatcher decided that the money was now legally his, and invested it for him, Widow Douglas meanwhile being intent on "making him respectable". But Huck found the discipline too much for him, and ran away. He encountered Tom, confessed what he had done, and implored Tom to help him. Tom persuaded him to go back to the Widow's, after having said he will make the Widow promise not to be so strict with him.

The book closes with the two boys planning to organize a band of robbers.

No brief précis of the story can ever hope to convey to the reader the quality of the style and the humour. The latter is all contained in the events, rather than in verbal wit. Except for the murder sequence, there is no story line; the entire value of the book lies in its recital of the ordinary everyday scrapes a small boy of spirit gets into, the way in which he reacts to them, the way in which he gets out of them. In Tom, Mark Twain has portrayed the universal boy, and in doing so he has, in a quite remarkable way, been able to put himself inside the boy's mind. This authenticity plays a major rôle in the appeal which the book has had in the ninety years since it first appeared.

THE BROTHERS KARAMAZOV

FEODOR DOSTOEVSKY

THE FOUR greatest writers of Western Europe, Shakespeare, Cervantes, Goethe and Dante, are matched by four giants in the East, Gogol, Turgenev, Tolstoy and Dostoevsky. Of the four Russians Dostoevsky is the greatest affirmer of life. Gogol laughs to hide his tears, Turgenev sadly contemplates the beauty of transitory existence and Tolstoy is preoccupied with the question what point there is in eating, drinking and loving when all living things sooner or later fall to dust. But Dostoevsky, despite his own harrowing experiences, never doubted that life is its own justification and that to love, to feel compassion, to have memories, even to suffer are better in all circumstances than non-existence. A passionate interest in life and in the heights and depths of human experience fill his novels and make them major works of art, crammed with fascinating characters, teeming with ideas on religion, nationality and politics, full of violent action, while behind all lurks a tragic sense that men are the victims of their own passions, driven by forces which they cannot control toward a fate they cannot foresee.

Of Dostoevsky's four most famous novels, *Crime and Punishment*, *The Idiot*, *The Possessed* and *The Brothers Karamazov*, the last is considered by some critics to be the best; others detect here a waning of his creative powers. However this may be, it is certainly the most involved and any reader coming fresh to Dostoevsky is liable to be somewhat baffled by his first glance at this long book. It seems to be full of interludes which have little to do with the main story: a scene in a monastery, for instance, where an Elder, Father Zossima, gives spiritual advice to some peasants, a long chapter on his early life and conversion, a digression about some schoolboys, one of whom is dying of consumption, a long allegory headed "The Grand Inquisitor". But if we leave aside the digressions, the plot itself is fairly simple. An old man, Fyodor Karamazov, a drunken sensualist and buffoon, lives on the outskirts of the small town of Skotoprigonyevsk. He has three sons, Dimitri and, by his second wife, Ivan and Alexey, known as Alyosha. These sons have strongly contrasting characters, though they share with their father a kind of primitive force, a thirst for life said to be typical of the Karamazovs which makes them extremists in their various ways: Alyosha a near-saint with intense spiritual awareness, Dimitri a reckless debauchee who squanders money on women and riotous escapades, and Ivan, a passionate intellectual, a prey to strange and conflicting ideas with a mind both sceptical and idealistic.

These young men, all in their twenties, pursue parallel lives, though they touch at critical moments. One such occasion quickly arises over a young woman named Grushenka, a typical Russian beauty, plump and rosy, with a bold, determined, proud and insolent character. Old Karamazov, whose amorous escapades arouse his eldest son's disgust and contempt, is pursuing Grushenka, but so is Dimitri, and his hostility to his father, already intense owing to early neglect and because he believes that the old man has cheated him of 3,000 roubles left to him by his mother, flares into feverish hatred. Both he and Ivan, in fact, would be glad to see their father out of the way and their hatred for him is fanned for purposes of his own by their illegitimate half-brother, Smerdyakov, a secretive, sinister and intensely ambitious young man employed as old Karamazov's valet.

After an ambiguous conversation with Smerdyakov, Ivan leaves the town, half believing that in his absence the valet will kill the old man. Dimitri, too, is led by Smerdyakov to contemplate murder, and one evening, when he has reason to suspect that Grushenka will be visiting his father, his jealousy and hatred boil over. He goes to the old man's house, taking a heavy pestle with him in his pocket, and listens beneath his lighted bedroom window, then climbs up some creeper and peers inside. His father, in a striped silk dressing-gown, is obviously awaiting his visitor. But there is no sign of Grushenka. Dimitri lures the old man to the window with prearranged signals that Smerdyakov has told him about, and as he sees his father's sagging Adam's apple, his hooked nose, his lips smiling in greedy expectation, fury suddenly surges up within him and he pulls the brass pestle from his pocket. . . .

In escaping from the garden, Dimitri fells one of the household servants with the pestle and later is found, babbling incoherently and covered with blood, by one of his friends. He goes to a neighbouring village, ostentatiously buying cases of champagne to take with him – with part of the 3,000 roubles, perhaps, which he knew were under his father's pillow – and there discovers Grushenka carousing with some friends. Later in the evening he finds himself alone with her and she murmurs: "I love you. I love only you." But he is troubled with remorse over the old servant he wrongly believes he has killed. The idyll has come too late and soon he is arrested in the tavern for his father's murder. A long and impressive trial scene follows, with cogent speeches for the prosecution and defence, and the story ends with his conviction and sentence to twenty years' hard labour in Siberia.

But Dimitri did not, in fact, kill old Karamazov. The murderer and thief of the 3,000 roubles was the utterly amoral and bitterly resentful Smerdyakov. Before the trial he surrenders the stolen money to Ivan and confesses to the crime. Next day he hangs himself, but this is not in atonement for the murder. Cynical and embittered though he is, Smerdyakov needs an idol in life, someone to look up to whom he can believe is all strength, all ruthlessness, all fixity of purpose. This person is Ivan, and when he reveals himself to be even weaker than Smerdyakov himself, the disillusioned valet commits suicide.

This is the main plot of *The Brothers Karamazov*, but the theme of the book is faith versus atheism, a spiritual as contrasted with a materialistic view of life, a contrast which is worked out in the characters, very subtly portrayed, of the three brothers. Not that there is all white on one side and all black on the other; Dostoevsky is too profound a psychologist for that. But broadly speaking, Alyosha represents the pure flame of spiritual awareness, while Dimitri and Ivan are trapped in the mire of materialism. Dimitri is the most involved character in the book and vies for central place with Alyosha whose adult life was to be portrayed by Dostoevsky in a further novel which he had no time even to start. Brimming with the Karamazov lust for life, but neglected by his father in childhood, Dimitri grows up with a burning conviction that the world owes him happiness and he is determined to win it in the shape of Grushenka despite all obstacles, degradations and even crimes. He does possess a yearning for what he dimly thinks of as a virtuous life, but virtue and decency must be put on ice until he has gained his heart's desire. Meanwhile, he believes they are unattainable, for he sees himself as the victim of circumstances, a nice fellow at heart who has never had a chance. So for Dimitri life is not a continuous process from which men must learn, in good days and bad, but a lottery in which all must be staked on the winning ticket. His conviction at the end of the book of a murder he never committed stands as Dostoevsky's solemn warning to those who hold such immature and dangerous views.

If Dimitri is the reckless, perpetual adolescent, Ivan is the haughty, austere and would-be self-sufficient young intellectual, also with dim strivings toward the good life, but whose brain gets in the way of his heart. He has spiritual faith of a kind, but his intellect refuses to concur and he is another example of a split personality which is a danger to itself and others. He is rather a colourless character and perhaps for that reason Dostoevsky connects with him two long digressions, magnificent in themselves but extraneous to the plot.

The first is the story of the Grand Inquisitor, a prose poem in allegorical form. It tells a story full of meaning for us today. In the sixteenth century, at the time of the Inquisition, Christ comes to Seville on the morrow of an *auto da fe* when a hundred heretics have been burnt. The Grand Inquisitor arrests him, puts him in prison and explains why it will be necessary to burn him at the stake next day. Christ, he says, came to bring men freedom, to draw their minds to God of their own free will, to claim their allegiance without the aid of miracles which could so easily, as the Devil suggested in the wilderness, have given Christ all the Kingdoms of the Earth. But this gift of freedom, asserts the Inquisitor, is the very thing which men are unable to bear. They do not want free choice. Freedom of choice may be all right for the ten thousand elect, but for the rut of humanity, weak, rebellious and timid, it is poison. If Christ had loved men more he would not have given them this intolerable gift but have turned stones to bread and so compelled their allegiance. And so, the Inquisitor claims, he and his fellows have corrected Christ's work. They have set up their own authority as supreme, they surround it with a mystical aura and they teach men to serve in perfect contentment the laws and decisions of the Inquisition. Their aim is to take a realistic view of human nature, to give men a goal, to supervise their work and their play, to say to them "Follow us and everything will be simple. You need nothing more in life." Of course, such creatures, enjoying this robot form of happiness, have nothing but death to expect in the Hereafter, but the Inquisitor freely admits that he is following the Devil's and not God's teaching. In fact he does not believe in God. . . .

And here, at the end of the allegory, we have a touch of pure Dostoevsky, reflecting his belief that evil even of this blatant kind somehow contributes to the Grand Design. The Inquisitor stops speaking and expects that Christ will answer. But instead, "He suddenly approached the old man in silence and softly kissed him on his aged bloodless lips." The old man shudders. His lips move. He goes to the door, opens it and says to Him: "Go, and come no more . . . come not at all, never, never!" And he lets him out into the dark alleys of the town.

This sombre interlude, with its disturbing vision of modern authoritarianism, takes place early in the book. Later, in Ivan's dream interview with the Devil, when he is being driven mad by the belief that he connived in his father's murder, we are offered a different perspective. The Devil, the product of his subconscious mind, appears to him in the guise of a shabbily dressed but genteel man of the world whom he suddenly finds sitting on his sofa. The Devil argues in favour of a world where men have finally abandoned the idea of God. How glad they would be to exploit the dictum which Ivan has preached throughout his life: "All things are lawful." But even the Devil – and here another part of Ivan speaks – is obliged to tell an anecdote about a sceptic who died and much to his indignation found that a future life lay before him. The man was told that he had to walk a quadrillion miles to reach paradise. For a thousand years he squatted on the road and refused to budge, then he finally got moving, reached paradise after aeons of time and had only been two seconds there when he declared that to enjoy them was worth walking a quadrillion times the distance.

In Ivan and Dimitri, though they are both knavish, the longing for virtue and faith keep breaking through. With Alyosha, the youngest brother, religion is the perpetual climate of his mind. Alyosha lives in a monastery and would like to spend the rest of his life there as pupil of the saintly Father Zossima. But he is urged to go out into the world, marry and live the life of a normal individual and he does this after Father Zossima's death. His later years Dostoevsky intended to trace in the sequel to this book which he never wrote. Here Alyosha figures as a physically robust young man of wide tolerance and love of humanity, spiritually unshakable and intelligent. He is convinced of the immortality of the soul and swears to live for the future life. He plays no active part in the main plot beyond helping his brothers to know their better selves, but it is through him and Father Zossima that some of Dostoevsky's most profound beliefs are brought to the reader and there can be no better ending to this brief survey than to quote two short examples. The saintly Elder on his death-bed is giving advice to his monks:

"Brothers, have no fear of men's sin. Love a man even in his sin, for that is the semblance of Divine Love and is the highest love on earth. Love all God's creation, the whole and every grain of sand in it. Love every leaf, every ray of God's light. Love the animals, love the plants, love everything. If you love everything, you will perceive the divine mystery in things. Once you perceive it, you will begin to comprehend it better every day. And you will come at last to love the whole world with an all-embracing love. . . ."

And at the very end of the book, the charming, fourteen-year-old Kolya, who has just witnessed the funeral of Ilusha, one of his beloved school-fellows who has died of consumption, cries to Alyosha: "Karamazov, can it be true what's taught us in religion, that we shall all rise again from the dead and see each other again – all, Ilusha, too?" And Alyosha, and with him Dostoevsky in his last words to us at the end of a life full of suffering, replies: "Certainly we shall all rise again, certainly we shall see each other and shall tell each other with joy and gladness all that has happened."

PIERRE ET JEAN

GUY DE MAUPASSANT

WITH CHEKHOV, Guy de Maupassant ranks as the world's greatest writer of short stories, for variety and fascination of plot, excellence of characterization, swiftness of narrative and clarity of style a master of his craft. But apart from these qualities his stories contain something even more valuable. Their perfection of form conveys a sense of beauty that is related to something eternal, that seems to mirror the unity of life as a whole and lifts a small corner of the veil that shrouds human destiny itself. The impression may strike people in different ways, they may have different definitions for it, but it is the same in essence as that derived from any great work of art.

Maupassant, indeed, was a superb artist and he held strong opinions about his work. Unlike modern writers who like to plumb the depths of the psyche, he believed that the writer should confine himself to portraying impressions that can be received through the organs of sense, in other words, he describes what his characters do or say, how they look, but only where strictly necessary what they think or feel and he never indulges in psychological dissection. This technique, which makes the writer an observer of life, but not an omniscient god, has been called objective realism. In keeping with it, Maupassant held that the writer must be sincere and tell the truth about life and human beings as he sees them and he abhorred romantic literature which distorted observable truth in order to comfort, console or divert the reader. Finally, like Flaubert, his intimate friend whom he looked on as a father, he believed in a scrupulous process of selection so that only what is essential to an understanding of the characters and action appears in the best of his stories and nothing can be taken from the finished work without destroying the harmony of the whole. These principles, carried into effect with instinctive genius, help to explain the compelling power of his stories.

The best of Maupassant's work is compact and flawless as a jewel, but his life was chaotic. He wrote with ease, producing masterpieces with the same natural simplicity as apples fall from a tree. But this round-headed, heavy-featured, broad-shouldered young man, who looked more like a soldier than a writer, led a restless existence with one foot in the gutter and the other in high society which would have exhausted men with even more stamina than himself.

Born in 1850 of parents sprung from the Norman gentry, he became, after spasmodic early schooling, a clerk in the Naval Ministry in Paris where he stayed until the age of thirty, writing his first story in 1875, but filling most of his leisure in these years with long boating trips on the Seine and bouts of revelry among the workers and prostitutes who crowded its banks. He was alone in Paris; his younger brother, who ultimately went mad, lived in the country with their mother, a gifted but hysterical woman, abandoned by her husband in Maupassant's childhood and mutually devoted to her eldest son who, as sometimes happens in such cases, could only find erotic release in the arms of less worthy females.

In Paris he made many friends among students and workers as poor as himself, but from 1880 when he resigned his clerkship and took up writing as a career his fortunes rapidly improved. In the next few years, besides pouring out articles for the daily press, he wrote bawdy tales for a notorious periodical called *Gil Blas*, and some of his more famous stories, such as *En Famille* and *La Maison Tellier*, were published. By 1884, literary success enabled him to move to Normandy where he built a house with a splendid garden and kept a parrot – typical Maupassant touch! – trained to shriek rude greetings at lady visitors. By 1889, when his output began to fall off, partly as a result of syphilis for which no effective treatment was known in those days, he had written nearly 250 short stories and six novels.

He died in July, 1893, deeply mourned by the public and his friends, for whom Émile Zola spoke by the Paris graveside: "He had only to appear and tell his stories and instantly everyone loved him. He became a celebrity overnight. Readers accepted everything he wrote: things that would have shocked them had they come from others, from him made them smile. He satisfied all intelligences, he touched all sensibilities, and we had the extraordinary spectacle of a robust, frank talent, making not the slightest concession and yet immediately capturing the admiration and even the affection of the reading public."

It is difficult, in the case of a writer whose fame now rests on his stories, to discuss these effectively in a short article, but he also wrote novels and it is a curious fact that in his lifetime his reputation was even greater as a novelist. Among the six he wrote in the eleven years of his literary life it is possible, up to the fourth which is easily the best, to discern his increasingly successful struggle to adapt the short-story technique to the longer form, so that the novels start as a loosely connected series of scenes, culminating in the masterpiece, *Pierre et Jean*, written in 1888, where a single situation affecting a small number of characters and a single problem fill the whole short book.

Because of its concentrated action, *Pierre et Jean* is best described as a long story rather than a short novel and it shows up every one of Maupassant's merits: his extreme economy of style, his skill in characterization, rapid development of plot, and that added sense of beauty which derives from the perfection of the whole. It is a sombre tale, set near the port of Le Havre with its evening mists and wailing sirens, about a young man who has strong reasons to suspect that his younger brother is not his father's son. We meet the family when they are out fishing: Monsieur Roland, a rather doltish retired jeweller with a passion for small boats; his sentimental and still pretty wife; their elder son Pierre, restless and imaginative, who has recently qualified as a doctor; the younger son Jean, about to start practice as a lawyer; and finally their neighbour, Madame Rosémilly, a young and attractive widow in whose presence latent jealousy springs up between the brothers.

In the evening startling news arrives: a Monsieur Maréchal of Paris, former friend of the Rolands, has died and left all his money, a considerable fortune, to Jean. Monsieur Roland is naïvely delighted. His wife says simply: "That proves he was very fond of us," and Pierre is naturally prompted to ask: "Did you know him very well, then, at one time, this Maréchal?" Yes, very well, replies Roland effusively. He was very kind to both the boys when they were small. He was in the house when Jean was born and even ran to fetch the doctor. No doubt his thought was: "I have helped at the birth of this child so I will leave him my fortune." This explanation seems to satisfy everyone, but after the two sons have gone out and Monsieur Roland has retired to bed, his wife stays downstairs, gazing dreamily at the oil lamp beside her table....

So ends the first chapter. From now on, Pierre is filled with a feeling of unease. Pacing to and fro by the harbour he interprets it at first as jealousy of his brother, but then a visit to a friend, a Polish refugee pharmacist, sows the seed of greater distress. "That will not make a good impression," says the old man on being told of Jean's inheritance and on being pressed he merely repeats the remark, adding that in such cases both brothers should benefit equally. Next day, Pierre is too busy looking for rooms where he can set up his medical practice to ruminate, but he is deeply upset by a comment from a waitress in a café. Hearing about Jean's good fortune, she smiles enigmatically and says: "Well, he's lucky, your brother, to have friends like that. No wonder he's so unlike you!" For a time, Pierre refuses to believe the insinuation and his only thought is to warn his brother not to accept the inheritance for the sake of his mother's reputation. He finds it impossible to speak to Jean that evening as a noisy party takes place at home to celebrate the windfall. As he sits surrounded by champagne and laughter, however, resentment digs deeper into his mind.

Next day, after firmly lecturing himself, he manages to dispel the feeling for a while, but the discovery that his brother, with his new-found wealth, has rented the very apartment he would have liked for his medical practice, but could not afford, brings anger bubbling to the surface and with it the desire to probe deeper into his parents' friendship with Monsieur Maréchal. How did they get to know him, he asks, and when? The answer, given by his garrulous father, is devastating. He had first got to know Maréchal well when Pierre was three and Jean had not yet been born and the reason for the intimacy had been Maréchal's great assistance in helping the child over an attack of scarlet fever. How delighted the good man had been when the little boy recovered, how he had smothered him with attention! "From that moment on," says Monsieur Roland, "we became great friends." And yet Maréchal left his fortune to Jean. Why?

Obsessed with this question, Pierre goes out to the harbour and wanders about in a thick fog matching the fog in his mind. With agonized intensity he tries to work out a definite answer to the question: was Jean the son of Maréchal? He recalls the man's elegance and refinement and realizes he could never have made a friend of Monsieur Roland. He remembers that he gave his mother roses and, with a shaft of pain, that he was blond like Jean and that there used to be a miniature of him in the house. Where is it now? Has Pierre's mother hidden it? The thought makes him groan with distress and almost in his face the siren on the quay gives a desolate wail. . . .

Next morning, Pierre creeps into his brother's room when he is asleep, examines his face and notes a complete lack of resemblance to Monsieur Roland. He asks his mother about the miniature. She hesitates for a moment, then says she thinks it may be in her desk. That evening she produces it and Pierre notices at once a slight similarity between Jean and Maréchal. He studies the portrait long enough for his mother to become uneasy and from now on a silent struggle takes place between them and they eye one another, each trying to fathom the other's mind.

In the following weeks the conflict continues: Madame Roland becomes ill with suffering, while Pierre cannot refrain from torturing her with a word or a glance. In this state of tension the family go for a day to the seaside where Jean becomes engaged to Madame Rosémilly and then, after a house-warming at Jean's new apartment, he and Pierre find themselves alone together in the salon. A quarrel flares up between them, culminating in a taunt flung at Jean for accepting the fortune of one man when he is supposed to be the son of another. Jean is horrified, but the tumour in Pierre's mind now bursts and he pours out all his rage and despair before rushing out of the house in deep humiliation, leaving his mother, who has overheard all from a neighbouring room, to tell her illegitimate son that the accusation is true. To her state of collapse Jean reacts with pity and intensified love and against her first inclination persuades her to stay with him, provided something can be done about Pierre who obviously can no longer live at home.

From this point, the intolerable strain affecting everyone in the home but the stupid Monsieur Roland ebbs away as a solution is found. Pierre will go away as a ship's doctor. An appointment is obtained, preparations for departure are made and heavy at heart he takes leave of his friends in the town. To the end he does not know whether his mother confessed or denied the accusation to Jean. He himself is almost but not completely certain of the truth. Between himself and his mother there is nothing now but resentment on one side and a guilty sadness on the other. She loves him, but knows he cannot stay. So, on the morning when his liner sails, the family gathers in his cabin to say good-bye, his mother in black and her hair, grey till a few months ago, now completely white. To cover a painful silence he discourses on the pharmaceutical properties of the drugs in his cupboard. Then Monsieur Roland, still blithely oblivious of the tragedy, suggests that the party take a boat to wave good-bye as the liner reaches the sea. *Vite, vite, en voiture!* he cries. There is not a moment to be lost. And the last scene is of Pierre standing alone at the stern of his ship as she leaves the harbour, waving to his family in the little row-boat where his mother, in reply, stretches out her arms to him. Then, on shore again, she looks out over the water, but the liner has gone and there is nothing to be seen now but a little grey smoke, so distant, so light that it looks like mist. Thus she is left with her guilt and suffering, Jean with his inheritance, father Roland with his illusions and it is Pierre, the innocent victim, who has to leave home for the sake of the others.

Henry James pronounced this tale to be faultless and Maupassant's latest biographer calls it the longest piece of fiction in which he is all but continuously in top form. The famous critic Jules Lemâitre wrote to him: "Nothing you have done is sharper, better planned, better composed and arranged, more masterly." And here Lemaître was praising what Lytton Strachey defined in later years as the one high principle which, through the ages, has guided like a star the writers of France: "the principle of deliberation, of intention, of a conscious search for ordered beauty." But Maupassant himself was content to tell his mother: "I am sure that the book is good".

THE GOLDEN BOUGH

SIR J. G. FRAZER

DEEP IN the Alban Hills to the south of Rome is the Lake of Nemi.
The ancients called it "Diana's Mirror", and it is easy to imagine the
goddess still haunting its lonely shore. On its banks there used to
stand a temple dedicated to Diana Nemorensis, or Diana of the
Wood, and adjoining the temple was a sacred grove. The nearest
town was Aricia, some three miles off, and both lake and grove are
sometimes given this name.

The scene is surpassingly beautiful, and Turner's famous painting
has but done it justice. And yet "in antiquity this sylvan landscape
was the scene of a strange and recurring tragedy". For "in this sacred
grove there grew a certain tree round which at any time of the day,
and probably far into the night, a grim figure might be seen to prowl.
In his hand he carried a drawn sword, and he kept peering warily
about him as if at every instant he expected to be set upon by an
enemy. He was a priest and a murderer; and the man for whom he
looked was sooner or later to murder him and hold the priesthood in
his stead. Such was the rule of the sanctuary. A candidate for the
priesthood could only succeed to office by slaying the priest, and
having slain him, he retained office till he was himself slain by a
stronger or a craftier."

This passage is taken from the first page of one of the most remarkable books to be published in the last century. Its name – *The Golden
Bough*; its author – Sir James George Frazer.

In the reference books Frazer is described as a social anthro-
pologist, and this is true as far as it goes. But he was very much more.
He was a singularly graceful writer. He was one of the greatest
classical scholars of his country and age. Still more, he was possessed
of a penetrating intelligence and a most sympathetic understanding
that enabled him to bring light into some of the darkest and most
perplexing fields of human culture and religious experience.

Born in Glasgow in 1854, where his father was the senior partner
in a firm of chemists, he did not die until 1941. From Glasgow
University he proceeded to Trinity College, Cambridge, where in
1879 he was elected to a fellowship which he retained to the end of

O

his life. The first volume of *The Golden Bough* appeared in 1890, and subsequently other volumes were published until the book was completed in 1915 with the twelfth. An abridgement in one volume without the copious notes, was issued in 1922, and most readers will find this adequate to their purpose.

Now, what was the "golden bough"? To put it simply, it was a branch broken off from a certain tree in that grove beside the lake at Nemi. According to the age-old custom of the sanctuary, the man who succeeded in penetrating to the grove and breaking off a branch from that tree, might claim the right to fight the priest in single combat. If he won, then he became priest in the stead of the man whom he had slaughtered; he became the "King of the Wood", and reigned in lonely terror until he was defeated and killed in his turn. This strange rule of succession had its origins in the mists of the past but it survived into historical times, since we learn that the Emperor Caligula (1st century A.D.), thinking that the then "King of the Wood" had reigned long enough at Nemi, hired a more stalwart ruffian to waylay and assassinate him.

The sanctuary where the priest officiated was dedicated to Diana who was revered as the goddess of woodlands and wild creatures and was also believed to bless men and women with offspring and to aid mothers in childbed. Being thus intimately concerned with sexual matters, it was supposed that she should have a male companion, and in the classical legend this divinity's name was Virbius. In historical times Virbius seems to have been represented by the line of priests at Nemi, the Kings of the Wood who regularly perished by the sword of their successors and whose lives were in a manner bound up with that particular tree in the grove from which the "golden bough" had to be plucked by a venturesome newcomer. For so long as that tree was uninjured, the priest was safe from attack.

Frazer was fascinated by this ancient custom, and the problems involved in its explanation presented themselves as a challenge. The first question he put to himself was: Why was the priest at Nemi called the King of the Wood? Why was his office spoken of as kingdom? He knew, of course, that in the ancient world many kings were commonly priests as well, and that their rôle as intercessor between man and God had led in many cases to their being worshipped as gods themselves. This was one way in which the idea of man-god had been arrived at. But there was another. In early society the king is frequently a magician as well as a priest, and often he appears to have attained to power by virtue of his supposed proficiency in the black or white art.

Frazer analyses the "principles of magic" into two. The first is the law of Similarity, that like produces like, or that an effect resembles its cause; the second is the Law of Contact or Contagion, that things which have once been in contact with each other continue to act on each other at a distance after the physical contact has been severed. Magic, he concludes, is "a spurious system of natural law as well as a fallacious guide to conduct; it is a false science as well as an abortive art". He fills many pages with illustrations of these two principles in action, illustrations drawn from many lands and many peoples, mostly savage or barbarous. And here it may be remarked that Frazer never saw a savage in the flesh, he never visited a country where he might stand a reasonable chance of coming across one. All that he knew of savage life he obtained from books and what other people told him; with the result that he is inclined to take a kindly view of savage folk – even though he allows that sometimes they display such deplorably bad manners as to kill and eat one another.

Perhaps if he had met an African medicine-man, Frazer might not have written so appreciatively of the magician? The public profession of magic (he writes), being one of the roads by which the ablest men have risen to supreme power, has rendered no small service to humanity. "If the black art has done much evil, it has also been the source of much good; if it is the child of error, it has yet been the mother of freedom and truth." Magic is older than religion in the history of humanity, and belief in its efficacy is the "universal faith, the truly Catholic creed".

Magic is nearer to Science than it is to Religion, argues Frazer, and he defines Religion as "a propitiation or conciliation of powers superior to man which are believed to direct and control the course of nature and of human life". Priests endeavour to *persuade* these powers, by the offering of sacrifices, the recitation of prayers and other outward ceremonies, and sometimes by displaying that "pure religion and undefiled" of which St. James speaks. Magicians, on the other hand, are fully persuaded that they can *compel* the supernatural powers to do their bidding, provided they employ the correct formulas and perform the appropriate rites.

In no sphere is this compulsion more sought after than that of fertility. One of Frazer's most pregnant chapters is on "The Influence of the Sexes on Vegetation", and he argues that the spring and summer festivals of Europe, by representing the marriage of the sylvan deities in the persons of a King and Queen of May, a Whitsun Bridegroom and Bride, and so forth, were attempts by our rude forefathers to quicken, on the principles of imitative magic, the growth of trees and plants. "Such representations were no mere symbolic or allegorical dramas, pastoral plays designed to amuse or instruct a rustic audience. They were charms intended to make the woods to grow green, the fresh grass to sprout, the corn to shoot and the flowers to blow." And it was only natural to suppose that the more closely the mock marriage of the leaf-clad or flower-decked mummers aped the real marriage of the woodland sprites the more effective would be the charm.

From this Frazer goes on to suggest that our May Day, Whitsun and Midsummer celebrations are survivals of prehistoric rites in which the actors consciously performed the parts of gods and goddesses.

To take the case of Diana, for instance. As we have just seen, she was not a mere goddess of trees, but in her sacred grove at Nemi was worshipped as a goddess of fertility. Now on the principle that the goddess of fertility must herself be fertile, it was supposed that she entered into sexual union with her male partner, Virbius. By their marriage, the fruitfulness of the earth, of animals, and of mankind would be promoted; and "it might naturally be thought that this object would be more surely obtained if the sacred nuptials were celebrated every year, the parts of the divine bride and bridegroom being played either by their images or by living persons".

In all such practices everything is seen to depend on the virility of the goddess's male partner, and in the nature of things he will grow old and weak. Then the "king" is slain when his strength fails, and another is appointed in his place. In this way we may perhaps account for the barbarous rite at Nemi, when a stronger and fiercer kills the priest and so provides the goddess with a more potent consort.

If the growth and decay of vegetation and animal life be taken as dependent upon the waxing and waning of such "divine kings" as the King of the Wood at Nemi, the alternations of the seasons will also be interpreted in terms of gods and goddesses who are born and die and are born again in fresh life and vigour. This belief has found expression in the great seasonal dramas associated with Attis, the Phrygian god, and his consort Cybele, and of Osiris and Isis in Egypt.

Some of Frazer's best writing is to be found in his chapters describing these fertility cults of the ancient world. His conclusion is that they were all worshippers of a great Mother Goddess, the personification of all the reproductive energies of nature; that associated with her was a lover, or series of lovers, divine yet mortal, with whom she mated year by year, their sexual union being deemed essential to the propagation of plants and animals; and further, that the fabulous union of the divine pair was simulated and, as it were, multiplied on earth by the real, though temporary, union of the human sexes at the sanctuary of the goddess, thereby ensuring the fruitfulness of the ground and the increase of man and beast. In this way Frazer accounts for the religious prostitution that was a feature of some of the ancient heathen worships.

From this examination of the practices of the classical civilizations, Frazer passes to an investigation of similar customs in northern Europe – the cults of the Corn-Mother and the Corn-Maiden in particular – and in many other lands. One chapter is devoted to the Corn-Spirit as an Animal, another to Vegetation Gods that were supposed to take animal forms, and a third to the sacrament of "Eating the God". From this he proceeds to a study of Scapegoats, which involves an account of the Saturnalia in Ancient Rome and one of human sacrifices among the Aztecs of ancient Mexico. After this we have several chapters on the Fire-Festivals of Europe and their interpretation. The connexion between some of these subjects and his original theme is sometimes by no means obvious, and there is ground for the charge that Frazer included in his great work anything and everything that excited his particular interest.

Frazer's final volumes bear the title of "Balder the Beautiful", and they are concerned in the main with the Norse god Balder, the best and wisest and most beloved of the Scandinavian immortals, who was slain by a mistletoe-bough thrown at him by Loki the Mischief-maker. Frazer retells the ancient myth, and seizes the occasion to explore all that has been told about the mistletoe, that peculiar plant which grows and flourishes without having roots in the earth. Balder was invulnerable against everything but a mistletoe bough, and Frazer concludes that he, in Scandinavian belief, was nothing more nor less than a personification of the mistletoe-bearing oak. From this he goes on to argue that the Golden Bough was the mistletoe.

At last we have come back to the sacred grove at Nemi. There are grounds for believing (says Frazer) that the priest of the Arician grove – the King of the Wood – personified the tree on which grew the Golden Bough. Hence if that tree were the oak, the King of the Wood must have been a personification of the oak-spirit. It is easy to understand in this case why, before he could be slain, it was necessary to break the Golden Bough. As an oak-spirit, his life or death was in the mistletoe on the oak, and so long as the mistletoe remained intact, he, like Balder, could not die. To slay him, therefore, it was necessary to break the mistletoe, and probably to throw it at him

But why is the mistletoe called the Golden Bough, when its berrie are not golden but whitish-yellow? Frazer is ready with his answer In the first place, the mistletoe bough assumes a rich golden yellow colour when it has been cut and kept for some months; and further there is also an old belief that the mistletoe is supposed to possess th property of disclosing treasures on earth, gold in particular.

And so, "our long voyage of discovery is over and our bark ha drooped her weary sails in port at last. . . ."

On the centenary of Frazer's birth, in 1954, *The Times* published special leading article by way of tribute. "Among the writings of Sir James George Frazer, who was born a hundred years ago today, it begins, "*Totemism and Exogamy* might have ranked as the *magnum opus* of a less encyclopedic savant, and the three volumes on *Folklor in the Old Testament* must have struck many of its first readers as revolutionary book. But for the general reader there is no doubt tha Frazer's reputation will stand or fall with *The Golden Bough*; an whatever the ultimate judgment upon it as science, it can be said on his centenary day that as literature it stands".

TESS OF THE D'URBERVILLES
THOMAS HARDY

F THERE is one thing that distinguishes Thomas Hardy from his
ellow novelists it is his sense of pity. This is the controlling note of
ll that he wrote – pity for the rabbit stalked by the blood-lusting
oat, and the bird fluttering to death in the house-cat's claws; pity
or the dumb brutes sent to the slaughter-house, and the wild crea-
ures torn to the music of the huntsman's horn; pity for the strong
man fallen from his high estate, such as Casterbridge's mayor, and for
ne Jude the Obscures predestined never to burst into flower on the
unghills of heredity and environment; pity for the sturdy young
loughman tippling his life away, and – yes – pity for the village
maiden undone beneath the moon.

Tess of the D'Urbervilles, his most famous novel, has for its heroine a
irl who in the first division of the book is "the maiden" and in the
econd "maiden no more"; and yet, with what some reviewers felt
vas an extraordinarily bold fling at the established moralities
f the time – the novel was published in 1891, when Victorianism
vas at its height – he appended to her name on the title-page the subtle, "A pure woman".

Tess was the daughter of a small local carrier or "haggler" named
ohn Durbeyfield, to whom we are introduced in the first sentence
f the book, when he is walking home one May evening from
haston to the village of Marlott, in the Vale of Blackmoor. It was
Thomas Hardy's somewhat curious habit to disguise his place-
ames, though ever so slightly, and Marlott has been identified with
Marnhull, a village in the north of Dorset on almost the northern-
nost edge of the Hardy Country, and Shaston is the ancient town of
haftesbury.

Durbeyfield was middle-aged, shiftless, and much too fond of his
lass, and nothing would have been heard of him, or indeed of his
aughter, if on this first evening of our acquaintance he had not had
is head turned by the information, imparted to him by a parson-
ntiquary whom he met riding along the road, that he was the
escendant of "the ancient and knightly family of the D'Urber-
illes", who in olden times had possessed estates in the county and

were commemorated in the church at Kingsbere (Bere Regis

The simple fellow's pride and pleasure at the news, and at bein
addressed, half in amusement and half in contempt, as "Sir John"
were somewhat diminished by the further information that n
mansions or lands, not a single acre, remained in the family now. Bu
all the same he felt justified in sending a boy to the Pure Drop Inn
with the request that a horse and carriage should be dispatche
immediately to fetch "Sir John" home – "and in the bottom o' th
carriage they be to put a noggin o' rum in a small bottle, and chalk
up to my account".

Tess's first appearance in the story comes a few pages later, when
walking with the other village maidens in the annual "club-walk
ing", a lingering reminder of the May Day dance of ancient time
she had her attention called to her father's homecoming. "I've-got-
gr't - family - vault - at - Kingsbere - and - knighted - forefathers
in-lead-coffins-there!" he was singing in a slow recitative, lazil
waving his hand above his head the while. The girls tittered, know
ing him of old – all but one of them, and she his daughter, wh
flushed and flared out at them so that they fell silent. She was a fin
and handsome girl, we are told, whose "mobile peony mouth an
large innocent eyes added eloquence to colour and shape", and in he
dark brown hair she wore a red ribbon, the only one of the whit
company of maidens who could boast of such an adornment.

The "walk" had its terminus at an open grassy space, where th
girls began dancing, at first with themselves and then, when wor
in the fields had finished for the day, with the young men of th
village. They were watched by a group of three young men of
superior class, who from the knapsacks strapped to their backs an
their stout sticks seemed to be on a walking tour. One wore the whit
tie of a clergyman, and the second had likewise a professiona
appearance; but the third and youngest had an "uncribbed un
cabined aspect in his eyes and attire". The three brothers, for that i
what they were, leant over a gate beside the highway, and after the
had inquired as to the meaning of the dance made as though t
continue their journey – but then the youngest declared his intentio
of "having a fling" with the girls for just a moment. His elders pro
tested at his ungentlemanly proposal, but he insisted and they wen
on without him. He entered the field, and had no difficulty i
obtaining a partner. The name of the girl he chose has not bee
handed down, but it was not Tess. She was disappointed, and a
Angel Clare at length quitted the dance he looked back and saw he
white figure standing there and thought he caught in her eyes th

faintest suggestion of reproach that he had not chosen *her*. He, too, was sorry, but was inclined to put the blame on her backwardness. Years later he was to be reminded of that first encounter. . . .

Tess was the eldest of a family of seven, and already she was "quite a Malthusian" when she reflected on the way in which her parents had provided her with such a number of brothers and sisters when they had not the means to provide for them. She was a thoughtful girl and had done well at the village school, and the more she looked about her the more she suspected that the world into which she had been introduced was like the occasional apple on the tree in their garden, a blighted one. She was confirmed in this opinion when, in the early hours of the day following her father's dramatic homecoming, she was obliged to take his place in the carrier's cart and met with an accident, the old horse on which their livelihood depended being killed. She blamed herself for the mishap, and so raised no great objection to her scheming mother's plan that she could claim acquaintance with a family bearing the name of d'Urberville who lived some little distance away. Dressed in her Sunday clothes and as pretty as a picture, she repaired to the d'Urberville home, and was found a job looking after the mistress's chickens. What she did not know was that these d'Urbervilles had not the slightest right to use the name, but had assumed it because it had such an aristocratic sound.

Mrs. d'Urberville was blind, and so got to know Tess only through her voice, and a charming voice it was. But her son, Alec d'Urberville, a "handsome, horsey young buck" who fancied a cigar between his teeth, from the first time he saw her thought her "a crumby girl" and, half in play and half in earnest, resolved on making her his own. In vain she resisted his advances, and indeed she could not help a sexual attraction. And so we are led up to the scene at night in Trantridge Chase, amid the primeval yews and oaks, the hopping rabbits and hares. Doubtless, writes Hardy, "some of Tess d'Urberville's mailed ancestors rollicking home from a fray had dealt the same measure even more ruthlessly towards peasant girls of their time", but even so, "why it was that upon this beautiful feminine tissue, sensitive as gossamer, and practically blank as snow as yet, there should have been traced such a coarse pattern as it was doomed to receive – why so often the coarser appropriates the finer thus", this was something which "many thousand years of analytical philosophy have failed to explain to our sense of order".

A few weeks later Tess returned to her old home. "What, isn't your cousin going to do the handsome thing?" demanded her mother. "He's not my cousin, and he's not going to marry me," replied the girl, and then she put her face on her mother's neck, and told. "And yet th'st not got him to marry 'ee! Any woman would have done it but you, after that!" The reply was charged with a poignant significance: "Perhaps any woman would except me."

So she thrust Alec d'Urberville behind her in her proud independence, and refused to let him be told of what had befallen her. A child was born, and the girl-mother took the baby with her to her work in the harvest field. It was a poor, puny little thing, and there came a night when she realized that it had only a short time to live. And it had not been baptized – it would be consigned to the nethermost corner of hell, as its double doom for lack of baptism and lack of legitimacy! Hurriedly she ranged her small brothers and sisters beside the washing-stand, and, imposing in her white nightgown and with a thick cable of twisted dark hair hanging down her back, she proceeded to christen her babe. "Sorrow, I baptize thee in the name of the Father, and of the Son, and of the Holy Ghost." Then, dipping her hand in the basin, she traced a huge cross on the infant, and all the children said, "Amen". A few minutes later little Sorrow had given up life's struggle before it had really begun.

So this first tragic chapter of Tess's life was closed, and in the next we find her employed as a milkmaid in Farmer Crick's dairy in the Valley of Great Dairies, as Hardy styles the valley of the Froom. The farm's name is given as Talbothays, and it would seem to have been situated not far from Weatherbury (Puddletown), on the fringe of Egdon Heath. This was the happiest time of Tess's life, and Hardy surpasses himself in his description of the dairyman and his milkmaids, working in conditions of pastoral happiness and plenty. And in this Eden was an Adam, in the person of Angel Clare, whom Tess recognized from the first as the young man who had caught her eye when, in her days as a maiden, she had danced on the village green at home. He for his part failed to make the recognition, but he soon found himself getting every day more and more in love with her. He was a pupil at the place, and intended before long to have a farm of his own; what better wife could he have than this beautiful girl, who was so part and parcel of country life, who was so good, so innocent, so utterly *pure*? His parents – Mr. Clare was a clergyman at a village in West Dorset – raised no great objection, and Angel made repeated protestations of love to Tess. To his surprise, she refused him, not once but time and again. He could not understand it, but she had her woman's reasons. She loved him passionately, as she had never loved before and never again, but she felt that her past was an irremovable obstacle. She wrote to her mother for counsel, and her mother strongly advised her to say nothing. Tess thought differently, however, and on several occasions she endeavoured to tell Angel of her early history. The last occasion was on their wedding-morn, and he laughingly refused to listen to her confessions – as if *she* could have anything to confess!

And so they were married, and that evening, as they sat side by side in the ancient house they had chosen for their honeymoon – it is generally identified with the house beside the bridge at Wool – she told him of her seduction, and its fruit, and how she had never loved anyone but "her dearest husband". He had some youthful escapades to confess, and she forgave him at once, and she in the simplicity of her heart and the fullness of her love believed that he would forgive her too. But Angel Clare was made in a different mould. He was so obsessed with anatomical integrity that he utterly failed to sense the essential purity of her nature. He rebuffed her, and at length left her, going off on a quixotic farming enterprise in Brazil.

Tess was left with some small allowance, but she soon dispensed this in helping her thriftless family, and she was working once more as a farm hand, doing the most laborious work in the fields, when Alec d'Urberville caught up with her. He was now a reformed character, moving from village to village as an evangelical missionary – and who should have effected his conversion but old Mr. Clare, Angel's father? The conversion was genuine enough, but it did not last long after Alec had once more met the girl whom he had seduced.

Very much against her will, Tess allowed him to render some help to the helpless Durbeyfields, but she wrote, time and again, to her husband, imploring him to come home to the woman who loved him and had never loved anyone but him. The letters were delayed, but at length Angel Clare returned to England. Hardship and sickness and opportunity for reflection had convinced him of his folly and worse, and he now realized the true worth of the girl whose love and devotion he had rejected. For some time he could find no trace of her, but at length he found her – when she was living at Sandbourne (Bournemouth) in furnished lodgings as d'Urberville's mistress. At first he failed to grasp the situation, and begged her to believe that he was a changed man, and deeply regretted his desertion. She pushed his hands away. "It is too late," she said; "too late, too late! No – you must not. Keep away." Then when he still did not understand, she informed him bluntly, sadly, tragically: "He has won me back to him." But she did not love him: on the contrary, she hated him, since he had told her a lie, told her that her husband would never come again, "and you *have* come".

Angel Clare staggered away from the house; and not long after the landlady heard strange sounds coming from the room overhead where her lodgers were. She could not distinguish the words, but there was a low note of moaning, "O – O – O!" Then a man's voice from the bedroom, and then words that she could distinguish, "O God – I can't bear this – I cannot!" Before long the woman came downstairs and went out, and the landlady went back to her chair and sat there until her eyes were arrested by a red spot in the middle of the ceiling. She reached up her hand and felt it: it was damp and she fancied that it was blood. . . .

Meanwhile Tess had caught up with her husband, and almost nonchalantly informed him that she had "killed him". He thought she was deranged, or at worst had attempted to kill Alec. But obviously flight was essential, and so the pair made their surreptitious way through the Hampshire woods. When night came on they found a large house, furnished but untenanted, and there, in a great old-fashioned four-post bedstead, they consummated at last their married love. For five days they stayed in their retreat, and then, suspecting that they had been discovered, they resumed their wanderings. Clare hoped that they might reach the north of England, where a way of escape across the sea might open, but by this time they were being sought everywhere. At nightfall they came to a great "Temple of the Winds", a place of giant pillars, and in the middle a stone like an altar on which Tess stretched herself and fell asleep with the innocent sleep of a child. Dawn, and Angel Clare heard the brush of feet. He jumped up, and all around were men. Her story was true then!

"It's no use, sir," said one of the pursuers, "there are sixteen of us on the Plain, and the whole country is reared". He implored them to let her finish her sleep, and they stood by her, among the pillars of Stonehenge, until she awoke. "What is it, Angel?" she asked; "have they come for me?" He replied, "Yes, dearest, they have come." And she said quietly, "I am ready."

So this most tragic tale, this almost savage tearing at the heartstrings, moves to its bitter end. In the concluding pages Angel Clare and 'Liza-Lu, his wife's young sister whom Tess had begged him to marry when she was gone, stand on the hill above Winchester, gazing across to the tower of the gaol. Upon the corner of the tower a staff is fixed, and just after eight has struck something moves slowly up the staff and extends itself upon the breeze. It is a black flag.

" 'Justice' was done, and the President of the Immortals, in Aeschylean phrase, had ended his sport with Tess. And the d'Urberville knights and dames slept on in their tombs unknowing. The two speechless gazers bent themselves down to the earth, as if in prayer, and remained thus a long time, absolutely motionless: the flag continued to wave silently. As soon as they had strength they arose, joined hands again, and went on."

THE INTERPRETATION
OF DREAMS

SIGMUND FREUD

SIGMUND FREUD, the oldest child of a second marriage of Jacob Freud, the Jewish owner of a small cloth-mill in the little Austrian town of Freiburg, was born on 6 May, 1856. Owing to the changes brought about in weaving by the industrial revolution, in 1860, Jacob Freud moved to Vienna and there set up as a cloth merchant.

Until he was eight Sigmund was taught at home by his father. He was clearly above the average in intelligence, so it came as no surprise to his family that at the end of his first semester at the Sperl High School in Vienna he should be top of his class, and remain there for the next eight years.

When he was fourteen he discovered Kant, and from him was led to the other great German philosophers, Hegel, Fichte and Schopenhauer. For a time he considered becoming a philosopher himself, but he realized that his father's financial circumstances made it necessary for him to adopt a career by which he could support himself, and after some thought he decided upon medicine.

In 1873 he entered the medical faculty of the University of Vienna. For the first two years, however, he found himself in considerable difficulties which arose from his inability to decide which branch of the natural sciences would most completely engage his interest. He wandered from department to department, and might have continued to do so had not a visit to his eldest half-brother, who had emigrated to Manchester, in some inexplicable way put new life into him. He had not long returned to Vienna when he discovered Ernst Brücke.

Brücke, an elderly man and a disciple of Robert Mayer, the famous physicist, whose discoveries relating to the conservation of energy had caused a tremendous sensation in scientific circles, was one of the greatest physiological investigators of his time. In Brücke's laboratory Freud believed that at last he had found what he had been searching for, and for the next six years he carried out research under his master's direction. So immersed did he become that he let the rest of his medical studies slide, and did not qualify until after eight years, instead of the usual five. He might not have done so even then had not Brücke told him bluntly that he had no intention of making him his assistant.

So after qualifying he became an intern at the Vienna General Hospital, and within a short time a junior resident physician. Here in the hospital he came under the influence of one of the leading psychiatrists of the day, Theodore Meynert. Under Brücke he had made a study of the nervous system, and now under Meynert he studied the central nervous system of the human being.

By this time he had become engaged to a cousin, Martha Bernays, and having rightly concluded that his work with Meynert would never lead to a post which would make marriage financially possible, he decided to study nervous diseases. Since there were few specialists in this branch of medicine in Vienna, Freud concluded that by hook or by crook he must go to Paris and study under Jean Charcot, then the greatest living specialist in nervous disorders.

Fortune favoured him, and he was awarded a travelling scholarship which made his plan possible. He studied under Charcot from the autumn of 1885 to the spring of 1886, then returned to Vienna, married and put up his plate as a specialist in nervous diseases.

Very soon Freud found himself in trouble with the more conservative elements of the profession. The Vienna Medical Society scorned the new ideas he had developed under Charcot, while Meynert banned him from his Institute of Central Anatomy because he objected to Freud's use of hypnosis in treatment. There was nothing for him to do, therefore, but withdraw from all academic activity and devote himself completely to his practice.

This proved a blessing in disguise, for though his professional colleagues might exclude him from their ranks, his patients were soon so loud in their praises of his work that within a short time his consulting-rooms were overflowing with neurotics eager to be cured by no matter what treatment so long as it was successful, and this Freud's was certainly proving to be. It was while he was treating these patients that he carried out the experiments which were to be the foundations of his later revolutionary discoveries and theories.

During the first ten years he concentrated on hysteria, and in 1895 published the results of his work in *Studies in Hysteria*, a landmark in the history of medical psychology, for it revealed that there existed an unconscious mind wherein lay the root of nervous illness. The treatment based on this discovery introduced a new medical discipline: psycho-analysis.

Such new concepts were bound to give rise to considerable controversy, but Freud was so convinced that he was right that he determined to carry on with his studies to discover the nature of the mind. Soon he was putting forward even more startling theories than his earlier ones had been.

Among these latest theories were those concerning dreams. When he published *The Interpretation of Dreams* in 1900, the controversy which had formerly raged about him in Vienna became worldwide, and his international reputation was assured.

In the days which might be termed pre-scientific, he began, men had no difficulty in finding an explanation of dreams. When, after waking, they remembered a dream, they regarded it either as a favourable or unfavourable manifestation of daemonic or divine powers. With the development of natural science, however, this earlier mythology was transformed into psychology and then only a small minority of educated people doubted that dreams were the products of the dreamer's own mind.

But from the time that the mythological hypothesis was discarded no new explanation of dreams had been put forward. "The conditions of their origin, their relation to waking mental life, their dependence upon stimuli which force their way upon perception during the state of sleep," all these, and a number of other questions, were in need of an answer, the foremost being the significance of dreams.

An investigation into the significance of dreams inquires, first, into the psychical significance of dreaming, into the relation of dreams to the mental processes and into any biological function dreams may have; while, second, it tries to discover whether dreams can be interpreted, whether the content of individual dreams has a "meaning" such as can be found in other psychical structures.

Having thus set out his problem, and referred to the more recent pronouncements on the nature of dreams by scientists and medical men, Freud points out that popular opinion has taken little heed of scientific judgments in this field, and persists in the belief that dreams have a meaning which relates to the prediction of the future and which can be discovered by some process of interpretation of a content which is often confused and puzzling. The methods of interpretation consist in transferring the content of a dream as it is remembered, either by replacing it piecemeal in accordance with a fixed key, or by replacing the dream as a whole by a certain series of symbols.

Serious-minded people were apt to smile at all this, but one day he was astonished to find that the view of dreams which most nearly approached the truth was not the medical one – that dreams are caused entirely by sensory and somatic stimuli – but the popular one. He had been led to this discovery by applying to dreams a new method of psychological investigation which had proved of great value in the solution of phobias, obsessions, delusions and so on – namely, psycho-analysis. Psychotherapy was the starting-point of the procedure which he used to determine the explanation of dreams.

To demonstrate his method, Freud recounts one of his own dreams, and analyses it by a process of psycho-analysis. This leads him to the introduction of a terminology, the first terms of which are "manifest dream-content" to describe the dream as it is retained in the memory after waking, and "latent dream-content" to describe the relevant material discovered by analysing the dream. He then proceeds to the solution of two problems arising out of this: (1) What is the psychical process which has transferred the latest dream-content into the manifest dream-content, which is known to the dreamer only from memory? (2) What are the motive or motives which have necessitated the transformation? The process which transforms the latent into the manifest dream-content he terms "dream-work". Having established this, he sets out, in the remainder of the work, to discuss the basis not of manifest dream-content, but of the newly discovered latent dream-content.

Dreams can be divided into three categories in respect of the relation between their latent and manifest content. First, those dreams which *make sense* and so can be fitted without difficulty into the content of our mental life. Second, those dreams which make sense in themselves, but which bewilder the dreamer because he cannot fit them into his mental life. Third, those dreams which have neither sense nor intelligibility, which seem *disconnected, confused* and *meaningless*. This is by far the largest of the three categories. Dreams of the first category present no problems at all to the analyst; those of the second, and particularly those of the third, demonstrate the contrast between the manifest and latent dream-content, for here the analyst seems faced with riddles which only disappear after the manifest dream has been replaced by the latent thoughts behind it.

Two important points now emerge. First, some part of the opposition between the manifest and latent dream-content is attributable to wish-fulfilment. Second, dream-work carries out compression or condensation on a large scale. The deeper dream-analysis goes, the more impressive this process appears; every situation in a dream seems to be put together out of two or more impressions or experiences, though there is a common element in all the components. If a common element is not present between the dream-thoughts, the dream-work sets about creating one. The most convenient way of bringing together two dream-thoughts which *prima facie* have nothing in common, is to alter the verbal form of one of them, and thus bring it halfway to meet the other, which may be similarly given a new form of words.

The process of condensation further explains certain constituents of the dream-content which are peculiar to it and are not found in the waking consciousness. These are "collective" and "composite figures" and "composite structures", the latter occurring in immense numbers and put together in an equal variety of ways. The same rules apply to their resolution.

The dream-work constantly represents two *contrary* ideas by the same composite structure. For example, a woman dreamt she saw herself carrying a tall spray of flowers, such as those often depicted in pictures of the Annunciation carried by the Angel. This stood for innocence. On the other hand, the flowers were like white camellias, and stood for the opposite of innocence, as associated with the Lady of the Camellias.

So far, much we have learned about condensation in dreams may be formularized thus: Each element in a dream-content is over-determined by material in the dream-thoughts. It is not derived from a single element, and these elements need not necessarily be closely related to each other in the dream-thoughts themselves. A dream element is the "representation" of all this disparate material in the dream-content.

Condensation, together with the transformation of thoughts into situations ("dramatization"), is the most important and peculiar characteristic of dream-work. But condensation and dramatization alone cannot account for the whole of the impression we gain of the dissimilarity between dream-content and dream-thought. A third factor also operates.

Analysis shows us that manifest dream-content deals with quite different material from latent dream-thoughts. This is only an appearance, for later we find that the whole dream-content is derived from the dream-thoughts, and that almost all the dream-thoughts are represented in the dream-content. Nevertheless, what stands out in the dreams as its essential content must play a very subordinate rôle among the dream-thoughts.

It can be put in this way: In the course of the dream-work the psychical intensity passes from the thoughts and ideas to which it properly belongs, to others which in our judgment have no claim to any such emphasis. No other process, which Freud terms "dream-displacement", conceals the meaning of a dream so much or contributes so much to making the connexion between dream-content and dream-thoughts unrecognizable.

If we unravel dream-displacement by analysis we obtain what appears to be completely trustworthy information about dream-instigators and the connexion of dreams with waking life. By analysis we find that every dream without exception goes back to an impression received during the last few days. The impression which acts as the dream-instigator may be such an important one that we feel no surprise at being concerned with it in the day-time. As a rule, however, if a connexion is to be found between a dream-content and an impression received the previous day, it is usually so trivial that we can recall it only with difficulty, and the dream-content seems concerned with trivialities. Analysis corrects this derogatory judgment, and we arrive at the following conclusions: Dreams are *never* concerned with things which we should not think it worth while to be concerned with during the day; and trivialities which do not affect us during the day are unable to pursue us in our sleep.

It is the process of displacement which is chiefly responsible for our being unable to discover or recognize the dream-thoughts in the dream-content, unless we understand the reason for their distortion. Nevertheless, the dream-thoughts are also submitted to another sort of transformation. The manifest content of dreams consists for the most part in pictorial situations, and the dream-thoughts must, therefore, be submitted first to a treatment which will make them suitable for a representation of this kind.

The psychical material of dream-thoughts habitually includes recollections of impressive experiences which are themselves perceived as situations having a visual subject-matter. The dream-situation is often nothing more than a modified repetition of an impressive experience.

But dream-content does not consist entirely of situations; it also includes disconnected fragments of visual images, speeches and even bits of unmodified thoughts. The dream-thoughts arrived at by analysis reveal themselves as a psychical complex of the most intricate possible structure, whose portions represent foreground and background, conditions, digressions and illustrations, chains of evidence and counter-arguments. Each train of thought is almost invariably accompanied by its contradictory counterparts.

Modification into a pictorial form, however, remains the

peculiarity of dream-work. But the heart of the problem lies in displacement, which is quite the most striking of the special achievements of dream-work, and if we enter deeply into the subject we begin to realize that the essential determining condition of displacement is a purely psychological one, something akin to *motive*, which more often than not is one of *repression*. Thus we are led to the concept of a "dream-distortion", which is the product of the dream-work and serves the purpose of disguise.

We are now in a position to express in general terms the principal findings to which analysis of dreams has led us. Dreams fall into three classes according to their attitude to wish-fulfilment: first, those which represent unrepressed wishes undisguisedly; second, dreams which express a repressed wish disguisedly; third, dreams which represent a repressed wish, but do so with insufficient or no disguise.

Freud now deals at some length with the psychology of repression, going with considerable detail into the dream-distortion which accompanies disguised "sexual dreams". This leads him to a discussion of dream-symbols, and finally concludes with an indication of the direction in which his exposition of dream-work calls for pursuit, maintaining that his work in this field is incomplete and must remain so "until analysis has clarified the origin of other psycho-pathological structures, such as hysterical symptoms and obsessional ideas".

This résumé of *The Interpretation of Dreams* perforce can give no indication of the true nature of that epoch-making and formidable work, which contains an accumulation of detailed observations, and above all the discussion of the bearing of Freud's study of dreams upon our understanding of the whole structure and functioning of the human mind. This was the great significance of the work; for out of Freud's efforts to understand the mind has emerged the modern view that insanity is a sickness no different from any other, and is as capable of treatment as any other.

KIM

RUDYARD KIPLING

RUDYARD KIPLING was born in Bombay in 1865, of English parents, and spent his early years in India, where his father, John Lockwood Kipling, an artist of considerable ability, was curator of the Lahore Museum from 1875 to 1893. After going to school in England, young Kipling returned to India at the age of eighteen and became a journalist, making a great study of native Indian life as well as of British officials and soldiers.

In 1886, when he was twenty-one, he published two volumes of light satirical verses, and followed them in 1887 with *Plain Tales from the Hills*, a collection of his journalistic articles. Six slim volumes followed which were a continuation of the *Plain Tales*, which had been a great success in India. He was immediately recognized as a new master of fiction, and by the time he was twenty-four he was famous. He returned to England via China, Japan and America in 1889 to find himself a literary figure.

He remained so until the end of his life, during which he produced a large number of short stories and verses. He spent some time in South Africa, where he became affected by a type of imperialism which did not have a good effect upon his writings. He lived the last part of his life in Sussex and died in 1936.

Kim was published in 1901. It was his second novel and his last tale of India. It has always been immensely popular, and many believe it to be his best work.

Kim started life as a street arab in Lahore. His father was Kimball O'Hara, a colour-sergeant in the Mavericks (an Irish regiment stationed in India), who married a nursemaid in a colonel's family. His wife died of cholera, after Kim's birth, and O'Hara took to drink and then opium which killed him. Kim, looked after by a woman of doubtful repute, ran wild in the streets of Lahore. He was as brown as many of the other boys in the bazaar, but he was white, and to prove it he carried around his neck a leather amulet case containing his birth certificate and his father's papers.

Kim was known as the Friend of the Stars who is the Friend of all the World, and before he had reached his teens he was wise in the ways of the world he lived in. Among his friends was Mahbub Ali, a well-known horse-dealer from beyond the Passes of the North, who travelled the British India of the 1890s and who was, unknown to Kim, a secret agent for the Indian Government.

One day when he was playing under the great gun Zam-Zammah near the Lahore Museum, Kim encountered a man such as he, with his great knowledge of the people of the Indian bazaars, had never seen before. Tall, stately and very old, he had the air and the accoutrements of a holy man, which indeed he was – a Tibetan Lama who was on a pilgrimage to the places in India where the sacred foot of Buddha had trod. In particular the Lama wished to find the River of the Arrow, which sprang from the place where the arrow of Buddha had fallen. This river washes away all taint of sin from those who bathe in it.

Kim became the Lama's disciple and offered to go with him on the pilgrimage to Benares to find the River of the Arrow. Kim, though fascinated by the Holy One, was at first cynical about the project, and indeed thought the Lama quite mad, but he was tired of Lahore and was eager to see the world. Besides, travelling with a Lama offered great advantages, for holy men were treated with great deference in India.

They were to leave in the morning on the pilgrimage, and Kim promised he could arrange a comfortable night's lodging for them. He took the Lama to Mahbub Ali who was staying with his caravan of horses and attendants at the Kashmir Serai, a kind of inn for travellers. Mahbub Ali was more than interested in Kim's journey with the Lama, and not only gave Kim and his revered companion bed and shelter for the night and some rupees to help them on their way, but he also entrusted Kim, whom he had known since a child, with a package to deliver to an Englishman in Umballa. Kim did not know that the package contained news of trouble being planned on the North-West frontier.

Before dawn Kim and the Lama were up and on the train to Umballa. In the crowded carriage the Lama was a venerable curiosity among the colourful passengers, and Kim enjoyed the hospitality which was lavished upon him and which he as the Holy Man's disciple shared.

At Umballa Kim delivered Mahbub Ali's package of papers to an Intelligence officer of the Indian Army, and, with his usual curiosity, remained behind to spy. He overheard the officer discussing the message with his Commander-in-Chief, upon whom it made a great mpression. Leave was to be cancelled, and the Pindi and Peshawar Brigades mobilized for action at once. Kim listened wonderingly to his momentous news, and then returned to the Lama at the house of one of the passengers on the train who had offered hospitality to the Holy Man and his disciple.

The local priest was invited to meet the venerable guest, and after earned discussion, the priest read the horoscope of the Lama's disciple. He told Kim that his future was ominously linked with "a red and angry sign of war", and that his destiny lay where a red bull would be found in a green field.

The next day Kim and the Lama left Umballa, laden with gifts and continued their search. Kim himself had a search now, as well as the Lama – for the red bull on the green field. Kim rapidly gained the respect of the Holy Man, who remarked of him, "He is not altogether of this world," meaning that Kim possessed spiritual qualities as well as very practical ones, for without the boy's worldly knowledge, the old man's journey would have been impossible. Kim skilfully protected him from cheats and robbers, and a great bond grew between them as they continued their marvellous journey. "Art thou spirit or imp?" asked the ancient philosopher after another of Kim's clever tricks to get them out of trouble.

And so mile after mile they walked along India's Grand Trunk Road, the Lama in silent meditation, Kim, bright-eyed, taking in everything on this "broad smiling river of life" as it flowed colourfully along the road, the endless stream of travellers providing a fascinating panorama of nineteenth-century India.

They spent the first night at a *parao*, a communal resting place. In this busy caravanserai they met a wealthy and rather formidable old lady who was travelling south with her retinue. This lady – the Sahiba – took a great interest in the Lama and his young disciple and they all travelled on together. Kim in particular was fascinated by the Sahiba, with her magnificent command of invective.

While on the road, Kim and the Lama – always looking for the River of the Arrow – made a detour and came across a camp of English soldiers. When Kim saw the regimental flag hoisted, he knew that he had reached the end of his search, for upon the flag was a red bull against a background of Irish green. That night Kim and the Lama returned to watch. Kim went on the prowl and was caught by the padre, and searched. When the padre examined the amulet case around Kim's neck which contained his father's papers with proof that he was not native but white, and that his father was a Mason to boot, there was no question of permitting Kim to go. He must be sent to the Masons' Orphanage. Kim was in agony and the Lama desolate. But there was nothing that either of them could do about it. They were faced with authority which they could not challenge. The Lama went on his way sorrowfully, knowing in his wise old heart that it was best for Kim to be among his own people.

And so Kim was thrust into a hot uncomfortable uniform and made to stay with the Mavericks. He was supremely unhappy, though his spirit was unsubdued. When the regiment started on the move, Kim told them they were going to war. They laughed at him until, suddenly, orders came through for them to go north ready for action.

Kim was left behind with the non-combatants and made to go to the military school. He was miserable and found it strangely lonely among his fellow whites whose ways he could not understand, and whose talk he found crude. He managed to send a message to Mahbub Ali, imploring his help.

Meanwhile the Lama had reached Benares and sent a letter offering to pay handsomely for Kim's education, much to the wonder of Kim and the priest, Father Victor. An order on one of India's best-known banks for the first year's fees quickly followed, and Father Victor arranged for Kim to go to St. Xavier's School at Lucknow.

Mahbub answered Kim's appeal, but would do nothing to help him get his freedom to go back to the gay and colourful life of the road. He must go to school, said Mahbub, and he introduced Kim to Colonel Creighton, an important officer in Indian Intelligence who was so impressed by the boy's extraordinary talents that he promised him a position in the Service after he had been to school.

Kim, greatly touched at what his friend the Lama had done for him, now went willingly to St. Xavier's which was a school for Anglo-Indians, and here Kim found himself quite at home, for the boys were more like him than the dull-witted oafs of the military school, with their very limited hard-swearing vocabularies. Kim's keen young brain quickly assimilated the learning which was necessary if he was to do anything with his life.

During the long summer holidays plans were made for him to return to the military barracks of the Mavericks, but this Kim would not have at any price. He just disappeared at term-end and took to the road.

Once more he fell in with Mahbub Ali, who was on one of his journeys of combined horse-trading and espionage in north-west India. Kim overheard a plot to kill Mahbub, warned him in time and thus saved his life.

During this memorable and exciting summer holiday he went to Simla to meet another colourful member of the Secret Service, Lurgan Sahib, who kept a shop of curiosities and precious stones. Here Kim saw many strange and mysterious things. He also met Hurree Babu, agent R.17, who was impressed by Kim's promise as a future member of the silent and Secret Service of India.

Kim's education at St. Xavier's proceeded and he did well, passing an examination in surveying, in between his happy vagabonding holidays on the Indian roads with Mahbub when horse-trading, espionage and military surveying were excitingly combined.

When he was sixteen Kim left St. Xavier's and began his life's work in the Secret Service. He returned eagerly to the Lama, to whom he was eternally devoted, and who was still engaged in his quest for the River of the Arrow.

Kim's final adventure involved Hurree Babu, who was on the trail of Russian agents, making military plans to set the North-West frontier aflame in the interests of the enemies of the Raj. The Lama, who had no knowledge of what was really going on, wished to return to the high hills, and Kim went with him as his disciple into the Himalayas. Kim planned to meet Hurree Babu who had already encountered the two spies from Russia, whose knapsacks were full of plans and drawings for the realization of the Russian campaign.

But the two foreigners were insufficiently informed about the country which they had been sent to spy upon. When they encountered Kim and the Lama, they treated the holy man with great disrespect, and went so far as to assault him and damage his sacred Chart of the Wheel which they tried to take from him. Horrified at such appalling sacrilege, their porters turned upon the Russians, and in the mêlée that followed Kim and Babu relieved the spies of all the plans and maps they had made, as well as secret letters and documents of great value to English Intelligence.

The experience was a violent shock to the venerable old Lama. He became ill and resolved to return to the plains to continue his search for the River of the Arrow. He was taken on a litter. The journey was such a tax upon Kim's strength, for he would not leave the old man, that he himself fell sick.

So they finally returned to the house of the kindly and hospitable Sahiba, who soon restored Kim to health by her devoted nursing. Here too the Lama came to the end of his search and found that the River of the Arrow flowed close by the house of the good Sahiba.

Kipling, though one of the most successful and popular authors of his day, was never a favourite with the critics, and his association with the type of imperialism of which Britain is no longer proud, has thrown nearly everything that he wrote into eclipse.

This is a grave injustice to such a work as *Kim*, in which there is none of the imperialism which we find so reprehensible today. Indeed the thing which stands out most in *Kim* is Kipling's deep love and understanding of the native Indians and their ways, and his undisguised scorn for most of the English, particularly Her Majesty's soldiery. His story, it is true, supports the *status quo* as it existed in the India of the 1890s, but his real hero, apart from Kim, the Lama, does not recognize the colour of a man's skin, but only the good and evil in him. A true sympathy and understanding of the races of differing colour, creed, customs and culture is something which all people today who have the love of humanity at heart wish to acquire. Kipling certainly had it. It shines like a beacon through the pages of *Kim*.

Kim is probably Kipling's best work and shows his genius for creating life and colour at its greatest. It also conveys an uncanny sense of strange knowledge. A very special and very complex world is revealed in this book with a breadth of vision and colour which is quite remarkable. It contains an infinite variety of characters, magically brought to life.

Kim himself, best when he is young and uncontaminated by schooling, is the apotheosis of the immortal boy which haunts the soul of every creative writer. His adventures are reminiscent of John Buchan at his best. Buchan once praised Kipling's sense of the subtle continuity of history. Kim is certainly an historical novel. Not to appreciate the genius of the man who created it is to have one foot still in the 1930s.

TYPHOON

JOSEPH CONRAD

JOSEPH CONRAD was born in Podolia in the Ukraine in 1857. His full name was Jósef Teodor Konrad Nalęcz Korzeniowski, and his parents were Polish. His father, a landowner and a man of letters, was deeply involved in the national Polish movement. Imprisonment for their political activities broke the health of both of his parents and young Conrad was orphaned when he was in his teens.

Conrad did not stay long in his homeland. At seventeen he was at Marseilles where he became a sailor, and for two years he served in French ships in the Mediterranean and on the South American coasts. In 1878 he came to Lowestoft and joined the British Merchant Service. He did not speak a word of English, though he spoke French fluently. In a few years he had mastered not only the art of seamanship, but also the English language sufficiently to pass examinations to become an officer in the merchant service.

He said that he never opened an English grammar in his life and denied that he had "mastered" the language, but rather "acquired" it. One has only to open his books to see how complete is his mastery of the language of which he could not speak a word until he was twenty.

In the eighties and nineties he served as an officer in several ships which took him to many parts of the world. In the nineties he began to write and he used his experiences to enrich a number of novels of sea and adventure which received the highest literary praise. He left his last ship, the famous clipper *Torrens*, in 1893, and settled down to a writing career in England. Though he spoke with a heavy foreign accent, he wrote English with an incomparable beauty. Among his most famous sea stories were *The Nigger of the Narcissus* (1897), *Lord Jim* (1900), *Nostromo* (1904) and *Typhoon* (1903). For most of his writing life Conrad lived in Kent and died in 1924, having gained a remarkable success in English letters.

Typhoon is probably the most brilliant and exciting storm-piece ever written. Conrad sets his scene quietly on the steamship *Nan-Shan* which is conveying two hundred Chinese coolies from

Singapore to some port in northern China. The Chinese are labourers returning home after their period of indenture to their native villages. Each man carries his packet of American dollars which he has earned.

The hero of the book is a commonplace, imperturbable sea-dog, Captain MacWhirr, one of Conrad's most successful creations. MacWhirr serves in the China Seas and only rarely goes home to his wife and two children in England, to whom he is almost a complete stranger. He writes long letters to Mrs. MacWhirr recounting his voyages which she reads with a yawn of boredom. "The only secret of her life was her abject terror of the time when her husband would come home to stay for good."

On this voyage from Singapore the cargo is unusual. The coolies live in a large bunker in the forepart of the ship, 'tween decks, and have the use of the foredeck. Captain MacWhirr does not dignify them with the name of passengers, for they are only coolies. Each Chinaman has with him his wooden box containing his meagre possessions and his small hoard of silver dollars.

The *Nan-Shan* ploughs her "vanishing furrow" across the South China Sea with Captain MacWhirr observing the steady fall of the barometer and realizing there is some dirty weather knocking about. The falling of the barometer is accompanied by an oppressive and clammy heat. The air is thick and lifeless. The sun becomes pale and pours down a leaden heat. The sticky oppressiveness affects everyone on board. A long oily swell, gradually becoming swifter and higher, makes the ship roll uncomfortably.

As the sun sets, the menacing rolling increases and dense banks of dark, olive-coloured cloud are seen to the north lying low and motionless upon the sea. Young Jukes, the Chief Mate, writes in the log: "Ship rolling heavily in a high cross swell. Sunset threatening."

After dark the swell increases, the barometer slides down and down the tube. The ship is secured, the coolies battened down for the night in their bunker in the 'tween deck. MacWhirr sits in the chartroom reading a chapter on storms in one of his books. Jukes suggests turning the ship's head into the enormous swell which is becoming more dangerous and uncomfortable every moment. But MacWhirr will not hear of it. "A gale is a gale, Mr. Jukes, and a full-powered steamship has got to face it." He goes to sleep in the chartroom telling Jukes to wake him at the slightest change.

The typhoon hits the *Nan-Shan* so suddenly and with such over-whelming force that Jukes is not able to get to the chartroom immediately. The officers stand on the bridge, holding on for dear life, in utter darkness, their senses blotted out by the battering, yelling wind. The *Nan-Shan*, enveloped from stem to stern in wastes of savage white water, begins "to jerk and plunge as though she had gone mad with fright".

Then at last the real thing comes. "It seemed to explode all round the ship with an overpowering concussion and a rush of great waters as if an immense dam had been blown up to windward. In an instant men lost touch with each other. This is the disintegrating power of a great wind: it isolates one from one's kind."

The typhoon is now at its height, and the only way for the men to communicate is to yell into each other's ears. It is a frightening experience, for none of them has been in a typhoon before. The Second Mate has collapsed in the wheelhouse in panic. Jukes is fighting a dreadful fear, convinced that the ship cannot survive the appalling fury of the storm. The responsibility lies on the shoulders of one man, MacWhirr, taciturn, obstinate and imperturbable.

"Will she live through this?" Jukes screams in his Captain's ears.

"She may."

The shock of the typhoon is so overwhelming that the ship's company only gradually recover from its stunning effect. Already the senseless fury of the storm has looted the ship of deck fittings, lifeboats and handrails. At any moment the steering gear would give way, the engines stop and the *Nan-Shan* would bury herself for the last time in the mountainous seas which assail her on every side. Jukes already perceives in her motion "the ominous sign of haphazard foundering. She was no longer struggling intelligently." He thinks it is the beginning of the end.

The boatswain manages to claw his way on to the bridge and yell in the Captain's ear that the Chinamen are fighting in the 'tween deck. MacWhirr sends Jukes to investigate.

With the decks of the *Nan-Shan* untenable and constantly awash with furious white water, Jukes and the boatswain crawl through the guts of the dark, madly rolling ship, with everything movable, including men, being hurled about in every direction. Eventually Jukes reaches the 'tween deck where the coolies are battened down and unable to get out. He sees a milling mass of terrified, yelling men. Some are fighting, some are being hurled backwards and forwards, helpless and bleeding, with the crazy motions of the ship, while others, clinging like flies to the hatchway ladder, are madly hammering at the battened hatch to try to get out. As the ship heels over, the coolies fall off the ladder like flies in tumbled screaming heaps. It is a nightmare scene.

In the engine-room Solomon Rout, the Chief Engineer, and his men are working desperately at the job of "coaxing the distracted ship over the fury of the waves" by controlling the speed of the engines as the ship bucks, rises and falls.

Jukes crawls into the engine-room and reports to MacWhirr on the bridge through the speaking tube. It is disaster in the Chinamen's quarters, he says. Some of them must already be dead. They will just go on fighting.

In the middle of this shouted conversation with his first mate, MacWhirr turns his eyes toward the bows of his ship and then leaps to the engine-room telegraph and rings to stop the engines. He has seen "a line of white foam coming on at such a height that he couldn't believe his eyes – nobody was to know the steepness of that sea and the awful depth of the hollow the hurricane had scooped out behind the running wall of water". This mountain of water races toward the *Nan-Shan*, which lifts her bows and leaps. This is the most terrifying moment of all. Swept from end to end with tons of water, the *Nan-Shan* crests the monstrous sea and then dives down the precipice beyond – "as if going over the edge of the world".

The ship finally lifts again, and Jukes resumes his talk with the Captain on the speaking tube, expecting to be told that everything must have been swept away in that enormous sea, the steering gear gone, the ship on the point of foundering. But MacWhirr just tells him in a calm voice to go to the 'tween deck and pick up those dollars.

Jukes is astonished, but he obeys. He rounds up the hands and they go in among the Chinese. Jukes stops the fight, rescues the money, rigs up lifelines for the coolies and then returns to the bridge.

They are in the eye of the typhoon, where it is dead calm, except for the sea which leaps up wildly in peaked mounds all around the ship as it "wallowed heavily at the bottom of a circular cistern of clouds". The barometer is lower than ever, and MacWhirr knows that the worst is yet to come.

"She will be smothered and swept for hours," says MacWhirr. "We must trust her to go through it and come out on the other side. That's plain and straight."

In the murmuring darkness they hear the distant shout of the typhoon racing toward them once more, "like the chant of a tramping multitude".

Days later the *Nan-Shan* arrives in the Chinese port of Fu-chau looking as though she had "been used as a running target for the secondary batteries of a cruiser".

What had happened is told in the various letters written home by the Captain and his officers. Mrs. MacWhirr only glances through hers and does not trouble to read the paragraph which tells her that between the hours of four and six on Christmas Day morning, her husband did not think that his ship could possibly survive another hour in such a sea, and that he would never see his wife and children again.

It is Jukes who tells about the incident of the Chinese coolies to a friend in the Western Ocean trade. He says that getting the dollars away from the coolies was a perilous job, because the Chinese obviously thought the white devils had come to rob them and if they had not been in such a state of terror he and the crew would have been massacred. When the storm died down the situation became very awkward, and he was all for keeping them under the hatches until they got to port, for letting them out when they believed they had been robbed would be extremely dangerous.

But MacWhirr thought differently, wrote Jukes. He let the coolies out, and a sorry lot they were, for they had had a terrible time and many of them were seriously injured. MacWhirr just lined them all up and divided the dollars equally between them. There were three dollars left over, and these were given to the three most damaged coolies, and everyone was happy.

Typhoon is a magnificent piece of descriptive writing. The tremendous storm is viewed from various angles. First it is seen from the bridge in the first shock of its terrible coming, the fear, the urgency, the sense of helplessness being vividly conveyed. The storm itself is seen, heard and felt in passages of great verbal beauty. Then the typhoon is viewed from below decks – the nightmare scene in the coolies' quarters, the desperate, purposeful efficiency in the engine-room, the wild figures stoking the furnaces in the lurching hold amid the hurtling coals.

Conrad gives a complete picture and tells a story which he first heard as a legend when he sailed the China Seas in the 1890s of a human conflict on board a ship at a moment of deadly peril from the elements.

Captain MacWhirr is a noble creation, a remarkable man of the sea who drove the *Nan-Shan* through the typhoon by the sheer force of his character and in defiance of the textbooks which he studied in his chartroom as the barometer ominously tumbled lower and lower. "MacWhirr is not an acquaintance of a few hours, or a few weeks, or a few months," writes Conrad in his Note on the book. "He is the product of twenty years of life. My own life. Conscious invention had little to do with him. It is true that Captain MacWhirr never walked and breathed on this earth (which I find for my part extremely difficult to believe). I can also assure my readers that he is perfectly authentic."

Conrad was a remarkable cosmopolitan writer whose adolescent language was Polish, who graduated in French, and did not begin the study and practice of English until his maturity. He delights in the use of words, and produces some remarkable effects which are poetically vivid.

He was a slow writer whose day's work was sometimes no more than a few sentences. But each sentence was fashioned with great care and with scrupulous avoidance of cliché. He has an irresistible style which carries the reader on with a clean vigorous rhythm which sometimes becomes sheer music.

THE FORSYTE SAGA

JOHN GALSWORTHY

MEET THE Forsytes! Here they all are, or all of them that matter, male and female, old, middle-aged and young, assembled on this afternoon of 15 June, 1886, in the drawing-room of Mr. Jolyon Forsyte's house in Stanhope Gate, Hyde Park.

Such meetings as this are a regular thing among the Forsytes when one of the family gets engaged, or married, or is born, and doubtless there will be one when a Forsyte dies. But up to now none of the Forsytes *has* died. Dying is against Forsyte principles. They are tough and tenacious, with the keenest sense of property, and they hold on to what they have got – money and houses and land and their women – and not least to life itself. The older members have lived so long that they might be excused for thinking that death has forgotten them. There they are mistaken, however. The oldest in this family gathering – Aunt Ann sitting over there in the corner: she was born in 1799 and remembers her father when he was still working his way up from stonemason to master builder – she has only a few more weeks left to her, for her knitting and reading and just quiet sitting. But at present there are no gaps in the family circle, and it must be admitted that the Forsytes make a formidable showing.

That man over against the piano, with a shaven, square old face the colour of pale leather, and wearing two waistcoats on his portly chest, is Uncle Swithin, formerly in the land and estate business. Near the window is his twin brother, Uncle James, senior partner in a highly esteemed firm of City solicitors; he is over six feet, but as lean as his brother is stout. Their elder brother Jolyon – Old Jolyon as he is called to distinguish him from his son Young Jolyon – calls them the fat and the lean. Seated in a row together are the three Forsyte old ladies, Aunts Ann, Hester and Juley, who for many years past have been living with their brother Timothy in his house on the Bayswater Road. Uncle Roger (he collects house property) and Uncle Nicholas (he puts his trust in mines and railways) are also here, and there in the middle of the room, under the chandelier as becomes a host, is the head of the family, Old Jolyon himself. He is

eighty, but bears himself well; and with his fine white hair, his little
dark grey eyes, and immense white moustache spreading below his
strong jaw, he has a patriarchal appearance and seems as though he
has learnt the secret of perennial youth. He is a strong character in
every way, but with his strength he combines a kindliness and a
sense of generosity that most of the Forsytes lack.

The present occasion of the Forsyte assembling is an "at home" to
celebrate the engagement of Miss June Forsyte, Old Jolyon's grand-
daughter, to that rising young architect Philip Bosinney. June is
seventeen, and the youngest one there; her parents have been long
separated – that is why Young Jolyon is not here this afternoon – and
since babyhood she has been Old Jolyon's ward and he has made her
his heiress. "A little bit of a thing," someone has described her, "all
hair and spirit," with fearless blue eyes, a firm jaw and a bright
colour and a crown of red-gold hair. Her function in life, as she sees
it, is to help lame dogs over stiles, and this goes a long way to explaining why she should have chosen this Bosinney, who is reputed to
have the most extraordinary ideas about architecture and no money
to speak of. He has also a strange taste in hats. There is a story going
round Forsyte Change that he paid his duty call on the Aunts wearing a soft, grey hat – a dusty thing with a shapeless crown – and
Aunt Hester, who is very shortsighted, seeing this hat on the chair
in their hall, shooed it off, mistaking it for a strange cat. . . .

George Forsyte, when the tale came round to him, grinned.
"Very haughty!" he remarked, thinking it likely that Bosinney had
worn the hat deliberately as a kind of practical joke at the expense of
the stuffy Forsytes, "the wild Buccaneer!" The name has stuck, and
indeed, Bosinney – just look at him now, standing talking with June
in the doorway – does look a bit of a pirate, with his untidy hair and
clothes that have the appearance of having been flung on anyhow.
Clearly he is most sadly deficient in that most cherished and typical
of Forsyte qualities, the sense of property, and it is feared that he will
prove as regardless of other people's property as of his own. But
little June thinks him the most wonderful fellow in the whole wide
world.

Two more of the Forsyte assembly remain to be introduced, and
they are the most important by far in the story that is to be told. One
is a woman, "a tall woman, with a beautiful figure, which some
member of the family once compared to a heathen goddess". Her
hands, gloved in French grey, are crossed one over the other. She is
holding her grave, charming face to one side, and the eyes of all the
men near her are fastened on it. Her figure sways, so balanced that

ie very air seems to set it moving. There is warmth in her cheeks,
ut little colour, and her eyes are dark and soft. But it is her lips that
ien look at most – sensitive lips they are, sensuous and sweet, and
irough them there seems to come warmth and perfume like the
armth and perfume of a flower. This lady – this young lady, for she
only twenty-three or four – is Mrs. Irene Forsyte, and has not long
een married. And there, following her about with his eyes, is her
usband – Soames Forsyte, only son of James and partner with him
the firm of solicitors; he is in his early thirties, "flat-shouldered,
at-cheeked, flat-waisted, yet with something round and secret
oout his whole appearance". He is a Forsyte of the Forsytes so far
the instinct for property goes and already a rich man, but there is
strong blend in his make-up of the connoisseur with his sense of
ossession.

These two, Soames and Irene, are at the heart and core of the
orsyte story: there would have been no *Saga* without them.

The Forsyte Saga comprises three novels – *The Man of Property*,
ublished in 1906, *In Chancery* (1920) and *To Let* (1921), and in
etween the first and second volumes of the trilogy is an interlude,
idian Summer of a Forsyte (1918). They were all republished to-
ether in one volume as *The Forsyte Saga* in 1922, by which time they
id become generally accepted as an incomparably exact and inti-
iate portrait of British upper middle-class society from the end of
ie 1880s to the 1920s.

Not that John Galsworthy had any such impressive end in view
hen he first set about the Forsyte story. *The Man of Property* was
inceived as a single work, and he wrote a number of novels and
lays before he returned to the Forsyte theme. And then it was
ecause, as he put it, "people wanted to hear some more about the
orsytes" – and what better reason could be given? So it came about
iat in the *Saga* the Forsytes are preserved for all time, with all their
enerally narrow sympathies but indomitable perseverance, their
isplay of the most commonly accepted prudential virtues and their
most fierce possessiveness, their relentless pursuit of a good profit,
id their determination to hold on to what they have got. And also
should be said of one or two of them but especially of Soames, an
ppreciation of something that money can seldom buy and still less
ften hold – Beauty.

That is what led Soames Forsyte to marry Irene Heron, the only
iild of an impecunious professor. He had never met a woman before
ho was so capable of inspiring affection, and for eighteen months

he pursued her with typically Forsytean tenacity before she at lengt
agreed to marry him. Very soon he was asking himself, "Why di
she marry me?", and if he was slow to admit it the reader may b
excused for suspecting that the reason was the not very complimen
tary one that she was tired of her home surroundings of gente
poverty and longed to have a home of her own. He gave her every
thing – or what he thought was everything: a fine house, money
clothes, jewels, servants, carriages, expensive holidays – he denie
her nothing. And yet she was soon treating him with something th
was too deeply felt to constitute indifference, a dislike that turned t
aversion and eventually to hatred. Perhaps today we might describ
it as sexual repugnance.

Very largely it was to provide his wife with something to intere
her that Soames decided to build a house in the country, at Robi
Hill on the northern edge of the Surrey countryside, from where o
a clear day you could see the grandstand at Epsom. (We may identif
the site as being on the Coombe hills overlooking Malden, whe
Galsworthy's father – the original of Old Jolyon – developed
housing estate in the 1870s.) At his cousin June's instigation, th
architect Soames appointed for what was a first-class commissio
was Philip Bosinney, and almost from the first there was trouble
Financial trouble – for Bosinney was always exceeding the limits th
Soames put on the expenditure, and later, personal trouble, for Iren
and Bosinney, being thrown much together, became involved in
shattering love affair. Soames heard whispers, and more tha
whispers, of what was afoot, and very likely it was not only a
offended business sense that induced him to take legal action again
Bosinney for having overstepped the financial limits that he had la
down. The case of Forsyte v. Bosinney was tried on a foggy No
vember day in 1887, and the verdict was, inevitably, in Soames
favour. Bosinney was not in court. The day before he had had wha
turned out to be his final interview with Irene, in the course of whic
she had allowed him to know that her husband had found her bed
room door unlocked and, as Galsworthy ironically puts it, had "a
last asserted his rights and acted like a man". In a mad fury of rag
and sexual jealousy Bosinney had then rushed out into the fog
bound streets and had been knocked down by a cab and killed.

From beginning to end of the novel Galsworthy's sympathies ar
very obviously with Irene, and the dispassionate reader may some
times wonder why. Soames may not be an endearing character, bu
he loved his wife in a way that was none the less sincere for being s
characteristically proprietorial. He was ready to do everything fo

er and to give her everything, save her freedom. As for Irene, she
ad made a bargain and, having made it, refused to keep her part in
. One of Galsworthy's contemporary novelists, Hugh Walpole,
vas so disgusted with her conduct that he described it as being from
rst to last that of a female cad. But Galsworthy did not see it in this
ght, for the excellent reason that he was by no means a dispassion-
te observer. For the original of Irene Forsyte was Mrs. Ada Gals-
vorthy, the wife of his cousin, Major Arthur George Galsworthy,
vith whom he was for a number of years on intimate terms until at
ength, in 1905, her husband secured a divorce and she and John
Galsworthy were married. Her influence on him was profound,
efore their marriage and after; it was she, indeed, who first realized
hat he had within him the makings of an author and encouraged
im to write. On one of their holidays together, in the very early
ays of their relationship, they were standing at a bookstall in the
Gare du Nord in Paris when she murmured to him, "You are just
he person to write; why don't you?"

But though Ada Galsworthy was the original of Irene Forsyte, the
man who was her husband was not the original of Soames. All who
vere in the best position to know Major Galsworthy were insistent
hat there was absolutely nothing in his composition of the hard,
omineering and possessive male.

Irene (it has been objected) never really does anything much save
ook beautiful; and for this she was amply rewarded. After her first
isastrous marriage she was treated by Fate, and the Forsytes,
emarkably well. She left Soames of course, but he refrained from
roceeding against her for a divorce. She had a small income of her
wn and kept herself afloat by music-teaching; and then, as we are
old in the *Indian Summer* interlude, she became the protégée of old
Uncle Jolyon, who was so appreciative of her companionship of a
w weeks, and of her beauty, that he left her £15,000 in his will.
This was in 1892, and she lived very comfortably until toward the
nd of the century when Soames, who had become set upon a son
nd heir, pestered her with his renewed attentions. After all, he
eminded her, she was still his wife in the eyes of the law. Feeling
orribly insulted and frightened, she found in Young Jolyon – he
vas now not so young, but in his early fifties, a widower with two
hildren besides June – a tower of strength. He fell in love with her
nd, when Soames now proceeded with his divorce, found himself
n the position of co-respondent. Irene married Jolyon in 1901, and
few months later a son was born to them, also Jolyon but called
on for short.

Meanwhile, what of Soames? In *The Man of Property* Galsworth did his best to make him out an abominable fellow, but in the fou teen years that elapsed between the publication of that novel ar that of *In Chancery* (the title is a reflection of Soames's unhapp marital status), his attitude toward him had mellowed considerabl and as the *Saga* proceeds he becomes more and more understandin so that Soames is revealed as being almost likeable. But his creat never permits him to be really happy.

When in middle life Soames was at length free to marry again h choice fell on Annette, the young and beautiful daughter of a Frenc restaurant proprietor in Soho, who soon made it plain that in h eyes the marriage was one of convenience, after the establishe French pattern. A child was born to them, but it was a girl, ar Annette went through such agonies in the process that the docto made it plain that there could be no more children. Soames receiv the blow with what in anyone else would be described as unflinchir courage, and when he saw the baby for the first time he showed hir self in an unexpected light. " '*Ma petite fleur!*' Annette said softl 'Fleur,' repeated Soames; 'Fleur! We'll call her that.' The sense triumph and renewed possession swelled within him. By God this this thing was *his*!'' (Note that even in this heartfelt moment Gal worthy makes him glory in his possessiveness.)

While Fleur was growing up she was all in all to her father, tl one human creature to whom he gave his heart; compared with h even his collection of pictures – he is revealed as a connoisseur deep understanding, who prided himself, however, on the fact th his choices were always "going up" in the market – was of secondar consideration. With Fleur to love, he could face with almost equan mity the infidelity of his wife, the death of old friends and relation the passing of an age. But Galsworthy shows him no mercy. In *7 Let* he is made to suffer one more ghastly blow, when Fleur fa madly, desperately, in love with Jon, the son of "that woman" ar his cousin Jolyon who had married her and made Robin Hill the home!

Neither Fleur nor Jon knew anything of the feud that had split tl Forsyte clan, except that it existed. But whatever it was, it had a happened a long time ago, and the only thing that mattered was th *they* were in love and were resolved on marrying. Soames migl (such was his love for his daughter) have been got to agree, althoug his love-hate feeling for his ex-wife was as strong as ever. But Jolyc knew full well that for Irene the marriage of her son to Soames daughter would be a death-blow; and so, a few hours before h sudden death through a heart attack, he wrote a letter to his son explaining that Fleur was "the daughter of the man who once owned your mother as a man might own a slave", and by marrying her "you enter the camp which held your mother prisoner and wherein she ate her heart out". Except for the two of them she had no one in the world, and soon she would have only Jon. . . . "Pluck up your spirit, Jon," he urged the boy; "don't break her heart. . . ."

Receiving such an appeal from, as it were, beyond the grave, Jon did indeed break away, but only after a soul-searing struggle. He went off to British Columbia; and Fleur – she married on the rebound bright and breezy young Michael Mont, heir to a baronetcy and a good deal else. And outside the empty shell of the house at Robin Hill they put up the board, "To let".

So *The Forsyte Saga* comes to a conclusion. But this is not the end of the Forsytes; and if you want to know what happened to Soames and the rest you will find it in that second trilogy (*The White Monkey, The Silver Spoon, Swan Song,* grouped under the title of *A Modern Comedy*) that completes John Galsworthy's evocation of a vanished age and people.

THE HISTORY OF MR. POLLY

H. G. WELLS

THE MIND or the heart? When, each day, we make – as make we must – our renewal of faith in ourselves and in mankind, where shall we place our ultimate hope? Each of us takes our Disputatious Choice as Mr. Polly ("who specialized in slang, and the disuse of English") might have said. Choice of either, of course, does not preclude the other. The human heart needs the human mind as its precision tool whereby to create an honourable destiny; the mind without the heart may well create the final arid desert where all is dust, not least the human spirit.

Herbert George Wells, who created Mr. Polly, had both heart and mind in vast degree yet he knew, in spite of the vastness of that mind, that the mind is bounded and that the heart is boundless, closer to the infinite, nearer to those fields of sleep from which we came, sensitive to messages, intimations, hunches – call them what you will – full sometimes of illogical reservations that infuriate the exactness of the mind. When anyone tried being too exact with Mr. Polly, tried too confidently to pin him down, he had the disconcerting habit of murmuring "Lil' Dog. . . ." and wriggling away. *The History of Mr. Polly* is a triumphant tribute to the human heart.

Yet, as we have said, it was written by a man of tremendous mind, who wielded a shining intellect like a rapier to prick the bubbles of stupidity, social dimness, cruelty and deprivation, ignorance, fear and "fear's three crippled brothers: dullness, indolence and appetite"; bubbles that for H. G. Wells festered like foul blisters on the body of what we like to call our civilization.

Born the son of a small shopkeeper in Bromley, Kent, himself for years a draper's assistant, he surveyed the world around him, felt the trappedness of most of mankind, himself included, and had many, many early tries at escaping. "It is an open question in my mind," he said in his Autobiography, "whether this dismay at the outset is the common experience of modern youth of the less fortunate classes, or whether because of the enlightenment of my previous starts I happened to see further and more clearly than most of my fellows. A considerable number, I think, get that caught feeling rather later." Mr. Polly is the eternal embodiment of that "caught feeling" and left it till almost forty before he decided to do something about it. H. G. Wells – not merely due to his previous starts, as he modestly explains it, but due to the driving talent within him – broke away early, spurred by the intensity and breadth of a vision of what life could be for all. He was *born* to "see further and more clearly than most" and all his life he devoted his talent, his skill, his mind and heart, to the task of trying to convey that vision to his fellow man, to make him conscious of the heritage which was his by virtue of the simple, wondrous fact of having been born a human being.

Books on science, economics, world history, wars in space and the shapes of things to come poured from his pen in a lifetime that began in 1866. Yet when he died shortly after the Second World War his last book was sadly called *Mind at the End of its Tether* – a mind, in fact, grown tired, baffled by what seemed man's constant inability to improve his destiny. But it was only the mind; it was Wells the thinker talking. Wells, the artist, had done much better than perhaps he realized. For among other things he had created Mr. Polly, whose history will be read when many other "histories" are lying mildewed on the shelf.

So sit with Mr. Polly on his stile, approaching forty, surveying his life and what had made it – Mr. Polly, his inborn geniality clouded with dyspepsia, trapped in small trade and approaching bankruptcy, enmeshed in matrimony with the wrong woman, "untrained, unwarned, confused, distressed, angry, seeing nothing except that he is nettled in greyness . . . a battle-ground of fermenting foods and warring juices . . . not so much a human being as a civil war . . . miserable with all the misery of a social misfit". In his own words, he'd had his Whack. Beastly home. Beastly Life. "Why had he never insisted on the things he thought beautiful? Never sought them, fought for them, taken any risk for them, died rather than abandon them?" There were good reasons. Therein is the heart-cry of so many Mr. Pollys, so many human beings whose lot is the more poignant because, like him, they feel that at bottom they are not at fault.

Consider first his education. "I remember seeing a picture of Education," said H. G. Wells, "a glorious woman with a wise and fearless face stooping over her children and pointing them to far horizons. She was telling of the great prospect of life that opened before them . . . the joys of skills they might acquire. The education of Mr. Polly did not follow that picture very closely. He went for some time to a National School. He left at fourteen and by that time his mind was in much the same state as you would be if you were operated upon for appendicitis by a well-meaning, boldly enterprising but rather over-worked and under-paid butcher's boy". There, indeed, lies one good reason why so many lives, like Mr. Polly's, are "apathetic and feebly hostile, ugly in detail and mean in scope". He left school, in short, like so many of the world's children "with the nice little curiosities and willingnesses of a child in a jumbled and thwarted condition". In that word "willingnesses" lies the poignancy, the human waste. A pity, for in our children lie each time our hopes and our beginnings.

The history of Mr. Polly from then on until we meet him sitting on his stile is, superficially, easily covered – life as an assistant in the Port Burdock Drapery Bazaar, first in Canterbury, then in Clapham; it was much the same wherever it was, described with the sardonic humour and bitterness that sprang from Wells's own early life and experiences in such cribs as, for the most part in those days, they were. Then came his father's death and, unexpectedly, a little money. Inevitably came marriage – marriage to Cousin Miriam and a little shop at Fishbourne. From the start "sunshine and laughter seemed things lost forever, picnics and shouting in the moonlight". Mr. Polly, true, approached the early days of marriage with determined optimism, even whistling round the shop – till Miriam complained "it went through 'er 'ead". Fifteen years of Fishbourne, then, dominated by "Zealous Commerciality" and dreams darkened by Miriam's cooking. It was more than enough for Mr. Polly sitting on his stile. "Kill myself," he said. "It won't hurt much."

If, up to this point, the story seems a sad one, then one must read it for oneself to restore the balance, discover the humour, the laughter that springs from the conflict between such a destiny and the unassuming courage, the growing refusal to accept that lay in Mr. Polly, full of what someone called "the wavering grace of common men". For Mr. Polly, in spite of trade and Miriam, would stand in front of his hosiery fixtures or, later, his own store and dream, "thinking of perennial picnics under dark olive trees in the everlasting sunshine of Italy". He always believed that beautiful, unexpected things "could and did happen – somewhere. Perhaps they happened south of Guildford, perhaps they happened just around the corner on weekdays when all good Mr. Pollys are safely shut up in shops". Read, too, of that glorious day in the Port Burdock Drapery Bazaar when young Parsons, Mr. Polly's fellow slave, full of "Joy de Vive", faced Mr. Garvace, symbol of respectable oppres-

THE HISTORY OF MR. POLLY

sion, with a bale of cloth at the ready; as the policeman put it later in court: "'e then 'it 'im on the 'ead – 'ard." To Mr. Polly it was like the storming of the Bastille, for he was the kind that did not get rises, he lost situations, "there was something in his eye employers did not like". Mr. Polly was not born to "get on"; he lacked appreciation of "the Shovaceous Cult or Smart Juniors full of Smart Juniosity".

Tears and laughter run very close together in *The History of Mr. Polly*. When his father died, he went for a solitary walk in the evening light, "and as he walked suddenly his dead father became real to him. He thought of things far away down the perspective of memory, of jolly moments when his father had skylarked with a wildly excited little boy." In that is the quiet stab to the heart that Dylan Thomas too expressed when he spoke of a child walking with his mother through the green chapels of childhood.

Yet, in the midst of the funeral, we find ourselves laughing. When Harold Johnson, his cousin, embodiment of all the boring virtues, expressed the opinion that all the relations should be invited. . . . " 'A bit vulturial, isn't it?' said Mr. Polly. A disagreeable feeling spread over his body as though he was blackening as he sat." Aunt Larkins and the girls (including Miriam), embodiment in turn of all female relations presiding over a corpse ("Should 'ave the contents of the stomach examined"), is confronted with old Uncle Pentstemon, picking his teeth. "You here?" he says. "You would be. Have you nailed him down yet? You always was in front of what was needful." But then Uncle Pentstemon had his own definite views on women. As he told Mr. Polly later at his marriage to Miriam: "Prize packets they are and you can't tell what's in 'em till you took 'em 'ome and undone 'em. A man's got to tackle 'em whatever they are. Good or bad, a man's got to tackle 'em."

Mr. Polly had his prize packet in Miriam. "At the sight of the bride Mr. Polly experienced a number of conflicting sensations – alarm, desire, affection, respect – and a queer element of reluctant dislike." Deep down inside him instinct murmured "Lil' dog" but it was too late and he was hooked. And even then at the peak moment of marrying, life was less for Mr. Polly than it might have been, something wonderful was killed at birth: "Pete arf me," said the clergyman, "Take thee Mirum wed wife . . . have hold this day ford . . . betworse . . . richpoo . . . leggo hands gort the ring . . . Pete arf me. . . . Withis ring Ivy wed . . ." Once again for Mr. Polly something that could have been "clothed in white samite, mystic, wonderful" was made to seem like "the momentary vision of an utterly beautiful thing seen through the smoke of a passing train."

So followed fifteen years of Fishbourne, but to the everlasting glory of Mr. Polly "the queer little flower of imagination still lived . . . an insatiable hunger for bright and delightful experiences, for the gracious aspect of things, for beauty". He sought refuge in what Wells called "thou world of books, happy asylum, refreshment and refuge from the world of everyday". He read and read "until his heart ached to see those sun-soaked lands before he died". And then one day it came to him that he would soon be forty – and thus we find him, sitting on his stile, full of sombre doubts and dark, dyspeptic plans. . . .

And, being Mr. Polly, at last he put them into action – well, most of them. The plan was twofold: burn down the shop and cut his throat. He did the first and did it well – so well that half the town was burnt down with it. Then he remembered an old lady who lived upstairs above one of the briskly burning shops and went and rescued her. "It's not what I'm used to," she said as he helped her over the tiles. And all the tradesmen hovering near bankruptcy watched, full of hope and thoughts of insurance. And Mr. Polly became a hero. But when the drama was over, the hero found himself getting ready for bed with Miriam. She, too, was full of thoughts of insurance. "We can easy begin all over again," she said. "H'm," said Mr. Polly. "It dawned on him for the first time that he had forgotten something. He ought to have cut his throat."

He did not cut his throat, however. He took a modest sum, left the rest to Miriam and took to the road, saw sunsets, re-discovered the simplicities of hedgerows, the beauties of his motherland, for no other lands, said Wells, with one of those sudden bursts of poetry, "have so mellow a sunlight nor so diversified a cloudland nor confess the perpetual refreshment of the strong soft winds that blow from off the sea as our Mother England does". And in his wanderings he found the lane, the old school wall where once so long ago in his youth "real romance came out of dreamland into life. And left him." It was only a schoolgirl and an innocent meeting. "Are you lonely?" she had asked. "I was sitting there in melancholy retrospectatiousness," he had answered. "She sat on the wall and all that was best and richest in Mr. Polly's nature broke like a wave and foamed up at that girl's feet and died and never touched her." And one day Mr. Polly had discovered three friends behind the wall listening and the bottom dropped out of his world . . . in complete humiliation he had stumbled and cut his head. . . . "He found his face was wet with blood which was none the less red stuff from the heart because it came from slight abrasions." Now all that was long ago. Mr. Polly surveyed the wall where once a young girl sat. "Was she a countess? Was she a queen? Children? Had sorrow dared to touch her?" Dear Mr. Polly, forever a knight, still seeking. What was it he wanted most in life? He knew the answer: "Fun . . . fun in companionship." Two simple, reasonable gifts to ask, so hard to find along a road we all seem determined to make darker.

But here is the glory of Mr. Polly. In spite of all evidence to the contrary, he *believed* and he persisted. "Deep down in the being of Mr. Polly, deep in that darkness like a creature which has been beaten about the head and left for dead but still lives, crawled a persuasion . . . that somewhere, magically inaccessible perhaps but still somewhere were pure and easy and joyous states of body and mind." And one day he found them. He turned a corner and there was the Potwell Inn. Inside was a woman who maintained that she was Fat but who Mr. Polly insisted was merely Plump. And again it is to the glory of Mr. Polly that he knew it when he saw it. "My sort," he said, and stayed to be barman, ferryman, bottlewasher and general factotum. This was to be his haven, this was where peace lay.

And then, one day, the name of Uncle Jim cropped up and "a mysterious shadow seemed to fall athwart the sunshine and pleasantness of the Potwell Inn". One last great hurdle still lay between Mr. Polly and his sunlit vision, one last lesson to be learnt, one last fierce dragon to be slain – Fear and Terror in the form of Uncle Jim, bully, thief, ex-reform schoolboy, "the Drorback to this place," as the Fat Woman said. "What sort of a size is he?" asked Mr. Polly. "I'm not one of your Herculaceous sort. . . . Nothing very wonderful biceptally." He was soon to know when Uncle Jim met him in the lane and warned him off. "Do I look reformed?" asked Uncle Jim as he stuck his fist beneath Mr. Polly's nose. "I'll make a mess of you . . . I'll do you injuries . . . I'll 'urt you in 'orrible, ugly ways."

Mr. Polly wanted to fly. "Eastward was the wise man's course. Mr. Polly saw himself going along it and tried to see himself going along it with all the self-applause a wise man feels." But Mr. Polly made his answer and of course it is H. G. Wells's answer to all that terrifies, makes ugly, comes between man and the light that he deserves. "He knew that if only he dared to look, the heavens had opened and the clear judgment on his case was written across the sky. He knew as much as a man can know of life. He knew he had to fight or perish. Man comes into life to seek and find his sufficient beauty, to serve it, to win and increase it, to fight for it, to face anything and dare anything for it, counting death as nothing so long as the dying eyes still turn to it." Mr. Polly was frankly terrified. " 'Oh

God, it isn't my affair,' he said, and so saying he turned his face towards the Potwell Inn."

And he vanquished Uncle Jim in his own Mr. Polly-ish way and thereafter the Potwell Inn was "as safe and enclosed and fearless as a child that has still to be born". And he sat in the evening by the river with the Fat Woman. "They were not so much thinking as lost in a smooth still quiet of the mind."

Sometimes they talked and because he had created them it was Herbert George Wells who talked, and if his ghost can read, it should read and find comfort in what he made them say in 1910, so many years before his Mind found Itself at the End of its Tether. "One seems to start in life expecting something. And it doesn't happen. And it doesn't matter. One starts with ideas that things are good and bad – and it hasn't much relation to what *is* good and what *is* bad . . . I've always been the Skeptaceous sort. . . ." That goes for brave new worlds and plans for Modern States. The Mind at the End of its Tether never lived to see the Modern State that it had done so much to fight for. "And it doesn't happen." One wants to repeat to H. G.'s ghost to comfort one who did so much: "And it doesn't matter." Wells spent the first fifty years of his life in a climate where it was possible to believe (with good reason) in swift social progress – the world of William Morris, Fabianism, Shaw. In the broad field of spreading enlightenment Wells did his stint and more . . . more than perhaps even he realized: "The larger part of my fiction was written lightly and with a certain haste," he said. "Only one or two of my novels deal primarily with personality and then rather in the spirit of the caricature-portrait. I doubt if Mr. Polly or these other persons have that sort of vitality which endures into new social phases. In the course of a few decades they may become incomprehensible."

Which goes to show how gloriously wrong the Mind can be. Mr. Polly has endured and will endure into new social phases and in a darkening world he becomes even more comprehensible. A caricature is larger than life and that is precisely the whole heart and meaning of Mr. Polly; his *belief* is the truth and what life is to so many is the caricature. For life will never be so large that the human heart will not dream to make it larger and that is why Mr. Polly will go marching on, caught forever in a kind of sunlit magic, meeting fate and fighting it, unassuming, greeting disaster with "Righto O' Man", dodging the moralizers and those with ready answers, too quick solutions with a muttered "Lil' Dog. . . ."

For *The History of Mr. Polly* is Wells the artist crying from the dark for those who cannot speak, full of quiet fury for their lot. And the cry will go on ringing, bursting with compassion yet shot with laughter, long after many, many minds have reached the end of their tether. Let Wells the thinker take consolation from Wells the story-teller and rest easy as he listens to his own immortal Mr. Polly seated forever outside the Potwell Inn: "It isn't what we try to get we get, it isn't the good we think we do is good. . . . There's a sort of char-acter people like and stand up for and a sort they won't." In Litera-ture as in Life, that goes for people, be it Mr. Polly on the one hand or, on the other, Uncle Jim or Adolf Hitler in whatever form he comes.

SONS AND LOVERS

D. H. LAWRENCE

"IF MY mother had lived, I could not have loved you, for she would never have let me go." These words spoken by D. H. Lawrence to his wife Frieda reveal to the full the nature of the relationship between Mrs. Lawrence and her son that only her death was to break.

Mrs. Lawrence had been a schoolteacher before her marriage to the gay, handsome young collier she had met at a party. She was refined, high-principled, deeply religious; he, barely literate, was easy-going, coarse in his ways, and fond of a glass. Totally unfitted to be a miner's wife, Lydia Lawrence soon lost her love for him.

David Herbert, the fourth of the five Lawrence children, was born on 11 September, 1885, in a mean brick house in Eastwood, a few miles from Nottingham. When he was two, the family moved to an even meaner home in The Breach – The Bottoms of *Sons and Lovers* – the mining settlement in the hollow below the town. Sickened by the squalid life, Mrs. Lawrence, a woman of indomitable will, vowed to herself that her sons should never follow their father down the pit. William Ernest, who was approaching the school-leaving age, became her first care, and unconsciously she transferred to him the passionate love she had once felt for her husband. Ernest was a clever boy, and her hopes for him were realized when he obtained a clerical job with good prospects.

Of all the Lawrence children, David, delicate and sensitive, most closely resembled his mother in temperament. He had inherited her love of natural beauty, and as well as a gift for words he had a talent for painting. From the local Board School he won a scholarship to Nottingham High School where he stayed for three years, thanks to Mrs. Lawrence's stubborn self-sacrifice. He did not distinguish himself in any particular way though he managed to win a prize for mathematics; when he was fourteen he left, and found himself a job in Nottingham with Haywood's, a firm manufacturing surgical appliances. It was shortly after he had started work that he met Jessie Chambers.

Jessie, the Miriam of *Sons and Lovers*, was a year younger than himself, a dreamy, dark-haired girl who shared his love of books and art. He became a frequent visitor at her father's farm where they would read poetry together in a corner of the kitchen or go for long walks through the beautiful countryside. It was Jessie who first awakened in him the desire to write, and it was to Jessie that he brought his first attempts at verse. Stimulated by her praise and encouragement, he began to try his hand at short stories.

Ernest died suddenly at the outset of a promising career in London, and David himself fell critically ill with pneumonia. (He was to die of tuberculosis at forty-five.) His mother nursed him back to health, and from then on he became the centre of her fierce, all-possessive love.

Young Lawrence never returned to Haywood's, for after his recovery he was given the opportunity to train as a pupil-teacher. The first part of the course was held in Eastwood.

The boy and girl idyll of David and Jessie did not ripen into lasting love. Lawrence's reasons for its failure to mature are recorded in Sons and Lovers, reasons very different from those given by Jessie in the memoir she wrote of him. According to her, she could never get close to him because of his mother, and she further averred that at this period of his life Lawrence was afraid of sex. As we know from Lawrence's words to Frieda, she was right on the first count; in all probability, she was equally right on the second.

Jessie herself was training to be a teacher, and although Lawrence was no longer emotionally involved with her, he continued to value her friendship. While he was at Nottingham University studying for his diploma, he fancied himself in love more than once; he even became engaged to one girl, but this affair, like the others, soon petered out.

Lawrence obtained his diploma, and started to teach at the Davidson Road School in Croydon in 1909. It was a memorable year for him; through Jessie, who had sent a batch of his poems to The English Review, he saw his name in print for the first time, and a month or two later the novel he had written, The White Peacock, was accepted by Heinemann's.

In 1910, Lawrence learnt that his mother was dying of cancer. He implored Heinemann's to print his book, and although The White Peacock was not published till 1911, he was able to put a copy into her hand a few days before her death. As Lawrence looked at her for the last time: "the world began to dissolve around me, beautiful, iridescent, but passing away. Till I almost dissolved myself, and became very ill. . . ." Weakened by grief, he went down with a second attack of pneumonia.

During his convalescence, he finished his second novel, *The Trespasser*, and wrote with burning enthusiasm to his publisher about "Paul Morel", the new book he had begun to write.

Lawrence showed the first draft of "Paul Morel", later to become *Sons and Lovers*, to Jessie Chambers, who rightly told him that much of it was melodramatic and that what had happened in real life was "far more poignant and interesting". She helped him with the second draft, and he included many incidents of which she reminded him. Lawrence saw Jessie for the last time in 1912, for in that year he met and fell lastingly in love with Frieda. The two went abroad together, and Lawrence finished *Sons and Lovers* in Italy.

Sons and Lovers was published in May, 1913, and Jessie was "bewildered and dismayed" when she read it, for she felt that Lawrence had "glorified his bondage to his mother" and had misrepresented their "desperate search for a right relationship". She was too involved to look at the book objectively and see it, not as a mere chronicle of events, but as a work of creative genius.

The first half of *Sons and Lovers* is entirely autobiographical, and it would therefore be repetitious to recount the early lives of Paul Morel (Lawrence) and his brother Willie (Ernest). It is important, however, for the understanding of the novel to convey an idea of the atmosphere in which their formative years were spent, and above all to give a picture of Mrs. Morel (Mrs. Lawrence) whose character is the key to the book.

Mrs. Morel, the ex-schoolteacher, is compounded not only of love and tenderness, but also of harshness and rigidity, and it is this side of her nature that widens the gap between herself and her collier husband until it becomes unbridgeable. As the result of her ceaseless efforts to make him more than he can be, Walter Morel changes for the worse; he stays out till all hours, drinking away his pay-packet with his cronies, comes home sodden and often violent, and no longer cares that his coarse ways offend and wound his wife's sensibilities. Yet he still retains flashes of his gaiety, his good humour, and these shine out most brightly when he is working with his hands, doing odd jobs about the house, cobbling the family's boots. At such times he tells the children about Taffy, the little brown pit-pony. "Yo' 'ear 'im sneeze . . . 'What's want, Taffy?' yo' say. And what does he want? A bit of 'bacca, my ducks!" But these moments are rare, and too often the children are woken by his tipsy shouting, the bang-bang of his fist on the table – small wonder that they shrink from him and cling to their mother who is all tenderness to them.

She makes every sacrifice for them, and is guilt-ridden on the one or two occasions when her beauty-loving nature tempts her into spending a few coppers on flowers, on a gaily patterned jug.

Physically small and fragile, Mrs. Morel has an indomitable will, and is fully determined that no son of hers shall follow his father down the pit. In this at least she is successful. . . .

Willie obtains a well-paid post in London. Mrs. Morel, however, by making him the object of the passionate love she had once borne for her husband, splits him in two; he cannot wholly love any woman but his mother, and so it is to a shallow, brainless, worthless girl that he becomes engaged.

At fourteen, Paul finds himself a job in Nottingham with Jordan's, a firm manufacturing surgical goods. While Willie is away, he draws closer and closer to his mother.

One day, Mrs. Morel decides to take Paul to visit a farmer's wife, Mrs. Leivers. She is wearing a new blouse for the occasion, and Paul exclaims: "You *are* a fine little woman to take for a jaunt!" The walk through the country lanes is a sheer delight to them both, and Paul is enchanted by the farm. Pretty, timid, Miriam Lievers, who shrinks from her rough brothers, is drawn to the delicately built Paul, but he prefers the company of the boys. Mrs. Lievers invites him to visit the farm as often as he likes.

Willie dies suddenly in London. In her grief, Mrs. Morel neglects Paul, who falls critically ill with pneumonia. She nurses him back to health, and now centres her fierce, all-possessive love on him.

Paul spends as much time as he can at the farm. He finds that Miriam shares his love for poetry and painting, and is drawn closer and closer to her. A boy and girl idyll develops between them, but when Miriam ripens into a beautiful girl and Paul's manhood awakens, shadows begin to dim the brightness. Miriam is too over-refined, too tense. "Why can't you laugh?" he asks her one day. "If only you could laugh at me just a minute, I feel it would set something free." He becomes increasingly conscious that he is "too damned spiritual" with her, and he does not want to be spiritual. Because of Paul's absorption with Miriam, Mrs. Morel has grown bitterly hostile to her, for she has summed her up as "one of those women who will suck out a man's soul". She suffers bitterly, and Paul, aware of her suffering and unable to bear it, is often cruel to Miriam. One evening he returns from seeing her to find his mother sitting in the kitchen, pale and drawn. She has had previous attacks which she put down to her heart, but "You were too wrapped up in Miriam to notice. There's no one else for you now. I could bear it with another woman, but not her – she'll leave me no room, not a bit of room." She flings her arms round his neck, and whimpers – she who has never whimpered before – "I've never had a husband, not really. . . ."

Paul knows he loves his mother best, but he cannot give Miriam up. One day he meets a visitor at the farm: Clara Dawes, a sensuously beautiful woman of thirty who is separated from her husband. Clara is as extrovert as Miriam is introvert.

Paul finally feels that his affair with Miriam is hopeless. "We agreed on friendship, and yet – it neither gets us there nor anywhere else," he tells her, and ceases to visit her.

Paul runs into Clara and tells her that Miriam only wanted a "soul-union" with him. Clara says: "She wants *you*."

Paul goes to Miriam and asks her to marry him at once. She says they are too young, but she does give herself to him, and Paul is filled with a wonder and delight that he never recaptures; when he takes her again, he finds that she cannot respond to his passion, and knowing that it is no good he makes the final break with her.

Paul and Clara become lovers, but as with Miriam, Paul finds that he cannot achieve fulfilment through her. Ultimately he restores her to her husband.

Paul has noted with growing anxiety his mother's increasing weakness. She has cancer, and the time comes when she lies agonizing. Yet she *will* not die, and at the end Paul releases her from her sufferings with an overdose of morphia. When she is at peace, he goes out, and returns late to find his father crouched, forlorn and lost, by the fire. "Sithee, lad, I've warmed thee a drop of milk," he says humbly, and Paul pities him deeply for the first time, for he realizes that his father, who has never known fear, has been afraid to go to bed, alone in the house with his dead.

Shortly after the funeral Paul runs into Miriam, and out of the depths of his loneliness he asks: "Will you have me?" Miriam says: "Do you really want to marry me?" and he answers painfully: "No".

They part for ever, and Paul walks toward Nottingham. It is as if his soul cannot leave his mother, and yet, when he leans on a stile, "there was his body, there were his hands on the bars". He turns away from death, and goes forward to the city "quickly".

Sons and Lovers is the first, and by far the finest, of the novels whose theme is the Oedipus complex. The tragic relationship between mother and son is handled with great restraint, without sentimentality or self-pity. The harshness, the pain are offset by passages of deep tenderness, and throughout there are passages of outstanding descriptive beauty which light up the Midlands countryside with Lawrence's unique vision. *Sons and Lovers*, written with passionate intensity, is in every sense a "lived" book, the book with which Lawrence liberated himself from the past.

Lawrence came to believe that he had treated his father too harshly in *Sons and Lovers*, but this belief was unjustified. The character of Walter Morel is drawn with deep compassion and understanding; the brutishness into which he has fallen is never allowed to obscure the bright side of his nature, his natural gaiety and good-humour, his tenderness with his children when they are ill. Walter Morel, indeed, compels our pity, for we see him not as the destroyer but as the destroyed. When, then, did Lawrence feel he had painted too dark a portrait? Clearly, it was because he had loved his father too little and his mother too much.

REMEMBRANCE OF THINGS PAST

MARCEL PROUST

IN 1905, after the death of both his parents, a rich young Parisian an assiduous visitor in fashionable houses, the author of some elegan literary trifles, intelligent and gifted but a very obvious dilettante began, gradually, to remove himself from the world and to spenc more and more time in bed in a cork-lined room, covered with jerseys, writing, in the midst of thick yellow fumigations then prescribed for his disease. The asthma from which he had suffered all his life had become worse; henceforward, for long periods of his life he never went out at all but at night, and only saw the sun through glass

Marcel Proust's asthma was the ally of his genius for, enforcing or him solitude, it gave him the time necessary to complete, before he died in 1922, an immense work of sixteen volumes, longer as he said himself with pride than the *Arabian Nights*, which is called *A La Recherche du Temps Perdu* – in its English translation by Scott Moncrieff, *Remembrance of Things Past*. Translations are inevitably inferior to the original; this translation is nearly an exception to the rule. The style of Proust in many respects lends itself to rendering in English.

But asthma was more than an ally of genius. It had set Marcel Proust from earliest childhood in a special position with regard to the outside world, quite different from that of his brother Robert who like his father was a doctor; and different from many of his friends who had careers in professions, as soldiers or diplomats. Proust had not to compete, for he could not compete. And he for long enjoyed the advantages of being an invalid without its disadvantages; late nights and amusements were not forbidden him. He was intensely selfish and self-regarding; yet so sensitive, so perceptive with regard to other people that he charmed everyone, including the people of his own age. Asthma, which is partly a nervous disease, helped to make him and keep him in his maturity a kind of child-monster. This child-monster preserved in himself the vitality of an artist, did not become in middle age merely a spoilt, failed character; and so it can be said that Proust's illness was more than the ally, it was the brother of his genius.

Remembrance of Things Past is an account of a life which the narrator had just lived and of memories of society which he had renounced.

Now the world Proust restores has something of the nature of a huge gossip column, written by a highly intelligent snob who has a sense of the comic, and, with all the attraction society exercises on him, a strong realization of its futility. This highly intelligent snob is also a man for whom music, painting and literature matter far more than society, and who is gifted with such powers of penetration into human passions that people have said that *Remembrance of Things Past* could not have been written before Freud.

In the first volume – *Swann's Way* – Charles Swann, a rich Jew who is a connoisseur of painting, is introduced as coming often to the house at Combray where Marcel's childhood was passed. To the narrator's family he is a curious, though agreeable, neighbour who brings them recipes and costly presents from abroad, but is not considered interesting enough to be asked to dinner to meet strangers when they are anxious to entertain particularly well. They have no idea of Swann's life in Paris beyond the fact that he lives in an unfashionable quarter. Swann, in fact, is a friend of the Duke and Duchess of Guermantes, admitted into the very highest aristocratic society and much liked by Edward VII. His noble friends consider him rather extraordinary because, suddenly, Swann is liable to be much more interested in their cook, whom he has seduced, than in them, and for a time will neglect them.

Swann falls hopelessly in love with a demi-mondaine, Odette de Crécy, not the kind of woman he normally likes at all. She leads him into the literary salon of Madame Verdurin, where Swann's life with the aristocracy, about which he speaks scarcely at all, is not guessed at. Hints of his acquaintance with this or that social celebrity are regarded as evidence that he is really a bore – which is what "the little clan" organized by Madame Verdurin call anybody who is not totally faithful to them. Which is the real Swann – the cultivated man of society, the man who really loves painting and art for its own sake, the seducer, the chaser after all fresh young females who seem comparatively easy game, or the hopeless lover of a woman who for all her superficial beauty is a commonplace creature?

The narrator falls in love with Swann's daughter by Odette de Crécy in his boyhood and then, in a collective way, with a group of young girls whom he meets at the seaside, one of whom, Albertine, is destined later to live with him. The next love of his life is the Duchess of Guermantes, whose husband's great house is near Combray. She, with her vivid blue eyes, aquiline nose and beautiful figure is like the heroine of a historical romance. The narrator at last penetrates into her world, becomes, like Swann, one of her familiars and accompanies her on the endless rounds of visits and receptions which she pretends to despise but in fact lives for.

But what the narrator mainly derives from the social round which, in a sense, represents the satisfaction of his love for the Duchess, is not that of living in an enchanted world, but acquaintance with a life full of vanity, egotism and cruelty. The Duchess going to a reception pretends not to understand that Charles Swann is telling them that he has cancer and is likely to die: she does not want to be late for the party. Important things in this world take second place to the trivial pleasures of meeting and exhibiting oneself. The inhabitants of this world, with their splendid names which reflect the history of France, are at bottom marionettes engaged in a combat of showing off – there is always some salon to which they would like to be admitted as intimates, some former close friends, country cousins maybe, who must be sloughed off in order that they themselves may become grander.

The key to this Proustian creation is that his world is made not of intellect but of *memory*. At the beginning the narrator, a young boy in Paris, is given a cup of tea and, dipped in the tea, a special kind of French bun called a madeleine. After two or three mouthfuls, he is aware of something happening inside him:

"An exquisite pleasure had invaded my senses, but individual, detached, with no suggestion of its origin. And at once the vicissitudes of life had become indifferent to me, its disasters innocuous, its brevity illusory – this new sensation having had on me the effect which love has, filling me with a precious essence; or rather this essence was not in me, it was myself. I had ceased now to feel mediocre, accidental, mortal. Whence could it have come to me, this all powerful joy?"

The memory aroused by the madeleine dipped in tea, which he used to be given when a child living in the country at Combray, had brought back to him all his childhood about which he had, naturally, often thought; but with the stimulus of the bun dipped in tea, his childhood and much else had returned in freshness and power – its soul restored. The recollections aroused by the madeleine, and by similar experiences, are different from those which are derived from a writer's notebooks (Proust also used notebooks to an extraordinary degree); they are the fruit of creative memory founded on sensation, which recalls the Past as it was, with all that the mind had forgotten of it. We can deliver the Past from the death which has absorbed it

so that it comes back in all its former freshness, variety and incon-
sistency which are the qualities of Life.

Remembrance of Things Past is not like Joyce's *Ulysses*, a difficult
work which, however important, is likely to appeal principally to
the specialist in literature. Proust may not appeal to all intelligent
readers but he is liable to entrap anyone – the simple-minded or
sophisticated, the well or ill-read – as no other author does. Reading
Remembrance of Things Past is liable totally to absorb one's mind for
quite a long period. For it is still the most original of all the great
novels of the world and its originality lies in that it has captured a
segment of life. One is not filled with the thoughts and emotions
aroused by characters or by a plot which an author intends the
reader to experience. The characters of Proust are more blurred,
more inconsistent, more ambiguous than those in other great works
of fiction, still alive and developing in our minds; they can continue,
when we think of them, to arouse questions, feelings of sympathy
and remorse, irritation, disappointment, disgust even; they are sometimes base, sometimes relatively noble, true and untrue to themselves,
and we can never be quite sure we have understood them.

At Baalbec, the seaside place where the narrator meets the band of
young girls, the narrator is introduced to a nobleman, the Baron de
Charlus, who impresses him by his real culture and by a sort of
brusque vitality which arouses the narrator's admiration and, to
some extent, fear. This Baron de Charlus, the brother of the Prince
and of the Duke of Guermantes, is in fact a far more original and
powerful character than the members of the high society whom he
frequently insults in the most gross fashion but who revere him for
his birth and fear him for his intellect.

The narrator sees the Baron from all sorts of angles; he admires his
hardness of mind, wonders at his rages, feels also, beneath his eccentricity, a great kindness. He knows nothing of the most significant
thing about Charlus until he overhears, by chance, a conversation
between the Baron and Jupien, an elderly homosexual waistcoat-
maker. The narrator acquires a new vision of the Baron, one which
it would be hard to avoid having later, for, as the years go on, the
Baron's thinking too fondly of men gradually makes him look like a
woman. He gets fatter and his behind protrudes almost symbolically;
he powders his nose and paints his lips; when he enters a drawing-
room, he flutters and seems to be wearing an invisible skirt.

As a result of his understanding about the Baron de Charlus, the
narrator suddenly becomes aware of the large fraternity of inverts in
the great world. Perhaps because Proust himself was a homosexual

he may have exaggerated the quantity of inversion, male or female, which was to be met with in the society of his time. As Proust writes: "The invert at first believes that he is alone of his kind in the world; only later does he come to think (another exaggeration) that the unique exception is the normal man."

Proust was the first great novelist to give inversion the place which it occupies in modern society. But the art of Proust has none of that sentimental desire to excuse, explain or proselytize which sometimes appears in the work of other authors who have treated this subject. The Baron's taste for footmen, young soldiers, and tramconductors is immensely important in the Baron's life. It leads him to a tragic love affair with a young violinist, a love affair which breaks him up and leads to the extraordinary decay which he presents in the last volume, and to the loss of all self-control. Swann's excessive promiscuity toward women leads him to spend the best of his mature years in love-admiration for one singularly unworthy woman whom he marries, is faithful to, and is betrayed by. But Love does not explain the characters of these two exceptional men, Charlus and Swann. Both have exceptional qualities and emotional vitality. Charlus, had he not been born in the Faubourg St. Germain, could have been a great musician or a politician; but, as it is, this excess of life-force in Charlus can only express itself in a form of dementia.

Proust's very faculty of creation forbids judgments and values. As a French critic, M. Revel, has pointed out, Proust is one of the very few great writers who are interested in seeing human nature as it is rather than explaining it. He has no preconceived ideas about people or events. Proust explains the superiority of a very great pianist to a merely very good one. People think that the first knows better how to interpret a sonata than the second. On the contrary, the very great pianist does not interpret the sonata at all, not even with genius: he merely knows how to abolish himself and through his fingers allow the music to convey its message.

Proust makes no judgments but submits himself to what he has seen. He professes no moral values. Yet this immense work of exploration of the past, in which human nature is shown as it is, leaves most readers with a feeling of exaltation, of life being enhanced and not diminished. Man is comic, much more like Caliban than Prospero. Love is not what it seems or is made out to be. Perhaps only grandmothers and mothers know love which is not hopelessly mixed with vanity, ambition or concupiscence. But in what a magic setting is man's life lived, how much variety, strangeness and beauty there is in the world of nature. Proust, like Matthew Arnold and Goethe, saw a truth which became fashionable, and was therefore travestied in what was termed at one time the doctrine of Art for Art's sake, according to which aesthetic values are held to be superior to moral values, and by which the aesthete who "walks down Piccadilly with a rose or yet a lily" is enabled to reckon of no account the daily human life he fears to live.

The truth which the work of Proust proclaims is that Art is one of the ways in which man saves himself. An absolute value emerges from a medley of relative and jarring force values. As André Maurois has written in his book *The Quest for Proust* the main subject of his novel is not the picture of the particular society to be found in France at the end of the nineteenth century, nor a new analysis of love; it is: "The struggle waged by the spirit of man with Time, the impossibility of finding in actual life a fixed point to which the self can cling, the duty of finding that point within oneself, the possibility of finding it in a work of art." That is the essential, the profound, the novel theme of *Remembrance of Things Past*.

THE REVOLT OF THE ANGELS

ANATOLE FRANCE

ANATOLE FRANCE was the pen-name of Jacques Anatole Thibault. The son of a bookseller whose shop was much frequented by literary men, he was born in Paris on 16 April, 1844. Educated at the Collège Stanislas in Paris, he resolved at an early age to be a writer, and joined literary circles, studied old manuscripts, wrote on bibliographical matters, contributed prefaces to French classics and wrote a monograph on Alfred de Vigny. He became a member of the staff of the Senate Library, and later of the famous Larousse *Dictionary*. But he was twenty-one before he published his first book, a collection of poems, *Poèmes dorés*.

Even now he seemed to be in no hurry to launch himself on his writing career, for six years were to elapse between the publication of these poems and his first prose work, a collection of tales called *Jocaste et le chat maigre*. This, however, seems to have opened the flood-gates of his inspiration, for there now came a long succession of books – novels, satires and criticism.

It was not until 1893 that his reputation was established with the publication of *La Rôtisserie de la reine Pédauque*. From now until 1914 there appeared annually at least one book, sometimes two, all of which more firmly entrenched France in popular literary esteem and at the same time made him the leading figure of his generation in French letters.

The origins of Anatole France – his father was of peasant stock and was unable to read or write until he joined the army and taught himself – are the clues to his character and his writings. He is the bibliophile, the classicist *and* the common man. The wit, sensuality and iconoclasm in his books may seem to go oddly with his love of the traditional. On the other hand, the greatness of his work is based on the alternating communion and conflict of learning and licentiousness, of reason and romanticism, of the worldly and the divine.

Sceptical, erudite and keenly interested in actuality, it is hardly fair to call him a novelist; he is rather a kindly satirist using the novel – the *récit* he would have called it – as his medium for dissertation and analysis. He took ancient and modern history as his theme, but what he most preferred was to turn ancient and legendary tales inside out and to show that the same characteristics are common to humanity of all ages. In a sense he resembled Shaw, or even Wells, but he was less ruthless and restless than either.

France's literary characteristics are nowhere more superbly revealed than in *The Revolt of the Angels*, which he always looked upon as his best book and is generally regarded so by the critics. Written and published just before the outbreak of the First World War in 1914, it is a prophetic satire of the world as it then was, and – proving France's thesis that humanity changes very little, if at all, with the passage of time – of the world as it is today.

"Beneath the shadow of St. Sulpice, the ancient mansion of the d'Esparvieu family rears its austere three stories between a moss-grown forecourt and a garden hemmed in, as the years have elapsed, by ever loftier and more obtrusive buildings, wherein, nevertheless, two tall chestnut trees still lift their withered heads."

Here, from 1825 to 1857, the great man of the family lived – Alexandre Bussert d'Esparvieu, Vice-President of the Council of State under the Government of July. Alexandre left as heir to his fame and fortune, Fulgence-Adolphe, senator under the Second Empire, "who added greatly to his patrimony by buying land over which the avenue de l'Impératrice was destined to pass, and who made a remarkable speech in favour of the temporal power of the popes".

Fulgence's third son, René, married, in 1888, Marie-Antionette, daughter of Baron Coupelle, iron-master of Blainville. "These perfect spouses, having married off their eldest daughter in 1908, had three children still at home – a girl and two boys."

Léon, the younger, aged seven, had a room next to his mother and his sister, Berthe. Maurice, the elder, lived in a little summer house comprising two rooms at the bottom of the garden. "The young man thus gained a freedom which enabled him to endure family life."

Good-looking, smart without too much pretence, and undeniably possessed of a certain charm, at twenty-five Maurice also "possessed the wisdom of Ecclesiastes". Doubting whether a man has "any profit of all his labour which he taketh under the sun", he never put himself out about anything. From early childhood his sole concern with work was devising the best ways and means of avoiding it, and it was while "still in ignorance of the teaching of the Ecole de Droit that he became a doctor of law, and a barrister at the Court of Appeal. But he neither pleaded not practised. He had no knowledge and no desire to acquire any, and in this he conformed to his genius "whose engaging fragility he forebore to overload; his instinct fortunately telling him that it was better to understand a little than to misunderstand a lot".

In this he was the opposite of his great-grandfather, Alexandre, for the latter, "desirous of embracing the whole circle of human knowledge and anxious to bequeath to the world a concrete symbol of his encyclopedic genius", had formed a library of three hundred and sixty thousand volumes, both printed and in manuscript. By a special clause in his will he had required his heirs to add to the library, and had apportioned part of his estate for this purpose. This, his two successors to date had faithfully done, so that the d'Esparvieu Library had become one of the finest private libraries in Europe.

The care of this magnificent collection had for many years been in the hands of Monsieur Julien Sariette, archivist and paleologue. Monsieur Sariette loved his library with a jealous love, and was there every day at seven in the morning, busy cataloguing at a huge mahogany desk.

As the story opens, Sariette is greatly perturbed by mysterious nocturnal visitations to the library. Precious books and manuscripts are taken from their shelves and left scattered about the tables in disarray.

At first he thinks that some member of the family must be responsible, but when all deny it, he becomes greatly alarmed. The books were an odd selection, in fact, for any member of the family to show an interest in, for they were "his most valuable Hebrew, French and Latin Bibles, a unique Talmud, Rabbinical treatises printed and in manuscript, Aramaic and Samaritan texts and scrolls from the synagogues – in fine, the most precious relics of Israel all lying in a disordered heap, gaping and crumpled".

The family, for their part, believe that the old man is either imagining things, or has himself consulted the books the day before and forgotten he has done so. They agree to humour him, however, by changing the locks and employing a firm of private detectives to keep watch. Neither measure does any good.

As the months pass into years, the family becomes convinced that old Sariette has really gone off his head, for presently he asserts that books come down from their shelves of their own accord, and one has even gone floating out of the library door, down the stairs, out of the house and across the garden to Maurice's summer-house.

Then quite suddenly one day the mystery is revealed.

Maurice rents a small flat at 126 rue de Rome, where he entertains his constantly changing mistresses. Here on Saturday, 30 January, he had been waiting for his latest acquisition, Madame des Aubels. She had arrived late, full of excuses which he obstinately rejected. But, "born to please and charm, she undressed leisurely, as a woman who knows that it becomes her to be naked and is prepared to show her beauty", and all his disagreableness vanishes.

Having made love once or twice, at half-past six she said, "We must be moving".

"Pricked by the touch of time's fleeting wing, Maurice was conscious of reawakened desire and reanimated powers. A white and radiant offering, Gilberte, with her head thrown back, her eyes half closed, her lips apart, sunk in a dreamy languor, was breathing slowly and placidly, when suddenly she started up with a cry of terrror.

" 'Whatever is that?'

" 'Stay still,' said Maurice, holding her back in his arms.

"In his present mood, had the sky fallen it would not have troubled him. But in one bound she escaped from him. Crouching down she was pointing with her finger at a figure. . . .

"Maurice at length turned his head, saw the figure, and perceiving that it moved, was also frightened."

Meanwhile Gilberte was recovering a little, and believing that the figure was another of Maurice's mistresses who had been with him earlier and had not been able to escape when she had herself arrived, began to upbraid him.

This was not true, and, in any case, he said, although he could not see the figure clearly, he could see enough to tell him that it was a man. This threw Gilberte into renewed panic.

Upon this the figure said, in a very sweet voice, "Have no fear, madame."

Slightly reassured, she asked who he was, and was told, "I am Maurice's guardian angel".

It took some minutes for both Maurice and Gilberte to be convinced of this, but eventually they allowed themselves to be, though they still could not understand what he was doing there.

The angel replied, "I am about to reveal to you a secret on which hangs the fate of the universe. In rebellion against Him whom you hold to be the Creator of all things, visible and invisible, I am preparing the revolt of the angels."

This is even more difficult to believe, but the angel, who has told them that his heavenly name is Abdiel, but that he prefers to be called Arcade, again convinces them, and from his arguments it suddenly dawns on Maurice that it has been Arcade who has been plaguing the librarian for the last two years, a charge which the angel admits.

They ask why he is plotting a revolt, and are told that Arcade has lost his faith. "I believe in the God of the Jews and Christians," he explains. "But I deny that *He* created the world; at the most *He* organized but an inferior part of it. . . . I do not think He is either eternal or infinite. . . . I think Him limited, even very limited. I no longer believe Him to be the only God. For a long time He did not believe it Himself; in the beginning He was a polytheist; later His pride and the flattery of His worshippers made Him a monotheist. His ideas have little connection; He is less powerful than He is thought to be. And, to speak candidly, He is not so much a god as a vain and ignorant demiurge. Those who, like myself, know His true nature, call Him Ialdabaoth."

Maurice and Gilberte implore Arcade not to go forward with his plan, but in vain, and since he has now revealed himself to them in human form, he tells them he can no longer be Maurice's guardian angel. So Maurice goes out and buys him some second-hand clothes, since he is naked, and says farewell to his former guardian angel.

It is now revealed that Arcade is not the only angel in revolt. There are living in Paris some three or four hundred of them, and they are conducting themselves on much the same lines as the Russian Nihilists were said to do. One of them, Théophile, lives with a little music-hall artiste, Bouchotte, another is Prince Istar, a maker of bombs and other instruments of destruction. Arcade, by degrees, contacts a number of these rebels and a kind of organization is formed.

Meanwhile Maurice feels lost without his guardian angel and begins a search for him. By chance he calls on Bouchotte one day to ask her to appear at a charity concert, and adds her to his company of mistresses. Through his association with her and her archangel lover, he re-encounters Arcade, and tells him that since Arcade can no longer be his guardian angel, he will be Arcade's.

As the plans for the revolt approach fruition, the angels hold a mass meeting in a small theatre. Naturally, the Security Police hear of it, and the Minister of Justice is at once convinced that a plot is being hatched aimed at the overthrow of the Republic. He orders the Security forces to keep the plotters under surveillance to gather evidence on which they may be arrested.

Maurice gets to hear of these official moves, and persuades Arcade to go into hiding in the rue de Rome apartment. A number of unfortunate events come of the move, affecting both Maurice and Arcade, but all are eventually satisfactorily resolved.

So the moment comes when the angels decide to launch their attack on heaven. "Doubtless they were but a few combatants to oppose the innumerable soldiers of the sultan of the heavens; but they counted on compensating for the inferiority of their numbers by the irresistible impetus of a sudden attack. . . . The celestial army had made no progress since its victory over the rebels before the beginning of time. As regards armaments and material it was as out of date as the army of the Moors. Its generals slumbered in sloth and ignorance. Loaded with honours and riches, they preferred to the delights of the banquet to the fatigues of war."

The rebels invite Satan to become their commander-in-chief, and he tells them he will sleep on it. During the night Satan has a dream in which he leads the rebellious army against the armies of Ialdabaoth, whom he defeats, and in whose place he is crowned king of heaven. But as he looked down on Ialdabaoth in Gehenna, "Lo, Ialdabaoth was now contemplating the earth and, seeing it sunk in wickedness and suffering, he began to foster thoughts of kindliness in his heart. On a sudden he rose up, and beating the ether with his mighty arms, as though with oars, he hastened hither and thither to instruct and to console mankind. Already his vast shadow shed upon the unhappy planet a shade soft as a night of love.

"And Satan woke bathed in an icy sweat.

"Nectaire, Istar, Arcade and Zita were standing round him. . . .

" 'Comrades,' said the great archangel, 'no – we will not conquer the heavens. Enough to have the power. . . . God conquered will become Satan; Satan, conquering, will become God. May the fates spare me this terrible lot. I love hell which formed my genius. . . . Now, thanks to us, the God of old is dispossessed of His terrestrial empire, and every thinking being on this globe disdains Him or knows Him not. . . . As to ourselves, celestial spirits, sublime daemons, we have destroyed Ialdabaoth, if in ourselves, we have destroyed Ignorance and Fear.' "

France strongly supported his country's entry into the First World War, and strove always to uphold the idealism of the French cause. By the end of the war he had become the Grand Old Man of French letters, and pilgrimages were made to his homes. Many portraits and photographs were made of him, all showing him in dressing-gown, skull-cap and slippers, the man of letters, the son of the people. From all of them one gets the impression of the thinker combined with a benign Puckish spirit, and above all, that in him was personified the spirit of the France of his times.

In 1921 he was awarded the Nobel Prize for Literature. He died at Tours on 13 October, 1924.

THE TOWN LABOURER

J. L. and BARBARA HAMMOND

IN THE seventy years, more or less, that extended from the latter part of the eighteenth century to well into the nineteenth, a great change came over England. From being an almost entirely agricultural country it became the factory and workshop of the world, buying the food for its ever-growing population from overseas with its exports of manufactured goods in immense variety. The name given to this transformation is the Industrial Revolution.

Many books have been written about it, starting with Arnold Toynbee's lectures at Oxford in 1881, but it is probably true to say that there is no name better known in this particular field than that of the Hammonds. The *two* Hammonds, for this was a case of a husband-and-wife literary partnership of a peculiarly intimate and useful kind.

To take the man first, John Laurence Le Breton Hammond (to give him his full name) was born in 1872 and died in 1949. He came of an old Jersey family, but was born in a Yorkshire village where his father was the rector. From Bradford Grammar School he proceeded to Oxford, and then embarked on a career in journalism in which he was chiefly connected with the *Manchester Guardian*. Although over forty at the time, he served for a year in the artillery in the First World War. In 1901 he married Lucy Barbara Bradby (1873-1961), the seventh and last child of Dr. Bradby, a notable headmaster of Haileybury. She went to Lady Margaret Hall at Oxford, where she proved a most brilliant student and was for four years a fellow before her most happy marriage to J. L. Hammond. As a young woman she was found to be suffering from tuberculosis, and for some years the pair read, wrote, ate, drank, and slept out of doors according to the methods of treatment then in vogue. To add to their difficulties Hammond lost his job as editor of a Liberal journal, and for a time was employed in a Civil Service post. Fortunately this left him with considerable free time, and it was under these conditions that the pair produced in 1911 the first of a number of volumes of social and economic history, concerned in the main with the period 1760 to 1832.

The Village Labourer, as this first volume was called, deals with the enclosure movement that resulted in the divorce of the farm worker from the soil, and the two authors made no attempt to disguise where their sympathies lay.

From a study of the village labourer the Hammonds went on to investigate the conditions of the town worker, and their first book on the subject, *The Town Labourer 1760–1832*, was almost ready for publication in the summer of 1914 when it had to be put on one side for the more pressing tasks of the war. It was published at length in 1917.

The book opens with a famous passage of purple prose from a speech made by Macaulay in the course of the great parliamentary struggle over the first Reform Bill. "Our fields are cultivated with a skill unknown elsewhere, with a skill which has extracted rich harvests from moors and morasses. Our houses are filled with conveniences which the kings of former times might have envied. Our bridges, our canals, our roads, our modes of communication fill every stranger with wonder. Nowhere are manufactures carried to such perfection. Nowhere does man exercise such a dominion over matter."

Fair and true enough, admit the Hammonds. There had been a most extraordinary transformation. Men born to poverty and degradation had by their own efforts attained to positions of wealth and influence. Whole regions had been developed as never before, new industries had been established, and a huge new population had come into existence – and even now we are not sure where all the fresh people came from. A great new middle class had been formed, and over a large part of society the standards of living had risen very appreciably. But what of the great mass of the people? A price had had to be paid for all this improvement and prosperity, and it was the working classes who had been called upon to pay it.

"Nowhere does man exercise such dominion over matter," Macaulay had boasted. The Hammonds summed up their impression of what the Revolution had meant for the "lower orders" in a transposition of Macaulay's words: "Nowhere does matter exercise such dominion over man."

In one chapter they described the new discipline to which the workers were subjected. By no means everything was as it should be under the domestic system, when a man combined a little farming with a little weaving. But he had some control over his own life. He could leave his loom for a while and go out into his garden for a smoke if he felt inclined. But now he was imprisoned in a factory for ten or twelve hours a day, he had to answer to the summons of the factory bell, he was the slave of the machine which worked on inexorably and never grew tired. For such trivial misdemeanours as breaking a thread or whistling at his work a spinner might be fined. Conditions in the mines were even worse than in the factories, for there men, women, and little children were not only employed in the most degrading circumstances but were exposed to constant danger of mutilation and death.

In another chapter we are given a picture of the New Town, of the massive congregations of jerry-built tenements that were what the workers had to come home to when the day's toil was over. There was no sanitation, but the waste products of human living were accumulated in noisome heaps. The streets were undrained and unpaved. There were no building regulations even in such a great town as Manchester or Liverpool. Few of the houses had even earth closets, and fewer still a piped water supply: a tap at the end of the row or street was turned on for an hour or two a day, and the inhabitants lined up with their baths and buckets. Some of the new towns were old villages that had grown out of their seams, others were ancient corporations, yet others were entirely new creations. But all were badly governed, nests of privilege and corruption. Means of recreation there were none. One of the most frequent complaints was that there were no places where a working man might go for a walk with his family on a Sunday afternoon – no parks, no open spaces, no allotments even.

The new towns, assert the Hammonds, "were not so much towns as barracks: not the refuge of a civilization but the barracks of an industry". Justice, so-called, was administered by local magistrates who were uniformly of the squirearchy and the employing class. There were no police forces until the very end of the period under review. Law and order was maintained by the army and the local militia. Another of the Hammonds' chapters is headed "The War on Trade Unions", and it is well to be reminded that from 1799 to 1824 anything and everything in the nature of trade-union activity was proscribed.

Coming now to the economic conditions, there is no doubt that the history of the early years of the Industrial Revolution is one of vast and rapid expansion. And yet, so the Hammonds assert, the wage-earners employed in the new industries did not obtain any part of the new wealth. While immense fortunes were being made in cotton, wool, iron and coal, the workers in these industries sank deeper in degradation and distress. On the one hand there emerged class of rich employers, and on the other a large and miserable proletariate.

For the mass of working people there was but one way of keeping body and soul together, and that was by sending their children to work in factory and workshop and mine, in order that their slender earnings might be made to help balance the family budget. Until the Hammonds wrote, the immense contribution made to industry by the labour of children, many of them not yet in their teens, was never properly appreciated, but anyone who has read their chapters on the employment of children in mill and mine will need no further convincing. The first factories were driven by water-power and were necessarily established on the banks of rivers and streams, generally in districts that were but sparsely populated. The manufacturers were hard put to it to obtain sufficient "hands", and they hailed with relief the proposal made to them by parish authorities in London and elsewhere that they might employ the thousands of children who filled the workhouses to overflowing. So began an infamous traffic which continued until, with the coming of steam-power, factories were established in towns and the so-called free children of the adult workers became available.

The first Factory Act, affording some slight protection to apprentice children from the workhouses, was passed in 1801; but as late as 1831, after years of Parliamentary agitation, children were left entirely unprotected except in the cotton industry; and even in the cotton industry masters might work children of nine years of age for twelve hours a day, exclusive of meal times. And even such regulations as were imposed were academic, since there was not one single factory inspector appointed to see they were carried out.

This is a dreadfully depressing picture, and it should be stated that it is relieved by not a few examples of employers who were fully aware of the evils of the factory system and did their best to remedy them. Not all the masters were tyrants, and not all the tyrants were masters: many parents showed themselves only too ready to exploit the labour of their children, and were responsible for some of the grossest cases of cruelty. But on the whole, it is still true to say that the upper classes treated the lower with a harshness, a lack of consideration, and even a measure of cruelty, which is hard to understand unless we realize the intellectual atmosphere of the time. This is analysed by the Hammonds in their chapters on the Mind and on the Conscience of the Rich. It was genuinely believed that the full and well-nigh unrestricted development of the capitalist system was in the best interests of the workers as well as of their employers, and the accepted guides in economic theory were almost at one in their agreement. Religion, too, threw its mantle of protection over the distresses of the poor. Such well-intentioned and benevolent people as William Wilberforce and Hannah More did not hesitate to console the poor with the intimation that their sufferings and deprivations in this life would be made up to them in the life beyond the grave.

Against these adverse influences the poor raised such defences as they could. Notwithstanding the opposition of the authorities, there was considerable development of trade unions, and friendly societies were established to afford their members some protection against the hazards of daily life. The Co-operative movement also made its first start in these depressing years. Then the poor also found relief and encouragement in what the Hammonds style the Spirit of Religion. The Established Church seemed all too certainly and exclusively on the side of the possessing classes, but in towns and villages throughout the land there were chapels of the Dissenting denominations, and specially of the Methodist movement, in which the doctrine was attuned to working-class ears, and where a man, however lowly his origin and humble his occupation, might find opportunities for exercising any gifts for organization and management that he might happen to possess.

One prominent omission in this survey of the intellectual forces at work in the new society will be noted. England was far behind the rest of the civilized world in the matter of the provision of schools for the children of the working classes. Many of those who prided themselves on their own educational attainments were quite content to deny to the poor even the rudiments, for fear of encouraging them in rebellious thoughts and inclinations; and even when schools were established under the auspices of the two societies associated with the names of Dr. Bell and Joseph Lancaster, the predominating motive was not the provision of education, even of the most elementary kind, so much as the making of proselytes for the rival camps of Church and Chapel.

In their last chapter the Hammonds revert to the prevailing intellectual climate in an England in which the Few still governed the Many. It was the conviction of all the classes that had acquired the new wealth that Property was the great civilizing force of the world. But the rapidly developing system of capitalist organization did not permit of a wide distribution of property: the masses, so it was believed, must ever remain propertyless and exposed to the mishaps of unemployment and a penurious old age. Until this depressing intellectual atmosphere could be banished – and it was banished in time – there could be no real hope for by far the greater part of the population.

So the Hammonds reached their conclusion, "that amid all the conquests over nature that give its triumphs to the Industrial Revolution, the soul of man was passing into a colder exile, for in this new world, with all its wealth and promise and its wide horizon of mystery and hope, the spirit of fellowship was dead".

Two years after the publication of *The Town Labourer*, the Hammonds published the third volume in their trilogy, *The Skilled Labourer 1760-1832*, and this was followed by a study of Lord Shaftesbury in 1923 and by *The Rise of Modern Industry* (1925), *The Age of the Chartists* (1930) and *The Bleak Age* (1934), which carry the story of the Industrial Revolution up to the middle of the last century. All these books are thoroughly documented, and at the same time intensely readable. For the Hammonds had a very special quality in their writing. Shortly expressed, they put the "humanity" into economic history.

ULYSSES

JAMES JOYCE

ULYSSES IS a unique book in English literature, being neither a straightforward novel, a fantasy, a satire nor a prolonged reminiscence, though it has elements of all these. It is the record of a day in the life of a Dublin Jew, Leopold Bloom, advertisement canvasser and husband of a singer, Marion Bloom. The day is 16 June, 1904, the happenings consist of preparing his wife's breakfast and his own, visiting various offices, going to a funeral, to the seashore, to pubs, to a brothel, talking in a cabman's shelter with a friend and finally returning home to his wife, once again lying asleep as she was, when the book opened, in the morning.

Joyce worked on this book from 1914–21, in Trieste, Zürich and Paris. Yet it is, like all Joyce's work, totally concerned with Ireland and particularly with Dublin. It is an exact recreation of Dublin as it was in Joyce's youth (he left Ireland in 1904), including the songs that were sung, the things that were talked about, the numbers of houses and the streets and, of course, all the pubs as they were. Joyce, born in 1882, only went to Ireland for a few short visits after he had left it, a penniless student, accompanied by a young girl from Galway, Nora Barnacle, who became his wife. But to a friend who once asked him why he never went back to Ireland he answered simply, "Have I ever left it?"

Other modern writers have concentrated on the re-creation of a city or milieu at a given period, though none so whole-heartedly as Joyce. The originality of the book lies in that Joyce not only re-creates the acts and conscious thoughts of his characters but the half-thoughts, the constant fantasies which the unconscious evolves all the time side by side with conscious activity; and, to do this, he evolved what is called the "stream of consciousness" method.

Many writers before Joyce used the interior monologue; none so thoroughly and with such technical daring and use of unconventional language and other devices. The last, and most celebrated passage in the book, a long description of what is going on in the mind of Marion Bloom as she lies, half asleep, around midnight at the end of "Bloomsday", consists of some twenty thousand words with, in all, but four full stops. This stream of consciousness method has enriched the technique of literature, enabling the writer to portray much more of the inner nature of man and woman, for the subconscious cannot be expressed in nicely balanced prose.

The stream of consciousness method is accompanied by the deliberate parodying of many kinds of English style in various episodes of the book. In recounting Bloom's visit to a maternity hospital, for example, the narrative consists of passages which trace the evolution of English style from middle English to Victorian prose. When Bloom wanders at one moment, by the seashore, he is observed by a young girl, Gertie McDowell, who has a limp; a long passage, which describes what is going on in her mind, as she sits on the sand and glances at Bloom, is deliberately written in the penny novelette Victorian woman's magazine style. Gertie starts by remembering an ineffectual lover:

"The night of the party long ago (he was still in short trousers) when they were alone and he stole an arm round her waist she went white to the very lips. He called her little one in the strangely husky voice and he snatched a half kiss (the first) but it was only the end of her nose and then he hastened from the room with a remark about refreshments. Impetuous fellow! Strength of character had never been Reggie Wylie's strong point and he who would woo and win Gertie McDowell must be a man among men. But waiting, always waiting, to be asked and it was Leap Year too and it would soon be over. No Prince Charming is her beau ideal to lay a rare and wondrous love at her feet; but rather a manly man with a strong quiet face who had not found his ideal, perhaps his hair slightly flecked with grey and who would understand, take her in his sheltering arms, strain her to him in all the strength of his deep passionate nature and comfort her with a long, long kiss. It would be like heaven. For such a one she yearns this balmy summer's eve."

Joyce's consummate mastery of the techniques of writing enabled him to use all the melodies of which the English language is capable. What seem like tricks of style, however, are not really tricks but the necessary colour components of a huge jigsaw puzzle, portraying a slice of life.

Ulysses was first published in Paris by the Shakespeare and Company Press, owned by Sylvia Beach, the benefactress of many of the best experimental writers of the time. It won immediate recognition from most, though not all, of the leading writers of England and France and the United States. However, it remained for long a work which few people had read. Just as the American postal authorities had largely suppressed editions of the *Little Review* which had published sections of the work before it was finished, so the copies of the limited edition of *Ulysses* brought out by the Egotist Press in London were seized and burnt by the British Post Office. In the United States a pirated version of *Ulysses* was printed; this led to a protest, on Joyce's behalf, signed by a great body of writers, including among the English writers men such as John Masefield, C. R. Trevelyan, Arnold Bennett, Galsworthy, Philip Gibbs, H. G. Wells, Walpole and Yates – as well as *avant-garde* writers of the time such as T. S. Eliot, Hemingway and many others.

The protest was followed by the appearance of an authorized unlimited edition for public sale by Random House, New York, who challenged the Federal authorities to make a judgment for or against the right of the book to appear on public sale. Judge John M. Woolsey in the United States District Court in 1933 finally ruled that the sale of the book was legal in the U.S. and this was followed by the first public edition in England in 1936, by the Bodley Head.

Strangely enough, *Ulysses* has become compulsory reading in many universities in Britain and in America, a fact which would perhaps have surprised Joyce and indeed might not altogether have pleased him. This highly intellectual book with its sordid and humorous matter is valued by young and old readers not perhaps for the reasons which have led it to be studied as a technical work.

Ulysses is much more than a thorough, daring and technically fascinating exploration of Dublin, some of its inhabitants and its underworld. George Moore, who never really liked Joyce's work, said that he thought *Ulysses* was an important book but he could not understand why Joyce had mixed it up with a lot of stuff from Homer. Now too much, perhaps, has been written by some intellectual admirers of Joyce about the relationship between Joyce's *Ulysses* and Homer's, and it is possible to read the Dublin work without a thought of the ancient Ulysses or the wine-dark Mediterranean. But the Homer parallel, present all the time in Joyce's mind and therefore necessary to the creation of his book, gives to this invocation of a Dublin of the past, to this laying bare of so much in the minds of ordinary people that is usually hidden, another dimension. Joyce's book has the quality of being a great panoramic view of mankind, in which the characters, for all the triviality of their lives, represent at moments the universal. The blowsy, amorous, sentimental, second-rate singer, Marion Bloom, is, in her reveries, all women, certainly the Penelope in Ithaca to whom

Ulysses returns inevitably for sustenance, and perhaps the Earth Goddess from whom women derive their strength. In her midnight monologue she returns again and again to her first love affair with Bloom, then a young man in Gibraltar, and her final answer to life is an affirmation that life is worth living – the word "Yes" resounds like the sound of a bell in the last passage:

"And the sea, the sea crimson sometimes like fire and the glorious sunsets and the fig trees in the Alameda Gardens, yes, and all the queer little streets and pink and blue and yellow houses and the rose gardens and the jasmine and geraniums and cactuses and Gibraltar as a girl where I was a Flower of the mountain yes, when I put the rose in my hair like the Andalusian girls used or shall I wear a red yes and how he kissed me under the Moorish wall and I thought well as well him as another and then I asked him with my eyes and asked again yes and he asked me would I yes to say yes to my mountain flower and first I put my arms around him yes and drew him down to me so he could feel my breasts all perfume yes and his heart was going like mad and yes I said yes I will yes."

Ulysses opens with a character who is of nearly equal importance to Leopold Bloom, Stephen Dedalus, who appears in Joyce's other works, The Portrait of the Artist as a Young Man and in Stephen Hero. Stephen is very largely Joyce himself. Like Joyce, he is the son of a family ruined by a father's extravagance, a brilliant scholar and who rebels against his country and against the Roman Catholic Church which educated him – from neither of which can he ever separate himself – an artist who has to fight for his integrity with the only weapons he possesses – silence, exile and cunning. Stephen, at the beginning of Ulysses, is living in a Martello Tower outside Dublin with Buck Mulligan – drawn from the young Oliver St. John Gogarty – he voices the rebellion and discontent of a young man who like Telemachus, the son of Ulysses in the Odyssey, feels he has lost his heritage. Stephen plays in the book the part of the man who sees clearly, even if imperfectly, compared with Bloom and his companions who spend their time in a daze of half-thought. Stephen is constantly epigrammatic and what he says represents the protest of the artist against muddle and illusion. Buck Mulligan lends him a cracked mirror to shave in, which he has picked up from his mother's house: "It is a symbol of Irish art. The cracked looking-glass of a servant," says Stephen. Talking to the pompous schoolmaster, Mr. Deasy, who says to him of the Irish, "We are a generous people but we must also be just", Stephen observes, "I fear those big words which make us so unhappy". And arguing still with the school-master he says: "History is a nightmare from which I am trying to escape."

Stephen's and Bloom's paths on 16 June cross each other. Bloom is the man, the only man who is really kind to Stephen.

The greatness of *Ulysses* is shown above all in the fact that its reader is very gradually made aware that Leopold Bloom is a hero of the modern world as Homer's Ulysses was of the semi-classical world of 1000 B.C. Homer's Ulysses is the man who became a great warrior but none the less whose instincts were against fighting, and an early legend shows Ulysses feigning madness to avoid going to the Trojan War. Whether brave or not, Ulysses is a master of craft, the wily Ulysses. Leopold Bloom is nothing of a warrior but he is also a wily man full of strange knowledge of himself and people. Joyce does not go out of his way to make the reader understand this; the reader has to discover it for himself. Joyce does the opposite of what most authors do to make his hero attractive. As Richard Ellman in his biography of Joyce has written:

"Joyce is the porcupine of authors. His heroes are grudged heroes, the impossible young man (Stephen), the passive adult (Bloom). It is hard to like them, harder still to admire them. Joyce preferred it so. Un-equivocal sympathy would be romancing. He denudes man of what we are accustomed to expect, then summons us to sympathize."

Bloom is shown in complete physical and mental nakedness. The most anodyne of his characteristics is that "Mr. Leopold Bloom ate with relish the inner organs of beasts and fowls. He liked giblet soup, nutty gizzards, a stuffed roast heart, fried ham and cod's roes. Most of all he liked grilled mutton kidneys which gave to his palate a fine tang of faintly scented urine." But we are shown into the depths of his unconscious mind. In the critical chapter of fantasy, he is, as it were, psycho-analysed, and we see the masochistic tendencies of this "womanly-man". Bloom appears an unusual man because we are told everything about him, yet the range of Bloom's peculiarities is probably not greater than that of other men. He is a nobody, al-though, to his cronies, who alternately admire and despise him, his power of expression and considerable, if slightly confused, know-ledge of matters of every kind make them admit "he is not one of your common or garden – he's a cultured all round man is Bloom".

We hardly notice Bloom's ordinary good points – he is devoted to his wife and daughter, he loves dogs and cats, feeds birds, helps a blind man across the street, subscribes more than he can afford to the children of a dead friend and looks after Stephen like a father. But when one has digested this many-sided character one realizes that, out of the mirk and triviality, the man is far more than the sum of his small, good, human qualities. Among a crowd of satisfied brutal chaps, strong in their Irishness or their religion or their prejudices, Bloom alone stands out as a complete human being. He is more than an Irishman or a Jew; he is devoid of narrow-mindedness, prejudice or pretence and therefore of fear or cruelty.

The great French critic Valéry Larbaud, one of the first admirers of Joyce, said that Bloom was as immortal as Falstaff. This may be true, although Bloom will remain a character known only to the comparatively few adventurous spirits who can master a book which, for all its exciting and amusing qualities, is an exceedingly difficult book to read – the most difficult, perhaps, of all the world's great works of fiction. For some, however, it is one of the most rewarding.

ARIEL

ANDRÉ MAUROIS

ANDRÉ MAUROIS, whose real name is Herzog, was born in July, 1885, son of a wealthy French textile manufacturer. Overnight he achieved popularity in this country with *The Silence of Colonel Bramble*, that immortal picture of the British army Blimp published soon after the First World War when he was attached to the British forces as interpreter. In this book, in the *Discourses of Doctor O'Grady*, in essays and other works, we find him an amused but benevolent observer of the English, their talk, manners and mentality, their soldiers, writers, aristocrats, a connoisseur of our country houses and the English countryside. But though feeling happy in England, Maurois has always remained the Frenchman, aware, despite his love for that country, of an irreducible something in his heart which could find no affinity with English life and held aloof, seeking the distant presence of his own land. In other words, he has always been a discerning admirer, which is the most flattering kind.

In his biographies of Disraeli, Marshal Lyautey, Byron, Dickens and Shelley, on which his fame also rests, Maurois has maintained the same detached and courteous observation, emphasizing not the greatness of these figures, but their humanity. In Lyautey he shows us the uncomplicated man of action, in Dickens the creative artist who finds release by transforming lived reality into a new and emotionally acceptable form. Byron is the genius at odds with himself. Disraeli is the visionary who tries and fails to turn his dreams into reality, while Shelley is the dreamer who revolts against reality and, with his head in the clouds, perpetually stumbles against the hard rocks of material existence.

Ariel, A Shelley Romance was first published in English translation in 1924. The book is as far from the conventional biography as a soufflé is from a suet pudding: scant mention of sources, no footnotes, no discussion, indeed barely a mention of his poems, a text empty of the details that give weight to more serious works; instead of awesome respect, ironic humour playing like summer lightning round the central character, the spotlight continually on Shelley and his immediate circle; no assessments, no mention of his place in English

494

literature. English critics found this novelistic approach, the lightness of touch enchanting. They praised the vivid picture of Shelley, Maurois's gift for the delineation of character, the fascinating originality of the book, and called it the fairest and most human portrait yet published. We have only to turn to more recent biographies to find that this is still true.

We first meet Shelley at Eton, an exceptionally beautiful boy, challenging, as a self-conscious individual in his own right, the conventions of school life – an unusual attitude in someone of his class, grandson of the wealthy Sir Bysshe Shelley and son of Timothy Shelley, Esquire, M.P., a vain, pompous, inoffensive yet exasperating gentleman who from the start eyed his girlish offspring with the gravest misgivings. Father and son could never get on; they did not speak the same language. Timothy was conventional; as a child Percy was already living in an unreal world, feeding on fantasies. At Eton he was bullied because he was different until, trembling with rage, too furious to be afraid, he fought his way free of tormentors and escaped to wander, lost in thought, through the Thames-side meadows, flinging himself down in the sun-flecked grass to watch the river glide past, fascinated by the tenuous fragility of willows reflected in the water, eyeing the massive towers of Windsor and Eton as symbols of a hostile world which he sensed would never change.

But in the holidays, at his opulent country home, he came into his own. "In the eyes of his sisters Shelley was a Superman. The moment he arrived from Eton the house was filled with fantastic guests, the park was alive with confused murmurs as in *A Midsummer Night's Dream*. The little girls lived in a continual but agreeable terror. Percy delighted in clothing with mystery the everyday objects of life. . . . What gave charm to these inventions was that the teller himself was not too sure he was inventing them."

Soon, at Oxford in the year 1810, the tall youth, his features afire with a vivid and preternatural intelligence, was voraciously reading philosophy and metaphysics. The variety of systems perplexed him and he amused himself by substituting for them "an aery edifice of crystalline theories, preferring to the real world, the incoherence of which terrified him, the more agreeable vision which the soul gains by looking at facts through the vaporous meshes of clouds". "What an extraordinary creature!" thought his friend Jefferson Hogg, with whom he argued until the small hours. "The grace of a young girl, the purity of a maiden who has never left her mother's side, and nevertheless an indomitable force, the soul of a Benedictine monk, with the ideas of a Jacobin."

From Oxford, Shelley inundated his beautiful cousin, Harriet Grove, with love letters full of inflammatory ideas, including an advocacy of free love. Appalled, she turned him down, leaving him to fulminate against the intolerance she personified. A month later, in the midst of theological Oxford, he published *The Necessity of Atheism*. "Although", writes Maurois, "he had an ardent belief in a Spirit of Universal Goodness, the creator and director of all things, the word 'Atheist' pleased him because of its vigour. He loved to fling it in the face of Bigotry. . . ." He and Hogg, who stood by him, were expelled from Oxford: he refused the conditions his father placed on his return home and the two young men took lodgings in London, without friends or occupation and practically penniless.

For Shelley there now began an extraordinarily chaotic and vagabond existence. A delightful child of sixteen swam into his ken, Harriet Westbrook, a retired publican's daughter, small, delicately formed with an air of delicious freshness. In her he saw the vessel into which all his idealism could be poured and soon they were eloping to Edinburgh with a few pounds borrowed from a friend. The marriage prospered, Shelley read the classics with Harriet and then a larger scheme loomed: work for Catholic emancipation in Ireland. He showered the Dubliners with pamphlets, but reaped only mockery and disillusionment, for his expectations had been high.

Maurois traces Shelley's erratic wanderings with his wife, her sister Elizabeth and Miss Hitchener whose soul he was "directing" from Wales to Lynmouth and back to London, where a friendship was struck up with William Godwin, author of *Political Justice*, which Shelley much admired, and a circle of young ladies was soon listening to the poet's fiery eloquence with ecstatic attention. Money was always a problem. Shelley borrowed, not for his own needs so much as to help Godwin and other impoverished writers. But happiness reigned. Shelley was writing *Queen Mab* and initiating Harriet, who was with child, into Horace and Vergil.

After the birth of the child, a girl named Ianthe, a shadow fell between husband and wife. Harriet was not really an intellectual. Horace had been a great strain and now she wanted to enjoy herself, buy bonnets and clothes – with the money he thought better spent on Godwin and worthless scribblers. These tastes seemed to him scandalous and he made her feel it. A house-party in Bracknell, where he spent long hours reading Petrarch with the daughter of his hostess, set the seal on the estrangement. Harriet was furiously jealous. The jealousy made her appear more stupid than she was. Shelley was disgusted. She returned alone to London. He pursued her, but found her haughty and cold. So the marriage foundered and Shelley's dream-world was temporarily shattered.

But "he needed for his happiness to embody in the form of a beautiful woman the mysterious and benevolent forces which he imagined as scattered throughout the Universe". Ripe for new love, he now met Mary Godwin, daughter of the philosopher's first wife, the brilliant Mary Wollstonecraft. This delicate young girl, sensitive, courageous and intelligent, aroused his ecstatic adoration. He resolved to elope with her, summoning Harriet to London and calmly, with much kindness, explaining his intention. Four months gone with child and already unwell, she now fell into despair. Shelley nursed her with devotion, then resumed his implacable argument. "The union of the sexes is sacred only so long as it contributes to the happiness of husband and wife, and it is dissolved automatically from the moment that its evils exceed its benefits. Constancy has nothing virtuous in itself. . . ." So with cruel and fallible argument Harriet was cast aside and Shelley, in extreme agitation but still firm in his resolve, dosed himself heavily with laudanum.

A few months later he eloped to Switzerland with Mary and her sister Jane as companion. They returned to London, deliciously happy despite frowns from the Godwin family, pressing creditors and the inexplicable sulks of Harriet when they met her. Mary, now pregnant, responded well to instruction in Greek and Latin. They sailed paper boats on the Serpentine and the only shadow was the continued presence of Jane, who had renamed herself Claire, and had long intellectual (?) talks with Shelley when Mary was unwell. Then the child was born and died within a month and with Claire still in the house Mary became seriously vexed. She was certain that Claire was in love with Shelley.

Claire left, to pursue and conquer Lord Byron, and the spring of 1816 found her with the Shelleys in Switzerland awaiting the advent of her lover who crossed the Continent in the most sumptuous of travelling carriages to join them. Byron and Shelley got on well together and Shelley, the least vain of men, did not notice Byron's admiration for him as someone whose "will was a force, a bent bow, while his own floated loose on the current at the mercy of his passions and his mistresses".

In England again, two tragedies smote the Shelleys. Mary's half-sister, Fanny, committed suicide and, soon after, Harriet in advanced pregnancy was found drowned in the Serpentine. She had fallen from despair, living first with an army officer who had left her on being ordered to India and then with a humble protector, allegedly a groom, who had deserted her. Absolutely alone, she had chosen death rather than face the approaching scandal.

A fortnight later, having convinced himself that he was in no way responsible for the tragedy, Shelley and Mary were married in a London church. He then sought the custody of Harriet's two children, but this, in the Court of Chancery, was denied him on account of his atheistic and morally subversive writings. The decision was very bitter to him. It seemed to sanction his exile from the community of civilized men and "was like a brevet of incurable folly".

He, Mary, their children and the inevitable Claire, escaped to Italy. There was vexatious business with Byron, installed with his mistresses in Venice, over the custody of Claire's daughter by him, Allegra. Shelley's youngest child died. He and Mary felt friendless and alone. He worked hard on *Prometheus Unbound*, but the joy of creation only banished melancholy for a time. "It seemed to him that in the frail bark which carried beneath an alien sky his group of youthful exiles Misery stood at the helm." To cheat their sorrow, the couple went to Rome and on to Naples, where another of the family, William, his father's darling, died of dysentery. Disconsolate, they moved to Florence and Mary gave birth to a son.

When winter came they went to Pisa, where they made interesting friends, and Emilia, the daughter of a Florentine nobleman, immured in a convent aroused all Shelley's instincts of knight-errantry. He visited her, fell mystically in love, and Mary, the mother, housekeeper, a drier and more practical version of the girl he had carried away to Switzerland, had to watch while his soul revelled in this new vision of perfect womanhood. Unfortunately, while Shelley was still writing a magnificent love-poem, Emilia was married off to an unattractive gentleman and the disenchanted poet was left to mourn: "I think one is always in love with something or other; the error consists in seeking in a mortal image the likeness of what is, perhaps, eternal."

There were more meetings with Byron in Ravenna, painful gossip regarding Shelley and Claire and much heartache for the mother over the fate of Allegra, in Byron's custody but neglected by him. Then Byron arrived in Pisa with five carriages and a menagerie of animals. The place became a social and literary centre. Byron was lionized, but Shelley, who did not hide his boredom at balls and dinners and was so uncomfortably absolute in his opinions, was cold-shouldered by English visitors. It did not worry him in the least.

And now, in the over-intellectualized, somewhat sultry atmosphere, a breezy sailor, corsair and pirate suddenly appeared, who had led a life of adventure the world over, Trelawny by name, desperately anxious to meet the two poets. But it was they who were most impressed. Trelawny was a man of action, not a dreamer, to Byron and Shelley a strange and enviable phenomenon. Soon Shelley was consulting him about nautical terms, drawing keels, sails and sea-charts on the sandy banks of the Arno.

Dazzled by the dashing Trelawny, Shelley now wanted a boat. One was built in Genoa and delivered to him at Lerici on the coast – she sailed and worked well, he was told, but she was a difficult craft to manage and needed tons of iron ballast to make her safe. She was christened *Ariel*. Afloat, though he tangled himself up in the rigging, read Sophocles while trying to steer and several times nearly fell overboard, Shelley was deliriously happy. His joy was increased by the addition of a dinghy which frequently capsized and gave him a ducking. The water, the breezes, the azure sky stimulated him as nothing else. Far out at sea, with a boatload of children, to their mother's horror he fell into a deep reverie from which he awakened to exclaim joyfully: "Now let us together solve the great mystery!"

For a whole glorious summer, nothing could mar his joy. He sailed the *Ariel* by moonlight, Mary sitting at his feet, her head against his knees. Then, in July, 1822, a month before Shelley's thirtieth birthday, came tragedy. The heat was suffocating. On the 8th, Shelley, with two friends, arrived in Leghorn where the *Ariel* was moored, intending to sail her back, a seven hours' trip, across the Bay of Spezia to Lerici. They set off in the afternoon across a leaden sea. Some time later, a heavy storm blew up with thunder, torrential rain and a gale-force wind. When it cleared, no sign of their boat could be seen from shore. It was a week before Mary could bring herself to suspect the worst and further days passed before certainty came when a corpse, half-eaten by fishes, was washed ashore in the Bay. In one coat pocket was a volume of Sophocles and Keats's poems in the other. At intervals the bodies of the two companions were also found.

As sanitary laws forbade the removal of the corpses, they were burned on the shore, with incense, oil and salt thrown on the flames and village children watching wide-eyed with awe.

Mary Shelley never married again. She lived in Italy for a long time and then in London. Her sister Claire spent the evening of her life in Florence and it was there, in the spring of 1878, that a young man seeking information about Shelley came for reminiscences. She confessed she had never loved Byron.

"There was a silence. The visitor, hesitating a little asked: 'Have you never loved, Madame?'

"A delicate blush diffused the withered cheeks, and this time she made no reply, gazing on the ground.

" 'Shelley?' he murmured.

" 'With all my heart and soul,' she replied, without raising her eyes. Then, with charming coquetry, she gave him a tap on the cheek with her closed fan."

So Maurois ends his book. There have been more learned volumes about Shelley, but none which conveys in a shorter space, with more insight or delicacy of touch the poetic truth about this strange spirit clothed in human shape, to whom the lines so well apply in the closing days of his life: "*Ariel*: Wast well done? *Prospero*: Bravely, my diligence. Thou shalt be free."

THE MAGIC MOUNTAIN
THOMAS MANN

THE SON of a German grain merchant, Thomas Mann was born in Lübeck; but on his father's death the family moved to Munich. His studies embraced literature, art, history and political economy. He developed special interest in Russian, Scandinavian and French nineteenth-century novelists.

Leaving school at nineteen, he took an unpaid post with an insurance company and surreptitiously wrote his first book, a love story called *Fallen*.

At twenty-five he achieved fame with an autobiographical novel *The Büddenbrooks*, following this three years later with *Tonio Kröger*, his own favourite work.

In 1912 he spent three weeks in a Swiss sanatorium with his wife who had a lung affliction. This brief experience was to bear remarkable fruit some twelve years later; but first came the First World War, during which he wrote some soul-searching treatises and published, in 1918, *Reflections of a Non-Political Man*.

In pre-war days he had enjoyed a happy family life and was held in high esteem and had homes in Munich, Tolz and at Nidden in Memelland. *The Magic Mountain*, which stemmed from his experiences in Davos, appeared in 1924, set the seal upon his literary reputation, and won him the Nobel Prize for Literature.

When the Second World War threatened he was on the crest of the wave. He was, in fact, lecturing in Holland when the Nazis burned the Reichstag. He did not return to Germany, but made for Zürich to continue work on *Joseph and His Brothers*, for which he had already conducted much research.

For denouncing the Nazis in newspaper articles he was deprived of German citizenship. An honorary doctorate at the University of Bonn was rescinded and his works were banned in his homeland.

Mann went to the U.S.A., and there the erstwhile "non-political man" became actively anti-Fascist, lecturing widely, and publishing (in 1938) *The Coming Victory of Democracy*.

He was appointed Fellow of the Library of Congress, consultant in German Literature. Making a home in Princeton, New Jersey, he continued his lecturing and writing, and, in 1941, was able to build himself a house at Santa Monica, California. He became an American citizen in 1944; and in 1949 revisited Germany to receive a "Göethe Prize" at Frankfurt-am-Main and a second Göethe award in Weimar. He died in Zürich in 1955.

It is not possible in this short sketch to list more than a few of his published works which included his various Joseph novels, *Lotte in Weimar*, *The Transposed Heads*, *Doctor Faustus*, *The Holy Sinner*, *This Peace*, *This War* and many, many more. A writer of great artistic and intellectual power, his international reputation is assured and books seeking to interpret his work and influence have multiplied almost yearly since his death.

Hans Castorp, son of a wealthy Hanseatic family, an average sort of person in intellect and tastes, is sent to a Davos sanatorium for three weeks and remains for seven years. The book tells how his personal horizon is widened and how he undergoes physical, moral, intellectual and spiritual development entirely as a result of his human encounters and personal reactions during those seven years in the rarefied atmosphere of the Swiss Alps.

The narrative pattern is formed by a clever interweaving of multiple strands of thought and experience. Castorp may stand as a sort of "Mr. Everyman", and the book's wider implication becomes apparent as his story unfolds. Many people have pointed out that the book may be read on several levels – as a distinctive novel in its own right; as a dialectic work or as an allegory in which the isolated mountain resort may be taken as a microcosm of Europe and the sick world below. It does not really matter. The abundance of ideas and the incisively drawn characters carry the reader on.

Also under treatment at the sanatorium is Hans Castorp's cousin, Joachim Ziemssen, and as other patients appear Hans is brought face to face with the stark realities of sickness and disease. Mann does not spare his hero the repulsive physical details of tuberculosis in all its manifestations; nor does he spare the reader. Stark realism prevails, especially in the early chapters, when Hans finds that among his fellow-patients is a select coterie known as The Half Lung Club.

Pervasive characters make their appearance. There is Dr. Krokowski, exponent of psycho-analysis, who asserts that all disease is merely love transformed; and Settembrini, the garrulous Italian, who discourses eloquently and endlessly on liberal capitalism, bourgeois nationalism and rationalism, spicing his talk with ideas borrowed from Petrarch, Voltaire, Schiller, Mazini and many others; Settembrini it is who cheerfully christens the patients "horizontallers" for the obvious reason that they spend so much time recumbent.

Among the women patients, most of whom are well drawn, is a particularly seductive Russian – Clavdia Chauchat. She catches Castorp's eye quite early in the tale. After she has figured in his dreams twice in a single night he falls in love with her, and it is she who occupies his thoughts for nearly half the book. An opportunity to make advances to her comes in a chapter called Walpurgis Night; but just as he has screwed up courage to declare his passion there is a characteristic touch of the author's irony – she leaves the sanatorium next day.

From this point the book becomes more given over to the ideas and theories most of which are bandied between another character, Leo Naphta, and Ludovico Settembrini. They are perfect foils for each other and enter into long and lively arguments on sickness and health, life and death, war and peace, history, philosophy, religion and what have you. They dispute a good deal over what freedom is, without coming to any conclusion. Hans and others sometimes attempt to participate in these discussions, but they seldom get in a word when these two star talkers are hard at it.

Hans vaguely buoys himself up with expectation of Clavdia's return, but it is hardly surprising that, sated with so much daily disputation on abstract topics, he yearns for a break. He plans to get away from it all, if only for a time, to give himself a chance to take stock and think a little for himself. He buys some skis and makes himself sufficiently proficient to venture up the mountain. It is a break for the reader, too, as Hans, alone on the silent, snow-clad heights, at last feels the freedom that Naphta and Settembrini had failed to define in words. Recklessly he goes on and on. This is reality; and very nearly fatal reality, for he is caught in a sudden snowstorm and is forced to shelter in the lee of a locked hut. There he falls into a kind of dream or delirium in which his mind is a prey to a jumble of the mixed impressions gained in his sojourn in Davos to date. He wakes to an echoing phrase: "For the sake of goodness and love, man shall let death have no sovereignty over his thoughts." It is fair weather; he makes his way safely back to Davos, his dream already fading from his mind.

And now comes a new excitement with the introduction of a forceful character, a most colourful creation, Mynheer Pieter Peeperkorn, who dominates the stage for a time. His entry is a dramatic surprise, for he arrives in company with Clavdia Chauchat; they share a sleigh from the station; they sup together. The intimacy of their association is apparent.

Hans, who has waited so expectantly for his Clavdia, had not bargained for this. It is another example of the author's love for an ironic touch. But, possibly because of his lone adventure in the snow, Hans now has enough character to get over this shock and he even strikes up a friendship of sorts with his victorious rival, a jovial extrovert whose talk is reminiscent of Alfred Jingle's, for it consists of short, staccato utterances. But he is usually much less explicit than Jingle and often his sentences are quite meaningless. But he loves life and has special zest for wine and food and women. He is also an exhibitionist and announces loudly: "Pieter Peeperkorn will now take unto himself a glass of Hollands," as he prepares to swallow a glass of gin. He is great fun, but he does not stay the course. When his vigour fails there are no resources left in life for him and he commits suicide. Though the way seems clear for Hans to renew his claim on Clavdia, she goes away again and passes from his life forever.

Hans is in the dumps. He sees on every side "the uncanny and the malign . . . life without time, life without care or hope, life as depravity, assiduous stagnation; life as dead".

At a loose end, he joins with other patients in various hobbies, photography, stamp-collecting and games with pencil and paper. It is futile, stop-gap stuff at best.

A gramophone is provided for patients and Hans draws satisfaction from music for a time, working his way "in undisturbed enjoyment" through the record albums. He comes to cherish such favourites as "Aïda," "Carmen," "L'après-midi d'un Faune" and Gounod's "Faust," drawing something from all of them.

In his unsettled state he is ready to clutch at any straw of experience. When Dr. Krokowski extends his field from psycho-analysis to hypnotism, telepathy and spiritualism, Hans takes a passing interest in the occult, only to be reprimanded by his friend Settembrini, who tells him to have respect for his humanity. "Confide in your God-given power of clear-thought," says the Italian, "and hold in abhorrence these luxations of the brain, these miasmas of the spirit!"

In time Hans is disillusioned, and the old restlessness returns. He is far from being the only one affected. Tension is general in the isolated mountain resort, just as it is throughout Europe and the rest of the world. The First World War is near. Arguments are many; people are on edge, and in this atmosphere the perpetual wrangling between Naphta and Settembrini boils over in an open quarrel.

"I am in your way and you are in mine!" cries Naphta after one stormy session. "We will transfer the settlement of our differences to a suitable place ... You will hear from me."

"And you will find a hearing, sir!" is the Italian's dramatic retort.

Hans strives to avert the threatened duel without success. Pistols are prepared; the men meet. Settembrini, unable to bring himself to kill, discharges his weapon in the air. Naphta angrily calls upon him to fire again, and when Settembrini steadfastly refuses, Naphta's reaction is to turn his own pistol on himself.

After this intimate tragedy comes word of another shooting with wider implications – the assassination at Serajevo. As war engulfs Europe, Hans, restored in health, decides to return to his native land to play his part.

Mann gives his readers a brief glimpse of Hans in the midst of a fierce attack on the Western front, and ends with a soliloquy reminiscent of those moralizing interpolations so beloved by Thackeray.

"Farewell, Honest Hans Castorp. Life's delicate child! Your tale is told. . . .

"Farewell, and if thou livest or diest! Thy prospects are poor. The desperate dance in which your fortunes are caught up will last many a sinful year; we should not care to set a high stake on thy life by the time it ends. We even confess that it is without great concern we leave the question open. Adventures of the flesh and in the spirit, while enhancing thy simplicity, granted thee to know in the spirit what in the flesh thou scarcely couldst have done. Moments there were, when out of death, and the rebellion of the flesh, there came to thee, as thou tookest stock of thyself, a dream of love. . . ."

And echoing, perhaps, the waking thoughts of his hero after the delirious dream in the snow, Mann concludes:

"Out of this universal feast of death, out of this extremity of fever, kindling the rain washed evening sky to a fiery glow, may it be that Love one day shall mount?"

Thomas Mann is regarded as a master of irony, and *The Magic Mountain*, as has been shown, provides him with plenty of scope for the indulgence of this gift. Yet he himself was a prey to ironic influences when committing this masterpiece to paper. He has confessed that in his first conception he envisaged little more than a light, humorous book touching on "the fascination of death, the triumph of extreme disorder over a life founded upon order and consecrated to it ... a droll conflict between macabre adventure and bourgeois sense of duty".

But, somehow, once he had begun to write, the creation ran away with the creator and the manuscript grew and developed into an epic study of a civilization in decay. Instead of the slight personal narrative he had conceived, he found himself depicting with earnest Teutonic thoroughness a comprehensive picture of the contemporary world scene until the thing grew into a massive work of more than 700 pages.

Into this mighty creation crept much of the earnest soul-searching displayed in earlier treatises and essays. Ideas with which he had already experimented helped to mould the expanding theme of The Magic Mountain, as did remembered reading among Russian, French and Scandinavian literature and among philosophic writers like Göethe, Schopenhauer, Nietzsche and others.

A further ironic touch which is evoked by reading The Magic Mountain is that though a powerful stylist with a great gift of expression, his work in general, and this masterpiece in particular, has bred a whole group of would-be interpreters, all of whom have striven, according to their lights, to unravel the complex strands of the story.

Certain critics have traced evidence of the Schopenhauer influence in specific passages; others, again, have produced "interpretations" which sometimes seem more obscure than the matter they are seeking to clarify.

Mann, with his tendency toward mysticism, allows himself free range in The Magic Mountain. He was known to have been superstitious where numbers are concerned and some interpreters have noted that the number seven crops up repeatedly in this tale, though the significance of this is not clear.

Such things hardly matter. The wide sweep of this great book sets before the ordinary reader an impressive feast of reading. First, it tells an unusual, absorbing story, with some memorable characters and stimulating dialogue. Every reader, whatever his limitations, can count upon adding appreciably to his knowledge of human nature, of life and of the world. Even those who may be baffled by some passages, or who may grow impatient when ploughing through some of the endless discussions between certain characters, cannot fail to be deeply stirred by what they read. The Magic, in fact, lies just as much in the author's powerful pen as in the Mountain of his tale.

THE GREAT GATSBY

F. SCOTT FITZGERALD

IN THE 1920s America was sick, very sick indeed. The United States had just come through the first great European war in which she had taken part, and already the fruits of victory were turning sour. There was a spirit of disillusion in the air. Old ways of life had been disrupted, old ideals shattered, a new order was coming in, and there were many who dreaded its impact. Millions of young men who had gone out to battle for "democracy" and the rest, were now putting off their uniforms and seemed to have no higher objective than to have a good time before they had to settle down to the harsh reality of getting a living.

Perhaps the effects of the war were greater on the women than on the men. Millions of young women were experiencing an intoxicating feeling of emancipation and release from the conventional restraints that still wrapped round their mothers. Women had just been granted the suffrage, but most of the new voters were much more interested in what they called "life" than in politics. Their skirts got tighter and rose a few more inches toward the knee, while their "waists" began to show just a suggestion of a "V". They dabbed powder on their faces; and their cigarettes, when they took them out of their mouths, were marked with a tell-tale ring of crimson.

Prohibition had just come in also, and a great new industry sprang up almost overnight. Vile gin was manufactured in bakehouses, "speakeasies" blared and blazed in almost every street, and the bootlegger was added to the list of American occupations. Men who had never taken a drink before now gloried in becoming "criminals", and young women (and the not so young) who wanted to be "in the swim" made a boast of the number of times they had been "blotto". Since by no means everybody had an automobile, a ride in a car was something of an event, and it became quite the recognized thing, after a session at the movies watching Chaplin or Mary Pickford, to spend an hour or two on the back seat of an open car (most of the cars were "open" in those days) "necking" with the latest boy-friend, who might be expected to have had the foresight to bring with him a bottle of "rye".

One of the brightest of the bright young men of the period had a name for it. He called it "the Jazz Age" – the "he" in the case being Francis Scott Fitzgerald, who when the twenties opened was writing short stories which he couldn't sell.

Scott Fitzgerald knew what he was writing about. He had been through it all, and, as he might say, had seen through it all. He was a most typical member of that "new generation" as he called it, that "new generation which had grown up to find all Gods dead, all wars fought, all faiths in man shaken". He was a Middle Westerner, born of wealthy parents in Minnesota, but he became an Easterner by adoption, finding the scenes and characters of his stories in New York and the Atlantic seaboard. He was twenty-one in 1917, the year in which the U.S.A. joined in the war, and he served for a short time in the American Army. Before joining up he had been a student at Princeton, and that distinguished centre of education was the scene of his first novel. *This Side of Paradise* it was called; it came out in 1920, and after its publication there were no more rejection slips to be pinned on the frieze in his room. It is about young students who went to the war, the girls they were in love with, and the things they got up to. At the time it was thought awfully "advanced". We may smile at the girl who confessed that "I've kissed dozens of men, and I suppose I'll kiss dozens more," but when the parents of America's young womanhood read that they blanched, and Ada and Clara had to think up some really good excuses when they arrived back home a few minutes after ten.

Five years later, in 1925, Scott Fitzgerald published *The Great Gatsby*. In those years he had grown to maturity – in his writing, that is; in his life he never managed to throw off the irresponsibility of youth, and he died, "burnt out", in 1940. It is a short book as great novels go, but there is no doubt about the "great". It is sparkling often, sour at times, frequently witty and brilliant, and through it runs a note of unusual tenderness.

The story is told in the first person, the narrator being a young man named Nick Carraway, who had some sort of job in New York but lived at West Egg, a small place on the shore of Long Island Sound, twenty-five miles from the great city. Carraway's house was modest enough, but next door was a great garish mansion, the scene of almost interminable parties. Across the bay, in the more fashionable East Egg, lived Nick's cousin Daisy, who was married to a big beefy fellow named Tom Buchanan. Daisy was beautiful and charming, and not lacking in intelligence: what made her, then, marry such a brutal lump? Buchanan had money, pots of it.

That summer, reports Nick Carraway, "there was music from my neighbour's house through the nights". Guests arrived at all hours between nine in the morning and after midnight. Cars from New York were parked five deep in the drive. Buffet-tables were set up in the gardens, a full-size orchestra performed almost non-stop, the champagne corks seemed never to cease popping. There were guests everywhere, and (so it transpired) most of them were uninvited, since you didn't have to have an invitation to one of Mr. Jay Gatsby's parties.

Nick was one of the few who did actually get a card of invitation, and out of curiosity he went along. He had never met his host, and nobody seemed to know anything much about him, except that he was very obviously a man of wealth, and knew how to spend it. At the party Nick met a girl friend of his, Jordan Baker, a professional golfer, and he inquired what she knew about their host. "Somebody told me they thought he had killed a man once." Another girl came up with the suggestion that he had been a German spy in the war, and a man nodded in confirmation. Later in the evening Nick met Gatsby, although he did not know it was he at first. They happened to be sitting at the same table, and they got talking about their war experiences. Then his new acquaintance said that he had bought a hydroplane, and invited him to join him in trying it out. "Want to go with me, old sport?" he asked, and Nick agreed. Then Nick went on to say that he had not even seen their host: "I live over there – and this man Gatsby sent over his chauffeur with an invitation."

For a moment the man looked at him as if he did not understand. Then, "I'm Gatsby," he said, "I thought you knew, old sport. I'm afraid I'm not a very good host." And then, as he brushed aside Nick's apologies, the "elegant young roughneck, a year or two over thirty, whose elaborate formality of speech just missed being absurd", smiled. And such a smile it was, "one of those rare smiles with a quality of eternal reassurance in it, that you may come across four or five times in life". It created in Nick an immediate liking, that was to grow into something very near affection.

Not that he ever got to the bottom of Gatsby's character. He was always a man of mystery. Once he told Nick that he was the son of some wealthy people in the Middle West, he had been educated at Oxford, and when his parents had died he had come into a good deal of money and had lived like a rajah in all the capitals of Europe – Paris, Venice, Rome; he had collected jewels, he had hunted big game, he had had a disappointing love affair, after which he had "joined up" and seen active service as an infantry lieutenant. In the battle of the Argonne Forest he had held up three German divisions with the remains of his machine-gun battalion. Whereupon he had been given a decoration by every European government, "even Montenegro, little Montenegro down on the Adriatic Sea!" Of course Nick didn't believe him – but what a story it made! Then Gatsby reached in his pocket, fished out a piece of metal slung on a ribbon, and put it in his palm. It bore the legend, "Montenegro, Nicolas Rex", and the inscription, "Major Jay Gatsby. For Valour Extraordinary".

When their acquaintance had ripened, Nick learned something of the truth about Gatsby. His real name was James Gatz, and he had changed it when as a down-and-out youth he had done a good turn to a rich yachtsman named Dan Cody on Lake Superior. Cody had taken him up, employed him in a succession of ever more responsible jobs, and left him twenty-five thousand dollars in his will. He didn't get the money: he was swindled out of it by his dead patron's favour-ite mistress. But he had learnt a great deal through his contacts with the copper millionaire. He had learnt to keep off drink, he had learnt how to use women for his purposes, he had made shady friends who put him in the way of making a fortune. So he *was* a bootlegger, mused Nick as he listened to the tale; but he was not all phoney. He *had* served in the War, he *had* fought in the Argonne, he *had* been decorated.

Eventually Nick learnt the most revealing confession of all. Gatsby, in the days before the war, had been the lover of Daisy, Nick's cousin, and had every reason to hope that when he came back they would be married. But when he did return, he found Daisy married, although she confessed that she still loved him and never had loved anyone else; but Gatsby was poor and jobless, and Tom Buchanan was rolling in dollars, and to a girl such as she was, money was everything – or almost. So that is why he had come to West Egg, just to be able to look across the bay to the light on the pier of the Buchanans' mansion....

Through Nick's instrumentality, Gatsby and Daisy were enabled to meet again, and the beautiful young woman and the intensely virile Gatsby were at once caught up in the grip of a tremendous passion that they could hardly be bothered to hide, and certainly took no pains to keep under control. They became lovers, and talked of getting married if Tom Buchanan could be induced to give his wife a divorce. Buchanan was no model husband. For some time past he had been paying regular visits to a mistress – Myrtle Wilson, the big, richly sensuous and intensely vital wife of George Wilson, who kept a garage beside the ash-dump on the road to New York. But Buchanan was also deeply devoted to his wife – she was the principal display-stand of his wealth – and he had no intention of letting her go. Somehow he got to know something of what was going on, and at length the matter was brought right out into the open.

It was an excessively hot day in late summer, and Daisy insisted that they should make up a party to enjoy themselves in New York. So they set off, Daisy and her husband, Gatsby, Jordan Baker and Nick Carraway. On their way there, they stopped for some "gas" at Wilson's garage, and in conversation with him Buchanan learnt that the man had come to suspect that his wife was carrying on with some unknown, and he was resolved to get rid of his business and take her away somewhere in the country. Buchanan thus realized that he was threatened with the loss not only of his wife but of his mistress.

Arrived in New York, the party took a room in an hotel and ordered drinks. Then Buchanan embarked on a goading operation against Gatsby. He reminded him that he had once said he had been to Oxford, and there was sneering unbelief in the remark. Gatsby got out of that one: he *had* been to Oxford – for five months, in 1919, when there had been a scheme to send selected young officers there on short courses. This did not improve Buchanan's temper, and he now moved on to discuss Gatsby's way of life: "I suppose" (he snarled) "you've got to make your house into a pigsty in order to have friends – in the modern world." Now it was Gatsby's turn. "I've got something to tell *you*, old sport –." Daisy guessed what he was about to say, and implored him not to say it. But Gatsby persisted. "Your wife doesn't love you," he told Buchanan. "She's never loved you. She loves me."

"You must be crazy!" cried Buchanan. "Daisy's leaving you," said Gatsby. "I won't stand this," cried Daisy; "oh please, let's get out."

Gatsby tried to induce Daisy to admit that she had never loved her husband, but this was further than she was willing to go. She *had* loved him once, but she loved Gatsby now. "Isn't that enough?" she demanded of him; "I can't help what's past." Then Buchanan raked up some supposedly unsavoury incident in Gatsby's business career – the case of a bootlegger who had been employed by Gatsby's crowd and then left in the lurch in New Jersey gaol. "He came to us dead broke," rejoined Gatsby: "he was very glad to pick up some money, old sport."

"Don't call me 'old sport'!"

After this the party broke up and they set off home. Buchanan felt so sure that Daisy would never dream of leaving him for good, that he urged that she should go in Gatsby's car, and this she did. And out of that boastful gesture, tragedy sprang. Gatsby's car (with Daisy driving) swept down the road from New York, touching as much as fifty at times. They were approaching the garage now, and here Wilson had been keeping his wife a prisoner for fear that she would escape him and make for her lover. Just as Gatsby's car came in line with the garage, Myrtle Wilson suddenly burst out into the road. The car caught her, ripped her open, flung her aside like a piece of refuse – and sped on. A few minutes later the second car with Nick and the rest stopped outside the garage to see what was the trouble, and Buchanan was confronted by the dead body of his mistress.

The rest of the story is melodrama. Wilson, distraught with grief, went in search of the men who had "murdered" his wife, and in the course of his inquiries he called at the Buchanans' and was told by Tom that it was Gatsby's car that had run his wife down. So Wilson, thinking that Gatsby was the person responsible, moved on to Gatsby's garish mansion, found its master taking his ease on a pneumatic mattress in the bathing-pool, and shot him dead. Then he walked a little distance away across the grass and shot himself.

Nick Carraway arranged the funeral, and he was almost the only mourner, for he was unable to persuade any of Gatsby's "friends" to risk the possible reflection on their characters. Nick recalled the last time he had seen Gatsby, on the morning after the tragic happening on the highway. It was then that Gatsby had told him of his early love for Daisy. As they had shaken hands and Nick had turned away to go, he had looked back and shouted across the lawn. "They're a rotten crowd. You're worth the whole damn bunch put together." Gatsby had nodded, and then his face broke into that radiant and understanding smile of his. "I disapproved of him from beginning to end," Nick is made to say, but "I've always been glad I said that."

Toward the end of the year Nick decided to give up his house at West Egg and return to New York. He couldn't stand the place any more: it had quite got on his nerves. The house was empty now, but he kept on seeing the gleaming, glittering parties that Gatsby had given there, he heard the music and the laughter, the crunch of car wheels on the gravel of the drive. On his last night there he went over and looked at "that huge incoherent failure of a house" once more. Some boy had scrawled an obscene word with a piece of brick on the white steps: Nick erased it with a rasping movement of his

Coming as he did from the lower middle class, H. G. Wells (*above*) was completely fitted to describe the aspirations and experiences, humorous and pathetic, of struggling youth. Yet it was not with such human documents as *Mr. Polly* and *Kipps* and *Ann Veronica* that he first made his name but with romances that paved the way for the science and space-fiction of our own day. Most of the great inventions that have characterized our present age were anticipated by this nimble-minded little man. Aldous Huxley (*left*) came of one of the most cultured stocks of British intelligence, but he, too, chose to write on sociological themes. While his witty and satirical essays and novels and books of travel are the delight of innumerable readers, it is probable that *Brave New World* will maintain his fame.

Notwithstanding the tortured eccentricities of its style, its baffling absence of plot, its exuberance of unpunctuated paragraphs, James Joyce's *Ulysses* has always had its devotees on both sides of the Atlantic. When it was first published (in 1922, in Paris) it achieved notoriety on account of its alleged obscenities. Then it became the fashion to admire Joyce's "stream of consciousness" technique. Now when the uproar has subsided, the book is chiefly valued for its inimitably nostalgic picture of life in Dublin, almost street by street and hour by hour, on a particular day in June 1904. This photograph of Joyce (*left*) was taken at Lucerne in 1935, when he was in his early fifties; he died in 1941.

A Nottingham miner's son, D. H. Lawrence (*right*) was much more the son of his mother, from whom he inherited his artistic capacities and leanings, his love of literary expression and, perhaps above all, his tender understanding of the human animal, woman in particular. He wrote novels, verse and short stories, and perhaps the book by which he will be longest remembered is his novel *Sons and Lovers*, in which he incorporated so much of his own life with his mother, his girl friends and the father with whom he was never able to effect a satisfactory relationship.

shoe. Then he wandered through the garden down to the beach, and sat there brooding and thinking of Gatsby's wonder when he had first managed to pick out the green light shining on the end of Daisy's pier.

Gatsby had come a long way to arrive at this place, and it must have seemed to him that his dream had come so close that he could hardly fail to grasp it. He had believed in that green light, and in the "orgiastic future" that it promised. It had eluded him, however, and (so Nick Carraway mused) it had eluded *us*, not getting any nearer but receding year by year. "But that's no matter – tomorrow we will run faster, stretch out our arms further . . . And one fine morning—." But no more than for the "Great Gatsby", for Scott Fitzgerald and his generation that "fine morning" never came.

AN AMERICAN TRAGEDY

THEODORE DREISER

IN 1844, a young German, John Paul Dreiser, emigrated to America, married the daughter of a Moravian farmer, and rose to become the owner of a mill. During the years of prosperity, his wife bore him eleven children, but the mill burnt down uninsured, his fortunes declined as rapidly as they had risen, and when his son Theodore was born on 27 August, 1871, in Terre Haute, Indiana, he was a broken man of fifty. By the time "Dorsch" was six, the Dreisers were so bitterly poor that they had to split up; the older children struck out for themselves, and while her husband went from city to city looking for work, Mrs. Dreiser became the mainstay of the three youngest children, taking in washing and renting rooms to provide for them.

For Theodore these were the happiest years of his life, for his gay, courageous, warm-hearted mother (he was to immortalize her in *Jennie Gerhardt*) filled even the poorest home with sweetness. It was thanks to her that he received any education, for when he was thirteen she sent him to a state school.

A new world opened for "Dorsch", who up to this time had been forced by his bigoted father to attend one hopeless Catholic parish school after another where he was taught virtually nothing. Books became his passion, and he showed such a high grade of intelligence that one teacher, Miss Fielding, convinced he would go far, urged him to keep on with his studies. Despite her encouragement, however, Theodore at fifteen was so filled with "a wild enthusiasm for the colour of life" that one day he announced: "Ma, I'm off to Chicago".

Chicago cast a spell over Theodore, who eagerly absorbed every detail of its teeming life. His first job was that of a dish-washer in a filthy Greek restaurant; later, he became a clerk at five dollars a week. Unexpectedly, when he was seventeen, his former teacher, Miss Fielding, came to him with the money she had saved to send him to the University of Indiana. Ill-equipped for studying, Theodore did not feel that he had learnt enough at the end of the year to accept Miss Fielding's offer of a second; accordingly he returned to Chicago and took another clerical job. It was shortly after this that his adored mother, who had been failing for some time, collapsed and died in his arms. Her death was the "biggest psychologic shake-up" of his life.

The clerical job folded up, and Theodore became a laundry-truck driver, then a collector for a hire-purchase firm. It was at this time that he began to write pen-pictures of Chicago, and while he did not envisage himself as an author, he felt he ought to try to get on a newspaper. In 1892, when extra reporters were needed to cover the Democratic National Convention, one paper gave him a temporary assignment, but his actual journalistic career began when an article he had written won him a place on the *Globe*. He had a flair for "human interest" stories, and John McEnnis, the editor, impressed by his potentialities, decided to give him a chance to broaden out; accordingly, he sent young Dreiser to St. Louis to work for a much larger newspaper, the *Globe-Democrat*.

Theodore's main assignments were feature stories and interviews; it was his ambition to become a dramatic critic that led to his downfall. His routine review of three shows duly appeared, but the shows had not, and he hastily fired himself!

Dreiser worked for a number of newspapers after leaving the *Globe-Democrat*, and was finally persuaded by his eldest brother, Paul, to go to New York.

Paul, a well-known composer of popular songs[1], secured for "Dorsch" the editorship of the magazine his publishers were bringing out. After running it successfully for two years, Theodore resigned, and took to free-lancing. He made enough money to marry Sally White to whom he had become engaged in St. Louis, but his work did not satisfy him, and his close friend, Arthur Henry, a journalist like himself, suggested that he should try his hand at short stories. His first effort was bought by Ainslee's Magazine for 75 dollars, and Henry challenged him to write a novel. With no idea how to set about it, Dreiser jotted down a title, *Sister Carrie*, and to his own surprise the words came tumbling out of him.

Sister Carrie, based on the life of one of his sisters, was accepted by Doubleday in the absence of Mr. Doubleday, who when he read the manuscript thought it utterly immoral since the author had neither censured nor punished Carrie for her "fall". Obliged to honour the contract, he refrained from advertising the book of which he issued a mere 1,000 copies; despite a few favourable reviews, only 650 were sold.

The virtual suppression of *Sister Carrie* spelt ruin to Dreiser. No publisher would consider the further two books he had planned, and,

[1] Dreiser wrote the lyric for his brother's greatest hit, "By the Banks of the Wabash Far Away".

with no money coming in, he was forced to send his wife back to her father and move into one small room. But his state of mind was such that he could neither write nor sleep; he became subject to hallucinations, and finally broke down completely. His friend Arthur Henry came to his rescue and sent him to a sanatorium for treatment. Once he had recovered, Dreiser returned to journalism.

His career during the next few years was spectacular. From 35 dollars a week he rose to 10,000 dollars a year as managing editor of Butterick's three fashion magazines. By this time he was so divorced from his own work that he wrote to one contributor: "We cannot admit stories which deal with immoral relations or such degrading themes as drunkenness". The irony of it was that Dreiser was dismissed by the Butterick organization for an affair with a girl on the staff, an affair that also broke up his marriage.

Amazingly, from this inglorious end to his journalistic career, the real Dreiser emerged. He set to work on one of the two books he had planned before the Doubleday debacle, changing the title from *The Transgressor* to *Jennie Gerhardt*.

Jennie Gerhardt was published in 1911. The theme of this novel was much the same as that of *Sister Carrie*, but times had changed and it was an immediate success. Dreiser, now that he had at last "risen above the wind", followed it up with *The Financier*, *The Titan* and *The Genius*, and early in the 1920s began on his sixth novel, partly a documentary since the core of his material was a murder committed in 1906, the drowning in Moose Lake of Grace Brown by Chester Gillette. *An American Tragedy* was published in 1923, and instantly acclaimed as a masterpiece.

Twelve-year-old Clyde Griffiths is uncomfortable and ashamed when he takes part in the street services his parents conduct in Kansas City. He hates the dreary mission and has little faith in religion, for although his mother is always saying "God will provide", their poverty remains unchanged. His thoughts dwell continually on the wealthy uncle he has never seen, his father's brother, Daniel Griffiths, a collar manufacturer in Lycurgus.

At fifteen, Clyde is a refined-looking, handsome boy, weak and shallow, consumed with a craving for material prosperity. His is the type of mentality that never matures.

Clyde becomes a bellhop at the Green-Davidson Hotel, and gets his first taste of opulence. He is careful to keep from his mother the amount he makes in wages and tips. The bellhops, a wild lot, initiate him into the gay life, and take him to a brothel where he has his first sexual experience. Through one of them he meets Hortense Briggs, a flashy, gold-digging shopgirl; he falls heavily for her, and instead of helping his mother, lavishes presents on her. A youth named Sparser "borrows" his employer's car, and Clyde and Hortense are among the party of bellhops and their girl-friends that he takes for a joy-ride. On the reckless ride back, Sparser knocks down a child, but instead of stopping he jams down the accelerator, hurtles into a deserted side street and overturns the car. All but Sparser and one girl manage to scramble out; police-sirens are heard approaching, and Clyde, leaving Hortense to fend for herself, makes for the railroad, jumps a freight and skips the city. Next morning he reads of the child's death, and sees his own name in the paper; Sparser, charged with manslaughter, has given his companions away.

Clyde goes to Chicago and lives under an assumed name until he deems it safe to use his own. When he is twenty, he gets engaged as a bellhop at the exclusive Union League Club for Gentlemen. It is here that at last he meets his uncle. Samuel Griffiths, struck by his resemblance to his own son, Gilbert, favourably impressed by his modest demeanour, decides to take him on in the collar factory.

Full of hope, Clyde arrives in Lycurgus, and presents himself at the factory where he is interviewed by his cold, arrogant cousin who contemptuously assigns him to the lowest-paid, meanest job. It is only after weeks that Clyde is invited to his uncle's palatial home; while he is there, Sondra Finchley, a chic, beautiful flapper whose parents are almost as wealthy as the Griffiths', drops in. Clyde is dazzled by her, he cannot get her out of his head.

The snobbish Griffiths do not invite him again. However, Mr. Griffiths feels that "it won't do" for a Griffiths to work in the shrinking-room at a wage that doesn't allow him to dress properly; accordingly he is put in charge of the girls in the stamping department, with a warning from Gilbert that any familiarity with them will lead to his dismissal.

The wealthy families spend the summer at a fashionable lakeside resort. Clyde, continually dreaming of Sondra, reads about her avidly in the society columns. Bored and lonely, still cherishing the hope that he may one day be admitted to her set, he learns to paddle a canoe and becomes a powerful swimmer.

Clyde takes on another hand, Roberta Alden, the daughter of a poor farmer who has come to Lycurgus to better herself. Clyde is strongly attracted by her delicate beauty, her refinement, and Roberta, as lonely as he is, daydreams about her handsome young boss. A chance encounter with Roberta triggers off Clyde's feelings, and in defiance of the rule he gets her to meet him secretly.

Inevitably, they become lovers, but once Roberta is his, Clyde's feelings change; she is only a factory girl, no fit wife for a Griffiths. . .

One day Sondra Finchley sees Clyde gazing wistfully at his uncle's house and mistakes him for Gilbert. She realizes her error, but insist on driving him back to his boarding house. She is touched when Clyde tells her he has never ceased thinking about her, and finds him so attractive, so presentable that she decides to take him up. At last Clyde enters the glittering world of the Bright Young Things, the centre of which is his wonderful Sondra who soon begins to return his feelings.

It is now that Roberta tells him she is pregnant. Clyde, appalled buys her pills which fail to work, takes her to a doctor who refuses to perform an operation. Roberta says he must marry her – she with nothing is asking him all, while Sondra with everything is offering all. To gain a short respite, Clyde persuades Roberta to go back to the farm for a rest.

Clyde does not keep his promise to come for Roberta, and in desperation she writes that she will come to Lycurgus and reveal her plight. Clyde realizes that if he does not get rid of her he will lose Sondra. He recalls Great Bittern, a lonely lake, he had visited with Sondra, and plans to murder Roberta. He hastens to the farm, and tells Roberta they will have a holiday together and then get married.

Clyde behaves with the utmost ineptitude. He spends the night with Roberta at the tiny inn at Great Bittern where he registers as "Clifford Golden and wife". Next morning he suggests a row on the lake, and under the pretext that it will hold the tripod of his camera he takes his bag with him and leaves it on the shore. Once out on the lake, however, the eerie atmosphere overcomes him, his courage oozes away, and he realizes he cannot murder Roberta. He looks so strange that she thinks he is ill, and moves toward him; Clyde, shrinking from her touch, pushes at her face with his camera; she topples back, overturns the boat and plunges them both in the water. Clyde swims ashore, leaving her to drown, and flings his hat on the lake to make it appear that he, too, has drowned. He changes into the dry suit he has brought in his bag, stuffs his sodden suit inside it, and walks through the woods to join Sondra at the lakeside resort where she is staying.

When the "Goldens" do not return, the inn-keeper raises the alarm; the overturned boat, the straw hat are seen on the lake, and Roberta's body is recovered. A letter addressed to her mother found in her pocket, establishes her identity; her bruised face is taken as evidence of murder. Clyde has left so many clues pointing to himself that he is soon arrested and charged. The prosecution has no difficulty in presenting a damning case against Clyde, and though legally innocent he is condemned to death.

In the Death House, the minister sent by Clyde's mother seeks earnestly to save his soul. In his terror Clyde clutches at the straw of salvation, and proclaims his conversion, his contrition. Yet he never understands why he should be punished for his human – if all too human and perhaps wrong hungers – yet from which so many others along with himself suffered", and he does not know whether he believes in God or not as he is pushed forward to the electric chair.

It has only been possible to skim the surface of this vast book with all its many currents and undercurrents. Slowly and surely, using his heavy, lumbering prose to a maximum effect, Dreiser has assembled the countless pieces of a giant jigsaw and locked them into the inevitable tragic pattern. Although Clyde himself is a mere pawn, it is the measure of Dreiser's achievement that we see him as pathetic, as the victim of a crude society whose values are assessed in terms of wealth. As Eisenstein wrote[1]: "*An American Tragedy* is a work of cosmic veracity and objectivity . . . as broad and shoreless as the Hudson . . . as immense as life itself."

[1] Eisenstein's script of the book did not meet with Hollywood's approval.

IF IT DIE

ANDRÉ GIDE

ANDRÉ-PAUL-GUILLAUME GIDE was born in Paris on 22 November, 1869. Paul Gide, his father, was a very distinguished lawyer from the Cévennes, and his mother, Juliette Rondeaux, was the daughter of a wealthy industrialist from Normandy.

Just before André Gide was eleven his father died, and he was brought up by his mother, a woman of great character, a Protestant – as her husband had been – narrow-mindedly puritanical, and of determined views. Though everything she did for her son she did with the best intentions in the world, there can be little doubt that but for his own strong personality, the life she planned for him could have frustrated utterly what was to prove one of the finest flowerings of modern French literature.

Paul Gide had left his wife comfortably off, while she herself possessed more than ample means from the Rondeaux. There would never be any necessity for Gide to have to work for a living, and this influenced both mother and son. While still in his teens, however, he formed the determination to become a writer, but though she had no alternative to offer, Madame Gide strongly opposed him.

Fortunately, he was not aiming at being a dilettante in letters, and since the born writer cannot be prevented by any obstacle placed in his way from eventually achieving his ambition, his mother's opposition was doomed to be overcome. In fact, while he had always had the most profound respect for his mother, in this he was prepared to disregard her wishes entirely.

He received encouragement for his ambition from a friend of his schooldays, Pierre Louis (who later spelt his name Louÿs). Louis found the means of introducing him to the literary life of Paris, and in particular to Mallarmé. He also launched him on his literary career by presenting to the public his first book, *Les Cahiers d'André Walter*.

In 1895, when Gide was twenty-five, his mother died, leaving him very comfortably off. He had formed a lifelong attachment to his cousin Madeleine, and a few months after Madame Gide's death they married.

Unfortunately, despite the fact that there was love, admiration and tenderness on both sides, there was a gulf between husband and wife – which will be described later – which could not be bridged. It is against this background of private tragedy that the story of the flowering of his rare literary genius (until Madeleine's death in April, 1938) must be viewed.

If the quality of the writing is disregarded for the time being, the book which launched him on his literary career is little different from any other adolescent production, for its material is commonplace, its manner lacking in maturity. Despite this, however, there is no doubt that *Les Cahiers d'André Walter* is a work of genius. The technical mastery of the great works of the mature Gide may be absent, but there is almost no theme treated in the later works which is not present in *André Walter*.

Les Cahiers d'André Walter was followed by a number of works to which Gide himself has applied the term "treatises". They were slight works, but nevertheless showed a rapidly developing mastery of the writer's art and craft. It was not until 1895 that he published his first work that could be considered a masterpiece, *Paludes*, a satire on the sterility of the cult of letters when it is separated from life.

In the meantime, however, Gide had made a journey to North Africa, in the course of which he had made certain discoveries concerning himself and had yielded to them. After he returned from this journey he wrote *Les Nourritures terrestres*, which, he declared, was misunderstood at the time, and was not properly appreciated for twenty years. In fact, the book seems to be an invitation to unbridled sensuality, but as in *André Walter*, Gide is still searching for God. The difference is that whereas in *André Walter* the search demanded not only a great and continuous effort of will, but the deliberate shutting-out of ordinary, everyday realities, in *Les Nourritures terrestres* the reverse applies. It is sufficient to accept, for since God is everywhere, there is no need to search.

Seven and fourteen years respectively were to pass before the real sequels of *Les Nourritures terrestres* appeared in the twin books *L'Immoraliste* and *La Porte etroite*. In the intervening years several works were published, all of which developed Gide's mastery of his art, and established his reputation as one of the most important French writers of the day. Subsequent books were to enhance his reputation.

On the outbreak of the First World War, Gide threw himself wholeheartedly into work for an organization whose task was caring for the Belgian refugees who fled before the German invaders of their country, into northern France. It was work that was hard both on the nerves and the emotions, and eventually Gide had to give it up through sheer physical exhaustion. It was while he was engaged in this work that he experienced the religious crisis in which he seemed to be returning to abandoned Christian beliefs. *Numquid et tu?*, published in 1922, however, revealed that it was not toward Christianity that he was moving but toward a Dostoievskian mystical evangelism.

In 1924 he produced what he always regarded, until his death, as his most important work. This was *Corydon*, an apologia for homosexuality. But it was more than apologia; it was a public avowal of his own sexual inclinations, an act of courage, therefore; and besides, it was an expression of faith by a great artist, and *per se*, a work of art. The public impact was merely one of astonishment that a man of such gifts and high reputation should seem to take delight in exposing his own abnormality, moreover an abnormality detested by all right-minded folk above all others!

This homosexuality was the gulf which had come between Gide and his wife. Madeleine, of course, had secure grounds for divorce; that neither of them ever sought a separation at once reveals that notwithstanding the great unhappiness both suffered, there was something in the union which has still not been disclosed satisfactorily, despite the efforts of Gide-scholars to discover what it was.

Since in *Corydon* Gide was exposing himself as no modern man of letters so far had done, and since *Corydon*, which is not a straightforward tract, but is presented as an argument between two fictitious characters, precluded a personal explanation of how Gide's own homosexuality had developed, he published, as a companion volume to *Corydon*, an autobiographical fragment called *Si le grain ne meurt.* . . . This book achieved a far wider circulation than *Corydon*, for reasons which will become obvious presently.

Si le grain ne meurt. . . . (in the English translation, *If It Die*), merits inclusion in this collection of the world's great books on several counts. First, as a work of art it is a distillation of Gide's maturity as a writer; second, the delicacy with which the incidents are described and the matching fineness of the language; and third, and perhaps most importantly, the author's aim sets the book apart from all other internationally great works in the *genre*, for it is to tell all about himself without reserve.

The title, which expresses the author's motive for doing this, is taken from verse 24 of the twelfth chapter of St. John's gospel:

Except a corn of wheat fall into the ground and die, it abideth alone:
but if it die, it bringeth forth much fruit.

The intention is akin to Rousseau's, who wrote at the beginning of his
Confessions: "I am embarking on an undertaking, the conception of
which is without precedent and the execution of which will find no
imitator. *I intend to show my fellow-men a man in all the truth of nature;
and that man will be myself*".

The affinity between Rousseau and Gide is a close one. Both
claim sincerity; both at the very outset offer "scandalous" revelations
as though in proof of this sincerity; both are eager to unburden
themselves notwithstanding the indignity they may bring upon themselves in the process; both display the same underlying vanity.

"I realize perfectly," says Gide in the fifth paragraph of the book,
after having already revealed that he and a small friend indulged
in simultaneous masturbation under the dining table, "I realize
perfectly . . . that I am harming myself by recounting this and other
things that follow; I foresee what use will be made of them against
me. But the sole reason for my story is to be truthful. Let us say that
I am writing it as a penance."

As the book progresses, however, it becomes apparent that although only the truth is being revealed, it is a selected truth. When
one knows the work of Gide, one realizes that it could not be otherwise. For though he is writing the story of his life, his art demands
that this story shall have form, form that is visible in patterns, proportion, balance and clarity, which few, if any, actually lived lives
have.

He begins with memories of his childhood, unattached, uncon-
nected, but which at once envelop the reader in the atmosphere
which will enclose him in his reading of the whole book. He was
born in Paris in a flat in the rue de Médicis, which his parents left for
a second-floor flat at 2, rue de Tournon, on the corner of rue Saint-
Sulpice, when he was only a year or two old.

His father, who was a lecturer in the Faculty of Law, had very
little time to devote to his son, but he left the boy with an impression
of extreme gentleness. André went to his father's study only on
express invitation, and then his father would read aloud to him. "My
father had special ideas about what he should read to me – ideas that
were not shared by my mother; and I used often to hear them discuss what was proper nourishment for a child's mind." Sometimes,
on a fine sunny evening, when Paul Gide was not too busy, he would
say, "Would my little friend like to come for a walk?" He never

called his son anything but "my little friend". As the time they could spend together was so little, the few things they did in company had "an unfamiliar, solemn and rather mysterious air about them which delighted me". But his supreme contribution to his son's future was his passing on early his own love of good literature.

When he was five, Gide embarked upon an educational career that was to prove highly irregular, scrappy, disorganized. He was sent first to some classes held by a Mademoiselle Fleur and Madame Lackerbauer. Two years later these classes were to be supplemented by piano lessons from a Mademoiselle de Goecklin.

"I mean to write down," says Gide, "my recollections just as they come, without trying to arrange them in any order. The most I can do is to group them round places and persons; my memory seldom goes wrong about places but often confuses dates."

This he does, but with a skill which produces a work of art. Nevertheless, the method makes it very difficult to extract a straightforward biographical account of his childhood. Memories of places and people, and especially relations, come upon the scene in a profusion that does nothing to aid the composition of a formal progression. The memories, however, all contribute to the portrait of the boy out of whom the man will develop.

Besides his parents one person had an outstanding influence on his early life. Anna Shackleton, a young Scottish woman of Madame Gide's own age, had entered the Rondeaux family as Juliette Rondeaux's (Madame Gide's) governess. She had remained to become her companion, and after her marriage to remain her most intimate friend.

Anna embroidered interminably and painted a little; but "her dearest study was botany". She went on botanical excursions, and as Madame Gide thought this would be a good opportunity for her son to get some exercise, he accompanied Anna. Thus it was that he became imbued with Anna's enthusiasm, and developed a passion for the natural sciences that was to play such a large part in his thinking and his art.

Presently the time came when he was considered to have outgrown the Lackebauer lessons and he was sent to the Ecole Alsacienne. Unfortunately, he had not been there long when one day he was observed by a master to be masturbating during class, and he was rusticated for three months. Paul Gide was shocked not so much by the incident as by the harsh punishment it incurred, while his wife, horrified, dragged their son to doctors all over France in the hopes of finding a "cure".

Then began for him a succession of private tutors, for he became the victim of a series of psychological and nervous disorders that prevented him from returning to the Ecole Alsacienne, and from attending any other school, except for brief periods. The tutors were a very odd assortment and taught the boy practically nothing, until eventually a Monsieur Richard was found, somewhat better than the rest, who prevented him from remaining quite so illiterate than he might otherwise have been. It was more than fortunate that his father's introduction to literature and Anna Shackleton's to botany had provided him with two passionate interests; but for these it would not have been surprising had international letters been deprived of one of its geniuses.

Gide recounts his childhood – his strange education, his constantly recurring illnesses, his friendships, his relatives (his cousin Emmanuele – Madeleine – in particular), the places he visited, the childish adventures he indulged in – with a curiously selective choice of incident which at times seems to be trivial, yet one finds oneself in the grip of a compulsive desire to know more and more about even the most minute details. But the skill with which it is done is suddenly perceived when there appears before us, as the boy merges into the young man, a striking portrait of an exciting personality. It is now that one realizes the success Gide has had in his expressed object of telling the truth and nothing but the truth about himself, for only the relation of truth could produce such a portrait in depth as we now realize it to be.

The major influence in his life up to this point has been his mother, and the portrait of her that emerges is inevitably the most important after his own. The strange vagaries which her Protestantism provoked are summed up in the occasion when she would not allow Gide to go to a recital devoted to Chopin played by Rubinstein, because in her view the music of Chopin was "unhealthy", and in her refusal to allow the adolescent boy the use of his father's library until an older cousin intervened.

It is clear that Gide always had a profound respect for his mother and greatly admired her. At the same time it is equally clear that there was a lack of warmth in their relationship, emanating solely from her rigid adherence to the strict standards she had set herself which inevitably, so we can see, provoked an irritation in Gide which at times he makes no attempt to conceal.

Roughly three-quarters of the book are employed to produce the portrait of the young man as he had developed at the age of twenty-five, and to bring us to the fateful African journey.

In 1893, a young artist friend, Paul Laurens, had been awarded a travelling scholarship which obliged him to go and work abroad for a year. Gide had been considering making a journey out of France, and was on the point of accepting an invitation from a cousin to accompany a scientific expedition to Iceland, when Laurens "chose me as his travelling companion".

They embarked from Marseilles for Tunis in October, 1893. In Marseilles Gide caught a cold but said nothing about how ill he felt. By the time they reached Africa, however, he was really ill and even the slightest movement exhausted him. Presently he began to recover a little, and then he would join Laurens while he was painting. It was while he was being guided to the spot where Laurens had one day set up his easel that his young Arab guide made it clear that he would be hurt if Gide did not have sexual relations with him.

It was not until this very moment of confrontation that he suddenly realized that his inclinations were entirely homosexual. Up to this point in his life he had had no inkling that this might be the case, and the realization and the acceptance of the invitation there and then brought him tremendous relief.

There was reaction, however, and he tried to resist what all his upbringing had subliminally taught him was wrong, by sharing with Laurens the sexual favours of an extremely beautiful Arab girl of the very special prostitute class known as Oulad Naïl. For a time he seemed to be successful, but the arrival of his mother to look after him and her discovery of the young men's activities provoked a crisis, and he accepted what he now realized was his destiny.

"I heard, I saw, I breathed as I had never done before. . . . 'Take me, take me body and soul,' I cried, sobbing out my worship to some unknown Apollo. 'I am thine – obedient, submissive. Let all within me be light! Light and air! My struggle against thee has been vain. But now I know thee. Thy will be done! I resist no longer. I am in thy hands. Take me!'"

"And so, my face wet with tears, I entered an enchanting universe full of laughter and strangeness."

His illness passed.

The book ends with the death of his mother, and his engagement to Madeleine, but the penultimate section contains a fascinating encounter with Lord Alfred Douglas and Oscar Wilde, who was shortly to return to England to confront so disastrously the Marquess of Queensbury.

Having made the discovery of his homosexuality, it seems strange that he should have persisted in marrying Madeleine; and it would appear that in this marriage he had hoped he would find a "cure". He and Madeleine had no children, but in 1923 Elisabeth van Rysselberghe gave birth to his daughter, Catherine.

In 1925 he went to the Congo, where the treatment of the natives by the concessionary companies appalled him. His subsequent exposé, *Voyage au Congo*, led to a commission of inquiry being set up and the introduction of some reforms.

For a brief period, round about the time of the Spanish Civil War, he formed an attachment with Communism, but disillusionment followed a visit to Russia in 1936. The Second World War he spent in North Africa, returning to Paris in 1946, and there passing his remaining years.

He was awarded the Nobel Prize for Literature in 1947, and died in Paris on 19 February, 1951, universally recognized as one of the truly great literary geniuses of modern France.

TO THE LIGHTHOUSE

VIRGINIA WOOLF

BORN IN 1882, Virginia Stephen was the daughter of the compiler of *The Dictionary of National Biography*, Sir Leslie Stephen, and his second wife. In 1912 she married Leonard Woolf, a writer and sociologist, and together they founded the Hogarth Press, which published all her books, except the first two, *The Voyage Out* and *Night and Day*. Her first three novels were moderately successful and her reputation was further enhanced in 1925 when she published *Mrs. Dalloway*, in which she first attempted the style of writing later to become known as the "stream of consciousness" technique. This was described by the novelist E. M. Forster, who was her contemporary and friend, as "analagous to a sensation. It was not about something: it *was* something". She herself, describing her method of approach in an essay published posthumously in *The Moment* (1947), wrote:

"You have a crowded day, let us suppose, sightseeing in London. Could you say what you have seen and done when you come back? Was it not all a blur, a confusion? But after what seemed a rest, a chance to turn aside and look at something different, the sights and sounds and sayings that had been of most interest to you swam to the surface, apparently of their own accord; and remained in memory; what was unimportant sank into forgetfulness. So it is with the writer. After a hard day's work, trudging around, seeing all he can, feeling all he can, taking in the book of his mind innumerable notes, the writer becomes – if he can – unconscious. In fact, his under-mind works at top speed, while his upper-mind drowses. Then, after a pause, the veil lifts; and there is the thing – the thing that he wants to write about – simplified, composed."

Virginia Woolf was not concerned with writing a plain narrative which would simply tell a story. What fascinated her, and what she perpetually tried to re-create, was the interplay of feeling and ideas within the human mind. It was by reproducing the pattern of this that she conveyed the personality of her characters. Most writers visualize and describe people from the outside; Virginia Woolf wrote almost entirely of their inner sensations and thoughts, and in this way gave them greater depth and a new dimension.

Writing *To the Lighthouse*, which was published in 1927, had great personal meaning for her. Referring to it years afterward she said: "I used to think of my mother and father daily, but writing *To the Lighthouse* laid them in my mind. I was obsessed by them both, unhealthily; and writing of them was a necessary act".

When she began it, she was forty-three: her mother had died thirty years before, and her father twenty. Working out its content in advance, she noted: "It is going to be fairly short; to have father's character done complete in it; and mother's; and St. Ives; and childhood; and all the usual things I try to put in – life, death, etc." Each year when she was a child she had been taken with the rest of the family for the summer to their house in St. Ives: the time there remained in her memory, said her husband in his notes to her *Diary*, when it was published after her death, "as summer days of immaculate happiness: and *To the Lighthouse* is bathed in this happiness". She changed the setting from St. Ives to the Isle of Skye, and the name of her parents to "Mr. and Mrs. Ramsay" (but gave them no Christian names). They are the central characters, as she intended; and round them move like satellites the other people in the house – their eight children, and the six guests.

As the book begins, on a sunny September afternoon, Mrs Ramsay is sitting by a window on the terrace, knitting a stocking; beside her is her youngest son, the six-year-old James, cutting pictures out of an Army & Navy Stores catalogue. She has just told him that if the next day is fine he will be able to go on a sailing-boat trip to the lighthouse across the bay; and her words "conveyed an extraordinary joy, as if it were settled the expedition were bound to take place, and the wonder to which he looked forward, for years and years it seemed, was, after a night's darkness and a day's sail, within touch". It is in this single sentence – only the third in the book – that the whole compass of the entire work is announced: the remainder of a day, a night, and part of another day.

But what Mrs. Ramsay says is heard by her husband who is walking with one of the guests, Charles Tansley, on the terrace, and he corrects her: it cannot possibly be fine the next day, he says, because the wind is blowing from the wrong direction. He resumes his stroll, quite unaware of the violent hatred with which his little son reacts to his destructive logic. But Mrs. Ramsay knows it: "Strife, divisions, difference of opinion, prejudices twisted into the very fibre of being; oh that they should begin so early," she says to herself.

As in a film scenes are changed by the camera cutting rapidly from one place to another, so in her writing Virginia Woolf switches without preamble from character to character. Sitting in a deck-chair on the lawn, basking in the sun, is the elderly poet Augustus Carmichael, his white moustache and beard streaked with yellow. Not far away from him, standing in front of her easel and canvas, is the thirty-three-year-old Miss Lily Briscoe, who is trying to paint a picture of the house and Mrs. Ramsay and James at the terrace window; at this moment she suddenly feels she is in love with the place and all the people in it. William Bankes, "a widower old enough to be her father", approaches and stands looking at her painting. They decide to go for a walk together, and pass another of the Ramsay's children, seven-year-old Cam, "wild and fierce", picking flowers. (This was probably Virginia Woolf's own re-creation of herself.) Of the children, William Bankes thinks that "as for being sure which was which, or in what order they came, that was beyond him. He called them privately after the Kings and Queens of England; Cam the Wicked, James the Ruthless, Andrew the Just, Prue the Fair. . . ."

Mrs. Ramsay thinks, as he and Lily Briscoe pass by, that perhaps one day they might marry, and it strikes her as "an admirable idea". Still strolling on the terrace, Mr. Ramsay has another brief discussion with her about whether it will be fine or not the next day, and then continues his walk, "slipping smoothly into speculation, suggested by an article in *The Times*. . . . If Shakespeare had never existed, would the world have differed much from what it is today? Does the progress of civilization depend upon great men? Is the lot of the average human being better now than in the time of the Pharaohs? Is the lot of the average human being, however, he asked himself, the criterion by which we judge the measure of civilization. . . ."

Going down the lane Lily Briscoe tries to explain her impression-istic style of painting to William Bankes; Mrs. Ramsay, showing a story-book to James, is thinking about two of the younger guests, Paul Rayley and Minta Doyle, who are out walking together also; she wonders if Paul is proposing marriage. Slowly the afternoon darkens into evening, and suddenly across the bay the lamp of the lighthouse begins to flash. Mildred the cook comes on to the terrace and leads James off to bed; as they go Mrs. Ramsay knows how disappointed he is at not being able to go to the lighthouse the next day: he will probably remember it, she thinks, all his life.

When her husband comes past again she gets up and takes his arm. They walk round the garden together, talking about their children, and stop to watch two of them, Prue and Jasper, playing with a ball. Returning, Lily Briscoe and William Bankes see them, and Lily thinks "That is marriage; a man and a woman looking at a girl throwing a ball".

From this point, time moves backwards slightly, to earlier in the afternoon. Paul Rayley and Minta Doyle are on the seashore with two of the other children, Andrew and Nancy, who are shocked when they see Paul and Minta kissing each other behind a rock. Minta loses a brooch; the incoming tide makes it impossible for a search to be made, and Paul promises her he will come at daybreak next morning to look for it. The afternoon ends, and they walk back toward the house. "As they came out on to the hill and saw the lights of the town beneath them, the lights coming out suddenly one by one seemed like things that were going to happen to him – his marriage, his children, his house. . . ."

Then follows the main scene of the book, an elaborate and extensive re-creation of the evening meal at the house, where fifteen people are seated round the table for dinner. Mildred serves her speciality, *Boeuf en Daube*, "a confusion of savoury brown and yellow meats, and its bay leaves and its wine". From the head of the candle-lit table, Mr. Ramsay happily surveys his family and guests; Lily Briscoe worries about a problem in the composition of her painting, but solves it, and moves the salt-cellar on the tablecloth to remind herself of how she wants to re-position a tree; Charles Tansley is sour and withdrawn, and has little to say; in love with each other, Paul Rayley and Minta Doyle chatter happily; Mrs. Ramsay watches them, then looks down the table at her eldest daughter Prue, and hopes one day she will be even happier than Minta is now.

When the meal ends Mrs. Ramsay moves out of the room, but in the doorway she turns back to look at the scene. "It was vanishing even as she looked, and then as she moved it changed, it shaped itself differently; it had become, she knew, giving one last look at it over her shoulder, already the past." She begins to go upstairs to see the youngest children, James and Cam, who are in bed; and as she goes she thinks of the people behind her in the dining-room, of the community of feeling between them all, and how in years to come they will all remember one another, and this house, and her. . . .

When she has said goodnight to the children, she comes downstairs again. Paul and Minta, and the other guests and the children, are all going down to the seashore again, to look at the waves in the moonlight. Mrs. Ramsay goes into the drawing-room, where her husband is. They sit opposite each other, reading, and from time to time look up at each other and smile, secure in each other's affection.

Soon the children and the guests return, and everyone goes to bed. The house is still, and there is darkness everywhere, except for the room where old Augustus Carmichael sits up in bed, reading Vergil by the light of a candle. After midnight he blows it out. All is quiet. The night begins to pass. . . .

But it is not only this night, but many nights which pass; not merely a few hours but, in a brilliantly sustained and imaginative piece of writing, a period of ten years. "What after all is one night? A short space. Night, however, succeeds to night. The winter holds a pack of them in store and deals them equally, evenly, with indefatigable fingers. They lengthen, they darken . . . the nights now are full of wind and destruction. . . ." Then, in a sudden sentence with a single blow, is removed one of the central characters; just as in life, often, death removes someone.˙. . . "Mr. Ramsay stumbling along a passage stretched his arms out one dark morning, but, Mrs. Ramsay having died rather suddenly the night before, he stretched his arms out. They remained empty."

And Prue, for whom her mother wished happiness, has married and died soon afterward, "in some illness connected with childbirth". In the Great War of 1914–18, Andrew Ramsay had been killed in the trenches. . . . As the years pass, the house stands silent and neglected, its only visitor old Mrs. McNab, who comes in occasionally to keep an eye on it, and to remember its past. "There were clothes in the cupboards: they had left clothes in all the bedrooms. What was she to do with them? They had the moth in them – Mrs. Ramsay's things. Poor lady! She would never want them again. She was dead, they said; years ago, in London. She could see her with one of the children by her, 'Good evening Mrs. McNab', she would say. . . ."

Damp and mouldering, the house crumbles: holes appear in the roof, the garden becomes derelict and overgrown with weed. Then one day a message comes: will Mrs. McNab please get the house ready for occupation, the Ramsays and their friends are returning to it again for the summer. Builders repair the brickwork, Mrs. McNab and her friend Mrs. Best clean and sweep and polish, Mrs. Best's son George brings a scythe and cuts the grass . . . the family, and life, returns.

Mr. Ramsay and the children arrive; so does Lily Briscoe; and Mr. Carmichael, even older, who is soon once again sitting dozing in his deckchair. "And it all looked, he thought, shutting his book, falling asleep, much as it used to look years ago."

Next morning Lily Briscoe coming down to breakfast finds herself alone in the dining-room. "What did she feel, come back after all these years and Mrs. Ramsay dead? Nothing, nothing – nothing that she could express at all." Suddenly she remembers how she had sat at the table ten years before, trying to resolve a problem of composition in a picture, and moving a salt-cellar to remind her where to re-position a tree. She never finished the painting. But she will do it now; after breakfast she goes out on to the lawn, and sets up her easel and canvas.

Sixteen-year-old James and seventeen-year-old Cam are going to sail with their father across the bay to the lighthouse. Before they leave Mr. Ramsay comes to talk to Lily: he thinks of how his wife once hoped she might marry William Bankes but nothing came of it. When Mr. Ramsay starts to talk to her about going to the lighthouse, Lily is angry and embarrassed, because she knows what he is really seeking is her sympathy for his bereavement. She can think of nothing to say, but suddenly looks at his feet and exclaims "What beautiful boots!" And immediately "She was ashamed of herself. To praise his boots when he asked her to solace his soul."

But Mr. Ramsay seems not to mind. He smiles, and shows her how he fastens the laces so they will not come undone. "Thus occupied he seemed to her a figure of infinite pathos. He tied knots. He bought boots. There was no helping Mr. Ramsay on the journey he was going." He goes off down to the harbour, to take James and Cam on their sailing trip.

Lily begins to try to paint her picture: near her, old Mr. Carmichael sits drowsing in his deckchair. Mr. Ramsay and the children get into the boat. Hating his father, James hopes the wind will not be strong enough to take the boat across the bay.

As she paints, Lily thinks of Mrs. Ramsay sitting on the shore one day; of how Paul and Minta's marriage has failed; and how Mrs. Ramsay will never know it. For a moment Lily feels almost triumphant, but the feeling goes, and sadness and a sense of loss make her begin to cry. "Mrs. Ramsay!" she says to herself; and "she remained a skimpy old maid, holding a paint-brush on the lawn".

Halfway to the lighthouse, James suddenly remembers the time, ten years before, when his hatred for his father welled up when he announced the weather was not going to be fine on the next day. . . .

Lily goes on painting: her old feeling of being in love with the house and the people in it returns. Thinking about Mr. and Mrs. Ramsay, she tries to imagine how they first met and fell in love; and she seems able to see Mrs. Ramsay again, a pale figure sitting at the window on the terrace. . . .

In the boat James and Cam and Mr. Ramsay eat their sandwiches; as the boat nears the rocks at the foot of the lighthouse, James at the tiller neatly steers it in. "Well done!" says Mr. Ramsay. They are the first words of praise he has ever given his son, and Cam knows how much they will mean. "His father had praised him. You've got it now, Cam thought. . . ."

Up on the lawn, Lily sees from far away that they have reached the lighthouse. "With a sudden intensity, as if she saw it clear for a second, she drew a line there, in the centre. It was done; it was finished. Yes, she thought, laying down her brush in extreme fatigue, I have had my vision."

And when she had finished writing it, Virginia Woolf commented in her *Diary*: "My present opinion is that it is easily the best of my books. It may mean that I have made my method perfect."

Her high opinion of it, and her satisfaction, were both completely justified. "Her genius", wrote one reviewer of the book when it was published, "is at once more difficult and more original than that of any other novelist of today". With the passing of time the difficulty of appreciation has disappeared; the originality and the genius remain.

THE SOUND AND THE FURY

WILLIAM FAULKNER

WILLIAM FAULKNER, widely acclaimed on both sides of the Atlantic as one of the greatest twentieth-century novelists, showed no early signs of any talent save that of playing truant from school. In Oxford, Mississippi, where his father owned a livery stable, he was the despair of parents and teachers alike, spending most of his days hunting and fishing with the sons of his father's Negro servants. He was, however, an avid reader and in adolescence took to haunting the town's book stores.

Deep within him the young Faulkner yearned to write, but lacking any power to put his thoughts into words, he covered endless sheets of cheap paper with jumbled, meaningless sentences. In despair he persuaded his parents to let him take a course in English Literature at the Mississippi State University in Oxford, and the happiest hours of his youth were spent in the great library there. In the evenings he would drift homewards, his head swirling with fragments of the day's reading; then by candlelight he would scribble crude attempts at poetry into a notebook. His verses were incredibly bad and he might have gone on bombarding editors with them for years if the outbreak of war in 1914 had not completely changed the course of his life.

To William Faulkner the conflict in far-away Europe was a crusade for freedom which he simply had to join, so somehow he made his way north and enlisted in the Canadian Air Force, later transferring to the Royal Air Force with the rank of lieutenant.

War pitchforked the dreamy introvert from Mississippi into a strange world of harsh reality, and as his body grew accustomed to discipline so his mind gradually digested the myriad snippets of learning it had gulped down. On demobilization the petty conventions of small-town life in Oxford irked him beyond measure and he moved to New Orleans, where he took cheap lodgings and wrote his war novel *Soldier's Pay*. His friend Sherwood Anderson, the playwright, kindly sent the manuscript to a publisher with a personal recommendation, and to Faulkner's surprise and delight the book was accepted. So soon as he received the modest advance due on it he boarded a freighter bound for Europe and spent a glorious year wandering around that continent.

He returned penniless in the beginning of 1926 to face bitter disappointment. Despite high praise from the critics and glowing reviews in both American and English papers *Soldier's Pay* had made him very little money. With his head full of another, far greater novel, he simply *had* to write. This time he could not leave Oxford, for the book concerned the very roots of his being which lay there; so for the next two years Faulkner worked as farmhand, hunter, fisherman and carpenter, and in the evenings wrote *The Sound and the Fury*. It was a labour of Sisyphus. Sometimes the words spilled out of him and he wrote furiously through the night; more often they came slowly, painfully, and he would take hours over one short paragraph. Somehow he finished the book and, secure in the knowledge that it contained the best that was in him, sent it off to his publishers. To his utter dismay they returned the manuscript, saying it was unpublishable in its present form, though they *might* consider it if it were entirely rewritten.

In his rage Faulkner nearly tore the manuscript to shreds; then he gritted his teeth, took a job as a night watchman and rewrote the novel kneeling at the upturned wheelbarrow which served him as a table. He had to do so, for it contained his deepest feelings about the problems of the land he knew so well. The publishers accepted the new version and in 1929 publication of *The Sound and the Fury* established Faulkner as what *The Spectator* termed, "One of the few living writers who may safely be accused of genius".

The novel also caused violent controversy, and re-reading it some thirty-five years later one understands why. *The Sound and the Fury* is a turbulent story which holds all the tragedy of the Deep South and is written in a style far in advance of its time. The main theme is the frightening disintegration of the Compsons, a fine old Mississippi family in whom inbreeding and self-indulgence have led to tainted blood. The underlying theme concerns their band of Negro servants and is perhaps the more important to present-day readers in view of the Bill of Civil Rights and the recent demonstrations against it.

Jason Compson and his wife Caroline refuse to believe times have changed. They live on in their huge, dilapidated old house, with the gardens a tangle of undergrowth, the stables housing only three aged horses and a broken-down surrey. They have four children, bright, handsome Quentin, lively Caddy (Candace), morose Jason and Benjy, an idiot, after whose birth his mother adopts the pose of semi-invalid, continually bewailing the unfairness of the Deity in making her give birth to such a son. The father shuts himself in his library and drinks, emerging at intervals to rage at the servants or the three elder children who grow to adolescence under the care of Mammy Dilsey, the cook-housekeeper, and old Roskus, the arthritic coachman.

Caddy, already showing signs of beauty, dominates Quentin and together they get up to all manner of mischief in which the Negro boys Versh and Luster gleefully join. Young Jason, a sullen lad with a chip on his shoulder, keeps aloof. At heart he is intensely jealous of the other two and by way of revenge torments Benjy. This rouses Caddy to fury, for her best trait is the motherly devotion she lavishes on the idiot boy. She alone can understand the weird grunts and cries he uses for speech and he adores her, knowing she will tend and protect him.

Disaster strikes when Benjy reaches puberty, for he chases and tries to rape a local schoolgirl. The town seethes with anger and the Compson parents, jolted out of their apathy for once and terrified lest he is sent to the county asylum, have the poor boy castrated. Benjy's tragedy draws Caddy and Quentin even closer – too close, for she is wanton at heart and he obeys her every whim. For several months they make love in secret; then their parents announce that they have entered Quentin at Harvard University, to which the Compsons have always gone. They stress they are making enormous sacrifices to do so; in reality, having sold all their land piecemeal over the years, they have robbed poor Benjy of some pasture land left him by a grandparent. There is a fearful scene, with the tortured Quentin raving about the beauty of incestuous love and his father raving about the awful sin of such a relationship. In the end Quentin is firmly taken to Harvard and his shocked parents decide that a husband for Caddy must be found without delay.

It is not in Caddy to be faithful to anyone, and while Quentin goes through the agonies of frustration at Harvard she amuses herself with several men. But the home atmosphere soon becomes unendurable: her mother nags continually, her father disapproves of her every action, Jason has developed into a malevolent youth who spends his time spying on her and telling tales to the parents. She chooses Herbert Head, rising young banker with plenty of money, and Mrs. Compson writes ecstatically to Quentin about how marvellous Herbert is, and how he will find openings in the bank for Jason and himself, and how he must come home for the wedding. As he reads her letter, in which she playfully encloses a formal printed invitation, something snaps in Quentin. Two days later his family learn that he has drowned himself. That he committed suicide is proved by the finding of a flat-iron in either trouser pocket.

Now the decay of the family sets in with a vengeance. Caddy marries her Herbert but finds herself haunted by the ghost of the brother she so bitterly betrayed. She calls her baby girl Quentin after him; then in an effort to blot out memory takes lover after lover. She goes home once for her father's funeral; but when Jason taunts her for weeping at the family grave where Quentin already lies she leaves abruptly, which is exactly what he wants. He is master of the house now and he means to extract full revenge for all the insults, the slights, the family have heaped upon him through the years.

With Caddy gone there is nobody to stop him. His mother has taken to her bed and lies sobbing weakly as he reminds her each evening that she and his father never sold any pasture land which was not legally theirs to send *him* to Harvard, never found him a job worthy of the name, never even gave him a decent education. He knows she has a little money of her own tucked secretly away and he means to get it. Worn out by his nightly tirades she at last gives him $5,000 to buy a partnership in a local hardware store. He hides the money in his room and works in the store as salaried manager.

Money becomes an obsession with Jason, because money means power. He saves most of his salary, his only major expense being his weekly visit to a brothel in the next town. He handles the housekeeping for his mother and saves on that too by keeping Benjy and the servants on short commons. The Negroes hate and fear him, yet submit to his tyranny. They are the direct descendants of the slaves bought by long-dead Compsons; faithful creatures to whom Emancipation means nothing and tradition all. Occasionally Luster and Versh, now grown men, threaten rebellion but are reminded by the aged Roskus that the white men are the masters. Mammy Dilsey suffers the full blunt of Jason's rages, for in addition to cooking and cleaning she has to dance attendance on her whining mistress and – hardest of all – keep poor Benjy quiet.

The girl Quentin is about twelve when Caddy brings her to the old house. Her marriage has broken up and she begs Mrs. Compson to keep the child, promising she will send money for her keep each month. After a humiliating scene with Jason she leaves the child and departs. Mammy Dilsey takes Quentin under her wing and she attends the local school; but every evening she has to come back to the shabby, tumbledown home with the creaking floorboards and the overgrown garden, where her grandmother lies sighing for vanished glories, and Mammy Dilsey shuffles about the kitchen while Benjy gibbers and moans in a corner. Worst of all she has to face her terrible Uncle Jason at the evening meal and submit to his bullying.

Like Caddy, Quentin lavishes affection on Benjy and he, believing his adored sister has returned to him, shambles after her everywhere. As the girl grows up she does indeed resemble her mother more and more and this infuriates Jason, for the mere sight of her brings back bitter memories of those years when Caddy and Quentin left him out of all their childish escapades. And, he warns Mrs. Compson darkly, Quentin will turn out a wanton too. He takes to spying on her every movement, watching her as she goes to and from school, noting her companions. Each night at supper he puts her through a searching cross-examination as to how she has spent every minute of the day and, when she tells him the truth, he shouts that she is a liar.

Quentin is seventeen when she reaches the limit of her endurance and writes to her mother begging to be allowed to join her. Caddy writes back at once, enclosing a goodly sum, but Jason intercepts the letter and pockets the money. The same day he learns that, despite his vigilance, Quentin is slipping out each night to meet a brash young man who is in town organizing the annual fair. In a towering passion he goes home, accuses her of being a whore like her mother, and locks her in her bedroom. He then drives off to seek solace in the brothel – but he has forgotten the old tree by the bedroom window, down which Caddy used to slither. Quentin uses the same means of escape and with her she takes the hoard of dollars which Jason has hidden so carefully in his room. By the time he returns home Quentin and the brash young man are far away, and although he chases them right across the county they manage to cross the state border.

The decay of the Compson family is complete. Mrs. Compson lies in her bed bewailing the fate which has overtaken her; Jason sits hunched in the library, a sick, crazy man nursing murder in his heart; in the kitchen old Dilsey tries to comfort Benjy, who cries and moans as he rocks to and fro clutching an old white satin slipper of his beloved Caddy's to his chest. They are all symbols of the greed, the corruption and the selfishness which the Confederate soldier whose statue stands in the market square tall and erect, shading his eyes with his hand as he gazes serenely into the bright future, fought and died to prevent.

The Sound and the Fury is regarded as Faulkner's finest work, though he himself preferred his novel *The Fable* (1954.) Throughout the thirties he lived quietly in Oxford with his wife Estelle and wrote steadily, being awarded the O. Henry Memorial prize in 1939. Ten years later came the crowning achievement of his career when he went to Stockholm to receive the Nobel Prize for Literature. In his short speech of acceptance we find the very essence of his artistry:

"I feel", he said, "that this award was not made to me as a man but to my work – a life's work in the agony and sweat of the human spirit, not for glory and least of all for profit, but to create out of the materials of the human spirit something which did not exist there before. Man will endure because he has a soul, a spirit capable of compassion and sacrifice and endurance. The poet's, the writer's duty is to write about these things. It is his privilege to help man endure by lifting his heart, by reminding him of the courage and honour and hope and pride and compassion and pity and sacrifice which have been the glory of his past."

A FAREWELL TO ARMS

ERNEST HEMINGWAY

ERNEST HEMINGWAY was born on 21 July, 1899, in Oak Park, Chicago. The second of six children, whose father was a doctor and an enthusiastic sportsman, Hemingway was educated at Oak Park High School. Having twice run away from home, when he finally left school, in 1917, he became a cub reporter on the Kansas City *Star*. Here he remained only a few months before volunteering for an American ambulance unit in Europe in the First World War.

Sent to the Italian front, he was in time to witness the disaster which overtook the Italian armies at Caporetto in October, 1917. In July, 1918, he was severely wounded and invalided home. When he had recovered he became a feature writer for the Toronto *Star Weekly*. In 1921 he married and came to Europe as a roving correspondent, covering several of the famous post-war conferences. In 1924 he settled in Paris and began to devote himself to literature. In Paris he came into contact with a group of writers which included Gertrude Stein, Ezra Pound and James Joyce.

In 1923 his first book *Three Stories and Ten Poems* was published in France in a limited edition. Though it hinted at great literary talent, it made no impact outside his close circle of friends, and though small Paris editions of short stories were published in 1924 and 1925, he first attracted wider public attention with *The Sun Also Rises*, published in New York in 1926. His next book, a collection of short stories, *Men Without Women* (1927), greatly enhanced his reputation, but it was with his novel, *A Farewell to Arms* (1929), that he received world-wide acclaim and recognition as one of the outstanding writers to emerge since the war.

Here was not only a superb story-teller, but the master of a style that was tough, terse, peculiarly American – something, in fact, entirely new. Nor was it only the mechanics of his art which appealed. He reflected in his subject-matter and treatment the widespread disillusionment of the younger generations who found that the world, instead of being a place fit for heroes to live in, was in far worse straits than before the war, which had been fought to set all things right.

Underlying the apparent expression of disillusionment, however, was a somewhat complicated act of personal exorcism. In *The Sun Also Rises*, Hemingway had satirized the artistic scum then congregated in Montparnasse – the beats of the Lost Generation. At the same time he was proving to himself that he had freed himself of the spiritually blighting effects of the demoralization and degradation in which the Lost Generation delighted to wallow.

In much the same way *A Farewell to Arms* was a cathartic experience. By setting down the old war, as he had known it, in its humour and horror, Hemingway was attempting – and largely succeeding, though it was to take another war and another book, *Across the River and Into the Trees* (1950), to complete the process – to rid himself of the psychosomatic effects which his personal experience of war had had on him.

A Farewell to Arms is set on the Isonzo front in Italy. The narrator is an American, Frederic Henry, attached to an ambulance unit. He lives in an officers' mess situated in a house in Gorizia. Between the periodic offensives, defensives and counter-offensives, life is quiet. The usual distractions are sought, particularly the company of women.

In Gorizia there are English nurses. Henry's room-mate, Lieutenant Rinaldi, imagines himself to be in love with one of them, Catherine Barkley, and takes Henry to meet her. Henry likes her, and the following afternoon he calls on her alone. They see more and more of each other, and presently realize that they are in love, though Henry tries to convince himself that on his part it is not love, but merely the desire for female company, and the ultimate acquisition of female favours.

News arrives that an attack is to be launched above Plava, and Henry's unit is ordered up. Now that he must part from Catherine, though only temporarily, he has to confess to himself that perhaps he really does love her.

Italian losses resulting from the attack are heavy, as usual, and many of his friends in the mess are killed. While Henry is at the main dressing-station it receives a direct hit as he and his companions are having supper, and he is quite severely wounded in the legs.

After a short time in a field hospital, Henry is transferred to a hospital in Milan. When they arrive there they find that the hospital is not yet in commission. Nothing is ready and there are only two English nurses. Presently reinforcements arrive, among them Catherine Barkley.

Henry's legs prove to be more badly damaged than had at first been thought, and an operation is necessary. His recovery is pro-tracted, but with Catherine Barkley's ministrations his recovery is sure. As he approaches convalescence, they spend all Catherine's free time together. When she is on night duty, after she has settled down the other patients, she goes to his room and they make love.

"We said to each other that we were married the first day she had come to the hospital and we counted the months from our wedding-day. I wanted to be really married but Catherine said that if we were they would send her away. ... I wanted us to be married really, because I was afraid about having a child if I thought about it, but we pretended to ourselves we were married and did not worry much and I suppose I enjoyed not to be married, really."

So the summer passed for Henry and Catherine Barkley in con-tentment and quiet happiness. Occasionally they went out with Catherine's friend, Helen Ferguson, who was accompanied by a young American, Crowell Rodgers, who had been wounded in the eyes by the same explosion that had wounded Henry; but they pre-ferred being on their own.

The day comes, however, when their summer idyll has to end. Henry is informed that he is to have three weeks' leave after which he is to return to duty at the front. When he tells Catherine this news, she says that she will try to get leave, too. If it is refused, she will give up the work altogether.

Henry senses from the way she has spoken that there is something wrong, and under pressure she tells him that she is three months' pregnant. The confession brings her great relief, and she cheers up and begins to make plans for the baby's birth. In the meantime they will go together to Pallanza, on Lake Maggiore, for Henry's three weeks' leave.

Before he can go on leave, Henry is taken ill with jaundice. Their holiday has to be cancelled, because by the time he is better a new offensive is on the verge of being launched, and he is required to return to the front at once.

The night he has to return to duty, on an impulse they go to an hotel. They have only time for an hour or two, and when they leave in the small hours it is to go to the station so that he may board the troop-train. He will not let her stay to see him off, but puts her in a carriage which is to take her back to the hospital.

Henry has been ordered to the Bainsizza sector of the front, where he has not been before. On this sector the little town of Caporetto is situated. Before the Italians can launch their offensive, the Aus-trians attack and at Caporetto break through the Italian lines.

German troops have been sent to help the Austrians in an offensive for the first time. They are very different soldiers from those whom the Italians have faced up to now. Their reputation is even greater than their actual prowess, but it is the reputation that the Italians recall, and seized by an inferiority complex they go into retreat.

Unfortunately, administrative difficulties arise at Italian command. Communications are dislocated, generals disobey the orders of the Commander-in-Chief and within a very short time the retreat has become a rout.

Henry and his ambulance unit are caught up in the retreat and Hemingway's descriptions of the disorders, the strange behaviour of soldiers who have cast all discipline to the winds, the ruthless and callous attempts of some of the officers to stop the rot, the plight of civilian refugees and of the wounded, make the chapters concerned the most brilliant section of the book. Here Hemingway is giving full rein to his personal catharsis; here the horrors, the stupidities, the brutalities, the hopelessness of war are depicted with a realism that cannot fail to make a tremendous impact on the reader.

Through all the horror of the retreat, Henry's thoughts are constantly of Catherine and her baby to come. Overwrought by his experiences, driven by his passion for the woman he loves, disillusioned by the events around him, he decides to leave his unit, and take a train to Milan in search of Catherine.

On going to the hospital in Milan, he finds that she is no longer there. She has left two days before with Helen Ferguson, and the porter believes they have gone to Stresa. Henry acquires some civilian clothes and follows them. Since the porter has no knowledge of their address in Stresa, Henry is faced with the task of searching the hotels. He has little difficulty, however, in tracking down two English nurses.

After a short but embarrassing scene with Helen, who does not wish to be left on her own, Catherine joins Henry at his hotel. For the first time they can behave normally as man and wife. But unknown to Henry, the townspeople believe him to be a deserter, and late one night the hotel barman warns him that he is to be arrested in the morning. The only way he can avoid this is by going up the lake to Switzerland.

The barman can provide a rowing-boat, so Henry and Catherine set out in darkness, wind and driving rain. After rowing for the remainder of the night, they eventually reach the safety of Switzerland. Here they rent a chalet surrounded by pine trees on the mountainside above Montreux.

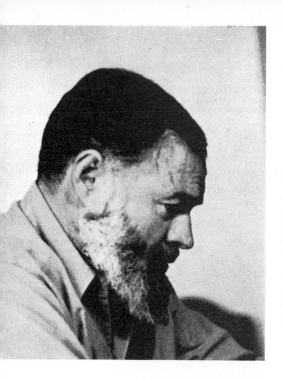

One of the most memorable novels to come out of the First World War was *A Farewell to Arms* by Ernest Hemingway (*left*). Against the background of the terrible disaster that overtook the Italian armies at Caporetto in October, 1917 is told the love story of an American lieutenant in the ambulance service and an English nurse. At the cost of tremendous humiliation and suffering and loss, the military defeat is reversed, but for the young officer and the woman he loved there is nothing but the heartbeats of tragedy. The poignant note struck by Hemingway in this most moving novel may be heard in most of his later work, until his life, too, came to an end in tragic disillusionment.

other of the books evoked the War of 1914–18 was bert Graves's *Goodbye to That*, published in the ne year (1929) as Hemingy's *A Farewell to Arms*. Still his teens when the War ted, Graves (seen here on right, working at his k) promptly enlisted and s soon under fire in nce. Through battle after tle he passed, he was unded, and most of his nds became casualties. hen the Armistice was nded at length, he was at heart and disillusioned, the memory of his dead nrades was ever with him. t until ten years had passed ld he succeed in putting wn on paper something of at his generation had been made to go through.

That young fellow on the right of this group of British soldiers taken prisoner by the Boers in the South African War – who can it be other than Winston Churchill? He is twenty-six, and already he is famous. Ahead lie more than sixty years of struggle and striving and immense achievement in a variety of fields. *Below* is a scene from the film of John Steinbeck's classic novel, *The Grapes of Wrath*, in which two half-maddened cotton farmers put up a futile show of resistance to the tractor that relentlessly moves forward to expropriate them and theirs from the Dust Bowl region of Oklahoma in the heart of the American Continent.

Throughout the winter they pass an idyllic existence here. Henry once again suggests marriage, but Catherine resists because she is too plainly pregnant.

In March they move to Lausanne, where they put up at an hotel, and here Catherine goes into labour. There are complications, and a Caesarian operation is necessary. The baby, a boy, is born dead. A little later Catherine has a number of serious haemorrhages, which the doctors are unable to stop, and she too dies.

The cathartic processes of these two first novels, and especially of *A Farewell to Arms*, were clearly successful, for throughout the rest of his life the main themes of Hemingway's work are the extolling of physical courage and the projection of a stoical acceptance of violence in sport and war.

In 1932 his next considerable work appeared. *Death in the Afternoon* was the result of ten years' study of the Spanish bull-fight, and is a history, a guide, a report and a descriptive analysis of the sport bound into one. He had been drawn to the subject because it seemed to him to promise an opportunity to gain "the feeling of life and death".

From the literary point of view, it showed that *A Farewell to Arms* was not a single *tour de force*, but the work of a writer of particular genius.

His style attracted many imitators, and as John Wain was to observe later, "Though there were many imitators there was never truly a 'School of Hemingway', because the standard he set was too severe". Nevertheless, he had a great influence on the development of style. His short sentences, the colloquial flavour of much of his descriptive work, his use of conversation as a means of underlining the development of his theme, all appealed to his contemporaries, writers and readers alike, for they seemed to provide, with their air of callous detachment – which was really the reverse of sentimentality – an antidote to the paradoxical juxtaposition of intellectual and physical softness with great human suffering which marked the 1920s and 1930s.

In his own person Hemingway projected the toughness of his writing. The study of bull-fighting was followed by big-game hunting in Africa, which formed the subject of *The Green Hills of Africa*, published in 1935. Early in his lifetime he had already become something of a legend as a tough, even ruthless man.

The love which he had acquired for Spain over the many years he had spent there collecting material for *Death in the Afternoon* naturally caused the Spanish Civil War to make a deep impression on him. *For Whom the Bell Tolls* (1940) is outstanding among all the books, both fictional and factual, that were spawned by that conflict.

Besides his major works, Hemingway poured out an almost ceaseless stream of short stories. In this very special literary form he proved himself a master comparable with Somerset Maugham, though in a very different genre. For his work in this field he was awarded the Pulitzer Prize.

It was not until some years after the Second World War that he received the accolade of the Nobel Prize for Literature. This was given to him in 1954, two years after the publication of his *novella*, *The Old Man and the Sea*.

After the Second World War he settled in Cuba. Though he had admired and had been a close friend of Fidel Castro, he was disillusioned by the course which the Cuban revolution subsequently took. He returned to Sun Valley, Idaho.

His health began to fail, and it was necessary for him to make frequent visits to the hospital for treatment of diabetes. From one of these visits he returned unusually depressed, and the following morning, 2 July, 1961, his wife heard a shot and found him dead on the floor with a shotgun by his side.

ALL QUIET ON
THE WESTERN FRONT

ERICH MARIA REMARQUE

ALL OF Erich Maria Remarque's deeply humanitarian novels reflect the fact that, as a writer and as a man, he has never forgotten the horrors he witnessed and experienced at the front during the First World War. The shock must have been all the greater, as he was born – in 1898 – into a quiet middle-class family in Osnabrück in Hanover. His people had maintained the Roman Catholic faith of their ancestors who had settled in the Rhineland after the French Revolution. In this connexion it should be stated that Remarque was his real name, though, for years, hoping to discredit him among his anti-Semitic compatriots, the Nazis asserted that he was of Jewish origin and had assumed the name of Remarque.

When he was eighteen Remarque left his high school, the local Gymnasium, to join the army. He then served as a private soldier for two years, until the end of the war. He was wounded five times, the last time very seriously, and he left the army a disillusioned man, still young in years, but old and weary in his mind.

The Latin, Greek, history, all the book learning acquired as a lad, seemed far away and long ago. The only energy he had seemed to be directed toward mechanical pursuits, but nevertheless he was at first persuaded that teaching was the only way he could earn his living. He accepted a scholarship for a teachers' course offered to discharged soldiers by the Weimar Government. He then taught for a year, but hated teaching and abandoned the profession to do odd jobs. In the meantime he had been developing his mechanical bent, and he found employment as a test driver for a Berlin tyre manu-facturing company. He also began contributing to a Swiss motor-car magazine and wrote advertising copy for his tyre firm. Writing came more easily than he had hoped and he found a job as assistant editor of an illustrated sports journal.

Work never for a moment really helped Remarque to forget the tragedy which the war had inflicted on his generation everywhere in Europe. He longed to bear witness to this tragedy and to warn his fellow-countrymen never again to unleash a war. He finished *All Quiet on the Western Front* and, after the manuscript had been rejected by many publishers, it was finally published in 1929 by the Ullstein Verlag in Berlin. The book was a sensation and sold over a million copies in the first year.

Suddenly Remarque, who hated publicity and fuss, became a rich and famous man. By 1932 it was obvious to perceptive Germans that the Nazis would soon be in power. He decided to leave the country and, as one of his lungs was affected as a result of a war wound, he chose Switzerland as his new home. He acquired a house in Porto Ronco, on the Lago Maggiore, and went there to live. His private life had been restless for some years: he had married in 1923, but he and his wife Ilse were divorced before he moved to Switzerland. They were remarried in 1938.

Soon after Remarque settled down in Porto Ronco his voluntary exile from Germany became permanent. His hatred of militarism and war made him a natural target for the goose-stepping and war-loving Nazis. They were particularly resentful toward Remarque as outwardly he was a perfect specimen of what they called "Aryan": he was tall, blond and athletic in appearance.

At the outbreak of war in 1939 Remarque went to live in New York and he became an American citizen in 1947. Since the war Remarque has divided his time between New York and his home in Switzerland; he has always travelled extensively. As a hobby he collects paintings and beautiful *objets d'art*, but as his many novels – including the most recent one *Night in Lisbon* – indicate, his humanitarianism has remained as strong as it was when he wrote his first book.

The scope of *All Quiet on the Western Front*[1] – still one of the most famous books about the Kaiser's war – was most clearly defined by Remarque himself in an introductory note.[2] "This book," he wrote, "is to be neither an accusation nor a confession, and least of all an adventure to those who stand face to face with it. It will try simply to tell of a generation of men who, even though they may have escaped its shells, were destroyed by the war."

All Quiet is simply and straightforwardly written in the first person. The narrator is Paul Bäumer, a lad of nineteen, who with his friends in the sixth form of their Gymnasium, had joined up a year before this account begins. The boys had been persuaded to volun-

---

[1] First published in English by G. P. Putnam & Sons, 1929, London.
[2] Passages quoted from A. W. Wheen's translation as published by Putnam's.

teer by Kantorek, one of their masters. He was one of those civilians, Bäumer records, "who continued to talk and to write," while "the young soldiers at the front saw the wounded and the dying". Bäumer is equally bitter about Corporal Himmelstoss, in civil life a postman, who had given Bäumer and his friends a brutal basic training before they went to the war. Now, a year later, it is obvious that this training had done little good, for a number of Bäumer's classmates were already dead or crippled for life. Bäumer no longer dreams of one day writing plays; he is overwhelmed by memories of the slow death of Kemmerich and some of his other friends.

Now the four survivors from the Gymnasium cling to each other: Müller still carries a few of his schoolbooks in his knapsack and harbours the illusion that, one day in the future, he will sit for examinations. Albert Kropp tries to make the best of the situation and has advanced to the rank of Lance-Corporal. Leer, once a promising mathematician, now occupies his mind with thoughts about the whores in the officers' brothel.

The educational standards and ambitions of these young men are forgotten. Comradeship in common hardships and dangers is all that matters, and the former scholars have become increasingly attached to men in their unit who come from quite different backgrounds. There is Tjaden, a locksmith before the war, a skinny little man who needs protection from the officers and non-commissioned officers for he has a tragic affliction: he is a bed-wetter. There is Haie Westhus, a peat digger, whose strong hands are often helpful, and Dettering, a peasant farmer, who can think of nothing but his farm-yard and his overworked wife at home.

The leader of all these young men is Stanislaus Katczinsky, a cobbler, whom the boys call "Kat". Kat, a man of forty, is shrewd and kind, cunning and resourceful. He is, as Bäumer writes affectionately, a man "with blue eyes, bent shoulders, and a remarkable nose for dirty weather, good food, and soft jobs". Kat comforts and scolds the younger soldiers as though he were their father; he sees humour in the grimmest situation. He is what men in the Second World War would have called an "organizer": in the winter he somehow finds and takes away a small stove and wood to burn in it; he knows where to get straw for himself and his friends to use as beds; and he is a genius when it comes to stealing food. If there are geese or chickens anywhere he will find them. And he is always practical; he can cook horseflesh or vegetables; he makes excellent bandages for wounds.

Kat is an extraordinarily stabilizing influence on his young friends. They have lost their sense of reality. Life seems vague, a fluctuating blur. Older men at the front have a settled background: they have wives and children, they have known a regular job. Bäumer and his contemporaries, on the other hand, have no roots, they seem to live in a vacuum surrounded by death and danger. For us, Bäumer writes, everything was swept away. For the older men the war is merely "an interruption. We, however, have been gripped by it and do not know what the end may be. We only know that in some strange and melancholy way we have become a waste land."

There are fleeting moments when Bäumer thinks of home, but the memory is vague as something seen in a picture. "I am in the cathedral cloister," he writes, "and look at the tall rose trees that bloom in the middle of the little cloister garden where the monks lie buried. Around the walls are the stone carvings of the stations of the Cross . . . I stand there and wonder whether, when I am twenty, I shall have experienced the bewildering emotions of love."

And when Bäumer has home leave, there is only sadness. His mother is dying of cancer, and he must tell her cheerful fairy tales about the front. His father asks many questions which Bäumer has not the heart to answer. He is also afraid to answer them, for if he did so he is sure that his fears and doubts would become gigantic and utterly overwhelm him. Bäumer is glad when his leave has ended.

It is clear to him and his friends that their companionship cannot last. The chances of survival grow less and less, and in the end Bäumer loses all of his friends. Dettering, the peasant, runs away from the unit, but is caught and shot as a deserter before he reaches his farm. Leer, Müller, and the others are horribly wounded in battle and die of their wounds. Kat is shot "only in the knee", but is then shot in the head by a sniper while Bäumer is carrying him to safety.

Bäumer, too, is seriously wounded, but after months in hospital at the base he is returned to the front line. He is fully aware that the war is lost for Germany. "Only the General Staff and the factory owners who are growing richer and richer want to continue the conflict." Bäumer is no longer afraid of enemy fire. Without his friends and without hope there is nothing for which to live.

The book ends with a postscript not written by Bäumer. This postscript says: "He fell in October, 1918, on a day that was so quiet and still on the whole front, that the army report confined itself to the single sentence: All quiet on the Western Front.

"He had fallen forward and lay on the earth as though sleeping. Turning him over one saw that he could not have suffered long; his face had an expression of calm, as though almost glad the end had come."

All Quiet on the Western Front is certainly an outstanding book which has stood the test of time, and which would have been given special notice whenever it appeared. The simplicity and unpretentiousness of the style, and the obvious sincerity of the author, create for the reader a real and lasting impression of an ordinary soldier's experiences. Besides, in this, his first work, Remarque already demonstrated his unusual ability to bring the people about whom he writes vividly to life. There is no ponderous delineation of character: Bäumer and his friends emerge as living men from the very beginning of the book.

Another remarkable quality of *All Quiet* is that it does not date. The background of Germany's rigid militarism during the Kaiser's war is excellently described, but Remarque's soldier-characters, with their sufferings, frustrations and despair, might have served in any war, in any country, and at any time. *All Quiet* is thus a timeless book.

And yet the time at which this book was published was extremely important as far as its success was concerned. During the decade immediately after 1918, people everywhere tried to forget the suffering brought about by the conflict. Men who had known the trenches disliked discussing their shattering experiences, except among themselves. Men and women who had lost sons, husbands, or brothers, too, were inarticulate as they could not bear to recall what this "lost generation" had undergone. The memory of the war was thus a hidden sore in the minds of men. Ordinary soldiers did not write books about the war, and the memoirs of admirals, generals and statesmen told readers little about what the war had been like.

Then, ten years after the Armistice, *All Quiet on the Western Front* made the breakthrough; it was the first war book written by a then anonymous soldier. The manuscript of Remarque's book had been rejected by many publishers not only in Germany but in England as well before it was finally accepted. It was followed by other war books: at last the general public was told what war meant to the soldiers who had fought it. The actual facts about war were brought out into the open, people talked frankly about it and this was a relief after years of silence.

GOODBYE TO ALL THAT

ROBERT GRAVES

ROBERT GRAVES was born in 1895, at Wimbledon, and educated at Charterhouse School. During the First World War he became a Captain in the Royal Welch Fusiliers. He has a great reputation for his poetry, which he regards as his prime activity and an "obsession". Graves's historical novels include *I, Claudius, Claudius the God* and *Wife to Mr. Milton*, and he has written non-fiction books on a variety of themes. In *The White Goddess* he discusses the origins of the poetic impulse. Penguin Books published his two-volume dictionary of Greek mythology, which combines exhaustive learning with a most unexhausting charm of style.

In 1929 Graves's frank autobiography, *Goodbye To All That*, won success and has remained a classic; he then left for Majorca, where he has since lived almost continuously, in his later years building up a circle of younger writers and artists there. For the usual one-year period Graves had the honour of being Professor of Poetry at his old University, Oxford. Cambridge has honoured him, too, by inviting him to deliver the Clark Lectures on English poetry.

Such is the brilliant and ever-searching personality who is at the centre of *Goodbye To All That*. From his father, Alfred Perceval Graves, the popular poet, he had Irish and Aberdonian blood; from his mother, Amalia von Ranke, daughter of a Radical refugee and niece of the great historian, he inherited German and Danish strains. Scholars and clergy abounded on both sides. His father, with five children already by a former marriage, was 49 at Robert Graves's birth, and his mother 40.

An inspector of schools, his father was busy but kindly; his mother and nurse brought the children up in strict honesty, moral scruples without hypocrisy, and a wide but censored reading. Energy and work were inculcated. Graves remembers holidays in Germany with relatives there. How rich and spicy was Bavarian food! He found a natural human sense of home in Bavaria, its woods and mountains; while his mother's house at Harlech in Wales yielded a personal peace beyond history or geography.

Of schools the boy had plenty: a dame's school, King's College

School at Wimbledon, and a Welsh school at Penrallt. At Copthorne in Sussex: "I learned to keep a straight bat at cricket and to have a high moral sense." Then he won the top scholarship to Charterhouse. German blood, shortage of pocket-money, prudish innocence, and a liking for work, all made for unpopularity. His friendship with Raymond Rodakowski, also a member of the tiny Poetry Society, was perilous, for no friendship was allowed between boys of different houses or ages. Raymond, a fellow-rebel and questioner of religious dogma, was Robert's junior. Then in his fourth year he formed a deep friendship with a boy three years younger than himself, an exceptionally intelligent and high-spirited lad.

His other great human contact was George Mallory, a twenty-six-year-old master, who really treated the boys as equals; he it was who revealed to the young Graves modern literature, and in his rooms he met the appreciative Edward Marsh. Mallory later taught him climbing and they enjoyed many climbs together. These were oases in the rule-bound Philistinism of Charterhouse. Robert Graves had just finished with school when the First World War began, and he enlisted.

Three weeks at the Wrexham depot of the Royal Welch Fusiliers were followed by supervision of an internment camp for enemy aliens – harmless mostly. An inconvenient accident happened: during a midnight telephone conversation about rationing, the line got struck by lightning; an electric shock spun Graves round, and he could not use a telephone for twelve years without sweating and stammering.

Impatient for real action, he was drafted to France. Four or five hours daily were spent sentencing men for breaking King's Regulations at the rate of one "crime" every three or four minutes; some cases were amusing or grotesque, but Graves found the business dispiriting. Yet he congratulated himself on one thing: the choice of this particular regiment, with its twenty-nine battle honours, its insistence on the spelling *Welch*, and its flash, a fan-like bunch of five black ribbons, attached to the back of the collar at an exactly prescribed angle.

On arrival in France, Graves and his comrades found themselves posted to the Welch Regiment, Second Battalion, which was in the trenches at Cambrin, some ten kilometres from Béthune. Rifle-fire he found more trying than shell-fire. His battalion H.Q., a dug-out in the reserve line, about a quarter of a mile behind the front companies, was comfortable, as the previous French occupants had a local armistice with the Germans opposite. Graves's first sight at the front line was of a soldier who had accidentally blown his face to pieces and soon died. Once a German soldier, disguised as an R.E. corporal, was discovered and shot. Two Welsh miners, hating their bully of a platoon sergeant, planned to kill him, but shot the sergeant-major instead; they were shot by a firing squad of their own company against a convent wall. In June, 1915, for the first time, Graves saw human brains splashing the cap of a man who took three hours to die.

With the advance of summer came new types of bombs and trench-mortars, heavier shelling, improved gas-masks and a general tightening up of discipline. Despite casualties, Graves and his men felt on the defensive; pessimism and superstition were rife. At the Red Lamp, the army brothel, 150 men would queue, each to have his brief turn with one of the three prostitutes. Then Graves found himself alone with Lieutenant the Prince of Wales in the Béthune public bath, and agreed with him that the water was bloody cold. Graves was often on night patrol and would journey through the small No Man's Land of 200 yards, barbed wire and all, in over two hours.

If a German found a wounded man he might well kill him, depending on the time-risk involved in bringing him back alive. Indeed opinion varied about saving the lives of enemy wounded; the Canadians, at one extreme, delighted in finishing them off. In general, all calculated the risks to be taken. Holding a position, taking life, saving one's life – each involved a different formula. In the midst of this, for some error in saluting, Graves was condemned to "parade every morning before breakfast for a month under Staff-Sergeant Evans and do an hour's saluting drill". And his dug-out at Cuinchy was rat-ridden – "I remember a new officer finding two rats on his blanket tussling for the possession of a severed hand."

Meanwhile sporadic fraternization occurred with the enemy; Graves's battalion had no political feelings; duty meant fighting as the King ordered; journalists, profiteers, pacifists and politicians were loathed; but the Germans were strangely conceived of as one patriotic block without individual opinions. The French were disliked for their inhospitality and graspingness.

In September, 1915, the great offensive against La Bassée had begun; a disaster occurred in a gas-attack, with vast confusion – one man's body was hit in seventeen places. A subsequent raid found Graves's mind a blank, except for the recurrence of the phrase "S'nice S'mince S'pie". The attack was called off. From the morning of 24 September to the night of 3 October he had only eight hours' sleep;

whisky kept him awake and alive. Every night he and his men went out in drenching rain to fetch in the dead of other battalions – "those we could not get in from the German wire continued to swell until the wall of the stomach collapsed. . . ." Once the Highlanders mistook Graves's men for the enemy, and fired wildly. The Germans started firing and Graves's men retreated in a panic (mistaking "Cease fire!" for "Retire!") and were chased back at bayonet point by a sergeant, who was decorated for this feat.

Soon Charles Sorley, a twenty-year-old poet, was killed (as later Isaac Rosenberg and Wilfred Owen). On 15 October Graves was gazetted a Special Reserve captain; in November he received orders to join the First Battalion, now reorganizing after the Loos fighting. At Locon he met Siegfried Sassoon, who had already published poems, while Graves was putting together his first volume, *Over the Brazier*. Their discussions started a lifelong friendship. Graves admired in him both his creative mind and his intense, active personality: his nickname was "Mad Jack".

Meanwhile the whole battalion had to build a strong reserve line in a temperature of 10 degrees below zero. Round about this time Graves also witnessed Field Punishment No. 1 which was "awarded" to one Private Fahy for drunkenness in the field. Fahy was spread-eagled to the wheel of a company limber for several hours a day for twenty-eight days. As to "atrocities", both sides seemed to be equal: rape, "accidental-on-purpose bombing", machine-gunning of civilians from the air, and the killing of prisoners or cutting their ears off.

Then Graves's friend David Thomas got killed. Graves felt empty and lost, while Siegfried Sassoon went mad with hatred of Germans. Home leave in 1916 did nothing to calm Graves or restore him: paraded as he was by his parents at a jingoistic Good Friday service, and introduced in London to Lloyd George with his sleepwalker's eyes. Yet his German mother and her sisters in Germany would correspond via Zürich. And some officers had hinted that Graves was a spy!

He then entrained for the Somme. "Unforgettable" was the sight of a Briton and a German "who had bayoneted each other simultaneously". One day an enemy barrage wiped out a third of Graves's battalion before the "show" began and Graves himself was one of the casualties. He was cut above the eye; a finger-wound burst the bone; a piece of shell had pierced his right shoulder-blade and come out through the chest; another pierced the left thigh near the groin. He was judged to be dead and his parents received the routine note of condolence. Then he was found to be breathing and, eventually, after an agonizing journey, Graves arrived home.

At Highgate the lung healed, and the doctors saved his finger. *The Times* published free of charge, under "Court Circular", a contradiction of the report of his death. Sassoon, in England through suspected lung trouble, joined Graves at Harlech, where they got their poems in order. Next January (1917) Graves was passed fit for France. There he found that the brothels saved the lives of scores by incapacitating them for future service, owing to V.D. The bayonet instructors excelled themselves in venom, obeying the War Office command to hate the foe. Executions for cowardice or desertion were frequent, though in the House of Commons such happenings were flatly denied.

But soon Graves broke down with bronchitis, and was sent to hospital – by his own request – at Oxford. Staying at Garsington with the pacifist Morrells, he told Bertrand Russell that he would order his men to fire on munition-workers who went on strike, and that fire they would. Transferred to the Isle of Wight, Graves made friends with the French Benedictine Fathers. But now Siegfried Sassoon was in England again and on the verge of nervous collapse. At last he had trumpeted forth his pacifism in a refusal to serve further. This was addressed to his commanding officer and printed in the *Bradford Pioneer* as *Finished with the War: A Soldier's Declaration*.

Graves, alarmed, felt that he must save Sassoon from a court-martial; he cajoled the doctors into passing himself fit for home service, and then intrigued – through many authorities – that Sassoon, who had hallucinations of corpses strewn on the London pavements, be given indefinite medical leave. Siegfried Sassoon stood by his statement and rejected his friend's prudence. In the end Graves was detailed to escort him to a convalescent home for neurasthenics, under the friendly and perceptive Professor Rivers. There Sassoon began the sequence of war poems which won him fame.

In 1916 Graves had met Nancy Nicholson; in January, 1918, they were married, and a year later a daughter, Jenny, was born. Sassoon had returned to France, though still a "pacifist" according to his oscillating type of heroism. He seemed beset by opposite impulses, each of them heroic. Graves comments: "I was both more consistent and less heroic than Siegfried." The Armistice saw Graves cursing and sobbing and thinking of the dead.

Demobilized after brief service in Limerick, he was still mentally and nervously organized for war: shells burst into his marital bed; strangers seemed like friends who had been killed; truth-telling was difficult; while requisitioning of objects and also endurance (though not of train-travel) were easy. Oxford allowed Graves to study English there, and the little family lived on the Parnassus of Boar's Hill, near Robert Bridges, John Masefield (a charming acquaintance) and Gilbert Murray. A son, David, was born, but Nancy's feminism (could they not be dis-married, so as to live together without legal or religious ties?) became more pronounced.

For six months they even managed their own general store, enjoying the patronage of Mrs. Masefield. But failure faced them and Graves's mother bought them a cottage just outside Islip village. Here they befriended ex-servicemen, tramps, beggars, but otherwise lived a hard, domestic life. Contacts with writers – with de la Mare, the Sitwells, Bennett, even the aged Hardy – increased, and Graves published his degree-thesis, "Poetic Unreason". His closest new friend was T. E. Lawrence. Life with him was an adventure, mental or practical. Delightfully eccentric, at times a furtive practical joker, generous, interested in modern poets, half scholar, half active leader, Lawrence would work through the night in his rooms at All Souls.

Nancy Graves's health now deteriorated. Both to meet her needs and his own, Graves became Professor of English Literature at the new Cairo University. His family, scandalized at the young couple's frankly socialist activities, hoped he would reform in the air of Empire. His elder brother Dick and sister Mollie had each been living in Egypt for years. Frenchmen dominated the Faculty of Letters (through interpreters), and Graves's weekly lectures (when the students were not on strike) were good-natured pandemonium. After a year he resigned. His memories of Egypt remained rich and contradictory, some comic; but he always received generous hospitality. The British Raj was omnipresent and uncomprehending.

Graves returned home. Dramatic but undisclosed events ensued before Nancy and he parted in 1929. He settled in Majorca, leaving it only during the Spanish Civil War and the Second World War. He married again and had four more children, enjoying good health and continuing his writing. He asks: "What else can I say, unless that my best friend is still the waste-paper basket?"

Graves's autobiography is important because of its frankness (more courageous in 1929 than now), its dry humour and warm humanity, its portraits of unusual people (among them Siegfried Sassoon and Lawrence of Arabia), and above all the filtered picture, realistic yet poetic, of the First World War. *Goodbye To All That* combines a broad sweep, with a mosaic of tiny pictures, acute observations and incidents gay and tragic. In short, it is a masterpiece.

MY EARLY LIFE

SIR WINSTON CHURCHILL

By the time he was twenty-five Winston Churchill was already famous, indeed the most famous young Englishman of his generation. He could look back on years filled with the most exciting adventures. He had seen active service in Cuba. He had played polo in India, and had served in a couple of small wars on the North-West Frontier. By hook and by crook he had managed to get sent out to Egypt, and as a subaltern in the 21st Lancers had charged the Mahdi's dervish hordes in the battle of Omdurman. Then he had gone to South Africa at the outbreak of the Boer War, and although technically a newspaper correspondent had been taken prisoner when the armoured train in which he was travelling across the veldt was captured by the Boers. Then to crown all he had made a dramatic escape from the prison-camp at Pretoria, and got safely away across hundreds of miles of enemy-held territory. When he got back to England he was given a hero's welcome, and what was to prove a long and chequered career in Parliament was opened by his triumph at Oldham. These are the highlights of the story that he had to tell when in his middle fifties and about to enter upon a lengthy period in the political wilderness. He called his book *My Early Life*, and it was first published in 1930.

Needless to say, there is not a page in it that fails to interest, but to the discerning reader the most absorbing pages may well prove to be those in which he tells not of martial exploits but of his battles to educate himself. For Winston Churchill, greatly favoured as he was in birth and lineage and family influence, and great as he was to prove in the mastery of words both spoken and written, was in the main a self-educated man.

"Menaced with education" is how he describes his first contact with the world of letters. The approach of a "sinister figure" called a governess was announced, and in preparation for her arrival his nurse put him through a course of study in a book called *Reading without Tears*: "it certainly did not justify its title in my case." With the governess he toiled every day, not only at letters but with what was very much worse – figures. When he was seven he was sent to boarding-school. The school selected by his parents was one of the most expensive and fashionable in the country; it modelled itself upon Eton, "but I am sure no Eton boy, and certainly no Harrow boy of my day, ever received such a cruel flogging as this Head-master was accustomed to inflict upon the little boys who were in his care and power". For two years Winston was a pupil there, and he hated it.

Fortunately for him, he had already discovered the joys of reading. His father had given him a copy of *Treasure Island*, and he remem-bered the delight with which he devoured it. But his masters, when they saw him reading books which they thought beyond his years and at the same time he was backward in his lessons, so that he was often at the bottom of his form, were offended and strove to make him learn Greek and Latin by the "large resources of compulsion" that were at their disposal. But "where my reason, imagination or interest were not engaged, I would not or I could not learn".

After this unhappy experience, the boy went to a school at Brighton kept by two ladies, one that was cheaper, smaller and less pretentious, and here he remained for three happy years: happy, since he was allowed to learn things which interested him, French, history, lots of poetry by heart, and above all riding and swimming. Then at twelve he was sent to Harrow, where he remained three times as long in the Fourth Form as anyone else. But this was no bad thing. He learned English thoroughly as a result of spending so much time on it. "I got into my bones the essential structure of the ordinary British sentence – which is a noble thing." When in after years he saw schoolfellows who had won prizes for writing Latin poetry and pithy Greek epigrams, compelled to come down to writing common English to earn their living or make their way, he did not feel him-self at any disadvantage. "Naturally I am biased in favour of boys learning English. I would make them all learn English: and then I would let the clever ones learn Latin as an honour, and Greek as a treat. But the only thing I would whip them for is not knowing English. I would whip them hard for that."

Looking back on his schooldays, Churchill declared that these years formed not only the least agreeable but the only barren and unhappy period of his life. He hardly ever was asked to learn any-thing which seemed of the slightest use or interest, or allowed to play any game which was amusing. Harrow was a very good school, with some first-rate masters, and most of the boys seemed to be happy enough. But *he* was the exception. "I would far rather have been apprenticed as a bricklayer's mate, or run errands as a messenger boy, or helped my father to dress the front windows of a grocer's shop. It would have been real; it would have been natural; it would have taught me more; and I should have done it much better. Also I should have got to know my father, which would have been a joy to me."

After three tries, Churchill managed at length to pass the entrance examination at Sandhurst (thanks mainly to a very efficient "crammer") and started on his army career. He went to India, as a subaltern in the 4th Hussars; and it was there, in the winter of 1896, when he was almost twenty-two, "that the desire for learning came upon me". He had plenty of spare time on his hands when the parades were over and it was too hot to play polo, and he thought it a good idea to fill some of the gaps that his education had left in his mental equipment. He had "picked up a wide vocabulary and had a liking for words and for the feel of words fitting and falling into their places like pennies in the slot", but of so many of the words he did not know their meaning. Just before he left England a friend had said that "Christ's gospel was the last word in Ethics", and this had sounded good at the time, but – what were Ethics? Out in Bangalore there was no one who could tell him, for love or money: "I would have paid some scholar £2 at least to give me a lecture of an hour or an hour and a half about Ethics." Then one day someone used the phrase, "the Socratic method": what on earth was that? Who was Socrates anyhow? A very argumentative Greek who had a nagging wife. . . . But beyond any doubt a considerable person. . . . Then there was history. Once he had been given a hundred pages to read of *The Student's Hume* as a holiday task, and his father (who was the eminent Tory statesman Lord Randolph Churchill) had tested him to see how much he understood of it. And very little it had proved to be. His father was quite concerned about it, as though the history of Charles I really mattered: "I was puzzled by his concern: I could not see at the time why it should matter so much".

Now his father was dead, and the young man was left to his own resources. He "resolved to read history, philosophy, economics, and things like that", and his mother was delighted when she received a letter from him asking for a number of books he had heard of and thought he ought to read. Every mail thenceforth brought him a substantial package of "standard" works. Someone had told him that his father had read Gibbon with delight, that he knew whole pages of it by heart, and that it had greatly affected his style of speech and writing. Without more ado he set upon Dean Milman's edition of Gibbon's *Decline and Fall of the Roman Empire*; it was in eight volumes, and from the first page he was dominated both by the story and the style. "All through the long glistening middle hours of the Indian day, from when we quitted stables till the evening shadows proclaimed the hour of Polo, I devoured Gibbon. I rode triumphantly through it from end to end and enjoyed it all. I scribbled all my opinions on the margins of the pages, and very soon found myself a vehement partisan of the author against the disparagements of the pompous-pious editor. I was not even estranged by his naughty footnotes. On the other hand, the Dean's apologies and disclaimers roused my ire." So pleased was he with the *Decline and Fall* that he began at once on Gibbon's Autobiography, which luckily was bound up with it in the same edition.

From Gibbon he went on to Macaulay and learnt all *The Lays of Ancient Rome* by heart, and loved them; after which he embarked on Macaulay's *History* – "that splendid romance", he calls it. He accepted all Macaulay wrote as gospel, and was grieved to read his harsh judgments of Churchill's ancestor, the great Duke of Marlborough. "There was no one at hand to tell me that this historian with his captivating style and devastating self-confidence was the prince of literary rogues, who always preferred the tale to the truth, and smirched or glorified great men and garbled documents according as they affected his drama. I cannot forgive him for imposing on my confidence. . . ." Many years later, Churchill had the satisfaction of presenting his ancestor in a better light, in his own massive volumes on *Marlborough*.

Not less than in his *History*, he revelled in Macaulay's *Essays*, Chatham, Frederick the Great, Hampden, Clive, Warren Hastings and the rest. From November to May while he was in India he read for four or five hours every day the great classic works on history and philosophy – Plato's *Republic*, Aristotle's *Politics*, Malthus *On Population*, Darwin's *Origin of Species* . . . all interspersed with books of lesser standing. "It was a curious education. First because I approached it with an empty, hungry mind, and with fairly strong jaws; and what I got I bit; secondly because I had no one to tell me: 'This is discredited.' 'You should read the answer to that by so and so; the two together will give you the gist of the argument.' 'There is a much better book on that subject,' and so forth." For the first time he began to envy "those young cubs at the university" who had fine scholars to tell them what was what. But later he pitied them, "when I see what frivolous lives many of them lead in the midst of precious fleeting opportunity. After all, a man's Life must be nailed to a cross either of Thought or Action. Without work there is no play."

This was something that he felt very deeply about. Sometimes when he was "in the Socratic mood and planning my Republic" he thought of the drastic changes that he would make in the education of the sons of well-to-do citizens. When they were sixteen or seventeen they would begin to learn a craft and do healthy manual labour, with plenty of poetry, songs, dancing, drill and gymnastics in their spare time. They could thus let off their steam on something useful. Only when they were really thirsty for knowledge, longing to hear about things, would he let them go to the university – as a favour, as a coveted privilege, to be given only to those who had either proved their worth in factory or field or whose qualities and zeal were pre-eminent. "However, this would upset a lot of things; it would cause commotion and bring me perhaps in the end a hemlock draught," such as Socrates had been compelled to drink.

Of course his "various readings" were bound to lead to questions about Religion. Hitherto he had dutifully accepted everything he had been told. At Harrow and at home he had gone regularly to church every Sunday, and in the army there were regular church parades, when sometimes he marched the Roman Catholics to their church and sometimes the Protestants to theirs. But now he began to read a number of books which challenged the religious education that he had been given at his public school. The first of these books was *The Martyrdom of Man* by Winwood Reade, which he describes as "a concise and well-written universal history of mankind, dealing in harsh terms with the mysteries of all religions and leading to the depressing conclusion that we simply go out like candles". At first he was much startled and even offended by what he read, but then he found that Gibbon evidently thought on very much the same lines as Winwood Reade, and so did Mr. Lecky, whose *Rise and Influence of the Spirit of Rationalism in Europe* and *History of European Morals* he read in the course of one winter.

The "difficulties" that such books aroused in other minds left Churchill cold. He could not understand why bishops and clergy should make such heavy weather over reconciling the Bible story with modern scientific and historical knowledge. "Why do they want to reconcile them? If you are the recipient of a message which cheers your heart and fortifies your soul . . . why should you worry about the shape or colour of the travel-stained envelope; whether it is duly stamped, whether the date on the postmark is right or wrong?" These matters might be puzzling, but they were certainly not important. The really important thing "is the message and the benefits to you of receiving it". So he worked out his own very individual philosophy. "Quite early in life I adopted a system of believing whatever I wanted to believe, while at the same time leaving reason to pursue unfettered whatever paths she was capable of treading."

One final recommendation remains to be mentioned. "It is a good thing for an educated man to read books of quotations. Bartlett's *Familiar Quotations* is an admirable work, and I studied it intently. The quotations when engraved upon the memory give you good thoughts. They also make you anxious to read the authors and look for more." Well said; and if *that* has not yet found its way into the books of quotations it surely ought to, along with many another small reflection of this great man's thought and experience. And all expressed in such simple, sturdy, forthright English.

CAKES AND ALE

W. SOMERSET MAUGHAM

W. SOMERSET MAUGHAM was one of the most distinguished of that rich generation of English writers which included such giants as Wells, Arnold Bennett, John Galsworthy, D. H. Lawrence, Joyce and Virginia Woolf; the generation which flourished between the last years of the last century and the thirties of the present one. His acute sense of character, his brilliant wit, and above all his tremendous narrative ability, placed him above almost all his novelist contemporaries.

He was born in Paris on 25 January, 1874, and was educated at King's School, Canterbury, and Heidelberg University, having been brought up by an uncle and aunt who lived at Whitstable, in Kent. He qualified as a doctor at St. Thomas's Hospital in London, but was unable to resist the compulsion to write, which is the hallmark of every writer worth his salt.

In 1897, his first year of practice as a doctor, he published his first novel, *Liza of Lambeth*. The immediate and pronounced success which the book had led him to abandon medicine and devote all his time to writing; and over the next four decades a river of novels, plays and short stories came from his pen, all of which received wide acclaim, with the exception of his last play, *Sheppey* (1933).

In 1930 he published *Cakes and Ale*, in which his art was revealed in full maturity. In it all the distinguishing marks of Maugham as a brilliant writer are to be seen with almost shattering clarity; his pre-eminence as a story-teller, his brevity, his wit, his gift of eliminating inessentials which gives point and meaning to every sentence, the cynicism which, in fact, conceals a deep understanding of human nature, his tolerance of human weaknesses.

William Ashenden, the narrator, himself a writer, was invited to lunch by Alroy Kear, one of the leading novelists of the day. Ashenden knew Kear well enough to realize that behind the invitation lay a motive, and though he was really reluctant to accept, his curiosity got the better of him.

At lunch, Kear appeared to be in no hurry to reveal his motive. Over coffee, however, he remarked casually that the last time

Edward Driffield, the Grand Old Man of English Letters, who had recently died, visited London, he had lunched with Kear here at his club. Equally casually, he told Ashenden that he had just returned from a short stay with Driffield's widow – his second wife – who sent him "all sorts of messages".

Ashenden replied that he would not have thought that the second Mrs. Driffield would have remembered him. Kear reminded him that, six years before, he had lunched with the Driffields at Ferne Court, their house at Blackstable, as one of a small party which had gone over from the house nearby where Ashenden was staying.

They discussed Driffield's work for a time, but when Ashenden said that he must go, Kear had clearly not seemed able to mention the real reason for his having asked Ashenden to lunch. Their conversation about Driffield, however, had recalled to Ashenden his acquaintance with Driffield and his first wife, Rosie, in the days before the famous author had achieved his later eminence.

As a boy, Ashenden was brought up by an uncle who was vicar of Blackstable, in Kent. His German aunt came of a noble but poor family. But despite the fact that "the only portion she brought her husband was a marquetry writing-desk . . . and a set of tumblers" she could not forget that she was high-born. "When a rich banker from London, with a name that in these days is famous in financial circles, took a neighbouring house for the summer holidays, though my uncle called on him . . . she refused to do so because he was in trade." It was on this basis that she and his uncle tried to inculcate into the boy a sense of his own position in relation to society.

One day when he was home for the summer holidays – he was fifteen – Ashenden met his uncle's curate in the street, and stopped to have a word with him. The curate was walking with a smallish bearded man dressed in rather loud brown knickerbockers, navy blue stockings, black boots and a billy-cock hat. Though the man was unknown to the boy, the curate did not introduce him, and he took him to be a summer visitor from London.

Later in the day, when the curate visited the vicarage, Ashenden asked him who the man was. Replying that he had not introduced him because he did not think his uncle would approve, the curate told him that the man was Edward Driffield, a Blackstable man, whose father had been bailiff at Ferne Court, one of the big Blackstable houses. The boy also learned that Driffield, who was a writer, had married a Blackstable girl, who had been a barmaid. Ashenden could understand his uncle's finding Driffield an unsuitable acquaintance for his nephew.

Driffield, despite his humble origins, had been educated at Haversham School, where he had won a number of prizes. He had also won a scholarship to Oxford, but instead of taking it up had run away to sea. He had not stayed long at sea, and after a variety of jobs had taken up writing.

Ashenden had been given a bicycle which he was having some difficulty in learning to ride. He was determined to master it, however, and was out one day in a quiet Blackstable lane when he saw a man and a woman, also on bicycles, approaching. As they drew level with him, the woman fell off. Naturally, the man stopped, and Ashenden saw that he was Edward Driffield, who was teaching his wife to bicycle.

The encounter led to Driffield helping Ashenden also, and to an invitation to accompany the Driffields on brass-rubbing expeditions to local churches. Despite, or perhaps because of, his uncle's reactions to his becoming friendly with the Driffields, the boy determined to accept the invitation; but Driffield insisted that he should obtain his uncle's permission.

Because of the object of the expeditions, the uncle did not object, though he made it clear that he would not approve the boy's becoming at all intimate with the couple. Somewhat naturally, this was to prove impossible, and the boy took to visiting the Driffield's in their cottage without telling his guardians.

Curious to know why the Driffields were particularly unacceptable to the vicar, the boy asked the cook if she knew anything about them. From her he learned that Mrs. Driffield had been Rosie Gann before she married, and had been a barmaid at public houses in Haversham, where her "carryings on" with the customers raised a local scandal.

Among these customers was a coal-merchant, George Kemp, always referred to by the inhabitants of Blackstable as Lord George Kemp. Rumour had it that though Kemp was married and had children, he and Rosie were lovers. It came as something of a surprise, therefore, when she married Edward Driffield; but not such a surprise, when you thought about it, because he had not a very savoury reputation either. All that had happened several years before Driffield had become a writer, and before their sudden reappearance in Blackstable.

Ashenden continued to visit the Driffields in their home during his school holidays, keeping the visits secret from his uncle. Very often the curate would be there, and sometimes Lord George Kemp (whom the boy, unseen, had once watched secretly meeting Rosie and walking off with her with his arm round her waist) and the four of them would play whist while Driffield worked or read, or occasionally took down his banjo and sang popular songs of the day.

Then, coming home for the Easter holidays, he was met with the amazing news that a few days before the Driffields had "bolted", leaving behind numerous debts. Blackstable was agog and scandalized. It was hinted that Kemp had helped them to get away during the night, but he denied it, and still went about the town with his customary swagger.

All this William Ashenden, the writer, recalled after having his memory revived by his discussion of Driffield's work with Alroy Kear when they had lunched together. Because he was convinced that Kear had not asked the favour which had been the ulterior motive for the luncheon invitation, Ashenden was not surprised when Kear called on him again the following day.

Now at last Ashenden learned what Kear wanted of him. Driffield's widow had asked Kear to write a "Life" of her husband. Since her marriage to him, at the time when his fame was beginning to increase, she had kept records, but there was nothing for the years in Blackstable and a little later, and since Ashenden had known the Driffields during those periods, Kear asked him if he would allow him to use what reminiscences he had for his biography.

While not refusing, Ashenden pretended that there was very little he had to tell; and, at all events, the interlude at Blackstable had contained certain episodes which could not possibly be used in a panegyric. Kear replied that he had heard of "some unpleasantness", but was sure he could gloss over it satisfactorily, while not sacrificing professional integrity. The greatest problem to be overcome, as he saw it, was the unfortunate marriage to the common Rosie Gann and her subsequent scandalous behaviour. But in order to solve this problem, Kear maintained, he must have the full facts, and Ashenden was the only one who could supply them.

Under Kear's coaxing, Ashenden eventually agreed that he would give the matter some thought, and Kear suggested that he should accept Mrs. Driffield's invitation to stay at Ferne Court for a day or two, when all three of them could discuss the problem. To this Ashenden also reluctantly agreed.

This promise "sent my thoughts back to my first years in London". On leaving school, he had joined the medical school at St. Luke's Hospital. He had taken rooms with a Mrs. Hudson in Vincent Square, which was convenient for the hospital. He had been living in Vincent Square for nearly two years, and one evening in June, having left St. Luke's early, he was walking down the Vauxhall Bridge Road when he met Rosie Driffield, who greeted him happily and entirely without embarrassment, declaring how glad she was to see a Blackstable face.

Now almost twenty-one, Ashenden observed her with more mature eyes. He estimated that she must be at least thirty-five. She looked very smart, and for the first time he realized how pretty she was.

She and Driffield were living in a flat not far from Vincent Square, and she pressed him to return with her now to meet Driffield who, though still producing his novels, was the literary editor on a newspaper.

Ashenden enjoyed meeting them again, and dropped into the habit of attending their "at homes" which they held every Saturday afternoon. At these "at homes", Ashenden was surprised to discover that Driffield was regarded as a distinguished person. Though the twenty books he had written never earned him more than a pittance, "the best judges admired them and the friends who came to his house were agreed that one of these days he would be recognized".

Driffield's work for his paper was mostly done at night which prevented him from taking Rosie out in the evenings. Rosie, however, did not see why her husband's pre-occupations should deprive her of the diversions which she found to be indespensable for her enjoyment of life, and was prepared to accept any invitation to dine or indulge in any other amusement made to her. There were many men proud to be seen with her and willing to relieve her tedium. They were mostly artists and writers – and young Willie Ashenden.

One night when he and she had been to a music-hall, and he had walked her home, as they said goodnight she had kissed him on the mouth. Taken unawares, he had accepted her kiss stupidly. As he walked back to his lodgings he realized she was fond of him. Within a short time they had become lovers.

Their relationship had lasted a year before Ashenden realized that he was not Rosie's only lover. She slept with all the men who entertained her. When he taxed her with it, she revealed her philosophy to him. "Oh, my dear, why d'you bother your head about any others? What harm does it do you? Don't I give you a good time? Aren't you happy when you're with me? . . . you must take me as I am, you know." "All right," he agreed.

Among those who had come to the Driffields' "at homes" was a Mrs. Trafford, who had a flair for discovering literary geniuses. About six months after Ashenden had agreed to accept Rosie "as she was", he received a note from Mrs. Trafford one day, asking him to call urgently. When he did so, it was to learn that Rosie had run away from Driffield with Lord George Kemp.

At Mrs. Trafford's request, Ashenden went to Blackstable to try to discover what was known there about the affair. It seemed that Kemp's business had failed, and that he was not only bankrupt, but in danger of being arrested. The story was that he had scraped together about £1,500 and had decamped with Rosie, some said to Canada, some to Australia.

Rosie's leaving him had a profound effect on Driffield. He had known of her many infidelities, but until this happened had rejected the fact of them. Mrs. Trafford persuaded him to go to live at her house, and from this point she began to project him as the genius she knew him to be. His reputation gradually began to increase until he was recognized as the outstanding writer of the age.

After this, Ashenden lost touch with Driffield. He saw in the papers that he had divorced Rosie, of whom nothing more was heard. Then came the news that Driffield, who had been ill, had married his nurse.

All this Ashenden recalled before he went down to Blackstable with Alroy Kear. During their discussions, Mrs. Driffield attacked Rosie's character so fiercely that Ashenden sprang to her defence, to the embarrassed disbelief of both his hearers. "She was naturally affectionate. When she liked anyone it was quite natural for her to go to bed with him. . . . It was not vice; it wasn't lasciviousness; it was her nature."

It was believed that Rosie had died some ten years ago. Ashenden discovered that this was untrue when, some time later while, on a visit to New York for the production of one of his plays, he received a note from her asking him to call. She was now seventy, but still vivacious, still loving life. Kemp had made a new start in New York and had done very well. He had died ten years before, leaving her comfortably off. She still had many beaux, and had received many offers of marriage, but she was quite happy as she was.

Ashenden asked her why she had run off with Kemp, and learned that the Blackstable version was virtually correct. He had gone to her, told that he was bankrupt, but was escaping to America with what little money he had. "I couldn't let him go all that way by himself."

"I sometimes think he was the only man you ever cared for," Ashenden suggested.

"I dare say there's some truth in that," she agreed.

"I wonder what it was you saw in him."

"I'll tell you," said Rosie. "He was always such a perfect gentleman."

Cakes and Ale is entirely lacking in sentimentality, as is all Maugham's work. He was so aware of the suffering in the world that he had to keep his emotions rigidly under control. This realization, coupled with a temperamental fastidiousness, gave him a horror of gush.

The portraits he has drawn here of Driffield, Kear, the second Mrs. Driffield and the uncle and aunt are at times cruel. But there is no malice in the cruelty, for when Maugham is cruel it is because his scrupulous honesty compels him to present life as he views it, with uncommon acuteness.

The outstanding characters of the book are Rosie and Kear. They represent two diametrically opposed aspects of humanity. In the view of many, Maugham demonstrates in his characterization of Rosie, as in none of his other characters, his deep understanding of human frailties, his enveloping tolerance and his comforting sympathy.

But it is not only the characterization which makes *Cakes and Ale* the great book it is. The main object of the story is to remove the false image of Driffield as the Grand Old Man of Letters and replace it with the real Ted Driffield, the man. The delicacy of touch with which this is done, now with direct narration, now with a memory or a snatch of gossip, reveal Maugham's narrative mastery.

Had Thomas Mann treated the subject, one can imagine the long psychological probing and the intricacies of structure which, brilliantly done though they would have been, would have involved the reader in a profound collaboration with the author. Maugham achieves the same effect with clarity, economy and wit, requiring of the reader only a subconscious appreciation of his art.

Somerset Maugham died in December, 1965, in his villa at Cap Ferrat. His ashes were buried in the grounds of his old school at Canterbury.

THE KNOT OF VIPERS

FRANÇOIS MAURIAC

FRANÇOIS MAURIAC was born on 11 October, 1885, in Bordeaux, where his family had deep roots, and which provided the background and the essential atmosphere of many of his novels. He studied at the University of Bordeaux, and in 1906 entered the Ecole de Chartes, in Paris, remaining there for a short time.

He began his literary career in 1909 with a volume of poems, *Les Mains jointes*, which brought him to the notice of Maurice Barrès, that other grand old man of French letters contemporary with Anatole France. He published his first novel, *L'Enfant chargé de chaînes*, in 1913, and followed it with *La Robe prétexte* in the following year. Though these two books reveal that he had not yet mastered his technique, they indicate very clearly his insight into troubled human relationships.

He established his reputation as a major novelist in 1922 with *Le Baiser au lépreux*, in which he described the tragic incompatibility of a husband and wife, and with his following books demonstrated his ever-increasing mastery of his art. During this period, 1923 to 1930, Mauriac went through a period of religious unhappiness in which two problems faced him – the reworking out of his individual faith; and how he might reconcile his integrity as a novelist with his obligations as a Catholic, that is to say, how to portray the evil in human nature without implanting temptation in his readers' minds.

How well he was able to overcome the pitfalls inherent in this last problem is nowhere better demonstrated than in *Le Noeud de Vipères* (*The Knot of Vipers*), published in 1932, which is generally recognized as his masterpiece. Underlying his descriptions of human passions, frustrations and weaknesses, particularly pride, avarice, jealousy and to a certain extent sensuality, are the doctrines of grace and redemption. This is the constantly recurring theme of all his books, but in none is it so intensely portrayed nor with such concentration as in the story of the old lawyer, Louis, aged sixty-eight, liable to die at any moment of a weak heart, who is whiling away his time pouring out in a confession all the hatred he has felt nearly all his life for his wife, children and grand-children.

At one point he exclaims, "I know my heart, this heart, this knot of vipers: stifled by them, saturated with their venom, it continues to beat. ... This knot of vipers that it is impossible to untie, that must be cut with a knife, with a stroke of the sword: 'I am not come to bring peace but the sword.' "

The narrator was an only child. His father, who had died when he was very young, had been a high official at the prefecture of Bordeaux; the mother had inherited a small estate at Calèse, not far from Bordeaux, and other property, which brought her an income of 50,000 francs a year, which, in the provinces in the 1880s was quite a good sum. The boy, however, had the impression that they were not well off, chiefly because of his mother's peasant astuteness and great care with money. The mother doted on her son and spoiled him. As he grew to adolescence he resented her over-abundance of love, and contrived every means he could to let her know how he felt, even to the extent of courting a most unsuitable girl.

While at school he made no friends, and spent all his time studying. His constant poring over books made him round-shouldered and added to his generally unprepossessing appearance, which was responsible for his severe inferiority complex.

In the August of 1883 mother and son visited Luchon. Staying in the same hotel was the Fondaudège family, who were fairly considerable merchants. Their second daughter, Isa, soon began to show she was attracted to Louis, and at last he forgot he was ugly and unwanted. A marriage was arranged, despite the differences in social position, and the young man's character completely changed.

The mother wished the young couple to share the houses in Bordeaux and at Calèse with her, but when she saw that they did not wish to she built herself a small chalet on one of her other properties. The marriage was a happy one; the law practice of the young husband flourished; and all was well until one night Isa confessed that before meeting her husband she had been very much in love with a young man called Rodolphe, the son of an industrialist. His parents, however, had forbidden an engagement because they had heard that two of Isa's brothers had died of consumption on the threshold of adolescence and feared that Isa might contaminate their son.

The Fondaudèges had been very upset, not so much by the action of Rodolphe's parents, but because they feared no one would be prepared after this to marry their daughters. They had found an old man, a Baron Philipot, willing to marry the eldest, Marinette, and when Isa had trapped Louis they had been only too pleased to approve a marriage in spite of the social inequality.

The effect of this confession on Louis was profound, when he realized that it was not love which had attracted Isa to him. His emotion was not jealousy, but hatred. Nevertheless, he was able to dissemble, and he continued to sleep with Isa until she had had three children, a boy, Hubert, and two daughters, Geneviève and Marie.

From the birth of Hubert, Louis claimed, Isa rejected him. She showed herself to be a mother, and only a mother. As for him, he had no paternal instinct at all. To compensate, he devoted himself to his work, and became a creature of habit.

As the children grew up, he included the two eldest in his hatred for their mother. They were afraid of him; and yet, as the old dying man, he says, "What a terrible thing it is to make one's children afraid of one". Only little Marie was not afraid of him, and he loved her deeply.

He fostered this hatred of wife and family deliberately, and indeed revelled in it. He began to think that everyone hated him, and when anyone, as, for example, the young student-priest, who was engaged to tutor the children, once told him that he was a good man, he could not believe it.

At the same time he began to hoard his money. He did not keep his family short, but he kept a strict watch on all expenditure.

He had a number of affairs, all of which he abandoned as soon as his mistresses, in his view, began to demand too much. By one of these liaisons in 1909 he had a son, Robert.

Throughout the narration, which mixes the past with the present, runs the constant theme of the old man's hatred of his wife and children, and the revelation of his grand obsession – to give all his money away before he dies so that they shall not benefit by a single sou. This, and the leaving of the confession to be read after his death, is to be his revenge on them and on the world.

The death of his little daughter Marie, the result of a wrong initial diagnosis, after only a few days' illness, widened the breach between husband and wife still more. Isa accused him of having caused the child's death by refusing to call in a specialist at the very beginning. She had no conception of the depth of his love for the child, and when he refused to visit the cemetery after the funeral she interpreted it as a terrible indication of his hatred of his family and mankind, when, in fact, it was his love for the living child which made him reject the idea of the dead child.

Shortly before Marie's death, the ancient Baron Philipot, Marinette's husband, had died leaving a will which provided that should his widow remarry, she would be deprived of his fortune. She had come to stay at Calèse for a time. Though older than Isa, she was gayer and more vivacious, and it was a crime that having sacrificed by her marriage to the old man all the pleasures that are a young woman's right, she should now be placed under such a ban. Somewhat strangely Louis had consoled Marinette during her stay at Calèse and there is a faint suggestion that they had been lovers.

Suddenly, however, she left Calèse on the pretext that a friend at Biarritz needed her help, and shortly afterwards her family learned that she had married a journalist there. She died in childbirth, leaving a little son, Luke, whom the father looked after until he remarried, and then had given into the care of Marinette's mother. When Madame Fondaudège had died, Isa had taken over her responsibilities toward the boy, who visited Calèse every year for the long summer vacation.

Louis found in the boy, who showed no fear of him, and laughed at the rest of the family because they were so afraid, all the qualities that had made him love little Marie. So he planned to leave Luke all his money. But Luke was called up in 1917, sent to the front and shortly afterwards posted missing.

As his children grew up and married his hatred of them increased and was extended to his children-in-law, and to Geneviève's daughter Janine and her good-for-nothing husband Phili. Phili was becoming involved in business difficulties and needed capital to see him through the crisis. Cruelly the old man let Geneviève plead for his help, and then took delight in refusing her.

With the disappearance of Luke, his next plan was to leave his fortune to his natural son Robert. By this time Louis had already aged considerably and was suffering from heart trouble. He had retired from business and had been advised by the doctors to go nowhere on his own. So when he suddenly announced that he was going to Paris, Isa and the rest of the family tried to dissuade him, but in vain. (There is a poignant scene between Louis and Isa before he goes, in which it is seen that despite all the skilfully built-up picture of hatred, after all these years the old man does not wholly hate his wife.)

In Paris he met Robert for the first time, and was unpleasantly surprised by the physical likeness to himself, his son, now in his middle thirties, possessed. He was angered, however, by the reaction of the plump, elderly simple woman into whom the pretty girl he had made love to had grown, and of her son to his proposal to transfer all his immense fortune to Robert. They suspected that he was not quite in his right mind, that his family knew what he was proposing to do and were having him watched, and that if he did as he proposed they themselves would be bound to be involved in a law suit with the family. They were quite happy as they were, they told him.

They were so convinced that they were right, that they even refused to meet him except in the most outlandish places. While on his way to one of these rendezvous, by chance he saw his son and son-in-law with Robert go into a church, and when he challenged the young man, Robert admitted that they had said that if he would refuse the old man's offer they would not ask the law to intervene, and, into the bargain, would pay him an annuity of 12,000 francs a year from the moment they came into their inheritance.

He had accepted the arrangement, but now he had changed his mind. But the old man, disgusted by the scene Robert made, in turn changed his mind. However, if Robert did not tell the brothers-in-law that he knew what they were doing, he would pay Robert an annuity of 15,000 francs a month for life, beginning on 1 August. All the hopes he had had of loving this son of his had been shattered.

It was necessary for Louis to remain a day or two in Paris to make arrangements for the payment of the annuity to Robert; and on one of these he went to the post office to collect any letters there might be for him. There were one or two letters and three telegrams. Since it was raining he went into a near-by *bistro* to read them while having a meal.

The first telegram he opened read, "Mother's funeral tomorrow 23rd July nine o'clock St. Louis church". It was dated that morning. The others, sent at intervals the previous afternoon and evening, read, "Mother very ill come back" and "Mother died. . . ."

Crumpling up the telegrams he went on eating, his mind completely occupied by the thought that from somewhere he must find the strength to take the train to Bordeaux that evening. Presently these thoughts were replaced by others which for the time being stupefied him – he had survived Isa, he, the old man, expected to die any day, had survived his wife. All his planning and plotting had been based on the expectation that he must die first. He had always thought of his wife as a widow. . . . Then the businessman reasserted himself and he began to re-examine the situation.

Alfred met him at the station, and explained how Isa had had a stroke while walking in the public gardens. She had remained conscious most of the night, and though unable to speak had several times signed that she wished to see him. Then she had lost consciouness and died.

He was in a state of collapse by the time they reached the house, and had just entered the hall-way when he fainted. On coming to, he found himself surrounded by his children, and there was a terrible scene in which he let them know that he knew they had followed him to Paris and discovered where he was staying. He reproved them for not sending the first telegram direct to him, though he realized that they could not have done so without betraying what they had done.

He was too ill to go to the funeral, but paid his last respects to Isa in her coffin. After the funeral, when he was more composed, Hubert and Geneviève came to him again. Hubert launched himself on a prepared speech in his defence. All they had wanted to do was to protect their rights of inheritance. He let them both go on for a time, and then told them that he had decided to divide his fortune between them immediately.

At first they thought that this was another cruel but typical trick. But at last he was able to persuade them that he was in earnest, and then they, in their turn, insisted that they would wait until he died.

So he returns to Calèse, where he is looked after by old servants. His character has completely changed, and he is shown doing small kindnesses to those whom he had formerly considered his enemies, particularly Janine, who, deserted by her husband, comes to live at Calèse with him.

Suddenly the narration stops in the middle of a word.

Two letters follow. One from Hubert to Geneviève describes how the old man had been found dead by the servants sprawled over the extraordinary document he is enclosing; the other from Janine to Hubert, asking for his permission to read the document. Hubert finds in the "confession" complete justification for their and Isa's counter-plots; while Janine tries to persuade Hubert that the old man changed during the last months of his life, that he regretted what he had done, and was sincere in the amends he tried to make.

Following on the publication of *The Knot of Vipers*, Mauriac was elected to the Academie Française. During the 1930s he intervened vigorously in the ideological conflicts of the times. Throughout the Second World War he worked with the writers of the French Resistance under the pen-name of Forez, and when the war was over continued to be engaged in political discussion, first as an editorial writer for *Figaro* and then as a contributor to *L'Express*. Some of his shorter stories of the post-war period had met with unequal success, but in 1952 he was awarded the Nobel Prize for Literature, an honour he certainly deserved.

BRAVE NEW WORLD

ALDOUS HUXLEY

ALDOUS LEONARD HUXLEY was born in 1894 and died in 1963. Brother of Sir Julian Huxley, the famous zoologist, he was a son of Leonard Huxley who edited *The Cornhill Magazine*, and a grandson of Thomas Henry Huxley, the great scientist who was in his own time the most prominent champion of Darwin's Theory of Evolution.

After being educated at Eton and Balliol College, Oxford, Aldous as a young man worked on the editorial staff of *The Athenaeum* and later became drama critic of *The Westminster Gazette*. He published his first book, a small collection of poems, when he was in his early twenties; three more volumes of verse followed, and then came a book of short stories, *Limbo*, in 1920. His first novel, *Crome Yellow*, published in 1921, immediately established him as an important writer; his three subsequent novels – *Antic Hay* published in 1923, *Those Barren Leaves* in 1925 and *Point Counter Point* in 1928 – consolidated his reputation.

His writing was witty, sardonic and satirical, typical in outlook of the post-war generation to which he belonged, and to many of his contemporaries he appeared by far the most stimulating and exciting writer of the day. The way in which he wrote too was itself a novelty: he frequently used a cross-cutting technique from scene to scene or conversation to conversation, that almost paralleled the then newly-developing technique of film-making. In contrast to the established older writers of that time – John Galsworthy, Arnold Bennett and H. G. Wells – Aldous Huxley seemed refreshingly sophisticated and original: and, in his comparatively outspoken treatment of sexual matters, attractively shocking to his readers. Some of the circulating libraries refused to stock his books, and this helped to create an unjustified reputation for his works as obscene: as a result more people took the trouble to read them than might otherwise have done so.

If he had written nothing else but those stylishly-mannered early works he would probably have gained for himself a modest but significant position in the history of English literature, as a writer concerned mainly to entertain and amuse by his displays of wit and erudition. But after the publication of the technically-experimental *Point Counter Point* he seemed suddenly to grow in stature: he became an original thinker, occupying himself less with satirizing men and more with the future of Mankind, less with mordant observation and more with the posing of moral dilemmas and the attempt to discover an eclectic philosophy. Until the end of his life he continued to produce a stream of novels, short stories, anthologies and books of essays which dealt learnedly with aspects of science, religion, ethics, music, painting and many other subjects. But although he wanted to instruct rather than merely to entertain, he never lost his great gift for stimulating mental exercise and provoking argument: he became, in fact, almost a popularizer of pure intellectualism.

Yet it is possible to see, even in the comparatively immature works of his early twenties, the beginnings of ideas which flowered in his later works. One of the characters in his first novel *Crome Yellow*, for instance, summarizes in this way what he fears the future of the world might be. . . .

"An impersonal generation will take the place of Nature's hideous system. In vast State incubators, rows upon rows of gravid bottles will supply the world with the population it requires. The family system will disappear; society, sapped at its very base, will have to find new foundations; and Eros, beautifully and irresponsibly free, will flit like a gay butterfly from flower to flower."

It is this ironic description of a possible scientific Utopia which Aldous Huxley developed at length as the subject of his most famous novel, *Brave New World*, which was published eleven years and twenty books later in 1932.

It is prefaced by a quotation (in French and untranslated – for Huxley made no concessions to those whose education had not been as good as his own) from the writings of Nicolas Berdiaeff, a Russian Idealist philosopher who had become disillusioned with Marxism and founded an "Academy of the Philosophy of Religion" in Paris. "Utopias would appear to be much more likely to be realized than anyone has so far thought possible," wrote Berdiaeff: "and we find ourselves actually faced with an agonizing question – how can their logical development be prevented? Perhaps a new era is beginning, when intellectuals and cultured people will dream of trying to prevent utopias and turn instead to a society which is not utopian – less 'perfect' and more open. . . ."

In the Central London Hatchery and Conditioning Centre, the

Director is showing round "a troop of newly-arrived students . . . he always made a point of personally conducting his new students round the various departments."

This device allows Huxley to explain the entire background of his new world in minute detail as the Director's remarks and his students' questions continue. The year is set at the vague time of A.F. (After Ford) 632, though the names "Ford" and "Freud" have become inextricably confused in men's memories.

In the Centre the science of creating human beings "in vast State incubators" has been refined to perfection. Five different standard grades are produced – Alphas, Betas, Gammas, Deltas and Epsilons – each with its predestined social position and its allotted tasks. Alphas are the intellectuals, the brain workers: at the other end of the scale, the Epsilons are mentally sub-normal beings, created to do nothing but carry out menial tasks and any hard physical labour.

The system of producing standard beings of different mental capacity is described by the Director as "one of the major instruments of social stability", and his remarks are reinforced by one of the factory-workers in the Centre who adds his own description of the processing of the eggs in the various test-tubes and containers in the Social Predestination Room. "We decant our babies," he says, "as socialized human beings, as Alphas or Epsilons, as future sewage workers or – as future Directors of Hatcheries": and the Director acknowledges the compliment to himself with a modest smile.

After the embryos have matured into infants, neo-Pavlovian conditioning takes place. Those who are destined to be workers are taught an instinctive dislike of such things as books and flowers, so that they will never be distracted from labour by abstract thoughts of beauty or pleasure. While they sleep, loudspeakers under the pillows in their cots keep up a continual whisper of ideas to condition them into acceptance of their social status. . . . "I'm so glad I'm like I am, I'm glad I'm not an Alpha, Alphas have to work much harder than we do because they're so clever. . . ."

"The disappearance of the family system" has also come about: in the past Ford (or Freud) plainly revealed "the appalling dangers of family life when the world was full of fathers – was therefore full of misery; full of mothers – therefore of every kind of perversion from sadism to chastity; full of brothers, sisters, uncles, aunts – full of madness and suicide". Indeed, words like "parent" are now considered obscene, and "father" and "mother" are two of the most embarrassing subjects that can ever be imagined.

In the new scientific Utopia, as one of its inhabitants reflects, "the world's stable now. People are happy; they get what they want, and they never want what they can't get. They're well off; they're safe; they're never ill; they're not afraid of death; they're blissfully ignorant of passion and old-age; they're plagued with no mothers or fathers; they've got no wives or children or loves to feel strongly about; they're so conditioned that they practically can't help behaving as they ought to behave. And if anything should go wrong, there's *soma*. . . ." *Soma* is the universally-used palliative, a mild tranquilizer taken at any time of stress.

For entertainment people visit such places as "the newly-opened Westminster Abbey Cabaret, with Calvin Stopes and his sixteen Sexophonists, together with London's Finest Scent and Colour Organ, and all the latest synthetic music". Or they can go to the "feelies", cinemas in which the viewers, by placing their hands on metal knobs by their seats, can experience the actual sensations of the protagonists in the films. . . . "The stereoscopic lips came together and the facial erogenous zones of the six thousand spectators tingled with almost intolerable galvanic pleasure." Or, when a character in the story falls on his head – "Thump! What a twinge through the forehead! A chorus of 'ows' and 'aies' went up from the audience."

Great care is taken, both by encouraging the constant use of *soma* and by rigorous censorship of all reading, that no one should ever become unhappy or dissatisfied. "Ideas might easily decondition the more unsettled minds among the higher castes – make them lose their faith in happiness as the Sovereign Good and take to believing instead that the goal was somewhere beyond, somewhere outside the present human sphere; that the purpose of Life was not the maintenance of well-being, but some intensification and refining of consciousness, some enlargement of knowledge."

Huxley lingers for nearly the entire first half of *Brave New World* over the details of the future he imagines: like many other writers who have dealt with similar subjects, he was as much fascinated as repelled by his own thoughts of what might be. The characters he uses to carry forward the plot of the novel are hardly important, and the story itself is not a very clever one. It concerns at first a young man called Bernard Marx who, owing to a slight defect in his conditioning, falls mildly in love with a girl named Lenina Crowne. He finds the universally-practised promiscuity distasteful, and begins to want to keep Lenina for himself – an unheard-of desire in the new "stable" society, and one which causes both him and the girl extreme embarrassment. "When the individual feels, the community reels", she tells him reprovingly, using one of the dozens of catch-phrases with which they have both been indoctrinated since they were created. Yet Bernard cannot avoid an awareness of the spiritual inadequacies of their materialistic existence. "We are adults intellectually and during working hours," he says, "but infants where feeling and desire are concerned."

They go for a holiday together to the Reservation in New Mexico where, for historical interest, a few "savages" have been kept living in "pre-civilized" conditions. They meet one of them, a youth called John, who once discovered and read an ancient book called *The Works of William Shakespeare*. He talks to Bernard and Lenina about it, quoting passages – which they find impossible to understand, because the words describe individual relationships, which are beyond their experience and comprehension. But they are intrigued by the young Savage; they tell him about their own society, and offer to take him back with them when they return to it. John is enthusiastic after their description of it – "O brave new world," he quotes, from *The Tempest*, "That has such people in't!" "You have a most peculiar way of talking," says Bernard, staring at the young man in perplexed astonishment. "And anyhow, hadn't you better wait till you actually see the new world?"

"Civilization" soon sickens the young Savage when he experiences it. Worse, completely unconditioned as he is, he falls helplessly in love with Lenina. Where Bernard found her promiscuity irritating, he finds it unbearable, rages with jealousy and calls her "a whore". To try and placate him, Lenina offers herself to him: and is incapable of understanding, of course, why this drives him into an even greater fury. In disgust he goes off to live the life of a penitent in an abandoned "air-lighthouse" in Surrey. But there he can find no peace, plagued by a stream of laughing visitors whose idea of an afternoon's entertainment is to fly over in helicopters and watch how the comic Savage behaves. Eventually he hangs himself.

Fourteen years later, after the Second World War, Aldous Huxley wrote a Preface for a new edition of his book. "*Brave New World*," he wrote, "is a book about the future, and a book about the future can interest us only if its prophecies look as though they might conceivably come true. How plausible do its prognostications seem? One vast and obvious failure of foresight is immediately apparent. *Brave New World* contains no reference to nuclear fission. . . .

"Assuming that we are capable of learning from Hiroshima as much as our forefathers learned from the Thirty Years' War, it may be assumed that nuclear energy will be harnessed to industrial uses.

The result, pretty obviously, will be a series of economic and social changes unprecedented in rapidity and completeness. These far from painless operations will be directed by highly-centralized totalitarian governments, and a really efficient totalitarian State would be one in which the all-powerful executive of political bosses and their army of managers control a population of slaves who do not have to be coerced because they love their servitude."

And he still foresees, as one of the necessities of this kind of society, "a foolproof system of eugenics, designed to standardize the human product, and so to facilitate the task of the managers. And all things considered," he concludes, "it looks as though Utopia were far closer to us than anyone, only fifteen years ago, could have imagined".

Whether the kind of Utopia he dreaded will ever arrive and, if it does, whether it will have as few redeeming aspects as Aldous Huxley the austere intellectual could imagine, is debatable. But cold and at times almost devoid of human feeling and warmth as *Brave New World* is, nothing can alter the fact that when it was first written it was undoubtedly one of the great and exciting pioneering works of the 1930s. It brought sharply into public consciousness the necessity for questioning contemporary attitudes of self-satisfaction. For all its chilling unawareness of the power and variety of common humanity, it still made many who read it begin to think out for themselves what society could be, might be, and ought to be. Clinical and detached, fundamentally contemptuous of the non-intellectual, Huxley by his very clarity and coldness made the re-thinking of the human condition an important and almost inescapable necessity for his readers. If the world was not to become as he described it, what was it to be? How could his vision be proved wrong? Few books of our time have even attempted to stimulate thought, through the medium of the novel, about so profoundly disturbing a theme.

THE SEVEN PILLARS OF WISDOM

T. E. LAWRENCE

THOMAS EDWARD LAWRENCE, the second of five brothers, was born in Tremadoc, Caernarvonshire, in 1888. Until he was eight, the family moved about a good deal, so little Ned, who was later to become famous as the legendary Lawrence of Arabia, travelled to Scotland, Jersey, France and Hampshire before his parents finally settled down in Oxford. He was brought up in an atmosphere of Victorian piety and no doubt the strict discipline that prevailed in the Lawrence household during his formative years was the basis of the iron self-control he was to display subsequently in the deserts of Arabia.

A precocious child, young Lawrence possessed a remarkably retentive memory. Books fascinated him, especially those which dealt with ancient castles and sieges. He did well at the City of Oxford School and then went up to Jesus College, where his academic interests covered a wide field. It is significant that among the out-of-the-way subjects that attracted his attention were medieval castles and fortifications. His extra-mural activities included the exploration of underground rivers and roof-climbing. He was physically strong, good at any contest requiring fortitude and endurance, but saw little point in organized games. One of his most outstanding traits was his desire to be "different".

After touring the old castles of France and Wales, Lawrence studied Arabic for a time and then went to Syria to have a look at the castles of the crusading period. When he came back to England captivated by the Middle East, he was perhaps dimly aware of the unusual mission awaiting him in that "Garden of the Enchantress". At any rate, it was not very long before he was out there again, on this occasion visiting two places that were destined to feature prominently in the forthcoming Arab revolt against the Turks – Deraa and Damascus. It is also relevant to mention Lawrence's archaeological probes along the banks of the Euphrates, for even then he was living far more roughly than he need have done, training himself to exist on bare necessities in the way of food and drink.

At the beginning of 1914, Lawrence formed one of a party

employed by the Palestine Exploration Fund to explore and survey from Gaza and Beersheba southwards and eastwards as far as Akaba. Consequently when war broke out he was able to help the map department of the War Office by preparing a useful map of Sinai. A few months later he was serving in the Middle East where he was eventually fully occupied in giving shape and substance to the Arab revolt. *The Seven Pillars of Wisdom* is a personal account of his heroic achievements among the Arabs.

Soon after Feisal's army had swept triumphantly into Damascus, Lawrence returned to London and reported to the War Office. For the next three years he advocated Arab independence, but the politicians had other views. Deeply affected by this betrayal of the Arabs, Lawrence blamed himself for the way they had been used and then rejected. It was during this period of nervous tension and strain that he wrote *The Seven Pillars of Wisdom*.

In 1921, under Winston Churchill in the Colonial Office, Lawrence was given every opportunity of furthering Arab interests. His personality and drive would have carried him to high office, but in the following year he resigned and enlisted in the R.A.F. under the name of John Hume Ross. When he was recognized and turned out of the Air Force, he toyed with the idea of becoming a lighthouse keeper or a soldier in the Irish Free State army. Instead he changed his name to T. E. Shaw and joined the Royal Tank Corps.

Although he was the most popular man in Bovington camp, Lawrence disliked army life and went back into the R.A.F. For five years he was happy, keeping up a voluminous correspondence with his many friends and cruising round the countryside on his Brough motor-cycle, but then came disaster. In May, 1935, when riding to his cottage on Egdon Heath, he swerved to avoid an errand-boy on a pedal cycle, shot over the handlebars of his machine and was fatally injured.

Best remembered as the young fair-haired Englishman, superbly mounted on a high-stepping camel and resplendent in the "white silk and gold embroidered" Arab dress presented to him by Feisal, Lawrence has now become a legendary figure. For most of us, too, he still remains an enigma, for there are many facets of his personality that have never been satisfactorily explained. Those who would seek to pluck out the heart of his mystery must turn to Lawrence's own revelations as set down in his masterpiece, *The Seven Pillars of Wisdom*. He might have abbreviated it thus:

Sent out to the Arabs during the 1914–18 war to encourage them in any move against the Turks, I try to efface my English self and to adopt the Arab mentality and outlook. I realize that although there are many social and economic differences between the various tribes, fundamentally their minds work the same way. They are dogmatic, narrow-minded, imaginative, accepting the gift of life without query or compromise. Most important of all, they are always ready to follow "the prophet of an idea".

I know that under the Turkish yoke the Arabs have formed secret freedom societies, all of which are awaiting the propitious moment to turn on their masters and overthrow them. I am also aware that when the Turks became involved in the 1914 war, their policy was to despatch possibly rebellious Arab officers and men to distant battle fronts.

Although the Sultan held Sherif Hussein ibn Ali a prisoner in Constantinople, the Sherif's sons – Ali, Abdulla, Feisal and Zeid – have all been educated in the modern manner and are ready to lead the Arab armies in a revolt against Turkish rule. After the young Turks take control, they send Hussein to Mecca as Emir. Feisal, then in Damascus, has every confidence in the immediate success of a rebellion in Syria. When the Allies move to the Dardanelles instead of to Alexandretta, however, Feisal's Syrian supporters are arrested or scattered, so he pretends loyalty to Turkey, advising his father to postpone offensive action until more favourable conditions obtain.

Meanwhile, as soon as Turkey allies herself with Germany, the British appreciate that the Arabs could have tremendous nuisance value in the Middle East. British policy henceforth is to persuade the Arab tribesmen to unite against their common enemy and to win their independence.

As a staff captain in the Intelligence Section, I at first busy myself with the distribution of the Turkish army and the preparation of maps. I also run the Arab bulletin, a secret weekly record of politics in the Middle East. Later on, I am transferred to the Arab Bureau to do a more useful job of work. My task is to look for a possible Arab leader and, through him, to weld the tribes together into an effective military force.

At Jidda I meet Abdulla, an astute politician. He is determined to gain independence for his country, but I do not see him as the master-spirit of the Arab uprising. I go to Rabegh and quietly assess the capabilities of Ali and Zeid. They possess certain qualities that will advance our cause, but neither is the leader I am seeking. Accompanied by a guide, I set out by camel along the old pilgrim road leading to Feisal's camp.

Crossing the Wadi Mared we are joined by Khallaf, who is obviously curious about my intentions and history. We learn afterward that he is a spy working for the Turks. The guide and I ride on to Wadi Safra, stopping at one of the larger houses in the village of Wasta. From there we continue our journey as far as Hamra, where at last I come face to face with Feisal. I know immediately that he is the man who will "bring the Arab revolt to full glory".

Feisal's nominal A.D.C. complains that the Arabs are ill-equipped. They need flour, rice, barley, rifles, ammunition, machine-guns, mountain guns, technical help and information. I tell him that I have come to learn what they want and to report shortages, but before I can act I must examine the general situation. Feisal himself traces the history of the revolt from its inception. He then introduces me to the other Arab leaders, all of whom are "fighting to get rid of an Empire, not to win it".

I inspect Feisal's troops and I am suitably impressed, although they strike me as being good for defence but not built for attack. They are, for instance, terrified of cannon-fire. Clearly their morale will be boosted if they can be supplied with more artillery.

A large escort conducts me to Yenbo on the west coast. The *Suva* takes me to Jidda, and thanks to the friendly co-operation of Admiral Wemyss, I am given a passage to Khartoum in the *Euryalus*. I make for Cairo, submit my report and my chiefs seem delighted with the optimistic picture I present. General Clayton, head of the Military Intelligence in Egypt, commends my efforts and sends me back to Yenbo, Feisal's new army base. There I meet Garland, who is already instructing the Arabs how to blow up railways with dynamite. He teaches me to be familiar with high explosive. "Sappers handled it like a sacrament, but Garland would shovel a handful of detonators into his pocket, with a string of primers, fuse, and fusees, and jump gaily on his camel for a week's ride to the Hejaz Railway."

I find Feisal patient, self-controlled, full of humour, and always ready to give audience to anyone with a complaint. He informs me that the Turks have planned a surprise attack on Yenbo. To distract the enemy while Yenbo is being strengthened, he moves his army to a northern village. I spend two days in the Arab camp, wearing Arab clothes at Feisal's request, and then we return to Yenbo to attend to the port's amphibious defences. The Turks approach, but menaced by the naval guns of British ships in the harbour they quickly withdraw.

After reviewing the situation, I advise Feisal to seize Wejh, higher up the coast. I am also in favour of an attack on Turkish-held Medina, so Feisal gets Abdulla to head for Wadi Ais, a hundred miles north of the town, and threaten Turkish communications with Damascus. I go carefully into the question of what naval help will be required for the Wejh operation. The transfer of our forces from Yenbo northwards implies that as a precautionary measure the port must be emptied of stores. Everything appears to be in our favour. The initiative has passed so completely to the Arabs that I predict our entry into Damascus within twelve months.

The Wejh garrison, although ordered to defend the town "to the last drop of blood", pulls out as we draw near. We march in unopposed. "First rode Feisal in white, then Sharraf at his right in red head-cloth and henna-dyed tunic and cloak, myself on his left in white and scarlet, behind us three banners of faded crimson with gilt spikes, behind them the drummers playing a march, and behind them again the wild mass of twelve hundred bouncing camels of the bodyguard, packed as closely as they could move, the men in every variety of coloured clothes and the camels nearly as brilliant in their trappings."

I now undertake a gruelling journey across the desert to help Abdulla sabotage the railway line north of Medina. We destroy the track near Aba el Naam station, take thirty prisoners and kill or wound seventy of the Turkish garrison.

On returning to Wejh, I am overjoyed to discover that Auda the warrior, one of the desert's greatest fighters, has thrown in his lot with Feisal. He supports my contention that Akaba would be a more valuable prize than Medina. Its capture would not only extend the Arab front; it would also link us with the British. Consequently we cross the desert in a north-easterly direction, gathering more and more voluteers *en route*, sweep round to Bair, where the Turks have blown all the wells but one, and carry out a number of diversionary raids on bridges and railways. As we drop down toward Sinai, we come across several abandoned enemy outposts. Such Turkish soldiers as are still in the town surrender and Akaba is ours. Feisal's army under General Allenby can now take part in the military deliverance of Syria, that "country of tireless agitation and incessant revolt".

We continue to advance northwards, attacking Turkish garrisons, blowing up bridges and trains, cutting telephone wires, and constantly enlisting new recruits. Very little goes wrong until I am captured in Deraa and dragged into the Bey's bedroom. When I resist his amorous advances, he has me beaten up and whipped. I manage to escape and make my way back to our base at Azrak.

My next journey is to Akaba, where I report to General Allenby. While I am with him, news arrives that Jerusalem has fallen. Dressed as a British major, I enter the city in the rôle of General Clayton's staff officer. This ride into Jerusalem is my supreme moment of the war.

When I rejoin the Arab army we begin operations against the knot of villages north of Akaba and push ahead with our latest mission – to stop Turkish traffic through the Dead Sea. Our recces in force (using armoured cars and Talbots) prove so effective that the Turks offer a hundred pounds for any British officer dead or alive. I am flattered to learn that they have put a special price on me of £20,000 alive, £10,000 dead. I set little store by these figures, but nevertheless I provide myself with a powerful bodyguard.

With Jericho in Allenby's hands and British reinforcements pouring in, the big offensive against Damascus and possibly Aleppo is about to be launched. When Allenby places two thousand camels at our disposal, we know that victory is not far away. The Sheikhs assemble and we harangue them for the last time.

We first attack Deraa, blowing the railway bridge south of the town, then capturing ten miles of the only line between Damascus and Palestine. Jealous for Arab honour, I reject the suggestion that the Arabs should fall back and allow the British to occupy Deraa. Instead we capture the town and then race north to Damascus, "the climax of our two years' uncertainty".

On November 1st, 1918, we drive into Damascus. "Every man, woman and child in this city of a quarter-million souls seemed in the streets, waiting only the spark of our appearance to ignite their spirits. Damascus went mad with joy. The men tossed up their tarbushes to cheer, the women tore off their veils. Householders threw flowers, hangings, carpets, into the road before us: their wives leaned, screaming with laughter, through the lattices and splashed us with bath-dippers of scent."

The liberation of Damascus, however, is a sad occasion for me. Now that my mission is accomplished, I ask Allenby to release me. To begin with he is reluctant to let me go, but "in the end he agreed; and then at once I knew how much I was sorry".

Lawrence's *The Seven Pillars of Wisdom*, an epic and a classic, will never be surpassed as a chronicle of war and adventure. Whatever the author's virtues or vices (and in this book he can be as embarrassingly frank as Rousseau), there is one quality that cannot be denied him. He is a born story-teller. In simple language and with a sort of youthful exuberance, he describes the highlights of the Arab revolt as seen through the eyes of a particularly sensitive Englishman. The reader is swept along from incident to incident at such a breathtaking pace that he can be forgiven if he asks himself afterward whether this sensational exposure of the horrors of modern war is fact or fiction.

Critics have indeed suggested that Lawrence was a liar, supporting their arguments by quoting contradictions, discrepancies and occasional impossibilities that appear in the text. Nothing that they say, however, can detract from the book's essential truthfulness. It is common knowledge that the artist very often creates truth after his own image and that is precisely what Lawrence has done in his *Seven Pillars of Wisdom*. It would be doing him a disservice to single out for praise or blame a purple passage here or a slight exaggeration there. This tale of men under strain, of that curious *camaraderie* found among warriors, of relentless heart-searching and masterly analysis must be considered as an artistic whole.

As Gertrude Bell said, the author lights "so many fires in cold rooms". He reveals his own weaknesses against the "vast and lurid backcloth of the history that he helped to make", and is honestly trying to understand other men and himself at the same time. His standards were high, for he aimed at perfection.

Lawrence tells us himself that he had one craving all his life – "for the power of self-expression in some imaginative form". When he wrote *The Seven Pillars of Wisdom*, that power was undoubtedly his.

BRIGHTON ROCK

GRAHAM GREENE

GRAHAM GREENE, who wrote this thriller which has become a modern classic, was born in 1904. Educated at Berkhamsted School, where his father was Headmaster, and Balliol College, Oxford, where he distinguished himself by winning an exhibition in Modern History and publishing a book of verse, he joined the editorial staff of *The Times*. He married in 1927 and published his first novel, *The Man Within*, in 1929.

He quickly gained distinction as a novelist and left journalism to devote his full time to writing. Between 1935 and 1939 he travelled to Liberia and Mexico and became film critic of the *Spectator*. He investigated religious persecution in Mexico and as a result wrote *The Lawless Roads* and later *The Power and the Glory*. In 1940 he became literary editor of the *Spectator*, and also worked for the Ministry of Information. He joined the Foreign Office, who sent him to Sierra Leone, where he worked from 1941–43. In 1950 he published *The Third Man*, which was filmed by Carol Reed, and from which a series of television thrillers of the same name was derivated. In 1941 he became a director of Eyre and Spottiswoode, the publishers. *Brighton Rock* was first published in 1938.

He became a Roman Catholic in 1926, and much of his writing reflects his concern with the Catholic faith. He has published some thirty novels, "entertainments," plays, children's books and collections of short stories.

Brighton Rock begins on a Whit Monday in the mid-1930s, when all the world is on holiday in Brighton. The central figure of Part One of the book is "Fred" Hale, a lonely neurotic man, who as Mr. Kolly Kibber of the *Daily Messenger* travels the seaside resorts leaving cards at various places, the finder of which gets a small prize. A larger prize is reserved for the person who, carrying a copy of the *Messenger*, successfully challenges his identity.

Hale is sick with fear. He has come down to Brighton to do his job for the paper, knowing that an attempt will be made to murder him. He finds it difficult to hide, for he has to stick closely to the route mapped out for him, which covers all the familiar Brighton spots – the Aquarium, the two piers, the sea front, Castle Square and Queen's Road. Hale is soon aware that "they" are following him. Desperately, he mixes with the crowds in an endeavour to shake them off, but in vain.

He goes into the friendly refuge of a pub where he meets Ida Arnold, a plump and agreeable woman, "full of beer, good fellowship and no regrets". But there is no escape for Hale, for it is here also that we meet Pinkie, the anti-hero of the book, seventeen years old, undersized, in a "shabby-smart" suit. Pinkie has a "face of starved intensity, a kind of hideous unnatural pride". He is pure evil.

Pinkie looks at Hale with hatred, and Hale, knowing the boy is there to kill him, tries feebly to buy him off by offering him the prize for recognizing Kolly Kibber. Pinkie rejects the offer with vicious scorn, and Hale knows that "they" will be waiting for him outside.

In vain he tries to pick up Ida and take her to lunch at the Old Ship Hotel, but Ida, a little in her cups, declines to leave the pub before closing time.

So Hale continues his wretched peregrination through Brighton, determined to do his job at the risk of his life. Following him are Pinkie and his gang. Desperately Hale tries to pick up girls, knowing they would not dare to strike if he had a girl with him. But all the girls scorn him.

Eventually he comes across Ida again, sitting on a deckchair on the front. Warm-hearted and sympathetic, she is easily picked up, for she has lost her handbag. Hale gives her ten shillings to tide her over, and a hot tip for Brighton Races on Saturday.

They set off together in a taxi to the Palace Pier, followed by Pinkie and his gang in their ancient Morris which Hale observes through the back window of the taxi while he is kissing Ida. At the Palace Pier Ida leaves him for a few minutes to go to the Ladies, impressed by his ardour that she should not leave him for a moment longer than she must. She hastens to return, to find that he has disappeared.

The scene now changes to Pinkie in a café on the Palace Pier with the members of his gang, Spicer, Cubitt and Dallow. All are older than this cold-blooded boy, who makes them sit at the table and eat, "like children before his ageless eyes".

They tell him that Hale has been killed. To establish an alibi they have distributed the cards which Hale was supposed to have deposited on his route. Spicer has left one under a tablecloth at Snow's restaurant, and Pinkie is furious at this, for a waitress might have noticed that the man who left the card was not Kolly Kibber, whose picture was in the paper.

Pinkie goes to retrieve the card himself, but finds that Rose, the new waitress at Snow's, has already found it and is bent on claiming the reward. Rose is a thin, pathetic, immature creature from a desperately poor home. She has a bony face, a large mouth, and eyes which are too far apart. When she tells Pinkie that she well remembers the face of the man who left the card, the boy fixes his "dangerous, unfeeling eyes" on her. "You an' me have things in common," is his sinister remark.

Pinkie makes a mistake in thinking that Rose would be dangerous to him. The real danger is Ida, whom the gang knows was with Hale just before the murder. But Pinkie dismisses her as just "a buer" – a tramp Hale had casually met, and thus makes the first of a series of disastrous blunders, which he deceives himself into thinking are clever moves to protect himself against the eternal enemy – the police.

Back in London, Ida reads about Hale's death in the newspaper and is overwhelmed by the tragedy of it. The papers say he died from heart failure, but Ida is not satisfied, for she knows there was more to it than what was revealed in the Coroner's Court. She goes to the funeral at the crematorium and weeps a sentimental tear for Hale, remembering his kisses in the taxi and his telling her that he was going to die and that he was scared.

She recollects the menacing way Pinkie had behaved in the pub and she knows that a crime of some sort has been committed against Hale. Ida passionately believes in life, and she believes also in an eye for an eye.

Down in Brighton, Pinkie meets Rose on the Palace Pier during a thunderstorm. There is a bottle of vitriol in his pocket. He decides not to use it on her, but merely demonstrates the corrosive effects of the acid on the pier rail.

He makes his point. Rose is cowed, and fascinated, regarding him with "horror and admiration". They discover they are both Roman Catholics, and this creates an immediate bond between them.

That night at his bedroom at Billy's, Pinkie meets his gang, who deal in protection. Kite, the late-lamented leader of the gang, had been betrayed by Hale to Colleoni, a smooth prosperous gangster who has moved into Brighton. Kite was attacked by Colleoni's razor boys as a result of Hale's action, and one of the Colleoni gang was too enthusiastic with his razor, and so Kite died by mistake. This is why Kite's betrayer was murdered by the gang, now taken over by Pinkie.

That night Pinkie and Dallow go to collect an overdue "subscription" from a bookmaker named Brewer, but Brewer tells them he is now being protected by Colleoni. Pinkie slashes Brewer brutally with his razor and Brewer pays up, warning Pinkie that Colleoni will get even with him.

Pinkie, furious at Colleoni's intrusion into his territory, goes to see his prosperous rival at the latter's luxury suite at the "Cosmopolitan". Colleoni tells the seventeen-year-old boy contemptuously to keep out of his way. Pinkie leaves in angry frustration, muttering threats. Envious of Colleoni, he is determined to become the powerful gangster of legend – and one has to start somewhere.

Distrusting Spicer, who could compromise him in Hale's murder, Pinkie arranges to have him razored at the Races, but it is Pinkie who gets slashed by Colleoni's men in revenge for the attack on Brewer. Bleeding but unbeaten, the single-minded young psychopath sets about the killing of Spicer himself, pushing him down the staircase – the bannister of which is notoriously rickety – at Billy's where they all live. The verdict is accidental death. Thus Pinkie gets away with his second murder.

Ida had also been at the race meeting. She wins £250 on the tip Hale had given her, and on the proceeds of this she stays at the "Cosmopolitan", sharing a room with an ardent admirer, Phil Corkery, who finds her amorous demands rather exhausting for a man of his age.

But Ida is single-minded about getting justice for Hale. She relentlessly pursues Rose, well aware that the girl knows enough to make the police reopen inquiries into Hale's death. But Rose is desperately loyal to Pinkie, and refuses to answer Ida's awkward questions.

Solely for the reason that a wife cannot be made to give evidence against her husband, Pinkie marries the wan, pathetic Rose in the register office. The marriage is contrived by a broken-down lawyer named Drewitt, as they are both under age.

After the wedding they wander around Brighton and Rose stops at one of those make-a-record-of-your-voice machines. He has bought her nothing on her wedding day. He could at least make a record for her and give it to her. They have no gramophone, but perhaps one day he would be away and she could borrow a gramophone and play it, and then he would speak to her, and she would hear his voice.

After irritably refusing, he finally agrees and goes into the automatic booth and closes the door and speaks his message to her into the mouthpiece: "God damn you, you little bitch, why can't you go back home for ever and let me be?"

He then gives her the record, saying, "Here, take it. I put something on it – loving."

Rose goes to live with Pinkie in his wretched digs at Billy's, where on the morning after her sexless wedding night – sex to Pinkie is horror and sin, as it is to many murderers – Ida calls and tells her that Hale was strangled by Pinkie and his gang, but he had a heart attack as they closed in for the kill, which was the reason why it was thought to be a natural death. Ida warns Rose that Pinkie will probably kill her too. But Rose is unmoved, and in her tragic and reasonless devotion to Pinkie cannot believe that he would kill her.

Pinkie now knows Ida is as much a danger to him as Rose. "Have I got to have a massacre?" he asks Dallow. Dallow, though a thug, has more normal instincts than Pinkie, and is shocked at the idea of killing Rose. "There's nothing wrong with the poor kid, except for liking you."

Pinkie takes Rose to Peacehaven in the old Morris, having half talked her into a suicide pact with him, though he intends that only she shall die.

Meanwhile, the clever Ida has bluffed Dallow into thinking that Drewitt has betrayed them, and has persuaded a policeman that Pinkie has gone off in a stolen car. She arrives with Dallow and the policeman at Peacehaven just in time.

Pinkie, thinking Dallow has betrayed him, throws the bottle of vitriol at Dallow, but the policeman is quicker. He hurls his truncheon straight at Pinkie, smashing the bottle of vitriol into the boy's face. Pinkie turns, screaming with agony, and runs to the edge of the cliff, and is gone – "as if he'd been withdrawn suddenly by a hand out of any existence – past or present, whipped away into zero – nothing".

In her passion of misery, Rose goes to Billy's to collect the only thing he gave her – his voice on the record. "She walked rapidly in the thin June sunlight towards the worst horror of all."

Brighton Rock is perhaps the best crime novel written during that golden age of the crime story – the 1930s. It is doubtful whether a better one has been written since.

The Brighton scene is beautifully realized, and though the backstreet atmosphere of crime and squalor engulfs the story, there is a feeling that Brighton itself is untouched by it. Pinkie and his shabby little crowd are no more than vicious flies on the window of a splendid room.

Pinkie is a terrible and memorable character. To him the finest sensation of all is the infliction of pain. Cruelty "inflames him like lust". He has consciously chosen evil, and as a Catholic he takes a bitter pride in the prospect of his own damnation. His involvement with Rose, whom he hates and despises, creates an atmosphere of ironic bitterness which is unforgettable.

Rose herself is the most pathetic, the most touching of heroines. Yet, while your heart goes out to her, you flee in despair from her hopeless desolation and her shameful humility. Her fierce loyalty to the wanton caricature of youth whom she married arouses pity rather than admiration.

Brighton Rock is one of those books you do not forget.

THE GRAPES OF WRATH

JOHN STEINBECK

THE NAME of one novelist is lastingly linked to the Great Depression in America, the terrible years of mass unemployment and starvation that preceded the Second World War; it is that of John Steinbeck, who opened the eyes of the nation with *The Grapes of Wrath*.

John Steinbeck was born on 27 February, 1902, in Salinas, California. His home was full of books, for his mother had been a schoolteacher, and his reading had ranged from *Crime and Punishment* to *Madame Bovary* by the time he entered high school. Young Steinbeck spent his holidays working on different ranches, and in this way he came to know more and more of the country he was to write about. In 1920 he began to read English at Stanford University, but left without a degree in 1925. This was hardly surprising since he continually abandoned his studies to take a variety of jobs; at one time he worked in a haberdasher's shop, at another he swung a pickaxe with a gang of navvies who were constructing a road, and at yet another he was an assistant chemist in a beet factory.

From Stanford he went to New York hopeful of earning his living as a writer, but the hope proved vain. His short stories were all returned with the editor's regrets, and he was obliged to work his passage back to California as a deckhand via the Panama Canal.

After this ignominious experience, Steinbeck took a job as caretaker of an estate on Lake Tahoe, high up in the Californian Sierras, and it was here that he wrote his first novel *Cup of Gold*, a historical romance based on the life of the pirate Henry Morgan. *Cup of Gold* came out in 1929, the year of the Wall Street collapse, and was almost ignored; Steinbeck, however, heartened by the very fact that it had been published, decided to stick to writing.

His next three books, *To a God Unknown*, *The Pastures of Heaven* and *The Long Valley*, marked his development as a regional novelist, but they failed to achieve the recognition they have since been accorded, and in all sold only 3,000 copies.

Success came to Steinbeck in 1935 with *Tortilla Flat*. The rich folk-humour of *Tortilla Flat*, which is not so much a novel as a loosely-linked series of stories about the *paisanos* of the Salinas Valley, exactly hit the public taste, and was on the best-seller list for months.

It must have been obvious to Steinbeck that if he continued to write books similar in character to *Tortilla Flat* the royalties would come pouring in; characteristically, however, he did nothing of the kind. His next two novels, *Of Dubious Battle* and *Of Mice and Men*, different though they were from one another, were both deeply involved with the misery and chaos of the Depression. *Tortilla Flat* had been a popular success, but it was *Of Dubious Battle* and *Of Mice and Men* that established Steinbeck as one of America's most important writers.

Steinbeck's dramatized version of *Of Mice and Men* opened on Broadway on 23 November, 1937, but he was not there to hear the applause when the curtain came down, for as soon as he had finished the play he had bought a car and had driven to Oklahoma, where he joined a party of migrants heading south-west. In California, he lived with them in the fearful camps, and worked with them on the land, and what he saw and experienced filled him with burning indignation and pity. "In the interior valleys of California there are 5,000 families, not just hungry but starving to death," he wrote to his agent, "the death of children in our valleys is just staggering . . . I'll do what I can . . . funny how little books become in the face of such tragedies". Steinbeck was referring to the novel he had recently completed: *L'Affaire Lettuceberg*, which he had refused to publish because he felt it was altogether too slick. With *L'Affaire Lettuceberg* out of the way, Steinbeck became absorbed in another book about the migrants, a book that, far from being "slick", was to rouse the nation with its anger and compassion. It was while he was writing it that *Time Magazine* asked him to accompany a photographer to the valleys and supply the necessary material; Steinbeck accepted the commission, but refused to take more than would cover his expenses. "I can't make money on these people," he wrote to his agent. "The suffering is too great for me to cash in on." This was the man who, a few months later, was to face, among other charges, that of "literary opportunism".

The Grapes of Wrath was published in 1939, and instantly provoked a storm of controversy. It was denounced as obscene by many prominent men of the day, among them Archbishop (now Cardinal) Spellman, and was not only banned but publicly burnt in various states throughout America.[1] It was attacked with equal violence on

---

[1] Exception was taken to the deeply moving scene with which the book closes.

political grounds, and the book's central message, an appeal to the "haves" to behave with common humanity to the "have-nots", was misinterpreted as a deliberate attempt to stir up class warfare, to incite the working-class to rise against the owning-class. *The Grapes of Wrath*, in fact, was passionately discussed and debated purely as a documentary, and it was not until the tumult had died away that it was seen in its true light as a work of creative art infused, as J. F. Watts has rightly said in his book on Steinbeck, "with an imaginative power and generosity of heart rarely equalled in American literature".

Oklahoma during the Depression. Young Tom Joad, released on parole after having been in prison for killing a man in self-defence, found the Joad place half-stove in. A man saw Tom standing there, and told Tom how the companies and banks had turned the share-croppers off the land because the tenant-system didn't pay, and how the tractors had come and crushed the houses. "Your fam'ly's over to your Uncle John's," he said.

The Joads, Grampa, Granma, Uncle John, Ma and Pa and their children, Noah, Al, teen-age Rose of Sharon, heavy with child, her husband Connie, and the Joad's two little 'uns, Ruthie and Winfield, were going to California where, the handbill said, thousands of workers were needed. Ma was afraid she would never see Tom again, and it was an answer to prayer when he walked in and put his arms round her. With Tom was Preacher Jim Casy, whom he'd met on the road, only Casy wasn't a preacher no more because he'd figured out that the Holy Spirit wasn't God or Jesus but the human spirit and that all men were part of one big soul.

Ma, who had known and accepted all pain, was the citadel of the family, the strong place that couldn't be taken. Now that Tom was back, she was eager to start, so they slaughtered the hogs and salted down the meat, and only took with them such things as they couldn't do without. They clambered into the old Hudson Al had bought, and Pa looked doubtfully at Jim Casy and said: "Kin we fill an extra mouth?" Ma said: "It ain't kin we, it's will we – as far as 'kin,' we can't do nothing, but we can do what we will." As they started off, Al asked Ma if she was scairt, and Ma said: "No. When somepin' happens I got to do, I'll do it."

Route 66. Overcrowded, battered old cars and lorries all going westward. Broke down on the way, many of them did, the jalopies couldn't make the terrible journey. But the Joad's Hudson made it – made it across the last terrible stretch, the Painted Desert, but

Grampa and Granma died on the way, and Noah, he left the fam'ly when they reached the Colorado river, and Ma's heart was heavy because the fam'ly was beginning to break up.

When they had crossed the desert, they saw the green and fertile valleys of California lying below. It was late when they left Bakersfield, and dusk had fallen when they reached the migrants' camp. They shuddered when they saw the filthy huddle of huts and shacks, but they couldn't go any farther that day. The camp was a Hooversville[1] and there was a Hooversville outside every Californian city. A man called Floyd told Tom that this wasn't no Promised Land. "It's this way," he said. "When the owners need pickers, they advertise for maybe a thousand men when they only need a hundred – with so many men and so few jobs, they can always find plenty willing to work for a low rate, and supposin' as they walk off, there's others that desperate by then that'll they'll work for a crust of bread for their fam'lies. There's so many of us workless and starving," Floyd said, "that they keep moving us on so that we can't go on relief and because they're scairt we'll organize ourselves". A line of starving children watched Ma as she ladled out the supper, and though she couldn't spare the food, she gave them all a taste, knowing it wasn't near enough. Connie, Rose of Sharon's husband, he'd never dreamed there were such places as Hooversville, and he couldn't take it, and during the night he ran off. When morning came, a man arrived, and with him was a deputy sheriff. The man said: "You'll all get work in Tulare County," but when Floyd asked what they were paying, he called him a Red agitator, and the deputy sheriff fired at Floyd but missed him and blew off a woman's hand. Then Jim Casy knocked him down and seized his gun, but the vigilantes rushed into the camp and overpowered Jim Casy and Floyd. "We're taking them two to jail," they said, "and you all had better get out, 'cause we're a going to burn down this here camp to-night." Rose of Sharon screamed that she wouldn't leave without Connie, but Ma said: "We got to go – we'll meet up with him on the road." But Connie had gone for good.

The Joads were lucky – they found room in a Government camp. It was a fine, clean place with toilets and showers, and a committee of migrants ran it for the good of them all. But there was no work to be had, and Ma said: "We got to move on."

On the road they were stopped by a man who told them peach pickers were wanted. There were police at the plantation gates, but

---

[1] Called after President Hoover, who was in office at the time of the Wall Street collapse. He was defeated at the election of 1932 by Roosevelt.

they were let through and taken on. Once inside, they weren't allowed out because there had been a strike, and the strikers were picketing the place, but Tom got through the wire fence and found it was Casy who was leading the strike. "You're helping to keep wages down by working here," Casy said. "If we all joined together, they'd have to pay us the rightful wage." The guards heard them talking, and one of them came at Casy. "You're starving children – you don't know what you're doing," Casy said, and those were his last words, for the guard smashed his skull with his club. Tom felled the man and knew he had killed him, and another guard split open his cheek, but Tom got away in the dark and told Ma what he'd done. "You didn't aim to kill him," she said. "We got to leave here soon as it's light." They hid Tom under a mattress in the Hudson, and left that place safely.

They came to a sign "Cotton pickers wanted", and Tom hid up in a culvert and Ma made the little 'uns promise not to tell. They got taken on and shared a box-car with another family, and Ma took Tom food at night. But one day Ruthie told about Tom, so Ma went to him and told him he must go away. Tom said: "Don't fret, Ma. Maybe like Casy said, a fella ain't got a soul of his own but on'y a piece of a big 'un, and then – why, it don't matter, I'll be everywhere, I'll be where people are being starved or beaten up, and when our folks live in their own houses and eat the stuff they raise, I'll be there." Ma didn't understand, but she was comforted. . . .

Rose of Sharon didn't fret and whine no more, she had grown womanly. Her time came, and in the box-car her baby was born dead. The rains came, the water washed over the steps of the box-car, and Ma said: "We got to get Rose of Sharon out of here." Al wouldn't come because he'd found a girl he wanted to marry. There was no one to drive the Hudson, so Pa and Uncle John carried Rose of Sharon along the highroad. They saw a barn, and Ma said: "Rose of Sharon kin rest up on the hay." But inside the barn, they found an old man lying with a boy bending over him. The boy said: "He ain't ate for days – reckon he'll die unless he gets soup or milk." Ma looked at Rose of Sharon, and she said "Yes". Ma took the others outside, and Rose of Sharon laid down by the old man, undid her dress, and pulled his poor head down to her breast. "You got to," she said, and her face lit up with a mysterious smile. . . .

If Steinbeck had contented himself with merely relating the story of the Joad family, *The Grapes of Wrath* might have been no more than a deeply moving documentary. It is the scriptural structure of the book, sustained throughout by a complexity of symbolism, that raises it to the height of an epic. The action takes place in three stages: the departure from the Land of Oppression and the oppressors (Oklahoma, the owners of the land, the companies and banks); Exodus (the journey); and the sojourn in the Promised Land (California) amidst the hostile tribes of Canaan (the Californians). In this Biblical context, the significance of Jim Casy's initials is plain. The title, taken from "The Battle Hymn of the Republic", is itself a reference to Revelation, and it is with the most powerful symbol of the grape that Steinbeck fuses the two themes into one in the terrible and beautiful closing scene. Rose of Sharon, giving life to the old man in the barn, is the Beloved of the Song of Songs "whose breasts are like unto a cluster of grapes", the Beloved who says: "Take, eat: this is My Body. . . ."

John Steinbeck, undoubtedly America's major living novelist, was awarded the Nobel Prize in 1962.

1984

GEORGE ORWELL

GEORGE ORWELL (whose real name was Eric Blair) was born in India in 1903. His versatile career ranged from Eton, the Burmese Police Force, and Paris, to teaching in England and fighting for the Republicans in Spain. He later became famous as a journalist and writer, and died in 1950. Personal experience gave vigour to his books: *Down and Out in Paris and London, Burmese Days, The Road to Wigan Pier, Coming Up for Air* and *Homage to Catalonia*. In 1945 he won great success with *Animal Farm*, a political satire in the form of a beast fable. Four years later came *1984*, which has been produced on film and television. Orwell, an independent radical, hated Fascism and Communism. He was a born fighter for social causes and an individualist with the courage to see the faults in these causes themselves. His mind was of a sceptical cast and he expressed himself pungently. Orwell's death from tuberculosis in 1950 was caused partly by his injuries in the Spanish Civil War and the deliberately chosen hardships of his later life.

London, Airstrip One, Oceania: that was the setting in which, on a cold April day, thirty-nine-year-old Winston Smith left his dingy flatlet in Victory Mansions to go to work in the Records Department at the Ministry of Truth. At every corner flamed the portrait of a magnetic Face, with the caption – Big Brother is Watching You. And on the Ministry's frontage were inscribed the three slogans of the Party: War is Peace, Freedom is Slavery and Ignorance is Strength. Other Ministries were those of Peace (dealing with war – such was the *doublethink*), of Love (dealing with law and order), and of Plenty (concerned with economics). The Revolution of some decades earlier had produced *Ingsoc* (meaning English Socialism), where the Inner and Outer Party ruled, the mass of Proles being left largely to their own devices. The world consisted of Oceania, Eurasia and Eastasia. War was continuous and indecisive; at the moment Oceania and Eurasia were at war, but the ganging-up between the three Powers was always changing.

Yet such changes were never admitted (another *doublethink*), and fanatical effort went into erasing or perverting the past; this was Winston's job. Telescreens recorded almost every word and movement of each citizen. Winston's parents had disappeared, and may even have been vaporized after arrest by the Thought Police, like the husband of the woman working in the cubicle next to Winston's – yet she calmly continued her work of distortion and *goodthink* (orthodoxy). Daily there is a Two Minutes Hate, in which crowds shout abuse at pictures of Eurasian prisoners (or the prisoners themselves, when publicly hanged), while their supreme hatred is cast at the renegade leader, Emmanuel Goldstein, the focus of all that is evil. Children are taught to betray their parents for unorthodox words or deeds; at six they join the Spies. Winston himself was threatened by the nine-year-old son of his acquaintance Parsons, a good-natured, sweaty fool with a mania for "community-efforts". The parents even showed pride in their children's skill as sneaks.

But Winston has dreams of both future and past; in a junk shop he sees a pad of lovely cream parchment (a relic of the evil past), and buys it to write a diary of heretical and personal thoughts. Even during the exhausting compulsory P.T. which brings on his coughing fits he meditates: is there not some dim association of rebels, known as the Brotherhood? And what about that Inner Party official, burly but sensitive O'Brien, who had murmured to Winston: "We shall meet in the place where there is no darkness." Meanwhile, who was that young, athletic, dark-haired girl, screaming behind him during the Two Minutes Hate? He transferred his hate to her, yet had also half fallen in love.

Winston had a "comrade" called Syme, the philologist who worked on the 17th edition of the Newspeak dictionary. (Syme, he felt, would surely be vaporized: he was too subtly clever.) Newspeak, which would become compulsory by 2050, aimed to destroy words, to diminish the range of thought. "Bad" became *ungood*, "very good" *plusgood*; and a whole system of neat compounds were brought into being: *Ingsoc, doublethink, goodthinkful* ("orthodox"), *speakwrite, recdep* (Records department), *Minipax* (Ministry of Peace), *ownlife* ("individualism"), *sexcrime, oldthink* (objective or rational thought), *bellyfeel* (emotional approval of *Ingsoc*), *joycamp* (Forced Labour camp), and so on. And by 2050 the literature of the past will have been so "translated" as to be destroyed.

Meanwhile, the Telescreen booms out statistics of a non-existent plenty; and the chocolate ration (just reduced from 30 grammes to 20) is now announced as being *raised* to 20 – with cheers. But Winston was troubled by his own private problems: he recalled his

priggish, frigid wife Katharine (long disappeared, perhaps vaporized, like his parents); prostitution was easy with the Proles but, if
caught, one got five years; desire itself was "thoughtcrime", and
adolescents had their Junior Anti-Sex League. Perhaps hope, in all
spheres, lay with the Proles, 85 per cent of the population? As to the
Party, "the heresy of heresies was common sense". Winston in his
unease sought the company of an old Prole, and pumped him for
memories of pre-Revolution days. But the old man was disappoint-
ingly vague and incoherent. Winston found himself outside the junk
shop where he had bought the diary, and guiltily went in. Elderly
Mr. Charrington, gentle, fussy and somehow himself an antique,
sold him a glass paperweight containing a coral, to Winston a most
beautiful object. And the unused, old-fashioned, dilapidated room
upstairs might be just right for his private needs. As he left, he
glimpsed the dark-haired girl from the Fiction Department. An
official pursuer? How he desired her! Yet he feared her and could
strike her dead!

Suddenly one morning in the corridor he saw her approach. Her
arm in a sling, she slipped on the floor. As he helped her up, she
thrust a note into his hand and disappeared. Terrified that the
message was connected with the Thought Police, he delayed opening
it; at last he read its three words: *I love you.* A mixture of emotions
assailed him: delight, fear both of love itself and of the Police,
sensual curiosity about the girl, and a fever lest he lose her. But how
could he make contact? Perhaps in the canteen, where a few vital
words would be lost in the general buzz. For a week she either passed
him unnoticed or failed to appear. At last he managed to sit at a table
with her, but inconspicuously, in case the Authorities might suspect.

Now they could exchange simple confidences: she suggested and
he agreed to meet her near the monument in Victory Square; he
must not come up to her till she was among a lot of people. The
rendezvous was successful; and she gave him detailed instructions
how to reach a certain tree in a lonely field, starting with a journey to
Paddington. Clearly she was used to such complications.

Sunday afternoon saw Winston travelling briskly but cautiously
(how lucky no Patrols were out!) to the lonely field, there to find the
girl's love and the calm of nature. Their own nature followed its
course, and Winston and Julia – she now revealed her name – progressed in knowledge of each other. She told him she recognized
him some time ago as one who "doesn't belong" – "I knew you were
against them." Winston, still filled with vague uneasy memories as
of "a landscape seen in a dream", became enthralled with this natural,

easy girl: how welcome her hatred of the Party! How clever her double life: outward orthodoxy, thrice weekly working for the Junior Anti-Sex League, yelling with the crowd, yet cheerfully promiscuous and adoring the present moment of love!

Further furtive meetings followed, but never twice in succession at the same place. "Never go home the same way as you went out," she advised. Along the poorer streets they would talk casually, breaking off a sentence on the approach of a Party uniform. And both were busy (his working week of sixty hours was even less than hers), while their free days seldom coincided. But during May they did make love once, in the belfry of a ruined church. There she told him more about herself. Aged twenty-six, she lived in a hostel with thirty other girls, and she worked on the novel-writing machine in the Fiction Department, servicing a large electric motor. But she was no reader, and not clever enough for the Planning Committee or the Rewrite Squad; it was through her excellent moral and athletic record (troop-leader in the Spies, for example) that she had been picked to work in Pornosec, where the kaleidoscopes turned out cheap pornographic rubbish for the sex-hungry proletarian youths. His deeper nature felt drawn to her gay, practical love of pleasure; her first lover (when she was sixteen) was a Party member of sixty who later killed himself to avoid arrest, thus saving Julia from exposure. She had always wanted a good time, and so kept the small rules of the Party, in order secretly to break the big rules. The Party was unalterable; the pre-Revolution world she had never known, and of the Brotherhood she had never heard. How could anyone be so stupid as to imagine that revolt could succeed?

Then Winston described his life and his wife; he spoke of her succinctly as *goodthinkful*, deadly correct, frigid in sex. Julia understood only too well and enlarged on the Party's sexual puritanism. Not only was sex a world of its own, outside official control; more important still to the Party was the way that the hysteria of sex privation could be transformed into war fever and the leader cult. "All this marching up and down, and cheering and waving flags is simply sex gone sour." Were not the Party equally cunning to educate children into spying on their parents night and day? To Winston's resigned mood ("We are the dead"), she replied with her robust love of life, though she foresaw that one day the Thought Police would have her vaporized.

Winston had hired the shabby but attractively old-world room above Mr. Charrington's shop. Waiting for Julia's arrival, he gazed from the window at an enormous woman, "stumping to and fro between a washtub and a clothes line," and booming out the latest pop song. He envied her proletarian contentment. Quickly Julia arrived. bringing him sugar, "real Inner Party coffee" and real tea. In a few minutes she made up her face, and then climbed into the huge mahogany bed. But soon a large rat peeped out of the wainscoting – to Winston, the ultimate horror. Julia stuffed up the hole; and, left alone, Winston compared the coral in his glass paperweight to Julia's life and his own.

By now Syme had vanished. He was missing from work, and "had never existed". Preparations for Hate Week were in hectic swing. Julia's unit rushed out atrocity pamphlets, a new Hate Song was plugged on the Telescreens, rumours circulated, photographs faked; processions, lectures, film shows and the rest were frantically organized, and the streets festooned. The rocket bombings increased, and an old couple, suspected of foreign ancestry, were suffocated in their own house. Julia and Winston continued to enjoy their private room, but such happiness could not last for ever. Winston told her of his strange *rapport* with O'Brien. Julia's mind half accepted the conventions and half probed the truth. She startled Winston by denying that the war was "happening"; probably the Government of Oceania itself dropped bombs on London "just to keep people frightened".

Soon the expected message came from O'Brien and at last Winston stood with Julia in O'Brien's well-appointed Inner Party flat. In this sinister atmosphere, O'Brien swore them into the Brotherhood, with its ruthless rules. In its interest they must be prepared to perpetrate any evil, but they must not expect any help from the Brotherhood. O'Brien lent Winston *the book*, Goldstein's.

Suddenly it was announced that Eastasia, not Eurasia, was the enemy: Eurasia was an ally and always had been. The public ranters changed the names in the middle of a sentence. But records had to be altered or excised, history twisted, so that Winston and the others worked an eighteen-hour day. Then he opened Goldstein's *Theory and Practice of Oligarchical Collectivism*, which started with "Ignorance is Strength". In detail it described the lay-out of power. Science and technology are valued only when they diminish liberty. The state of war is perpetual, both the outward stalemate of the three blocs, and the mental condition of *doublethink*. Goldstein outlined the history of the nineteenth and twentieth centuries up to the Ingsoc régime, and its destruction of personal freedom.

Suddenly the Thought Police arrived and arrested Winston and Julia. Among them stood a rejuvenated, alert-looking Mr. Charrington! Winston was imprisoned in the Ministry of Love, in a high, windowless and crowded cell. Even if he put his hand in his pocket, a voice from the Telescreen would yell prohibition. Criminals came and went, but the "politicals" – like Winston or his friend, the poet Ampleforth – were treated as dirt. Everything was stench and hunger. Even Parsons was a prisoner, betrayed by his own daughter. A protesting man was removed to the dreaded Room 101.

Then O'Brien entered, and Winston, subdued by blows, found himself in a room of interrogation and torture, where he was beaten and kicked until he fell like a sack on the stone floor. He gradually confessed to false and monstrous crimes. Then followed Room 101, where O'Brien stood over him in varying moods. Under torture, Winston was drilled into first perverting the truth and then into *believing* his lies. He learned to distort his own memories. He was taught that Power demanded suffering, not mere obedience.

Stripping to order, Winston stood aghast at his own filthy, bruised body. For the final test, his ultimate horror – rats – became a reality. As rats gnawed his face he screamed: "Do it to Julia! Not me! I don't care what you do to her." Released, he sat in the Chestnut Tree Café. Julia appeared and each admitted the betrayal of the other. The ardour had gone, but they agreed to meet again. Suddenly the trumpet blared the news of Victory, "the greatest in human history". Sitting in a blissful dream, he was glad. Winston at last "had won the victory over himself. He loved Big Brother."

In this grim satire Orwell has enriched our language with memorable terms: "Big Brother," "doublethink" and others. The novel itself is a most original vision, though related to the satirical tradition of Swift, Voltaire (who is more humorous) and modern writers like Aldous Huxley with his *Brave New World*. We may also find a kinship with certain trends in science fiction. The story is well built up, though the actual style is not always really effective. Orwell depicts the Oceania tyranny as absolute, but intuitively he also portrays the resistance of human beings who value dignity and enjoyment. The structure of his society is deadly clear and is a terrible warning. *1984* has the magnetism and drive of an important creative work.

THE KON-TIKI EXPEDITION

THOR HEYERDAHL

IT HAD been a clear, beautiful, tropical evening, with the golden moon spreading its path across the Pacific, and they had sat in silence, watching.

Then she spoke. "It's queer – but there are never breakers like this on the other side of the island."

It was true: there were not. Here they rolled in, regular as clockwork, to burst in white spray in front of them: on the other side, half a mile away, there were no waves at all. But this was hardly a remarkable idea: there was a prevailing wind, throwing waves in, week after week through the year. It left the other side of the island in the lee, untouched.

But when young Thor Heyerdahl considered this in the context of an islander's remark that "Tiki was both God and chief, it was Tiki who brought my ancestors to these islands——" and of the fact that the huge stone figures of this god Tiki on the island were remarkably like other figures he had seen in South America, a theory began to take shape.

He had come with his wife to this island in the Marquesas group to study the culture of people who had lived there hundreds of years before, had left weird stone relics and vanished. Now there was something quite different to consider.

Could the ancestors of the Polynesian people inhabiting these Pacific islands have come right across this far-from-pacific ocean, from the west coast of South America? Was it possible? There were many clues to suggest that it was, quite apart from the stone figures. These island people were a distinct type, unrelated to the inhabitants of Asia or Australia, and their type and their language were scattered over many hundreds of islands, islands which had practically no communication among themselves. For a language to be so dispersed, *yet so nearly identical*, between islands which had no contact, suggested strongly that migration had taken it there. And not long enough ago for the language to develop differently on different islands.

The theory grew in Thor Heyerdahl's mind, even after he and his wife had ended their year of study in the Marquesas. But before he had a chance to do anything about it, it was 1940 and his native Norway had been overrun by the Germans.

At the end of war, after service in the Norwegian Air Force, Heyerdahl found himself in America. He ran out of money, had to move into the Norwegian Sailors' Home in New York, and it was in these bleak surroundings that he made up his mind to prove his theory. After all, he was in the New World, from which the migration he intended to prove had set out (even though he was a thousand miles, and more, too far north) and there was also a chance that he might get financial backing in the United States.

But at first there was little but ridicule for his theory: *of course* the Polynesians couldn't have crossed thousands of miles of ocean in the sort of craft they had: it was impossible. The Norwegian dreamer should stick to his natural history.

He did nothing of the sort: he studied the rafts the South American Incas had used, made of fantastically light balsa wood; he collected charts of the Pacific, studied and plotted the effects of tides and currents, drew a line from the coast of Peru to the Tuamoto Islands.

He even worked out a rate of travel. To go from Peru to the islands, sailing and drifting, on a raft, would take not a hundred days, not ninety – but ninety-seven.

This, to all who heard his theory, was the most ridiculous part of all. That a man should decide, not only to drift across an impossible ocean, but to take an exact time over it, was as near lunacy as made no difference.

Yet Heyerdahl managed, from New York, to recruit a team of five keen young Scandinavians to go with him. From various parts of the world they agreed to come, help build a raft, and sail it clear across the largest ocean in the world.

Financial backing was organized, lists of stores and equipment were drawn up, rejected, drawn up again, plans were made for building the raft. It would be of balsa, which is lighter than cork, and as in Peru it grows only inland they would have to do as the Incas had done: travel up the coast to Ecuador and fell the giant trees there, where they grew to the water's edge.

They flew to Ecuador – and it was more complicated than they had thought. There were no balsas big enough. Eventually, though, they got hold of the twelve big ones they needed, got them laboriously to the port of Callao in Peru, whence they would sail. If the raft ever got built.

And so, for the first time in perhaps a thousand years, a balsa raft was built in Callao. Heyerdahl had calculated that the earlier trips – if they had taken place – would have begun from here. As the present-day inhabitants were fascinated and amused by the mad scheme, and the dockyard was efficient, the raft took shape rapidly. Nine of the thickest logs were chosen for the raft itself, the longest being forty-five feet in length. These were dropped in the water to see how they floated together, then lashed together with rope. (Nails or wire would be cheating, could not possibly be used.) The forty-five-foot log formed the centre fore-and-aft line of the raft, with shorter ones laid on either side, down to a length, on port and starboard, of thirty feet. A deck of split bamboo was laid and lashed on top of this, and above that a small cabin of bamboo, thatched with banana leaves. Forward of this were two masts, side by side, made of hard mangrove wood, and leaning toward each other. They were lashed together at the top, and to them was attached a large square-sail.

The raft as it grew day by day became an exact replica of the type used a thousand years before, along the South American coast.

There was much public enthusiasm, private discouragement. Each of the young mariners was, at one time or another, taken aside and urged, by an ambassador, a politician, a sailor, a friend, to give up the mad idea. But no one had the slightest intention of abandoning it now, and excitement mounted as the raft neared completion.

At last, by 28 April, the *Kon-Tiki* as they now had christened her, after the Polynesian Sun-god, was ready to sail. They finished loading stores and embarked.

There was a huge crowd of people around Callao Bay as they set off, towed for the first few miles by a tug, a tug steaming as fast as it could go, anxious, perhaps, to get this mad enterprise out of the way and return to more normal work. When they were clear of the coast they were given the tug's relieved blessing, and set adrift.

They had followed the old design of raft to the last detail but had worried about several aspects of the design. For one thing, would the ropes which bound the logs together fray, come apart, leaving *Kon-Tiki* to collapse in mid-Pacific and become a bundle of logs drifting off in every direction, its crew to be devoured by sharks?

But now, to their delight, they saw just why the ancient mariners of Peru had stuck to rope: the balsa wood, being soft, wore slowly and the ropes, instead of fraying, bit slowly into it, then lodged firm, in a stouter joint than even bolts would have made.

The trip – and it took, incredibly enough, the ninety-seven days Heyerdahl had calculated – is one of the great epics of human courage and imagination. Many times they were on the verge of disaster, as storms struck and flung the paper-light craft over the sea, as sharks came and nudged them, as men and equipment fell off and had to be rescued. But they managed, like all good adventurers, to impose a sane pattern on their lives. The ordinary day began much as a day might begin in less strange surroundings: the last of the night watch shook up the cook, who then emerged, protesting, from his sleeping bag and began to gather the flying fish which had landed on the deck during the night, a new crop each morning, like mushrooms. These he carefully fried over a Primus stove. They had made concession to the twentieth century in the considerable quantity of tinned and dried food they brought with them, stowed under the bamboo deck, but they subsisted, for much of the time, on the fish they either caught with rod or net, or collected from the deck. Another concession – which at first Heyerdahl had been reluctant to make – was the little radio transmitter and receiver they brought, with which they sent out weather reports for all who might care to listen.

After two months their supplies of fresh water had become almost unbearably stale, but by this time there was sufficient regular – and sometimes terrifying – rainfall to keep containers brimming with it. And the fish grew daily more plentiful, it seemed, with the big bonitos which made superb eating, actually swimming on board, waiting to be killed and cooked.

To starve to death, Thor Heyerdahl realized, was quite impossible.

But there were several even less attractive alternatives. Their greatest fear was an invasion at night by octopuses, for in this part of the Pacific they might easily encounter monsters as big as the raft, able to grab anything or anyone off *Kon-Tiki* without actually getting on board.

Many times they held breath as a whale, longer than *Kon-Tiki* herself, cruised alongside: a sudden whim and it could have capsized them with a flick of its tail. But this mammal, this distant cousin, "like a jovial, well-fed hippopotamus," gave them the greatest pleasure, just by his presence: he was a peaceful fellow, they could hear him breathing. Somehow, to hear an animal – not a fish, after all – breathing in mid-Pacific, made that vast ocean seem less wide.

And there were the dolphins, leaping and bounding joyously beside them, for hours on end.

The description of their adventures in Heyerdahl's fine book is exciting enough as it stands, but it is helped enormously by the photographs they were able to take and which accompany it. They had a rubber dinghy which, on calm days, they used for little trips around *Kon-Tiki*, taking photos of it as it drifted serenely westwards over the Pacific. There are other pictures: a huge shark being held by its tail until the wicked jaws stop snapping; a whale a yard behind them in the water; an almost unknown "snake mackerel" held in a crew member's arms, like an indignant pike.

On 30 July – just over three months after leaving Callao – there is great excitement as they see land. It is an island, of course, and they drift, as they had planned, right past it, giving it only a passing wave, delighted to know they are on the right course. And on 7 August, after the precise ninety-seven days they had calculated, they reach the encircling reef of another island and wait for a canoe to come out and guide them in.

They wait as the two brown men approach in the little boat. Then, as they reach the raft, one jumps on board. He holds out a hand, grins, says, "Goodnight".

It is English: the only non-Polynesian word he knows.

The story of *Kon-Tiki*'s adventure will go down in history – worthy in its way to be ranked with the feat of Heyerdahl's compatriot Amundsen, who first reached the South Pole, a few weeks before the arrival of the tragic Scott. In sheer impudence, it surpasses almost any other true story we know.

The book of this exploit was first published, in Norwegian, in 1948, and then (by Allen & Unwin) in English translation in 1950. For any lover of adventure it is a "must".

Its author, Thor Heyerdahl, was born in 1914 at Larvik in Norway. Almost from the start of his life he took the greatest interest in natural science. He studied it at Oslo University, married young and then went out, with his equally adventurous wife, to the Marquesas.

They returned and he went out to do important excavations in British (Columbia). It was while he was working there, in the west of Canada, that war broke out, and he rushed to join the Norwegian Air Force. Later he transferred to a parachute unit.

As soon as he could, after the war, Thor Heyerdahl went back to research and in particular to his plans for the trip across the Pacific. For he realized now that the best – indeed, the only way – to prove such a theory was to do the journey oneself.

As we have seen, he achieved it. Not all experts, however, have been convinced that this is the way the Polynesians crossed the Pacific – if indeed they crossed it, in that direction, at all.

But whether Heyerdahl's theory is correct or not, he has left us with an epic narrative of courage and imagination.

THE MASTERS

C. P. SNOW

BORN IN Leicester in 1905, Charles Percy Snow began his career as a scientist. Winning a research scholarship to Cambridge, he worked on molecular physics and became a Fellow of Christ's College in 1930. He remained in academic life until the outbreak of the Second World War, when he joined the Civil Service, where he was principally concerned with the selection of scientific personnel. In 1964, as Lord Snow, he was given a junior post in the Labour Government.

Just before leaving Cambridge C. P. Snow began the sequence of novels to be known on completion by the title of the first volume, *Strangers and Brothers* (1940). *The New Men* won the James Tait Black Memorial Prize for the best novel of 1954. *The Conscience of the Rich* was widely acclaimed in 1958, and *The Affair* (1960) was a Book of the Month choice in the U.S.A. *Corridors of Power* appeared in 1964. C. P. Snow is also well known for his views on education: these were forcibly expressed in his Rede Lecture at Cambridge, *The Two Cultures and the Scientific Revolution* (1959).

C. P. Snow's *The Masters* (1951) opens on a depressing winter evening in Cambridge. The narrator, Lewis Eliot, has just learnt that the illness of Vernon Royce, the respected Master of the unnamed College, is incurable. He has but a few months to live; yet his wife – Lady Muriel in her own right – has begged everyone to keep the truth from him. Their daughter Joan opposes this. Soon the thirteen Fellows begin to wonder who the new Master will be. Gradually, canvassing and intrigue arise; personal idiosyncrasies, rancours and loyalties cut across views on scholarship and even Party politics.

Lewis Eliot tried to keep his head (and perhaps this came naturally to a specialist in Law), though he had decided his vote within a few days. His choice was Paul Jago, the Senior Tutor, Anglo-Irish, warm, proud, inconsistent, cursed with disappointments, self-doubts and a tactless wife. Jago had come to see him on the night they knew of the Master's fatal condition, and had pleaded for his vote. The biologist Crawford, quiet, conceited and narrow, was the alternative candidate.

Jago's side was led by Brown, the Senior Fellow, a shrewd

peace-maker with a tolerance for less-disciplined natures. Snow says of him: "In the depth of his heart he loved Jago's wilder outbursts, and wished he could have gone that way himself." Brown was supported by his friend Chrystal, the Dean, a more aggressively organizing type. Neither Jago nor Chrystal could abide the bitterly tactless yet not inhuman Bursar, Winslow, who doted on his scatter-brained son whom Brown was desperately striving to coach into a bare pass degree. Winslow wanted Crawford to win, as did the wizened Chaplain and Master's Deputy, Despard-Smith.

Another Crawford man was Eliot's friend Francis Getliffe, a physicist. Getliffe and Eliot were both Left-wing (like Crawford), but Getliffe was unwilling to put Jago's human qualities above his stiff Conservatism. On the other hand, the embittered physicist Nightingale decided for Jago out of jealousy toward Crawford.

There remained four doubtful voters: old Professor Gay, an expert on Nordic sagas, amiable but with a failing memory; the delightful aesthete Pilbrow, a young seventy-four, known all over Europe as an art patron; and the two youngest, and temporary, Fellows: Luke, a scientific genius, and Eliot's closest friend, Roy Calvert. Calvert, not yet twenty-seven, was already internationally famous as an Orientalist. Rich and handsome, he divided his life between mockery and God-seeking melancholy, between ancient manuscripts, drink and women. Snow seems especially fond of him and Calvert dominates the novel *The Light and the Dark*. Roy Calvert and Joan Royce were more or less in love, and Lady Muriel treated him like a son. He readily agreed to vote for Jago.

Imagine all these personalities in continual conference or clashing, either in each other's rooms or drinking wine in the Combination Room. The Jago "caucus" frequently assembled in Brown's solidly tasteful rooms, with Chrystal as boss. Both Pilbrow and Luke announced their support for Jago, and it was hinted that Gay preferred Crawford.

Chrystal and Brown were engaged on a scheme to benefit all. They hoped to charm the "business knight", Sir Horace Timberlake, into giving a large benefaction to the College. Chrystal was fascinated by the power exercised by Sir Horace. It was urgently necessary that the magnate's nephew should get a good degree (a pathetic parallel to Winslow's son) and that Sir Horace himself be well dined and entertained. In this intrigue Chrystal and Brown worked indefatigably, by-passing the irascible and "difficult" Winslow who might have offended Sir Horace.

Meanwhile, the Master continued his slow death, and yet they talked to him of how soon he could come into Hall. Throughout this period of tension Roy Calvert had become Lady Muriel's mainstay; being her confidant touched dangerously on his own melancholia, but everyone felt the strain of having to deceive the Master. Mixed motives urged them to hope that Lady Muriel would steel herself to tell him the truth – but not just yet, not before the Feast, fixed for Shrove Tuesday, when Sir Horace was to be prodded.

As Lewis Eliot took Sunday tea with the Jagos, Joan Royce, also a guest, repeated emphatically that her father ought to be told the truth. But even more disturbing was the notorious personality of Mrs. Jago – how could her snobbish tactlessness, her mania for collecting snubs and brooding on them, her all-round complaining and pseudo-grand manner fit the Master's Lodge? Brown and Chrystal agreed with Eliot that she was a millstone around Jago, and nobody liked the task of telling this bluntly to her husband. A further complication arose when Nightingale hinted that he would vote for Jago only if promised the Junior Tutorship.

Tuesday brought the Commemoration of Benefactors and Sir Horace joined the smart attendance in Chapel. The succeeding Feast brought gaiety, and afterward the Fellows were ready to listen to Sir Horace and tackle him. The guest talked on endlessly about his nephew ("character is what counts"), and at last veered to the real subject – the endowment of new Fellowships for scientists, the men of the future. Masterfully vague, he left them with nothing concrete. Next morning Sir Horace, taking a fancy to Roy, spent hours examining his "wonderful" manuscripts. He left and the general mood became tense: Jago despised himself for his prevaricating tact with Nightingale, and Calvert was sad because Lady Muriel had at last told her husband the truth, and she was upset at the psychological distance that separated them, even at such a moment. Then Francis Getliffe told Eliot that Nightingale had gone over to the Crawford side, making the votes 6–5, with neither party in a clear majority.

Nightingale explained his change of front venomously: frustrated ambition, jealousy and personal dislike for the Jagos came out in every word. Telling Jago was no pleasant task for Brown, Chrystal and Eliot; Jago seemed despairing and thought of resigning, and yet they had to risk hurting him further by warning him about his wife and the gossipy airs she put on as if the Lodge drawing-room were already hers.

The atmosphere among the Fellows became nearly intolerable and good companionship seemed a thing of the past; Nightingale's furious attacks on Calvert's amorousness gave an ironically raffish tint to the Jago faction; members of each party would cut their opponents, and few of them imitated Crawford in his imperturbability. Then he and Jago made a joint announcement that each would abstain from voting, thus rendering a sufficient vote for *either* side unlikely. Eliot noted the "electric attraction of rivalry" which almost brought Jago and Crawford into momentary intimacy.

Nor was the mood improved when it was learnt that the Master's disease was slowing down, and that even September might see the problem still on the Fellows' hands. Delay edged their nerves; each side, in near-hysteria, came to hold the other as collectively guilty of the crimes or tactlessness of any member, such as Nightingale's blackmailing of young Luke – if Luke did not vote for Crawford, Nightingale would see that Luke lost his temporary Fellowship. Only Chrystal seemed absorbed in devices to bring Sir Horace to heel. The summer slid by in delicious scents, and Brown's claret party, guided by Pilbrow's expertise, did bring some comradeship to members of both sides.

Suffering, too, produced strange momentary friendships. The Tripos results came out, and Sir Horace's nephew luckily scraped through with a third-class but Winslow's son failed. Seeing Winslow sitting in misery, Calvert impulsively sympathized with him, told him to ignore those who gloated over his suffering, and spoke of his own distress at the erotic rumours spread about him. Calvert's nerves were so keyed up – with these rumours, with comforting the wife of the dying Master, with being in love with his daughter and now with seeing his companions gloat over the wretched Winslow – that he actually wrote down on paper what truth there was in the erotic rumours, so that Winslow could realize that "what people say doesn't matter". This is one of the most moving scenes in *The Masters* and reveals the author at his psychological best; and it firmly establishes the character of Roy Calvert.

Left alone with Lewis Eliot, Winslow even hinted at using this document to spoil both Calvert's reputation and Jago's chances. But he relented. Eliot sought out Calvert, knowing that his frantic act, induced by melancholy, would now release his gaiety and good sense. Eliot was not so successful with his old friends, Francis Getliffe and his wife Katherine. Their failure to draw him into voting for Crawford – did not the times demand a liberal-minded Master? – they felt as political and personal betrayal. But Getliffe did agree to curb Nightingale's blackmailing of young Luke.

The Summer Vacation found Calvert lecturing in Berlin, Pilbrow roaming in the Balkans and Eliot having a strangely serene talk with the Master as he lay in bed.

October brought the whole of this tightly-knit little group back to residence, except for Pilbrow, whose vote was still undecided. His vote would add Jago's score up to 6 against Crawford's 6: even this would mean stalemate unless Gay or Despard-Smith were won over. Otherwise the decision would be left, by statute, to the "Visitor", a northern Bishop whose interference no one desired. Suppose the Bishop appointed an outsider!

Therefore Chrystal proposed that the two candidates be forced to vote for each other; Brown opposed, as always, any arrangement with the other side. Chrystal's intrigue and perseverance won and a conference, including Winslow and Despard-Smith, ended in a notice being sent to all the Fellows, urging Jago and Crawford to vote for each other, under the threat of a *third* candidate being chosen from inside the College. The two candidates agreed, but Jago smouldered into indignation at the underhand methods involved. His vulnerable nature, so less assured and simple than Crawford's, made him in Eliot's eyes the better candidate.

The Master died on 4 December and the funeral was suitably attended. The veteran Gay rose to the occasion with admirable youthfulness and arranged for a meeting on 20 December to elect the new Master. Meanwhile Jago was twisted by doubts, by ambitious greed and timid resignation. As always, Snow stresses the man's complexity. Then Sir Horace offered the College the largest benefaction ever – £120,000 for six Fellowships, one of which was to encourage "the wonderful work of Mr. Roy Calvert". Everyone reacted differently to the news: most depressing of all was Winslow's complaint that, as Bursar, he should have been consulted by Brown and Chrystal who had kept him in the dark about their plan. Nothing could now move his determination to resign.

Pilbrow, back from the Balkans, insisted on voting for Crawford in view of the increasing menace of the world situation. The next day Calvert and Eliot had an embarrassing visit: suddenly Alice Jago burst into Eliot's room and into tears. She let forth a torrent of feelings: she explained how she had read the hints and insults to herself circulated by Nightingale, she felt she was letting her husband down and had always done so, and she confessed her belief that she could never be loved – hence her awkward mannerisms. The two men consoled her and escorted her home, where Jago, bitter at Pilbrow's change of front, said he would withdraw from the election but for the threat to humiliate him through Alice. That evening he confronted Crawford with Nightingale's doings and Crawford sensibly promised to write to Alice Jago and confer later with the offender.

The next evening Roy Calvert and Eliot set out for an amusing interview with old Gay. After showing off his Scandinavian exhibits and revealing a peculiar youthful acuteness, he almost agreed to vote for Jago. The two friends arrived back to find tension rising between another pair of friends. Chrystal inclined toward a meeting with the other side and a possible third candidate, while Brown remained solid for Jago and was angrily hurt at Chrystal's "betrayal".

Chrystal talked on until 2 a.m., plugging the possibilities of one "third man" after another. Brown angrily refused to stand and left, but it finally became apparent that he was the only possible third choice. The next day Eliot sounded old Despard-Smith. His reasons for voting for Crawford were indeed curious, and he summed them up in the words: "I have had a disappointing life." He saw Jago as the same type of failure as himself, whereas Crawford's scientific eminence would win honour for the College.

The day before the election passed with dragging slowness. Chrystal now declared he would vote for Crawford, was angry with himself for his propaganda on Jago's behalf and sad to quarrel with Brown. Eliot noted these mixed motives – and indeed here we have Snow wryly commenting on human two-sidedness, or the kind of ambivalence commonly mistaken for betrayal.

Crawford was duly elected. After dinner Jago came in, pale-faced, to drink Crawford's health. He asked for one privilege only: that he and his wife should be the first to entertain the new Master, the next evening. Then "in the blustering night, under the college lamps, he walked away", an isolated, defeated, unhappy man.

Snow's concern in *The Masters* is with men attempting self-fulfilment through power, and the self-knowledge and responsibility power sometimes brings. In the struggle that precedes the election of a new Master strong emotions, normally in England kept under control, come to the surface and occasionally explode.

Here, then, in this Cambridge struggle for power one glimpses the whole business of practical politics. It happens every day at all levels, whether in running a tennis club or at Westminster. *The Masters* is C. P. Snow's most artistically successful novel, for it more surely coheres than any of the others. Because of the intensity of the plot, Snow's style, normally serviceable rather than memorable or individual, is frequently heightened into something near to poetic statement; and the author's insight into human motivation is never less than excellent.

THE ALEXANDRIA QUARTET

LAWRENCE DURRELL

LAWRENCE DURRELL was born in India on 6 February, 1912, the son of a civil engineer. He was educated at St. Joseph's College, Darjeeling, and St. Edmund's School, Canterbury.

After the death of their father, Mrs. Durrell, who had not been left very well-off, brought up her family on a Greek island. The story of these days is very amusingly told by Lawrence's younger brother Gerald, in his book *My Family and Other Animals*.

On leaving school, Durrell entered the Foreign Service as a Press Officer, serving in Athens and Cairo. Later he worked for the Government of Cyprus during a phase of the difficult pre-independence period. His experiences here he describes in his beautiful book, *Bitter Lemons*.

Lawrence first attracted notice as a poet of outstanding lyric qualities, and if his prose works were also admired, it was only by a small discerning circle of connoisseurs.

In 1957, however, he suddenly achieved universal acclaim with the publication of the first of a series of four novels which taken together are known as *The Alexandria Quartet*. They excited the literary world because they were an entirely new experiment with the novel form, and though they also aroused some controversy among the so-called experts, they were generally recognized as one of the outstanding English literary achievements of the immediate post-war period.

Set in Alexandria, they concern a small circle of characters dominated by Justine, the protagonist of the first book.

JUSTINE

The narrator is an English teacher named Darley, who while aspiring to be a writer ekes out a poverty-stricken existence in Alexandria on the pittance he earns from his teaching. He has a small room in the flat of Georges Pombal, a minor official in the French Consulate-General.

One summer, while he is on leave, Pombal lets the flat to Purse-warden, a successful novelist, who gives many parties. During one of these, Pursewarden comes to Darley's room, saying that he has heard that he is a doctor, and will he please come and attend to one of his women guests who has been taken ill.

Darley did once embark on a medical career, and on going to the girl, who is a dancer in a second-rate night-club, realizes that she is very ill indeed, and urges Pursewarden to call a doctor without delay. An old Greek doctor living near by is sent for. While they are awaiting his arrival, Darley and Pursewarden carry the girl, Melissa, to Darley's room.

After examining her, the doctor says she is riddled with tuber-culosis, which must eventually kill her. He arranges for her to enter the Greek hospital. Melissa is grateful to Darley, visits him when she leaves hospital, and becomes his mistress, installed in his tiny room.

One evening Darley gives a lecture to a small literary club, whose members are gifted amateurs of the arts. On his way home after the lecture he stops at a shop to eat some olives, and while there Justine comes in to ask him a question arising from his lecture.

Justine is a strange, enigmatic Jewess, who had had countless lovers before she married Nessim, a wealthy Coptic banker. She takes Darley home, and this marks the beginning of a friendship for him with both Justine and Nessim. Eventually he and Justine become lovers.

Justine is widely known in Alexandria, and many men spend much of their time trying to unravel her character. The French Consul-General is particularly interested in her, and during his probings comes upon a small book written by a Jacob Arnauti, who was once married to Justine, in which, among many sketches of the Alexandria he knows and the people there with whom he is acquainted, he gives a portrait of his wife and of their marriage as they have appeared to him.

In it Arnauti discloses that when a child, Justine was raped by a relative and suggests that this experience lies at the root of her behaviour. Clea, an artist, does not agree with Arnauti's assessment of Justine. She tells Darley: "The true whore is man's real darling – like Justine; she alone has the capacity to wound one. . . . After all Justine cannot be justified or excused. She simply and magnificently *is*; we have to put up with her, like original sin. But to call her a nymphomaniac or to try to Freudianize her, my dear, takes away all her mythical substance – the only thing she really is. Like all amoral people, she verges on the Goddess."

Among Darley's friends is Balthazar, a homosexual Jewish doctor, to whom he is introduced by Justine, when she takes him to a small study circle called the Cabal. From Balthazar Darley discovers that Justine has had a child by a lover before she married Arnauti, which, when it was six, was kidnapped.

The Cabal, which studied the Cabbala, a secret Jewish philosophy transmitted orally, met in a small disused curator's hut, near Pompey's Pillar, a somewhat desolate district of the city. It consisted of about twenty people, among whom were Nessim and a money-lender called Capodistria. Balthazar was the titular leader of the group.

Before Melissa became Darley's mistress she had been the mistress of Cohen, an old Jewish furrier. News reaches Darley that Cohen is in hospital dying and that the old man has been asking to see her. When Darley gets home, he finds Melissa sleeping exhausted, so goes to the hospital alone. The old man tells him that he wished to make amends to Melissa by marrying her now and gives him some rings for her.

Among Darley's acquaintances is Scobie, a seventy-year-old former Lieutenant-Commander and paederast, who has served in the Alexandria Vice Squad and the C.I.D., and is now living on a small pension. Clea supplies him with tobacco, and Darley with admiration, company and brandy. Clea is Scobie's greatest friend. She has painted a splendid portrait of him in his uniform, "and spends much of her time with the old pirate".

As for Clea herself, she has great beauty, enough money to be independent, skill as an artist. "She lives without lovers or family ties, without malices or pets, concentrating with single-mindedness upon her painting, which she takes seriously, but not too seriously."

Working, seeing his friends, writing; living with Melissa, making love with Justine; so Darley's life passes, but dominated always by the enigma of Justine.

Presently, Hamid, his one-eyed servant, tells him of a mysterious caller who has told him that his master is in great danger "from some highly-placed personage", clearly Nessim. Nessim's attitude toward him has changed, he has shed some of his former reserve, and when he speaks to him uses unfamiliar endearments. Both Darley and Justine know that Nessim is aware of their being lovers, but their follies are increased rather than diminished by all the warnings, and during Melissa's absence in Palestine they have some narrow escapes.

One night an Egyptian officer calls on Darley and takes him to Scobie, who tells him that he has been made head of the Secret

Service. There is going to be war, Scobie goes on, "the enemy is working night and day right here among us. We want to take you on our strength. The most dangerous gang of all is right here, in Alexandria. All friends of yours." Nessim, Justine and their leader Balthazar.

Scobie's people cannot break the code the gang is using and that is why they want Darley to join them. "What could I say? The idea was too delightful to be allowed to melt." But when he did join them and tried to quieten his conscience by telling Scobie's office that the Cabal was a harmless sect, he was told that he must not believe their obvious cover-story, and that while Scobie's men continue trying to break the code, he must attend and report on the Cabal's meetings, which he faithfully does.

Meanwhile Nessim is beginning to behave even more strangely. He gives reception after reception, he is always hearing noises, the fires begin burning in extraordinary shapes, and one night he awakes and sees sitting on his bedrail a bat-like creature with the head of a violin. But when the time comes for the yearly great shoot on Lake Mareotis, he changes and becomes like a man who has taken a decision.

Darley is invited to the shoot. Justine implores him not to tempt Providence by accepting, for she is sure that Nessim means to kill them both.

Unknown to them, it is Melissa who has been responsible for goading Nessim to this extreme. Overwhelmed by her own unhappiness caused by Darley's unfaithfulness to her, she has blurted out to Nessim, "Your wife is no longer faithful to you". Immediately aghast at what she has done, she is nevertheless unable to refuse Nessim's invitation to go with him.

Driving her out to the dunes beside the sea, he takes out his cheque-book and asks, "What is the price of your silence?" Putting a timid hand on his arm she says, "I am so ashamed. Please forgive me. I did not know what I was saying."

"For a minute it was almost as if they had fallen in love with each other from sheer relief."

The time for the shoot comes and, the evening before, the guests, including Darley who has been unable to refuse, drive out to the lake. At dawn each is allotted a punt and a gun-bearer. Darley is given Faraj, the most experienced and reliable of the bearers. Darley is successful for him, though he bags only eight brace. He returns in high spirits to learn that there has been an accident. Capodistria has been killed.

On arriving home, Hamid tells him that Justine has fled.

The night after Justine's disappearance, Darley calls on Clea and from her learns that the man who has raped Justine as a child was Capodistria. Some time later, Clea tells him that she has heard from Justine, who is working on a *kibbutz* in Palestine.

Darley is now faced not with the problem of Justine but of Melissa. Pursewarden, who has recently killed himself, has left him £500, which is still in the bank. It is enough for them to live on cheaply for two years. Instead, he goes off by himself to a teaching job in Upper Egypt.

Two years go by, then Clea one day telephones him to tell him that Melissa is in hospital very ill. When he reaches Alexandria she is already dead. He now learns that she has had a child by Nessim, a little girl whom Nessim is trying to get adopted as he thinks Justine will never come back to him while he has Melissa's child.

In the early summer, Darley receives a letter from Clea telling him that a few weeks previously she has met Justine who has told her that she suspects Nessim of having killed Capodistria. As for Darley, Justine has said, "I had to put him out of my mind."

Taking Melissa's child, Darley goes to live on an island in the Mediterranean.

In the second novel,

BALTHAZAR

Darley is still the narrator. He is using notes supplied by Balthazar. *Balthazar* is not a sequel to *Justine*. All the characters of the first novel appear here also, but we learn much more about them; and many of the incidents of the first book are repeated, but from a different angle.

The first character to be expanded is old Scobie, who confesses to Darley that at the time of the full moon he cannot prevent himself from dressing up in women's clothes. To save him from disaster he begs Darley to take away the clothes and keep them for him. Darley agrees.

It has been hinted in *Justine* that Clea has been in love with Justine, and this is now shown to be true. She had been painting Justine who at this time – after her divorce from Arnauti – was poor and had to earn a little money by modelling. and they had become lovers.

Not long afterward Nessim has asked Justine to marry him. He may want other women, he tells her, but he *needs* her. She agrees, because she needs his money to help her in her search for her kidnapped child.

As soon as he has her agreement, Nessim finds himself over-whelmed by shyness, "an acute unwillingness to face his mother and confront her with his intentions". But he knows he must, and drives out to the old country house where his mother Leila and his brother Narouz live.

Nessim's family, the Hosnanis, is ancient and wealthy, and its fortunes are "deployed in two directions, separated into two spheres of responsibility and each brother had his own". While Nessim con-trolled the banking-house, Narouz lived the life of a Coptic squire, looking after the large estate.

Their mother has periods of mental instability. For the past two months, however, she has been well, and now is particularly happy because Mountolive, an Englishman who had been sent to Egypt while waiting to be appointed to a diplomatic post, and had re-mained for many years, has now returned as Sir David, High Commissioner. During her late husband's illness, Mountolive had become Leila's lover.

Nessim is Leila's favourite son. Putting off telling her of his intention to marry Justine, he talks of politics. "Now Mountolive is back," he says, "for the first time what we are trying to do will be understood." He leaves the house still not having told her his news, and commissions Narouz to do it for him.

It now becomes clear that Nessim is involved in some deep poli-tical undertaking, for which the greatest secrecy is required.

The character, however, who is most expanded here is Purse-warden. He is not only a novelist, but appears to be an undercover agent of some kind. Justine has found him attractive and would readily have slept with him, but he has resolutely refused to become sexually involved with her. She talks to him of her private diffi-culties, and tells him how, to rid herself of the Capodistria succubus, she has asked Capodistria to sleep with her again, but that Capo-distria has refused and has been quite unable to recall having raped her. The finding of Pursewarden's body by Nessim after his suicide is also described, but the reasons for his death are not given.

Next we are shown Narouz to be a strange young man, slightly unhinged, consulting clairvoyants, from whom he has discovered that Justine's child is dead, secretly nursing a violent love for Clea.

Scobie's death is then described. He has been kicked to death by a naval rating, while dressed as a woman.

Narouz only comes to Alexandria once a year, for the carnival. This year, one of Pombal's young colleagues, Toto de Brunel, is murdered at the masked ball, no one knows how. He is found to be wearing Justine's ring. Justine believes that Nessim has killed him, mistaking him for her. The incident causes widespread concern in many Alexandrian circles for a variety of reasons.

Finally we learn that after the discovery of the body, Narouz has gone to Clea and told her that he loves her and that he must now give himself up to Nessim. Asked why, he confesses that he has killed Justine, because she has betrayed his brother, and it transpires that he has killed Toto, believing him to be Justine.

In the third book,

MOUNTOLIVE

events described in *Balthazar* are developed. *Mountolive* is written in the third person, and the first third of it describes the career of David Mountolive and his relationship with Leila Hosnani.

Pursewarden's suicide is also explained. Melissa, to raise money to buy herself a new coat, has offered to sleep with him. Afterwards she tells him that her old lover, Cohen, unguardedly told her that he was acting on behalf of the Hosnani family, running guns to Palestine for use in ejecting the British. This information confirms the theories of his predecessor. He writes to Mountolive, telling him this and explaining that because Nessim is his friend he cannot face the consequences of his "betrayal" of his friend, and so intends to kill himself.

Mountolive does not act at once, and many more details of the Hosnani plot are given, among them the fact that Justine knows all about it and is deeply involved herself.

The book closes with the mysterious death of Narouz.

The final book of the quartet is

CLEA

In it the story gradually unfolded in the previous three books is advanced and resolved. Once more the narrator is Darley, who has returned from his island with Melissa's child. It is wartime. They are met by Nessim who had abandoned his plans in Palestine when war became imminent. Justine is back and living with him. She is a much changed Justine, however, and when Darley visits her "he can hardly wait to be gone".

Darley visits Balthazar and learns that the Cabal has been disbanded, and that Capodistria is not dead after all, but that his "death" was arranged by Nessim so that he might collect the insurance, as he was on the verge of bankruptcy. Balthazar provided the corpse.

Next he calls on Clea. She tells him that Scobie has been beatified, and takes him to the old man's former flat which has been turned into a shrine. He goes home with Clea, and during an air-raid they go to bed and make love. Later she tells him more about Pursewarden, who has been in love with his blind sister Liza, and been her lover. Liza had come out to be with him shortly before his death.

Liza is about to be married to Mountolive. She asks Darley to go through letters which had passed between her and her brother, and it would seem that it was their relationship which really made Pursewarden kill himself. Darley advises her to burn the letters and they do so together.

Clea goes to France to paint, and the book closes with a letter from her to Darley in which she tells him she has recently encountered Justine and Nessim. They are planning to settle in Switzerland from where they intend to direct an international plot on the lines of the Hosnani plot. Justine has claimed that she is happy at last.

Durrell has explained what he has tried to achieve in the *Quartet*.

"Modern literature offers us no Unities, so I have turned to science and am trying to complete a four-decker novel whose form is based on the relativity proposition.

"Three sides of space and one of time constitute the soup-mix recipe of a continuum. The four novels follow this pattern.

"The first three parts, however, are to be deployed spatially (hence the use of 'sibling' and not 'sequel') and are not linked in a serial form. They interlap, interweave, in a purely spatial relation. Time is stayed. The fourth part alone will represent time and be a true sequel."

The central theme of the book is an investigation of modern love, he claims. But this is closely rivalled by the portrait he has given of his Alexandria.

Whether he has succeeded in what he set out to do; whether he has shown that his method of construction is not the Proustian or Joycean method illustrating the Bergsonian theory of Duration, but one of Space-Time; these are matters still debated among the literary cognoscenti. One thing, however, emerges – the *Quartet* represents a massive literary achievement. And not only in the field of literary experiment, but in the field of style.

Durrell is essentially a poet. In these four books he has written with a poet's sensitivity and a poet's imaginative insight, using words, images and symbols in a way that no purely prose-writer could. For many this alone makes the reading of the *Quartet* a thrilling experience.

DOCTOR ZHIVAGO
BORIS PASTERNAK

MANY READERS will remember David Lean's film of *Doctor Zhivago*, while those who did not see it may have gathered that they missed a wonderfully sad and romantic tale. But whatever opinions may be of the film, nothing could be conveyed in this medium of the freshness and precision of Pasternak's poetic insight, particularly into nature, nor of his philosophy, and not much of the novel's originality and power.

Boris Pasternak was born in Moscow in 1890, the son of cultured parents. After graduating in law at Moscow University he realized that poetry was his vocation and devoted almost his whole life to writing. Always an inner emigré and an opponent of the Soviet regime, he showed courage on several occasions by dissociating himself from its actions and for a period after 1945 his work was banned. At this time he began writing *Doctor Zhivago*, and it first appeared in 1957 in Italian translation and in English in 1958, in which year he was awarded the Nobel Prize for Literature. This released a storm of condemnation by the Soviet authorities and he was obliged to renounce the prize for the sake of staying in his homeland. He died in 1960.

The novel presents a graphic panorama of life in Russia during the Revolution, the Provisional Government and the Civil War, with many characters from all sections of the population caught in the turmoil and struggling to survive, Pasternak showing them in action, suffering and trying to define their attitudes in an upheaval both terrifying and creative. It is raw existence which is portrayed and the disjointed character of the novel mirrors the roughness of life itself which, as Pasternak insists, cannot be manipulated but has to be lived, "renewing, remaking and transfiguring itself". In this process, visible to him in nature of which he is an integral part, the individual must cooperate; that is his destiny, indeed in Pasternak's view his religious task as a focal point of creation itself.

Life breaks in with elemental force in the public aspect of the novel, but also in the private world of two characters, Yuri Zhivago and Larissa ("Lara") Guishar, and it is their story, running parallel to and influenced by political events, which provides the main thread. Just as Russia is fated for revolution, so they are predestined for each other.

We first meet Yuri in 1901 as a child weeping at his mother's funeral outside Moscow. His father, once a millionaire, has long since abandoned his family for a life of dissipation and has been impelled to suicide by an unscrupulous lawyer named Komarovsky who has battened on him. The orphaned Yuri goes to live in Moscow with the Gromekos, a cultured family of intellectuals who have a daughter Tonya, the same age as himself.

These are wealthy people, but in a poor part of the city another much impoverished family has come to live, Amalia Guishar, widow of a Belgian engineer, and her young daughter Lara. Komarovsky, who was a close friend of her husband, becomes Amalia's lover, but his eyes are already on the warm-hearted and beautiful Lara. ˙

Meanwhile, railway workers are organizing a lightning strike, among them Antipov, a track overseer, who is later given a long prison sentence for his involvement. His son Pasha, an intelligent, obsessively tidy boy, then goes to live with another working class family and soon, amidst rioting all over Moscow, is lucky to escape with his life when caught in a mob being dispersed by Cossacks.

But now something terrible happens. We gather that by a mixture of skilful flattery and self-abasement Komarovsky has succeeded in seducing Lara. The scene is not described, only its effects: Lara's conscience-stricken regret and her sense of a stain that can never be expunged.

Three years pass during which, to escape Komarovsky, Lara works as governess to a wealthy family. She now leaves, intending to set up on her own somewhere, perhaps as a teacher, and ask Komarovsky for the necessary money which she feels he ought in partial reparation to give her. If he refuses or tries to humiliate her, she resolves to kill him. It is Christmas, 1911, and knowing that Komarovsky can be found at a party given by some friends of the Gromekos she sets out through the snow-bound city with a pistol hidden in her muff. On the way she calls on Pasha Antipov, with whom she has been friendly since childhood. Pasha, now grown into a politically idealistic student, adores her. She finds him dressing for the party and on impulse asks him to switch off the electricity and light a candle. "The flame spluttered . . ., then sharpened to an arrow and steadied. . . . On the window-pane, at the level of the flame, the ice melted, leaving a black chink like a peep-hole." She tells him she is in serious trouble and asks him to marry her as soon as possible, to which he joyfully agrees.

Meanwhile, in the intervening years Yuri Zhivago has qualified as a medical practitioner and developed a strong poetic imagination. Having grown up together, he and Tonya have become engaged. Now, muffled in furs, they are being driven to the same party, past the very house where Lara and Pasha are talking. Yuri looks up and notices the candle-flame shining through the window. It seems to be waiting for someone. " 'A candle burned on the table, a candle burned', he whispered to himself—the confused, formless beginning of a poem; he hoped that it would take shape of itself, but nothing more came to him."

At the party Lara does not speak to Komarovsky, but fires a shot at him which misses, and she is arrested. Fearing a scandal, he uses his influence to settle the matter out of court and Lara then marries Pasha, leaving with him for the Urals where they mean to take up teaching. Tonya meanwhile bears Yuri a son and he continues working at a Moscow hospital until, a year after the outbreak of world war, he is drafted to the Galician front as a doctor. By now Lara, too, has had a child, a girl, but there are domestic difficulties and Pasha joins the army while, leaving the baby Katya in the care of friends, Lara volunteers for nursing at the front. Eventually she arrives at the hospital where Yuri is working and he recognizes her at once.

With subtlety Pasternak describes how the first threads between Yuri and Lara are spun. They both sense that something lies in wait for them and are reluctant to accept it. After all, both are married and have children. But, talking enthusiastically of the Russian revolution now beginning, Yuri then turns to "private, individual revolutions" and suddenly something in his voice betrays him. "This is what I've been afraid of," says Lara softly, as if to herself, and with kindness pleads with him to "be as I've known you till now and as I want you to be".

A week later Lara goes back to the Urals to teach at the town of Yuryatin and soon Yuri returns to his family in Moscow. It is the time of the Provisional Government under Kerensky and there is fighting in the streets. Food and fuel are hard to come by and through a harsh winter the Zhivago family, including Tonya's father, only just manage to survive. In the spring they decide to migrate to the Varykino estate outside Yuryatin, once owned by Tonya's grandfather, where they can hope to be self-supporting. After a nightmare journey in freight-trucks across the war-torn countryside they settle in a part of the abandoned house. Yuri becomes unofficial doctor to the neighbourhood and they dig, barter and scrape to keep alive. But Yuri has long since realized that people of his class are destined for destruction and their days are numbered. Once he wrote poetry, but nothing comes to him now: the spirit of the age is against him and the revolution is going sour. At the same time in his dreams he hears a woman's voice calling to him and when spring comes the nightingales seem to be singing: "Wake up!"

One day he rides into Yuryatin to visit the town library and sees Lara there. He does not speak to her at once, but then calls on her at her flat and when they meet, sensing the future and now accepting it, feeling sure of one another, they talk in plain, unextravagant language and when Lara shows him where she hides the key to the flat she says merely: "You might come one day when I'm out—you can open the door and make yourself at home till I come back."

After many trips to see Lara in the following weeks, always returning to Varykino in the afternoon, there comes a time when Tonya does not see him till the following morning, to be told he has been detained on business. Yuri is acutely conscious of his offence against Tonya, but is powerless in the grip of his love for Lara until one day, returning from Yuryatin, he resolves to break with her and make a full confession to his wife. But at that moment, as he rides home, three horsemen suddenly block his way and he is taken prisoner to serve as doctor to a group of Red partisans.

For two years Yuri perforce shares in the desperate misery of warfare against the Whites in the Siberian forest and Pasternak scathingly contrasts the bombast of political catchwords with the realities of starvation, treachery and slaughter. Yuri thinks of Lara and of Tonya: "Tonya, you are my everlasting reproach". Then one day he manages to escape.

After a terrible journey on foot across Siberia, he eventually staggers, half-starved, into Yuryatin and learns that, fearing attack by bandits, the people up at Varykino—his family—left some weeks ago for Moscow. Greatly depressed he manages to reach Lara's flat, finds her out and falls into a sleep of exhaustion, dreaming pathetically of his son. He wakes to find her bending over him and nearly faints with joy. He soon recovers and Pasternak tells us: "They loved one another greatly. . . . To them—and this made them unusual—the moments when passion visited their doomed human existence like a breath of timelessness were moments of revelation, of ever greater understanding of life and of themselves."

Lara tells him of the blight cast on her life by Komarovsky and also speaks of a certain Strelnikov, a ruthless ally of the Bolsheviks whom Yuri once met in awkward circumstances on the train journey to Varykino. Strelnikov, who slaughters by the book to achieve his ideals, is none other than her husband, Pasha Antipov, who returned from a German prison camp after the war and made himself useful to the Reds. She senses that he lives only on sufferance and his days, too, are numbered.

Yuri's early enthusiasm for the revolution has evaporated, not for personal reasons but through bitter contempt for the men of blood and doctrine, hostile to life, who have climbed to power. Their idealism has given way to witch-hunting and he and Lara are now in danger, particularly in Yuryatin where there is a revolutionary tribunal, so they decide to go back to Varykino. But before they can leave, out of the blue Komarovsky appears and urges them to go with him to the eastern maritime provinces where an independent government is to be set up. But they both refuse.

So Yuri, Lara and Katya go to Varykino. Amid the full rigour of the Siberian winter they busy themselves in the house till an illusion of ordered domesticity is created and they enjoy a brief taste of life as it might have been. Yuri feels an urge to write and at night, while Lara and her daughter are sleeping, composes poetry. In particular, those lines that came to him long ago complete themselves: "A candle burned on the table, a candle burned . . .", and he knows now that it burned for him and symbolized the love awaiting them. (Under the title "Winter Night" this and other poems are printed at the end of the novel.)

But within a fortnight Komarovsky seeks them out again and this time there is not a moment to lose. A train for the Far East is under steam at Yuryatin station, and if they do not catch it the chance may never recur. Lara, for the sake of the child, agrees to go with Komarovsky, but not without Yuri; so Yuri, determined in fact to go to Moscow to find his family, invents a pretext to follow their sledge in a few minutes on another horse. Thus there is no farewell to Lara, only a wave of the hand, and he waits with death in his heart to catch a last glimpse of her as the sledge climbs a distant hill. When it has finally vanished he turns to the house with his back to the world and something inside him is saying: "My bright sun has set".

The last eight years of Yuri's life are told in a single chapter. He goes to Moscow, again on foot, finds that his family has been expelled from Russia and gone to Paris. He tries and fails to obtain a visa to join them, and then "marries" the daughter of the former steward at the Gromeko home. All the time his grip on life and himself is disintegrating till finally he can neither write nor work as a doctor. One day, in a crowded tram, he has a heart attack, struggles out into the fresh air, collapses in the street and dies (the film incident where he imagines he sees Lara is not in the novel).

But by coincidence Lara is in Moscow and visits the house where Yuri is laid for friends to take their last farewell. In simple, familiar words she takes her leave, talking as she has always talked to him: "... your going, that's the end of me ... the riddle of life, the riddle of death, the beauty of loving—yes, that we understood ... as for such trifles as re-shaping the world—no, thank you, these things are not for us ... Good-bye my dear one, my own, my pride. Good-bye my swift deep river ...".

In a single short paragraph we are now told that soon after this Lara is arrested in the street, as so often happened in those days, and vanishes into a concentration camp, or dies somewhere, "forgotten as a nameless number on a list which was afterwards mislaid". But his poems have survived and, as we now learn, their child survives. There is an epilogue, the scene being the Russian front during the Second World War. Tanya, a laundry girl working with the troops, meets a Major General Zhivago and tells him the story of her hard life as an orphan and, guessing who she is, he promises to send her to college and look after her. He is, in fact, Yuri's half-brother on his father's side, illegitimate son of a Kirghiz princess and, though appearing only occasionally in the narrative, always to help Yuri over some difficulty, a character of mystical importance, real yet symbolic. He it is who is both the spirit of Yuri's death and his guardian angel and, recognizing this, Yuri is for a long time puzzled about his role. How can death be a help to life? But finally, as we hear from the mouth of Lara, they both understand the riddle, for they have lived it: they have lost parents, home, family, career, comfort, possessions, security, have become penniless waifs, yet in dying to all this have for that very reason, being stripped of everything but themselves, found deep and enduring love.

Here, it seems to me, lies the essence of this great novel, and a greater hope springs from it that, not despite but because of their sufferings the Russian people will one day be able to use their glorious talents more fully than ever before and the candle still burning among them will shed a wider and stronger light.

Another thought is prompted by *Doctor Zhivago*, so important that it should be mentioned. Many of us are inclined to ask: "What do I want from life?", but Pasternak tells us that the question should be put the other way round: "What does life want from me?"

INDEX

Acknowledgements

The editor and publishers express their acknowledgements to publishers, agents and literary trustees for their courtesy in permitting condensations and quotations from the following books:

Allen and Unwin Ltd., *The Interpretation of Dreams* by Sigmund Freud, *The Kon-Tiki Expedition* by Thor Heyerdahl; The Bodley Head Ltd., *The Revolt of the Angels* by Anatole France, *Ariel* by André Maurois, *Ulysses* by James Joyce; Jonathan Cape Ltd. and the Executors of Ernest Hemingway's Estate, *A Farewell to Arms* by Ernest Hemingway; Jonathan Cape Ltd. and the Executors of T. E. Lawrence's Estate, *The Seven Pillars of Wisdom* by T. E. Lawrence; Chatto and Windus Ltd., *Remembrance of Things Past* by Marcel Proust, *To the Lighthouse* by Virginia Woolf, *The Sound and the Fury* by William Faulkner, *Brave New World* by Aldous Huxley; William Collins, Sons and Co. Ltd. and Pantheon Books Inc., *Doctor Zhivago* by Boris Pasternak; J. M. Dent and Sons Ltd. and the Trustees of the Joseph Conrad Estate, *Typhoon* by Joseph Conrad; Eyre and Spottiswoode Ltd., *The Knot of Vipers* by François Mauriac; Faber and Faber Ltd., *The Alexandria Quartet* by Lawrence Durrell; Editions Gallimard, *If It Die* by André Gide; William Heinemann Ltd., *The Forsyte Saga* by John Galsworthy, *Cakes and Ale* by W. Somerset Maugham, *The Grapes of Wrath* by John Steinbeck; William Heinemann Ltd. and The Viking Press Inc., *Brighton Rock* by Graham Greene; Longmans, Green and Co. Ltd., *The Town Labourer* by J. L. and Barbara Hammond; Macmillan and Co. Ltd. and the Trustees of Thomas Hardy's Estate, *Tess of the d'Urbervilles* by Thomas Hardy; Macmillan and Co. Ltd., *The Masters* by C. P. Snow; Laurence Pollinger Ltd., The Estate of the late Mrs. Frieda Lawrence, William Heinemann Ltd. and The Viking Press Inc., *Sons and Lovers* by D. H. Lawrence; Laurence Pollinger Ltd., The Bodley Head Ltd. and the Estate of F. Scott Fitzgerald, *The Great Gatsby* by F. Scott Fitzgerald; Laurence Pollinger Ltd., the Dreiser Trust, Mrs. Myrtle R. Butcher and Harold J. Dies, *An American Tragedy* by Theodore Dreiser; Putnam and Co. Ltd., *All Quiet on the Western Front* by Erich Maria Remarque; Secker and Warburg Ltd., *1984* by George Orwell, *The Magic Mountain* by Thomas Mann; A. P. Watt and Son, Macmillan and Co. Ltd. and Trinity College, Cambridge, *The Golden Bough* by Sir J. G. Frazer; A. P. Watt and Son, Macmillan and Co. Ltd. and the Estate of Mrs. George Bambridge, *Kim* by Rudyard Kipling; A. P. Watt and Son and Cassell and Co. Ltd., *Goodbye to All That* by Robert Graves; A. P. Watt and Son and the Trustees of H. G. Wells's Estate, *The History of Mr. Polly* by H. G. Wells.